SAP PRESS e-books

Print or e-book, Kindle or iPad, workplace or airplane: Choose where and how to read your SAP PRESS books! You can now get all our titles as e-books, too:

- ▸ By download and online access
- ▸ For all popular devices
- ▸ And, of course, DRM-free

Convinced? Then go to **www.sap-press.com** and get your e-book today.

ABAP® Development for SAP HANA®

 PRESS

SAP PRESS is a joint initiative of SAP and Rheinwerk Publishing. The know-how offered by SAP specialists combined with the expertise of Rheinwerk Publishing offers the reader expert books in the field. SAP PRESS features first-hand information and expert advice, and provides useful skills for professional decision-making.

SAP PRESS offers a variety of books on technical and business-related topics for the SAP user. For further information, please visit our website: *www.sap-press.com*.

Michael Pytel
Implementing SAP Business Suite on SAP HANA
2016, 596 pages, hardcover and e-book
www.sap-press.com/3895

Brian O'Neill
Getting Started with ABAP
2016, 451 pages, paperback and e-book
www.sap-press.com/3869

Ankisettipalli, Chen, Wankawala
SAP HANA Advanced Data Modeling
2016, 392 pages, hardcover and e-book
www.sap-press.com/3863

Paul Hardy
ABAP to the Future
2015, 727 pages, hardcover and e-book
www.sap-press.com/3680

Hermann Gahm, Thorsten Schneider, Christiaan Swanepoel,
Eric Westenberger

ABAP® Development for SAP HANA®

Rheinwerk®
Publishing

Bonn • Boston

Editor Hareem Shafi
Acquisitions Editor Kelly Grace Weaver
Translation Lemoine International, Inc., Salt Lake City, UT
Copyeditor Julie McNamee
Cover Design Daniel Kratzke, Graham Geary
Photo Credit Shutterstock.com/71555557/© Max Earey
Layout Design Vera Brauner
Production Kelly O'Callaghan
Typesetting SatzPro, Krefeld (Germany)
Printed and bound in the United States of America, on paper from sustainable sources

ISBN 978-1-4932-1304-7

© 2016 by Rheinwerk Publishing, Inc., Boston (MA)
2nd edition 2016

Library of Congress Cataloging-in-Publication Data
Names: Schneider, Thorsten. | Gahm, Hermann. | Swanepoel, Christiaan. | Westenberger, Eric.
Title: ABAP development in SAP HANA / Hermann Gahm, Thorsten Schneider, Christiaan Swanepoel, Eric Westenberger.
Description: 2nd edition. | Bonn ; Boston : Rheinwerk Publishing, 2016. | Previous edition: ABAP development for
SAP HANA / Thorsten Schneider, Eric Westenberger, and Hermann Gahm. 2014. | Includes index.
Identifiers: LCCN 2016015191| ISBN 9781493213047 (print : alk. paper) | ISBN 9781493213054 (ebook) |
ISBN 9781493213061 (print and ebook : alk. paper)
Subjects: LCSH: ABAP/4 (Computer program language) | SAP HANA (Electronic resource) | Database management.
Classification: LCC QA76.73.A12 S36 2016 | DDC 005.74--dc23 LC record available at https://lccn.loc.gov/2016015191

Contents at a Glance

Dear Reader,

What does SAP HANA mean for you? From high-speed in-memory processing to real-time calculation capabilities, SAP HANA is changing the world of SAP. For many developers it means new concepts to learn, and old concepts to apply to new scenarios. For me, it means a wonderful book to work on and an inspiring author team to collaborate with.

Thorsten Schneider, Eric Westenberger, Hermann Gahm, and Christiaan Swanepoel have made it their mission to make sure that, whatever SAP HANA means for you as a developer, you are prepared to meet its challenges head-on. With thorough examples, they introduce you to the intricacies of ABAP development for SAP HANA, and ensure that as you make your way through this book you will become a more confident user of the SAP HANA development environment.

What did you think about *ABAP Development for SAP HANA*? Your comments and suggestions are the most useful tools to help us make our books the best they can be. Please feel free to contact me and share any praise or criticism you may have.

Thank you for purchasing a book from SAP PRESS!

Hareem Shafi
Editor, SAP PRESS

Rheinwerk Publishing
Boston, MA

hareems@rheinwerk-publishing.com
www.sap-press.com

Contents

9

PART III   Advanced Techniques for ABAP Programming for SAP HANA

Foreword

SAP HANA has been in the market for more than five years and has stirred up the database market considerably. Column-based main-memory databases have established themselves as major players, and all major database manufacturers either have integrated a version already or have announced their intention to do so. Compared to most other approaches, the main difference with SAP HANA is that the main memory column store is also used for transactional applications, which prevents multiple representation.

We could not have foreseen this development back in 2002 when we integrated the first version of a pure main memory-based (non-transactional) column store into the TREX search engine. For the document world, column-based storage of metadata (e.g., author, creation date, etc.) delivered added value because it was possible to add metadata in a flexible and easy manner and to query this data efficiently.

Things got interesting when we started using the technology to aggregate large volumes of data. Initial performance results were phenomenal and produced an air of disbelief within SAP, quickly followed by immense euphoria. Production continued until 2005; in that year, we delivered the SAP BW Accelerator (BWA) as an accelerator for our SAP Business Warehouse (SAP BW) systems. The benefits were obvious: no additional database aggregates, as well as extremely good and, above all, consistent access times because the risk of accessing undefined aggregates had disappeared.

The major breakthrough in relation to main memory-based column stores occurred in 2009 when Hasso Plattner had the vision to postulate joint column storage for Online Analytical Processing (OLAP) (reporting) queries and the Online Transaction Processing (OLTP) load. This proposal was revolutionary due to Hasso's suggestion to place OLAP and OLTP in one system and to supplement this system with database storage in the form of a main memory-based column store. At first, the research community was very skeptical, but soon after, the sheer number of high-quality publications on this topic proved that it had well and truly arrived.

To turn this vision into a viable product, SAP HANA was established in 2009 when three groups (P*Time, MaxDB, and TREX) were merged and later joined by the Sybase team. The goal was—and remains—to build a database management platform that offers much more than traditional databases and to make this platform available to a wide range of applications, including SAP application platforms. At the end of 2010, SAP delivered the first "data-mart variant" of SAP HANA, followed by SAP HANA for BI and SAP HANA for SAP BW. A major event and final confirmation of Hasso's vision was the announcement of SAP Business Suite powered by SAP HANA in January 2013 and its delivery to our customers. The sales figures of SAP Business Suite 4 on SAP HANA (S/4HANA) and SAP HANA itself speak for themselves.

Our customers, partners, and internal development groups can now implement a large range of options that incorporate SAP HANA's speed and functionality into their applications and thus reap the rewards of deploying SAP HANA. ABAP is and will be one of the substantial development environments for SAP HANA, but as the developer, you must rethink whether you want to exploit the potential of SAP HANA fully. This book will certainly help in this regard.

SAP HANA will remain SAP's innovation platform. We can therefore all look forward to exciting times ahead with lots of new features, innovations, and opportunities to build new types of never before conceived applications.

Franz Färber
Executive Vice President SAP PI HANA Platform, SAP SE

Preface

SAP HANA turns five! Hard to believe, but this technology has been on the market for almost five years now. During this time, its use potential has increased significantly, from an in-memory database for data marts, which supplements SAP Business Warehouse (SAP BW) and the SAP Business Suite, to all types of data warehouse applications, and a platform for analytical and transactional systems. Today, SAP HANA is a complete, high-end database for all SAP applications and, at the same time, an innovation platform for completely new types of real-time applications (in the area of healthcare, for example).

I had the opportunity to accompany this rapid development, from its origins in the SAP BW environment right up until the present day, and to do so from the perspective of an internal user. Never before had I witnessed the energy within the walls of SAP that greeted the arrival of SAP HANA. In addition, the best thing about it is that this is just the beginning. Anyone who has experienced this enthusiasm from customers, partners, and employees—or seen the wealth of ideas for developing completely new applications for the software—will know exactly what I mean.

SAP BW (since the end of 2011) and the SAP Business Suite (since the start of 2013) can now run productively on SAP HANA. Porting and optimizing these systems for the in-memory database technology was one of SAP's key strategic projects in recent years. In parallel, and as an additional support for this project, we developed a new SAP NetWeaver release—SAP NetWeaver 7.4—in mid-2012. As part of this development, we systematically optimized ABAP technology for use with SAP HANA and ported the Java-based SAP NetWeaver hubs (for example, SAP Enterprise Portal and SAP Business Process Management) to SAP HANA in particular, thus giving each and every customer the opportunity to run SAP NetWeaver productively on SAP HANA—a key milestone for not only SAP but our customers as well. In the meantime, SAP NetWeaver 7.4 is used widely. The presentation of the new SAP Business

Suite 4 SAP HANA (SAP S/4HANA) in early 2015 laid the foundation for the next generation of SAP business applications with full utilization of the in-memory technology.

The new features in SAP NetWeaver AS ABAP 7.4 support the application developers at SAP in optimizing existing ABAP programs for SAP HANA and implementing completely new applications based on SAP HANA. Of course, our customers and partners can also benefit from these opportunities. A nondisruptive way of migrating existing business processes to SAP HANA, while at the same time developing completely new applications, now exists for the entire ABAP ecosystem.

In this book, Thorsten Schneider, Christiaan Swanepoel, Eric Westenberger, and Hermann Gahm describe the importance of SAP HANA for ABAP development, as well as the new opportunities presented by ABAP 7.4 in the context of in-memory database technology. Thorsten, Chris, Eric, and Hermann not only discuss program acceleration as a result of moving the calculation logic to the database but also the innovative features that SAP HANA makes available to you—thus making this book a must-read for every ABAP developer.

I hope that you enjoy reading this book.

Andreas Wesselmann
Senior Vice President SAP Products & Innovation Technology,
SAP SE

Introduction

Today's business world is extremely dynamic and subject to constant change, with companies continuously under great pressure to innovate. SAP HANA's vision is to provide a platform that can be used to influence all business processes within a company's value chain in real time. However, what does this key term *real time* mean for business applications?

In technological terms, real time describes, in particular, the availability of essential functions without *unwanted* delays. The environment in which a technology is used and the time when this occurs strongly influences the functions needed and what is deemed to be an *acceptable* delay. Before we discuss the software currently used for enterprise management, we want to illustrate this using an example from daily life, namely telecommunications.

Early forms of communication (e.g., telegraphs) were very limited in terms of their usage (range, availability, and manual effort). At that time, however, it was an immense improvement in terms of the speed at which messages were exchanged previously. Then, with the advent of the telephone, it became possible to establish flexible connections over long distances. Once again, however, users of this technology had to allow for various delays. Initially, it was necessary to establish a manual connection via a switchboard. Later, and for a very long time after, there were considerable *latencies* with overseas connections, which affected and complicated long-distance telephone conversations. Today, however, telephone connections can be established almost anywhere in the world and done so without any notable delay. Essentially, every leap in evolution has been associated with considerable improvement in terms of real-time quality.

Example: real time in telecommunications

In addition to a (synchronous) conversation between two people, asynchronous forms of communication have always played a role historically (e.g., postal communication). In this context, real time has a different meaning because neither the sender nor the receiver needs to wait.

Asynchronous communication has also undergone immense changes in recent years (thanks to many new variants such as email, SMS, etc.), which, unlike postal mail, facilitates a new dimension of real-time communication between several people. Furthermore, there is an increasing number of nonhuman communication users such as devices with an Internet connection, which are known as *smart devices* (e.g., intelligent electricity meters).

Most people will testify to the fact that, today, electronic communication is available in real time. Nevertheless, in our daily lives, some things still cannot occur in real time despite the many advances in technology (e.g., booking a connecting flight during a trip). It's safe to say that in the future, many scenarios that are inconceivable now will be so widespread that currently accepted limitations will be completely unacceptable.

Real time in business

The preceding telecommunications technology example contains some basic principles that are also applicable to business software. On one hand, there are corporate and economic developments, such as globalization, the increasing mobility of customers, and employees who are the driving forces for new types of technology. Companies operate globally and interact in complex networks. Furthermore, customers and employees expect to be able to access products and services at all times, from anywhere in the world.

On the other hand, there are technological innovations that pioneer new paths. The Internet is currently a catalyst for most developments. Enormous volumes of data are simultaneously accessible to a large part of the world's population (i.e., in real time). The Internet also provides a platform for selling all types of products and services, which has led to a phenomenal increase in the number of business transactions conducted each day. Companies can gain a massive competitive advantage each time a business process (e.g., procurement, production, billing) is optimized. In most industries, the great potential here can be realized by establishing a closer link between operational planning and control in real time.

Today's customers also expect greater customization of products and services to their individual wishes (e.g., to their personal circumstances).

In particular, companies that are active in industries subject to major changes (e.g., the energy industry, financial providers, or specific forms of retail) are under a great deal of pressure to act.

Real time shapes the evolution of 40 years of SAP software. Even the letter "R" in SAP's classic product line, R/3, stood for *real time*. SAP's initial concepts in the 1970s, which paved the way for the development of R/1, facilitated the on-screen entry of business data, which, compared to older punch card systems, provided a new quality of real time. Consequently, processes such as payroll accounting and financial accounting were the first to be mapped electronically and automated. With SAP R/2, which was based on a *mainframe* architecture, SAP added further SAP ERP modules, for example, Materials Management (MM), to these applications areas. As part of this release, SAP introduced the reporting language ABAP. ABAP *reports* were used to create, for example, a list of purchase orders, which was filtered according to customer and had *drilldown options* for line items. Initially, this was available in the background only (*batch mode*). However, it later became available in *dialog* mode.

Real time at SAP

Thanks to the *client/server architecture*, in particular, and the related scaling options in SAP R/3, a large number of users within a company could access SAP applications. Consequently, SAP software, in combination with consistent use of a database system and an ever-growing number of standard implementations for business processes, penetrated the IT infrastructure of many large companies, thus making it possible to use an integrated system to support transactional processes in real time (e.g., a *just-in-time production process*).

Parallel to these developments is the fact that over the past 20 years, it has become increasingly important to analyze current business processes to obtain information continuously in order to make better operational and strategic decisions. Within this business intelligence trend, however, it soon became clear that in many situations, it's technically impractical to perform and integrate the required analyses into a system that already supports business processes. Parallel processing of analyses and transactions involving extremely large amounts of data overloaded most systems, with the database, in particular, emerging as a limiting

Importance of business intelligence

factor. This was one of the reasons SAP created a specialized system for analytical scenarios, which you currently know as *SAP Business Warehouse (SAP BW)*. In addition to new options for consolidating data from multiple systems and integrating external data sources, the use of the data warehouse system for operational scenarios is, unfortunately, fraught with losses when data are processed in real time. First, data needs to be extracted and replicated, which, in practice, can cause a time delay, ranging from several hours up to one week, until the current data is available at the correct location. This was SAP's starting point for SAP HANA, that is, no more delays in receiving key information for a business decision.

SAP HANA as a database

SAP likes to describe SAP HANA as a platform for real-time data management. To begin with, SAP HANA is a high-end database for business transactions (*Online Transaction Processing*, OLTP) and reporting (*Online Analytical Processing*, OLAP), which can use a combination of in-memory technology and column-oriented storage to optimize both scenarios. In the first step, SAP HANA was used as a *side-by-side scenario* (i.e., in addition to an existing traditional database) to accelerate selective processes and analyses. Soon after, it was supported as a new database for SAP BW 7.3 (or higher). In this way, SAP demonstrated that SAP HANA not only accelerates analytical scenarios but can also serve as a primary database for an SAP NetWeaver system. With the availability of *SAP Business Suite powered by SAP HANA*, it's now finally possible for customers to benefit fully from SAP HANA technology within standard SAP applications. The SAP NetWeaver release 7.4 SP 05 underlying this constellation (in particular, SAP NetWeaver Application Server ABAP 7.4 [AS ABAP]) will therefore play a key role in this book. Furthermore, the sample programs in this book require ABAP 7.4. However, we'll always indicate which functions you can also use with earlier releases of SAP NetWeaver. A cloud-based trial version of ABAP 7.4 on SAP HANA is available. For more information, see Appendix E.

SAP HANA as a platform

Furthermore, SAP HANA provides many more functions that go beyond the usual range of functions associated with a database. In particular, these include extensive data management functions (replication; extraction, transformation, loading [ETL]; etc.) and data analysis functions (e.g., *data mining* by means of a *text search* and *predictive analysis*).

Many of these technologies and functions aren't exclusively available to SAP HANA. In fact, many software systems now manage data in the main memory or use column-oriented displays. SAP itself developed and used in-memory technology long before SAP HANA came into being (e.g., in *SAP BW Accelerator [BWA]*). Similarly, a number of software manufacturers (including SAP) are involved in data analysis, especially in the context of *business intelligence* and *information management solutions*. One key benefit of SAP HANA is that it offers this function in the same system in which business transactions are running. If, for example, you want to run SAP Business Suite on SAP HANA, these enhanced functions are available to you immediately, without the need to extract data. Furthermore, because SAP HANA incorporates the key data structures of the SAP Business Suite, installed functions already exist for some standard operations (e.g., currency conversion).

Therefore, what does SAP HANA mean for standard SAP applications that run on the ABAP application server? What changes are occurring in ABAP programming? What new options does SAP HANA open up in terms of ABAP-based solutions? These three questions will be at the heart of this book. Furthermore, we'll use examples to explain the relevant technical backgrounds and concepts, rather than simply introducing the technology behind the new tools and frameworks. In particular, we'll focus on the basic functions of ABAP development and database access via ABAP. We will introduce existing or planned supports for SAP HANA in ABAP-based *frameworks* as an overview or outlook because a detailed description generally requires an introduction to how these components work. (Examples here include *Embedded Search* and *BRFplus*.) In the examples contained in this book, we'll use simple ABAP reports as the user interfaces for the most part. In some cases, however, we will also create web-based interfaces with Web Dynpro ABAP and HTML5.

ABAP development on SAP HANA

As you'll see, this book is divided into three parts. In Part I, we'll introduce you to the basic principles of in-memory technology. Here, you will get to know the development tools as well as refresh your knowledge of ABAP database programming. In **Chapter 1**, we'll start with an overview of the components of SAP HANA and potential usage scenarios in conjunction with ABAP. In **Chapter 2**, we'll introduce you to the

Structure of the book: Part I

development environment, which includes SAP HANA Studio and the ABAP development tools for SAP NetWeaver (also known as ABAP in Eclipse). **Chapter 3** discusses the use of Open SQL and Native SQL to access the SAP HANA database from ABAP programs.

Part II
In Part II of the book, you'll learn how to store data from an ABAP application (e.g., certain calculations) in SAP HANA, thus achieving considerably better performance. Here, the focus initially will be on programming and modeling SAP HANA, as well as accessing SAP HANA from ABAP programs. In **Chapter 4**, we'll discuss the various options for using data views and SQLScript procedures to conduct comprehensive calculations and analyses in relation to ABAP table content directly in SAP HANA. Then, in **Chapter 5**, you learn how to integrate and transport the objects you've created in the previous chapter in ABAP. **Chapter 6** presents various new technologies of ABAP 7.4 that allow you to relocate more logic to the database within ABAP programs without having to continuously create native SAP HANA objects. Together with the tools in **Chapter 7**, you now have the basic tools you need to know within the context of SAP HANA. Part II concludes with **Chapter 8**, where we'll use the technologies and tools introduced earlier in this book to optimize an existing ABAP implementation for SAP HANA, step by step.

Part III
In Part III, we'll introduce you to some advanced SAP HANA functions that aren't available in classic ABAP development. Even though the chapters contained in Part III of this book are based on the content of the preceding part, Part III can be read in isolation.

Then in **Chapter 9**, we'll introduce you to the capabilities of the embedded SAP BW technology in conjunction with ABAP developments on SAP HANA and existing SAP BusinessObjects Business Intelligence (SAP BusinessObjects BI) products. In **Chapter 10**, we'll discuss the usage of *fuzzy search* in SAP HANA, including how to use it to improve, for example, input helps within an ABAP application. You can then use decision tables, whose usage we'll discuss in **Chapter 11**, to use rules that enable you to design parts of an application in a very flexible manner. In **Chapter 12**, we'll show how you can, for example, incorporate statistical functions for *predictive analysis* into an ABAP application. As a final element, in **Chapter 13**, we'll use the Geo-Spatial Engine in SAP HANA for geographical operations in conjunction with external maps. The book concludes with **Chapter 14**, which contains our recommendations for optimizing ABAP applications on SAP HANA as well as some new developments in relation to ABAP applications on SAP HANA.

As you'll see while reading this book, the SAP HANA platform provides a whole host of options. You don't necessarily have to use all of the elements introduced here in ABAP custom developments on SAP HANA. For some new types of functions, the use of low-level technologies, which you may only have used occasionally in the past, is currently necessary in the ABAP application server (e.g., Native SQL). However, we are convinced that the use of new options holds great innovation potential in terms of new developments. For this reason, we strive to adopt a certain pioneering approach, which is evident in some of the examples provided in this book.

Deploying new technologies

As an example, we will use the *flight data model* in SAP NetWeaver (also known as the SFLIGHT model), which was and remains the basis for many training courses, documentation, and specialist books relating to SAP ERP. Thanks to its popularity, the new features and paradigm shifts involved with SAP HANA can be explained very well using this example. The underlying business scenario (airlines and travel agencies) is also very well suited to explaining aspects of real time because, in recent years, the travel industry has been subject to great changes as a result of globalization and the Internet. Furthermore, the volume of data in the context of flight schedules, postings, and passengers has continued to grow.

Sample data model

Throughout this book, you will find several elements that will make it easier for you to work with this book.

How to use this book

Highlighted information boxes contain helpful content that is worth knowing but lies somewhat outside the actual explanation. To help you immediately identify the type of information contained in the boxes, we have assigned symbols to each box:

[+] *Tips* marked with this symbol will give you special recommendations that may make your work easier.

[»] Boxes marked with this symbol contain information about *additional topics* or important content that you should note.

[!] This symbol refers to *specifics* that you should consider. It also warns about frequent errors or problems that can occur.

[Ex] In addition, you'll find the *code samples* used throughout as a download on this book's web page at *www.sap-press.com/3973*.

This book provides a comprehensive tool that will support you in using the SAP HANA technology in ABAP programs, and we hope you enjoy reading it.

Acknowledgments

We would like to thank the following people who supported us by partaking in discussions and providing advice and feedback during the writing of this book:

Arne Arnold, Dr. Alexander Böhm, Ingo Bräuninger, Stefan Bresch, Adolf Brosig, Ralf-Dietmar Dittmann, Franz Färber, Timm Falter, Markus Fath, Dr. Hans-Dieter Frey, Boris Gebhardt, Dr. Heiko Gerwens, Andreas Grünhagen, Dr. Jasmin Gruschke, Martin Hartig, Vishnu Prasad Hegde, Rich Heilman, Thea Hillenbrand, Mike Hirsch, Dr. Harshavardhan Jegadeesan, Thomas Jung, Horst Keller, Christiane Kettschau, Kilian Kilger, Bernd Krannich, Dr. Willi Petri, Eric Schemer, Joachim Schmid, Sascha Schwedes, Welf Walter, Hong Wang, Jens Weiler, Stefan Weitland, Tobias Wenner, Andreas Wesselmann, Sigrid Wortmann, Katja Zavozina, Klaus Ziegler

Thank you so much—this book would not have been possible without your help.

**Hermann Gahm, Thorsten Schneider,
Christiaan Swanepoel, Eric Westenberger**

PART I

Basic Principles

SAP HANA is more than just a database. It provides a platform with a myriad of libraries and tools for information management, complex analyses, and application development. Using SAP HANA, you can optimize existing applications as well as develop new applications from scratch.

1   Overview of SAP HANA

At its core, SAP HANA is a modern, main memory-based relational database (*in-memory database*) that is optimized both for analytical and transactional scenarios and is designed for usage in business-critical areas. Both SAP Business Warehouse (SAP BW) and the entire SAP Business Suite can use the SAP HANA database and benefit from the advantages it provides. Based on the underlying in-memory technology, SAP HANA comprises a multitude of libraries and tools that can be deployed independently or in combination with other SAP solutions for business applications. For this reason, SAP HANA is referred to as a *platform* both for its own applications and for customers and partners.

Meaning of the Name SAP HANA   [«]

Originally, the name HANA officially stood for *High Performance Analytical Appliance* because it was possible to process large amounts of data in real time for analytical scenarios, and SAP HANA was exclusively provided as an *appliance* (combination of hardware and software). In recent years, however, the usage scenarios have considerably increased and changes have occurred in the appliance model, so SAP no longer uses HANA as an abbreviation but as a separate brand name for various products.

In the first part of this chapter, we introduce the individual components of SAP HANA. We then describe the basic principles of the in-memory technology and the architecture of the SAP HANA database. To conclude this chapter, we present application cases for SAP HANA and explain the impact SAP HANA has on application development.

1.1   Software Components of SAP HANA

This section presents the components of the SAP HANA platform based on Service Pack Stack (SPS) 9. The SAP HANA basic package comprises the following software components, which we'll discuss in more detail in the following subsections:

▸ **SAP HANA database**
The actual SAP HANA database with its core components.

▸ **SAP HANA Client**
Database driver for various programming languages and tools.

▸ **SAP HANA Studio**
The central Eclipse-based tool for administration and development.

▸ **SAP HANA XS**
The embedded web server for native SAP HANA applications and tools.

The following sections explain the structure of the basic components and their usage. In this context, we'll focus on aspects that are relevant for application development.

1.1.1   SAP HANA Database

Relational database

As a full relational database, SAP HANA provides functions similar to other traditional relational databases that are supported by SAP. Like these traditional databases, SAP HANA provides functions for data *backup* and *recovery*, supports the SQL standard (SQL 92 Entry Level and some SQL 99 extensions), and guarantees data consistency by following the ACID principle(atomicity, consistency, isolation, durability) when executing transactions.

Differentiation

In contrast to other relational databases, SAP HANA can place all relevant business data in the main memory. It combines row-, column-, and object-based database technologies and has been optimized to use the parallel processing functionality provided by modern hardware technologies. With this, you can use multi-core and multi-CPU architectures to their fullest potential. You can thus optimize existing applications for the new technology and develop applications that you could only dream of with traditional database technologies. Section 1.2 and Section 1.3 discuss the internal architecture of the SAP HANA database in more detail. The abilities of the SAP HANA database (and their usage in ABAP programs) are presented later in this book.

There are various *lifecycle management tools* for using and operating SAP HANA. You can perform most system administration tasks using SAP HANA Studio; for some tasks, access at the operating system (OS) level is necessary or desirable:

Lifecycle management tools

▶ You use the *SAP HANA Lifecycle Manager* tool (Program HDBLCM) for adapting the SAP HANA system. With this tool, you can make all adaptations to the system layouts, including the installing optional components, implementing updates, and adding further hosts for scale-out.

▶ To install or update native SAP HANA applications, you must use *SAP HANA Application Lifecycle Manager* (Program HDBALM). You can call it in SAP HANA Studio or in a browser; access is also possible using the command line, which is useful for automation, for example. Application Lifecycle Manager isn't used for ABAP applications on SAP HANA, however. Here, you still deploy the regular ABAP transport system for the lifecycle of applications.

▶ Each SAP HANA host runs the *SAP Host Agent*, which makes it possible to monitor the individual hosts and their corresponding instances. This information is then made available for central monitoring via web services (e.g., via the *SAP Management Console*).

In case of urgent support is need, you can set up a connection between your SAP HANA installation and the SAP Support that provides restricted access via the SAP standard support infrastructure (especially *SAProuter*). Using the *Diagnostics Agent* on the SAP HANA appliance, SAP Solution Manager provides comprehensive options for technical monitoring of your SAP HANA system in the context of standard Application Lifecycle Management (ALM) processes (e.g., *root cause analysis* or *SAP EarlyWatch Alert*).

Support access and landscape integration

1.1.2   SAP HANA Studio

Eclipse develop-
ment environment

SAP HANA Studio is comprised of the administration and development environment. This solution is based on the Eclipse platform, which SAP strategically intended as a new development environment. AnEclipse-based development environment is now also available for ABAP (*ABAP Development Tools for SAP NetWeaver*). We'll primarily use this environment for the tasks described in this book.

[»]

The Significance of Eclipse for SAP

Eclipse is a platform for development tools and environments (e.g., for Java, C/C++, or PHP). The platform is maintained and further developed by the Eclipse Foundation (see *http://eclipse.org*). As an active member of the Eclipse Foundation, SAP supports the organization in several projects.

In addition to SAP HANA Studio and the ABAP Development Tools for SAP NetWeaver, the following SAP development environments are based on Eclipse:

▸ SAP NetWeaver Developer Studio (Java)

▸ SAP Eclipse Tools for SAP HANA Cloud Platform

▸ SAP UI Development Tools for HTML5

▸ SAP Gateway Plug-in for Eclipse

One of the main advantages of the Eclipse platform is the capability to integrate different tools into one installation so that the user benefits from a homogeneous development environment. Particularly useful is the capability to install the ABAP Development Tools in SAP HANA Studio, which is described in Section 1.3.

Usage areas

As an example, administrators can use SAP HANA Studio for the following tasks:

▸ Starting and stopping database services

▸ Monitoring the system

▸ Specifying system settings

▸ Maintaining users and authorizations

▸ Configuring the audit log

Administering SAP HANA isn't the focus of this book. Please refer to the documentation at *http://help.sap.com/hana* for this information. As a developer, however, you can create *content* (e.g., views or database processes) using SAP HANA Studio. These development artifacts are stored in the *repository* of the SAP HANA database. The development environment of SAP HANA Studio is explained in detail in Chapter 2 and Chapter 4.

SAP HANA Cockpit and SAP HANA Web Workbench   **[+]**

Besides SAP HANA Studio, administrators and developers can also use web-based tools that are executable in every Internet browser (and thus on mobile devices).

For some administrator tasks, you can also use the *SAP HANA Cockpit*, which you start via the URL *https://<host>:<port>/sap/hana/admin/cockpit*.

In addition to SAP HANA Studio, *SAP HANA Web Workbench* is available for native development, which we'll briefly discuss in Section 1.1.4. For ABAP development for SAP HANA, however, this environment only plays a minor role.

1.1.3   SAP HANA Client

Using the SAP HANA Client, you can connect to the SAP HANA database via a network protocol. The following standards are supported (see Figure 1.1):

Connection protocols

▶ Open Database Connectivity (ODBC) and Java Database Connectivity (JDBC) for SQL-based access

▶ OLE DB for OLAP (ODBO) for multidimensional expressions (MDX) access

Internally, in particular the proprietary *SQL Database Connectivity (SQLDBC) library* from SAP is used.

Because the Eclipse platform is Java-based, SAP HANA Studio uses the JDBC client to establish the connection. This variant is also used in Java-based application servers, such as SAP NetWeaver AS Java.

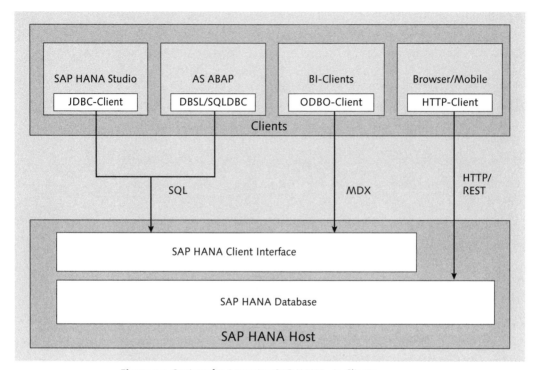

Figure 1.1 Options for Accessing SAP HANA via Clients

SAP HANA SQL Command Network Protocol

SAP has published the specification of the network protocol for access to SAP HANA via SQL under *http://help.sap.com/hana*. This allows for implementations of SAP HANA drivers for other programming languages. For example, there's a freely available implementation of an SAP HANA Client for *node.js* under *https://github.com/SAP/node-hdb*.

Connecting
AS ABAP

The SAP NetWeaver AS ABAP uses the *Database Shared Library* (DBSL), which is embedded in the SQLDBC client, to connect to the SAP HANA database. The database interface architecture of the AS ABAP is explained in detail in Chapter 3.

BI clients

Special business intelligence (BI) clients, such as add-ins for Microsoft Excel, frequently use MDX-based access for multidimensional queries that are executed via the ODBO client.

In addition, SAP HANA provides direct HTTP access via the *XS Engine*, which is discussed in the next section.

1.1.4   SAP HANA Extended Application Services

The SAP HANA Extended Application Services (SAP HANA XS) allow you to develop applications directly in SAP HANA without an additional application server. For this purpose, SAP HANA XS provides a complete development environment consisting of a web server, a development model, and supporting tools.

SAP Internet Communication Manager (ICM) and *SAP Web Dispatcher* are used as web servers, which are also used for all SAP NetWeaver application servers (ABAP and Java). Inbound HTTP requests are accepted and then transferred to the SAP HANA XS runtime, which assumes the processing of the associated program code in conjunction with the SAP HANA database.

Web servers

Applications are developed with SAP HANA XS using several development objects that cover everything form defining a data model to developing user interfaces (UIs). The individual objects are defined as normal text files; you can use package structures for grouping. In this context, each development object has its predefined syntax, whereas the type is distinguished through the file extension. The objects are managed in the SAP HANA repository, and the repository can generate objects (e.g. a database table) in the database catalog upon activation. For the definition of data models (tables, views, etc.), for example, the *Core Data Services* (CDS) description language is available, which is stored in the files with the extension *.hdbdd*. The CDS description language is also supported in ABAP as you'll learn in Chapter 6. Further central elements of programming using SAP HANA XS include writing application logic using server-side JavaScript as well as defining REST-based interfaces for web applications. Within the scope of this book, we won't further detail the development using SAP HANA XS because for ABAP-based applications, the primary access to SAP HANA is made via ABAP development objects for logical reasons.

Development model

There are two options for development using SAP HANA XS: SAP HANA Studio or SAP HANA Web Workbench, which is executable in a regular

Tools for development

Internet browser and thus doesn't require any installation. In both cases, you're provided with practical editors and graphical tools for defining the individual development objects. Additionally, the two environments provide options for syntax checks, debugging, and application configuration.

1.1.5 Additional Options

Based on the core components, several additional options enable more usage scenarios. The following grouped list gives an overview of the options. Note, however, that we highlight those options that are addressed within the scope of this book.

Engines and Libraries

The functional scope of SAP HANA can be enhanced through *engines* (components with a separate runtime environment) and libraries (collections of algorithms). These enhancements are either part of the standard SAP HANA database or are installed later on as plug-ins.

Available packages   The following packages are available in SAP HANA SPS 9:

▸ **SAP HANA Predictive**
This option permits the usage of various functional libraries for mathematical operations, such as the creation of models for statistical predictions. In addition, this option comprises an integration with the statistical software package R. Chapter 12 discusses the actual use of the *Predictive Analysis Library* (PAL) that is contained in this option.

▸ **SAP HANA Spatial**
With this option, you can process geographical information in SAP HANA. This opens up interesting new options for business applications, which we'll present in Chapter 13.

▸ **SAP HANA Advanced Data Processing**
This package comprises advanced search and analysis options in structured and unstructured data, including functions for extracting information from texts and documents (*text mining*). The options are presented in Chapter 10.

Replication and Integration of Data

As you'll see in Section 1.4, you sometimes have to transfer data from existing systems to SAP HANA. The source systems can be, for example, SAP Business Suite, SAP BW, or any other data source. | *Source systems*

This is referred to as *data replication* if the data structures and data records are basically transferred without modifications. Tools for data replication usually support both the initial data transfer (*initial load*) and the subsequent synchronization of changes (*delta load*), and they usually have the goal of transferring changes in *near real time*. | *Data replication*

If you require additional transformations and other steps for data consolidation or improvement of data quality, this is referred to as *data integration* (or *information management*). For this purpose, you specifically require tools for *extraction, transformation, and loading (ETL) processes*. These tools are designed for *batch operation* so that data are available with a certain time delay. In some cases, human interaction is required, for example, to cleanse data records manually. | *Data integration*

SAP provides several tools for data replication and data integration. However, we can't offer a full product overview here. The following presents the most critical options and technologies used directly in SAP HANA: | *Available options*

▶ **SAP HANA Real-Time Replication**
This additional option comprises several tools for data replication from various data sources to SAP HANA in real time. This specifically includes SAP Landscape Transformation Replication Server (SAP LT Replication Server) and SAP Replication Server (SRS). SAP LT is the standard option for the replication of tables from ABAP systems and is based on *database triggers*.

▶ **SAP HANA Enterprise Information Management (EIM)**
This package offers various options for efficient transfer of data from heterogeneous sources with data transformation and cleansing options. You can define your own adaptors and processes using a development environment and thus control the data flow flexibly.

▶ **Smart Data Access (SDA)**
You can use the SDA technology to access other systems from SAP HANA. This can involve another relational database or other data sources, such as a *Hadoop cluster*. The data is made visible in SAP HANA as virtual tables so that direct SQL access is possible.

▶ **Direct Extractor Connection (DXC)**
This technology allows you to use a direct HTTP connection to transfer data to SAP HANA using extractors that were developed using the SAP BW technology.

Recommendations   Selecting the right technology and the right tool for data replication/ integration strongly depends on the usage scenario and the qualities required. We won't discuss further the selection and operation of these components within the scope of this book. For extensive, up-to-date information on these variants and their usage scenarios, please see the SAP HANA Master Guide (available at *http://help.sap.com/hana*).

Further options

Besides the packages we mentioned previously, additional enhancement options are available:

▶ **SAP HANA Smart Data Streaming**
By using this option, you can efficiently process continuous high-frequency data flows as they emerge in the context of machine data, for example. SAP HANA Smart Data Streaming is based on the SAP Event Stream Processor that is also available as a stand-alone product.

▶ **SAP HANA Dynamic Tiering**
This option allows you to enhance the in-memory capacities of an SAP HANA database through disk-based storage (*extended storage*). This is based on the same technology as the column-based *SAP IQ database* and is primarily used for *data aging scenarios* so that older data can be swapped from the main memory to more cost-efficient media.

▶ **SAP HANA Accelerator for SAP ASE**
If you operate the applications on the *SAP Adaptive Server Enterprise (ASE) database*, you can use this variant of SAP HANA as an accelerator for high-performance analyses to attain benefits without implementing a database migration.

▶ **SAP HANA Data Warehousing Foundation**
This option provides tools to obtain even data distribution on individual database servers in distributed SAP HANA systems.

As you've seen, SAP HANA provides several components and add-on packages in addition to the actual in-memory database to provide comprehensive data management. The following section now discusses the core concepts of SAP HANA in more detail with a special focus on the basic principles of in-memory technology.

1.2   Basic Principles of In-Memory Technology

This section describes some of the basic principles of in-memory technology and special innovations in SAP HANA with regard to both hardware and software. Although not all of these aspects have a direct impact on the development of ABAP applications for SAP HANA, it's important to explain the basic concepts of SAP HANA and their implementation to help you understand some of the design recommendations within this book.

In recent years, two major hardware trends dominated not only the SAP world but also the market as a whole:

Hardware trends

▶ Instead of further increasing the clock speed per CPU core, the number of CPU cores per CPU was increased.

▶ Sinking prices for the main memory (RAM) led to increasing memory sizes.

Section 1.2.1 further explains the hardware innovations of SAP HANA.

For software manufacturers, stagnating clock speeds are somewhat problematic at first. In the past, we assumed that clock speeds would increase in the future, so software code would be executed faster on future hardware. With the current trends, however, you can't safely make that assumption. Because you can't increase the speed of sequential executions simply by using future hardware, you instead have to run software code in parallel to reach the desired performance gains. Section 1.2.2 introduces such software optimizations in SAP HANA.

Software optimizations

1.2.1 Hardware Innovations

Hardware partners To benefit from these hardware trends, SAP has been working in close cooperation with hardware manufacturers during the development of SAP HANA. For example, SAP HANA can use special commands that are provided by the CPU manufacturers, such as single instruction, multiple data (SIMD) commands. Consequently, the SAP HANA database for live systems only runs on hardware certified by SAP (see information box).

[»] **Certified Hardware for SAP HANA**

The SAP HANA hardware certified for live systems (appliances and Tailored Datacenter Integration [TDI]) are listed at *https://global.sap.com/community/ebook/2014-09-02-hana-hardware/enEN/index.html*.

In addition to the appliances (combination of hardware and software) from various hardware manufacturers, there are more flexible options within TDI to deploy SAP HANA. SAP HANA also supports variants for operation in virtualized environments. Both options are summarized in the following box.

[»] **Tailored Datacenter Integration and Virtualization**

Within the scope of TDI, you can deploy different hardware components that go beyond the scope of certified appliances. For example, it's possible to use already existing hardware (e.g., storage systems) provided that they meet the SAP HANA requirements. More information on TDI is available at *http://scn.sap.com/docs/DOC-63140*.

SAP HANA can be operated on various virtualized platforms. More information is available in SAP Note 1788665 at *http://scn.sap.com/docs/DOC-60329*.

The premium segment for hardware currently uses Intel's Haswell EX architecture (Intel XEON processor E7 V3 family), which contains up to 16 CPUs per server node with 18 CPU cores each and up to 12TB RAM. Older systems still use the Intel IvyBridge EX architecture (Intel Xeon processor E7 V2 family) with up to 16 CPUs and 15 cores each and up to 12TB RAM or the Intel Westmere EX architecture (Intel Xeon processor E7 V1 family) with up to 8 CPUs with 10 cores each and up to 4TB RAM.

For SAP BW (see Section 1.4), a *scale-out* is possible, where up to 16 server nodes (some manufacturers even allow for up to 56 server nodes) can be combined with up to 3TB RAM. This way, systems with up to 128 CPUs; 1,280 CPU cores; and 48TB RAM can be set up. For internal tests, systems with up to 100 server nodes are currently already combined. Table 1.1 summarizes the data previously discussed.

Hardware Layout	Intel Westmere EX	Intel IvyBridge EX	Intel Haswell EX
Scale-up for SAP Business Suite on SAP HANA (1 server node)	Up to: ▸ 8 CPUs ▸ 10 cores ▸ 4TB	Up to: ▸ 16 CPUs ▸ 15 cores ▸ 12TB	Up to: ▸ 16 CPUs ▸ 18 cores ▸ 12TB
Scale-out (up to 56 server nodes)	Up to: ▸ 8 CPUs ▸ 10 cores ▸ 1TB	Up to: ▸ 8 CPUs ▸ 15 cores ▸ 2TB	Up to: ▸ 8 CPUs ▸ 18 cores ▸ 3TB

Table 1.1 Hardware Examples for Appliances in the Premium Segment

Table 1.1 shows the growing number of CPUs and CPU cores as well as the increasing main memory, which might increase in the future too.

> **SAP HANA on Power** [«]
>
> Since version 9, SAP HANA is also available for the IBM Power platform. You can find more information in SAP Notes 2133369 and 2055470.

Due to the large RAM size, the I/O system (persistent storage) is basi- Access times
cally no longer accessed for reading accesses to SAP HANA (at least, not if all data is loaded into the main memory). In contrast to traditional databases, data transport from the I/O system to the main memory is no longer a bottleneck. Instead, with SAP HANA, the speed of the data transport between the main memory and the CPUs via the different *CPU caches* (there are usually three cache levels) is of central importance. In the following sections, these access times are discussed in more detail.

Hard disks Current hard disks provide 15,000 rpm. Assuming that the disk needs 0.5 rotations on average per access, 2 milliseconds are already needed for these 0.5 rotations. In addition to this, the times for positioning the read/write head and the transfer time must be added, which results in a total of about 6 to 8 milliseconds. This corresponds to the typical hard-disk access times if the actual hard disk (i.e., not a cache in the I/O subsystem or on the hard disk) is accessed.

Flash memory When using flash memory, no mechanical parts need be moved. This results in access times of about 200 microseconds. In SAP HANA, places performance-critical data in this type of memory and then loads the data into the main memory.

Main memory Access to the main memory, (dynamic random access memory, DRAM) is even faster. Typical access times are 60 to 100 nanoseconds. The exact access time depends on the access location within memory. With the nonuniform memory access (*NUMA*) *architecture* used in SAP HANA, a processor can access its own local memory faster than memory that is within the same system but is being managed by other processors. With the currently certified systems, this memory area has a size of up to 12TB.

CPU cache Access times to caches in the CPU are usually indicated as *clock ticks*. For a CPU with a clock speed of 2.4 GHz, for example, a cycle takes about 0.42 nanoseconds. The hardware certified for SAP HANA uses three caches, referred to as *L1*, *L2*, and *L3* caches. L1 cache can be accessed in 3 – 4 clock ticks, L2 cache in about 10 clock ticks, and L3 cache in about 40 clock ticks. L1 cache has a size of up to 64KB, L2 cache of up to 256KB, and L3 cache of up to 45MB. Each CPU comprises only one L3 cache, which is used by all CPU cores, while each CPU core has its own L2 and L1 caches (see Figure 1.2). Table 1.2 lists the typical access times.

The times listed depend not only on the clock speed but also on the configuration settings, the number of memory modules, the memory type, and many other factors. They are provided only as a reference for the typical access times of each memory type. The enormous difference between the hard disk, the main memory, and the CPU caches is decisive.

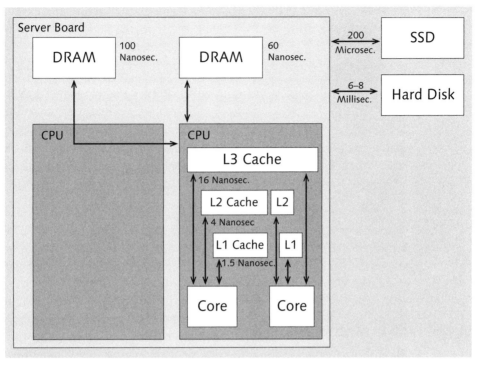

Figure 1.2 Access Times

Memory	Access Time in Nanoseconds	Access Time
Hard disk	6.000.000 – 8.000.000	6 – 8 milliseconds
Flash memory	200.000	200 microseconds
Main memory (DRAM)	60 – 100	60 – 100 nanoseconds
L3 cache (CPU)	~ 16 (about 40 cycles)	~ 16 nanoseconds
L2 cache (CPU)	~ 4 (about 10 cycles)	~ 4 nanoseconds
L1 cache (CPU)	~ 1.5 (about 3 – 4 cycles)	~ 1.5 nanoseconds
CPU register	< 1 (1 cycle)	< 1 nanosecond

Table 1.2 Typical Access Times

When sizing an SAP HANA system, you should assign enough capacity to place all frequently required data in the main memory so that all critical reading accesses can be executed on this memory. When accessing

Main memory as the new bottleneck

the data for the first time (e.g., after starting the system), the data is loaded into the main memory. You can also manually or automatically *unload* the data from the main memory, which might be necessary if, for example, the system tries to use more than the available memory size.

In the past, hard disk accesses usually caused the performance bottleneck; with SAP HANA, however, main memory accesses are now the bottleneck. Even though these accesses are up to 100,000 times faster than hard-disk accesses, they are still 4 to 60 times slower than accesses to CPU caches, which is why the main memory is the new bottleneck for SAP HANA.

The algorithms in SAP HANA are implemented in such a way that they can work directly with the L1 cache in the CPU wherever possible. Data transport from the main memory to the CPU caches must therefore be kept to a minimum, which has major effects on the software innovations described in the next section.

1.2.2 Software Innovations

The software innovations in SAP HANA make optimal use of the previously described hardware in two ways: by keeping the data transport between the main memory and CPU caches to a minimum (e.g., by means of compression), and by fully leveraging the CPUs using parallel threads for data processing.

SAP HANA provides software optimizations in the following areas:

- Data layout in the main memory
- Compression
- Partitioning

These three areas are discussed in more detail in the following subsections.

Data Layout in the Main Memory

In every relational database, the entries of a database table must be stored in a certain *data layout*—independent of whether this representation is done in the main memory (e.g., in SAP HANA) or by following the traditional approach using a physical medium. Two completely different options are available for this: *row-based* and *column-based* data storage. SAP HANA supports both approaches. The concepts and their differences are explained next.

We'll first take a look at row-based data storage in the *row store* of SAP HANA. In this store, all data pertaining to a row (e.g., the data in Table 1.3) are placed next to each other (see Figure 1.3), which facilitates access to entire rows. Accessing all values of a column is a little more complex, however, because these values can't be transferred from the main memory to the CPU as efficiently as in column-based data storage. Data compression, which is explained in the next section, is also less efficient with this storage approach.

Row store

Name	Location	Gender
...	...	...
Brown	Chicago	M
Doe	San Francisco	F
Smith	Dallas	M
...	...	...

Table 1.3 Sample Data to Explain the Row and Column Store

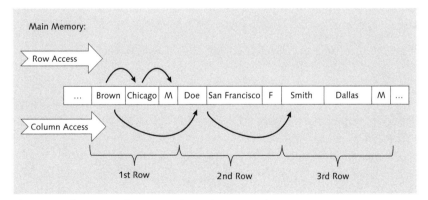

Figure 1.3 Illustration of Row-Based Data Storage in the Row Store

Column store   Let's now take a look at column-based data storage in the *column store*. Column-based data storage is nothing really new; rather, this type of storage was already used in data warehouse applications and analysis scenarios in the past. In transactional scenarios, however, only row-based storage had been used thus far (such as in the row store described already).

Refer to Table 1.3 for a schematic representation of the sample data from Figure 1.4 in column-based storage. The contents of a column are placed next to each other in the main memory. This means that all operations accessing a column will find the required information nearby, which has favorable effects on the data transport between the main memory and the CPU. If a lot of data or all data from a row are needed, however, this approach is disadvantageous because this data isn't nearby. Column-based data storage also facilitates efficient compression and aggregation of data based on a column.

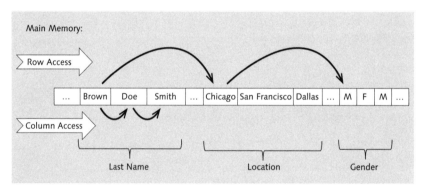

Figure 1.4 Illustration of Column-Based Data Storage in the Column Store

Flexible data storage   As you can see, both approaches have advantages and disadvantages. With SAP HANA, you can specify the storage approach to be used for each table. Business data are almost always placed in column-based storage because the advantages of this approach outweigh its disadvantages. This particularly applies if you need to analyze large amounts of data. However, some tables (or their main access type) require row-based data storage. These are primarily either very small or very volatile tables where the time required for write accesses is more important than the time required for read accesses, or in tables where single-record accesses (e.g., via ABAP command `SELECT SINGLE`) are the main access pattern.

Compression

The SAP HANA database provides a series of compression techniques that can be used for the data in the column store, both in the main memory and in the persistent storage. High data compression has a positive impact on runtime because it reduces the amount of data that needs to be transferred from the main memory to the CPU. SAP HANA's compression techniques are very efficient with regard to runtime, and they can provide an average compression factor of 5 to 10 compared to data that hasn't been compressed.

The compression techniques listed next are based on *dictionary encoding*, where the column contents are stored as encoded integers in the attribute vector. In this context, encoding means "translating" the contents of a field into an integer value.

Dictionary encoding

To store the contents of a column in the column store, the SAP HANA database creates a minimum of two data structures:

► Dictionary vector

► Attribute vector

The *dictionary vector* stores each value of a column only once. This means that the GENDER column for our sample data from Table 1.3 only contains the values "M" and "F" in the corresponding dictionary vector. For the LOCATION column, there are three values: Chicago, San Francisco, and Dallas. The contents of the dictionary vector are stored as sorted data. The position in the dictionary vector maps each value to an integer. In our example, this is 1 for gender "F" and 2 for gender "M". In the dictionary vector for the location, integer 5 stands for Chicago, integer 6 for Dallas, and integer 7 for San Francisco. Because this value can implicitly be derived from its position (first value, second value, etc.), no additional storage is required.

Dictionary vector

The dictionary vectors for the sample data from Table 1.4 are displayed in the upper half of Figure 1.5. Only the data shaded in gray are explicitly stored in memory.

Attribute vector The attribute vector now only stores the integer values (the position in the dictionary). Like traditional databases, the order of the records isn't defined.

Record	Last Name	Location	Gender
…	…	…	…
3	Brown	Chicago	M
4	Brown	San Francisco	F
5	Doe	Dallas	M
6	Doe	San Francisco	F
7	Smith	Dallas	M
…	…	…	…

Table 1.4 Sample Data for Dictionary Encoding and Compression

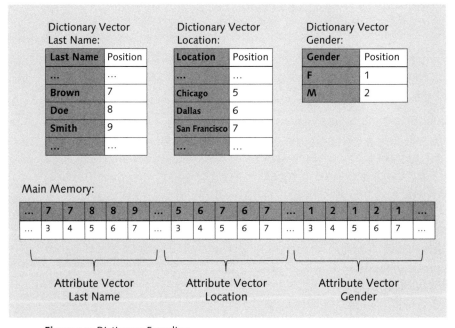

Figure 1.5 Dictionary Encoding

48

The last name "Smith" was placed in the dictionary vector for last names. From its position in this vector, a value can implicitly be derived (the value "9" in our example). This value, again, is now always stored at the position for the last name "Smith" in the attribute vector for the last name; in our example, this is the seventh record of the sample data from Table 1.4. Another example is the location "San Francisco", which is stored at position 7 in the dictionary vector for the location and appears for rows 4 and 6 in the attribute vector for the location (Table 1.4). The attribute vectors are shown in the lower part of Figure 1.5. In this figure, all three attribute vectors are shown consecutively to show that all data (also the dictionary vectors) are stored in a data stream in the main memory and addressed via memory references and offsets. Here, only the sections shaded in gray in Figure 1.5 are actually stored in the main memory. The row numbers displayed below those sections don't need any storage space and are again derived implicitly from their position in the attribute vector. They correspond to the position in our example of Table 1.4 (first record, second record, etc.).

The fact that the data are only stored as integer values in the attribute vectors provides the following advantages:

> **Advantages of storing integer values**

► Lower storage requirements for values that occur several times

► Accelerated data transfer from the main memory to CPU caches because less data needs to be transported

► Faster processing of integer values (instead of strings) in the CPU

Moreover, additional compression techniques can be used for both dictionary vectors and attribute vectors. These are introduced in more detail later on.

For the dictionary vector, *delta compression* is used for *strings*. With this compression technique, every character from a string in a block with 16 entries, for example, is stored only once in a delta string. Repeated characters are stored as references.

> **Compression in the dictionary vector**

Delta Compression   [Ex]

The following entries are present: Brian, Britain, Brush, Bus. After delta compression, this results in the following: 5Brian34tain23ush12us. The first digit indicates the length of the first entry (Brian = 5). The digit pairs between the other entries contain the information for reconstruction. The first digit indicates the length of the prefix from the first entry; the second digit indicates the number of characters that are appended by the subsequent part. Consequently, "34tain" means that the first three characters from Brian ("Bri") are used and that four more characters are added ("tain"). "23ush" means that the first two characters from "Brian" are used and three more characters ("ush") are added. "12us" means that one character from "Brian" is used and that two more characters are added ("us").

For the attribute vector, you can use one of the following compression techniques:

▸ **Prefix encoding**
Identical values at the beginning of the attribute vector (prefixes) are left out; instead, a value and the number of its occurrences is stored only once.

▸ **Sparse encoding**
The individual records from the value with the most occurrences are removed; instead, the positions of these entries are stored in a bit vector.

▸ **Cluster encoding**
Cluster encoding uses data blocks of perhaps 1,024 values each. Only blocks with a different value are compressed by storing only the value. Information on the compressed blocks is then stored in a bit vector.

▸ **Indirect encoding**
Indirect encoding also uses data blocks of 1,024 values each. For every block, a mini-dictionary is created that is similar to the dictionary vector in the dictionary encoding described previously. In some cases, a mini-dictionary may be shared for adjacent blocks. This compression technique provides another level of abstraction.

▸ **Run-length encoding**
With run-length encoding, identical successive values are combined into one single data value. This value is then stored only once together with the number of its occurrences.

SAP HANA analyzes the data in a column and then automatically chooses one of the compression techniques described. Table 1.5 presents a typical application case for each compression technique.

Compression Technique	Application Case
Prefix encoding	A very frequent value at the beginning of the attribute vector
Sparse encoding	A very frequent value occurring at several positions
Cluster encoding	Many blocks with only one value
Indirect encoding	Many blocks with few different values
Run-length encoding	A few different values, consecutive identical values
Dictionary encoding	Many different values

Table 1.5 Overview of Compression Techniques

The memory structures presented so far (consisting of sorted dictionary vectors and attribute vectors with integer values), which might still be compressed in some cases, are optimized for read access. These structures are also referred to as the *main store*. They aren't optimally suited for write accesses, however. For this reason, SAP HANA provides an additional area that is optimized for write access: the *delta store*. This store is explained in detail in Appendix C. In this appendix, another memory structure is also described: indexes. Moreover, Appendix C explains why SAP HANA is called an *insert-only database*.

Partitioning

Let's now take a look at the third area of software innovation: partitioning. Partitioning is used whenever very large quantities of data must be maintained and managed.

This technique greatly facilitates data management for database administrators. A typical task is the deletion of data (such as after an archiving operation was completed successfully). There is no need to search large amounts of information for the data to be deleted; instead, database administrators can simply remove an entire partition. Moreover, partitioning can increase application performance by only reading those partitions in which the data required occur (*partition pruning*).

There are basically two technical variants of partitioning:

- ▶ **Vertical partitioning**
  Tables are divided into smaller sections on a column basis. For example, for a table with seven columns, columns 1 to 5 are stored in one partition, while columns 6 and 7 are stored in a different partition.

- ▶ **Horizontal partitioning**
  Tables are divided into smaller sections on a row basis. For example, rows 1 to 1,000,000 are stored in one partition, while rows 1,000,001 to 2,000,000 are placed in another partition.

SAP HANA supports only horizontal partitioning. The data in a table are distributed across different partitions on a row basis, while the records within the partitions are stored on a column basis.

The example in Figure 1.6 shows how horizontal partitioning is used for a table with the two columns—NAME and GENDER—for column-based data storage.

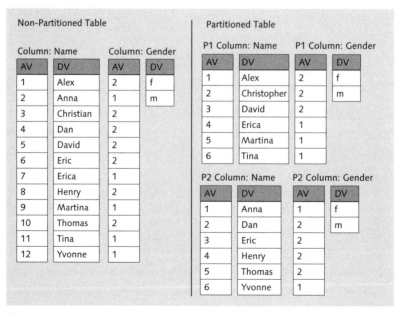

Figure 1.6 Partitioned Table

On the left side, the table is shown with a dictionary vector (DV) and an attribute vector (AV) for both the column NAME and the column GENDER. On the right side, the data was partitioned using the round-robin technique, which is explained in more detail next. The consecutive rows were distributed across two partitions by turns (the first row was stored in the first partition, the second row in the second partition, the third row again in the first partition, etc.).

Partitioning should be used in the following application scenarios: Application cases

▸ **Load distribution**
   If SAP HANA runs on multiple servers, the data from very large tables can be distributed across several servers by storing the individual partitions of the tables on different servers. Table queries are then distributed across the servers where a partition of the table is stored. This way, the resources of several computers can be used for a query, and several computers can process the query in parallel.

▸ **Parallelization**
   Parallelization is not only possible across multiple servers but also on a single server. When a query is run, a separate thread is started for each partition, and these processes are processed in parallel in the partitions. Note that parallelization across partitions is only one variant of parallelization in SAP HANA. There are other types of parallelization that can be used independent of partitioned tables.

▸ **Partition pruning**
   With partition pruning, the database (or the database *optimizer*) recognizes that certain partitions don't need to be read. For example, if a table containing sales data is partitioned based on the SALES ORGANIZATION column so that every sales organization is stored in a separate partition, only a certain partition is read when a query is run that needs data just from the sales organization in that partition; the other partitions aren't read. This process reduces the data transport between the main memory and CPU.

▸ **Explicit partition handling**
   In some cases, partitions are specifically used by applications. For example, if a table is partitioned based on the MONTH column, an application can create a new partition for a new month and delete old

data from a previous month by deleting the entire partition. Deleting this data is very efficient because administrators don't need to search for the information to be deleted; they can simply delete the entire partition using a *Data Definition Language (DDL) statement.*

[»] **Partitioning to Circumvent the Row Limit**

The SAP HANA database has a limit of two billion rows per table. If a table should comprise more rows, it must be partitioned. Each partition must again not contain more than two billion rows. The same limit applies to temporary tables that are, for example, used to store interim results.

Partitioning types in SAP HANA

Now that you're familiar with the concept of partitioning and suitable application scenarios, let's consider the types of partitioning available in SAP HANA:

▶ **Hash partitioning**
Hash partitioning is primarily used for load distribution or in situations where tables with more than two billion records must be maintained. With this type of partitioning, data is distributed evenly across the specified number of partitions based on a calculated key (*hash*). Hash partitioning supports partition pruning.

▶ **Round-robin**
With round-robin partitioning, data are also distributed evenly across a specified number of partitions so that this type is also suitable for load distribution or for very large tables. Round-robin partitioning doesn't require a key; instead, the data are simply distributed in sequence. If a table is divided into two partitions, for example, the first record is stored in the first partition, the second record is stored in the second partition, the third record is again stored in the first partition, and so on (see Figure 1.6). Round-robin partitioning doesn't support partition pruning.

▶ **Range partitioning**
With range partitioning, the data are distributed based on values in a column. You can, for example, create a partition for every year of a YEAR column or create a partition for three months of a MONTH column. In addition, you can create a partition for *remainders* if records

are inserted that don't belong in any of the ranges of the partitions you created. Range partitioning supports partition pruning.

These partitioning types can be combined in a two-step approach. For instance, you could use hash partitioning in the first step and then, in a second step, use range partitioning within this hash partitioning.

1.3 Architecture of the In-Memory Database

This section introduces important aspects of the SAP HANA database architecture. Figure 1.7 shows the main components of the architecture.

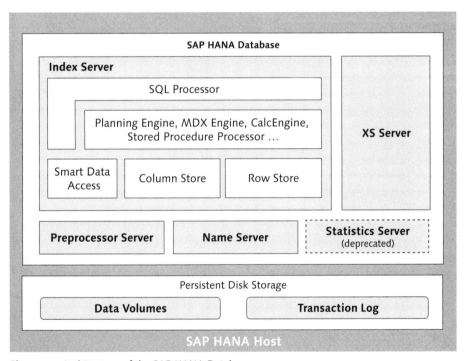

Figure 1.7 Architecture of the SAP HANA Database

The following section provides a detailed description of all these architecture components, which can be subdivided into two component types:

Server and engine components

▸ **Server**

Server components are processes and services that are run on the OS.

▸ **Engines**

Engine are functional components within a server that are used to handle certain queries.

Structure
An SAP HANA system consists of an instance (or several instances in case of scale-out), which each run on a host system. This instance comprises a disk memory that is used for secure persistence of data and log files, for example, to read data again from the main memory after a system restart. We'll discuss the individual server processes of an SAP HANA instance in more detail in the following.

[»] **Multitenant Database Container**

As of SAP HANA SPS 9, you can manage several independent databases within an SAP HANA system. This allows you to separate independent applications and assign resources to the respective databases. This installation option is particularly beneficial for operation in a cloud environment because it allows you to organize the usage of SAP HANA hardware efficiently by several users. We won't discuss these *multitenant database containers* in more detail within the scope of this book. Suffice it to say that while the OS and the database software are used jointly by the individual databases, the content of the databases is completely separated, and they thus implement a different approach than the client supports in the ABAP AS.

Index server
An SAP HANA database comprises several server components; the most important one is the *index server*, which is used to process SQL commands. The index server itself contains several components: The *SQL processor* receives and accepts the SQL commands and either runs them directly or forwards the commands to a subordinate component. These subordinate components can be either central data storage (i.e., the column store or the row store) or one of the engines. All data that are currently being used are either stored in the column store or in the row store. These data are read directly from these stores or, for complex queries, processed via one of the engines. Multiple engines can be used for activities such as planning functions, MDX, or database procedures

(*stored procedures*). These engines all were optimized for special data processing tasks that can be called if required.

The *preprocessor server* is used for the text-search function integrated in SAP HANA and primarily analyzes text data. If needed, this server is called by the index server.

Preprocessor, statistics, and name server

The *statistics server* is used for monitoring the SAP HANA database. It collects information on status, performance, and resource consumption of the individual components, and it creates historical views based on this data in a dedicated schema (_SYS_STATISTICS). SAP HANA Studio accesses this information via the statistics server.

Embedded Statistics Server as of SAP HANA SPS 7   **[+]**

As of SAP HANA SPS 7, you can operate the recording of statistics data as part of the index server and not as a separate server process. SAP recommends using this option, but it requires a configuration setting for compatibility reasons. You can find details on the changes in SAP Note 2092033.

The *name server* manages the information via the topology of the SAP HANA system; that is, it knows the various hosts and the distribution of data to the hosts.

Section 1.1.4 already discussed the application sever that is included in SAP HANA. The *XS server* comprises the HTTP server and the XS runtime environment that distributes queries to the respective components. Therefore, functions that are implemented with server-side JavaScript are executed within an embedded JavaScript runtime. Here the XS runtime efficiently interacts with the index server and particularly with the SAP HANA repository, which manages the development objects.

XS server

Integration with an External User Administration   **[«]**

Besides the local administration of users, you can also integrate SAP HANA with an external user administration and specifically support single sign-on (SSO) scenarios. In this context, SAP HANA supports established standards such as *Kerberos* and *Security Assertion Markup Language (SAML)*. Details on this topic are available in the SAP HANA Security Guide.

1.4   Application Cases and Deployment Options for SAP HANA

This section provides an overview of the various application cases and deployment models for SAP HANA.

1.4.1   Application Cases

The following describes four application cases for SAP HANA:

▶ Real-time analyses

▶ Accelerators

▶ Data warehousing

▶ New applications

Real-Time Analyses

Historically, the SAP HANA database was primarily used for analyzing large data volumes in real time. This application case is still widespread today. Here, SAP HANA serves as a data mart in which you store partial datasets for reporting and data analysis.

Side-by-side scenarios
Frequently, the data that is required for real-time analysis is replicated from SAP systems and particularly from SAP Business Suite. SAP HANA is then used as a *secondary database* in addition to an existing traditional database (*primary database* of the SAP system), which is why this is often referred to as a *side-by-side scenario*.

Figure 1.8 shows the architecture of side-by-side scenarios and visualizes the accelerators that are described in the next section.

You can often achieve significant speed benefits by shifting the data analysis from a traditional database to the SAP HANA database.

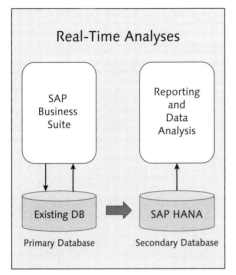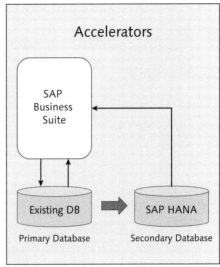

Figure 1.8 Architecture of Side-by-Side Scenarios

SAP HANA Live [«]

SAP HANA Live is a virtual, multilevel data model in the database tables of SAP Business Suite for usage within the scope of a data mart. SAP provides predefined reports and analytical applications based on this data model. They enable enterprises to evaluate the data of SAP Business Suite in real time. Here it's irrelevant whether SAP HANA is used as a primary or secondary database.

You can find more detailed information on SAP HANA Live at *http://help.sap.com/hba*.

Accelerators

Accelerators (which also represent a side-by-side scenario) are used to accelerate selected business processes. They are usually represented by ABAP programs or transactions within SAP Business Suite.

For acceleration—as in the previous application case—data are replicated from the traditional database to the SAP HANA database, and then selected reading database accesses within the application are redirected to SAP HANA (see Figure 1.8). The redirection of database accesses can

59

be implemented using various procedures. In most cases, this redirection is done via separate database connections and small changes to the ABAP source code.

SAP CO-PA Accelerator

The SAP Cost Profitability Analysis (CO-PA) accelerator is used to implement an accelerator scenario and is probably one of the best-known examples of a side-by-side scenario. However, there are more implementation examples. An overview can be found in SAP Note 1761546.

You can also accelerate customer-developed ABAP programs using an accelerator scenario. For the *SAP Business Application Accelerator powered by SAP HANA* (see Appendix D), redirection is done via a special SAP kernel and adjustments in Customizing. Note that it's not necessary to change the ABAP source code for this accelerator.

Data Warehousing

The next important application case for the SAP HANA database is data warehousing. By using the SAP HANA database as a database for SAP BW, you can usually improve performance and simplify administration.

The performance of SAP BW benefits from the in-memory technology. By deploying SAP HANA, you can often accelerate not only queries but also load processes. The option of avoiding "unnecessary" database aggregates frequently simplifies the data modeling.

New Applications

The last application case involves applications that were developed specifically for SAP HANA or were migrated to SAP HANA and subsequently optimized.

SAP Business Suite

First, we should mention SAP Business Suite. Since 2013, SAP Business Suite has been available on the basis of SAP HANA (*SAP Business Suite on SAP HANA*). Since then, SAP has incrementally optimized parts of the SAP Business Suite code for the in-memory technology. However, besides the SAP HANA database, SAP Business Suite also supports traditional databases as persistence storage.

This spring, SAP announced *SAP S/4HANA* (*SAP Business Suite 4 SAP HANA*). This is a new product that only supports SAP HANA as persistence storage. From the technical perspective, SAP S/4HANA corresponds to SAP Business Suite on SAP HANA and add-ons that are based on this suite. These add-ons are referred to as *exchange innovations* because they gradually replace and optimize the system's entire code. Wherever possible, the data model of SAP S/4HANA waives aggregates and index tables. This results in significant simplification and reduces the memory required.

In addition to SAP Business Suite or SAP S/4HANA, SAP has developed numerous other applications based on the in-memory technology, such as the following two examples:

Completely new applications

- *SAP Fraud Management* for uncovering, examining, and preventing fraud
- *SAP Integrated Business Planning for Sales and Operations* for planning the supply chain

In many cases, the completely new applications partially use data from SAP Business Suite and write results back to the suite. For this reason, this is often also referred to as a side-by-side scenario.

1.4.2 Deployment Options

Roughly speaking, two deployment models can be distinguished for SAP HANA:

- On-premise deployments
- Cloud deployments

Both models are discussed next.

On-Premise Deployments

Enterprises can install and operate SAP HANA in their own datacenters. As described in Section 1.2.1, appliances, TDI, as well as virtualization are available for this purpose. On-premise deployments provide enterprises with maximum flexibility and control of their SAP HANA database.

Cloud Deployments

In simple terms, cloud computing enables enterprises to use "remote" datacenters for the installation and operation of SAP HANA. We won't define cloud computing and particularly the various technical implementation at this point. Three cloud offers are relevant for SAP HANA:

▸ **SAP HANA Cloud Platform**
  SAP HANA Cloud Platform is a *Platform-as-a-Service (PaaS)*. On this platform, enterprises can develop new applications or enhance existing applications (e.g., SAP Business Suite or SAP SuccessFactors). SAP HANA Cloud Platform provides most functions that SAP HANA also offers on-premise. In addition, it offers numerous application services, for example, a cloud-based portal, a cloud-based identity provider, and an integration service.

▸ **SAP HANA Enterprise Cloud**
  SAP HANA Enterprise Cloud is a *managed cloud offer* where interested enterprises have SAP operate entire system landscapes that consist of SAP Business Suite, SAP BW, and customer-specific applications. They are provided with numerous services from which they can compile a "tailored" offer.

▸ **Usage of Infrastructure-as-a-Service providers**
  Enterprises that don't install SAP HANA on-premise and don't want to use a PaaS or managed cloud offer either can operate the SAP HANA database at various *Infrastructure-as-a-Service (IaaS) providers*. In this context, we particularly want to mention the offers of *Amazon Web Service s (AWS)* and *Microsoft Azure*. More information is available on the websites of the respective providers.

This book focuses on the usage of SAP HANA in the context of ABAP-based applications, specifically SAP Business Suite on SAP HANA and SAP S/4HANA. We won't discuss the specifics of deployment models, however.

1.5   How SAP HANA Affects Application Development

Having explained the basic principles of the in-memory technology, the architecture of the SAP HANA database, as well as application cases and deployment models, you may now be asking yourself how the described hardware and software innovations affect application development with ABAP. This question is answered in the following section.

Note that not everything changes when implementing SAP HANA. Like in the past, you can develop powerful applications using ABAP even if these applications use SAP HANA as a database. Many of the rules for ABAP programming that you're familiar with (e.g., the rules for efficient database access, that is, the *five golden rules*; see Chapter 14, Section 14.4) will essentially still be valid.

Many rules are still valid

So what changes for application development in ABAP? In the following section, we'll describe the technical options that benefit ABAP developers when using SAP HANA, and we'll explain the *code pushdown* concept. You'll learn why the database can no longer be considered a *black box* in the future, and which skills you should acquire.

1.5.1   New Technical Options

Using SAP HANA, you can support several application scenarios—as described in Section 1.4.1. From an ABAP developer's point of view, using SAP HANA provides the following new technical options:

Optimization potential

▶ **Accelerate**
Using SAP HANA, you can accelerate existing ABAP programs. On the one hand, this allows you to reduce the time needed to run background jobs significantly. On the other hand, you can improve the immediate response time for queries triggered by end users within dialog transactions.

▶ **Extend**
You can use SAP HANA to customize and extend existing applications in a way that goes beyond solely accelerating these applications. Some ABAP programs that could only be run as background jobs in the past

due to their response behavior can now be converted into interactive dialog transactions with SAP HANA. Moreover, you can enhance usability and functionality of ABAP dialog transactions by implementing SAP HANA. Such improvements include embedded analyses and fault-tolerant full-text searches.

▸ **Innovate**
Finally, you can develop new, innovative applications and application types using ABAP and SAP HANA. In this context, convergence of *Online Transaction Processing* (OLTP), *Online Analytical Processing* (OLAP), and *hybrid applications* are often mentioned. Hybrid applications combine transactional and analytical functions within a single system so that end users can take direct steps based on insights gained in real time from data analyses (e.g., supported by statistical algorithms for predictions based on historic data).

1.5.2 Code Pushdown

For applications that take advantage of the hardware and software innovations in SAP HANA described in Section 1.2, at least part of the application logic must be executed in the database. This is especially important if complex calculations with large data amounts must be performed. The process of moving application code from the application layer to the database layer is often referred to as *code pushdown*.

Various paradigms
Traditionally, ABAP-based applications use the *data-to-code paradigm*. Applications optimized or developed specifically for SAP HANA, however, use the *code-to-data paradigm*. The remainder of this subsection describes the differences between the two paradigms.

Data-to-code
As you can see in Figure 1.9, the application data is placed in the database layer when using the data-to-code paradigm. Basically, the application logic—comprised of orchestration logic and calculation logic—is executed entirely in the application layer. The presentation logic is executed in the presentation layer.

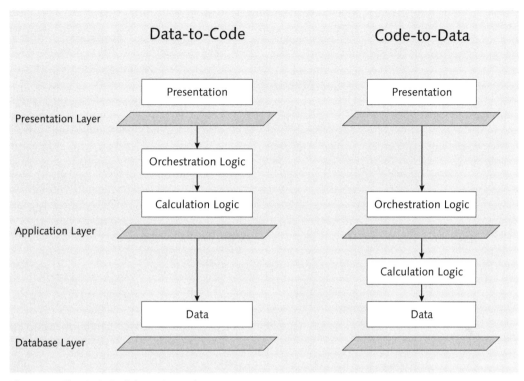

Figure 1.9 The Code Pushdown Principle

Elements of the Application Logic   **[«]**

In the following, the application logic is subdivided into two sections:

▸ The *orchestration logic* controls business processes and the data flow and determines how calculation results are combined and further processed.
  Example: After a flight booking is saved, the system automatically sends an email to the traveler.

▸ The *calculation logic* identifies algorithms used to perform calculations based on the application data.
  Example: To suggest the "best" flight to a traveler, the system analyzes historical flight and booking data prior to a booking and then calculates a score per flight.

For ABAP programs, the following occurs: A data-to-code application reads the records from the database. The records are then buffered in internal tables of the application server. The application logic is implemented based on this principle. For presentation, the records or the data calculated based on these records are transferred to the frontend—SAP GUI, SAP Enterprise Portal, or SAP NetWeaver Business Client (NWBC). With this procedure, it's possible to send millions of records from the database to the application server, even though only a few hundred calculated key figures will be displayed for the end user.

Code-to-data   When using the code-to-data paradigm, the application data is also placed in the database layer. However, some of the application logic is executed in the application layer, while some of it's implemented in the database layer. In an extreme case, the entire application logic can be executed in the database layer. Nothing fundamentally changes in the execution of the presentation logic.

When applying this paradigm to an ABAP program, the following occurs: The data of a code-to-data application is stored in the database. The orchestration logic is implemented on the application server. The calculation logic is usually executed in the database. The more complex a calculation is and the more records needed for the calculation, the more valuable is the execution in the database. With this approach, the amount of data transferred from the database to the application server can be kept to a minimum. Even if millions of records are needed for a calculation, the system only transfers the few hundred calculated key figures that the user should see.

1.5.3   Database as White Box

Thanks to the architecture of AS ABAP and the database independence of *Open SQL*, you can develop ABAP applications without knowing database-specific details. Chapter 3, Section 3.2 describes all important elements of database access from ABAP applications in detail.

Open SQL   Using Open SQL, you can perform operations on the database of the application server. Open SQL provides a unified syntax and unified semantics for all database systems supported by SAP. The result of the operations and potential error messages are independent of the database system, which means programs that only use Open SQL can be run on all database systems supported by SAP.

In addition to Open SQL, Native SQL can also be used. With Native SQL, you can use database-specific operations that aren't supported by Open SQL. However, the disadvantage of Native SQL is that programs using database-specific operations can't be run on all database systems supported by SAP. This is probably the reason why you've only used Native SQL and database-specific operations in exceptional cases in the past. The database was usually a *black box*, or a closed system with an internal structure that didn't need to be considered.

Native SQL

However, if the application logic, or at least part of it, is now to be executed (and possibly implemented) in the database, knowledge of database-specific (or better, SAP HANA-specific) details is very helpful. To really benefit from SAP HANA and achieve optimum performance, the database must become a *white box*. In particular, you must understand the following aspects:

From a black box to a white box

▸ How can application code be moved from the application layer to the database layer?

▸ To what extent is moving the application code possible when using Open SQL?

▸ What options are provided by the SQL standard and SAP HANA-specific extensions in this regard (e.g., modeled or implemented SAP HANA Views and SQLScript)?

▸ How can you use these options in ABAP?

When optimizing programs for SAP HANA, you should always ask yourself if these programs should also be used on different database systems (which is often the case). If a program is to be used not only on SAP HANA but also on other systems, you carefully need to weigh the pros and cons of optimizing it with SAP HANA Views or SQLScript (as you had to when using Native SQL in the past). You could, for example, have significantly better performance. A disadvantage, however, is the database-dependent application code that results from this optimization.

The risk of complexity

In general, you should only use Native SQL, SAP HANA Views, and SQLScript if optimization using Open SQL doesn't result in the desired outcome (e.g., with regard to the response behavior) (see Chapter 14). Here you should consider that the functional scope of Open SQL was significantly enhanced in ABAP Release 7.4. Furthermore, as of this release, the CDS provide you with manifold options for view creation in ABAP. For more details, see Chapter 6.

Modularization
units

Within a program—or generally speaking, within modularization units—you can distinguish between application code for SAP HANA and application code for other database systems using case distinctions, that is, by using `IF... ENDIF`. In some cases, if the application code would otherwise become too complex, you might need to create several alternative implementations of a modularization unit. In the extreme case, you have to develop a separate program for every database system.

[Ex]

Alternative Implementations

Alternative implementations for a modularization unit might look like the following:

- One implementation for SAP HANA that uses SAP HANA-specific options and one Open SQL-based implementation for all other database systems supported by SAP.
- One implementation for SAP HANA, one implementation for Oracle, one implementation for IBM DB2, and so on. With this approach, each implementation is optimized for the respective database system.

Code pushdown might lead to greater complexity of programs that are to support both SAP HANA and other database systems. Chapter 14, Section 14.1, will pick up this topic again.

1.5.4 Required Qualifications for Developers

How should ABAP developers deal with the impact of SAP HANA on application development? It's certainly not enough simply to understand the impacts described. To optimize existing applications and develop new applications or application types based on ABAP and SAP HANA, developers need to gain expertise. You should make sure to acquire this knowledge at an early stage.

SQL and
SAP HANA

From our point of view, you should gain detailed knowledge of the latest options of Open SQL and CDS (if you're not already highly skilled with these two options), but should also familiarize yourself with technologies of the SQL standard and the SAP HANA database that go beyond Open SQL. You should know how to model SAP HANA Views and how to use SQLScript for more complex requirements both in SAP HANA Views and within database processes.

To optimize existing applications for SAP HANA—especially with regard to their performance—you need to know which programs and *code patterns* within these programs are particularly suitable candidates. You should familiarize yourself with the development tools used to identify suitable programs for code pushdown, and you should be able to perform a runtime analysis to examine the identified programs thoroughly.

Performance analysis and optimization

Altogether, we assume that sound knowledge in the areas of performance analysis and performance optimization with regard to the in-memory technology will become (even) more important than in the past for traditional databases.

To develop new applications that process large data amounts using SAP HANA, the application architecture must be designed accordingly from the start. The performance of SAP HANA must be noticeable for the end user. It might not be sufficient to perform calculations with a high performance. The results of these calculations must also be displayed to the user very quickly and in simple and intuitive views. You should therefore also familiarize yourself with technologies for developing modern UIs.

New UI technologies

And finally, you should understand the impact SAP HANA has on the known rules of ABAP programming. As already mentioned at the beginning of Section 1.5, many rules are essentially still valid. However, some rules now have a different priority; for instance, compared to using traditional databases, they are now more or less important when implementing SAP HANA. For example, avoiding many individual SQL statements (such as in a loop) is now more important than in the past.

Old and new rules

At the same time, new guidelines will help you create several alternative implementations of a modularization unit so that a program can be run optimally, for example, both on the SAP HANA database and on traditional databases. ABAP developers should be familiar with those new guidelines as well. Details on all of these guidelines are provided in Chapter 14.

ABAP development for SAP HANA is closely linked to SAP's latest development tools, which are based on the Eclipse platform. ABAP developers require a basic understanding of this platform and, in particular, should become familiar with both the ABAP Development Tools for SAP NetWeaver and SAP HANA Studio.

2   Introducing the Development Environment

In the past, ABAP developers used the SAP GUI-based ABAP Workbench to develop, adjust, and test programs. However, SAP's new development tools are based on the Eclipse platform. Furthermore, SAP is migrating some of its existing development tools to Eclipse.

At the start of this chapter, we'll explain Eclipse and the significance of this platform for SAP. We'll then introduce you to the ABAP Development Tools for SAP NetWeaver, which is the new Eclipse-based development environment for ABAP—as well as SAP HANA Studio, which is the administration and development environment for the SAP HANA database. We'll also discuss how to install these development environments.

2.1   Overview of Eclipse

Eclipse is an open-source framework with which you can develop any type of software. IBM developed Eclipse originally, but it has been maintained and developed by the Eclipse Foundation (*http://eclipse.org*) since 2004. Eclipse is known particularly as a platform for development tools and environments.

Open-source framework

One of the main strengths of Eclipse is the capability to integrate different tools—such as *Java Development Tools* (JDT), *C/C++ Development*

Tools (CDT), or ABAP Development Tools—into one installation so that the user benefits from a homogeneous development environment.

Enhancement options and plug-ins

Eclipse technically defines *enhancement options*, which can be used by plug-ins to integrate with Eclipse. A plug-in enhances the functional scope of Eclipse. Every plug-in is described by an XML file (the *manifest*) and is implemented in Java. Every plug-in can also provide its own enhancement options for other plug-ins that are based on this plug-in.

Eclipse SDK

Eclipse provides the *Eclipse Software Development Toolkit* (Eclipse SDK) for developing plug-ins—and for developing Java applications in general.

Figure 2.1 shows the structure of the Eclipse SDK and how the tools integrate in Eclipse on various levels and through enhancement options. As you can see, Eclipse SDK has three components:

- Eclipse platform
- Plug-In Development Environment (PDE)
- Java Development Tools (JDT)

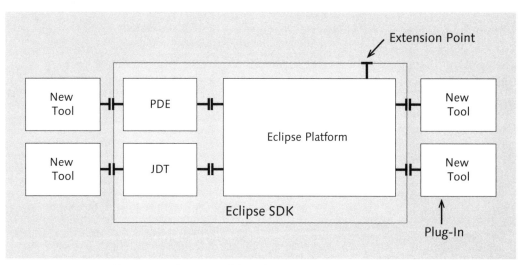

Figure 2.1 Architecture of the Eclipse SDK

The Eclipse platform provides a framework for development tools and contains reusable user interface (UI) modules. This is helpful, for example, when implementing help systems and connecting version control systems.

You use the PDE to create the manifest for a plug-in, while you use the JDT to implement the plug-in in Java (and for Java development in general). Technically, the PDE and JDT are also implemented as plug-ins for Eclipse.

The Eclipse Foundation coordinates the maintenance and further development of Eclipse. In particular, it handles the following:

- ▶ IT infrastructure
- ▶ Copyright
- ▶ Development process
- ▶ Ecosystem

The Eclipse Foundation organizes the development process on the basis of projects. These projects, known as *Eclipse projects*, handle the further development of the Eclipse platform, PDE, and JDT, among other things. There are also a number of other projects (e.g., Eclipse Modeling Project, the Mylyn Project, and the Eclipse Web Tools Platform Project). We don't examine these projects here, but further information is available at *www.eclipse.org/projects/*.

Each year, in an effort to synchronize the various projects, the Eclipse Foundation releases all projects at the end of July in one composite release (known as the *Eclipse Release Train*). The current composite release is called *Luna*. Figure 2.2 provides an overview of the past six composite releases and their scope in terms of the number of projects involved and the number of program lines (*lines of code*, LOC). Sources are the *2014 Annual Community Report* as well as the Eclipse Foundation's press release, "Eclipse Luna Release Train Now Available" on June 26, 2014.

The composite releases are important for ensuring that all development tools based on Eclipse can work together without any problems (at least while they follow the Eclipse Foundation's development process).

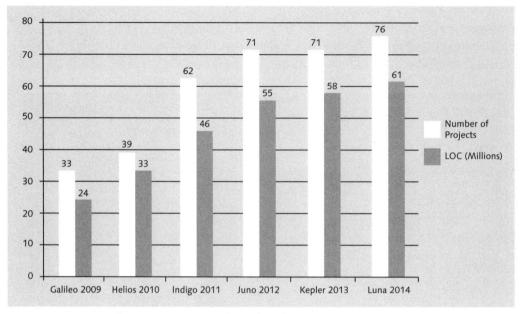

Figure 2.2 Composite Releases by Eclipse

2.2 SAP's Eclipse Strategy

Heterogeneous tools

Today, developers have to work with different tools to develop SAP applications. The tools, for example, *ABAP Workbench*, *SAP NetWeaver Developer Studio*, and *Enterprise Services Repository* (part of *SAP Process Integration*), are based on different technologies. They sometimes don't follow the same operating concept, have different underlying lifecycle management concepts, and occasionally don't (ideally) work together.

Desktop and web Eclipse as a strategic platform

In the future, SAP wants to follow a dual strategy with regard to development tools via desktop-based and web-based development tools. For ABAP development for SAP HANA, however, only the desktop-based tools play a role. For this reason, we want to discuss briefly the approach that SAP is taking for those tools.

To achieve a holistic operating concept and lifecycle management for all desktop-based development tools deployed in the SAP context and integrate them optimally, SAP decided to use the Eclipse platform as a strategic basis for new desktop-based development tools. Additionally, SAP migrates some of the existing development tools to Eclipse.

However, the decision to develop new development tools based on Eclipse doesn't solve the problem of heterogeneous tools. It's good if various development tools are based on Eclipse and even follow the same operating concept. However, if the tools use different Eclipse versions, the users are forced to provide several Eclipse installations. That is why SAP, similar to the Eclipse Foundation, provides a composite release for Eclipse-based development tools: the *SAP Release Train for Eclipse*.

SAP Release Train for Eclipse

The purpose of the SAP Release Train for Eclipse is to ensure that various development tools can coexist in an Eclipse installation, to ensure the unbundling of Eclipse and SAP software, and to provide a central update site for installing and updating development tools.

2.2.1 Unbundling of Eclipse and SAP Software

In the past, SAP frequently delivered Eclipse-based development tools in the form of installation programs (they still exist today for some tools). These installation programs generally don't make it possible to integrate different development tools into one Eclipse installation. Instead, each installation program generates its own Eclipse installation, and, as a result, the user has to switch among multiple development environments to use different tools (even if the tools are based on the same version of Eclipse).

Problem of installation programs

However, the use of other installation mechanisms, specifically a *repository* or update site, enables Eclipse and SAP software to be unbundled. Consequently, all of the tools following the SAP Release Train for Eclipse are available in one development environment.

2.2.2 Central Update Site

Equinox P2
Update Sites

Equinox P2 is a platform for adding or updating software components in an existing Eclipse installation (see also *http://projects.eclipse.org/projects/rt.equinox.p2*). The basic concept here is that a software component is stored in a self-descriptive repository that is typically made available as an *update site* on an HTTP server. However, it can also be stored in a file system as a compressed archive file. If the Eclipse installation recognizes the repository, it can install or (automatically) update the software from there. If Eclipse identifies dependencies on software components stored in another known repository during the process of adding or updating software, it can automatically download these from the repository. Figure 2.3 provides a graphical representation of the update site concept.

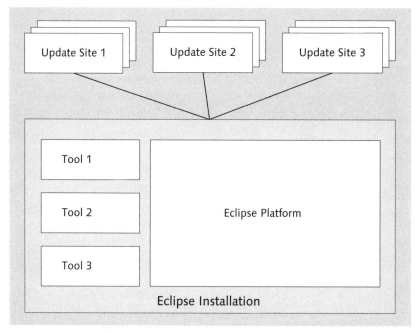

Figure 2.3 Update Site Concept

SAP provides the following central update site for tools associated with the SAP Release Train for Eclipse: *https://tools.hana.ondemand.com/*. To some extent, however, you can also download the repositories for the development tools from SAP Service Marketplace and then run your own update site, for example.

At present, the following development tools are affiliated with the SAP Release Train for Eclipse and are available on the update site:

- ABAP Development Tools for SAP NetWeaver
- Modeling Tools for SAP BW powered by SAP HANA
- SAP HANA Cloud Platform Tools
- SAP Mobile Platform Tools
- SAP HANA Tools (i.e., SAP HANA Studio)
- SAP HANA Cloud Integration Tools
- SAP Identity Management Configuration Lifecycle Tools
- UI Development Toolkit for HTML5

2.3   Installing the Development Environment

Now that we've given you some background information about Eclipse and its significance for SAP, we'll explain how you can set up a development environment for ABAP development for SAP HANA. We'll consider the installation of a development environment only conceptually. In other words, our explanations will in no way replace the installation guides valid at the time of installation.

We'll install Eclipse (Luna release) first. Then we'll add SAP HANA Studio and ABAP Development Tools for SAP NetWeaver to the Eclipse installation. As already mentioned in the introduction, our consideration is based on the following: SAP NetWeaver Application Server (AS) ABAP 7.4 (SP 10), ABAP Development Tools for SAP NetWeaver 2.44, and SAP HANA 1.0 (SPS 9). We'll assume that you've already installed the ABAP AS and the SAP HANA database.

Steps

2.3.1   Installing the Eclipse IDE for Java Developers

Eclipse IDE for Java Developers is the basis of your development environment for ABAP development for SAP HANA. You can download it readily

Download and unpack

77

at *www.eclipse.org/downloads/*. It's available for various system environments (Windows, Linux, Mac OS).

After you've successfully downloaded the development environment, you must unpack the zip file to any directory on your PC or laptop. You then run the *eclipse.exe* file to start Eclipse.

2.3.2 Installing SAP HANA Studio

Availability of SAP HANA Studio

At present, you can install SAP HANA Studio in the following system environments:

▶ Windows XP, Vista, 7, and 8

▶ Linux (SUSE, Red Hat)

▶ Mac OS X 10.9 or higher

It supports both Eclipse 4.3 and 4.4 and requires *Java Runtime Environment (JRE)* 1.6 or higher as well as *Microsoft Runtime DLLs VS2010* (for an installation on Windows; the Microsoft Runtime DLLs VS2010 will be installed automatically if you use the Program HDBSETUP or Program HDBINST installation mechanisms described next).

Installation and update

The following three installation mechanisms are available:

▶ Installation in the form of a graphical installation program (Program HDBSETUP)

▶ Installation via the command line (Program HDBINST).

▶ Installation using a repository or an update site (if a compatible Eclipse installation already exists)

You can also use the same mechanisms to update an existing SAP HANA Studio installation. This is always necessary if you or an administrator update the SAP HANA database.

Components

SAP HANA Studio comprises the following components:

▶ **Administration**
Tools for the administration of the SAP HANA database.

▶ **Application Development**
All tools required for creating native SAP HANA *Extended Application Services* (SAP HANA XS) applications.

▶ **Database Development/Modeler**
Tools that are particularly required for developing data marts and ABAP-based applications on the basis of SAP HANA.

▶ **Sample Applications and SAP HANA Cloud Platform Tools**
Sample applications and components for using SAP HANA Studio in combination with cloud-based SAP HANA databases.

More detailed information and a step-by-step guide to installing SAP HANA Studio is available at *http://help.sap.com/hana_appliance*.

2.3.3 Installing the ABAP Development Tools for SAP NetWeaver

ABAP Development Tools for SAP NetWeaver are currently available for the following system environments:

Availability of ABAP Development Tools

▶ Windows XP, Vista, 7, and 8

▶ Linux (SUSE, Red Hat)

▶ Mac OS X 10.8 or higher

Analogous to SAP HANA Studio, ABAP Development Tools support Eclipse 4.3 and 4.4. They also require JRE 1.6 or higher as well as Microsoft Runtime DLLs VS2010 (under Windows).

Unlike SAP HANA Studio, there is no installation program for the ABAP Development Tools. Both the installation and the update of an existing installation are done via a repository or an update site. A prerequisite for the installation is that you have a compatible Eclipse installation on your computer.

Installation and update

The ABAP Development Tools for SAP NetWeaver include the following components:

Components

▶ **ABAP Core Development Tools**
Editors for editing ABAP source code, debuggers, transport connections, and so on.

▶ **ABAP Development Tools for Web Dynpro**
Tools for developing UIs with Web Dynpro ABAP.

▶ **ABAP Development Tools for Web Dynpro**
Tools for ABAP development on SAP HANA.

▶ **ABAP Connectivity and Integration Development Tools**
Tools for integrating systems.

▶ **ABAP Business Objects Tools**
Tools for implementing business objects using the *Business Object Processing Framework (BOPF)* (see *http://scn.sap.com/community/abap/bopf*).

More detailed information and a step-by-step guide to installing the ABAP Development Tools for SAP NetWeaver are available at *http://service.sap.com*.

2.4   Getting Started in the Development System

Now that you've set up a development environment for ABAP development on SAP HANA, you can get started in the system. We'll therefore provide you with sample developments that you can install on SAP NetWeaver AS ABAP 7.4 (as of SP 10, by using the description provided in Appendix E).

[»]   **Note**

If this is your first time working with Eclipse, we recommend that you look at other sources of information in addition to this book. We'll refer you to these additional sources at the relevant stages in this section.

2.4.1   Basic Principles of Eclipse

Start the newly set up development environment as described in Section 2.3. Run the *eclipse.exe* program file for this purpose.

Workbench   If the Welcome tab page is displayed when you start the program, use the button at the top-right of the screen to navigate to the Workbench. Choose Window • Open Perspective to open the ABAP perspective. You should now see a screen similar to that shown in Figure 2.4. We'll use this figure to explain the key elements of the Eclipse development environment.

Figure 2.4 Eclipse Workbench (with the ABAP Perspective Opened)

In Eclipse, you can work with one or more *windows* in parallel. If you want to open an additional window, choose the menu option, WINDOW • NEW WINDOW.

Windows and perspectives

Within a window, Eclipse only ever shows exactly one *perspective* at any given point in time. The name of the perspective currently displayed by the system is shown in the window's title bar ❶. A perspective describes the layout of screen elements for a particular purpose. For example, the ABAP perspective is available for ABAP development, while the JAVA perspective is available for Java development.

In the following text, we'll discuss in detail the most important screen elements within a perspective:

▸ Views ❷ and ❸

▸ Editors ❹

▸ Menu bars ❺

▸ Toolbars ❻

Eclipse automatically saves any changes that you make to the screen elements of a perspective (e.g., layout and size). If you exit a perspective and then open it again (via the menu path, WINDOW • OPEN PERSPECTIVE), the perspective will look exactly as it did when you exited it.

If you want to reset a perspective to its original state, choose the menu option, WINDOW • RESET PERSPECTIVE. You can also create your own perspectives, if necessary, by choosing WINDOW • SAVE PERSPECTIVE AS.

Views   A *view* (❷ and ❸) makes certain information available to you. For example, the PROBLEMS view displays warnings and errors that occurred when you activated a program. You can view the properties of a program (e.g., title, package, and original system) in the PROPERTIES view and change them to some extent. To open a view, choose WINDOW • SHOW VIEW.

Editors   An editor ❹ is used to edit a development object. Editors are frequently *source code-based*. However, *form-based* editors also exist.

[»]   **Differences between Views and Editors**

When developers work with Eclipse for the first time, they often ask what the difference is between a view and an editor. The main differences between views and editors are as follows:

▸ Within a window, a view can only be opened once, while an editor can be opened several times (e.g., to edit different programs in parallel).

▸ Unlike a view, an editor can't be positioned anywhere.

▸ When an editor is open, it can be viewed in every perspective.

▸ Changes within a view are saved immediately. Changes within an editor must be saved explicitly.

Further information is available at *http://wiki.eclipse.org*.

Menu bars and toolbars   Menu bars and toolbars contain commands that you can execute in the current context (e.g., saving a program or activating a program). The main menu bar ❺ is located at the very top of the Eclipse development environment. Views and editors can have additional menus, especially context menus (which you open by right-clicking). However, you can also add additional commands to the main menu bar.

The main toolbar is located below the main menu bar ❻. Frequently used commands are located there. Views and editors can have additional toolbars. You can also add additional commands to the main toolbar.

Finally, we want to explain the purpose of *workspaces*. You likely noticed that the system prompted you to specify a workspace upon initial startup of the development environment.

Workspaces

Put simply, a workspace is a directory on your computer's hard drive in which Eclipse stores your personal settings (e.g., layout and size of the screen elements in a perspective) and your project data (e.g., system connections to the ABAP AS). Eclipse only works with exactly one workspace at any given point in time. In the case of workspaces, you can configure the following settings:

▶ You can use the file *eclipse.ini* to control which workspace Eclipse will automatically open at startup.

▶ You can configure Eclipse in such a way that, at startup, you're asked which workspace you want to use. This is Eclipse's default behavior.

▶ You can change the workspace within Eclipse at any time. To do this, choose FILE • SWITCH WORKSPACE.

Further information about Eclipse is available at *www.eclipse.org/documentation/*.

2.4.2 ABAP Development Tools for SAP NetWeaver

We'll now discuss the ABAP Development Tools for SAP NetWeaver in more detail. When working with the ABAP Development Tools, use the following views/perspectives:

Available perspectives

▶ ABAP
Use this perspective to edit development objects (e.g., programs, classes, and interfaces). You can also perform code checks and module tests here.

▶ ABAP CONNECTIVITY & INTEGRATION
Use this perspective to develop integration between systems. An enhanced programming model enables you to create your own ABAP

application irrespective of the communication protocol that is used later on.

▶ ABAP PROFILING
Use this perspective to conduct performance analyses.

▶ DEBUG
Use this perspective to analyze program errors. (The DEBUG perspective isn't delivered with the ABAP Development Tools. Rather, it's a standard component of Eclipse and is also used, for example, to debug Java programs or SQLScript.)

Authorizations

In the ABAP backend, you require the relevant authorizations for working with the ABAP Development Tools. The following authorization roles are available by default:

▶ SAP_BC_DWB_ABAPDEVELOPER
This role enables you to create, change, activate, and delete development objects.

▶ SAP_BC_DWB_WBDISPLAY
This role enables you to display development objects.

Both roles contain the authorization object S_ADT_RES, which is needed for working with the Eclipse-based development environment. If you want to use your own roles to assign authorizations to ABAP developers, make sure that these roles consider the authorization object S_ADT_RES.

We'll now explain the steps involved in creating a program with the ABAP Development Tools. We'll provide some background information for each step as well.

Creating a Project

Connection to the
ABAP backend

To work with the ABAP Development Tools, you need an *ABAP project* that connects the Eclipse-based development environment with the ABAP backend. To create an ABAP project, choose FILE • NEW • ABAP PROJECT, and then provide:

▶ **A connection from the SAP Logon Pad.** Alternatively, you can also maintain the connection data manually without a corresponding entry in the SAP Logon Pad.

- **A logon client and language.**

- **A user name and password.** You only enter the password if single sign-on (SSO) isn't set up for the connection from the SAP Logon Pad. Because the password isn't saved, you must enter it again any time you restart Eclipse.

- **Optionally, include a list of your favorite packages.** You should always include the TEST_A4H_BOOK package here, which you'll use in conjunction with this book. (To install the package, refer to the information contained in Appendix E.)

The project data is saved to your current workspace (see also Section 2.4.1). You can create any number of projects within a workspace and therefore work with multiple ABAP backends simultaneously.

After you've saved the project data, the ABAP project is displayed in the PROJECT EXPLORER view (❷ in Figure 2.4). A tree structure is displayed below your project, and the uppermost level of this tree structure contains the following two nodes:

Project Explorer

- Your FAVORITE PACKAGES and their development objects

- The SYSTEM LIBRARY, which you use to access all packages and their development objects on the connected application server

If you double-click a development object in PROJECT EXPLORER, the relevant editor opens. In addition, the OUTLINE view ❸ displays the structure (e.g., the global variables and methods for a program), while the PROPERTIES view displays the properties of the development object. Not all development objects have an editor that is implemented natively in Eclipse. If a development object doesn't have an editor, the SAP GUI opens. For a data element, Transaction SE11 (ABAP Data Dictionary) opens, for example. The OUTLINE and PROPERTIES views aren't available in this case.

Editors and SAP GUI integration

You can use SAP GUI integration to execute any development objects in the SAP GUI, even if they aren't displayed in the PROJECT EXPLORER view at present. To do this, choose RUN • RUN ABAP DEVELOPMENT OBJECT, and select the relevant development object. This is particularly useful if you want to execute a standard program or transaction (e.g., Transaction SM50).

ABAP resource URLs

ABAP resource URLs are interesting for all development objects, irrespective of whether the ABAP Development Tools provide native editor development objects. They enable you to generate hyperlinks for development objects and integrate them into websites or emails, for example. You can click the hyperlink to open the relevant development object directly in the ABAP Development Tools.

To generate an ABAP resource URL, choose SHARE LINK from the context menu of a development object (or choose SHARE LINK FOR SELECTION in the source of a development object). Note that you can't open a development object via a hyperlink unless you've registered your Eclipse installation. Keep reading for more information.

No check-in/ check-out

Unlike other Eclipse-based development tools, the ABAP Development Tools don't use a *check-in/check-out mechanism*. As a result, you can't work with the ABAP Development Tools *offline* (i.e., without a connection to the ABAP backend). As soon as you edit a development object, this is automatically locked against editing by another user. Therefore, unlike in the SAP GUI, you don't explicitly toggle between DISPLAY and CHANGE. The following tasks always occur in the ABAP backend: save, perform syntax check, and activate.

User-Specific Settings

You should be familiar with choosing UTILITIES • SETTINGS to configure user-specific settings in the ABAP Workbench, and therefore adjust the (SAP GUI-based) development environment to your personal requirements.

General settings

In Eclipse, user-specific settings are available under WINDOW • PREFERENCES. Many of the options provided here are general settings for Eclipse. They aren't specifically used for ABAP development but influence it nonetheless. The specific settings for the ABAP Development Tools are available under the ABAP DEVELOPMENT node (see Figure 2.5).

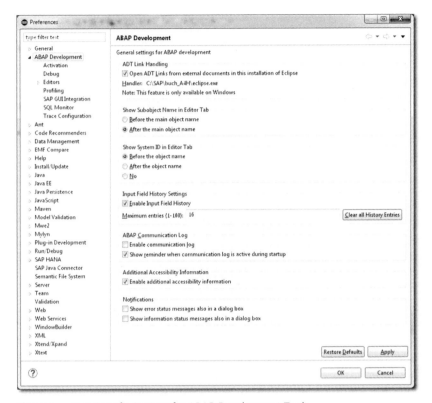

Figure 2.5 User-Specific Settings for ABAP Development Tools

You should be familiar with the following setting options:

▶ Directly on the ABAP DEVELOPMENT node, you can set the OPEN ADT LINKS FROM EXTERNAL DOCUMENTS IN THIS INSTALLATION OF ECLIPSE checkbox. You can't use ABAP resource URLs (see the previous section) unless this checkbox is set.

Edit the source code

▶ You can make settings for activation using the ACTIVATION node.

▶ You control debugging via the DEBUG node.

▶ With the EDITORS node, you can manage code templates and control *Pretty Printer*, among other things.

▶ The PROFILING node allows you to parameterize performance analyses, and the SQL MONITOR node allows you to influence the behavior of the SQL Monitor.

Creating a Program

The next step is to create a new development object by choosing FILE •
NEW. If you want to create a program that outputs the flight schedule for
a given airline, for example, choose FILE • NEW • ABAP PROGRAM. Then
enter the program name, title, and package. Select a transport request, if
necessary.

The editor for the program now opens. As an example, insert the source
code from Listing 2.1.

```
REPORT zr_a4h_chapter2_first_report.

DATA: lt_spfli TYPE STANDARD TABLE OF spfli, "#EC NEEDED
      lv_spfli TYPE string. "#EC NEEDED
FIELD-SYMBOLS: <ls_spfli> TYPE spfli. "#EC NEEDED
PARAMETERS: p_carr LIKE <ls_spfli>-carrid OBLIGATORY.
SELECT * FROM spfli UP TO 50 ROWS INTO TABLE lt_spfli
        WHERE carrid = p_car. "this line contains
                              "a syntax error
LOOP AT lt_spfli ASSIGNING <ls_spfli>.
  lv_spfli = |{ <ls_spfli>-carrid } | &&
  |{ <ls_spfli>-connid } { <ls_spfli>-airpfrom } | &&
  |{ <ls_spfli>-airpto }|.
  WRITE: / lv_spfli.
ENDLOOP.
```

Listing 2.1 Simple ABAP Program

[»] **Note on Listing 2.1**

To restrict the program runtime, use the UP TO n ROWS addition. Consequently, the program doesn't output the entire flight schedule. Instead, it
outputs a maximum of 50 connections.

Editing functions When editing the source code, you're supported by numerous functions
in ABAP Development Tools (just like in the SAP GUI), including the following three functions:

▸ **Code completion**
  You can use the key combination ⌨Ctrl+⌨Space to ensure that the system proposes valid keywords and identifiers at a particular location
  within the source text.

- **Code templates**

  You can also use the key combination [Ctrl]+[Space] to insert code *templates*) in the source code. Alternatively, this also works by dragging templates from the Templates view and dropping them in the editor. Also in the Templates view, you can also define your own code templates that are then saved to your current workspace.

- **Pretty Printer**

  The *Pretty Printer* helps you to standardize source text formatting (especially with regard to uppercase/lowercase and indentations). As is the case in the SAP GUI, you use the key combination [Shift]+[F1] to call the Pretty Printer in the ABAP Development Tools.

When editing the source text, you can perform a syntax check at any time by pressing [Ctrl]+[F2].

Check

As shown in Figure 2.6, warnings and errors are displayed in both the Problems view and in the editor (specifically in the left and right column spaces). For Listing 2.1, the syntax check should issue a reminder about an error in program line 8. Correct this error.

Available perspectives

Figure 2.6 Result of the Syntax Check

If you want the source text to undergo more extensive checks, you can use the *ABAP Test Cockpit* for this purpose. To do this, call the context menu in your program: Run As • ABAP Test Cockpit.

Saving and activating programs
Following a successful syntax check, choose FILE • SAVE to save your program (in principle, you can also save erroneous development objects). When you save your program, an inactive version of the program is generated in the ABAP backend.

If you then choose EDIT • ACTIVATE to activate the program, an active version of the program is generated in the ABAP backend (assuming that the program doesn't contain any syntax errors).

As a result of your work with the ABAP Workbench, you have no doubt become familiar with—and have come to appreciate—the extensive navigation options available there. Forward navigation and the where-used list are also available to you in the Eclipse-based development environment.

Forward navigation
For forward navigation, select an identifier in the source text, and choose NAVIGATE • NAVIGATE TO (or press the ⌐F3⌐ key). For our sample program, you can execute the following actions:

▶ Forward navigation to the variable LV_SPFLI in program line 14: The system navigates to the definition of the variable in program line 4.

▶ Use the mouse pointer to select database table SPFLI, and then press the ⌐F3⌐ key: The system opens the definition of the database table in the SAP GUI.

Where-used list
The where-used list works in the same way. First, select an identifier in the source text. Then, choose GET WHERE-USED LIST in the context menu. The result of the where-used list is displayed in the SEARCH view (see Figure 2.7).

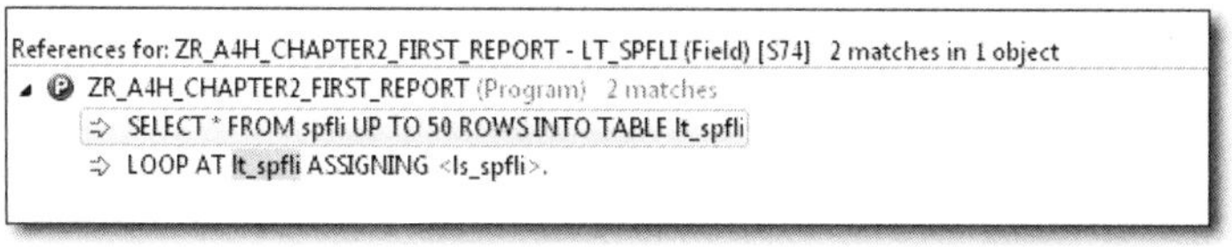

References for: ZR_A4H_CHAPTER2_FIRST_REPORT - LT_SPFLI (Field) [S74] 2 matches in 1 object
▲ ⓟ ZR_A4H_CHAPTER2_FIRST_REPORT (Program) 2 matches
  ⇨ SELECT * FROM spfli UP TO 50 ROWS INTO TABLE lt_spfli
  ⇨ LOOP AT lt_spfli ASSIGNING <ls_spfli>.

Figure 2.7 Result of the Where-Used List

You can double-click a line in the result to navigate to where the object is used.

Executing the Program

Now that you've learned how to create a program and are familiar with the editing options available in the ABAP Development Tools for SAP NetWeaver, you'll most likely want to execute the program for testing purposes. To do this, choose RUN AS • ABAP APPLICATION from the program's context menu, and execute the sample program shown earlier in Listing 2.1. The selection screen for the program is then displayed in the SAP GUI. Here, enter the code of an airline. Press F8 to display the corresponding flight schedule.

Executing the program in the SAP GUI

If you want to debug a program to analyze program errors, you can set one or more breakpoints in the ABAP Development Tools. Here, you can choose between static and dynamic breakpoints:

Debugging

- ▶ *Static breakpoints* refer to a specific program line. You set a static breakpoint by double-clicking the left column space in the editor.

- ▶ *Dynamic breakpoints* refer to a specific ABAP statement or exception class. To set a dynamic breakpoint, choose RUN • ABAP BREAKPOINTS.

Figure 2.8 shows how static breakpoints are displayed in the left column space in the editor and in the BREAKPOINTS view. Dynamic breakpoints are displayed in the BREAKPOINTS view only.

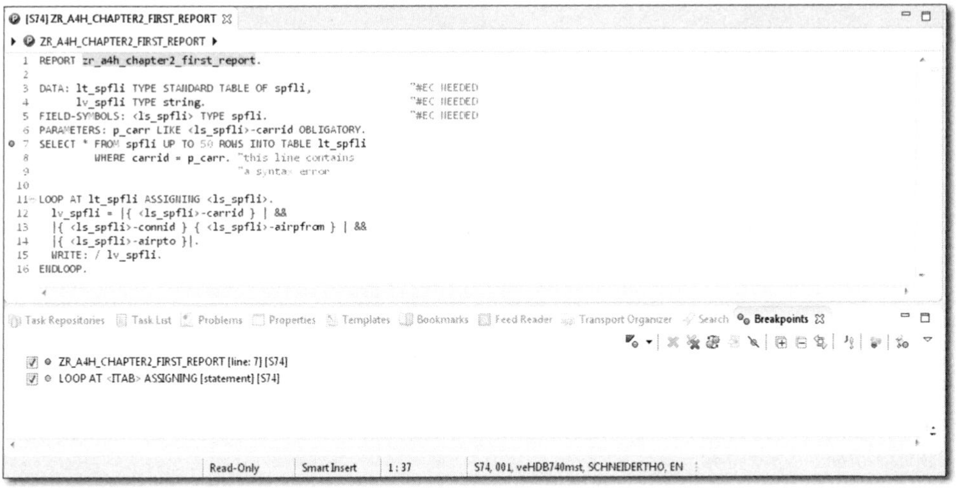

Figure 2.8 Displaying Breakpoints That Have Been Set

External
breakpoints
From a technical perspective, the ABAP Development Tools work with *external breakpoints*. These apply to all programs in your current user session, which are executed under your user on one of the application servers on the ABAP backend (defined by the system and client in the ABAP project).

If the system encounters a breakpoint when executing a development object, it automatically opens the DEBUG perspective. Similar to the SAP GUI-based debugger, you can analyze the call hierarchy and the contents of the variables, as well as debug the source code step by step. Figure 2.9 shows the DEBUG perspective for our sample program.

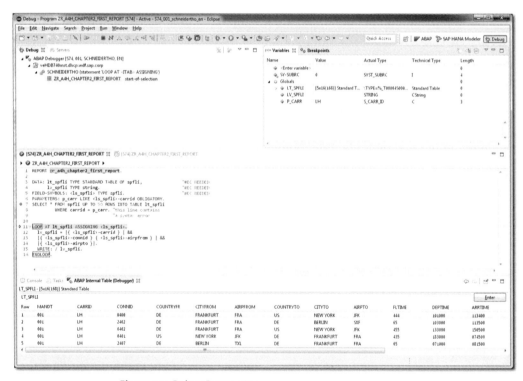

Figure 2.9 Debug Perspective

Additional
information
The following are some additional sources of information related to the ABAP Development Tools:

- If this is your first time working with the ABAP Development Tools, we recommend that you complete the tutorials in the SAP Community Network at *http://scn.sap.com/docs/DOC-31815.*

- You can call the online documentation at any time by choosing HELP • HELP CONTENTS.

- SAP has provided some *cheat sheets* to help you get started with the ABAP Development Tools. They are located under HELP • CHEAT SHEETS.

You're now ready to use the ABAP Development Tools for SAP NetWeaver. In the next section, we'll introduce you to SAP HANA Studio.

2.4.3 SAP HANA Studio

Just like the ABAP Development Tools for SAP NetWeaver, SAP HANA Studio also includes different perspectives:

- SAP HANA ADMINISTRATION CONSOLE
  In this perspective, you or an administrator can monitor the system, configure system settings, and manage users and authorizations, among other things.

- SAP HANA MODELER (MODELER)
  In the modeler, you can access the database catalog and create views and database procedures in the *SAP HANA Repository.*

- SAP HANA PLANVIZ
  This perspective is used to visualize execution plans (see Chapter 7).

- SAP HANA DEVELOPMENT
  This perspective is used for development in SAP HANA. In particular, it's intended for *SAP HANA XS.* It communicates with the SAP HANA Repository.

Similar to working with AS ABAP, you require the relevant authorizations for working with SAP HANA Studio, specifically in the SAP HANA database.

Authorizations for SAP HANA Studio

[»] **Authorizations in SAP HANA**

The authorizations in SAP HANA are divided into the following areas:

- *Analytical authorizations* control access to attribute views, analytic views, and calculation views.
- *Object authorizations* define specific authorizations that users have for particular database objects.
- *System authorizations* define the system operations that users are permitted to perform.
- *Package authorizations* control access to the packages in the SAP HANA Repository.
- *Application authorizations* control access to applications that are developed with SAP HANA XS Engine.
- *User authorizations* are required within the scope of debugging of SQLScript from other users.

Authorizations can be grouped into roles or assigned directly to users.

We won't discuss the authorization concept for the SAP HANA database in detail here. Instead, we'll focus on the authorizations that you require, as an ABAP developer, to work with SAP HANA Studio.

Roles for ABAP developers

If you're already working with ABAP release 7.4 and using the SAP HANA database as the primary persistent storage, you can use the following standard roles to assign authorizations to ABAP developers who will work with SAP HANA Studio:

- ABAP_DEV
  This role enables you to edit development objects in the SAP HANA Repository.

- ABAP_READ
  This role enables you to display development objects.

- ABAP_ADMIN
  This role allows system administrators to assign the ABAP_DEV and ABAP_READ roles to other users.

Settings in the SAP HANA Modeler perspective

In this section, we'll focus on the SAP HANA MODELER perspective, which is relevant for you as an ABAP developer. Based on this, Chapter 4 will provide more detailed information.

Creating a System Connection

To work with SAP HANA Studio, you require a system connection between SAP HANA Studio and the SAP HANA database. You can create a system connection in the SAP HANA MODELER perspective, for example. In the SYSTEMS view, use the ADD SYSTEM option in the context menu for this purpose. Then, provide the following information for the system connection:

Connect to the database

▸ Server name and instance number

▸ Description

▸ User name and password

The system data is saved to your current workspace (see also Section 2.4.1). You can create any number of system connections within a workspace. This enables you to work with multiple databases simultaneously.

After you've saved the system data, the system connection is displayed in the SYSTEMS view (see Figure 2.10).

Figure 2.10 Modeler Perspective in SAP HANA Studio

Navigator

A tree structure is displayed below your system connection, and the uppermost level of this tree structure contains the following four nodes:

▸ The CATALOG node ❶ contains *database objects* ❷, such as database tables, views, and database procedures.

▸ The CONTENT node ❸ represents the packages in the SAP HANA Repository, which is used for development organization.

▸ The PROVISIONING node is used for integrating other data sources.

▸ The SECURITY node ❹ is used for managing roles and users.

User-Specific Settings

Similar to the ABAP Workbench or ABAP Development Tools, you can also configure some user-specific settings in SAP HANA Studio. The relevant settings for the SAP HANA MODELER perspective are located under WINDOW • PREFERENCES • SAP HANA • MODELER. Of particular interest here are the data preview settings (under the DATA PREVIEW node) and the rules for validating development objects (under the VALIDATION RULES node).

Working with the Database Catalog

Database schemas

The database catalog in the SAP HANA database has a similar structure to the catalogs in other databases. It manages the database objects in *database schemas* (❷ in Figure 2.10). A schema groups logically related database objects together (comparable with a *namespace*). In principle, each database user has his own database schema.

The ABAP application server generally uses exactly one technical database user to communicate with the database. This user also has a corresponding database schema, known as the *system schema* or *ABAP schema* (for more information, see Chapter 3, Section 3.1). In Figure 2.10, this is schema SAPS74.

Technical schemas

Some database schemas are used internally by the SAP HANA database. In particular, these include the database schema SYS and all database schemas that start with _SYS.

Technical Database Schemas in SAP HANA [«]

Immediately after the installation, SAP HANA contains a set of database schemas that play a major role in different scenarios, so we've included some background information about some of the schemas used internally by the SAP HANA database:

▸ _SYS
  This schema contains technical tables and views for managing and monitoring the system. It doesn't play any role in application development.

▸ _SYS_AFL
  Database objects for function libraries are stored here. The schema is first created when function libraries are installed (see Chapter 12).

▸ _SYS_BI
  This schema contains special tables and views for analysis scenarios (e.g., fiscal year data).

▸ _SYS_BIC
  When you activate development objects, the associated runtime objects are generated in this schema (we'll discuss this in more detail next).

▸ _SYS_REPO
  The development objects for the SAP HANA Repository are stored here (we'll also discuss this in more detail later in this section).

▸ _SYS_XS:
  This schema is used by the SAP HANA XS Engine.

Database schemas contain database objects. The SAP HANA database recognizes the database objects listed in Table 2.1.

Database objects

Object	Description
COLUMN VIEW	Column views are special views in SAP HANA based on tables in the column store and are usually created in the SAP HANA Repository.
FUNCTION	A *user-defined function* performs calculations and can be integrated into SELECT statements.
INDEX	An index facilitates searches and sorting. Note the information about indexes in Chapter 10 and Chapter 14.
PROCEDURE	You can use database *procedures* to encapsulate and reuse algorithms that are to be executed in the SAP HANA database. Further information is available in Chapter 6.

Table 2.1 Objects in the Database Catalog

Object	Description
SEQUENCE	You can use a *sequence* to generate unique, consecutive numbers in accordance with certain rules. This concept is very similar to number ranges in ABAP.
SYNONYM	Synonyms can be defined as aliases for database tables, data views, procedures, and sequences. We'll discuss these later in this chapter.
TABLE	Data is saved to database *tables*. As part of your ABAP development work in SAP HANA, you frequently use the ABAP Data Dictionary (DDIC) to create database tables.
TRIGGER	Database *triggers* are functions called for certain changes made in the database.
VIEW	*Views* are saved queries (across one or more tables) that can be called via SQL in the same way as a database table.

Table 2.1 Objects in the Database Catalog (Cont.)

As part of your ABAP development work in SAP HANA, you generally won't create any database objects directly in the catalog. You'll typically create objects only indirectly, for example, via the DDIC, SAP HANA Repository, or SAP Landscape Transformation Replication Server (SAP LT Replication Server). In certain circumstances, however, you may want to view database objects directly in the catalog. We'll now use the example of table SPFLI, which you already used in Listing 2.1, to explain how this works.

Table definition
Open the ABAP schema under the CATALOG node. Here, you see nodes for the different database objects. If you want to search for a specific database table, choose the FIND TABLE option in the context menu for the TABLES node. Then, enter "SPFLI" in the search dialog box. Make sure that the SHOW DEFINITION checkbox is set, and choose OK.

The system now opens the table definition (see Figure 2.11). Here, you see that table SPFLI uses *column-oriented data storage* (known as the *column store*). You can also check columns, indexes, and runtime information for the database table, among other things.

Table contents and data preview
Similar to the table definition, you can also use the FIND TABLE option in the context menu to display the table contents. Alternatively, you can

use the context menu for the TABLES node to set a filter for the table name. The NAVIGATOR view then displays only those tables that satisfy the filter condition. You can now right-click to select the OPEN CONTENT option in the context menu. Note that the system displays only the first 1,000 data records (and not the entire contents of the database table).

HDB (SCHNEIDERTHO)	10.66.182.236 02								

Table Name: SPFLI Schema: SAPS74 Type: Column Store

Columns | Indexes | Further Properties | Runtime Information

	Name	SQL Data Type	Di...	Column Store Data Type	Key	Not Null	Default	Comment
1	MANDT	NVARCHAR	3	STRING	X(1)	X	000	
2	CARRID	NVARCHAR	3	STRING	X(2)	X		
3	CONNID	NVARCHAR	4	STRING	X(3)	X	0000	
4	COUNTRYFR	NVARCHAR	3	STRING		X		
5	CITYFROM	NVARCHAR	20	STRING		X		
6	AIRPFROM	NVARCHAR	3	STRING		X		
7	COUNTRYTO	NVARCHAR	3	STRING		X		
8	CITYTO	NVARCHAR	20	STRING		X		
9	AIRPTO	NVARCHAR	3	STRING		X		
10	FLTIME	INTEGER		INT		X	0	
11	DEPTIME	NVARCHAR	6	STRING		X	000000	
12	ARRTIME	NVARCHAR	6	STRING		X	000000	
13	DISTANCE	DECIMAL	9,4	FIXED		X	0	
14	DISTID	NVARCHAR	3	STRING		X		
15	FLTYPE	NVARCHAR	1	STRING		X		
16	PERIOD	SMALLINT		INT		X	0	

Figure 2.11 Table Definition Using the Example of Table SPFLI

You can use the *data preview* to analyze more than 1,000 data records. To access the data preview, choose the OPEN DATA PREVIEW option in the context menu. Figure 2.12 displays the data preview using the example of table SPFLI.

Data preview

The data preview comprises the following tab pages:

▸ The RAW DATA tab page displays the table's raw data. Here, you can filter, sort, and export the data, among other things.

▸ On the DISTINCT VALUES tab page, you can analyze which different values exist for a field in the database table and the frequency with which these values occur, thus enabling you to draw conclusions in relation to data distribution.

▸ The ANALYSIS tab page has a similar structure to a pivot table. You can create simple analyses here. Both a tabular and graphical display are available here.

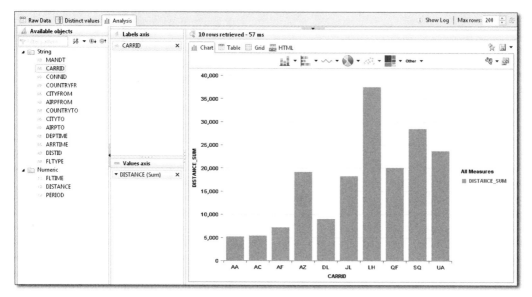

Figure 2.12 Data Preview Using the Example of Table SPFLI

SQL console   We'll now introduce you to one more tool—the *SQL console*—that can be very useful when working with the database catalog. This enables you to quickly and easily execute read and write SQL statements on the SAP HANA database. If, for example, you want to add the name of an airline to the flight schedule from Section 2.4.2, you can use a *join* (see Chapter 3). You can test the JOIN statement (see Listing 2.2) in the SQL console. To open the SQL console in the NAVIGATOR view, choose the OPEN SQL CONSOLE option in the context menu for the ABAP schema. You can then enter the relevant SQL statement. Similar to the ABAP Development Tools, you can also use Ctrl + Space to revert to code completion and templates.

```
select spfli.carrid, scarr.carrname, spfli.connid,
       spfli.airpfrom, spfli.airpto
       from spfli
       join scarr on scarr.carrid = spfli.carrid;
```
Listing 2.2 Simple Join

Then, choose EXECUTE to execute the SQL statement. The result is shown in Figure 2.13. In addition to the result list, the system provides some information about the runtime and number of data records read.

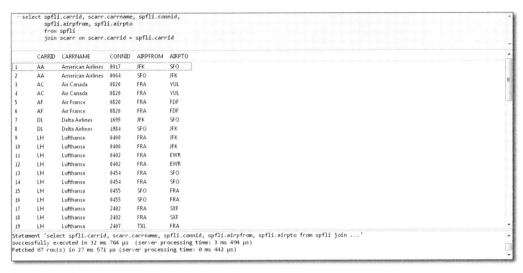

```
select spfli.carrid, scarr.carrname, spfli.connid,
       spfli.airpfrom, spfli.airpto
  from spfli
  join scarr on scarr.carrid = spfli.carrid
```

	CARRID	CARRNAME	CONNID	AIRPFROM	AIRPTO
1	AA	American Airlines	0017	JFK	SFO
2	AA	American Airlines	0064	SFO	JFK
3	AC	Air Canada	0820	FRA	YUL
4	AC	Air Canada	0820	FRA	YUL
5	AF	Air France	0820	FRA	FDF
6	AF	Air France	0820	FRA	FDF
7	DL	Delta Airlines	1699	JFK	SFO
8	DL	Delta Airlines	1984	SFO	JFK
9	LH	Lufthansa	0400	FRA	JFK
10	LH	Lufthansa	0400	FRA	JFK
11	LH	Lufthansa	0402	FRA	EWR
12	LH	Lufthansa	0402	FRA	EWR
13	LH	Lufthansa	0454	FRA	SFO
14	LH	Lufthansa	0454	FRA	SFO
15	LH	Lufthansa	0455	SFO	FRA
16	LH	Lufthansa	0455	SFO	FRA
17	LH	Lufthansa	2402	FRA	SXF
18	LH	Lufthansa	2402	FRA	SXF
19	LH	Lufthansa	2407	TXL	FRA

```
Statement 'select spfli.carrid, scarr.carrname, spfli.connid, spfli.airpfrom, spfli.airpto from spfli join ...'
successfully executed in 32 ms 764 µs  (server processing time: 3 ms 494 µs)
Fetched 67 row(s) in 27 ms 571 µs (server processing time: 0 ms 442 µs)
```

Figure 2.13 SQL Console

If you enter several SQL statements in the SQL console, each separated by a semicolon, you can execute them by choosing EXECUTE once. If you want to execute only one or some of the SQL statements, select them before you choose EXECUTE.

Working with the SAP HANA Repository

This brings us to the SAP HANA Repository, which helps to organize *development objects* (known as *content*) in a flexible and expansible manner. The development objects contained in the SAP HANA Repository are organized along a package hierarchy. In terms of their notation and significance, these packages are very similar to Java packages. Because a package defines a namespace, the identifier for development objects must only be unique within the package (unlike the global uniqueness of the identifiers for ABAP objects).

Development objects

SAP delivers content below the `sap` root package. Parallel to this package, you can establish your own package hierarchy for your development objects. You can group multiple packages together to form a *delivery unit*, which you can then transport. We'll examine the package concept and application transport in detail in Chapter 5.

Content types   In the MODELER perspective, you can create the development objects described in Table 2.2. These are also known as *content types*.

Object	Description
PACKAGE	A *package* groups development objects together. We'll discuss this in Chapter 5, Section 5.3.1.
ATTRIBUTE VIEW	You can use *attribute views* to connect multiple database tables or to select a subset of the columns in a database table. For more information, see Chapter 4, Section 4.4.1.
ANALYTIC VIEW	In particular, you use *analytic views* to quickly aggregate data. Details are available in Chapter 4, Section 4.4.2.
CALCULATION VIEW	*Calculation views* are available for requirements that can't be mapped using attribute views and analytic views. They can be modeled or implemented using SQLScript. Details are available in Chapter 4, Section 4.4.3.
ANALYTIC PRIVILEGE	You can use *analytic privileges* to restrict—line by line—access to views. They aren't directly relevant for access from ABAP because this is done using a technical database user.
PROCEDURE	You can use database *procedures* to encapsulate and reuse algorithms that are to be executed in the SAP HANA database. More information can be found in Chapter 4, Section 4.3.
DECISION TABLE	You can use *decision tables* to store business rules in SAP HANA. We'll discuss this in Chapter 11.

Table 2.2 Development Objects in the SAP HANA Repository

You can create additional development objects in the SAP HANA DEVELOPMENT perspective. This is particularly relevant for any development work based on SAP HANA XS. For the moment, we won't discuss these development objects further.

Example: We'll now use a specific example to explain some key concepts associ-
Flight schedule   ated with the SAP HANA Repository: Figure 2.14 shows the editor for the attribute view AT_FLIGHT_SCHEDULE in the package TEST.AH4. BOOK.CHAPTER02.

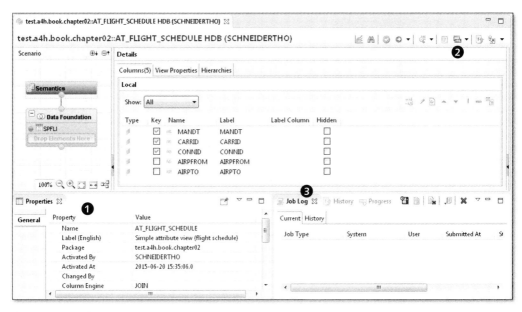

Figure 2.14 Attribute View AT_FLIGHT_SCHEDULE

Without discussing the specific features of attribute views, we'll explain the following concepts:

- Creating development objects
- Validating development objects
- Activating development objects
- Testing development objects
- History and version management

Each development object in the SAP HANA Repository is described by different properties (❶ in Figure 2.14), some of which you can specify when creating the object, and some you can also change later. Examples include the unique identifier within the package (NAME), description (LABEL), and DEFAULT CLIENT. Other properties are automatically set by the system, for example, the last user who changed the object (CHANGED BY).

Storage

The system creates an XML file for each development object and ultimately stores it as a *Character Large Object* (CLOB) data type in the database schema _SYS_REPO. You can choose DISPLAY XML to display the XML file for an object ❷.

Figure 2.15 shows the XML representation of the attribute view AT_ FLIGHT_SCHEDULE. In this figure, we've highlighted some parts of the XML document, namely the identifier for the view, the description of the view, the columns in the view, and the database table underlying the view.

Figure 2.15 XML Representation of an Attribute View

Similar to ABAP development objects, the development objects in the SAP HANA Repository also have a status (either INACTIVE or ACTIVE). If you create a new object or change an existing object, the system generates an inactive version first.

You can validate an object before you activate it. In addition to syntax checks (e.g., correct syntax of SQLScript within a database procedure), the validation can also consider some aspects of quality (e.g., performance). This is similar to the (enhanced) syntax check in ABAP. We'll discuss some of these aspects in greater detail in Chapter 14.

Validate

To start validation, choose SAVE AND VALIDATE CHANGES TO THIS OBJECT. The validation result is displayed in the JOB LOG (❸ in Figure 2.14). If warnings or errors occur when validating an object, you can display them by double-clicking the corresponding row in the job log.

Job log

Figure 2.16 shows an example of what would happen if you were to validate the attribute view AT_FLIGHT_SCHEDULE without defining at least one key attribute first. This is a mandatory requirement for attribute views.

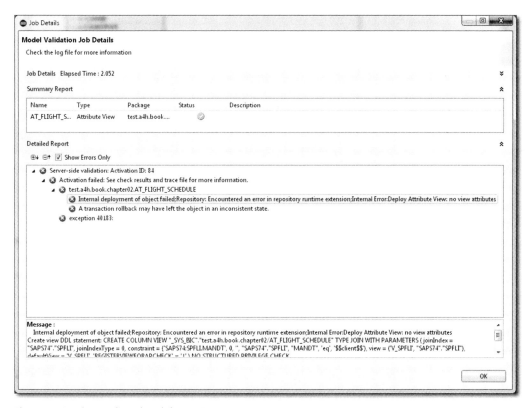

Figure 2.16 Job Details with Validation Errors

Activate
When you activate an object, you generate an active (i.e., executable) version of a development object. An object is automatically validated when it's activated. To start activation, choose SAVE AND ACTIVATE. The result is displayed in the job log.

Design time and runtime objects
Following successful activation, the system usually generates one or more database objects in the schema _SYS_BIC. The development objects in the SAP HANA Repository represent the *design time objects*, while the database objects in the database catalog represent the *runtime objects* (see Figure 2.17).

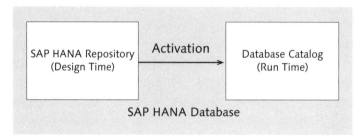

Figure 2.17 Design Time and Runtime

[»]

Authorizations for the User _SYS_REPO

The internal user _SYS_REPO (the owner of the SAP HANA Repository) generates the runtime objects in the database schema _SYS_BIC. This user must have read access to the schemas used in the development objects. In other words, the user requires the SQL SELECT with GRANT authorization on the schema.

Column view
For the attribute view AT_FLIGHT_SCHEDULE, the system generates (among other things) a column view and a public synonym for this column view in the database catalog. A column view is a special data view in SAP HANA. In our example, the name of the column view comprises the package and identifier for the attribute view (see Figure 2.18).

Synonym
A *synonym* is an alias. A *public synonym* is an alias that is unique across all database schemas and can be used by all users. If, for example, you use the relevant public synonym to access the column view, you avoid having to name the schema _SYS_BIC explicitly. In our example, the name of

the public synonym comprises the package and name of the attribute view (see Figure 2.19).

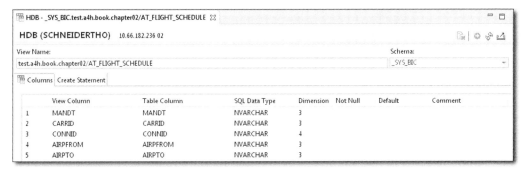

Figure 2.18 Runtime Object for an Attribute View

Figure 2.19 Public Synonym for a Column View

When you want to test objects in the SAP HANA Repository, it's best to use the data preview and the SQL console. You're already familiar with both of these tools, which we explained when we discussed the database catalog previously. To start the data preview for a development object, choose DATA PREVIEW. This preview is available for attribute views, analytic views, calculation views, and decision tables.

Testing

Because we've already used the example of database table SPFLI to explain the data preview, we won't discuss it in further detail here. However, take a look at the SHOW LOG button in the data preview. You can use this button to call a selection log, which helps you quickly find the corresponding runtime object for a design time object (see Figure 2.20). This enables you to determine the runtime object for a development object.

Selection log

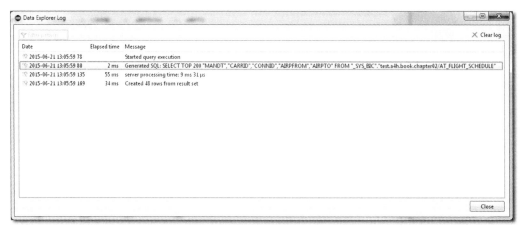

Figure 2.20 Selection Log with a Database Object

SQL console

Alternatively, you can conduct tests directly in the SQL console. In our example, you can use the following objects here: the name of the column view generated (i.e., `test.a4h.book.chapter02/AT_FLIGHT_SCHEDULE` in the schema `_SYS_BIC`) and the public synonym (`test.a4h.book.chapter02::AT_FLIGHT_SCHEDULE`).

History and version management

Similar to ABAP, development objects are put under version control. Each time an object is activated, the system creates a new version of the object. You can display existing versions in the version history. To access the version history, choose HISTORY. However, you see only the time when a version was created (i.e., the time when an object was activated). You can't see the actual changes made to each version.

If there is an inactive version, you can choose SWITCH VERSION to execute the following actions:

▸ Switch between displaying active and inactive versions.

▸ Drop the version that is currently inactive, and revert to the last active version.

You now know the relevant tools for ABAP development on SAP HANA, and you've taken your first steps toward getting started in the system. In the next chapter, we'll discuss ABAP database programming. For more information on working with SAP HANA Studio, see Chapter 4.

To develop ABAP applications for SAP HANA, it's essential to have a basic knowledge of the SAP NetWeaver AS ABAP architecture—and especially Open SQL—as well as the corresponding development tools. Moreover, native database access takes on greater importance when working with an SAP HANA database.

3 Database Programming Using SAP NetWeaver Application Server ABAP

When using ABAP in combination with SAP HANA, database accesses from ABAP programs play a decisive role; after all, they are the interface between application and data. The main difference between SAP HANA and traditional databases is the available set of queries and operations that you can execute on the existing data.

This chapter introduces database programming in ABAP and, in particular, explains the specific aspects that are significant for development on SAP HANA irrespective of the ABAP version. While the basic ABAP database architecture for SAP HANA doesn't differ from other SAP-supported database systems, we'll describe the options (and limitations) of classic ABAP database programming in this chapter. Chapter 6 will introduce some additional technologies that require ABAP 7.4 (with a sufficiently high support package level).

Let's start by contemplating a simple ABAP program as shown in Listing 3.1.

```
DATA: wa TYPE scarr.
SELECT-OPTIONS: carrier FOR wa-carrid.
SELECT * FROM scarr INTO wa WHERE carrid IN carrier.
  WRITE: / wa-carrid , wa-carrname.
ENDSELECT.
```

Listing 3.1 Simple Database Access from ABAP via Open SQL

Based on a selection of codes for airlines (e.g., "LH"), the full names of these airlines (e.g., "LH Lufthansa") are displayed.

Qualities of ABAP database access

This simple example shows some fundamental qualities of database access from ABAP that aren't available in this form in most other development environments:

- Database access is integrated into the programming language.

- Manually opening or closing a database connection isn't required.

- Knowledge of the underlying database system isn't required.

- You can iterate directly over a result set.

- A complex selection on the database can be derived directly from an input mask (e.g., via the SELECT-OPTIONS command and the IN clause).

In this chapter, we'll first describe the technical aspects of a connection between the SAP NetWeaver AS ABAP and the database. We'll then explain how ABAP developers can access the database efficiently based on a few examples. And, finally, we'll describe tools that can be used when developing database accesses.

Components of database access

Two components play an important role when accessing the database from ABAP:

- **ABAP Data Dictionary (DDIC)**
  ABAP tables and views are created and maintained in the database via the DDIC, as described in Section 3.2.1.

- **SQL options**
  SQL support in ABAP makes it possible to read and modify data. There are two options for SQL access: *Open SQL* (see Section 3.2.2) and *Native SQL* (see Section 3.2.4). It's an essential aspect of this book that you understand the capabilities and usage options of these two variants.

Because database access is of paramount importance in the context of SAP HANA and is enhanced by some new aspects, it's important to understand fully the interaction of ABAP and the SAP HANA database.

Experienced ABAP developers may already be familiar with some of the information provided in this chapter.

For the examples throughout this book, we used a model that is available in every ABAP system—the well-known SAP NetWeaver flight data model (SFLIGHT). Appendix A introduces the technical details and business aspects of this application and describes the database tables and their relationships. This chapter only uses the tables SCARR (airlines), SFLIGHT (flights), SCUSTOM (flight customers), and SBOOK (flight bookings).

3.1 SAP NetWeaver Application Server ABAP Architecture

The database plays an integral role for the ABAP AS. This server can't be operated without a running database. Ultimately, all technical and business data (except for a few configuration and log files of the server components) are database contents in AS ABAP; even the ABAP source code and other development objects are maintained in database tables.

In this section, you'll find a short description of the basic structure of an ABAP system. An ABAP system can comprise one or several application servers. Several application servers are deployed for a scale-out scenario to provide high availability and avoid overload situations. To coordinate several application servers, central services such as the *start service*, the *message server* (load distribution), or the *enqueue server* (lock management) are available.

SAP system

Requests received on a server are forwarded to a *work process* by the dispatcher, where the request in question is processed by an ABAP program. There are different types of work processes, such as *dialog* (running ABAP programs in the dialog), *update* (executing *update modules* in case of a COMMIT WORK), *background* (running batch jobs), or *enqueue* (executing lock operations to synchronize database operations). You can configure the number of available work processes, which depends on the hardware resources and scenario requirements (e.g., the number of concurrent users).

Work processes

ABAP runtime
environment ABAP programs are executed by the runtime environment in the *ABAP kernel*. Within the kernel, several components are in use when executing ABAP statements; not all of those components will be explained in detail within this book, but here are a few sample scenarios:

▸ When calling a function module using `CALL FUNCTION <...> DESTINATION`, the Remote Function Call (RFC) library is used.

▸ If an ABAP data structure is serialized to XML (or JSON) via `CALL TRANSFORMATION`, the kernel support for XML stylesheets is used.

▸ When accessing the database via the ABAP `SELECT` statement, the kernel's database interface is used.

Database access using the `SELECT` statement is explained in detail in the next section. In the next section as well, Figure 3.1 shows the basic server architecture of an ABAP system. Further details on installation and operation of the components are available in *SAP NetWeaver AS ABAP—System Administration* by Frank Föse, Sigrid Hagemann, and Liane Will, (SAP PRESS, 2012).

3.1.1 Database Interface

This section describes in detail how the ABAP application server accesses the database. In this context, there are three important components:

▸ Database interface (DBI)

▸ Database-specific library (Database Shared Library [DBSL])

▸ Database client (driver)

Database interface
(DBI) Every ABAP work process is connected to the database via an active connection. If the database is accessed from an ABAP program, the DBI in the ABAP kernel is responsible for the first processing steps. The DBI is independent of the concrete database system.

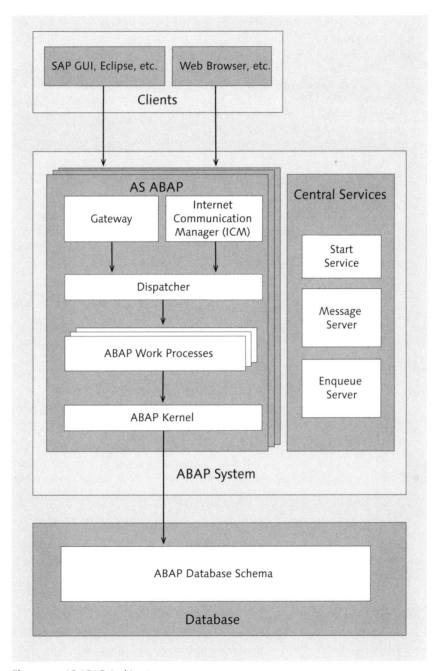

Figure 3.1 AS ABAP Architecture

One of its main responsibilities is translating Open SQL (see Section 3.2.2) into native SQL, which is then passed to the database via the DBSL (and the database driver).

In addition to processing SQL queries, the DBI provides the following functions:

- **Automatic client handling**
  If Open SQL is used to access client-dependent tables, the client is included automatically (e.g., in the WHERE clause), as explained in Section 3.2.2.

- **ABAP table buffer**
  In the DDIC, you can specify if table contents should be buffered on the application server to avoid unnecessary database accesses. These buffers are maintained and synchronized by the database interface.

[»]   **Database Systems Supported by SAP NetWeaver**

The AS ABAP currently supports the following vendors' database systems:

- SAP databases (SAP HANA, Sybase ASE, SAP MaxDB)
- IBM DB2
- Oracle database
- Microsoft SQL Server

Current details are provided in the Product Availability Matrix (PAM) at *http://service.sap.com/pam*.

Database Shared Library (DBSL)
There is a specific library for every database system supported by SAP: the *DBSL*. This library is linked dynamically to the ABAP kernel and integrates the respective database driver for the technical connection to the database.

Secondary database connections
You can install several of those libraries on an application server. This makes it possible to establish connections to other databases besides the ABAP system database. This is important in the context of SAP HANA when implementing the side-by-side scenarios described in Chapter 1, Section 1.4. The technical aspects of such *secondary* connections are described in more detail in Section 3.2.5. The prerequisites and steps for installing the SAP HANA DBSL on an existing system are described in

SAP Note 1597627. Figure 3.2 shows how the DBI, DBSL, and database driver interact.

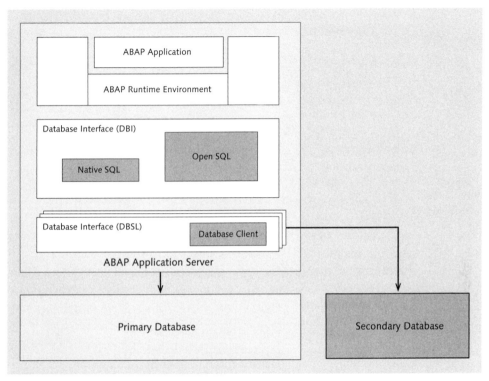

Figure 3.2 Interaction of the DBI, DBSL, and Database Client

3.1.2 Role of the Database for the ABAP Application Server

AS ABAP stores all data in exactly one specific schema within the data- ABAP schema base catalog. This schema is also referred to as the *system schema* or *ABAP schema*. You can think of a schema as a kind of namespace within the database. In traditional ABAP development, the database schema is irrelevant. In the context of SAP HANA, however, the schema is relevant for two reasons: First, when replicating tables to SAP HANA, the replicated data are often stored in different database schemas to separate them from the system data. Second, a series of technical schemas in SAP HANA play an important role in native development in SAP HANA (see Chapter 2, Section 2.4.3, and Chapter 4).

As mentioned already, every ABAP work process is connected to the database. For the standard database connection, a technical database user is used.

ABAP Schema and Technical Database User

The name of the ABAP schema is usually composed of the system ID (SID) and the prefix "SAP". The default schema name of the ABAP system "NSP" would be SAPNSP, for example. ABAP tables such as the SFLIGHT table can thus be addressed in the database catalog using SAPNSP.SFLIGHT.

This schema also comprises a database user SAPNSP, which is used by the AS ABAP to establish the standard database connection.

Transaction concept of the database

Every database uses a transaction concept to consider the consequences of interactions as a logic unit (*logical unit of work [LUW]*) and guarantee atomicity, consistency, isolation, durability (ACID) qualities for this unit. Database transactions are usually relatively short-lived operations and are always focused on the technical consistency of table contents (during parallel access, in error situations, etc.). Business transactions (e.g., creating a new customer in the system), on the other hand, are often associated with a longer lifetime and additional requirements with regard to data consistency because the data must also be consistent from a business perspective. The transaction concept of the database is hardly suitable to meet these additional requirements.

SAP LUW concept

To ensure consistent changes to data models in business applications, ABAP provides the *LUW concept*. With this concept, changes to data records are collected first and are then, at a defined point in time, either written to the database by a COMMIT WORK statement or discarded by means of a ROLLBACK WORK. By collecting changes, changes in transactions that comprise several dialog steps or even several application servers can be bundled (see Section 3.2.2). Because there is currently no equivalent concept in SAP HANA, only the transaction concept of the database can be used for native implementations in SAP HANA (e.g., via SQLScript). For recommendations on this topic, please read Chapter 14.

Lock concept

Physical locks are used automatically by every relational database system to synchronize parallel changes to table contents. In addition, AS

ABAP uses a logical lock concept that is focused on business aspects. With this concept, *lock objects* can be used to indicate that a data record is unavailable for certain accesses (e.g., for changes) for a certain time period. Locks can be created or queried at runtime using special function modules that manage lock entries via the enqueue work process.

For example, when booking a flight, it isn't possible to perform another booking for the same flight to make sure it's not overbooked. Because these logical locks don't lead to physical locks on the database (so tables can technically still be changed), the effectiveness of the locks is based on conventions and guidelines for application development. These aspects must also be considered when modifying ABAP tables outside the context of an ABAP program (e.g., with SQLScript in the case of SAP HANA).

3.1.3 Data Types

As an ABAP developer, you may not have given data types a lot of thought in the past and simply used the types that were available. In many situations, however, complex conversions and interpretations are performed in the background that can lead to unexpected results if they aren't used properly.

Before you learn about the different types of systems and their properties, we'll introduce the topic briefly using a few examples. We start in Listing 3.2 with a simple database access using Open SQL.

Implicit type conversions

```
DATA: lv_carrier TYPE string.
SELECT SINGLE carrname FROM scarr INTO lv_carrier
WHERE carrid = 'LH'.
```
Listing 3.2 Implicit Data Type Conversions

This simple ABAP program already uses different data types and conversions. The CARRNAME column of table SCARR is based on the S_CARRNAME data element in the DDIC, which is defined as type CHAR (i.e., string) with a length of 20. In the database, the data type of this column is NVARCHAR(20) (NVARCHAR is a string of variable length). A selection is made into an ABAP variable of type String; in addition, a constant (literal) LH is used in the WHERE clause, which is checked against the CAR-RID column of type CHAR(3). The result of this selection is the name of the airline "Lufthansa." If you now replace the filter condition in Listing 3.2 with the expression WHERE carrid = 'LH abcd', the result may not be obvious at first glance. Because the CARRID field contains only three characters, the record is found in this case as well.

Data types with semantics

For character-type data types with special semantics (e.g., a date or a number as a string), there are some aspects that need to be considered. Listing 3.3, for instance, determines the names of all passengers who booked a flight within the past 30 days (FLDATE column of type DATS) and received a discount of more than 20% (DISCOUNT column of type NUMC).

```
DATA: lv_date TYPE d,
      lv_name TYPE string.

lv_date = sy-datlo - 30.
SELECT DISTINCT name FROM sbook AS b
    INNER JOIN scustom AS c ON b~customid = c~id
    INTO lv_name
    WHERE fldate > lv_date AND fldate <= sy-datlo
    AND c~discount >= '20'.

  WRITE: / lv_name.
ENDSELECT.
```
Listing 3.3 Relevance of Semantic Properties of Data Types

When calculating a time difference in days or handling the string "20" as a number for the discount, this depends on the semantics of the data types. If you execute the corresponding expression in Native SQL via the SQL console in SAP HANA Studio, for example, you'll get different results.

For the *code pushdown paradigm* presented in Chapter 1, Section 1.5.2, where certain calculations are moved to the database, it's important that the data are semantically treated and understood identically; otherwise, the calculations may lead to wrong results. This is relevant, for instance, for the rounding behavior and internationalization aspects. You must especially make sure that there are no unexpected effects after changing an existing program to improve performance.

SAP HANA Supports Only Unicode   **[«]**

Another aspect of handling text data types is the technical encoding of characters using *code pages*. SAP HANA only supports Unicode installations. Non-Unicode installations must be converted to Unicode before migrating them to SAP HANA. The differences between Unicode and non-Unicode systems are beyond the scope of this book.

We'll now describe the different type systems. As an ABAP developer, you're probably already familiar with the type system of the ABAP language and the DDIC, but you may have paid little attention to the mapping of those types to the database's type system in the past.

The type system of the ABAP language defines the data types that can be used in ABAP programming. It's designed in such a way that it can be mapped consistently to the supported operating systems for the application server. The following *built-in types* form the basic structure of the ABAP type system:

ABAP type system

- **Numeric types**: Integers (I), floating point numbers (F), packed numbers (P), and decimal floating point numbers (decfloat16, decfloat34)

- **Character-type data types:** Text field (C), numeric text field (N), date (D), and time (T)

- **Hexadecimal types:** X

- **Types with a variable length:** STRING for strings, and XSTRING for byte sequences

---

Usage of Numeric ABAP Data Types   **[«]**

For integers, you use the I data type. If the value range of this type isn't sufficient, you can use packed numbers or decimal floating point numbers without decimal places instead.

For fractional numbers with a fixed number of decimal places, packed numbers are used. This is the standard type for many business figures such as monetary amounts, distances, weights, and so on. This data type ensures an optimal rounding behavior.

Decimal floating point numbers (decfloat) were introduced with AS ABAP 7.02 to support scenarios where the value range of packed numbers isn't sufficient or where the number of decimal places is variable.

> Floating point numbers (F) should only be used for runtime-critical mathematical calculations where an exact rounding behavior isn't required.

Type system of the DDIC

The type system of the DDIC defines which data types can be used in structures, tables, and so on, in the DDIC. It's defined in such a way that it can be uniquely mapped to all supported database systems via SQL. This is the primary type system for database accesses from ABAP. The mapping of the DDIC types to the basic types of the ABAP language is described in Table 3.1.

Type system of the database

The internal type system of the database defines the possible column types for tables and the corresponding operations. It's the primary type system for queries or implementations in the database (e.g., by means of database procedures). Each database system uses slightly different data types or treats data types slightly differently.

Type mapping

Table 3.1 shows the mapping of DDIC types to ABAP types. The (fixed or variable) length of the corresponding ABAP type is indicated in parentheses.

Dictionary Type	Description	ABAP Type	Example
ACCP	Accounting period	N(6)	'201310'
CHAR	String	C(n)	'ABAP'
CLNT	Client	C(3)	'000'
CUKY	Currency key	C(5)	'EUR'
CURR	Currency field	P(n)	'01012000'
DATS	Date	D	'01012000'
DEC	Calculation/amount field	P(n)	100.20
DF16_RAW	Decimal floating point number (normalized; 16 digits)	decfloat16	100.20
DF16_SCL	Decimal floating point number (scaled; 16 digits)	decfloat16	100.20

Table 3.1 Mapping of ABAP Data Dictionary Types and ABAP Types

Dictionary Type	Description	ABAP Type	Example
DF34_RAW	Decimal floating point number (normalized; 34 digits)	decfloat34	100.20
DF34_SCL	Decimal floating point number (scaled; 34 digits)	decfloat34	100.20
FLTP	Floating point number	F(8)	3.1415926
INT1	1-byte integer	internal	1
INT2	2-byte integer	internal	100
INT4	4-byte integer	I	1.000
LANG	Language	C(1)	'D'
LCHR	Long character string	C(m)	'ABAP is …'
LRAW	Long byte string	X(m)	F4 8F BF
NUMC	Numeric text	N(m)	'123'
QUAN	Quantity field	P(n)	100
RAW	Byte sequence	X(m)	F48FBFBF
RAWSTRING	Byte sequence	XSTRING	27292745010801 8F8F8F8F
SSTRING	String	STRING	'ABAP'
STRING	String	STRING	'ABAP is …'
TIMS	Time	T	'123000'
UNIT	Unit key	C(m)	'KG'

Table 3.1 Mapping of ABAP Data Dictionary Types and ABAP Types (Cont.)

The example in Figure 3.3 shows the mapping of the DDIC types to SAP HANA data types (based on a custom technical table that uses most of the native DDIC types). As described in Chapter 2, Section 2.4.3, you can display the structure of a database table in SAP HANA Studio by double-clicking a table in the database catalog.

Mapping DDIC types to SAP HANA types

In addition to the SQL data type, this table also shows the specific data type used in the column store in SAP HANA. However, this type plays only a minor role for ABAP development on SAP HANA.

Table Name:

ZA4H_DATA_TYPES

Columns | Indexes | Further Properties | Runtime Information

	Name	SQL Data Type	Dim	Column Store Data Type	Key	Not Null	Default
1	CLNT	NVARCHAR	3	STRING	X(1)	X	000
2	ACCP	NVARCHAR	6	STRING		X	
3	CHAR10	NVARCHAR	10	STRING		X	
4	CUKY	NVARCHAR	5	STRING		X	
5	CURR	DECIMAL	10,2	FIXED		X	0
6	DATS	NVARCHAR	8	STRING		X	00000000
7	DEC10_2	DECIMAL	10,2	FIXED		X	0
8	DF16_RAW	VARBINARY	8	RAW		X	800000000000...
9	DF34_RAW	VARBINARY	16	RAW		X	800000000000...
10	DF16_DEC	DECIMAL	10,5	FIXED		X	0
11	DF34_DEC	DECIMAL	26,5	FIXED		X	0
12	DF16_SCL	VARBINARY	8	RAW		X	800000000000...
13	DF16_SCL_SCALE	SMALLINT		INT		X	0
14	DF34_SCL	VARBINARY	16	RAW		X	800000000000...
15	DF34_SCL_SCALE	SMALLINT		INT		X	0
16	INT1	SMALLINT		INT		X	0
17	INT2	SMALLINT		INT		X	0
18	INT4	INTEGER		INT		X	0
19	LANG	NVARCHAR	1	STRING		X	
20	NUMC	NVARCHAR	10	STRING		X	0000000000
21	QUAN	DECIMAL	10	FIXED		X	0
22	RAW100	VARBINARY	100	RAW			
23	RAWSTRING	BLOB		ST_MEMORY_LOB			
24	SSTRING	NVARCHAR	100	STRING		X	
25	STRING	NCLOB	21...	ST_MEMORY_LOB			
26	TIMS	NVARCHAR	6	STRING		X	000000
27	UNIT	NVARCHAR	3	STRING		X	

Figure 3.3 Mapping of ABAP Data Dictionary Types to SAP HANA Types

NULL value

It's important to note that there is no representation of the NULL value from SQL in the ABAP type system. However, there is an *initial* value for every ABAP and DDIC data type, for example, an empty string for string types or 0 for numeric types. This is particularly relevant for certain join variants (*outer joins*), as you'll see in Section 3.2.2.

Data types with a binary represen-tation

Certain data types with a binary representation usually can't be used directly in implementations in SAP HANA. These are, for example, floating point numbers of type DF16_RAW and DF16_SCL (as well as the corresponding types with a length of 34). Another example is the data cluster in ABAP, which is a special table type allowing you to read and write any kind of data record via the ABAP commands EXPORT TO DATABASE and IMPORT FROM DATABASE. The associated data is stored in the database in a column of type LRAW in a proprietary format that can only be unpacked via the ABAP kernel. You must take these aspects into account when considering moving parts of the logic to the database.

3.2 ABAP Database Access

Having introduced the basic database architecture of AS ABAP, we'll now describe the actual database access from ABAP. This includes both the definition of data models (tables, views, etc.) and write and read operations for data records.

The database is usually accessed via SQL. The SQL database language covers three intersecting categories, which are described in Table 3.2.

SQL

Type	Purpose	Examples
Data definition language (DDL)	Definition of data structures and operations	CREATE TABLE, DROP TABLE, CREATE VIEW
Data manipulation language (DML)	Read and write operations for data records	SELECT, INSERT, UPDATE, DELETE
Data control language (DCL)	Definition of access restrictions for database objects	GRANT, REVOKE

Table 3.2 Overview of SQL

In traditional ABAP application development, DML operations are implemented via Open SQL (see Section 3.2.2), while DDL is used indirectly via the DDIC (see Section 3.2.1). DCL, on the other hand, isn't relevant for *traditional* application development because the ABAP application server—as described in Figure 3.2—uses a technical user to log in to the database. In addition, the authorizations for the actual application user are checked using the ABAP authorization system (e.g., using the AUTHORITY-CHECK command). When using SAP HANA for implementing part of the application logic inside the database and accessing data outside the ABAP schema, you must also consider the authorization concepts of the database.

3.2.1 ABAP Data Dictionary

Using the ABAP Data Dictionary (DDIC), you can create data models in the database. These data models can be enriched with semantic aspects such as texts, fixed values, and relationships. This metadata, which is particularly important for business scenarios, plays an important role for developments in SAP HANA because it can be used for modeling and implementation tasks in SAP HANA.

Qualities of the DDIC

Before we describe the individual types of development objects (tables, views, etc.), let's discuss two very important qualities of the DDIC:

▸ Because the DDIC is fully integrated with ABAP lifecycle management, you can transport the defined database objects and their properties into an SAP landscape.

▸ Objects in the DDIC can be extended; that is, SAP customers and partners can adjust these objects to their needs, for instance, by adding columns to a table.

The extensibility of DDIC objects is also important to consider when performing modeling and programming tasks in SAP HANA.

Object types in the DDIC

From a development perspective, Transaction SE11 is the main tool for using the DDIC. You use this transaction to define and maintain the following object types:

▸ **Table**
Tables define the structure for physically storing data in the database. A table consists of a number of fields (columns) and their corresponding data types. In addition to individual fields, you can also include predefined structures.

The DDIC supports different types of tables, for example, tables for application data, Customizing data, or master data, which differ in certain lifecycle management aspects. Moreover, you can maintain a series of technical properties for a table.

In addition to defining the mere field list, you can include additional metadata:

- *Foreign key relationships:* By specifying check tables for fields, you can define specific foreign key relationships. This information is used when modeling views in SAP HANA Studio (see Chapter 4, Section 4.4).

- *Currency and unit of measure:* To store monetary amounts or unit of measures, the currencies or units must be defined in addition to the numeric value. This is usually done via another column, and the DDIC allows you to define a relationship between the two columns.

- *Search helps:* By specifying a search help for a column, a generic input help can be provided in transactions without any programming effort.

▶ **View**
Views allow you to define specific views on several DDIC tables. The DDIC supports several view types for different usage scenarios:

- *Database views*: Used to define SQL views on the database. In ABAP 7.4, Core Data Services (CDS) views provide an additional variant that offers comprehensive capabilities (see Chapter 6, Section 6.2.1).

- *Projection views*: Used to hide fields of a table. These views don't exist physically in the database.

- *Help views*: Used as a selection method in search helps.

- *Maintenance views*: Facilitate a consistent entry of data records for interlinked database tables.

▶ **Data type**
Based on the basic types, user-specific types can be defined in the DDIC. These globally defined objects can be used when defining table columns and within ABAP programs.

The DDIC supports three kinds of data types:

- Elementary data elements
- Composite structures
- Table types

These data types can't be used directly for modeling and programming tasks in SAP HANA.

▶ **Domain**

Domains can be used to define value ranges. For an elementary data type, a length is specified (for numeric types, the number of decimal places may also be defined). In addition, you can limit the value range further by fixed values, intervals, or check tables.

Domains can't be used directly for modeling and programming tasks in SAP HANA.

▶ **Search help**

Search helps (also referred to as input helps or F4 helps) provide input options for fields in an SAP user interface. Using the DDIC, you can define such search helps based on tables, views, or a freely programmed Exit.

Implementing specific search helps on SAP HANA is described in more detail in Chapter 10.

▶ **Lock object**

Lock objects can be used to define logical locks in the database, as described in Figure 3.2.

Because views plays an important role in the context of SAP HANA, the possibility to define database views via the DDIC will be explained in more detail in Section 3.2.3.

Technical settings   In addition to pure data structures, you can maintain more properties in the technical settings for a database table, including the following two options:

▶ **ABAP table buffer**

Many tables used in application scenarios are suitable candidates for buffering on the application server because they contain a relatively small amount of data. Read operations are also executed much more often for those tables than write operations. The ABAP table buffer provides an efficient option for this purpose. You can activate buffering via the technical properties in the DDIC, and you can also configure whether single records, ranges, or the full table should be buffered. When using SAP HANA, where table contents are usually stored in the main memory of the database, the ABAP table buffer also plays an important role (see Chapter 14).

▸ **Data class and size category**
By specifying the data class and the expected table entries, the database system can efficiently reserve the required storage space. Moreover, you can use the size category of a table to analyze ABAP program performance issues that were detected in static code analyses.

As of SAP NetWeaver 7.4, the DDIC allows you to specify whether tables should be stored in the column store or in the row store in SAP HANA (see Figure 3.4). When selecting the default value UNDEFINED, the column store is used, which is recommended for basically all application cases. There are a few exceptions, which are described in Chapter 14 as well.

Row stores or column stores

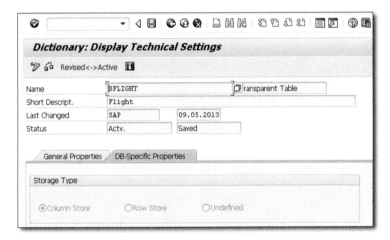

Figure 3.4 Database-Specific Settings for Tables

You can also define database indices in the DDIC. When doing so, you can create indices only for certain databases (*inclusion list*) or exclude them by specifying an *exclusion list*. During a database migration to SAP HANA, the system first creates entries for existing secondary indices in the exclusion list, so that the corresponding index on SAP HANA isn't created automatically. Instead, those indices should only be activated on a case-by-case basis. Technical background information and recommendations for index usage on SAP HANA can also be found in Chapter 14.

Indices

Figure 3.5 shows the index exclusion on SAP HANA for table SBOOK. In this case, the ACY and CUS indexes aren't created on SAP HANA because HDB is on the exclusion list.

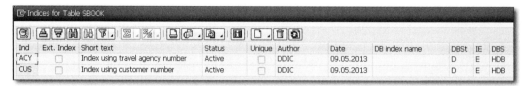

Figure 3.5 Index Exclusion for SAP HANA

Pool and cluster tables

In the past, some database versions came with severe restrictions on the maximum number of tables in the system and provided poor compression capabilities. To avoid these problems, you can create special table types in the DDIC—*pool* and *cluster tables*—where several logical tables are combined into one physical database table. These logical tables can be accessed from ABAP like normal database tables; however, there are also a number of restrictions to consider. Because pool and cluster tables aren't needed on SAP HANA, existing tables are converted into normal transparent tables when migrating to SAP HANA. The main advantage of this conversion is that the tables can also be used for modeling and programming tasks in SAP HANA, as described in Chapter 4. During migration, pool and cluster tables are compatible with existing applications. There is no need to adapt existing ABAP code. However, certain aspects must be considered with regard to the sorting behavior, which will be explained in more detail in Chapter 14.

3.2.2 Open SQL

Open SQL provides an option for database access that is integrated into the ABAP programming language. Both the supported syntax and the detailed semantics of Open SQL are database-independent, which makes it possible to write applications in ABAP without knowing the details of the underlying database system. This section provides an overview of the functional scope of classic Open SQL. The Open SQL enhancements, which are available as of ABAP 7.4, are discussed in Chapter 6, Section 6.4.

Read Access with Open SQL

SAP HANA mainly offers options to accelerate read accesses. Using Open SQL is the primary and simplest option to move data-intensive operations to SAP HANA.

In this section, we'll use examples to detail some of the advanced options of Open SQL that you may not have used in the past. Although the syntax of the ABAP command SELECT won't be explained in detail here, a comprehensive documentation of the Open SQL syntax can be found in the ABAP online help.

The examples deal with the following three aspects, which basically cover the advanced options for expressing calculation logic in Open SQL:

Express calculation logic in Open SQL

- ▸ Reading fields from several tables with foreign key relationships (use of *joins* and the FOR ALL ENTRIES clause)
- ▸ Calculating key figures based on the values of a column by using the aggregate functions (determining quantities, totals, average values, etc.)
- ▸ Selecting special entries of a table based on complex criteria using subqueries (*subselects*) and existence checks

In the first example, we'll use a join to read values from tables SCARR and SCURX (currencies). Depending on the table entries that should be included in the result, there are several options for creating joins in SQL. Open SQL supports *inner joins* and *left outer joins*. When we describe the process for modeling views in SAP HANA Studio in Chapter 4, Section 4.4, the different join variants are also explained in detail. Listing 3.4 uses the two variants that are supported in Open SQL and shows the differences between them.

Joins

```
REPORT zr_a4h_chapter3_open1.

TYPES: BEGIN OF result_type,
         currkey TYPE s_curr,
         currdec TYPE currdec,
         carrname TYPE s_carrname,
       END OF result_type.

DATA: wa TYPE result_type.

" Selection of all currencies and corresponding
" airlines. The inner join is used to select only
```

```
" currencies with a corresponding airline that
" uses this currency.
SELECT c~currkey c~currdec r~carrname FROM scurx AS c
    INNER JOIN scarr AS r
      ON c~currkey = r~currcode INTO wa.

  WRITE: / wa-currkey , wa-currdec , wa-carrname.
ENDSELECT.

" Selection of all currencies and corresponding
" airlines. The outer join is used to also select
" currencies without a
" corresponding airline.
" In this case, the value is initial.
SELECT c~currkey c~currdec r~carrname FROM scurx AS c
    LEFT OUTER JOIN scarr AS r
      ON c~currkey = r~currcode INTO wa.

  WRITE: / wa-currkey , wa-currdec , wa-carrname.
ENDSELECT.
```

Listing 3.4 Inner Joins and Left Outer Joins in Open SQL

NULL as the result of left outer joins As already mentioned in Section 3.1.3, there is no representation of the NULL value in ABAP. As shown in Listing 3.4, where no corresponding data record is found in the "right-hand" table, a left outer join generates the value NULL for the corresponding columns of the result set in the database. In ABAP, this value is converted into the initial value of the column. Consequently, whether no value was found or whether the corresponding value happens to be the initial value can't be determined. When executing the equivalent SQL statement via the SQL console in SAP HANA Studio, NULL values are displayed as question marks (?) as shown in Figure 3.6.

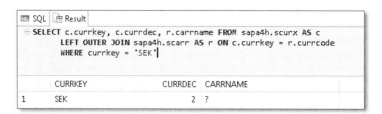

Figure 3.6 Representation of NULL Values in the SQL Console

In addition to the described inner join and left outer join, the expression FOR ALL ENTRIES provides another option in Open SQL to leverage foreign key relationships and use internal tables to create joins. This SAP-proprietary expression isn't part of the SQL standard and is a natural enhancement of the *ranges* that are used in selection options. A typical example of using this expression is shown in Listing 3.5. In this example, all airlines are first read, and then the airlines that can be displayed by the user are stored in an internal table. Subsequently, the FOR ALL ENTRIES clause is used for a type of inner join with table SFLIGHT.

"FOR ALL ENTRIES" expression

```
REPORT zr_a4h_chapter3_open2.

TYPES: BEGIN OF ty_carrid,
         carrid TYPE s_carrid,
       END OF ty_carrid.

DATA: ls_carrier TYPE ty_carrid,
      ls_flight TYPE sflight,
      lt_carrier TYPE TABLE OF ty_carrid.
SELECT carrid FROM scarr INTO ls_carrier.
  " Check authorization and, if
  " successful, add to internal table
  AUTHORITY-CHECK OBJECT 'S_CARRID'
      ID 'CARRID' FIELD ls_carrier-carrid
      ID 'ACTVT' FIELD '03'.

  IF sy-subrc = 0.
    APPEND ls_carrier TO lt_carrier.
  ENDIF.

ENDSELECT.

" Output of all flights of the airlines for which
" the user is authorized.
IF ( lt_carrier IS NOT INITIAL ).
  SELECT * FROM sflight INTO ls_flight
      FOR ALL ENTRIES IN lt_carrier
        WHERE carrid = lt_carrier-carrid.

    WRITE: / ls_flight-carrid,
             ls_flight-connid, ls_flight-fldate.
  ENDSELECT.
ENDIF.
```

Listing 3.5 Join of a Database Table with an Internal Table

[!] **Special Properties of FOR ALL ENTRIES**

For performance reasons, changing a nested SELECT statement into a FOR ALL ENTRIES expression can be useful. However, when doing so, you should pay attention to three important properties of the FOR ALL ENTRIES expression:

▸ If the driver table (i.e., the internal table following the FOR ALL ENTRIES expression) is empty, *all* values are returned as the result. If you perhaps forget the IF check before the selection at the end in Listing 3.5, you would, under certain circumstances, select data that the user might not be allowed to access.

▸ The driver table shouldn't contain any duplicates. This helps limit the number of accesses to a minimum and avoids the selection of identical data from the database.

▸ Selections with FOR ALL ENTRIES are always performed with an implicit DISTINCT so that no duplicates are returned. If you only select the columns CARRID and CONNID (instead of *) for the second SELECT statement in Listing 3.5, for example, far fewer results are returned (independent of the flight date, every connection is returned only once).

More information on SAP HANA is provided in Chapter 14, which also includes recommendations for optimizing ABAP programs.

Aggregate functions

In the third example, we'll use the aggregate functions (COUNT, SUM, MIN, MAX, AVG). Using an SQL query, you can determine inconsistencies within the data model. To do so, we'll execute a query to find out if there are more bookings for the economy class of a flight (based on the entries in table SBOOK) than occupied seats (attribute SEATSOCC in table SFLIGHT). In Listing 3.6, a join is combined directly with the calculation of a quantity (COUNT) and the limitation of the result set based on the result of the aggregation (HAVING).

```
REPORT zr_a4h_chapter3_open3.

TYPES: BEGIN OF ty_result,
         carrid TYPE sbook-carrid,
         connid TYPE sbook-connid,
         fldate  TYPE sbook-fldate,
         count_sbook TYPE i,
         count_sflight TYPE i,
       END OF ty_result.
DATA ls_result TYPE ty_result.
```

```
" Determination of all flights with more
" economy class bookings (table SBOOK) than
" occupied seats (table SFLIGHT)
SELECT b~carrid b~connid b~fldate
       f~seatsocc AS count_sflight
       COUNT( * ) AS count_sbook
  FROM sbook AS b
  INNER JOIN sflight AS f ON b~carrid = f~carrid
                         AND b~connid = f~connid
                         AND b~fldate = f~fldate
  INTO ls_result
  WHERE b~cancelled <> 'X' AND b~class = 'Y'
  GROUP BY b~carrid b~connid b~fldate f~seatsocc
  HAVING COUNT( * ) > f~seatsocc
  ORDER BY b~fldate b~carrid b~connid.
  WRITE: / ls_result-carrid, ls_result-connid,
           ls_result-fldate, ls_result-count_sbook,
           ls_result-count_sflight.
ENDSELECT.
```

Listing 3.6 Aggregate Functions in Open SQL

When using aggregations, it must always be noted that the GROUP BY expression lists all nonaggregated attributes; this also includes attributes that are used only in a HAVING clause.

As you can see, rather complex queries can be expressed via Open SQL. In the fourth example, we'll add another element: *subqueries*—and, as a special case, *existence checks*. A subquery is a SELECT statement in parentheses that can be used as part of the WHERE clause (both in reading and writing accesses). Typical use cases are existence checks with the following structure:

Subqueries

```
SELECT ... FROM ... INTO ...
  WHERE EXISTS ( SELECT ... ).
```

If only one column is selected in a subquery, this is referred to as a *scalar subquery*. In addition to simple comparisons (=, >, <) for a column, these queries support other operations as well (ALL, ANY, SOME, IN). The example in Listing 3.7 shows how subqueries can be used to implement a nested filter condition.

```
REPORT zr_a4h_chapter3_open4.

DATA: ls_flight TYPE sflight.
```

```
" Output of all flights from 2013 with more
" occupied seats than the average value for the
" same route in 2012
SELECT * FROM sflight AS f INTO ls_flight
  WHERE fldate LIKE '2013 %' AND seatsocc >
    ( SELECT AVG( seatsocc ) FROM sflight
              WHERE carrid = f~carrid
                AND connid = f~connid
                AND fldate LIKE '2012 %' ).

  WRITE: / ls_flight-carrid,
           ls_flight-connid, ls_flight-fldate.
ENDSELECT.
```
Listing 3.7 Usage of Subqueries

The approaches described previously provide a great variety of options for accessing database tables. Using joins, you can define relationships between several tables (and via FOR ALL ENTRIES, even between internal tables); use the aggregate functions for simple calculations; and use subqueries to allow nested selections. In addition to the SQL vocabulary, Open SQL provides further techniques to design database access flexibly and efficiently, which will be described next.

Dynamic SQL   Using Open SQL, you can also specify parts of an SQL statement *dynamically* so that, for instance, the table name or the selected columns can be controlled via a variable that has to be specified in parentheses (as shown in the example in Listing 3.8).

```
DATA: lv_table   TYPE string,
      lt_fields  TYPE string_table,
      ls_carrier TYPE scarr.

" Table name as a string
lv_table = 'SCARR'.

" Dynamic output of the columns
APPEND 'CARRID' TO lt_fields.
APPEND 'CARRNAME' TO lt_fields.

SELECT (lt_fields) FROM (lv_table)
  INTO CORRESPONDING FIELDS OF ls_carrier.
    WRITE: / ls_carrier-carrid , ls_carrier-carrname.
ENDSELECT.
```
Listing 3.8 Dynamic Open SQL

When working with dynamic Open SQL, note that the separating keywords (SELECT, FROM, WHERE, etc.) still have to be used statically in the code. This particularly helps prevent potential security vulnerabilities because certain attacks by means of *SQL injection* (introduction of unwanted database operations by an attacker) aren't possible. However, especially when using dynamic SQL, you should always make sure that the values of the variables are checked to avoid runtime errors or security issues. To do so, you can use a list of allowed values (*whitelists*) or *regular expression patterns*.

Using *cursors*, you can separate the definition of the selection from the data retrieval. For this purpose, you first have to open a cursor by specifying the selection, and you can then retrieve the data from the database using this cursor at a later point in time or elsewhere (e.g., in a FORM routine), as shown in Listing 3.9. Because the number of cursors that can be used in parallel is limited, you should always make sure to close a cursor after using it.

Using cursors

```
DATA: lv_cursor TYPE cursor,
      ls_flight TYPE sflight.

" Defining the cursor
OPEN CURSOR lv_cursor FOR
     SELECT * FROM sflight
              WHERE carrid = 'LH'.

" Retrieving a data record via the cursor
FETCH NEXT CURSOR lv_cursor INTO ls_flight.

" Closing the cursor
CLOSE CURSOR lv_cursor.
```
Listing 3.9 Simple Example of Using a Cursor

The data flow between the database and the application server can be controlled in Open SQL by defining package sizes via the PACKAGE SIZE addition (see Listing 3.10). When doing so, the specified number of rows is always retrieved from the database when selecting into an internal table within a loop.

Package sizes

```
DATA: lt_book TYPE TABLE OF sbook.

" Selection into packages of 1,000 rows each
```

```
SELECT * FROM sbook
          INTO TABLE lt_book
          PACKAGE SIZE 1000.

  " ...
ENDSELECT.
```
Listing 3.10 Selecting Data While Specifying a Package Size

Read operations in Open SQL

Before dealing with writing accesses, we'll briefly summarize the options for read access provided by Open SQL. Using the SELECT statement, you can efficiently read data records from a relational data model (tables with foreign key relationships). The aggregate function allows you to express simple calculations on a column. Data transfer from the database can be controlled using advanced techniques. However, it isn't possible to use complex filter expressions, case distinctions, or business calculations directly within the database. Furthermore, interim results can't be temporarily stored in the database because the result of a query is always transferred to the application server.

Write Accesses and Transaction Behavior

The basic principles of the ABAP transaction concept, and in particular the differences between the database LUW and the SAP LUW, were already discussed in Figure 3.2. To change database contents, Open SQL provides the statements INSERT (creating data records), UPDATE (changing existing data records), MODIFY (changing or creating data records), and DELETE (deleting data records). In addition to changing individual entries, you can also edit several rows at the same time. For example, you can use an Open SQL statement to create or update several data records based on the contents of an internal table in one go. This usually significantly improves the performance of a program because a lot fewer database accesses are necessary. The example in Listing 3.11 shows how these so-called *array operations* are used. Similarly, you can update all or only selected columns when changing a data record. This can also lead to increased performance. These two techniques are particularly recommended on SAP HANA (see Chapter 14).

```
REPORT zr_a4h_chapter3_modify_array.

DATA: lt_country TYPE TABLE OF za4h_country_cls.
```

```
" Select countries and number of customers
SELECT country COUNT(*) AS class FROM scustom
  INTO CORRESPONDING FIELDS OF TABLE lt_country
  GROUP BY country.

" Change table entries in one go
MODIFY za4h_country_cls FROM TABLE lt_country.

COMMIT WORK.
```

Listing 3.11 Modifying Table Contents via Array Operations

In Open SQL, the COMMIT WORK or ROLLBACK WORK statements are used for explicit transaction control. There are also situations where an implicit Commit (e.g., after completing a dialog step) or a rollback (e.g., in case of a runtime error) are performed automatically. To process database changes from several dialog steps in a single database LUW, the SAP LUW concept offers several bundling techniques. This primarily includes calling update modules (CALL FUNCTION ... IN UPDATE TASK) and bundling via subroutines (PERFORM ... ON COMMIT). If you perform direct writing operations on the database (e.g., with SQLScript), the programming model differs significantly from the traditional ABAP programming model (see Figure 3.2 and Chapter 14).

Even though Open SQL is database independent, it's possible to pass *hints* to the respective database system (or, more specifically, to the database optimizer) to specify how a statement should be executed. In practice, this variant offers tuning options for database experts and is used rather infrequently in normal ABAP development. Using hints, you can specify how the database should access the data (e.g., using a specific index). Because hints must be maintained manually (e.g., when performing a release upgrade or a database migration), this option should only be used if there are no other tuning methods.

Database hints

Although traditional Open SQL has a large functional scope, it only covers parts of the options available in the SQL standard. One reason for some commands not being available in Open SQL (e.g., UNION, CASE) is that they were implemented differently or not at all by the different database vendors. Moreover, proprietary SQL enhancements of databases via Open SQL can't be used due to database independence, which

Limitations of Open SQL

complicates the access to special engines particularly for SAP HANA. For this reason, SAP is working on both extending the scope of Open SQL (in cooperation with the manufacturers of supported databases) and providing specific capabilities of SAP HANA to ABAP developers. The chapters of Part II focus on these options.

3.2.3 Database Views in the ABAP Data Dictionary

Database views are a standard option for looking at data based on one or several tables in the database and thus predefining parts of a SQL query. In most database systems, views are created using SQL:

```
CREATE VIEW view_name AS SELECT ...
```

This section provides an overview of traditional options for creating views using DDIC. Chapter 4 will introduce you to SAP HANA-specific options that go beyond the wrapping of a simple SQL query.

Limitations
While you can define data views using the DDIC, not all options of Open SQL are available when following this approach. Basically, you can link several tables via an inner join and add fields to the projection list. You can't use other join types, aggregates, or subqueries, however.

Example: SFLIGHTS
Figure 3.7 shows the standard SFLIGHTS view, which defines a join to add fields from tables SCARR, SPFLI, and SFLIGHT. The corresponding CREATE VIEW statement can be displayed via the menu bar (EXTRAS • CREATE STATEMENT).

Access database views
These database views can be accessed like tables from ABAP coding using Open SQL and Native SQL. In this context, note that modifying operations can only be executed for views that access only one table. Similar to table access, you can configure buffering in the technical settings.

[»] **Core Data Services**

SAP currently works on a unified view creation process in SAP HANA and the DDIC called *Core Data Services* (CDS). The goal of this approach is to enhance the scope of functions significantly for defining views in the DDIC. Chapter 6, Section 6.2.1, presents the options of CDS in detail.

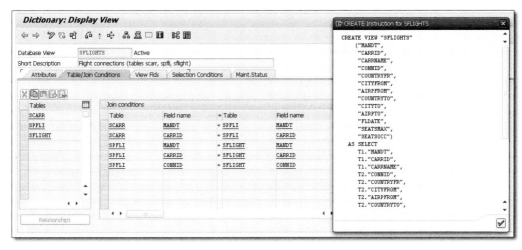

Figure 3.7 Dictionary View SFLIGHTS

3.2.4 Database Access via Native SQL

In addition to Open SQL, which enables database-independent access that is integrated into the ABAP programming language, there is another method for accessing the database from ABAP. With this variant, you more or less directly specify the native database commands. For this reason, this is also referred to as *Native SQL*.

Before we deal with the technical aspects of supporting Native SQL in AS ABAP, we'll explain why this variant plays a more important role in the context of SAP HANA than in the past. To benefit fully from the potential of SAP HANA, you must particularly use those functions that aren't standard relational database capabilities, includes using capabilities in SAP HANA-specific SQL beyond the SQL standard, and accessing development objects in SAP HANA beyond normal tables and SQL views. (Chapter 4 explains this in detail.) At this point, note that using Native SQL will play an important role in this context.

Native SQL and SAP HANA

There are two traditional options for using Native SQL in ABAP: either via the EXEC SQL statement or via *ABAP Database Connectivity* (ADBC)—an object-oriented interface available as of SAP NetWeaver 2004 (release 6.40). In this context, SAP recommends using ADBC because this approach provides greater flexibility and better options for trouble-

Variants for using Native SQL

shooting. Within the scope of this book, we'll therefore describe and use the ADBC variant. With regard to some of its concepts, ADBC is similar to Java Database Connectivity (JDBC), a standard database interface of the Java platform.

[»] **ABAP Managed Database Procedures**

In addition to the options mentioned, you can also create *ABAP Managed Database Procedures (AMDP)* for SAP HANA as of ABAP 7.4 SP 8. These database procedures are implemented with SQLScript and are realized as a special ABAP method. This important new technology is presented in Chapter 6, Section 6.5.

ADBC To use ADBC, essentially three ABAP classes are needed: CL_SQL_CON-NECTION, CL_SQL_STATEMENT, and CL_SQL_RESULT_SET. In the first step, you must use the constructor (or the static method GET_CONNECTION) of the CL_SQL_CONNECTION class to retrieve a database connection. If you don't specify any parameters, it will return the standard database connection, which is also used by default in Open SQL. However, you can also specify the name of a secondary connection (see Section 3.2.5). Using this connection, you create an object of type CL_SQL_STATEMENT via the CREATE_STATEMENT method, which can be used, for example, for reading database accesses via the method EXECUTE_QUERY by passing the SQL statement as a string. The result of this query is an instance of type CL_SQL_RESULT_SET. Similarly, writing accesses can be executed via EXE-CUTE_UPDATE, or DDL statements via EXECUTE_DDL.

Store the query result in an internal table To transfer the result of a query to an internal ABAP table, you'll first have to pass a reference to this table via the SET_PARAM_TABLE method. Then you'll be able to start the data transfer via NEXT_PACKAGE. When doing so, you can specify the package size, that is, the number of rows. The selected columns and corresponding data types must be compatible with the target structure for a call to be successful.

Error handling If an error occurs when executing the SQL statement, an exception of type CX_SQL_EXCEPTION is thrown, which can be used to obtain details such as the error code and error text. Possible runtime errors are described in detail in Chapter 7, Section 7.2.

The example in Listing 3.12 shows how the named classes are used for a   **Example**
simple read access. In this example, the SQL statement uses expressions
from the SAP HANA-specific SQL dialect, which can't be used in the
same manner in Open SQL.

```
REPORT ZR_A4H_CHAPTER3_ADBC.

" Variables for ADBC call
DATA: lv_statement  TYPE string,
      lo_conn       TYPE REF TO cl_sql_connection,
      lo_statement  TYPE REF TO cl_sql_statement,
      lo_result_set TYPE REF TO cl_sql_result_set.

" Definition of the result structure
TYPES: BEGIN OF ty_result,
         carrid TYPE s_carr_id,
         connid TYPE s_conn_id,
         fldate TYPE s_date,
         days   type i,
       END OF ty_result.

DATA: lt_result TYPE TABLE OF ty_result,
      lr_result TYPE REF TO data.

FIELD-SYMBOLS: <l> TYPE ty_result.
" Data reference
GET REFERENCE OF lt_result INTO lr_result.
" Native SQL Statement: sequence and data types
" of selected columns must match
" results structure
lv_statement =
     | SELECT carrid, connid, fldate, |
  && |   days_between(fldate, current_utcdate) as days |
  && | FROM sflight WHERE mandt = '{ sy-mandt }' and   |
  && |   days_between(fldate, current_utcdate) < 10    |.

TRY.
    " Prepare SQL connection and statement
    lo_conn = cl_sql_connection=>get_connection( ).
    lo_statement = lo_conn->create_statement( ).
    lo_result_set = lo_statement->execute_query( lv_
statement ).
    lo_result_set->set_param_table( lr_result ).

    " Get result
    lo_result_set->next_package( ).
    lo_result_set->close( ).
  CATCH cx_sql_exception.
    " Error handling
```

```
ENDTRY.

LOOP AT lt_result ASSIGNING <1>.
  WRITE: / <1>-carrid , <1>-connid , <1>-fldate, <1>-days.
ENDLOOP.
```
Listing 3.12 Native SQL Access via ADBC

The days_between function in SAP HANA-specific SQL determines the number of days between the parameters, that is, the number of days between the current date (which is obtained from the current_utcdate variable provided within SAP HANA-specific SQL) and the flight date in the example. The output of Listing 3.12 thus comprises all future flights and all flights within the past 10 days. For every flight, the system also displays the difference (in days) between the flight date and the current date. Because this query can't be expressed via Open SQL, the only traditional option is to load all data into the application server and calculate the dates via ABAP. Because we "pushed" a complex filter expression down to the database, this means that we implemented a so-called *code pushdown* via Native SQL.

Prepared statements and placeholders

If you want to use the same SQL statement consecutively with different parameterization, you should use prepared statements for performance reasons. These *prepared SQL statements* reduce the effort for subsequent executions. To do this, you create an instance of the CL_SQL_PREPARED_STATEMENT class (a subclass of CL_SQL_STATEMENT), while passing an SQL statement with placeholders that can be bound to a variable. Listing 3.13 shows the usage of prepared statements and placeholders using some of the ABAP language elements from ABAP 7.4 (see Appendix B). Note that you can use placeholders independently of prepared statements.

```
REPORT zr_a4h_chapter3_adbc2.

" Variables for the ADBC call
DATA: lv_sql    TYPE string,
      lo_result TYPE REF TO cl_sql_result_set.

DATA: lt_result TYPE TABLE OF scarr,
      lv_param  TYPE s_carrid.

" SQL statement with placeholder
lv_sql =
    | SELECT * |
```

```
&& |    FROM SCARR WHERE mandt  = '{ sy-mandt }' |
&& |                   AND carrid = ? limit 5|.

TRY.
    " Create prepared statement and set parameter
    DATA(lo_sql) =
          NEW cl_sql_prepared_statement( lv_sql ).
    lo_sql->set_param( REF #( lv_param ) ).

    " Execution with value for placeholder
    lv_param = 'LH'.
    lo_result = lo_sql->execute_query( ).
    lo_result->set_param_table( REF #( lt_result ) ).
    " Get and display result
    lo_result->next_package( ).
    lo_result->close( ).
    LOOP AT lt_result ASSIGNING FIELD-SYMBOL(<l1>).
      WRITE: / <l1>-carrid , <l1>-carrname.
    ENDLOOP.

    " Second execution with different value
    CLEAR lt_result.
    lv_param = 'UA'.
    lo_result = lo_sql->execute_query( ).
    lo_result->set_param_table( REF #( lt_result ) ).

    " Get and display result
    lo_result->next_package( ).
    lo_result->close( ).
    LOOP AT lt_result ASSIGNING FIELD-SYMBOL(<l2>).
      WRITE: / <l2>-carrid , <l2>-carrname.
    ENDLOOP.

    " Close prepared SQL statement
    lo_sql->close( ).
  CATCH cx_sql_exception INTO DATA(lo_ex).
    " Error handling
    lv_param = 'UA'.
    WRITE: | Exception: { lo_ex->get_text( ) } |.
ENDTRY.
```

Listing 3.13 Prepared SELECT Statement with ADBC

In addition, when working with ABAP 7.4, you can execute mass operations via the ADBC interface—just as you can when using Open SQL. For this purpose, the SET_PARAM_TABLE method is available in the CL_SQL_STATEMENT class, which can be used to pass an internal table as an input

Mass operations

143

parameter. This makes it possible to use the ADBC interface to fill a database table with the values of an internal table, for instance.

[+] **Using the SQL Console in SAP HANA Studio**

Usage of Native SQL is rather error-prone; this is especially true because syntax errors in SQL statements are only noticed at runtime. Before using a Native SQL statement in ABAP via ADBC, you should therefore first test the statement via the SQL console in SAP HANA Studio, which was introduced in Chapter 2, Section 2.4.3.

When implementing commands that were executed successfully in the SQL console in ABAP, note the following differences:

▶ To some degree, the execution of SQL statements is connected with the *session context*, that is, the state of the database connection. This particularly includes the default schema, the client, the language, and the application user. Depending on the query, this can potentially lead to different results.

▶ A Native SQL statement in ABAP can only contain a single SQL command. It isn't possible to execute several commands separated by semicolons.

Open SQL vs. Native SQL

In comparison to Open SQL, some capabilities aren't directly integrated into Native SQL. These include the ABAP table buffer (Native SQL doesn't read from the buffer), automatic client handling (when using Native SQL, the client must be inserted manually in WHERE or JOIN conditions, as shown in the example from Listing 3.12), and some other useful enhancements in Open SQL (IN, FOR ALL ENTRIES, INTO CORRESPONDING FIELDS, etc.).

[+] **Pitfalls When Using Native SQL**

There are some pitfalls with regard to the syntax when using Native SQL for the first time. To avoid unnecessary errors, consider the following.

Selected fields are separated by a comma:

▶ Open SQL: SELECT carrid connid FROM SFLIGHT

▶ Native SQL: SELECT carrid, connid FROM SFLIGHT

For table aliases, a period is used instead of the tilde character:

▶ Open SQL: SELECT f~carrid FROM SFLIGHT as f

▶ Native SQL: SELECT f.carrid FROM SFLIGHT as f

Moreover, the log and trace entries in different analysis tools (see Section 3.3) contain less context information for Native SQL. This means that the names of the tables or views aren't visible because the ABAP Compiler can't obtain this information from the Native SQL statement. On the other hand, when using ADBC, this context can be set using the SET_TABLE_NAME_FOR_TRACE method of the CL_SQL_STATEMENT class.

Log and trace entries

To conclude this section, we'll briefly explain some transaction-related aspects of Native SQL. If you use the standard database connection for Native SQL access, you must take into account that you share the database transaction within the ABAP session with other program components (e.g., classes from the SAP standard). To avoid inconsistencies, you should not run any commands for transaction control (e.g., COMMIT or ROLLBACK) via Native SQL.

Transaction-related aspects

Comprehensive Database Knowledge Required to Use Native SQL   [!]

Because incorrect usage of Native SQL can impact system stability, comprehensive database knowledge is required to use this language. Using the following Native SQL statement to set a schema context for the standard database connection of the AS ABAP leads to major problems:

```
SET SCHEMA <name>
```

The reason for this is that other database accesses within the same session no longer use the default schema of the AS ABAP but use the set schema instead. This can easily lead to inconsistencies within the system and should be avoided at all costs. In general, use Native SQL with great caution, and always take security concerns into account (e.g., the avoidance of SQL injection).

3.2.5 Secondary Database Connections

In addition to the primary database, that is, the database containing all tables maintained by the application server (including the actual ABAP code), AS ABAP can access other databases as well. These are referred to as *secondary databases* or *secondary database connections*. This section describes the technical steps to set up and use a secondary database connection.

Secondary connections are important in the context of SAP HANA, especially when implementing the side-by-side scenarios described in

Side-by-side scenarios

Chapter 1, Section 1.4.1. In those cases, complex database queries with very long runtimes are moved to SAP HANA. Secondary connections also form the basis for *Redirected Database Access* (RDA, see Appendix D), which is offered by the SAP Kernel 7.21. With this kernel release, not only can the secondary connection be maintained in the ABAP code but also in Customizing for specific programs and tables.

Database Shared Library (DBSL)

As a prerequisite for setting up a secondary database connection, the matching DBSL with the database driver must be installed; for SAP HANA, this means the DBSL must be installed with the SAP HANA Client. You can then create new connections in the Database Administration Cockpit (DBA Cockpit) via Transaction DBACOCKPIT (alternatively, you can also use Transaction ST04). The DBA Cockpit is the central starting point in AS ABAP for almost all database configuration and monitoring tasks. Within this book, we'll only discuss some of these aspects in the context of Chapter 7.

Create a connection

To set up a new connection, select DB CONNECTIONS and click ADD. You must then specify a unique name and the connection data (database system, host name, port, user, password, etc.), as shown in Figure 3.8. The schema associated with the specified user is always used as the default schema for this connection.

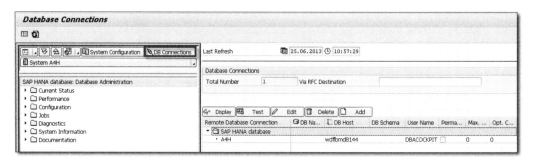

Figure 3.8 Setting Up a Secondary Connection in the DBA Cockpit

Configure the connection

You also can configure a set of parameters to define how the system should establish the created connections (see Figure 3.9):

- CONNECTION MAXIMUM
  Defines the maximum number of concurrent connections. If this limit

is reached, the system raises an error message when another connection is requested. If you don't set this parameter (initial value), the maximum number of supported connections (currently 255) is used.

▶ CONNECTION OPTIMUM
Defines an optimal number of open connections. If this number is exceeded, the system automatically closes existing connections after the transaction is completed.

▶ PERMANENT CONNECTION
Defines how to proceed if a connection is terminated. For permanent connections, the system tries to reestablish the connection for a running transaction so that, at best, the transaction can continue to run. You use this setting for critical and frequently used connections. The standard database connection of AS ABAP is flagged as permanent.

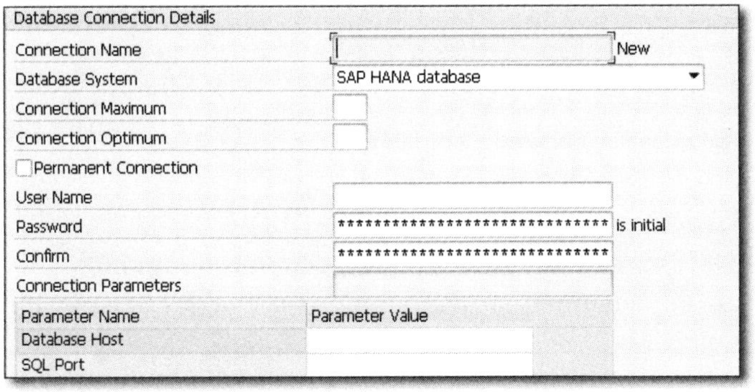

Figure 3.9 Configuring a Secondary Database Connection

After creating the connection, you can test it via the DBA Cockpit.

You can leverage secondary connections using both Open SQL and Native SQL. For Open SQL, the addition CONNECTION is used for this purpose (see Listing 3.14).

Secondary connections in ABAP programs

```
DATA: ls_carrier TYPE scarr.
SELECT SINGLE * FROM scarr CONNECTION ('SECONDARY') INTO
ls_carrier WHERE carrid = 'LH'.
```
Listing 3.14 Using Secondary Connections in Open SQL

To use Open SQL via a secondary connection, the tables and corresponding columns to be accessed must be known in the local DDIC, especially for any existing extensions.

In ADBC, you can specify the secondary connection when creating the connection (as shown in the example from Listing 3.15).

```
DATA: lo_statement  TYPE REF TO cl_sql_statement,
      lo_result_set TYPE REF TO cl_sql_result_set.

TRY.
    " Prepare SQL connection and statement
    lo_statement  = cl_sql_connection=>get_connection
      ( 'SECONDARY' )->create_statement( ).
    lo_result_set = lo_statement->execute_query(
      |SELECT SINGLE * FROM SCARR WHERE carrid = 'LH' AND
      mandt = { sy-mandt }| ).

    " ...
  CATCH cx_sql_exception.
    " Error handling
ENDTRY.
```

Listing 3.15 Using Secondary Connections in ADBC

Default schema

Both Open SQL and ADBC use the associated schema of the secondary connection, which is defined by the database user when configuring the connection, as the default schema. If table SCARR doesn't exist in this schema in the examples from Listing 3.14 and Listing 3.15, the program terminates. When using Native SQL, you can manually specify the schema; however, you should avoid this in productive scenarios.

Transaction behavior

Although generally secondary connections are used to accelerate queries by means of SAP HANA, we'll briefly discuss the transaction behavior for the sake of completeness. Secondary connections form their own transaction context so that data can be committed via a secondary connection (using COMMIT CONNECTION) without affecting the actual transaction. Secondary connections are terminated, at the very latest, after the actual transaction is closed or if a change in the work process is possible in the application program.

3.3 Analyzing Database Accesses Using the SQL Trace

In this section, we'll introduce some database programming tools. We'll focus on tools you can use for the database programming tasks described in this chapter. Tools for performance and error analysis are introduced in Chapter 7.

In the previous sections, we explained how the ABAP language, the database interface in the kernel (DBI, DBSL), and the database interact. We also described how SQL access from ABAP is used via primary or secondary connections. Using the SQL trace tool, you can track and check this procedure. In the following text, we'll use examples to demonstrate how you can analyze the following aspects directly within the system:

SQL trace

- Statement transformations (transformation of Open SQL into Native SQL via the database interface)
- Native SQL
- Usage of secondary connections and Native SQL (ADBC)
- Usage of the ABAP table buffer

3.3.1 Statement Transformations

Statement transformations of the DBI are described based on the example in Listing 3.16.

Sample program for DBI functions

```
"Variables for the result
DATA: ls_sflight TYPE sflight,
      lt_sflight TYPE TABLE OF sflight,
      ls_scarr TYPE scarr,
      ls_sbook TYPE sbook,
      lv_count TYPE i.

"Parameter for airlines
SELECT-OPTIONS: so_carr FOR ls_sflight-carrid,
                so_conn for ls_sflight-connid.
"Client handling and Open SQL -> Native SQL
SELECT *
  FROM sflight  UP TO 200 ROWS
  INTO ls_sflight
```

```
          WHERE carrid IN so_carr
          and connid in so_conn.

          APPEND ls_sflight TO lt_sflight.
          WRITE: / ls_sflight-mandt, ls_sflight-carrid,
                   ls_sflight-connid, ls_sflight-fldate.

      ENDSELECT.

      "Open SQL -> Native SQL
      MODIFY sflight FROM TABLE lt_sflight.
      COMMIT WORK.

      DELETE ADJACENT DUPLICATES FROM lt_sflight
      COMPARING carrid connid.

      "FOR ALL ENTRIES on SBOOK
      IF lines( lt_sflight ) > 0.
      SELECT *
        FROM sbook
        INTO ls_sbook
        FOR ALL ENTRIES IN lt_sflight
        WHERE carrid = lt_sflight-carrid
        AND connid = lt_sflight-connid
        AND fldate = lt_sflight-fldate.

      ENDSELECT.
      ENDIF.

      lv_count = sy-dbcnt.
      WRITE: / lv_count, 'SBOOK'.

      DELETE ADJACENT DUPLICATES FROM lt_sflight
      COMPARING carrid.

      "FOR ALL ENTRIES on SFLIGHT
      IF lines( lt_sflight ) > 0.
      SELECT *
        FROM scarr
        INTO ls_scarr
        FOR ALL ENTRIES IN lt_sflight
        WHERE carrid = lt_sflight-carrid.
      ENDSELECT.
      ENDIF.

      lv_count = sy-dbcnt.
      WRITE: / lv_count, 'SCARR'.
```

Listing 3.16 Sample Program 1 for DBI Functions

Using the SQL trace in Transaction ST05, you can record the SQL state-   Record SQL traces
ments that are sent to the database:

1. Start Transaction ST05 (see Figure 3.10).

2. Click ACTIVATE TRACE. Start the program and select a range of airlines.
   We want to display all airlines with an abbreviation from AA to LH,
   but not DL. Only the selection option for airlines (CARRID) is filled; the
   selection option for the connection numbers (CONNID) remains empty.

3. Click DEACTIVATE TRACE.

4. Click DISPLAY TRACE.

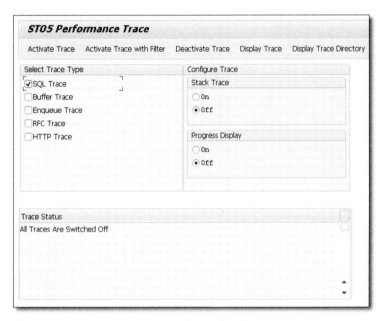

Figure 3.10 Transaction ST05: Recording an SQL Trace

A list with the recorded SQL statements is displayed. We'll now briefly   Record result
explain the most important columns; for more detailed information on
SQL traces, refer to Chapter 7. In the result list of the recorded SQL
statements (see Figure 3.11), the columns listed in Table 3.3 are important for the explanations in this section.

Figure 3.11 SQL Trace List

Column	Description
HH:MM:SS:MS	Time stamp of the execution in milliseconds
Duration	Duration of the statement in microseconds
Records	Number of records processed by the statement
Program Name	Name of the program where the statement is executed
Object Name	Name of the object to which the statement refers
Statement	The actual SQL statement
DB Conn.	Database connection used to execute the statement
User	SAP user who executed the statement

Table 3.3 Fields of the SQL Trace Analysis

Detail view

Further columns, which aren't shown in Figure 3.11, are the Client and Work Process Type where the SQL statement was executed. We'll now take a closer look at the first SQL statement for table SFLIGHT. When this statement was executed, the system read the first 200 rows (all columns) from table SFLIGHT that match the selected airlines.

Double-click the first statement for table SFLIGHT in the trace list to open the detail view shown in Figure 3.12. This view shows the SQL statement as it was sent from the DBI to the database.

Client handling and selection options

When comparing the Native SQL statement in the SQL trace to the Open SQL statement in the ABAP program, you'll notice the following:

▶ The client was inserted automatically in the WHERE condition of the Native SQL statement.

- The Open SQL addition UP TO <n> ROWS was translated into TOP 200 for the SAP HANA-specific Native SQL.

- The selection option IN so_carr was translated into a WHERE condition.

- The selection option IN so_conn wasn't sent to the database because it doesn't include any data.

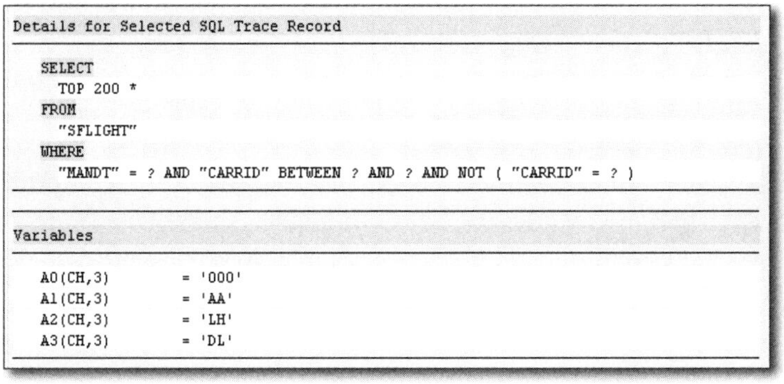

```
Details for Selected SQL Trace Record

  SELECT
    TOP 200 *
  FROM
    "SFLIGHT"
  WHERE
    "MANDT" = ? AND "CARRID" BETWEEN ? AND ? AND NOT ( "CARRID" = ? )


Variables

  A0(CH,3)          = '000'
  A1(CH,3)          = 'AA'
  A2(CH,3)          = 'LH'
  A3(CH,3)          = 'DL'
```

Figure 3.12 Detail View of the SQL Trace Record

Let's now look at the second SQL statement for table SFLIGHT in the list from Figure 3.11. The Open SQL MODIFY command was translated into an UPSERT statement by the DBI. The UPSERT command (a combination of the terms UPdate and inSERT) first tries to update the transferred records. If this isn't possible because the records don't yet exist, they are inserted via an INSERT statement.

Implementation of the MODIFY statement

Implementation of the MODIFY Statement in the Database [«]

On other database platforms and older SAP releases, the MODIFY statement is split by the DBI, which can also be traced and analyzed in Transaction ST05. In the SQL trace, you'll see two statements in this case: an UPDATE statement, and—if this first statement wasn't successful—an INSERT statement. However, an increasing number of database vendors provide native statements for this logic. The names of those statements are MERGE or UPSERT. As soon as such statements are available for a database, SAP will use them in the DBI. This means that the well-known UPDATE/INSERT sequence for the MODIFY statement will gradually disappear and be replaced by a Native SQL statement with the same function. This reduces the number of SQL statements sent to the database (round trips) and thus increases the performance.

FOR ALL ENTRIES statement

Let's now take a look at the two FOR ALL ENTRIES statements for tables SBOOK and SCARR (Listing 3.16). When analyzing the list of SQL statements in Figure 3.11, you'll notice that even though only one FOR ALL ENTRIES statement was written in the program for the two tables, table SBOOK is listed four times, while there is only one entry for table SCARR. This is because the driver table of the FOR ALL ENTRIES statement is divided into packages so that several statements are created if the driver table doesn't fit in one package.

OR combination

When comparing the FOR ALL ENTRIES statement for table SBOOK in the ABAP program's Open SQL versus the statement in the SQL trace's Native SQL, you'll notice that there are several references to the internal table (driver table) in Open SQL. The CARRID, CONNID, and FLDATE fields are compared to a column from the internal table. As a consequence, for every row of the internal table, an OR expression is created. Figure 3.13 shows such a chain of OR comparisons. This way, the comparisons are appended to the statement using OR operators. When the maximum package size (a certain number of OR operators) is reached (*blocking factor*), the first statement is sent to the database. Further packages are then created until all entries of the internal table are processed.

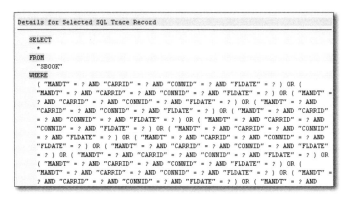

Figure 3.13 FOR ALL ENTRIES with OR Operators

IN list

For the second FOR ALL ENTRIES statement for table SCARR, there is only *one* reference to the internal table (for the CARRID field). This results in the statement being translated with an IN list. For every row of the internal table (driver table), an element is generated in the IN list (see Figure 3.14).

```
Details for Selected SQL Trace Record

  SELECT
     *
  FROM
     "SCARR"
  WHERE
     "MANDT" = ? AND "CARRID" IN ( ? , ? , ? , ? , ? , ? , ? , ? , ? , ? , ? , ? ,
     ? , ? , ? , ? , ? , ? , ? , ? , ? , ? , ? , ? , ? , ? , ? , ? , ? , ? , ? , ?
     , ? , ? , ? , ? , ? , ? , ? , ? , ? , ? , ? , ? , ? , ? , ? , ? , ? , ? , ? ,
     ? , ? , ? , ? , ? , ? , ? , ? , ? , ? , ? , ? , ? , ? , ? , ? , ? , ? , ? , ?
     , ? , ? , ? , ? , ? , ? , ? , ? , ? , ? , ? , ? , ? , ? , ? , ? , ? , ? , ? ,
     ? , ? , ? , ? , ? , ? , ? , ? , ? , ? , ? , ? , ? , ? , ? , ? , ? , ? , ? , ?
     , ? , ? , ? , ? , ? , ? , ? , ? , ? , ? , ? , ? , ? , ? , ? , ? , ? , ? , ? ,
     ? , ? , ? , ? , ? , ? , ? , ? , ? , ? , ? , ? , ? , ? , ? , ? , ? , ? , ? , ?
     , ? , ? , ? , ? , ? , ? , ? , ? , ? , ? , ? , ? , ? , ? , ? , ? , ? , ? , ? ,
     ? , ? , ? , ? , ? , ? , ? , ? , ? , ? , ? , ? , ? , ? , ? , ? , ? , ? , ? , ?
     , ? , ? , ? , ? , ? , ? , ? , ? , ? , ? , ? )

Variables

  A0(CH,3)        = '000'
  A1(CH,3)        = 'AA'
  A2(CH,3)        = 'AA'
  A3(CH,3)        = 'AA'
```

Figure 3.14 FOR ALL ENTRIES with the IN List

The FOR ALL ENTRIES clause is described in more detail with regard to performance and memory consumption in Chapter 14. In this section, we mainly wanted to show you how the DBI translates Open SQL into Native SQL, and how you can trace and analyze both variants in Transaction ST05.

You learned how Open SQL statements are modified for the SAP HANA database and translated into Native SQL statements. We mentioned automatic client handling, the selection options, and the FOR ALL ENTRIES clause. In addition to those aspects, there are further transformations (e.g., loading the table buffer or accessing number range buffers) that weren't presented in this chapter.

FOR ALL ENTRIES with the Fast Data Access Protocol   [«]

If the Fast Data Access (FDA) protocol is active, the DBI implements the FOR ALL ENTRIES statement in a different manner than described here.

FDA is an optimized protocol for exchanging data between the database and the database client. For FOR ALL ENTRIES using FDA, the data transport of the internal table to the database is run in an optimized form. Here, the internal table is transferred more efficiently to the database, where it's created as a temporary table. It's then joined with the database table of the FOR ALL

ENTRIES statement. The transport of results from the database to the database client is also run in an optimized form. The following parameters are prerequisites: rsdb/fda_level = 3 and rsdb/prefer_join_with_fda = 1. For more information, refer to SAP Note 1987132.

3.3.2 Secondary Connections

Example of database connections
We'll now use the example from Listing 3.17 to demonstrate how you can analyze accesses to a secondary connection. In the second sample program, all unique connections of table SFLIGHT are read once via a secondary connection (with the addition CONNECTION) and the standard connection.

```
DATA: ls_sflight TYPE sflight.

SELECT distinct connid
  FROM sflight CONNECTION ('QH3')
  INTO ls_sflight-connid
  WHERE carrid = 'LH'.
  WRITE: / ls_sflight-connid.
ENDSELECT.

ULINE.

SELECT distinct connid
  FROM sflight
  INTO ls_sflight-connid
  WHERE carrid = 'LH'.
  WRITE: / ls_sflight-connid.
ENDSELECT.
```
Listing 3.17 Sample Program 2 for Database Connections

Standard and secondary connection
In the SQL trace list in Transaction ST05, the name of the logical database connection is displayed in the DB CONN. column (Figure 3.15). In this list, R/3 always stands for the standard connection. Other connections are displayed using the name that was defined upon their creation.

Figure 3.15 shows that the statement was executed once for every connection and that table SFLIGHT contains different flight connections in the QH3 system. Transaction STAD, which will be described in Chapter 7, provides further information (e.g., the number of records read and the duration per database connection).

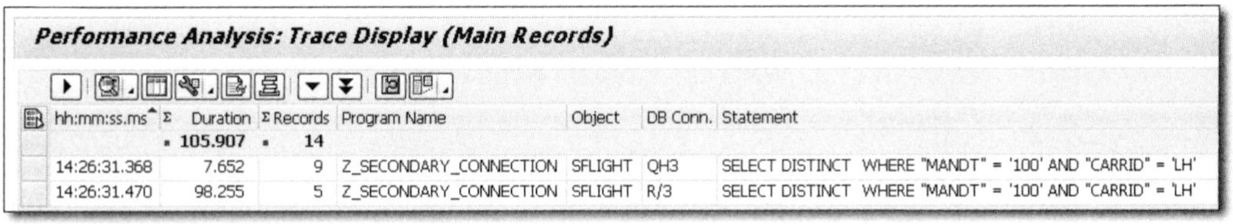

Figure 3.15 SQL Trace—Standard and Secondary Connection

3.3.3   Native SQL

Moreover, Transaction ST05 can be used to check whether ADBC was used. To do so, take another look at the source code shown earlier in Listing 3.12. The corresponding SQL trace analysis is shown in Figure 3.16. What's interesting in this analysis is the PROGRAM NAME, which refers to the CL_SQL_STATEMENT class. This indicates that ADBC was used for access. While the SQL statement is created as a string somewhere else within the program, it is first executed in the CL_SQL_STATEMENT class in this case (after the string was passed with the statement).

Track the use of ADBC

Figure 3.16 Analyzing Native SQL (ADBC) in Transaction ST05

The OBJECT NAME is the name of the table, which was set using the SET_TABLE_NAME_FOR_TRACE method. If no name is specified, the system tries to translate and display the object name from the FROM clause. In general, however, you should always define a table name because this is very important for other tools as well.

3.3.4   Buffer

You can also analyze table accesses to buffered tables using Transaction ST05. For this purpose, the table buffer trace (refer to Figure 3.10) must be activated. Otherwise, the SQL trace doesn't display table accesses processed via the table buffer. As an example, in Listing 3.18, we'll analyze the program from Figure 3.17 using the SQL and the table buffer trace.

Table buffer trace

```
" Variables for the result
DATA: ls_sflight TYPE sflight,
      ls_spfli TYPE spfli,
      lv_count TYPE i.

"Parameter for airlines
SELECT-OPTIONS: so_carr FOR ls_sflight-carrid.
" Read all flights
SELECT *
  FROM sflight
  INTO ls_sflight
  WHERE carrid IN so_carr.

" Details (buffered table)
  SELECT SINGLE *
    FROM spfli
    INTO ls_spfli
    WHERE carrid = ls_sflight-carrid
    AND connid = ls_sflight-connid.

  IF sy-subrc = 0.
  WRITE: / ls_sflight-mandt, ls_sflight-carrid,
           ls_sflight-connid,
           ls_sflight-fldate, ls_spfli-countryfr,
           ls_spfli-cityfrom, '->',
           ls_spfli-countryto, ls_spfli-cityto.
  ENDIF.

ENDSELECT.
```

Listing 3.18 Sample Program 3: Accesses to the Table Buffer

Trace result list   Figure 3.17 shows the common result list of the traces (for Listing 3.18). Database accesses appear in yellow (first row), while accesses to the table buffer appear in blue (second through fifth rows). In the STATE- MENT column, accesses to the database can be identified by the SQL syn- tax, while accesses to the buffer are only displayed using the technical keys. As you can see, no SELECT statement is displayed for the buffer accesses from our example.

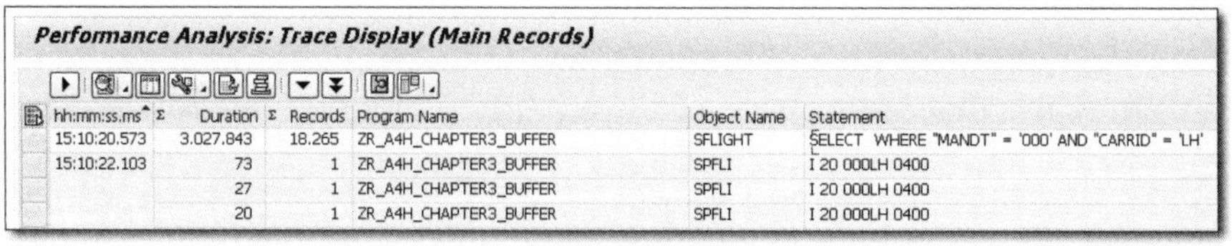

Performance Analysis: Trace Display (Main Records)

hh:mm:ss.ms ▲ Σ	Duration Σ	Records	Program Name	Object Name	Statement
15:10:20.573	3.027.843	18.265	ZR_A4H_CHAPTER3_BUFFER	SFLIGHT	SELECT WHERE "MANDT" = '000' AND "CARRID" = 'LH'
15:10:22.103	73	1	ZR_A4H_CHAPTER3_BUFFER	SPFLI	I 20 000LH 0400
	27	1	ZR_A4H_CHAPTER3_BUFFER	SPFLI	I 20 000LH 0400
	20	1	ZR_A4H_CHAPTER3_BUFFER	SPFLI	I 20 000LH 0400

Figure 3.17 Transaction ST05: SQL and Buffer Trace

PART II

Introduction to ABAP Programming with SAP HANA

Using SAP HANA, you can perform business calculations directly on the original data in the main memory without transforming data. SQL and SQLScript are available for this purpose. Calculations can be expressed using analytical models (modeled or implemented with SQLScript) or database procedures and can be used within ABAP.

4   Native Database Development Using SAP HANA

Having explained the basic principles of SAP HANA in the first three chapters of this book, this chapter now provides an overview of the native database development using SAP HANA. For this purpose, you'll first learn how the SAP HANA database enhances the SQL standard with some functions and particularly using *SQLScript*.

Subsequently, we describe how to implement database procedures using SQLScript in SAP HANA Studio, followed by a description of analytical models (*views*). We explain which view types SAP HANA supports and how to create and test these views using SAP HANA Studio.

4.1   Basic Principles of Native Database Development

Chapter 3, Section 3.2, discussed some basic principles of SQL as a central programming language in the context of databases and presented the usage via ABAP, particularly, via database-independent Open SQL. However, the Open SQL options aren't sufficient to execute more complex operations on data within the database and specifically in SAP HANA. For this reason, this section first deals with the *SQL dialect* of SAP HANA (including an overview of database objects). We use the term *dialect*

Overview

because although SAP HANA supports the fundamental SQL standard, it also defines other databases of proprietary SQL enhancements.

4.1.1 Objects in the SAP HANA Database Catalog

Before we deal with some SQL commands, we first provide an overview of all native database objects in SAP HANA. The *database catalog* of a database system contains the metadata of all objects included in a system, such as the names and the structure of all existing tables.

Overview You can find the database catalog in SAP HANA Studio when you open the CATALOG node for a system connection. Table 4.1 provides an overview of all types of database objects in SAP HANA. The SAP HANA-specific column shows whether you can find this object in SAP HANA only or also in other relational databases; the ABAP Support column shows whether you can use this object directly via the ABAP Data Dictionary (DDIC).

Object	SAP HANA-specific	ABAP Support	Description
Schema	No	No	A schema forms the namespace in the database.
Table	No	Yes (Chapter 3, Section 3.2)	Tables define the data structures (columns) in which you store data records (rows).
View	No	Yes (Chapter 3, Section 3.2)	Views (SQL) define a view on data that you can access like a table.
Procedure	No	Yes, (Chapter 5, Section 5.2, and Chapter 6, Section 6.5).	Procedures contain a summary of database commands, including input and output parameters.
Index	No	Yes (Chapter 3, Section 3.2)	An index is an additional storage structure for accelerating database accesses.

Table 4.1 Types of Database Objects in SAP HANA

Object	SAP HANA-specific	ABAP Support	Description
Function	No	No	Functions are user-defined operations that can be used within the scope of other SQL statements.
Trigger	No	No	Triggers allow you to respond to special events (e.g., changes to the content of a table) and run your own logic.
Sequence	No	No	Sequences enable you to generate unique consecutive numbers.
Synonym	No	No	A synonym allows you to address a table, a view, or a procedure via another name.
Column views	Yes	Indirect (Chapter 5, Section 5.1)	Column views are an SAP HANA-specific form of views generated during the creation of analytical models (see Section 4.4).
EPM models and query sources	Yes	No	Enterprise Performance Management (EPM) models and query sources are special artifacts in the context of the planning engine in SAP HANA. These objects won't be discussed within the scope of this book.

Table 4.1 Types of Database Objects in SAP HANA (Cont.)

An appropriate CREATE statement exists to create a database object of a specific type in the catalog using SQL. In the same way, you can remove objects again using DROP and make changes using ALTER. To create or delete a sequence, for example, you can use the CREATE SEQUENCE or DROP SEQUENCE statements, respectively. Within the scope of this chapter,

Create and change objects via SQL

we'll discuss the creation of tables, views, functions, and procedures in detail. For other objects, refer to the SAP HANA SQL reference at *http://help.sap.com/hana*.

Tools for development
In most cases, however, you don/t create the respective objects manually via SQL; instead, you use special tools in the ABAP development environment or SAP HANA Studio. This chapter focuses on procedures (Section 4.3) and column views (Section 4.4). You can also create the other objects of Table 4.1 using SAP HANA Studio. The objects that are supported in DDIC have already been described to some extent in Chapter 3, Section 3.2 (tables, views, indexes). This description is continued in Chapter 5 (proxies for column views and procedures) and Chapter 6 (CDS views and ABAP Managed Database Procedures [AMDP]). The objects of Table 4.1 form the basis in all cases.

Objects with related implementation
Object types such as views, triggers, functions, and procedures require an implementation in the associated logic. SQL and SQLScript are primarily used at these points, and there may be object-specific restrictions. You can define a normal view via SQL only and not via SQLScript. The functional scope of SQLScript is restricted for triggers.

4.1.2   SQL Standard and SAP HANA-specific Enhancements

SQL standards and enhancements
SAP HANA particularly supports the central SQL standards *SQL-92* and (with certain exceptions) *SQL:1999*. At this point, we can't provide a full overview of data types, statements, and operations, so please refer to the respective specifications. At this level, SAP HANA is fully compatible with other relational database systems. Based on these standards, SAP HANA provides numerous additional capabilities that can be used through SQL enhancements. The following text details some important SQL statements in SAP HANA that play a role within the scope of this book.

Create tables via SQL
To create a table in SAP HANA, you can use the CREATE TABLE statement (just like in the SQL standard). However, in this case, you create a table in SAP HANA's row store by default (see Chapter 1, Section 1.2.2). You can use the CREATE <table type> TABLE ... statement to create the desired table type. Table 4.2 shows the values permitted. The ABAP Support column shows whether you also can create such tables using the DDIC.

Type	ABAP Support	Description
ROW	Yes	Row store tables (standard).
COLUMN	Yes	Column store tables (recommended for most application scenarios).
HISTORY COLUMN	No	Special table type that supports a "time journey" function so that you can query the table content for a specific point in the past.
GLOBAL TEMPORARY (COLUMN)	No (internal in the ABAP kernel in the context of database procedures)	Global temporary tables (GTT) allow you to store interim results within a session. The table definition can be used by all users of the database; the contents, however, can only be viewed in the same database connection.
LOCAL TEMPORARY (COLUMN)	No	In contrast to GTTs, for local temporary tables, the metadata is also linked to the database connection. Thus, such tables can only be used within a database connection.
VIRTUAL	No	A virtual table is a reference to a table in another system that is linked with SAP HANA using the Smart Data Access (SDA) mechanism (see Chapter 1, Section 1.1.5).

Table 4.2 Types in SAP HANA

In most cases, you (or the DDIC) create tables in the column store, as shown in Listing 4.1. The additions UNLOAD PRIORITY 5 AUTO MERGE are SAP HANA-specific.

```
CREATE COLUMN TABLE "SCARR"
    ("MANDT" NVARCHAR(3) DEFAULT '000' NOT NULL ,
     "CARRID" NVARCHAR(3) DEFAULT '' NOT NULL ,
     "CARRNAME" NVARCHAR(20) DEFAULT '' NOT NULL ,
```

```
      "CURRCODE" NVARCHAR(5) DEFAULT '' NOT NULL ,
      "URL" NVARCHAR(255) DEFAULT '' NOT NULL ,
      PRIMARY KEY ("MANDT", "CARRID"))
UNLOAD PRIORITY 5 AUTO MERGE
```
Listing 4.1 Example: Definition of Table SCARR

Data types Chapter 3 already discussed the data types supported in SAP HANA. In addition to the default SQL data types such as INTEGER, VARCHAR, and so on, the column store in SAP HANA also offers several special data structures, which you'll get to know in subsequent chapters. These include the data types TEXT and SHORTTEXT (Chapter 10) as well as the geodata types of the ST_GEOMETRY family (Chapter 13).

Views Every relational database provides an option for defining views. These *standard views* (also referred to as *SQL views*) are defined in the database catalog using the CREATE VIEW statement essentially as an alias for a SQL query:

```
CREATE VIEW <name> AS SELECT <SQL query>
```

As a relational database, SAP HANA also supports SQL views; these views differ from the views of other databases only in the functional scope of the SELECT statement in SAP HANA, which we'll discuss in the following.

Example As you might expect, the SELECT statement provides the essential interface for the data access. This section can't detail all facets of this extremely comprehensive statement. Instead, it's limited to the various subject areas that play a significant role for creating views and procedures. The example in Listing 4.2 demonstrates various advanced capabilities that you don't know from classic Open SQL in ABAP.

```
SELECT
  concat (carrid,connid) as "Connection",
  passname as "Passenger",
  to_date(fldate) as "Flight date",
  to_date(order_date) as "Order date",
   convert_currency(amount=>loccuram,
   "SOURCE_UNIT_COLUMN" =>loccurkey,
   "SCHEMA" => 'SAPH74',
   "TARGET_UNIT_COLUMN" => 'EUR',
   "REFERENCE_DATE" =>CURRENT_UTCDATE,
   "CLIENT" => '001') as "Price (EUR)"
```

```
from sbook
where days_between(order_date, fldate) < 100
  and contains(passname, 'Idda Pratt', fuzzy(0.8))
order by fldate desc
limit 10
```
Listing 4.2 Example of a SELECT Statement

We'll use an example in the following to describe some functions in more detail so that you can get an idea of the functional scope.

If the result set of a query is very large, it's useful to retrieve the results in smaller packages, particularly if a user can't view all results at a glance. For this purpose, databases usually provide *paging* as an option for limiting the number of rows (LIMIT) and for defining the starting row (OFFSET). Listing 4.2 shows a usage example in which a maximum of 10 entries is read.

Paging

For some queries, you must convert data types to leverage certain operations. So if you treat a column of an ABAP table with the data type DATS (on database NVARCHAR(8)) as a real date using the SQL data type DATE, you can use the conversion function to_date (refer to Listing 4.2). There are also functions for converting other data types (e.g., to_int, to_decimal, etc.).

Conversion of data types

Several operations are available for manipulating character strings, for instance, concatenate texts (concat), read substrings (substring), or convert to uppercase or lowercase (upper/lower). In Listing 4.2, you read the airline and the flight connection as a combined field using the concat(carrid,connid) expression.

Character string operations

Date calculations play a role in many queries. In SAP HANA SQL, you can access the current data in various variants (e.g., using current_utc-date) or calculate with date values (e.g., using add_days). In the example shown earlier in Listing 4.2, the days_between function is used to compare dates.

Operations for date values

As a last example, we want to mention the conversion of currencies and units, which you can use by means of the functions convert_currency (for currencies) or unit_conversion (for units). In this context, the underlying logic is compatible with the respective logic in the ABAP AS

Conversion of units and currencies

and depends on the same Customizing tables (see the following information box). In Listing 4.2, we ran a currency conversion in euros for the current date. Within the scope of SQLScript and modeled views, this chapter will provide further options for implementing such conversions.

[»]

Currency Conversion and Unit Conversion in SAP NetWeaver AS ABAP

Currency conversion and unit conversion are standard functions in SAP NetWeaver AS ABAP. The customizing of the currency conversion in SAP Basis is done via the TCUR* tables in the SFIB package. To perform a conversion in ABAP, you can, for instance, use the function modules in the SCUN function group (e.g., CONVERT_TO_LOCAL_CURRENCY). In addition to the amount, the source currency, and the target currency, the key date and the exchange rate type are also important parameters for the conversion.

Unit conversion for ISO codes can be found in the T006* tables of the SZME package. To perform a conversion in ABAP, you can use the UNIT_CONVERSION_SIMPLE function module.

Joins Because joins will play a central role for subsequent modeling of column views, we'll briefly review the various join types in the SQL standard using examples. To do so, we'll use the known tables SFLIGHT (flights) and SCARR (airlines) with a foreign key relationship via the CARRID field (for the sake of simplicity, the client is disregarded in the excerpt in Table 4.3). The tables have an n:1 relationship and table SCARR may contain airlines for which no flight is entered in table SFLIGHT (e.g., the airline UA in Table 4.3).

Table SFLIGHT			Table SCARR	
CARRID	CONNID	FLDATE	CARRID	CARRNAME
AA	0017	20150101	AA	American Airlines
...	...	...	...	...
LH	400	20150101	LH	Lufthansa
LH	400	20150102	...	...
...	...	...	UA	United Airways

Table 4.3 Sample Data from the Tables SFLIGHT and SCARR to Explain Join Types

When defining joins, we differentiate between inner and outer joins. For an *inner join*, all combinations are included in the result if there is a matching entry in both tables. With an *outer join*, results that are present only in the left table (*left outer join*), only in the right table (*right outer join*), or in any of the tables (*full outer join*) are also included. To differentiate between left and right, the join order is used.

The differences between the join types will be explained based on the following SQL examples for selecting flights and the corresponding airline names. The first example comprises an inner join. Because the airline UA isn't present in the sample data for table SFLIGHT, there is no matching entry in the result set:

```
select s.carrid, s.connid, c.carrname from sflight as s
inner join scarr as c on s.carrid = c.carrid
```

For a right outer join, where table SCARR is the right-hand table, an entry for the airline UA is displayed in the result set, even though there is no corresponding entry in table SFLIGHT. The carrid and connid columns thus display the value NULL:

```
select s.carrid, s.connid, c.carrname from sflight as s
right outer join scarr as c on s.carrid = c.carrid
```

Similarly, UA is also included in the result set for a left outer join with table SCARR as the left-hand table. If the data model assumes that a corresponding airline exists for every entry of a flight (but not necessarily the other way around), the two outer join variants are functionally equivalent.

```
select s.carrid, s.connid, c.carrname from scarr as c
left outer join sflight as s on s.carrid = c.carrid
```

SAP HANA also provides advanced analytical operations in addition to the standard SQL aggregate functions COUNT, SUM, AVG, and so on (in combination with GROUP BY). These include more complex groupings via GROUPING SETS; support for expressions such as ROLLUP, CUBE, and so on; and calculation of subtotals. The following example for determining the flight prices groups by all combinations of airline, connection, and currency with subtotals in one single statement:

```
select carrid, connid, loccurkey, sum(loccuram)
  from sbook group by cube(connid, carrid, loccurkey) ;
```

[»] **Support of Multidimensional Expressions (MDX)**

Besides the analytical functions in SQL, which have already been mentioned, SAP HANA also natively supports *multidimensional expressions* (MDX). MDX is a powerful database query language for OLAP scenarios that was promoted by Microsoft and has become an industry standard. In contrast to SQL, MDX focuses on multidimensional access, with the terms *measures* and *dimension* playing a decisive role for selections on a *cube* that is based on a star schema.

You can find more detailed information on MDX support in SAP HANA under *http://help.sap.com/hana*.

Additional enhancements

In addition, SAP HANA offers some enhancements that we'll present in detail in subsequent chapters. These include, for example, the CONTAINS expression for the fuzzy search, which we'll discuss in Chapter 10. In Listing 4.2, shown previously, we searched for bookings where the passenger name is similar to "Idda Pratt" (which will find entries with the name "Idda Pratt"). Additional enhancements include geographical functions (e.g., for determining distances and areas), which are detailed in Chapter 13.

4.2 SQLScript

The previous section showed how SAP HANA enhances the SQL standard with some functions. Let's now discuss SQLScript.

SQLScript is an SQL-based programming language in SAP HANA whose goal is to move data-intensive calculations to the database with little effort and in their entirety. In the following, we'll first detail the qualities of SQLScript and then describe how SQLScript is processed in the SAP HANA database (Section 4.3 will then explain how to create procedures in SAP HANA.)

4.2.1 Basic Principles of SQLScript

Qualities of SQLScript

SQLScript has several advantages over Open SQL and the SQL standard. We'll use a specific example to illustrate the intrinsic qualities of SQLScript. Note that some details are omitted at first so that we can discuss them in later sections.

As was the case in the previous chapters, the example we'll use here is based on the SFLIGHT data model. For this example, we'll calculate two key performance indicators (KPIs) for an airline's top connections:

- ▸ **Total booking revenue**
  This KPI is calculated by totaling the field LOCCURAM field for all individual bookings that haven't been canceled from database table SBOOK (i.e., the CANCELLED field is blank).

- ▸ **Average number of days between the flight date and booking date**
  This KPI is calculated from the difference between the FLDATE and ORDER_DATE fields for all individual bookings that haven't been canceled from database table SBOOK.

We also want to identify those travel agencies that achieve the highest sales revenue based on an airline's top connections. The sales revenue for each travel agency is determined in the same way as the total booking revenue.

You can use SQLScript to implement database procedures and calculation views (see Section 4.4.3). Internally, calculation views implemented using SQLScript are represented as database procedures.

A database procedure comprises input/output parameters and the processing logic. You can use database procedures to modularize complex tasks. Figure 4.1 demonstrates how different database procedures can interact with one another to determine the KPIs and travel agencies associated with an airline's top connections.

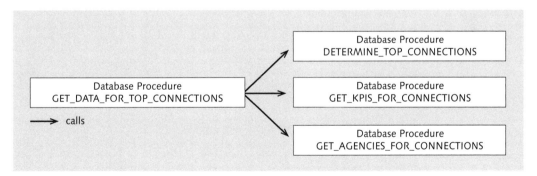

Figure 4.1 Using Multiple Database Procedures to Modularize Complex Tasks

Internally, the GET_DATA_FOR_TOP_CONNECTIONS database procedure uses the following:

- The DETERMINE_TOP_CONNECTIONS database procedure to identify an airline's top connections
- The GET_KPIS_FOR_CONNECTIONS database procedure to calculate the KPIs for an airline's top flight connections
- The GET_AGENCIES_FOR_CONNECTIONS database procedure to identify those travel agencies with the highest sales revenue for an airline's top flight connections

Thanks to modularization, you can simply reuse parts of the implementation for other tasks. For example, you can call the GET_KPIS_FOR_CONNECTIONS method for an airline's top connections as well as for any connections for multiple airlines.

Split up complex database queries

In addition to using multiple database procedures to modularize complex tasks, SQLScript also enables you to split up complex database queries within a procedure. There you can assign the result of a SELECT statement to a *table variable* and then use this table variable for subsequent SELECT statements. We'll now demonstrate this using the example of the GET_AGENCIES_FOR_CONNECTIONS procedure.

The purpose of this procedure is to aggregate all bookings that weren't canceled for a given set of flight connections, to identify the five travel agencies with the highest sales revenue, and then read the addresses of the five travel agencies identified. The corresponding database query can look as shown in Listing 4.3.

```
ET_AGENCIES = SELECT A.AGENCYNUM, T.NAME, T.POSTCODE,
  T.CITY, T.COUNTRY, A.PAYMENTSUM, A.CURRENCY
  FROM ( SELECT TOP 5 B.AGENCYNUM, SUM(B.LOCCURAM) AS
    PAYMENTSUM, B.LOCCURKEY AS CURRENCY
    FROM :IT_CONNECTIONS AS C INNER JOIN SBOOK AS B ON
    B.CARRID = C.CARRID AND B.CONNID = C.CONNID
    WHERE B.MANDT = :IV_MANDT AND B.CANCELLED <> 'X'
    GROUP BY B.AGENCYNUM, B.LOCCURKEY
    ORDER BY SUM(B.LOCCURAM) DESC ) AS A
  INNER JOIN STRAVELAG AS T ON
  T.AGENCYNUM = A.AGENCYNUM WHERE T.MANDT = :IV_MANDT;
```
Listing 4.3 Example of a Complex Database Query

Alternatively, with SQLScript, you can use one table variable to combine two database queries (see Listing 4.4).

```
LT_AGENCIES = SELECT TOP 5 B.AGENCYNUM,
  SUM(B.LOCCURAM) AS PAYMENTSUM, B.LOCCURKEY AS
  CURRENCY FROM :IT_CONNECTIONS AS C
  INNER JOIN SBOOK AS B ON B.CARRID = C.CARRID AND
  B.CONNID = C.CONNID
  WHERE B.MANDT = :IV_MANDT AND B.CANCELLED <> 'X'
  GROUP BY B.AGENCYNUM, B.LOCCURKEY
  ORDER BY SUM(B.LOCCURAM) DESC;

ET_AGENCIES = SELECT A.AGENCYNUM, T.NAME, T.POSTCODE,
  T.CITY, T.COUNTRY, A.PAYMENTSUM, A.CURRENCY
  FROM :LT_AGENCIES AS A INNER JOIN STRAVELAG AS T
  ON T.AGENCYNUM = A.AGENCYNUM
  WHERE T.MANDT = :IV_MANDT;
```
Listing 4.4 Splitting Up a Complex Database Query

The following advantages are associated with using SQLScript to split up complex database queries:

▸ Several relatively simple SELECT statements are frequently easier to read and therefore easier to maintain than one relatively complex database query.

▸ Interim results in the form of a table variable can easily be reused (e.g., to calculate KPIs and to identify travel agencies).

▸ Splitting up complex database queries may make it easier for the SAP HANA database optimizer to detect redundant subqueries and to prevent their repeated calculation.

The database optimizer decides how to execute multiple database queries (both within and across database procedures). Internally, it can combine multiple SELECT statements into one database query. Under certain conditions, the optimizer is able to process multiple SELECT statements in parallel (if the statements are independent).

We'll also demonstrate the parallel processing of independent database queries using the same example. As you know from the previous descriptions, several steps must be undertaken to complete the task:

Parallel processing

- ▸ Identify an airline's top connections.
- ▸ Calculate the two KPIs.
- ▸ Identify those travel agencies with the highest sales revenue.
- ▸ Read the addresses of the travel agencies identified.

Calculating the KPIs and identifying the travel agencies with the highest sales revenue (including reading their addresses) are dependent on identifying an airline's top connections but are fully independent of each other. Consequently, the SAP HANA database can process these database queries in parallel, as shown in Figure 4.2.

Parallel processing of database queries in SQLScript is a fundamental difference from Open SQL. If you use Open SQL to send multiple SELECT statements to the SAP HANA database (and use, e.g., the FOR ALL ENTRIES clause to connect them), they are processed in succession.

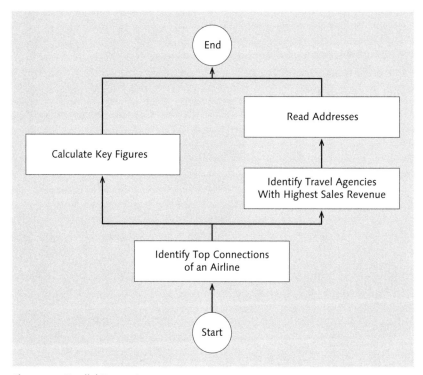

Figure 4.2 Parallel Processing

As a result of processing database queries in parallel, tasks can be accelerated considerably. However, this is only one form of parallelization in SAP HANA. The system can also use multiple threads to process individual database queries (e.g., calculating KPIs) in parallel (see also Chapter 1, Section 1.2.2). Open SQL also benefits from this form of parallelization.

SQL is a declarative programming language. Declarative programming focuses on the problem description (i.e., the "what"). SQLScript adds elements of imperative programming to the SQL standard. Imperative programming focuses on the problem solution (i.e., the "how").

Orchestrating the processing logic

The imperative language elements in SQLScript enable you to work, for example, with case distinctions (IF ... THEN ... ELSEIF ... ELSE ... END IF) and loops (WHILE ... ENDWHILE) in database procedures and calculation views, thus enabling you to orchestrate the (declarative) processing logic. Here, you also have options that extend far beyond the SQL standard.

Let's imagine that you want to identify an airline's top connections based on the sales revenue or percentage utilization. In this case, you can assign an input parameter to the DETERMINE_TOP_CONNECTIONS database procedure, and, depending on its value, you can execute different database queries (see Listing 4.5).

```
IF IV_ALGORITHM = 'P' THEN
  ET_CONNECTIONS = SELECT TOP 5 CARRID, CONNID
    FROM SFLIGHT
    WHERE MANDT = :IV_MANDT AND CARRID = :IV_CARRID
    GROUP BY CARRID, CONNID
    ORDER BY SUM(PAYMENTSUM) DESC;
ELSE
  ET_CONNECTIONS = SELECT TOP 5 CARRID, CONNID
    FROM SFLIGHT
    WHERE MANDT = :IV_MANDT AND CARRID = :IV_CARRID
    GROUP BY CARRID, CONNID
    ORDER BY AVG(TO_DECIMAL(SEATSOCC + SEATSOCC_B +
    SEATSOCC_F) / TO_DECIMAL(SEATSMAX + SEATSMAX_B +
    SEATSMAX_F)) DESC;
END IF;
```
Listing 4.5 Imperative Language Elements

Note that the use of imperative programming may prevent parallelization of database queries. In particular, we recommend that you avoid loop processing combined with the use of cursors as much as possible.

Access business
logic It's often a challenge to access business logic in the event of a code push-down from the application layer to the database layer. In ABAP application development, a large part of the business logic previously resided in the application layer and therefore was only available for data records transferred from the database to the application server. Currency conversion is a good example here.

SQLScript makes crucial business logic functions available in the database layer. In addition to currency conversion, SQLScript also supports the conversion of units of measure in accordance with Customizing for AS ABAP. You can also access the SAP HANA function libraries in database procedures and calculation views (see Chapter 12), which gives you considerably more options in terms of moving data-intensive calculations to the database than those available with Open SQL or Native SQL.

Process the
SQLScript Now that we've discussed the advantages of SQLScript, we'll explain how the SAP HANA database processes SQLScript. Here, we distinguish between processing when *activating* SQLScript and processing when *invoking* SQLScript.

Activate the
SQLScript When activating SQLScript, the SAP HANA database first checks the syntax of the database procedure. The system then checks the semantic correctness. It derives, among other things, the table variable types, which can be implicitly typed in SQLScript. The system checks whether the variables are being used consistently and whether all of the output parameters associated with the database procedure have been filled.

The system then optimizes the database procedures and creates a *calculation model* (possibly multilevel) that resembles a graphical calculation view. In this model, imperative language elements are generated as *L nodes*. L is a programming language that makes some language elements of C++ available and supports SAP HANA's system of data types. Internally, the SAP HANA database uses L as an intermediate language when compiling a database procedure to C++.

Finally, the system stores the database procedure in the database catalog and, if necessary, in the SAP HANA repository.

Invoke the
SQLScript Two phases are associated with invoking a database procedure: *compilation* and *execution*.

When compiling a database procedure, the SAP HANA database rewrites the database procedure call so that it can be executed by the *calculation engine*. Then, when executing the database procedure, the system binds the actual parameters associated with the call to the calculation model created when the procedure was activated. This process is known as *instantiating* the calculation model. During instantiation, the system possibly optimizes the calculation model further. Lastly, the system uses the engines available (see Chapter 1, Section 1.3) to execute the calculation model.

4.2.2 SQLScript Programming

Now that you're familiar with some basic principles of SQLScript, let's discuss the creation of database procedures and table types, variables, imperative enhancements, and calculation engine (CE) plan operators.

As discussed previously, a database procedure in SAP HANA consists of input/output parameters and the processing logic. From a technical perspective, SQL is used to generate, call, change, and delete database procedures. The SAP HANA database provides the following statements for this purpose:

▶ CREATE PROCEDURE
Statement to create a new database procedure.

▶ CREATE TYPE
Statement to create a table type for use in the database procedure interface.

▶ ALTER PROCEDURE
Statement to recompile the calculation model for a database procedure.

▶ CALL
Statement to call a database procedure.

▶ DROP PROCEDURE
Statement to delete a database procedure.

SQL console and SAP HANA Development perspective Even though you can execute these commands directly via the SQL console, we don't recommend this (with the exception of simple tests) because procedures created via the SQL console aren't stored in the SAP HANA repository. You therefore lose version management and transport management, among other things. Instead, we recommend that you create native database procedures in SAP HANA Studio in the SAP HANA DEVELOPMENT perspective and thus in the SAP HANA repository (see Section 4.3). If you want to use procedures from ABAP, you should use *ABAP Managed Database Procedures (AMDP)*, as described in Chapter 6.

Types of database procedures   SAP HANA distinguishes between two types of database procedures:

▸ **Read-only procedures**
Database procedures that only read data.

▸ **Read/write procedures**
Database procedures that can read and write data.

The use of INSERT, UPDATE, DELETE, and Data Definition Language (DDL) statements are prohibited in read-only procedures. Whereas read/write procedures can call any database procedure, read-only procedures can only call read-only procedures (see Figure 4.3).

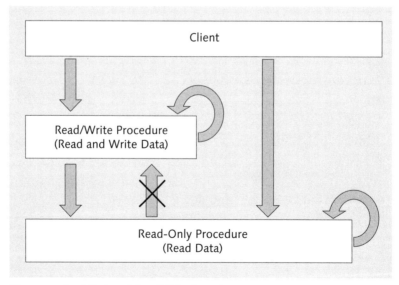

Figure 4.3 Read-Only and Read/Write Procedures

In general, SQLScript is used to implement database procedures. The SAP HANA database also supports two additional programming languages:

- ▶ **L programming language**
  L is based on C++. The use of L to implement database procedures is currently reserved for SAP itself.

- ▶ **R programming language**
  R is a free programming language for resolving statistical problems (*www.r-project.org*). Implementing a database procedure in R enables you to use the R language in SAP HANA and, if necessary, embed it into a more extensive calculation model. The programming language R is beyond the scope of this book.

User-Defined Functions   [«]

In addition to database procedures, *user-defined functions* are also available. User-defined functions are also implemented in SQLScript and are created or deleted using the `CREATE FUNCTION` and `DROP FUNCTION` statements. The user-defined function `DETERMINE_TOP_CONNECTIONS` is created in the following example:

```
CREATE FUNCTION DETERMINE_TOP_CONNECTIONS(IV_MANDT
   NVARCHAR(3), IV_CARRID NVARCHAR(3), IV_ALGORITHM
   NVARCHAR(1)) RETURNS TABLE(CARRID NVARCHAR(3), CONNID
   NVARCHAR(4)) LANGUAGE SQLSCRIPT SQL SECURITY INVOKER AS
BEGIN
   ...
END;
```

In contrast to database procedures, you can use user-defined functions directly in SQL statements. This can look like the following:

```
SELECT C.CARRID, C.CONNID, S.CARRNAME
   FROM DETERMINE_TOP_CONNECTIONS('000', 'LH', 'P') AS C
   INNER JOIN SCARR AS S ON S.CARRID = C.CARRID
   WHERE S.MANDT = '000';
```

Unlike database procedures (which include AMDP), user-defined functions can't be created directly in ABAP.

The following sections first describe which commands are available in the SAP HANA database for creating database procedures and table types (which can be used for defining the interface to the procedure).

Then we discuss variables, imperative enhancements, and CE plan operators.

Creating Database Procedures

CREATE PROCEDURE statement

You use the CREATE PROCEDURE statement to create a database procedure. The complete syntax is provided in Listing 4.6.

```
CREATE PROCEDURE <proc_name> [(<parameter_clause>)]
[LANGUAGE <lang>] [SQL SECURITY <mode>]
[DEFAULT SCHEMA <default_schema_name>]
[READS SQL DATA [WITH RESULT VIEW <view_name>]] AS
BEGIN [SEQUENTIAL EXECUTION]
  <procedure_body>
END
```

Listing 4.6 Syntax for the CREATE PROCEDURE Statement

Additions to the CREATE PROCEDURE statement

The CREATE PROCEDURE statement is followed by the name <proc_name> of the database procedure and a series of optional additions. Finally, the statement is enclosed between BEGIN and END, with the actual implementation in the form of source code <procedure_body> (i.e., the processing logic). The optional additions have the following meaning:

▶ After the name of the database procedure, you can define input and output parameters in the parameter list <parameter_clause>. Here, you can use *scalar parameters* based on *simple data types* (such as INTEGER, DECIMAL, or NVARCHAR) and *table parameters* based on database tables or *table types*. In the next section, we'll discuss table types in detail.

▶ After the parameter list, you can specify the programming language used to implement the database procedure. SQLSCRIPT and R are permitted for <lang>.

▶ You can use the SQL SECURITY addition to specify the user against which the system checks authorizations at runtime. DEFINER (creator of the procedure) and INVOKER (caller of the procedure) are permitted for <mode>.

▶ The DEFAULT SCHEMA is used for database accesses within the procedure if no explicit schema is entered.

▶ You use READS SQL DATA to indicate that a database procedure only reads data. If the read-only procedure returns exactly one table parameter, you can use WITH RESULT VIEW <view_name> to create a view. In this case, you can later use a SELECT statement to query the result of the database procedure.

▶ With the SEQUENTIAL EXECUTION addition, you can enforce the sequential execution of the database procedure (i.e., you can prevent the parallelization of database queries in SQLScript).

Creating Table Types

If you want to use table parameters in a database procedure interface, you can define them with reference to database tables or table types. Table types are an enhancement to the SQL standard and are part of the data type system supported by the SAP HANA database. Conceptually, table types are similar to the *structures* within the DDIC. The relevant command here is CREATE TYPE. The complete syntax is shown in Listing 4.7.

CREATE TYPE statement

```
CREATE TYPE <type_name> AS TABLE (<column_definition>
[{,<column_definition>}...])
```
Listing 4.7 Syntax for the CREATE TYPE Statement

The CREATE TYPE command is followed by the name of the table type <type_name> and individual columns. Each table type has at least one column, and each column definition (<column_definition>) comprises the name of the column and its data type (simple).

Using Table Variables

Table variables can be input/output parameters or local variables. They are based, either explicitly or implicitly, on a table type and can be linked to the result of an SQL statement or CE plan operator (see the upcoming section on the usage of CE plan operators) by means of the equals sign (=). The contents of the table variables are accessed using the relevant variable name supplemented by the prefix : (colon). This occurs in the same way in which database tables are accessed. We'll explain this a bit later via an example.

Explicit typing

If you want to define a tabular input or output parameter, you must type this explicitly. When you assign the result of an SQL statement or CE plan operator to a tabular output parameter, the system checks whether both are type-compatible.

Implicit typing

You *cannot* explicitly type a local table variable using the DECLARE statement. If required, the system automatically derives the required table type from the SQL statement or assigned CE plan operator. This simplifies programming and provides more flexibility but can also lead to unnecessary type conversions.

The example in Listing 4.8 shows how to use table variables. We've intentionally omitted some details from the source code (e.g., restricting the selection to one client).

```
CREATE PROCEDURE EXAMPLE_TABLE_VARIABLES (OUT
ET_FLIGHTS TT_FLIGHTS) LANGUAGE SQLSCRIPT SQL SECURITY
INVOKER READ SQL DATA AS
BEGIN
  LT_FLIGHTS = SELECT CARRID, CONNID, FLDATE
                    FROM SFLIGHT;
  ET_FLIGHTS = SELECT * FROM :LT_FLIGHTS;
END;
```
Listing 4.8 Using Table Variables

In this example, a SELECT statement is used to assign the CARRID, CONNID, and FLDATE columns in database table SFLIGHT to the LT_FLIGHTS local table variable, which is implicitly typed by the system.

Then, a second SELECT statement is used to assign the contents of the LT_FLIGHTS table variable to the ET_FLIGHTS table variable, which is an output parameter and is explicitly typed. It uses the TT_FLIGHTS table type.

Using Scalar Variables

Similar to table variables, scalar variables can be input/output parameters or local variables. They are based on a simple data type. Values are assigned using the assignment operator :=. Similar to table variables, the value of scalar variables is accessed using the variable name supplemented by the prefix :.

You must always explicitly type a scalar variable. For local variables, you
use the DECLARE statement (similar to local table variables). During the
typing process, you can refer to the SQL data types supported by SAP
HANA.

The following simple example shows how to use scalar variables. Once
again, we've intentionally omitted some details from the source code in
Listing 4.9.

```
CREATE PROCEDURE EXAMPLE_SCALAR_VARIABLES (IN
IV_CUSTOMID NVARCHAR(8) , IN IV_ADDITIONAL_DISCOUNT
INTEGER) LANGUAGE SQLSCRIPT SQL SECURITY INVOKER
READS SQL DATA AS
BEGIN
  DECLARE LV_DISCOUNT INTEGER;
  DECLARE LV_NEW_DISCOUNT INTEGER;

  SELECT TO_INT(DISCOUNT) INTO LV_DISCOUNT
         FROM SCUSTOM WHERE ID = :IV_CUSTOMID;
  LV_NEW_DISCOUNT := :LV_DISCOUNT +
                     :IV_ADDITIONAL_DISCOUNT;
END;
```

Listing 4.9 Using Scalar Variables

The database procedure in this example increases the customer discount
by a specific percentage by using multiple scalar variables. The variables
IV_CUSTOMID and IV_ADDITIONAL_DISCOUNT are input parameters,
whereas LV_DISCOUNT and LV_NEW_DISCOUNT are local variables.

Using Imperative Enhancements

If necessary, you can also work with imperative language elements in
SQLScript, which we'll briefly discuss here for the sake of completeness.
In general, however, you should only use imperative enhancements as
often as necessary, but as little as possible.

In particular, SQLScript is used to move data-intensive calculations to the
database. SAP HANA should process data-intensive calculations in parallel as much as possible. If you work with imperative enhancements, this
may prevent parallelization.

Control structures You can use control structures to control (orchestrate) a database procedure's process flow. SQLScript supports loops and case distinctions.

The WHILE... DO... END WHILE and FOR... IN... DO... END FOR statements are available for loop processing. If you want to end the current loop pass during loop processing, you can use the CONTINUE statement for this purpose. If you want to fully exit a loop, you can use the BREAK statement for this purpose. You can use the IF... THEN... ELSEIF... ELSE... END IF statement to implement case distinctions.

The sample database procedure in Listing 4.10 illustrates the use of control structures.

```
LT_SPFLI = SELECT MANDT, CARRID, CONNID FROM SPFLI
              WHERE MANDT = :IV_MANDT
                AND AIRPFROM = :IV_AIRPFROM
                AND AIRPTO = :IV_AIRPTO;
LV_DAYS := 0;
WHILE LV_DAYS <= IV_MAX_DAYS DO
  ET_FLIGHTS = SELECT P.CARRID, P.CONNID, F.FLDATE
    FROM :LT_SPFLI AS P
    INNER JOIN SFLIGHT AS F ON F.MANDT = P.MANDT AND
    F.CARRID = P.CARRID AND F.CONNID = P.CONNID
    WHERE TO_DATE(F.FLDATE) >=
      ADD_DAYS (TO_DATE(:IV_FLDATE), -1 * :LV_DAYS)
      AND TO_DATE(F.FLDATE) <=
      ADD_DAYS (TO_DATE(:IV_FLDATE), :LV_DAYS);
  SELECT COUNT(*) INTO LV_CONNECTION_FOUND
    FROM :ET_FLIGHTS;
  IF :LV_CONNECTION_FOUND > 0 THEN
    BREAK;
  ELSE
    LV_DAYS := :LV_DAYS + 1;
  END IF;
END WHILE;
```

Listing 4.10 Control Structures in SQLScript

The database procedure determines the flights available between two given airports (IV_AIRPFROM and IV_AIRPTO) for a given flight date (IV_FLDATE). If (and only if) no flight is available for the given flight date, the database procedure tries to find flights one day before and one day after. If (and only if) no flights are available for this date, the database procedure tries to find flights two days before and two days after. The IV_MAX_DAYS input parameter controls the maximum number of days searched before or after a given flight date. The database procedure uses a WHILE... DO... END WHILE loop combined with an IF... THEN... ELSE... END IF case distinction. It uses the BREAK statement to exit the loop prematurely, if necessary.

Similarly, as described for Open SQL in Chapter 3, Section 3.2.2, you can also work with *cursors* in SQLScript. The example in Listing 4.11 shows how to define a cursor in SQLScript and then use it to read data.

Cursor processing

```
DECLARE CURSOR LT_CONNECTIONS (LV_MANDT NVARCHAR(3),
  LV_CARRID NVARCHAR(3)) FOR
  SELECT CARRID, CONNID FROM SPFLI
  WHERE MANDT = :LV_MANDT AND CARRID = :LV_CARRID;
BEGIN
  FOR LS_CONNECTIONS AS LT_CONNECTIONS(:IV_MANDT,
    :IV_CARRID) DO
    /* DO SOMETHING */
    ...
  END FOR;
END;
```
Listing 4.11 Cursor Processing with SQLScript

Only use cursors if there is no other way to implement the required processing logic. The SAP HANA database can't easily optimize database procedures that contain cursors.

You can use dynamic SQL to construct SQL statements at runtime. The EXEC and EXECUTE IMMEDIATE statements are available for this purpose.

Dynamic SQL

The example in Listing 4.12 shows how you can construct a SELECT statement at runtime to determine an airline's flight connections. In this example, it isn't absolutely necessary to use dynamic SQL.

```
EXECUTE IMMEDIATE 'SELECT * FROM SPFLI
  WHERE MANDT = ''' || :IV_MANDT || ''' AND CARRID =
  ''' || :IV_CARRID || ''''';
```
Listing 4.12 Dynamic SQL

We advise you to refrain, as much as possible, from using dynamic SQL because it has limited optimization options. A database procedure that contains dynamic SQL may need to be recompiled for each call. With dynamic SQL, there is also a risk of *SQL injections*.

Using Calculation Engine Plan Operators

In this section, for the sake of completeness, we'll discuss *CE plan operators*, which you can use in database procedures as an alternative to SQL statements. SAP no longer recommends using them for implementing database procedures. Instead, you should always use SQL statements within database procedures whenever possible. For this reason, we only briefly discuss the principle of CE plan operators and provide an overview of existing functions.

Examples of CE plan operators

To help you understand the concept of CE plan operators, we'll consider a very simple database procedure for determining the sales revenue of all flight connections associated with an airline. When an SQL statement is implemented, this database procedure looks like that shown in Listing 4.13.

```
ET_PAYMENTSUM = SELECT CARRID, CONNID, CURRENCY,
  SUM(PAYMENTSUM) AS PAYMENTSUM
  FROM SFLIGHT
  WHERE MANDT = :IV_MANDT AND CARRID = :IV_CARRID
  GROUP BY CARRID, CONNID, CURRENCY;
```

Listing 4.13 Implementation Using an SQL Statement

The SQL statement selects data from table SFLIGHT. This statement uses a WHERE clause to restrict the selection to the specified airline. It also uses the SUM aggregate function combined with a GROUP BY expression to add the sales revenue for each airline, connection, and currency.

When CE plan operators are used, the same database procedure looks like the one shown in Listing 4.14.

```
LT_SFLIGHT = CE_COLUMN_TABLE("SFLIGHT");
LT_SFLIGHT_PROJECTION = CE_PROJECTION(:LT_SFLIGHT,
  ["MANDT", "CARRID", "CONNID", "CURRENCY",
  "PAYMENTSUM"], '"MANDT" = '':IV_MANDT'' AND
  "CARRID" = '':IV_CARRID'' ');
LT_SFLIGHT_AGGREGATION = CE_AGGREGATION(
  :LT_SFLIGHT_PROJECTION, [SUM("PAYMENTSUM") AS
  "PAYMENTSUM"], ["CARRID", "CONNID", "CURRENCY"]);
ET_PAYMENTSUM = CE_PROJECTION(:LT_SFLIGHT_AGGREGATION,
  ["CARRID", "CONNID", "CURRENCY", "PAYMENTSUM"]);
```

Listing 4.14 Implementation Using CE Plan Operators

The database procedure uses different CE plan operators, which are linked to one another by means of table variables:

1. First, the database procedure uses the `CE_COLUMN_TABLE` CE plan operator to bind the `LT_SFLIGHT` table variable to database table `SFLIGHT`.

2. It then uses the `CE_PROJECTION` CE plan operator to restrict the selection to the `MANDT`, `CARRID`, `CONNID`, and `CURRENCY` columns, as well as to restrict the selection to the connections associated with the specified airline. The `LT_SFLIGHT` table variable, which was bound in the first step, is used as the input, while the `LT_SFLIGHT_PROJECTION` table variable is used as the output.

3. The `CE_AGGREGATION` CE plan operator adds the sales revenue for each airline, connection, and currency. Here, the `LT_SFLIGHT_PROJECTION` table variable is used as the input, and the `LT_SFLIGHT_AGGREGATION` table variable is used as the output.

4. In a final step, the database procedure uses the `CE_PROJECTION` CE plan operator to perform a projection again. This projection is necessary because (due to the way the `CE_AGGREGATION` works) the sequence of the columns in the `LT_SFLIGHT_AGGREGATION` table variable doesn't correspond to the sequence of the columns in the `ET_PAYMENTSUM` output parameter.

CE plan operators are implemented directly in the calculation engine. They are divided into *data source* access operators, *relational operators*, and *special operators*.

Available
CE plan operators

You can use data source access operators to bind table variables to a database table or view. The access operators include `CE_COLUMN_TABLE`, `CE_JOIN_VIEW`, `CE_OLAP_VIEW`, and `CE_CALC_VIEW`.

Relational operators make the operations typically associated with relational algebra available to you. They work on the table variables that you've previously bound using the data source access operators, for example. SAP HANA currently provides the following access operators: `CE_JOIN`, `CE_PROJECTION`, `CE_AGGREGATION`, `CE_UNION_ALL`, and `CE_CALC`.

In addition to data source access operators and relational operators, the calculation engine currently makes the following three additional operators available:

▶ CE_VERTICAL_UNION
Enables you to connect columns in multiple table variables to each other (e.g., if this can't be done using a join). If necessary, you can rename the columns. It's important to note the sort order of the table variables used, or you may receive some unexpected results.

▶ CE_CONVERSION
Enables you to perform quantity and currency conversions.

▶ TRACE
Enables you to create traces. Don't use this one in live code.

[»]   **Note**

For more information on CE plan operators, refer to the SAP HANA SQLScript Reference at *http://help.sap.com/hana*.

4.3   Database Procedures

Now we'll describe how to implement database procedures in SAP HANA Studio using SQLScript.

Implement data-base procedures

In Section 4.2, you learned which commands are available in the SAP HANA database for creating database procedures and how you can use SQLScript within procedures. Now we'll discuss how to implement a database procedure in SAP HANA Studio.

SAP HANA Development Perspective

For this purpose, we use the SAP HANA DEVELOPMENT perspective. We won't detail the alternative usage of the MODELER perspective or the *SAP HANA Web Workbench* because we assume that as an ABAP developer, you'll create database procedures from ABAP in most cases (at least as of Release 7.4). Creating database procedures from ABAP is discussed in Chapter 6.

You particularly use the SAP HANA DEVELOPMENT perspective if you build applications based on SAP HANA Extended Application Services (SAP HANA XS; see Chapter 1, Section 1.1.4). If you create a database procedure in the SAP HANA DEVELOPMENT perspective, the system stores it in the SAP HANA repository—as in the MODELER perspective—and creates corresponding runtime objects for the procedure in the database catalog upon activation.

Now we'll cover the individual steps for creating and subsequently testing the read-only procedure DETERMINE_CONNECTION_UTILIZATION. The database procedure determines the percentage utilization for each flight connection. It has the following input and output parameters:

▶ The input parameter IV_MANDT (client) of the SQL data type NVARCHAR(3)

▶ The input parameter IV_CARRID (airline) of the SQL data type NVARCHAR(3)

▶ The output parameter ET_UTILIZATION

The output parameter ET_UTILIZATION is a table parameter that comprises the following columns:

▶ CARRID (airline) of the SQL data type NVARCHAR(3)

▶ CONNID (flight connection) of the SQL data type NVARCHAR(4)

▶ UTILIZATION (utilization) of the SQL data type DECIMAL(5, 2)

You need to create an *SAP HANA XS Project* and a *Repository Workspace* to create a database procedure:

Create project and Repository Workspace

1. Open the SAP HANA DEVELOPMENT perspective, and navigate to the PROJECT EXPLORER view.

2. Create an XS Project by choosing the menu path, FILE • NEW • OTHER.

3. The system displays the NEW XS PROJECT dialog window (see Figure 4.4). Enter a PROJECT NAME, for example, "chapter04". Then click NEXT.

Figure 4.4 Creating an XS Project

4. In the next dialog step, choose the ADD WORKSPACE button.

5. The CREATE NEW REPOSITORY WORKSPACE dialog window appears (see Figure 4.5). Select an SAP HANA system, and select the USE DEFAULT WORKSPACE checkbox. Then click FINISH.

6. In the NEW XS PROJECT dialog window, enter a package (in this example, "test.a4h.book"), and select the ADD PROJECT FOLDER AS SUBPACKAGE checkbox. Click NEXT.

7. In the last dialog step, deselect the two checkboxes, XS APPLICATION ACCESS (.XSACCESS) and XS APPLICATION DESCRIPTOR (.XSAPP), and then click FINISH.

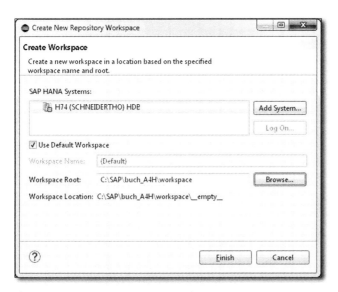

Figure 4.5 Creating a Repository Workspace

Next, you create the database procedure by following these steps:

1. Choose the menu path, FILE • NEW • OTHER. Then choose the STORED PROCEDURE wizard for creating a procedure.

2. Enter the name of the procedure in the FILE NAME field and fill in the TARGET SCHEMA field in the dialog window that opens (see Figure 4.6). In this example, the name is "DETERMINE_CONNECTION_UTILIZA-TION" and the target schema is "_SYS_BIC".

3. You must also specify the FILE FORMAT. TEXT and XML are available as file formats. You should usually use the TEXT file format because XML is outdated and is no longer recommended for use. However, the TEXT file format isn't supported if you use the *database procedure proxies* (see Chapter 5, Section 5.2) so that you don't have any choice when you use database procedure proxies. Close the dialog by clicking on FINISH.

4. Now the editor for editing the database procedure opens. Enter the source code of the procedure (for our example, you can find the complete code in Listing 4.15). Change the default schema if required.

Figure 4.6 Creating a Database Procedure

5. Copy the source code, and then activate the database procedure.

```
PROCEDURE "_SYS_BIC"."test.a4h.book.chapter04:
:DETERMINE_CONNECTION_UTILIZATION"
( IN IV_MANDT NVARCHAR(3), IN IV_CARRID NVARCHAR(3),
  OUT ET_UTILIZATION TABLE (
    CARRID NVARCHAR(3),
    CONNID NVARCHAR(4),
    UTILIZATION DECIMAL(5,2) )
)
  LANGUAGE SQLSCRIPT
  SQL SECURITY INVOKER
  DEFAULT SCHEMA "SAPH74"
  READS SQL DATA AS
```

```
BEGIN
  ET_UTILIZATION = SELECT CARRID, CONNID,
  AVG(TO_DECIMAL(SEATSOCC + SEATSOCC_B + SEATSOCC_F) /
  TO_DECIMAL(SEATSMAX + SEATSMAX_B + SEATSMAX_F) * 100)
  AS UTILIZATION FROM SFLIGHT
  WHERE MANDT = :IV_MANDT
    AND CARRID = :IV_CARRID
  GROUP BY CARRID, CONNID;
END;
```

Listing 4.15 Source Code for Sample Procedure

The system stores the database procedure in the SAP HANA repository and as a runtime object in the database catalog (within the _SYS_BIC schema in this example). You can check the creation of the runtime object as described in Chapter 2, Section 2.4.3.

Test database procedure

You can use the SQL console to test the database procedure (more information on the SQL console is also available in Chapter 2, Section 2.4.3):

1. Open the SQL console (e.g., by using the context menu of the SAP HANA SYSTEM LIBRARY node within the PROJECT EXPLORER view).

2. Use the CALL statement to call the database procedure. Figure 4.7 shows the result.

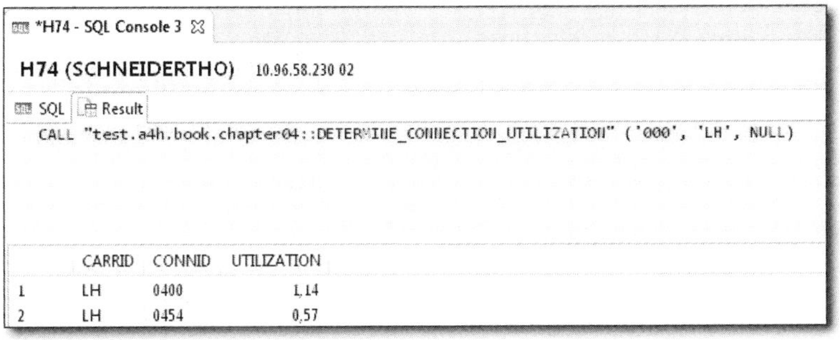

Figure 4.7 Testing a Database Procedure

You can find more information, for example, on debugging of database procedures, in the SAP HANA Developer Guide (for SAP HANA Studio) at *http://help.sap.com/hana*.

4.4   Analytical Models

This section deals with modeled views that are used for analysis. You may be wondering why this topic plays such a big role in the context of SAP HANA. To answer this question, we'll go back a little and briefly explain the underlying reasoning.

The business data of a domain are stored (usually in a normalized form) in a set of database tables that are connected via foreign key relationships (an *entity-relationship model*). Using this data model, single records can be efficiently created, selected, and modified. However, if data access becomes more dynamic and complex, or if certain analyses or checks are necessary, the data must be transformed.

The pattern most commonly used for these transformations is that the data are read from the database and used by a program for calculations before storing the results back in the database. This is referred to as *materialization* of the transformed data.

A simple example is the materialization of a totals calculation in a special column or *totals table*. In principle, the same pattern is used for data structures of a *business intelligence system*, where the original data is transformed into a form that can be used more efficiently for analyses (star schema). This materialization was primarily for performance reasons in the past because it wasn't possible to perform the transformations on the fly at runtime when users submitted a query. However, because the different data structures had to be synchronized (which is usually done with some time offset), this performance gain also led to higher complexity and prevented a real-time experience for users. Using SAP HANA, this redundancy can now be eliminated in many scenarios. From a technical perspective, this means that the transformations are performed in real time using the original data. Consequently, database views are an important element—in this context, to express transformations for read accesses—and SAP HANA offers a powerful and user-friendly tool through analytical models.

Reference example
for this chapter

In the scope of this section, we'll create relatively simple analyses of flight bookings and the seat utilization of flights based on the SFLIGHT data model. In addition to some master data of a flight connection (airline, departure, and destination location), statistical information on seat utilization, revenues, and baggage will also be displayed per quarter. To create these analyses, we'll use the different modeling options provided by SAP HANA and explain their properties and areas of use.

The following types of column views will be discussed:

View types

- ▸ **Attribute views**
  These views are used to define master data views (see Section 4.4.1). We'll introduce the different options available to create table joins and explain how calculated attributes can be added to a view.

- ▸ **Analytic views**
  These views can be used for calculations and analyses based on transaction data using a star schema (see Section 4.4.2). We'll explain how you can define simple and calculated key figures and add dimensions. As a special case of calculated key figures, we'll describe currency conversion and unit conversions.

- ▸ **Calculation views**
  These views are used to combine views and basic data operations in a flexible way (see Section 4.4.3). We'll describe both the modeling and the implementation of calculation views using SQLScript.

In this chapter, we first show how you can define and test these views in SAP HANA Studio. Chapter 5 describes how to access them via ABAP programs.

4.4.1 Attribute Views

Attribute views comprise a number of fields (columns) from database tables, which are linked through foreign key relationships. Moreover, attribute views provide a way to define calculated columns and hierarchical relationships between individual fields (e.g., parent-child relationships). They are significant particularly as components of other view types, especially as *dimensions* of analytic views (see Section 4.4.2) or for a more general purpose as *nodes* in calculation views (see Section 4.4.3).

In this section, we'll create a number of such views to demonstrate different functional aspects. We'll create several views because it's not possible or useful to use all functions for all tables. Table 4.4 provides an

Reference examples for this section

overview of the views used in the example together with a description and the corresponding functionality.

Column	Description	Functionality
AT_PASSENGER	Simple view for table SCUSTOM (passenger data)	First basic example
AT_FLIGHT	Flight data plus information from the flight plan and information on the airlines	Different join types, calculated fields, and hierarchies
AT_TIME_GREG	Pure time hierarchy (year, quarter, calendar week)	Attribute view of type TIME

Table 4.4 Sample Attribute Views Used in this Section

We'll reuse the views AT_FLIGHT, AT_PASSENGER, and AT_TIME_GREG in Section 4.4.2.

Basic Principles

Join views   Before describing how attribute views are modeled, let's take a quick look at the most important concepts. Because attribute views can be used to create data views based on several tables that are linked via different types of joins, they can also be referred to as *join views*. Because joins play a major role when dealing with attribute views, accesses to attribute views are handled by the *join engine* in SAP HANA.

Modeling concepts   When modeling attribute views, the following concepts are important:

▸ **Attributes**
These refer to the columns of the attribute view. You can add columns from one or several physical tables or define additional calculated columns.

▸ **Key attribute**
These attributes of the view uniquely specify an entry and play an important role when the view is used as a dimensions of an analytic view (see Section 4.4.2).

▶ **Filters**

Filters define restrictions applied to the values of a column (similar to a `WHERE` condition in a `SELECT` statement).

▶ **Hierarchies**

Hierarchies are relations defined for the attributes such as a parent-child relationship (see Section 4.4.1).

Special Join Variants   [«]

In addition to the standard joins presented in Section 4.1.2, two other special join types are used when modeling attribute views in SAP HANA:

▶ **Referential joins**
These joins provide a special way of defining an inner join. With this join type, *referential integrity* is assumed implicitly (which has advantages with regard to performance behavior). Therefore, when using a referential join without a query to a field from the right-hand table, no check is made for a matching entry. The data are assumed to be consistent. Referential joins are often a useful standard when defining joins in attribute views.

▶ **Text joins**
These joins can be used to read language-dependent texts from a different table. For this purpose, the column with the language key must be included in the text table; at runtime, a filter for the correct language is then applied based on the context.

Creating Attribute Views

Attribute views can be defined via the MODELER perspective in SAP HANA Studio, which was introduced in Chapter 2, Section 2.4.3. To create a view, select NEW • ATTRIBUTE VIEW from the context menu of a package in the CONTENT node. You first have to specify a NAME and a LABEL (description) in the dialog shown in Figure 4.8.

In this dialog, you can also copy an existing view as the basis for a new attribute view. When selecting SUBTYPE, you can create special types of attribute views (e.g., for time hierarchies, which are explained in more detail in Section 4.4.1). When you click the FINISH button, the attribute view is created, and the modeling editor opens.

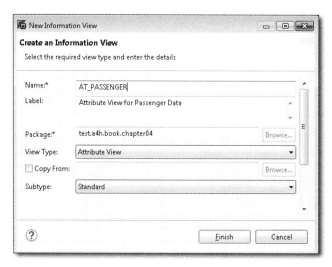

Figure 4.8 Creating an Attribute View

Modeling
editor

The editor used to define an attribute view has two sections: DATA FOUNDATION and SEMANTICS. These are displayed as boxes in the SCENARIO pane on the left-hand side of the screen (see Figure 4.9).

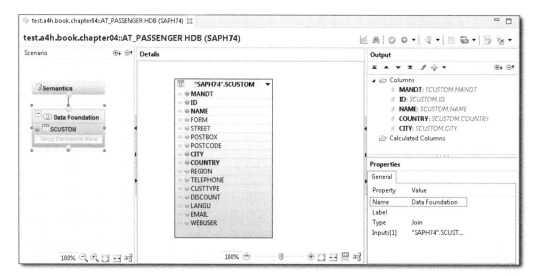

Figure 4.9 Definition of the Data Foundation

By selecting each node, you can switch between defining the data basis (Data Foundation) and the semantic configuration (Semantics). The Data Foundation is used to add tables, define joins, and add attributes. Figure 4.9 shows a simple example based on table SCUSTOM.

By selecting the Semantics node, you can maintain further metadata for the attribute view, such as the following:

Define metadata

- You can specify whether an attribute is a key field of the view. Note that every attribute view must contain at least one key field. In addition, you can define texts (*labels*) for attributes or hide attributes, which can be useful for calculated fields.

- You can specify how the client field is handled (static value or dynamically). Client handling is discussed in detail at the end of this section.

- You can define hierarchies.

The layout of the Semantics section is shown in Figure 4.10.

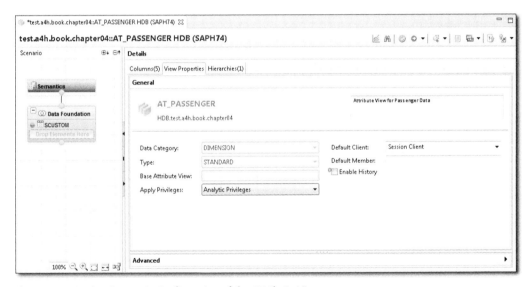

Figure 4.10 Further Semantic Configuration of the Attribute View

The selected columns from table SCUSTOM are marked as key fields. As described in Chapter 2, Section 2.4.3, you now have to save and activate the Attribute view to be able to use it.

Activation errors   If the view wasn't modeled properly, an error will be displayed during activation. Typical errors are caused by missing key fields, invalid joins, or calculated fields that weren't defined correctly. Figure 4.11 shows an example. The cause of an error may not always be as obvious.

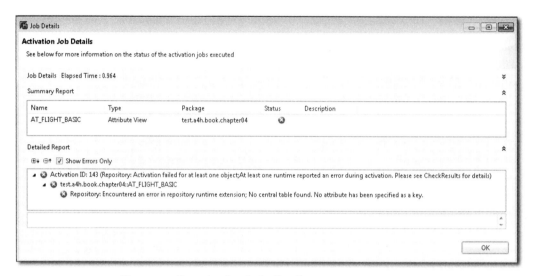

Figure 4.11 Example of an Activation Error

Client handling   If the tables used are client-dependent, you can specify if the client should be automatically included in the filter condition based on the current context (SESSION CLIENT). Alternatively, you can define the tables as CROSS-CLIENT to access the data for all clients. It's also possible to specify a static value for the client. Usage tips regarding this topic are provided in Chapter 5, Section 5.1.4.

[»]   **Determining the Client**

There is a *session context* for every database connection that stores certain properties of the current connection. In particular, this information comprises the current client, which is set by the Database Shared Library (DBSL) in case of a connection via AS ABAP. When using the DATA PREVIEW or a connection via the SQL console in SAP HANA Studio, the client is determined from the user settings. When configuring these settings, you can specify a default client for a user. If no client is specified, there is no client context, which means that all data is displayed (cross-client) when using the DATA PREVIEW.

Following this initial simple example, let's assume you now want to define a more complex attribute view. For this purpose, you want to define the SFLIGHTS view from the DDIC, which you've already seen in Chapter 3, Section 3.2.3, as an attribute view. To do so, you create a new AT_FLIGHT attribute view and add table SFLIGHT in the DATA FOUNDATION. You can either manually select those tables or have the system propose tables based on the metadata maintained in the DDIC. For the latter option, select the table, and then choose PROPOSE TABLES from the context menu. The selection dialog opens the screen shown in Figure 4.12.

View SFLIGHTS as an attribute view

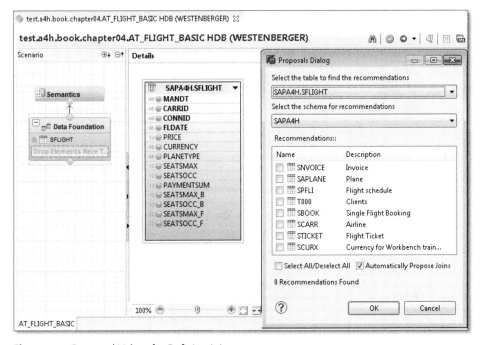

Figure 4.12 Proposed Values for Defining Joins

To reproduce the SFLIGHTS view, you'll add tables SCARR and SPFLI and define the joins as shown in Figure 4.13. If you want to define a new join, simply drag a connecting line between the corresponding attributes of two tables while holding the mouse button down. To define the properties of a join, you first have to select the join and then configure it in the PROPERTIES section (JOIN TYPE, CARDINALITY). For our example, a referential join and a cardinality of n:1 are used.

Select tables and define joins

[»] **Attribute Views Support Only Equi-Joins**

When formulating join conditions, you can use more expressions (e.g., <, >) in SQL that go beyond checking the equality of columns (*equi-join*), as shown in the following example:

```
SELECT ... FROM ... [INNER|OUTER] JOIN ... ON col1 < col2 ...
```

However, attribute views support only equi-joins.

Add attributes In the next step, you add the desired attributes from the tables via the context menu of the output structure of the view. The selected attributes are highlighted and displayed in the OUTPUT section in the right-hand pane of the editor.

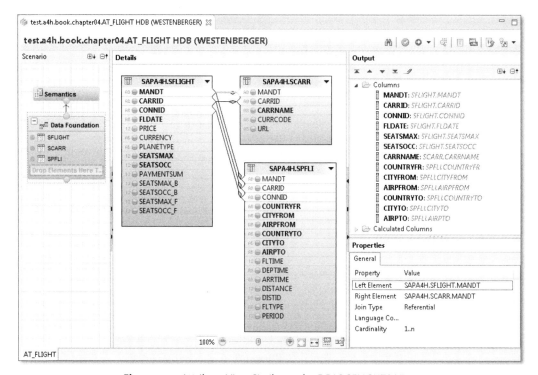

Figure 4.13 Attribute View Similar to the DDIC SFLIGHTS View

Activate/test For this example, choose the MANDT, CARRID, CONNID, and FLDATE columns as key attributes and then activate the view. The result shows the name of the airline and information on the departure and destination location for every flight (see Figure 4.14).

MANDT	CARRID	CONNID	FLDATE	SEATSM...	SEATSOCC	CARRNAME	COUNTRYFR	CITYFROM	AIRPFROM
001	LH	0400	20040101	280	257	Lufthansa	DE	FRANKFURT	FRA
001	AA	0017	20040101	220	174	American Airlines	US	NEW YORK	JFK
001	AZ	0555	20040101	189	150	Alitalia	IT	ROME	FCO
001	LH	2402	20040101	130	109	Lufthansa	DE	FRANKFURT	FRA
001	UA	0941	20040101	380	380	United Airlines	DE	FRANKFURT	FRA
001	AZ	0789	20040101	385	298	Alitalia	JP	TOKYO	TYO
001	LH	0402	20040101	380	321	Lufthansa	DE	FRANKFURT	FRA
001	QF	0005	20040101	385	361	Qantas Airways	SG	SINGAPORE	SIN
001	SQ	0015	20040101	220	187	Singapore Airlines	US	SAN FRANCISCO	SFO
001	SQ	0002	20040101	380	377	Singapore Airlines	SG	SINGAPORE	SIN
001	LH	0401	20040101	280	266	Lufthansa	US	NEW YORK	JFK
001	DL	0106	20040101	380	339	Delta Airlines	US	NEW YORK	JFK
001	JL	0407	20040101	380	315	Japan Airlines	JP	TOKYO	NRT
001	JL	0408	20040101	380	380	Japan Airlines	DE	FRANKFURT	FRA
001	AA	0064	20040101	380	331	American Airlines	US	SAN FRANCISCO	SFO
001	DL	1699	20040101	385	363	Delta Airlines	US	NEW YORK	JFK
001	DL	1984	20040101	280	266	Delta Airlines	US	SAN FRANCISCO	SFO
001	LH	2407	20040101	130	122	Lufthansa	DE	BERLIN	TXL
001	UA	3504	20040101	385	385	United Airlines	US	SAN FRANCISCO	SFO
001	AZ	0788	20040101	385	300	Alitalia	IT	ROME	FCO

Figure 4.14 Result of the Attribute View

As for normal SQL views, you can also specify filter values for columns when working with attribute views. To define the filter, you open the filter dialog for an attribute via the context menu item Apply Filter. Attributes with an existing filter are marked with a filter symbol, as shown in Figure 4.15. For this example, define a filter for the attribute PLANETYPE with an EQUAL operator and the VALUE "A330-300". Alternatively, you can also try other comparison operators.

Define filter values

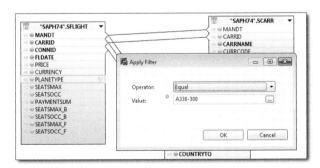

Figure 4.15 Filter for an Attribute

Calculated Fields

Virtual attributes

Now that you've seen how an attribute view can be used to read data from different tables using different join types, you can go one step further and dynamically calculate some of the view columns. Compared to classic DDIC views, these *virtual attributes* (i.e., attributes that don't belong directly to a column of one of the physical tables) are a new opportunity for expressing data processing logic. Chapter 6 introduces you to the new CDS views in ABAP, which offer this opportunity too.

As a first example, add a calculated attribute to the AT_FLIGHT attribute view (refer to Figure 4.13), which will contain the full flight connection (departure location and airport plus destination location and airport) as its value, for example, NEW YORK (JFK) – SAN FRANCISCO (SFO).

Define calculated attributes

To do so, define a calculated attribute in the DATA FOUNDATION via the CALCULATED COLUMNS node of the OUTPUT section, and specify a NAME, a LABEL, and a DATA TYPE (see Figure 4.16).

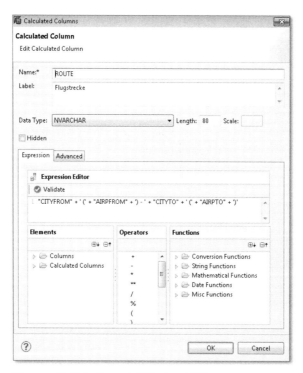

Figure 4.16 Definition of a Calculated Field

Using the EXPRESSION EDITOR, you can specify an expression that will be used to determine the value. This provides a variety of functions (conversions, mathematical operations, string operations, date calculations, and even simple case distinctions). In our example, we'll only use a simple concatenation of strings for now (see Listing 4.16).

Define expressions for calculations

```
"CITYFROM" + ' (' + "AIRPFROM" + ') -
' + "CITYTO" + ' (' + "AIRPTO" + ')'
```

Listing 4.16 Example of an Expression for a Calculated Field

Attribute References and Constants in Expressions

[!]

When defining *expressions* for calculated attributes, you must make sure to use the correct type of quotation marks. For references to attributes of the view (e.g., `"CITYFROM"` in Listing 4.16), double quotes must be used. It's recommended to use the drag-and-drop function via the formula editor. For text constants, by contrast, single quotes must be used (as shown in the parentheses in Listing 4.16).

Using the wrong quotation marks usually leads to an activation error.

After activating the attribute view, the calculated column is displayed in the output (see Figure 4.17). Calculated columns can be queried via SQL just like normal columns, which will be demonstrated in Section 4.4.4.

Output of the calculated field

CARRID	CONNID	FLDATE	CARRNAME	ROUTE
LH	0400	20040101	Lufthansa	FRANKFURT (FRA) - NEW YORK (JFK)
AA	0017	20040101	American Airlines	NEW YORK (JFK) - SAN FRANCISCO (SFO)
AZ	0555	20040101	Alitalia	ROME (FCO) - FRANKFURT (FRA)
LH	2402	20040101	Lufthansa	FRANKFURT (FRA) - BERLIN (SXF)
UA	0941	20040101	United Airlines	FRANKFURT (FRA) - SAN FRANCISCO (SFO)
AZ	0789	20040101	Alitalia	TOKYO (TYO) - ROME (FCO)
LH	0402	20040101	Lufthansa	FRANKFURT (FRA) - NEW YORK (JFK)
QF	0005	20040101	Qantas Airways	SINGAPORE (SIN) - FRANKFURT (FRA)
SQ	0015	20040101	Singapore Airlines	SAN FRANCISCO (SFO) - SINGAPORE (SIN)
SQ	0002	20040101	Singapore Airlines	SINGAPORE (SIN) - SAN FRANCISCO (SFO)
LH	0401	20040101	Lufthansa	NEW YORK (JFK) - FRANKFURT (FRA)
DL	0106	20040101	Delta Airlines	NEW YORK (JFK) - FRANKFURT (FRA)
JL	0407	20040101	Japan Airlines	TOKYO (NRT) - FRANKFURT (FRA)

Figure 4.17 Output of the Calculated Field

Calculated fields are also supported for the other view types (see Section 4.4.2), where these fields are used especially for the calculations and conversions of currencies and units that we already mentioned.

Hierarchies

Many types of data have hierarchical relationships. The place of residence or principal office of customers is structured geographically by country, region, and city; the hierarchical structure of a creation date comprises the year, quarter, and month; a product catalog can consist of several categories; and so on.

Data analysis
Hierarchies play an important role in data analyses. You can start with an aggregated view of the data and then navigate within the hierarchical structures. This is referred to as a *drilldown* (or drillup when data is aggregated).

Hierarchies in
SAP HANA
For attribute views, hierarchies are defined in the SEMANTICS section. SAP HANA currently supports two types of hierarchies:

▶ **Parent-child relationships**
For this type, two attributes with a parent-child relationship must be defined. For example, in the ABAP hierarchy of packages, the corresponding database table (TDEVC) comprises columns for the package name (DEVCLASS) and the name of the superpackage (PARENTCL). These two columns form a parent-child relationship because each superpackage itself constitutes a package in the table.

▶ **Level hierarchy**
With this hierarchy type, you define hierarchy levels based on the values of table columns or calculated attributes. If a table for example, comprises columns for the country and the city (e.g., table SPFLI), these two attributes define a hierarchy (the countries at the upper level and the corresponding cities at the lower levels). However, these attributes don't have a parent-child relationship because this would require the city values also to appear as countries.

Create hierarchies
Existing hierarchies are displayed in the SEMANTICS section, where you can also create new hierarchies. Figure 4.18 shows a level hierarchy based on the attributes of the departure location (country, city, airport)

from table `SPFLI`. You can also define hierarchies for *calculation views* (see Section 4.4.3).

Figure 4.18 Hierarchy of an Attribute View

There are various options for using the modeled hierarchies. This information is evaluated in particular by the supported business intelligence clients. One particular variant (access via Microsoft Excel) is shown in Section 4.4.5. SAP HANA thus provides basic support for simple hierarchies, but compared to the comprehensive hierarchy modeling that's available in SAP Business Warehouse (SAP BW), for example, the options are rather limited.

Attribute Views for Time Values

Most business data have a time reference (e.g., a creation date or a validity period). These references are usually implemented as date fields or time stamps in the data model. The flight data model, for example, comprises the flight date in table `SFLIGHT` and the booking time in table `SBOOK`. For many analyses, this point in time must be mapped to a certain time interval. In the simplest case, this can be the corresponding year, month, quarter, or calendar week. However, there are also more complicated or configurable time intervals such as the *fiscal year*, which is the calendar to be used for certain scenarios.

[»]

Customizing the Fiscal Year

Fiscal years and periods are configured via ABAP Customizing. Using ABAP Customizing, you can configure comprehensive settings or variants and also define special cases (e.g., a short fiscal year when a company is founded). These settings are configured via the MAINTAIN FISCAL YEAR VARIANT entry of Transaction SPRO.

The SAP standard provides several function modules to convert a normal date (e.g., of type DATS) into the corresponding fiscal year or period.

From a technical perspective, the corresponding Customizing is stored particularly in tables T009 and T009B. These tables were previously pool/cluster tables and therefore not available directly in the database. Such tables are converted into normal database tables when performing a migration to SAP HANA (see Chapter 3, Section 3.2.1) so that such data can also be accessed natively in the database.

Generate calendar data

SAP HANA offers a special attribute view type for handling time hierarchies. Before you can use this variant, you must first create time data once in special technical tables in SAP HANA. You can select GENERATE TIME DATA on the initial screen of the MODELER perspective for this purpose. Subsequently, you specify the details for the calendar type and time period.

Figure 4.19 shows the generation of time data based on days in the normal (Gregorian) calendar for the years 2000 through 2020. You can also define data in the fiscal calendar. Here, however, you must additionally specify a variant that was set in Customizing (see the preceding information box).

Attribute view of the "Time" type

You can then define an attribute view that uses this time data. To do so, you select the TIME type and specify the desired details for the calendar when creating an attribute view. Figure 4.20 shows how the attribute view AT_TIME_GREG is created for a day-based Gregorian calendar.

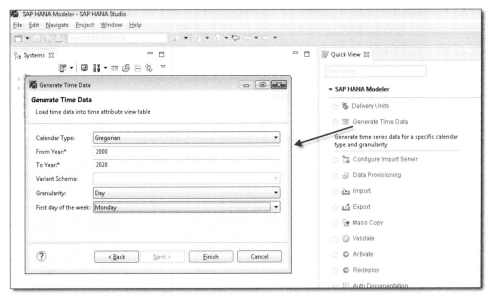

Figure 4.19 Generating Time Data

Figure 4.20 Attribute View for a Gregorian Calendar

Key attribute   Because the view contains the date as a key field, joins can be created for a date column in the business data. You use the attribute DATE_SAP of the attribute view for a join with a column of type DATS (e.g., FLDATE in table SFLIGHT).

This means that you can use these views as time dimensions in an *analytic view* if the date is part of the fact table. We'll discuss this in detail in the next section.

[»]   **Technical Tables for Time Data**

The time data is stored in special tables in the _SYS_BI schema, for example, tables M_TIME_DIMENSION and M_FISCAL_CALENDAR. These tables can also be used directly in attribute views (or general SQL statements).

4.4.2   Analytic Views

Analytic views are special views in SAP HANA that are used to calculate and analyze key figures. If you're already familiar with data warehouse or business intelligence applications, you can think of an analytic view as a *star schema*. We first provide a brief introduction of the most important concepts and then explain how you can create analytic views in SAP HANA Studio and define calculated key figures in particular.

Reference examples   In this section, two scenarios will be implemented as analytic views. In
for this section   the first example (AN_BOOKING), we'll model an analysis of the flight bookings based on attributes of the customer and the flight. In this analysis, the booking prices and the baggage weight are examined as key figures. For both figures, conversions must be considered due to different currencies and weight units. We'll also define another calculated figure based on the baggage weight, which specifies whether we're dealing with excess baggage (more than 20KG). In the second example, we'll define an analytic view called AN_SEAT_UTILIZATION to analyze the seat utilization of flights.

Both AN_BOOKING and AN_SEAT_UTILIZATION use the attribute views from the previous section. In Section 4.4.3, the two attribute views are combined for analysis.

Basic Principles

When using analytic views, you should be familiar with the most important concepts from the Online Analytical Processing (OLAP) environment, that is, from the field of data analysis. We'll therefore give you a short introduction based on an example in this section.

Analyses usually focus on transaction data (purchase orders, documents, invoices, etc.). The corresponding table is referred to as the *fact table*. This data includes one or several *key figures* or *measures*—for example, the invoice amount—which are relevant for data analysis. Fact tables usually contain a large number of entries. Moreover, fact tables can contain data from several database tables. The key figures must be from one table, and the attributes of the other table are, for instance, needed as foreign keys. Fact tables containing header data and line items are typical examples.

Fact table

The transaction data includes associations with master data (e.g., via the customer number of a purchase order) and other data such as time stamps (e.g., the purchase order creation date). Because this associated data can also be used to break down the fact table into data slices, the data are also referred to as *dimensions*, and an analysis along these dimensions are called *slice-and-dice* operations. An example of this is the determination of the total revenue in 2015 for customers from the United States. Within the dimensions, the data are usually structured hierarchically (e.g., by geographical regions or time intervals). This makes it possible to analyze these hierarchy levels (drilldown, drillup) further; for 2015 revenue in the United States, for example, you could analyze the data by state or quarter.

Dimensions

Let's now look at a concrete example based on our flight model. We'll use table SBOOK as the fact table and the LOCCURAM column (flight price in the airline's currency) as the key figure. The customer number, the flight date, and the flight connection comprise associations that allow you to perform the analysis based on several dimensions.

Example of a star schema

When looking at a graphical representation of the data model, it resembles a typical star schema (see Figure 4.21).

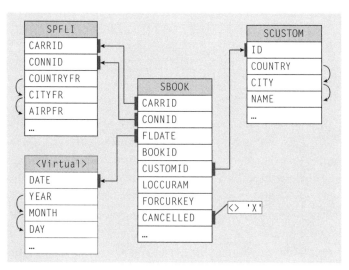

Figure 4.21 Example of a Star Schema with SBOOK as the Fact Table

Hierarchies within the dimensions

The data are usually structured hierarchically within the dimensions. The geographical data of the departure location, the customers' places of residence (country, city, etc.), and the flight date (year, month, day) represent the hierarchies in this example; the hierarchical relationship is defined by the columns, as shown in Figure 4.21. Because the flight data model doesn't contain a database table with time data, the time hierarchy is marked as virtual.

Filter variants

A star schema provides different filter variants. On one hand, there can be restrictions for the transaction data. When analyzing the flight bookings, for example, we only want to consider the bookings that weren't canceled. On the other hand, you can also define special key figures to directly apply restrictions within the dimensions (e.g., to consider only customers in the United States). These key figures are also referred to as *restricted measures*.

Creating Analytic Views

Similar to attribute views, analytic views are created in SAP HANA Studio via the context menu of a package in the MODELER perspective. After specifying a name and a description, the corresponding editor opens (see Figure 4.22).

Figure 4.22 Editor for Analytic Views

The editor for analytic views consists of three sections:

▸ Data Foundation
To define the fact table.

▸ Star Join
To add the dimensions defined by attribute views and to define calculated attributes and restricted measures.

▸ Semantics
To semantically enrich the selected attributes and define optional input parameters for the view.

The first example implements the star schema shown earlier in Figure 4.21 as an analytic view. To do so, you add table SBOOK as the fact table, select the required fields as you did for the attribute view, and define the filter for the CANCELLED column.

Then switch to the Logical Join section, and add the AT_FLIGHT, AT_PASSENGER, and AT_TIME_GREG attribute views from Section 4.4.1 as dimensions. When doing so, you draw a connecting line from the fact table to the attribute views. Figure 4.23 shows the resulting diagram.

As the final step, you select the measures in the Semantics section. In this example, the flight price in the local currency of the airline (LOCCURAM)

Editor for analytic views

Model the fact table

Add dimensions

Assign measures

and the baggage weight (LUGGWEIGHT) are used for these measures. After the view is activated, you can use the DATA PREVIEW for a first simple analysis of the result set. Figure 4.24 shows a sample breakdown of the revenue by year, quarter, and airline, with a filter set for the year 2013.

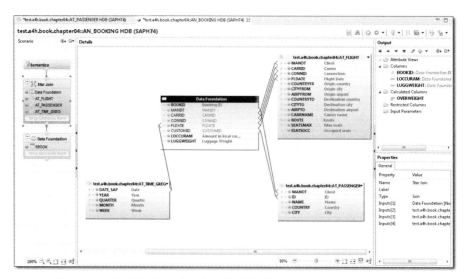

Figure 4.23 Analytic View Based on Booking Data

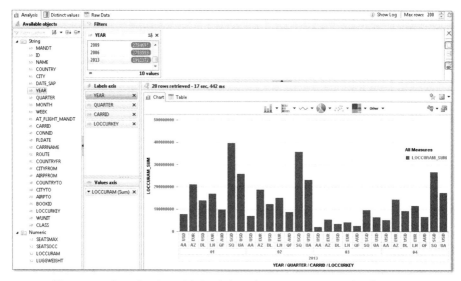

Figure 4.24 Data Preview with Breakdown by Year, Quarter, and Airline

Following the same procedure, you'll now create a second analytic view, AN_SEAT_UTILIZATION, which uses table SFLIGHT as the fact table instead of the flight bookings, but also uses AT_TIME_GREG as the time dimension so that the seat utilization can be analyzed by quarter. Figure 4.25 shows the resulting star schema.

Create another analytic view

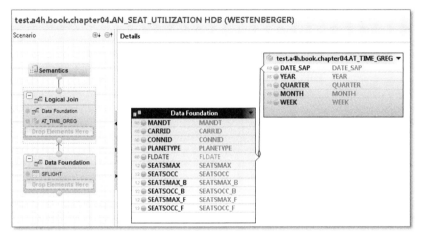

Figure 4.25 Second Analytic View, Based on Flight Data

Now that you know how to create and test analytic views, we'll discuss calculated key figures in the next section.

Calculated Key Figures

As with attribute views, you can also define virtual columns for analytic views. The values of those columns are determined by a calculation. For analytic views, you usually define calculated key figures, that is, numerical values such as amounts or units of measurement. A special case of such calculated values are conversions between different currencies and units. You'll calculate a key figure for each of the two analytic views from the previous section. For the AN_BOOKING view, you'll use an expression to identify the bookings with excess baggage; for AN_SEAT_UTILIZATION, the relative seat utilization will be determined as a percentage value based on the number of available and occupied seats.

Calculated key figures are basically defined following the same procedure that is used for attribute views. However, you must also flag the

Define calculated key figures

new column as MEASURE (via the COLUMN TYPE) and specify whether it's to be determined before or after an aggregation. In many cases, the calculation must be done using the raw data (i.e., before aggregation). Figure 4.26 shows the determination of all flight bookings with a baggage weight value of more than 20. Ignore the fact that the weight might be specified using different weight units for now. If a summation is done on this column, the number of bookings with excess baggage is determined because the value of the calculated column is null for all other bookings.

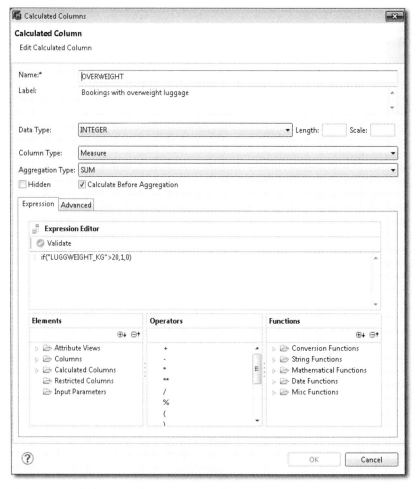

Figure 4.26 Calculated Key for the Number of Flight Bookings with Excess Baggage

Now follow the same steps to define a calculated key figure UTILIZATION (data type DECIMAL) in the AN_SEAT_UTILIZATION view, and use the following expression as the calculation formula:

```
if("SEATSMAX">0, decfloat( "SEATSOCC" + "SEATSOCC_B" +
  "SEATSOCC_F" ) / decfloat( "SEATSMAX" + "SEATSMAX_B" +
  "SEATSMAX_F" ),0)
```

As you can see, you divide the sum of the occupied seats by the sum of the available seats in the three booking categories. For the result to be handled as a decimal number, the type is converted using the decfloat function.

Currency Conversion and Unit Conversion

As a special case of a calculated key figure, the analytic view supports the conversion of monetary amounts and units of measure. We'll show you how this is done for the AN_BOOKING sample view to indicate the flight price in euros and the baggage weight in kilograms.

In addition to the modeled variant, you can also run a currency or unit conversion via the SQLScript CE_CONVERSION function or the SQL CONVERT_CURRENCY or CONVERT_UNIT functions, which you can also use in ABAP via CDS views (see Chapter 6).

There are two approaches for modeling currency or unit conversions: specify that the given conversion should be performed for every access on an existing column, or define an additional virtual column for the conversion result. When using the second variant, you can access both the original value and the converted value.

To use a calculated column for the conversion, you first define a calculated field of the type MEASURE and link it to the original column using the same data type. You can then configure the details on the ADVANCED tab.

You must specify whether the field contains a monetary amount or a quantity unit. Moreover, you must indicate the field where the corresponding currency or unit of measure can be found. Unfortunately, it's currently not possible to evaluate the corresponding information from the DDIC, where this relationship is also defined (CURRENCY/QUANTITY FIELDS tab in Transaction SE11).

The example in Figure 4.27 shows a currency conversion for the LOCUR-RAM column of table SBOOK into the target currency euro with the key date September 13, 2015. Here, the standard EXCHANGE TYPE M is used.

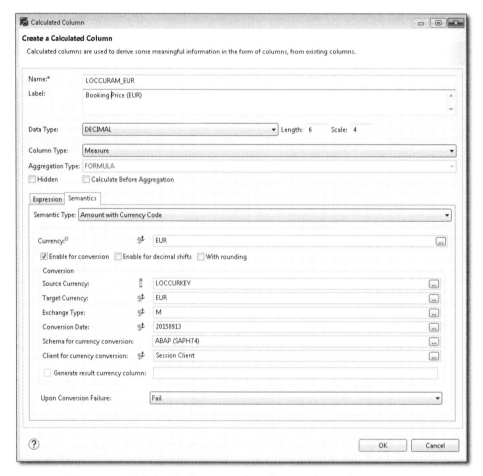

Figure 4.27 Defining the Parameters for a Currency Conversion

Parameterization for currency conversion In many cases, you want the target currency and the key date to be parameterized for the conversion. Unfortunately, this can't be done using the WHERE condition when accessing the view via SQL because it isn't possible to access the query parameters during modeling. For this reason, you can define input parameters for an analytic view, which can then be used as parameters for the conversion. You can define input parameters via the SEMANTICS section in the PARAMETERS/VARIABLES tab. These parameters can then be used as TARGET CURRENCY when configuring the conversion in Figure 4.27. The same procedure can be used to parameterize the key date.

The same principle is used for unit conversion. In our `AN_BOOKING` sample view, the baggage weight should always be considered in kilograms (KG) to identify bookings with excess weight. For this purpose, in Figure 4.27, you select the QUANTITY WITH UNIT OF MEASURE setting as the SEMANTIC TYPE, and define the parameters for the conversion.

Unit conversion

4.4.3 Calculation Views

In this section, we'll introduce the last view type, the calculation view, which is used whenever the capabilities of attribute and analytic views can't meet your requirements. This is especially the case in scenarios where it's necessary to combine several views in a flexible manner. Chapter 5 provides recommendations on how to use the various view types.

There are two variants of calculation views. You can either model calculation views or implement them using SQLScript. This section describes the usage of both variants.

In this section, we'll define two calculation views. We'll combine the two analytic views from the previous section in the modeled `CA_FLIGHT_STATISTIC` view and create a combined data view on the seat utilization and number of bookings with excess baggage for a flight. In the implemented `CA_SEAT_UTILIZATION_DELTA` view, we'll determine the average seat utilization and compare this result with the corresponding value from the previous year.

Reference examples for this section

Basic Principles

The main difference between calculation views and the other view types introduced so far is that calculation views can combine any other types of views. In case of attribute views, you can only link database tables via joins. Analytic views are always based on a star schema consisting of a fact table and dimensions. Calculation views have no such structural limitations.

Graphical modeling

A calculation view is based on a calculation model that consists of nodes and operations. These nodes can be tables or any type of view.

Calculation views are modeled graphically in a tree structure, with the leaves representing tables or views. The other nodes define operations on the data. The following operations are currently supported: JOIN, PROJECTION (definition of a field list), AGGREGATION (calculations), UNION, and RANK (sorting). The root node represents the output structure of the view and thus its external interface.

SQLScript provides a built-in function for each of these operations so that each graphical model has a canonical execution plan in the calculation engine in SAP HANA. This execution plan can be displayed using the *SAP HANA Plan Visualizer (PlanViz)* tool, which will be introduced in Chapter 7.

Like attribute views or analytic views, calculation views support the definition of hierarchies and input parameters.

Restrictions of graphical modeling

As with almost every graphical modeling approach, there are also certain limitations to modeling calculation views as described briefly here:

- ▸ **Restrictions with regard to possible SQL types**
  For example, it isn't possible to use the entire scope of functions in SAP HANA-specific SQL. Examples include calling the text search (see Chapter 10) or function libraries (see Chapter 12).

- ▸ **No free parameterization**
  You can't freely define the output structure of modeled views.

- ▸ **No options for performing calculations based on aggregates**
  There are also further scenarios that appear simple at first glance but can't be implemented by modeling a view in SAP HANA. Let's take a look at the example `AN_SEAT_UTILIZATION` from the previous section. In this case, you determined the seat utilization as a percentage per quarter for a flight connection. Let's assume you now also want to determine the variance from the previous year, that is, the difference

in use as a percentage. None of the presented modeling options can be used to directly perform this calculation.

To avoid these restrictions, SAP HANA provides the options to implement calculation views also via SQLScript, which we'll detail after the modeled variant.

Graphical Modeling of Calculation Views

Calculation views are created using the same procedure as attribute views and analytic views. To create a graphical calculation view, choose GRAPHICAL as the TYPE (Figure 4.28). The DATA CATEGORY defines the topmost node of the model and thus the primary usage scenario. Choose CUBE for a model that will be used as an analytical data source. You can leave this setting blank for a general view. Thus, the highest node in the model is a projection (see Figure 4.29).

Create calculation views

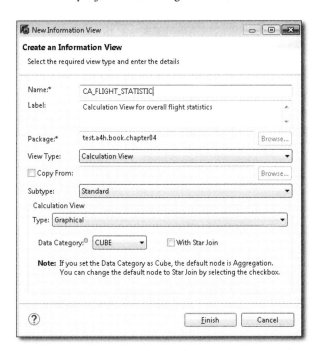

Figure 4.28 Creating a Graphical Calculation View

Figure 4.29 shows the resulting graphical calculation view.

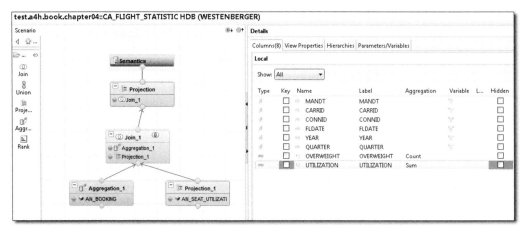

Figure 4.29 Graphical Calculation View CA_FLIGHT_STATISTIC

Layout of the editor

In the editor for calculation views, you can add tables and views as data sources and connect them using operations from the TOOLS PALETTE. These operations are PROJECTION, JOIN, AGGREGATION, UNION, and RANK. The editor displays both the data sources and the operations as nodes. The SEMANTICS node represents the output structure of the calculation view.

Integrate analytic views

For our example, we'll combine the data from the two analytic views. The output should include the number of bookings with excess baggage (calculated key figure OVERWEIGHT from AN_BOOKING) and the seat use (calculated key figure UTILIZATION from AN_SEAT_UTILIZATION). Because the data from AN_BOOKING is based on bookings, you have to first aggregate the key figure OVERWEIGHT and then create a join.

Connect nodes and add attributes

To create this view, you first add an AGGREGATION and a PROJECTION via the PALETTE and link them to the views as described previously. You must select the attributes needed for each of the nodes. Then select a JOIN node and link the nodes as illustrated earlier in Figure 4.29. Here, you define the join as you've done for the attribute views by selecting the node.

Result

After successful activation, the resulting CA_FLIGHT_STATISTIC calculation view is displayed (see Figure 4.30).

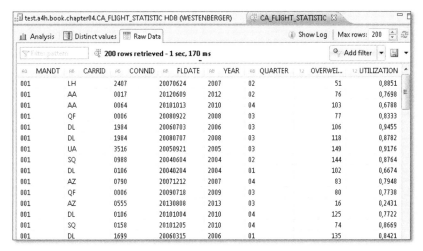

Figure 4.30 Data Preview for the Calculation View CA_FLIGHT_STATISTIC

Implementing Calculation Views via SQLScript

As previously mentioned, calculation views can also be implemented using SQLScript.

Implemented calculation views are created following a similar procedure as used for the modeled variant; however, you choose SQL SCRIPT as the TYPE (see Figure 4.31) in this case.

Create calculation views

Figure 4.31 Creating an Implemented Calculation View

Settings for SQLScript Views

The settings (PROPERTIES view in Eclipse) include three important parameters for calculation views that are implemented via SQLScript (the first two parameters have already been mentioned in Section 4.2.2):

▸ DEFAULT SCHEMA
Defines the default schema so that you don't have to specify a schema name when accessing tables or views using SQL. You should usually choose the standard schema of the ABAP system for this setting.

▸ RUN WITH
Configures the user for running the SQLScript code. The INVOKER'S RIGHTS setting indicates that the invoker (e.g., the ABAP database user) must have the required SQL authorizations.

▸ PARAMETER CASE SENSITIVE
Controls whether parameters are case sensitive.

SQLScript editor   After clicking the FINISH button, the system opens the editor for calculation views implemented with SQLScript (Figure 4.32).

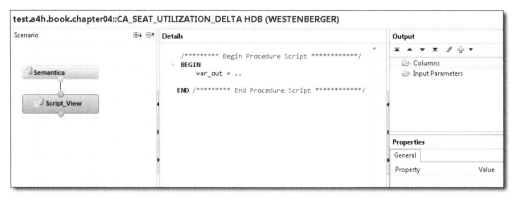

Figure 4.32 Editor for Implemented Calculation Views

The editor has two nodes:

▸ SCRIPT_VIEW
Here you implement the SQLScript logic and define the output structure in the OUTPUT area.

▸ SEMANTICS
Here, you can define more metadata such as label texts, hierarchies, and so on.

For our example, you first define the columns of the `var_out` output parameter. The result is displayed in Figure 4.33.

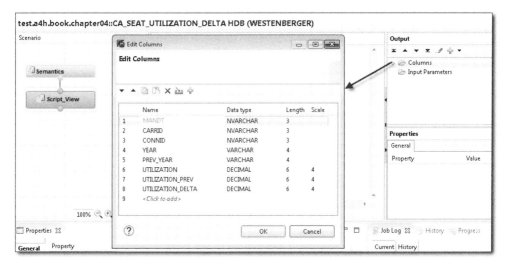

Figure 4.33 Structure of the Output Parameter var_out

In the next step, you can insert the SQLScript coding from Listing 4.17 as the implementation. Here, you perform a join of the `AN_SEAT_UTILI-ZATION` view with the same view (called a *self-join*). This defines the two *time slices* (data of the current and the previous year) needed for determining the variance in the average utilization. By means of SQLScript, you can first store an interim result in the `lt_data` table variable and use it in the second expression.

```
/********* Begin Procedure Script ************/
 BEGIN
   lt_data = select mandt, carrid, connid, year,
                avg(utilization) as utilization
     from "test.a4h.book.chapter04::AN_SEAT_UTILIZATION"
     group by mandt, carrid, connid, year;

   var_out = select c.mandt, c.carrid, c.connid,
        c.year, p.year as prev_year,
        c.utilization as utilization,
        p.utilization as utilization_prev,
        c.utilization - p.utilization as utilization_delta
     from :lt_data as c
     left outer join :lt_data as p
     on c.mandt = c.mandt and p.carrid = p.carrid and
```

225

```
         c.connid = p.connid and c.year - p.year + 1
         order by c.year desc;
END /********* End Procedure Script ************/
```

Listing 4.17 SQLScript Implementation of the Calculation View

The two time slices are called c (*current*) and p (*previous*) in the SQL statement, and the essential connection is implemented via the c.year = p.year + 1 join condition.

Define view columns
In the next step, you define the output structure of the view via the SEMANTICS section of the editor. You can select the columns of the var_out output parameter, which will be exposed by the calculation view. In addition, you specify whether the columns are exposed as attributes or as key figures. As with modeled calculation views, you can also create hierarchies and variables.

Result
After successful activation, you can display the result in the DATA PREVIEW. Figure 4.34 shows the percentage increase or decrease of the seat utilization for a time period of several years for connections of the airline LH.

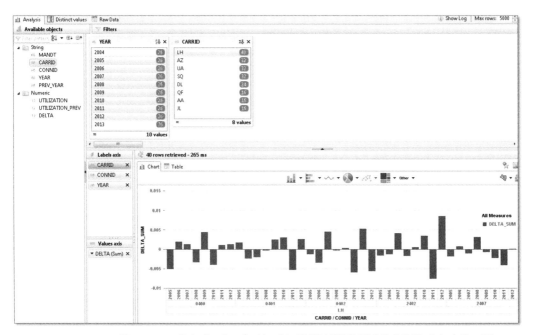

Figure 4.34 Data Preview for the CA_SEAT_UTILIZATION_DELTA Calculation View

4.4.4 Runtime Objects and SQL Access

As described in Chapter 2, Section 2.4.3, column views are created in the _SYS_BIC schema when activating views from the SAP HANA repository that can be accessed via normal SQL. These column views also form the basis for ABAP access, as shown in Chapter 5, Section 5.1. The exact runtime objects depend on the view type and the concrete modeling. Usually, there is a leading object that serves as the primary interface for data access and additional technical objects for specific aspects.

Addressing via SQL

Attribute Views

This section describes the specifics of attribute views. Every attribute view has a corresponding column view. In addition to this view, another column view is created for every hierarchy. For our AT_FLIGHT attribute view, the column views listed in Figure 4.35 exist in the database catalog in the _SYS_BIC schema.

Column views

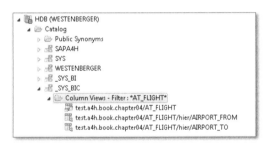

Figure 4.35 Column Views Generated for the AT_FLIGHT Attribute View

Note that the names of the runtime objects always contain the package names. This is necessary because you can create objects with the same name in different packages.

In addition, there is a *public synonym* that can also be used to access the views:

Public synonym

```
"test.a4h.book.chapter04::AT_FLIGHT"
```

Attribute views can be accessed using regular SQL. However, note that attribute views aren't optimized for calculations such as column aggregations, but rather for efficient join calculations. In other words, not every SQL statement should be used for every view type in SAP HANA.

Analytic Views

As is the case for attribute views, a primary runtime object corresponds to the analytic view. In addition, several additional column views are created depending on the occurrence of hierarchies, key figures, and calculated fields. However, for application developers, these objects play only a minor role. The primary runtime artifact of the AN_BOOKING analytic view in the test.a4h.book.chapter04 package can again be addressed via a public synonym:

```
test.a4h.book.chapter04::AN_BOOKING
```

Limitations when accessing views via SQL
When accessing a view via SQL, remember that analytic views aren't designed for single accesses but rather for aggregated accesses. For example, reading all rows using the following statement isn't supported:

```
; The following access results in an error message
SELECT * from "test.a4h.book.chapter04::AN_BOOKING";
```

Instead, you must always use an aggregation (COUNT, SUM, etc.) and the corresponding grouping. Moreover, because grouping can only be done via columns of the analytic view, analytic views can't be linked to other tables or views directly via SQL. We discussed this in Section 4.4.3 using an example.

Input parameter
If you defined input parameters for the view, you can pass them in an SQL query, as shown in the following example:

```
SELECT <Columns> FROM <View> ('PLACEHOLDER' = ('$$TARGET_
CURRENCY$$', 'EUR')) WHERE ... GROUP BY ...
```

Calculation Views

As is the case for attribute views and analytic views, there is a primary runtime object with a canonical name for calculation views as well; for our CA_FLIGHT_STATISTIC view, this is a public synonym with the following name:

```
test.a4h.book.chapter04::CA_FLIGHT_STATISTIC.
```

Moreover, when dealing with calculation views, there are also special column views for the hierarchies and key figures.

For implemented calculation views, the system also creates a database procedure and a table type for the `var_out` output parameter of the database procedure.

4.4.5 Accessing Column Views via Microsoft Excel

So far, you've only seen how the result of a view can be displayed using the DATA PREVIEW in SAP HANA Studio. While this is sufficient for first tests, the results aren't complete (there is a maximum number of rows), and the DATA PREVIEW provides limited options for analysis.

SAP provides many tools for accessing SAP HANA views. In particular, you can use the *SAP BusinessObjects Business Intelligence Platform* for analyses, dashboards, and so on, based on SAP HANA views. There is also a data modeling integration of the SAP HANA views in SAP BW. These advanced options are explained in more detail in Chapter 9.

In this section, we'll introduce a fairly simple method for accessing views from Microsoft Excel. To use this method, you only need the SAP HANA Client, which is part of SAP HANA. Installation details can be found in the corresponding documentation. After installing this package, the SAP HANA MDX PROVIDER should be available as an OLE DB PROVIDER (Object Linking and Embedding database interface) in the data import wizard of Excel (see Figure 4.36).

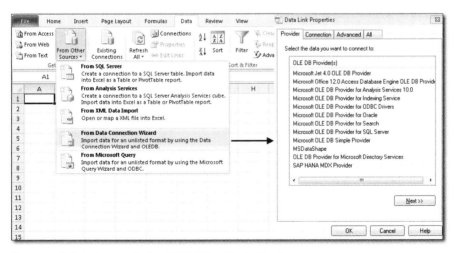

Figure 4.36 Data Import via the OLE DB Provider in Excel

Import data into a pivot table Using this provider, you can import the data from an analytic view or a calculation view into a *pivot table* in Excel. After the OLE DB driver establishes a connection, a selection dialog with the available SAP HANA views appears (see Figure 4.37).

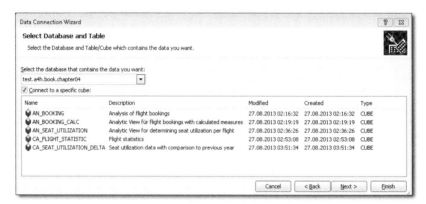

Figure 4.37 Importing SAP HANA Views into Excel

You can then use the pivot table functions in Excel on the data from the SAP HANA view. Figure 4.38 shows a representation of the data from the AN_BOOKING analytic view created in Section 4.4.2.

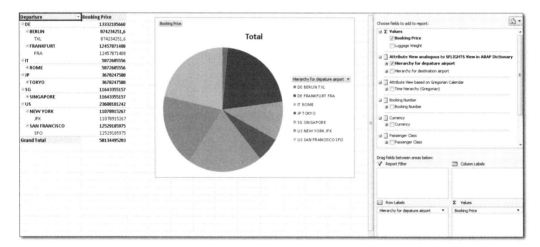

Figure 4.38 Pivot Table in Excel Based on the AN_BOOKING Analytic View

ABAP developers want to use views and database procedures that they've created in SAP HANA Studio in ABAP. Developers are also used to a high-performance transport system and expect consistent transport of native SAP HANA development objects via the Change and Transport System.

5   Integrating Native SAP HANA Development Objects with ABAP

Chapter 4 illustrated how you can create analytical models (views) and database procedures using SAP HANA Studio. Now we'll explain how you can call these native SAP HANA objects from ABAP.

We'll also discuss how you can transport ABAP programs that use native SAP HANA objects consistently in your system landscape.

5.1   Integrating Analytic Views

In the previous chapter, you learned how to model the different view types in SAP HANA Studio and how to access the results of a view using the Data Preview or Microsoft Excel. In Chapter 4, Section 4.4.4, we also explained how to address the generated column views via SQL.

This section describes how to access the views from ABAP. In this context, we have to differentiate between ABAP Release 7.4 and earlier versions. When working with earlier releases, only Native SQL can be used for access; this will be described briefly in Section 5.1.1. As of ABAP 7.4, you can import the views from the SAP HANA repository into the ABAP Data Dictionary (DDIC) and then access them using Open SQL (explained in detail in Section 5.1.2 and in Section 5.1.3). In the last section, you'll find some recommendations, tips, and tricks for SAP HANA view modeling.

Access with ABAP 7.4 and earlier releases

5.1.1 Access via Native SQL

When activating any of the presented view types in SAP HANA, a column view is created in the database catalog in the _SYS_BIC schema with a *public synonym*, for example, 'test.a4h.book.chapter04::AT_FLIGHT'.

Using these names, you can access this view from ABAP. Listing 5.1 shows how the AT_FLIGHT attribute view created in Chapter 4, Section 4.4.1, is accessed via ABAP Database Connectivity (ADBC).

```
" Definition of the result structure
TYPES: BEGIN OF ty_data,
         carrid    TYPE s_carr_id,
         connid    TYPE s_conn_id,
         fldate    TYPE s_date,
         route     TYPE string,
       END OF ty_data.

CONSTANTS:  gc_view TYPE string VALUE
                 'test.a4h.book.chapter04::AT_FLIGHT'.
DATA: lt_data TYPE TABLE OF ty_data.

" Access to the attribute view
DATA(lv_statement) =
   | SELECT carrid, connid, fldate, route |
&& |  FROM "{ gc_view }"|
&& |  WHERE mandt = '{ sy-mandt }' ORDER BY fldate|.

TRY.
   " Prepare SQL connection and statement
   DATA(lo_result_set) =
     cl_sql_connection=>get_connection(
        )->create_statement(
            tab_name_for_trace = conv #( gc_view )
        )->execute_query( lv_statement ).

   " Get result
   lo_result_set->set_param_table( REF #( lt_data ) ).
   lo_result_set->next_package( ).
   lo_result_set->close( ).
  CATCH cx_sql_exception INTO DATA(lo_ex).
    " Error handling
&& |  WHERE mandt = '{ sy-mandt }' ORDER BY fldate|.
    WRITE: | { lo_ex->get_text( ) } |.
ENDTRY.

LOOP AT lt_data ASSIGNING FIELD-SYMBOL(<l>).
```

```
WRITE: / <1>-carrid , <1>-connid, <1>-fldate,
          <1>-route .
ENDLOOP.
```
Listing 5.1 Accessing an Attribute View via ADBC

As you can see, this is a regular access using Native SQL. If an error occurs during execution, the text of the SQL exception points to the cause. In addition to SQL coding errors, which are also visible when accessing views via the SQL console, there may also be errors related to mapping the result to the ABAP data type. Recommendations regarding this topic are given in Section 5.1.4.

5.1.2 External Views in the ABAP Data Dictionary

In ABAP 7.4, *external views* are a new view type in the DDIC. Using such views, you can import column views defined in the SAP HANA repository into the DDIC. These views are called external views because they aren't fully defined in the DDIC but are used as a kind of *proxy* allowing the corresponding column view in the _SYS_BIC schema to be accessed from ABAP.

External views can only be defined using the ABAP Development Tools in Eclipse. To do so, you create a new development object of the DICTIONARY VIEW type. Figure 5.1 shows the NEW DICTIONARY VIEW dialog for the AT_FLIGHT attribute view.

Create external views in Eclipse

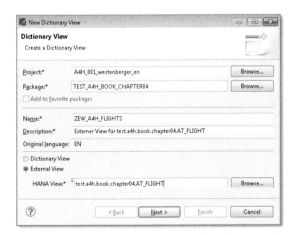

Figure 5.1 Creating an External View in the ABAP Data Dictionary

Check whether a
view can be
imported

When the view is created, the system checks whether it can be imported into the DDIC. Note that not all SAP HANA data types are supported in ABAP. When defining calculated attributes or accessing tables from views that weren't created using the DDIC, such potentially unsupported data types may appear. In this case, an error occurs when creating the external view, and the view can't be imported. The supported data types are listed in Table 5.1 later in this section and are described in Chapter 3, Section 3.1.3.

View structure and
synchronization

After successfully importing the SAP HANA view into the DDIC, the editor displays the structure of the view together with the data type mapping (Figure 5.2). In addition, you can use the SYNCHRONIZE button to synchronize the view after changing the structure of the corresponding view in SAP HANA Studio. Therefore, if you add attributes to the output structure, delete attributes, or change data types, you need to synchronize the external view to avoid runtime errors. Recommendations on synchronizing developments within a development team are provided in Chapter 14.

Figure 5.2 External ABAP Data Dictionary View Based on an Attribute View

Map data types

As you learned in Chapter 3, Section 3.1.3, SQL data types and DDIC types can't always be mapped uniquely. However, the data type is decisive for the correct handling of operations (e.g., the calculation of differences for a date). For this reason, the developer must manually map the correct ABAP data type.

Table 5.1 shows the possible data type mappings for some columns of the AT_FLIGHT sample view.

Column	SQL Data Type	Possible Dictionary Types
CARRID	NVARCHAR(3)	CHAR(3), NUMC(3), SSTR, CLNT, UNIT, CUKY
FLDATE	NVARCHAR(8)	CHAR(8), NUMC(8), SSTR, DATS
CARRNAME	NVARCHAR(20)	CHAR(20), NUMC(20), SSTR

Table 5.1 Possible Type Mappings

For the external view shown in Figure 5.2, we manually mapped the FLDATE column to the ABAP DATS data type. This may appear strange at first glance because this information is already present in the underlying DDIC table; however, the attributes of column views in SAP HANA don't have a reference to columns of existing tables that is recognizable by the DDIC. For instance, the FLDATE column could also be a calculated attribute.

Requirements

The procedure for defining external views based on an analytic or a calculation view is identical to the procedure used for an attribute view. Note that external views in the DDIC currently don't have a reference to the particular view type; that is, they are just pointing to an arbitrary column view in SAP HANA. The only prerequisite is that the view is defined via the SAP HANA repository. Column views, which solely exist in the database catalog (e.g., generated programmatically), can't be imported into the DDIC.

The transport of external views (and other SAP HANA-specific developments) is described in Section 5.3.

5.1.3 Options for Accessing External Views

Advantages   The main advantage of external views is that you can use Open SQL to access SAP HANA views. This allows you to benefit from the following advantages:

- Syntax checking by the ABAP Compiler and content assist during development (*code completion*)
- Automatic client handling
- Iterating through a result set within a SELECT loop
- Use of the INTO CORRESPONDING FIELDS expression for a matching selection in a target structure independent of the sequence in the projection list
- Use of IN for the WHERE condition to transfer selection options

Access via   Listing 5.2 shows how the access to the external view from Figure 5.2 is
Open SQL   implemented. From a functional perspective, this corresponds to the ADBC access variant from Listing 5.1. As you can see, the ABAP code required for access is significantly shorter and corresponds to the access for a standard DDIC view.

```
REPORT ZR_A4H_CHAPTER4_VIEW_OPEN.

DATA: wa TYPE zev_a4h_flights.
" Read data from external view
SELECT carrid connid fldate route
     FROM zev_a4h_flights
     INTO CORRESPONDING FIELDS OF wa.
  WRITE: / wa-carrid, wa-connid, wa-fldate, wa-route.
ENDSELECT.
```

Listing 5.2 Accessing an External View via Open SQL

[!]   **Possible Runtime Errors When Accessing External Views**

When using Open SQL to access an external view, an SQL query is executed for the corresponding column view in SAP HANA. The same rules apply as when accessing the view using Native SQL.

As explained in Chapter 4, Section 4.4.4, you must consider certain limitations when accessing analytic views via SQL. An unsupported query via Open SQL leads to a runtime error. Because these errors rarely occur when accessing ABAP tables using Open SQL, ABAP developers should use caution when following this approach. The troubleshooting tools and possible runtime errors during SQL access are explained in more detail in Chapter 7, Section 7.2.

In addition to Open SQL, you can also address external views using Native SQL. This variant, which seems somewhat awkward at first glance, is useful if you want to use an SQL query to access an SAP HANA view in a way that isn't supported using Open SQL, such as a *fuzzy search* in an attribute view (see Chapter 10, Section 10.4). Compared to accessing the generated column view in the _SYS_BIC schema via Native SQL, the external view has an advantage in that a suitable target structure for a selection via ADBC already exists in the DDIC.

Native access via ADBC

5.1.4 Recommendations

This section concludes with some recommendations for using SAP HANA views. These are limited to functional recommendations. Tools and recommendations for performance analysis are discussed in Chapter 7 and Chapter 14, where we'll also deal with design aspects such as naming conventions.

If the scope of functions provided by standard DDIC views is sufficient for your purposes and you've used these views in the past, there's no need to change your application using native SAP HANA views. The next chapter presents Core Data Services (CDS) views, which enable you to define complex views with calculated fields directly in ABAP.

Different view types

The modeled SAP HANA views provide simple access for special analytical scenarios. The following questions can help to determine the best view type in SAP HANA for your scenario:

▶ Are you dealing with master data views that might be extended by calculated attributes? In this case, you should start with an attribute view.

▶ Are you performing an analysis of transaction data based on a star schema? In this case, you should choose an analytic view and implement the dimensions as attribute views.

> ► Do you have to combine or adapt the results from different tables and SAP HANA views? In this case, you should use the modeled calculation view. If the modeled variant isn't sufficient for some part of your scenario, you can use a SQLScript-based implementation for that part.

Client handling   When modeling views, you should make sure that the client field is handled correctly. In particular, it's advisable to add the client field as the first field of the view and to make sure that the client is included in the join definition. In most cases, the SESSION CLIENT configuration value is the correct setting for views based on ABAP tables from the same system. If tables are replicated from a different system, it may be useful to use a fixed value for the client. Cross-client access is useful only in rare cases.

Schema mapping   You should always choose the correct default schema for analytic views and calculation views. This schema is taken into account in particular for the relevant Customizing for conversions, that is, if no special setting was configured for the attribute. Specifying the correct default schema is even more important when dealing with the implemented variant of calculation views.

Define external views   External views should only be defined for SAP HANA views that will be used for access via ABAP because these views have to be synchronized manually after changing the corresponding structures. Moreover, you should define a maximum of one external view for each SAP HANA view.

Troubleshooting   If error messages are displayed when activating an SAP HANA view, the error text usually includes information on the root cause. In some cases, however, you may need some experience to interpret the error message correctly. For this reason, we recommend following a heuristic approach to error analysis. As a first step, you should make sure that you mark at least one field of an attribute view as a key field and that you define at least one key figure for an analytic view. If your view contains calculated attributes, you should check if you correctly defined the corresponding expression.

If you come to a dead end during error analysis, you can try to remove the corresponding attribute (e.g., in a copy of the view). If an error message or unexpected data appears when calling the DATA PREVIEW, this is often an indication of a problem in the join modeling. For currency conversions, a missing client context may result in an error.

When accessing an SAP HANA view from ABAP using Native SQL, you should pass the name of the view (via the `tab_name_for_trace` parameter as shown in Listing 5.1 or via the `SET_TABLE_NAME_FOR_TRACE` method). This facilitates the error analysis in a support scenario.

5.2 Integrating Native Procedures with ABAP

In Chapter 4, you learned what SQLScript is and how you can use it for implementing database procedures. Now we want to explain how to call database procedures from ABAP. You have two options:

▶ Native SQL and ADBC (see also Chapter 3)

▶ Database procedure proxies

As of ABAP Release 7.0 and SAP Kernel 7.20, it's possible to use ADBC to call database procedures in SAP HANA. Database procedure proxies are available as of Release 7.4 and require that SAP HANA be used as the primary database. Moreover, database procedure proxies only support the XML file format (*.procedure*), which is actually outdated.

Requirements

5.2.1 Access via Native SQL

As already described in Chapter 4, Section 4.3, the system generates different runtime objects in the `_SYS_BIC` schema when activating a database procedure. It also generates a public synonym. Here, you can use Native SQL to access the database procedure from ABAP.

However, the use of Native SQL to call a database procedure is relatively time-consuming and prone to errors. Later in this section, you'll see how you can only use temporary tables to exchange tabular input and output parameters with the database procedure. Furthermore, SAP NetWeaver AS ABAP doesn't detect syntax errors in Native SQL statements until runtime. For more information, refer to the explanations provided in Chapter 3.

Disadvantages of
Native SQL

We'll now use several examples to provide a detailed description of how to use Native SQL to access database procedures. First, we'll consider a database procedure that determines the name of an airline on the basis of the ID. For the remaining examples, we'll revert to the database procedures from Chapter 4.

Example 1: Calling a Database Procedure

If you use ADBC to call a database procedure, the `CL_SQL_STATEMENT` class makes the `EXECUTE_PROCEDURE` method available. You can use this as long as a database procedure doesn't have a tabular input/output parameter.

Program ZR_A4H_CHAPTER5_CARRNAME_ADBC shows an example of the `EXECUTE_PROCEDURE` method (see Listing 5.3). It calls the `DETERMINE_CARRNAME` database procedure, which has the following input and output parameters:

- `IV_MANDT`: Client.

- `IV_CARRID`: ID of an airline.

- `EV_CARRNAME`: Name of an airline.

```
PARAMETERS: p_carrid TYPE s_carr_id.

DATA: lo_sql_statement  TYPE REF TO cl_sql_statement,
      lv_carrname TYPE s_carrname.

TRY.
  " create statement
  lo_sql_statement =
  cl_sql_connection=>get_connection(
  )->create_statement( ).

  " bind parameters
  lo_sql_statement->set_param( data_ref =
  REF #( sy-mandt )
  inout = cl_sql_statement=>c_param_in ).

  lo_sql_statement->set_param( data_ref =
  REF #( p_carrid )
  inout = cl_sql_statement=>c_param_in ).

  lo_sql_statement->set_param( data_ref =
  REF #( lv_carrname )
```

```
  inout = cl_sql_statement=>c_param_out ).

  " call procedure
  lo_sql_statement->execute_procedure(
  '"test.a4h.book.chapter04::DETERMINE_CARRNAME"' ).

CATCH cx_sql_exception INTO DATA(lo_ex).
  " error handling
  WRITE: | { lo_ex->get_text( ) } |.
ENDTRY.

WRITE: / lv_carrname.
```
Listing 5.3 Using Native SQL to Call a Database Procedure

First, the program generates an instance of the `CL_SQL_STATEMENT` class. Then, it calls the `SET_PARAM` method to bind the input and output parameters of the database procedures to the actual parameters. It then calls the `EXECUTE_PROCEDURE` method.

Explanation of the program

Example 2: Tabular Output Parameters

Alternatively, you can use the `EXECUTE_QUERY` method (together with the `WITH OVERVIEW` addition) to execute a database procedure. This also works for database procedures that have tabular input and output parameters.

Program ZR_A4H_CHAPTER5_TOP_ADBC in Listing 5.4 shows an example of the `EXECUTE_QUERY` method, in which the `DETERMINE_TOP_CONNECTIONS` database procedure is called. This database procedure determines an airline's top connections and has the following input and output parameters:

Example of output parameters

▶ `IV_MANDT`: Client.

▶ `IV_CARRID`: ID of an airline.

▶ `IV_ALGORITHM`: Controls how the top connections are determined.

▶ `ET_CONNECTIONS`: A table parameter that contains the airline's ID `CARRID` and connection code `CONNID`.

```
PARAMETERS: p_carrid TYPE s_carr_id.

" Definition of the result structure
TYPES: BEGIN OF ty_connections,
```

```
            carrid TYPE s_carr_id,
            connid TYPE s_conn_id,
          END OF ty_connections.

DATA: lt_connections TYPE TABLE OF ty_connections,
      lv_statement TYPE string,
      lo_result_set TYPE REF TO cl_sql_result_set,
      lo_connections TYPE REF TO data.

TRY.
    " Delete local temporary table
    lv_statement = | DROP TABLE #ET_CONNECTIONS |.
    cl_sql_connection=>get_connection(
  )->create_statement( )->execute_ddl( lv_statement ).
  CATCH cx_sql_exception.
    " The local temporary table may not exist,
    " we ignore this error
ENDTRY.

TRY.
    " Create local temporary table
    lv_statement = | CREATE LOCAL TEMPORARY ROW|
    && | TABLE #ET_CONNECTIONS LIKE "_SYS_BIC".|
    && |"test.a4h.book.chapter04::GlobalTypes.t|
    && |t_connections" |.
    cl_sql_connection=>get_connection(
  )->create_statement( )->execute_ddl( lv_statement ).

    " Call database procedure
    lv_statement = | CALL "test.a4h.bo|
    && |ok.chapter04::DETERMINE_TOP_CONNECTIONS|
    && |"( '{ sy-mandt }' , '{ p_carrid }', 'P'|
    && |, #ET_CONNECTIONS ) WITH OVERVIEW |.
    lo_result_set = cl_sql_connection=>get_connection(
      )->create_statement( )->execute_query(
      lv_statement ).
    lo_result_set->close( ).

    " Read local temporary table
    lv_statement = | SELECT * FROM #ET_CONNECTIONS |.
    lo_result_set = cl_sql_connection=>get_connection(
      )->create_statement( )->execute_query(
      lv_statement ).

    " Read result
    GET REFERENCE OF lt_connections INTO
      lo_connections.
    lo_result_set->set_param_table( lo_connections ).
    lo_result_set->next_package( ).
```

```
    lo_result_set->close( ).
  CATCH cx_sql_exception INTO DATA(lo_ex).

    " Error handling
    WRITE: | { lo_ex->get_text( ) } |.
ENDTRY.

LOOP AT lt_connections ASSIGNING
  FIELD-SYMBOL(<ls_connections>).
  WRITE: / <ls_connections>-carrid ,
           <ls_connections>-connid.
ENDLOOP.
```

Listing 5.4 Handling Table-Based Output Parameters

We'll now use the program to explain, in particular, how tabular input and output parameters are exchanged with a database procedure. Program ZR_A4H_CHAPTER5_TOP_ADBC uses *temporary table* #ET_CON-NECTIONS to transfer the ET_CONNECTIONS table parameter.

Temporary tables

Temporary Tables

[«]

Many databases, including the SAP HANA database, enable you to save *temporarily* the interim and final results of calculations in *temporary tables*. For this use case, temporary tables have many different advantages over conventional tables:

▸ The table definition and table contents are deleted automatically from the database if they are no longer required.

▸ The database automatically isolates data in parallel *sessions* from one another. It's neither necessary nor possible to place locks on temporary tables.

▸ The database doesn't write a transaction log for temporary tables.

▸ Generally, it's more efficient to use temporary tables than conventional tables.

SAP HANA supports global and local temporary tables:

▸ **Global temporary tables**
The table definition can be used in different sessions. The table contents can only be displayed for the current session. At the end of the session, the table contents are deleted from the database automatically.

▸ **Local temporary tables**
Both the table definition and the table contents are only valid for the current session. In other words, both are deleted from the database automatically at the end of the session.

Usage in AS ABAP

When using temporary tables to transfer data between AS ABAP and a database procedure, note the following:

▸ If you work with global temporary tables, you can create these once (because they can be used in different sessions). Organizationally, however, you must ensure that the table name isn't used for different use cases (that require a different table structure).

▸ You can create global temporary tables at design time. Then you must ensure that the tables are also available in the test and production systems after a transport.

▸ If you decide to create global temporary tables at runtime, you must ensure that—before you call a database procedure—the table structure is suitable for the interface of the database procedure called (because this may have changed in the meantime).

▸ You must create local temporary tables at least once for each session (also note the following explanations in relation to the ABAP work process and database connection). Consequently, you can only create local temporary tables when an ABAP program is running.

▸ Because each ABAP work process has only one connection with the database, multiple ABAP programs processed by the same work process subsequently, are one session for the database. Therefore, after an ABAP program ends, neither the definition nor the contents of local (and global) temporary tables are deleted automatically.

▸ For global and local temporary tables, you should delete the contents (of the current session) before you call the database procedure.

Explanation of the program

Program ZR_A4H_CHAPTER5_TOP_ADBC in Listing 5.4 works with a local temporary table. First, it uses DROP TABLE #ET_CONNECTIONS to delete local temporary table #ET_CONNECTIONS if it exists. It then uses the CREATE LOCAL TEMPORARY ROW TABLE statement to create a (new) local temporary table with the name #ET_CONNECTIONS. Here, the program refers to the table type that the system automatically created for the ET_CONNECTIONS output parameter when the database procedure was activated. This approach enables the program to ensure that, before the database procedure is called, the temporary table is empty and suitable for the current structure of the ET_CONNECTIONS output parameter.

244

The program now uses the EXECUTE_QUERY method to call the database procedure. It transfers SY-MANDT, P_CARRID, and 'P' to the input parameters, and it transfers temporary table #ET_CONNECTIONS to the output parameter for the database procedure.

After the database procedure has been called, the program reads the contents of temporary table #ET_CONNECTIONS, which correspond to the transferred airline's top connections.

Example 3: Tabular Input Parameters

If a database procedure has tabular input parameters, you can proceed in the same way as for tabular output parameters. Program ZR_A4H_CHAPTER5_KPIS_ADBC in Listing 5.5 shows how to call the GET_KPIS_FOR_CONNECTIONS database procedure for a set of flight connections. The database procedure determines some key performance indicators (KPIs) for each connection transferred.

The procedure has the following input and output parameters:

Example of an input parameter

▶ IV_MANDT: Client.

▶ IT_CONNECTIONS: A table parameter that contains the airline's ID CARRID and connection code CONNID.

▶ ET_KPIS: A table parameter that contains KPIs for connections.

```
...
LOOP AT lt_connections INTO ls_connections.
  lv_statement = | INSERT INTO #IT_CONNECTIONS VALUES
    ( '{ ls_connections-carrid }', '{ ls_connections-
    connid }' )|.
  cl_sql_connection=>get_connection(
    )->create_statement(
      )->execute_update( lv_statement ).
ENDLOOP.
" Call database procedure
lv_statement = | CALL "test.a4h.bo|
&& |ok.chapter04::GET_KPIS_FOR_CONNECTIONS|
&& |"( '{ sy-mandt }' , #IT_CONNECTIONS, #ET_KPIS )
  WITH OVERVIEW |.
lo_result_set = cl_sql_connection=>get_connection(
)->create_statement( )->execute_query( lv_statement ).
lo_result_set->close( ).
...
```

Listing 5.5 Handling Table-Based Input Parameters

245

Explanation of the program

Before the database procedure is called, the program fills local temporary table `#IT_CONNECTIONS` with the relevant flight connections. `EXECUTE_QUERY` is used to call the database procedure.

5.2.2 Defining Database Procedure Proxies

As of ABAP Release 7.4, you can define a *database procedure proxy* to access database procedures from ABAP. Note that only the XML file format (*.procedure*) is supported (see Chapter 4, Section 4.3).

A database procedure proxy is a *proxy object* that represents a database procedure in the DDIC.

[!] **Multiple Proxy Objects for One Database Procedure**

Technically, it's possible to create multiple database procedure proxies for one database procedure. However, we don't recommend this. In the DDIC, you should never create more than one proxy object for a database procedure.

Interface of the proxy object

The system also automatically creates an interface for each database procedure proxy. You can use this interface to influence the parameter names and data types used when calling the database procedure with ABAP:

▸ You can change the names of the input and output parameters as soon as they exceed 30 characters. In this case, the system initially abbreviates the parameter names. You can then overwrite these abbreviated names, if necessary.

▸ You can always overwrite the component names of table parameters.

▸ You can assign the relevant data type to each parameter. This is important because SQL data types aren't uniquely mapped to ABAP data types and DDIC types. Consequently, when creating a proxy object, the system can't (always) derive the correct ABAP data type and/or DDIC type.

Create a database procedure proxy

We'll now explain how to create a proxy object for the `DETERMINE_TOP_CONNECTIONS_XML` database procedure. To do this, open the ABAP Development Tools in Eclipse, and choose the menu option, FILE • NEW •

OTHER. Then, choose DATABASE PROCEDURE PROXY, and click NEXT. Figure 5.3 shows the window that opens.

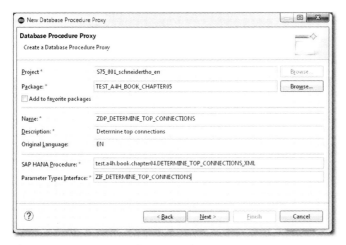

Figure 5.3 Creating a Database Procedure Proxy

In this window, enter the following data for the database procedure proxy:

Creation parameters

▶ NAME
Used to call the database procedure later in ABAP.

▶ DESCRIPTION
Piece of explanatory text.

▶ SAP HANA PROCEDURE
Name of the existing database procedure in the SAP HANA repository.

▶ PARAMETER TYPES INTERFACE
Name of the interface that is automatically created when you create the proxy object (see Listing 5.6).

After you choose NEXT and FINISH, the system creates the database procedure proxy and the corresponding interface.

The PROJECT EXPLORER contains the database procedure proxy in the corresponding package below the DICTIONARY • DB PROCEDURE PROXIES node. Just like the other interfaces, the parameter type interface is located in the corresponding package below the SOURCE LIBRARY node.

Adjust the interface

Figure 5.4 shows the database procedure proxy for the DETERMINE_TOP_ CONNECTIONS_XML database procedure. If you want to adjust parameter names or data types, you can do this in the ABAP NAME, ABAP TYPE, and DDIC TYPE OVERRIDE columns. For example, you can map the CONNID column in the table-based ET_CONNECTIONS output parameter to the S_ CONN_ID data element (and therefore to the ABAP data type N length 4).

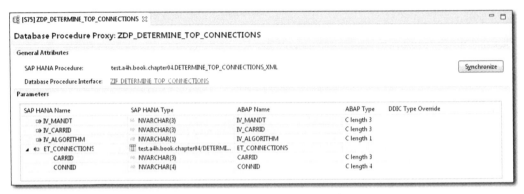

Figure 5.4 Database Procedure Proxy and Interface

Listing 5.6 shows the interface that the system automatically creates after the data types have been adjusted.

```
interface ZIF_DETERMINE_TOP_CONNECTIONS public.
types: iv_mandt type mandt.
types: iv_carrid type s_carr_id.
types: iv_algorithm type c length 1.
types: begin of et_connections,
         carrid type s_carr_id,
         connid type s_conn_id,
       end of et_connections.
endinterface.
```
Listing 5.6 Interface of the Proxy Object

5.2.3 Calling Database Procedure Proxies

Now that you've activated the database procedure proxy, you can use the proxy object to call the database procedure. Program ZR_A4H_ CHAPTER5_TOP_PROXY in Listing 5.7 shows an example of this usage.

```
PARAMETERS: p_carrid TYPE s_carr_id.

DATA: lt_connections TYPE TABLE OF
      zif_determine_top_connections=>et_connections.

TRY.
    CALL DATABASE PROCEDURE
      zdp_determine_top_connections
      EXPORTING
        iv_mandt = sy-mandt
        iv_carrid = p_carrid
        iv_algorithm = 'P'
      IMPORTING
        et_connections = lt_connections.

  CATCH cx_sy_db_procedure_sql_error
    cx_sy_db_procedure_call INTO DATA(lo_ex).
    " Error handling
        iv_algorithm = 'P'
    WRITE: | { lo_ex->get_text( ) } |.
ENDTRY.

LOOP AT lt_connections ASSIGNING
  FIELD-SYMBOL(<ls_connections>).
  WRITE: / <ls_connections>-carrid ,
          <ls_connections>-connid.
ENDLOOP.
```
Listing 5.7 Calling a Database Procedure Proxy

The program uses the CALL DATABASE PROCEDURE statement to call the
DETERMINE_TOP_CONNECTIONS_XML database procedure via the ZDP_
DETERMINE_TOP_CONNECTIONS proxy. When defining internal table LT_
CONNECTIONS, the program refers to the ZIF_DETERMINE_TOP_CONNEC-
TIONS interface. The program catches any problems that may occur
when calling the database procedure (exceptions of the type CX_SY_DB_
PROCEDURE_SQL_ERROR and CX_SY_DB_PROCEDURE_CALL).

Explanation of
the program

5.2.4 Adjusting Database Procedure Proxies

If you change a database procedure (or more accurately, the interface of
a database procedure) in SAP HANA Studio, you must synchronize the
proxy object with the SAP HANA repository via the SYNCHRONIZE button
(refer to Figure 5.4).

During the synchronization process, you can decide whether you want to retain or overwrite the adjustments made to the proxy object (component names or data types).

Chapter 6 introduces you to *ABAP Managed Database Procedures (AMDP)*. When used within the scope of ABAP, they have several advantages compared with procedures that you've created via SAP HANA Studio. For this reason, we generally recommend the usage of ABAP database procedures if you want to use SQLScript within ABAP.

5.3 Transport of Native Development Objects

In this section, we discuss how you can transport ABAP programs that use native SAP HANA objects consistently in your system landscape. For this purpose, we'll discuss *SAP HANA transport containers*. We won't outline the advanced *Change and Transport System (CTS+)*, which offers options too.

For our descriptions, we assume that you're already familiar with the development organization and transport in AS ABAP.

5.3.1 Digression: Development Organization and Transport in SAP HANA

To understand the functioning of the SAP HANA transport container better, this section provides some background information on the development organization and transport in SAP HANA.

Development Organization

The development organization in SAP HANA is similar in many ways to AS ABAP. However, it also differs in some essential aspects. As described in Chapter 2, the SAP HANA repository is the central storage of the SAP HANA database development objects.

Within the repository, SAP delivers content below the `sap` root package. Thus, no customer developments can be created under this package because they might be accidentally overwritten. You can build a parallel package hierarchy for customer developments instead. As a root package, for example, use your domain name.

The `system-local` package represents a special case. It's similar to the concept of local packages of AS ABAP. You can use it for development objects that won't be transported.

Transport

A transport usually takes place in SAP HANA on the basis of a *delivery unit*. A delivery unit combines packages that are to be transported or delivered together. Conceptually, it broadly corresponds to a software component in the sense of AS ABAP. While you usually work in AS ABAP with the `HOME` software component, you must always create your own delivery units for customer developments in SAP HANA. To do so, you or an administrator are required to have maintained, in advance, the `content_vendor` system parameter in the *indexserver.ini* file using the ADMINISTRATION CONSOLE of SAP HANA Studio.

Let's consider the assignment of a delivery unit and the subsequent transport using an `AT_CUSTOMER` attribute view. When you create the `AT_CUSTOMER` attribute view, you assign a package to it. You can maintain a delivery unit in the package properties. To do so, use the context menu entry EDIT of the package. You see all existing delivery units in the system in the QUICK VIEW using the menu entry DELIVERY UNITS. You can also create new delivery units there. Figure 5.5 shows the relationships among the development object, package, and delivery unit using the example of the `AT_CUSTOMER` attribute view (the `ZA4H_BOOK_CHAPTER05` delivery unit isn't part of the examples provided with this book).

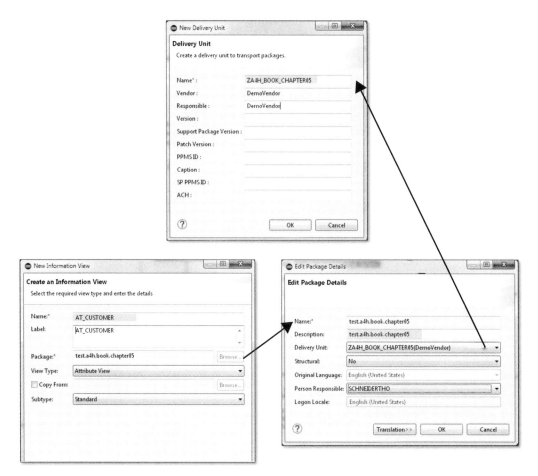

Figure 5.5 Development Object, Package, and Delivery Unit

Import and export In SAP HANA Studio, you have two options to transport development objects, that is, you can export and import them in the target system:

- Exporting/importing a delivery unit (optionally coupled with CTS+)
- Exporting/importing individual objects (the *developer mode*)

For a consistent transport of SAP HANA content (which isn't closely coupled with an ABAP development) in a production system landscape, we always recommend exporting/importing based on delivery units and CTS+.

Schema Mapping

Schema mapping is a special feature in transporting SAP HANA content. Schema mapping is necessary when the database schemas differ in the source system and target system of a transport. This involves mapping an *authoring schema* to a *physical schema*.

You maintain a schema mapping in the QUICK VIEW via the menu option SCHEMA MAPPING. Before we discuss more precisely when and how the system evaluates the mapping, we need to explain the need for schema mapping using the AT_CUSTOMER attribute view. Let's consider Figure 5.6 for this purpose.

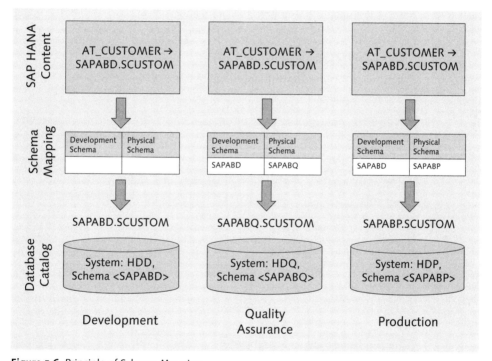

Figure 5.6 Principle of Schema Mapping

Remember that the AT_CUSTOMER attribute view reads customer data from database table SCUSTOM. This table is part of the flight data model of AS ABAP and is located in the development system in the SAPABD database schema (because the system ID of the ABAP system is ABD). As a result, the attribute view refers to SAPABD.SCUSTOM.

Schema mapping example

Table `SAPABD.SCUSTOM` doesn't exist in the quality assurance system or production system. Due to the different system IDs, the database table resides in the `SAPABQ` schema in the quality assurance system and in the `SAPABP` schema in the production system.

Schema mapping enables you to map the `SAPABD` schema to the `SAPABQ` schema in the quality assurance system and to the `SAPABP` schema in the production system.

Schema mapping maintenance

When maintaining schema mapping, you must consider the following:

► Schema mapping ultimately controls where—that is, in which database schema—an SAP HANA repository development object searches for a database catalog object.

► If no schema mapping is maintained, the authoring schema and physical schema are identical.

► You can map multiple authoring schemas to the same physical schema.

► You *cannot* assign multiple physical schemas to an authoring schema.

► The SAP HANA content stores references to database objects with the authoring schema. If this can't be clearly determined (due to a multiple assignment), the system stores the reference with the physical schema.

[»] **Schema Mapping When Installing SAP NetWeaver AS ABAP 7.4**

If you install AS ABAP 7.4 on a SAP HANA database, the installation program creates the `SAP<SID>` ABAP schema. Furthermore, the installation program also creates at least one schema mapping—that is, from the `ABAP` authoring schema to the `SAP<SID>` physical schema.

If you're interested in further information on the development organization and transport in SAP HANA, please refer to the documentation of the SAP HANA database.

5.3.2 Using the SAP HANA Transport Container

Let's now discuss the transport of ABAP programs that use native SAP HANA objects via the SAP HANA transport container. For this purpose, we use Program ZR_A4H_CHAPTER5_LIST_CUSTOMER, which accesses the AT_CUSTOMER attribute view of the SAP HANA repository via the ZEV_A4H_CUSTOMER external view of DDIC. The source text of the program is available in Listing 5.8.

```
REPORT zr_a4h_chapter5_list_customer.

DATA: lt_customer TYPE STANDARD TABLE OF
      zpv_a4h_customer,
      ls_customer TYPE zpv_a4h_customer.

IF cl_db_sys=>dbsys_type = 'HDB'.
  SELECT * FROM zev_a4h_customer
    INTO TABLE lt_customer.
ELSE.
  SELECT * FROM zpv_a4h_customer
    INTO TABLE lt_customer.
ENDIF.
LOOP AT lt_customer INTO ls_customer.
  WRITE: / ls_customer-id, ls_customer-name.
ENDLOOP.
```

Listing 5.8 Sample Report to Be Transported

Both Program ZR_A4H_CHAPTER5_LIST_CUSTOMER and the ZEV_A4H_CUSTOMER external view can be transported readily using the change recording and the transport system of AS ABAP (in principle, this occurs automatically). The AT_CUSTOMER attribute view that forms the basis of the external view, however, isn't subject to the change recording and transport system of the application server. For this reason, it isn't available in the target system after a transport (unless you take appropriate measures). Thus, a runtime error occurs in the target system when calling the report. The SAP HANA transport container provides relief here.

Problems during transport

Basic Functions

The SAP HANA transport container is available in SAP NetWeaver 7.31 as of SP 5 and as of Release 7.4. It can be used if SAP HANA is the primary database.

The SAP HANA transport container allows you to transport development objects created via SAP HANA Studio using the mechanisms of the

CTS of the ABAP AS (and without the need for a Java stack, which is required for CTS+).

From a technical perspective, the SAP HANA transport container is a logical transport object that acts as a proxy object for exactly one delivery unit. Figure 5.7 illustrates how the SAP HANA transport container works.

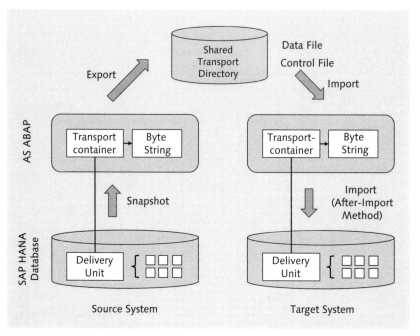

Figure 5.7 How the SAP HANA Transport Container Works

Create the transport container   You can only create a SAP HANA transport container using the ABAP Development Tools. In the ABAP perspective, for example, choose the menu path, FILE • NEW • OTHER • ABAP • SAP HANA TRANSPORT CONTAINER. Then enter the name of the delivery unit for which you want to create the transport container. The system automatically derives the name of the transport container (see Figure 5.8; the SAP HANA transport container ZA4H_BOOK_CHAPTER05 isn't part of the examples provided with this book).

Use a prefix namespace   If you want to use a prefix namespace in ABAP, you must assign the desired prefix name to the name of the content_vendor (refer to Section

5.3.1) before creating the transport container. To do so, you can fill database table `SNHI_VENDOR_MAPP` using the TABLE VIEW MAINTENANCE dropdown.

If the transport properties of the package that is used—in the example, `TEST_A4H_BOOK_CHAPTER05`—are maintained accordingly, the system records the creation of the transport container in a transportable change request.

Change recording

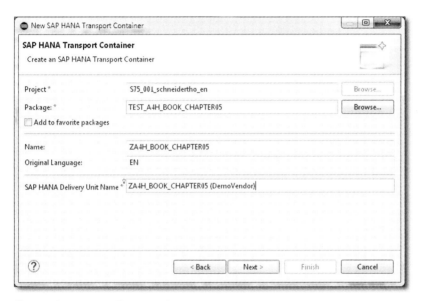

Figure 5.8 Creating a Transport Container

When you create a transport container, the system automatically synchronizes the contents of this container (once) with the contents of the delivery unit. This means that all objects of the delivery unit are loaded as a packed file on the ABAP AS and are stored there as a *byte string* in a database table (i.e., table `SNHI_DU_PROXY`). Strictly speaking, the content of the delivery unit then appears twice in the SAP HANA database:

Synchronization

▸ In the SAP HANA repository

▸ Via database table `SNHI_DU_PROXY`

If, after creating the transport container, you want to synchronize it with the delivery unit—because you've made changes to the `AT_CUSTOMER` attribute view, for example—you must do so manually. Use the TAKE SNAPSHOT AND SAVE link in this case. You can view the current content of the transport container using the CONTENTS tab (Figure 5.9).

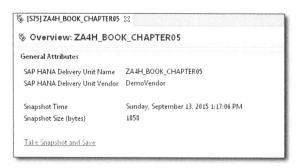

Figure 5.9 Synchronization and Content of a Transport Container

Exporting and importing

The transport from the development system to the quality assurance and production systems takes place via the CTS mechanisms:

▸ When exporting (more precisely, during *export release preprocessing*), the system writes the content of the transport container in the data file to the common transport directory of the systems involved in the transport.

▸ When importing (more precisely, in an *after-import method*), the system reads the transport container's content from the data file and imports the delivery unit in the SAP HANA database of the target system. Activation of content occurs only if you've activated this for the software component of the transport container in table SNHI_DUP_PREWORK (in the target system).

You can reproduce the two steps at any time using the transport log.

Mixed System Landscapes

Mixed system landscapes represent a special case of the ABAP development on SAP HANA. Imagine that as an ABAP developer, you want to optimize a program for SAP HANA and make use of specific SAP HANA database options. At the same time, however, this program should also be able to run on traditional databases, for example, because your employer uses SAP HANA as a database only in certain areas of the company. In this case, a simplified system landscape might look like that shown in Figure 5.10.

Using a case distinction, you can—to stick with the example of Program ZR_A4H_CHAPTER5_LIST_CUSTOMER—call the `ZPV_A4H_CUSTOMER` projection view once and the `ZEV_A4H_CUSTOMER` external view once (see Listing 5.8). As a result, you ensure that no errors occur at runtime.

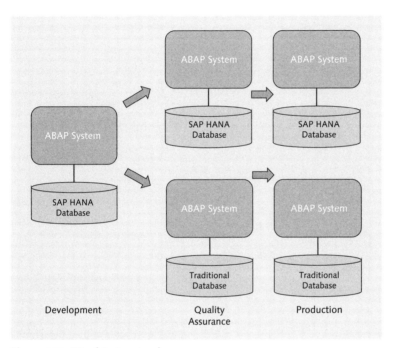

Figure 5.10 Mixed System Landscape

The implementation of the transport container ensures that no errors occur during the transport, and the SAP HANA content is only imported if the target system of the import is a SAP HANA-based system.

Systems without a SAP HANA database

Recommendations for Using the Transport Container

When using the transport container, you should note some restrictions:

Limitations

▶ When using the transport container, you always transport the complete delivery unit. You can't transport only the contents of a delivery unit that were changed in a specific time interval.

259

- Unlike development objects that are managed in AS ABAP, the system doesn't automatically record changes to the content of a delivery unit, and the objects of a delivery unit aren't locked exclusively for a transport request. It's thus your responsibility to synchronize the transport container with the delivery unit manually.

- When exporting the development objects from the source system, the transport considers only the active objects.

- The transport system doesn't recognize any dependencies between multiple transport containers that are transported simultaneously.

Within the restrictions, the transport container allows you to transport applications consistently that consist partly of ABAP objects and partly of SAP HANA content. We recommend its use if the prerequisites that are described at the start of Section 5.3.2 are fulfilled.

You don't require the SAP HANA transport container if you use the options described in Chapter 6.

To improve the support of code pushdown and the integration of the necessary database objects into the ABAP development process, SAP has enhanced the functional scope of Open SQL and ABAP database views even further since SAP NetWeaver AS ABAP 7.4 SP 5. In this chapter, we'll introduce the new features.

6   Advanced Database Programming with ABAP 7.4

To use the code-to-data paradigm in ABAP applications, you require the corresponding means to implement and execute the processing logic in the database. Chapter 5, Sections 5.1.2 and 5.2.2, described how you can use SAP HANA development objects for this purpose. However, you might have noticed that using these objects can also lead to problems.

In contrast to objects that are completely managed by AS ABAP, the following restrictions apply to the development of SAP HANA development objects and the usage of the corresponding replacement objects in ABAP (external view and database procedure proxies):

Disadvantages of SAP HANA development objects in ABAP

- ▶ SAP HANA development objects aren't integrated fully with ABAP Lifecycle Management.
  - ▶ If SAP HANA development objects are changed, the respective replacement objects and SAP HANA transport containers, which are managed by the ABAP Data Dictionary (DDIC), need to be synchronized manually.
  - ▶ SAP HANA development objects aren't linked to the ABAP version management.
- ▶ SAP HANA development objects aren't considered in the syntax check and activation of the ABAP application. The ABAP runtime environment doesn't display errors and warnings relating to SAP HANA

development object implementations. This often leads to runtime errors.

▸ SAP HANA development objects and consequently their replacement objects can't be extended.

▸ You can't map SQL data types to DDIC data elements in external views. If you use these replacement objects in user interfaces (UIs), the field labels and short descriptions are missing at first.

▸ To implement SAP HANA development objects, ABAP developers require an additional user for the SAP HANA database and the corresponding database authorizations.

This chapter introduces the new database programming and code pushdown options in ABAP. ABAP manages the resulting objects to ensure a familiar integration of the objects into ABAP Lifecycle Management, including version management and object extensibility. We'll discuss the following enhancements, which have been developed since ABAP 7.4 SP 5:

▸ **The advanced functional scope of ABAP database views within the scope of Core Data Services** (CDS; see Section 6.1)
CDS are used to define persistent data models.

▸ **New Open SQL features**
These include, for example, support of SQL expressions in the SELECT list and in the GROUP BY, HAVING, and WHERE clauses of SELECT statements (see Section 6.4).

▸ **Implementing SAP HANA database procedures in ABAP methods**
These *ABAP Managed Database Procedures (AMDP)* enable you to execute processing logic in the database (see Section 6.5). You can implement these database procedures in the normal ABAP development environment without requiring a user for the SAP HANA database.

6.1   Introducing Core Data Services

Core Data Services (CDS) are a specific SAP method of defining persistent data models. The specification is based on the SQL-92 and SQL:1999 standards. Just like SQL, CDS define a *data definition language* (DDL) and a *data control language* (DCL). They also define a query language (QL). You can use the DDL, for example, to describe database tables and structured types. The QL allows you to read data in a comfortable way and is used in combination with DDL to define database views. The DCL enables you to define access restrictions for CDS objects.

CDS additionally contain the following SQL enhancements that are necessary to create optimal data models for business applications:

SQL enhancements

▸ **Annotations**
These are used to enrich CDS objects with additional metadata, which can't be expressed in SQL. This metadata can also be queried and used by client applications. Client applications can also define their own annotations and store their own metadata together with the data model.

▸ **User-defined, scalar, and structured data types**
These are used to better illustrate the semantics of the data types used.

▸ **Associations**
These are used to define the relationships between CDS objects. During the modeling process and when data is read from the database, you can use path expressions to address relationships that have been described with associations.

The CDS specification is implemented in SAP NetWeaver AS ABAP and in SAP HANA. These implementations were made mainly independently of each other. Although the CDS implementation in AS ABAP (also referred to as *ABAP CDS*) leverages the infrastructure of the ABAP AS with mainly database-independent ABAP CDS objects, the CDS implementation in SAP HANA (also referred to as *SAP HANA CDS*) is fully bound by the conditions of the SAP HANA database. So currently, you can't use SAP HANA CDS objects in AS ABAP or ABAP CDS objects in SAP HANA.

CDS in ABAP and SAP HANA

Despite the different implementations, you can benefit from the shared specification: CDS describes a uniform and—due to the enhancements—expressive syntax for data modeling. If you are familiar with this syntax, you'll easily understand the models irrespective of where they are implemented. CDS also harmonize further data modeling aspects. For

Advantages of ABAP CDS

example, CDS define how you can enhance data models. This enables SAP customers and partners to adapt existing ABAP or SAP HANA CDS objects to their requirements in the same way. Finally, because CDS are based on the SQL-92 and SQL:1999 standards, many functions already familiar to you from SQL are available to implement the code pushdown in your data models.

6.2 ABAP Core Data Services

This section introduces the new ABAP CDS features in detail and uses examples to show you how to use these functions for your developments. For this purpose, we use the already known data model SFLIGHT.

CDS views

As explained in Section 6.1, ABAP CDS currently only implements a part of the CDS specification, that is, the requirements arising within today's scope of ABAP application development. Because the data from SAP solutions used in enterprises are already stored in the database system, it makes sense that the main focus of ABAP CDS is on creating views of already existing business data and not on defining new database tables. The resulting *CDS views* lay the foundation for the acceleration of existing ABAP programs and for the development of new, innovative applications. In SAP S/4HANA, for example, business data are provided by well-defined CDS views on SAP Business Suite database tables. These views allow new client applications to access clear and consistent interfaces and benefit from the code pushdown of these views. This is an important characteristic of ABAP CDS. You can also directly reuse your existing data models and DDIC objects (tables, views, data elements) in ABAP CDS. Therefore, the ABAP CDS specification is an extension of the DDIC and the SQL objects defined in the DDIC.

Database independence

Another important characteristic of ABAP CDS is its database-independent implementation. Similar to Open SQL, CDS views can run on all SAP-supported database systems on AS ABAP 7.4. This ensures that the database models you've modeled with ABAP CDS show a uniform functional behavior irrespective of your application case and system landscape. If you execute your CDS views on the SAP HANA database, you additionally benefit from the main memory data processing performance advantages.

The following sections introduce the CDS functions that have been provided since AS ABAP 7.4 SP 5. However, the further development of the CDS specification and implementation in AS ABAP is ongoing, so you can expect new and useful features in the future.

6.2.1 Core Data Services Views

In general, *views* are queries that are stored in the database. The structure and content of the data, which are returned as the query result, are based on other database tables or views. The results aren't stored; that is, each time a view is called, the respective query is executed again. You can use views for read accesses in ABAP everywhere where database tables can be used.

Views

In contrast to classic DDIC views, queries for CDS views are defined using the DDL of the CDS specification. This definition is written to a *DDL source*. When the DDL source is activated in ABAP, the query is stored as an SQL view in the database. In addition, the CDS metadata, for example, annotations and associations, are stored in the ABAP repository, and an entry is created for the view definition in the ABAP repository buffer. An entry is created in table TADIR for each DDL source. The respective transport object is called R3TR DDLS <DDL source name>.

DDL source

In addition to DDL sources and CDS views, you should know the following concepts in the ABAP CDS context:

Important concepts

- ▸ **CDS object**
  This is the generic term for all CDS artifacts that can be defined in DDL sources. This also includes CDS views.

- ▸ **CDS entity**
  This is a structured data type whose data are stored persistently. Therefore, a CDS view is also a CDS entity. Just like for DDL sources, an entry in table TADIR is created for each CDS entity. This entry has the R3TR STOB <entity name> key (STOB stands for "structured object"

here). CDS entities aren't transported; instead, they are generated when the DDL sources are activated.

▶ **SQL view**
This is the actual database view that is stored for the query. Although it's created in the DDIC, it's different from the classic DDIC view in that it's only a technical means and can't be directly used in ABAP programs. Because the SQL view doesn't have direct access to CDS-specific metadata, it isn't a standalone object but only a subobject of the CDS view. The SQL view isn't transported; instead, it's generated when the DDL source is activated.

▶ **Data source**
This is the persistence layer that forms the basis for the CDS view. Data sources can be database tables, classic DDIC views, other CDS views, or external views.

Creating Core Data Services Views

Development tools To demonstrate how to create a CDS view, we'll define the SFLIGHTS view from the DDIC, which we already used in Chapter 3, Section 3.2.3, as a CDS view. You can define CDS views using the ABAP Development Tools for SAP NetWeaver (introduced in Chapter 2, Section 2.4.2) in the ABAP perspective. You can't define CDS views using the ABAP Workbench.

Creating DDL sources To define a CDS view, you have to create a DDL source. For this purpose, open the context menu of a package in the PROJECT EXPLORER, and select NEW • OTHER ABAP REPOSITORY OBJECT. In the dialog window that opens, select DICTIONARY • DDL SOURCE. The creation wizard shown in Figure 6.1 opens. Enter a name and description for the DDL source.

Because it's currently not possible to define more than one CDS view in a DDL source in ABAP, it has become common practice to give the DDL source the same name as the CDS view that is defined in the source. This is very useful because only the name of the DDL source—not the name of the CDS view—is displayed in the PROJECT EXPLORER. For our example, we use the name "ZA4H_06_SFLIGHTS".

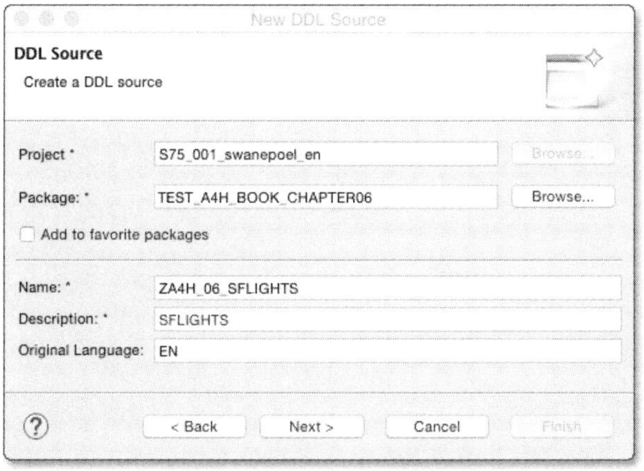

Figure 6.1 Creating a DDL Source

DDL Sources in AS ABAP 7.5   **[«]**

As of AS ABAP 7.5, you create DDL sources in the Project Explorer under
Core Data Services • Data Definitions instead of under Dictionary • ABAP
DDL Sources.

Perform all other steps in the wizard. In the last step, you can choose   Templates
between different creation templates. SAP provides these templates for
all CDS objects, which you can define in DDL sources. They form the
basic structure of your definition and are useful if you've just learned
how to use CDS syntax. Because they are delivered as *code templates* in
Eclipse, you can modify them or define your own templates. You can
manage the templates by choosing Window • Preferences • ABAP
Development • Editors • Source Code Editors • DDL Templates. For
our example, select the Define View with Join template as shown in
Figure 6.2.

After selecting the template, open the newly created DDL source in the   Code completion
DDL Editor in Eclipse. If no template is selected, the DDL source is
empty. In this case, you can assign a template retroactively by using the
code completion of the editor. To do so, press Ctrl+Space, and select
Define View with Join.

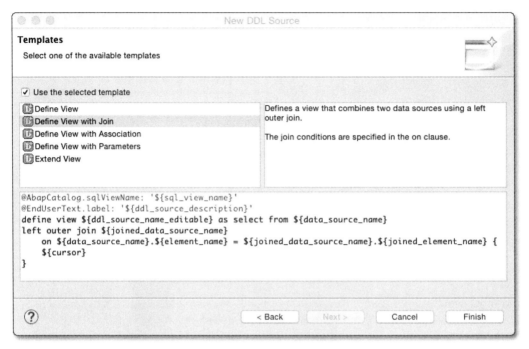

Figure 6.2 Selecting a Template for Creating a CDS View

Filling placeholders
The template only contains placeholders at first, which you have to fill (see Figure 6.3):

▶ sql_view_name

This view is stored for the query in the database management system. The name is specified using the @AbapCatalog.sqlViewName annotation. This annotation is mandatory for defining CDS views. You can find more information on annotations in Section 6.2.4. The SQL view name must be different from the CDS view name.

▶ Za4h_06_Sflights

The CDS view is often referred to as the *entity name*. The template inserts the name of the DDL source here by default. We recommend keeping this default setting.

▶ data_source_name

This is the first data source in the FROM clause on which the CDS view is based.

► joined_data_source_name

This is an additional data source in the FROM clause that is used in the query and linked to the first persistency via a join.

► element_name and joined_element_name

These data fields are used in the join condition (in the ON condition of the JOIN clause).

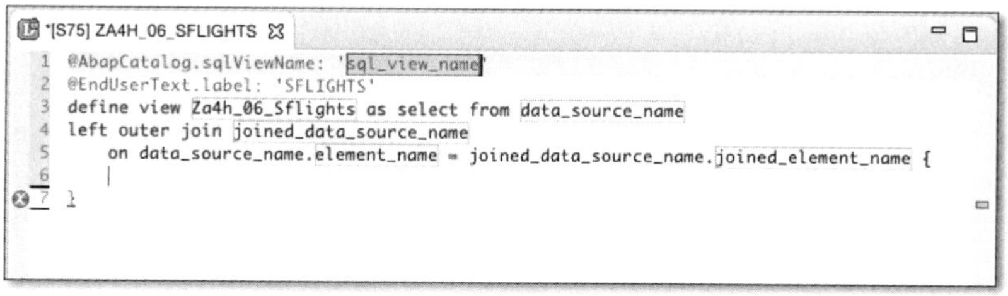

```
    [S75] ZA4H_06_SFLIGHTS ⊠
  1  @AbapCatalog.sqlViewName: 'sql_view_name'
  2  @EndUserText.label: 'SFLIGHTS'
  3  define view Za4h_06_Sflights as select from data_source_name
  4  left outer join joined_data_source_name
  5      on data_source_name.element_name = joined_data_source_name.joined_element_name {
  6      |
  7  }
```

Figure 6.3 Code Template: Define View with Join

You can use the Tab key to navigate from one placeholder to the next and then edit them. Listing 6.1 shows the structure of the Za4h_06_Sflights CDS view.

```
@AbapCatalog.sqlViewName: 'ZA4H06SFLIGHTS'
define view Za4h_06_Sflights as
select from scarr
    inner join spfli
        on  scarr.carrid = spfli.carrid
    inner join sflight
        on  spfli.carrid = sflight.carrid
        and spfli.connid = sflight.connid {
    scarr.carrid,
    scarr.carrname,
    spfli.connid,
    spfli.countryfr,
    spfli.cityfrom,
    spfli.airpfrom,
    spfli.countryto,
    spfli.cityto,
    spfli.airpto,
    sflight.fldate,
    sflight.seatsmax,
    sflight.seatsocc
}
```

Listing 6.1 Za4h_06_Sflights CDS View

CDS elements

The view query is made via a `SELECT` statement. Database table `SCARR` is called as the first data source. Database tables `SPFLI` and `SFLIGHT` are used as additional data sources. The data sources are linked via `JOIN` operators taking into account the defined `ON` conditions. The fields selected from the database tables are specified in the `SELECT` list between curly brackets. The fields that are separated from each other by commas define the structure of the returned data. In CDS, these fields are also called *elements*. As you'll see later, these elements can also be associations.

Now, check (via Ctrl+F2) and activate (Ctrl+F3) the DDL source. You can now test the automatically created view in the data preview in Eclipse via DATA PREVIEW by pressing the F8 key. Figure 6.4 shows the result set that our CDS view returns.

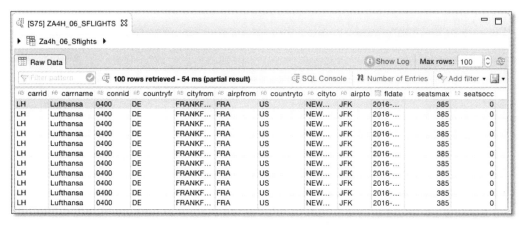

Figure 6.4 Result Set of Za4h_06_Sflights in the Data Preview

> [»] **Formatting DDL Sources**
>
> Currently, the DDL editor doesn't provide a Pretty Printer that you can call to format your DDL sources. However, when you save your DDL sources, the DDL editor automatically ensures that all names are formatted consistently. The names of all CDS entities and their elements are formatted according to their conventions in the definition (case preservation). All other names and CDS keywords are written in lowercase letters.

Joins

You might have noticed that we changed the left outer join, as provided by the code template, to an inner join in Figure 6.3. This was necessary to ensure that the process of querying the CDS view is identical to the process of querying the SFLIGHTS view. Compared to classic database views that are defined in the DDIC, ABAP CDS provides two new join options: left outer join and right outer join. The join type for linking two data sources highly influences the result set of the query:

Join types

- Inner joins merge data records of a *left* and of a *right* data source if the defined conditions are met. If the conditions aren't met, the result set is empty.

- Left outer joins always transfer all data records from the left data source to the result set. If a data record of the right data source and a data record of the left data record together fulfill the ON conditions, the data records are linked on a row basis and included in the result set. If there isn't a matching data record in the right data source, the fields that were supposed to be filled with data records from the right data source remain empty in the result set (NULL values). The fields of the left data source are always included, irrespective of the ON conditions.

- Compared to left outer joins, right outer joins function in exactly the opposite way. Right outer joins always transfer all data records from the right data source to the result set. They are linked to data records of the left data source if they meet the ON conditions.

NULL Values in CDS Views   [«]

Although the NULL value from SQL isn't represented in the ABAP type system, you still have to pay attention to NULL values when defining your views. Your CDS view queries are executed in the SQL engine of the underlying database, outside the control of the ABAP AS. Here, NULL values can occur if you use the new join types—left outer join and right outer join. You can work with comparison operators (IS [NOT] NULL) and functions (COALESCE) to handle NULL values when executing your query in the database system. Untreated NULL values in the results set are mapped by initial values in ABAP.

Link sequence Because we used an inner join, our view, `Za4h_06_Sflights`, only returns airlines that actually offer flights. To output all airlines, we should have used the `LEFT OUTER JOIN` operator. In this case, you should always consider the implicit link sequence. Joins in CDS view definitions are executed from left to right by default. You can determine the join sequence explicitly by sorting `ON` conditions and compounding `JOIN` clauses appropriately.

[»] **Join Sequence**

The join sequence can be defined solely via the sequence of the `ON` conditions. You don't have to compound `JOIN` operations using round brackets. However, you should always compound objects to enhance the readability of your definition and clarify the query's intention.

Client Handling

Another important difference between ABAP CDS and SAP HANA CDS is the automatic client handling feature in ABAP. Although the client field of the underlying data source hasn't been handled explicitly in the CDS view definition in Listing 6.1, the defined view is client-dependent. In the `CREATE` statement for the SQL view, the ABAP AS automatically considers client handling if the data sources are client-dependent.

Displaying the SQL CREATE statement Let's look at the SQL view definition that was created in the database for the CDS view from Listing 6.1. For this purpose, you can directly navigate from the DDL source in the ABAP Development Tools to Transaction SE11. To do so, position the cursor in the DDL source on the `ZA4H06SFLIGHTS` SQL view name in the `@AbapCatalog.sqlViewName` annotation, and press F3. The system then takes you to Transaction SE11 where you can call the `CREATE` statement of the SQL view in the menu via EXTRAS • CREATE STATEMENT. The statement is shown in Listing 6.2.

```
CREATE VIEW "ZA4H06SFLIGHTS" AS SELECT
  "SCARR"."MANDT" AS "MANDT",
  "SCARR"."CARRID",
  "SCARR"."CARRNAME",
  "SPFLI"."CONNID",
  "SPFLI"."COUNTRYFR",
  "SPFLI"."CITYFROM",
```

```
  "SPFLI"."AIRPFROM",
  "SPFLI"."COUNTRYTO",
  "SPFLI"."CITYTO",
  "SPFLI"."AIRPTO",
  "SFLIGHT"."FLDATE",
  "SFLIGHT"."SEATSMAX",
  "SFLIGHT"."SEATSOCC"
FROM (
  "SCARR" "SCARR" INNER JOIN "SPFLI" "SPFLI" ON (
    "SCARR"."MANDT" = "SPFLI"."MANDT" AND
    "SCARR"."CARRID" = "SPFLI"."CARRID"
  )
) INNER JOIN "SFLIGHT" "SFLIGHT" ON (
  "SPFLI"."CARRID" = "SFLIGHT"."CARRID" AND
  "SPFLI"."CONNID" = "SFLIGHT"."CONNID" AND
  "SCARR"."MANDT" = "SFLIGHT"."MANDT"
)
```

Listing 6.2 CREATE Statement for SQL View ZA4H06SFLIGHTS

Compared to the CDS view definition, in the SQL view definition, the client field of the first data source in the FROM clause was automatically added to the SELECT list, and the ON conditions of the JOIN clauses were also extended, respectively. As a result, the CDS view is client-dependent. The automatically added client field, however, isn't visible in the CDS view; that is, you can't address the MANDT field in Open SQL or in another CDS view definition if you use the CDS view as a client-dependent data source.

Explicit Client Handling   [«]

You shouldn't add the client field explicitly to the SELECT list of your view definition or handle the client fields in the join conditions. Client handling for CDS views with client-dependent data sources is implemented automatically in AS ABAP.

You can deactivate the automatic client handling function in CDS views as follows:

Deactivate automatic client handling

▸ The @ClientDependent: false annotation defines the CDS view as a client-independent view. The annotation must precede the DEFINE VIEW statement.

▸ The Open SQL CLIENT SPECIFIED addition doesn't change the client dependency of the CDS view but solely deactivates the automatic client handling function if the view is used in Open SQL. If you use this addition, a client column is automatically included in the result set, although it isn't a CDS view field. After the addition, you can assign a name to the automatically added client column and then address it in the SELECT statement in Open SQL.

The new CLIENT SPECIFIED addition for the TYPES ABAP statement enables you to declare an appropriate target area with an additional client column for the collection of results.

Listing 6.3 shows how you can use the CLIENT SPECIFIED additions in ABAP to read the flights of the '001' client via the Za4h_06_Sflights CDS view. We then output the flights using a WRITE statement.

```
TYPES: ty_result TYPE za4h_06_sflights
       CLIENT SPECIFIED clnt.
DATA: lt_results TYPE STANDARD TABLE OF ty_result
      WITH EMPTY KEY.

SELECT * FROM za4h_06_sflights
  CLIENT SPECIFIED za4h_06_sflights~clnt
  WHERE clnt = '001'
  INTO TABLE @lt_results.

LOOP AT lt_results ASSIGNING FIELD-SYMBOL(<flight>).
  WRITE: / <flight>-clnt,
           <flight>-carrid,
           <flight>-connid,
           <flight>-fldate.
  ENDLOOP.
```

Listing 6.3 Using the CLIENT SPECIFIED Addition for CDS Views

Associations

Improved compre-
hensibility

In the SFLIGHT data model, the relationships between database tables SCARR, SPFLI, and SFLIGHT are defined by foreign keys in the DDIC. We used these relationships to determine the data sources for our CDS view and to define the join conditions. Although the data model is simple, the foreign key relationships are still rather technical. They don't necessarily follow our natural way of thinking when working with this data model. We would presumably define an issue that we want to solve with the SFLIGHTS DDIC view as follows: "I want to view all flights of the airlines, including information on flight plans and names of the airlines." Of course, the requested information still needs to be detailed, but we would never say: "I want an INNER JOIN of SCARR and SPFLI for which the CARRIDs are identical and...." CDS and the associations in particular help you make the data model more comprehensible for users and experts.

Defining Associations

In this section, we again define SFLIGHTS as a CDS view, but we also use associations this time. For this purpose, we first define CDS views on database tables SPFLI and SFLIGHT in which we model the relationships between the data sources as associations. We then use these views as data sources for the Za4h_06_Sflights_Using_Assocs CDS view in which the associations are used. Table 6.1 provides an overview of the views to be defined and their associations.

CDS View	Data Source (Table)	Defined Association	Relationship Modeled by the Association
Za4h_06_ Flightplan	SPFLI	Airline	Za4h_06_Flight-plan (SPFLI) to SCARR
Za4h_06_Flight	SFLIGHT	Flightplan	Za4h_06_Flight (SFLIGHT) to Za4h_06_Flightplan (SPFLI)

Table 6.1 CDS Views and Associations for Database Tables SPFLI and SFLIGHT

First, we define the Za4h_06_Flightplan CDS view as shown in Listing 6.4.   Association definition

```
@AbapCatalog.sqlViewName: 'ZA4H06FLIGHTPLAN'
define view Za4h_06_Flightplan as select from spfli
association [1..1] to scarr as Airline
  on spfli.carrid = Airline.carrid
{
  carrid,
  connid,
  countryfr,
  cityfrom,
  airpfrom,
  countryto,
```

```
    cityto,
    airpto,
    fltime,
    deptime,
    arrtime,
    distance,
    distid,
    fltype,
    period,
    //Display association for external usage
    Airline
}
```

Listing 6.4 CDS View Za4h_06_Flightplan with Definition of the AIRLINE Association

Link between the data sources

The Airline association is defined through the ASSOCIATION keyword. It models a link between the data source in the FROM clause (table SPFLI) and the data source after the TO keyword (table SCARR). The data source after TO is referred to as the *target data source*. The condition for the link is defined in the ON clause. All fields of the data sources that are specified in the FROM clause and used in the ON condition must also be added to the SELECT list. The name of the association is also used as an alias for the target data source in the association definition. This alias must be used in the ON clause. You don't have to assign an association name. If you don't assign a name, the association is given the name of the target data source.

Conversion into database joins

At first glance, the association definition looks similar to the join definition in Listing 6.1. Actually, you can generate a join in the database from this association definition; however, this is only implemented when the association is used. When the DDL source is activated, AS ABAP converts the association into an SQL join before the SQL view is created in the database.

Visibility

Associations can be used locally in the CDS view in which they are defined and externally by other CDS views that leverage the view as a data source. For this purpose, you must make the association visible by adding it to the SELECT list. Otherwise, it remains hidden from other CDS views.

Cardinality

Finally, association definitions also include the cardinality of the target data source, which is specified in square brackets ([<min>..<max>]). This information is supposed to help users understand the relationship between the data sources and can also be used for the generation of SQL joins for optimizations in the SAP HANA database. To express that a flight plan belongs to *exactly one* airline, for example, the cardinality is defined with [1..1]. If a flight plan could belong to *no* airline *or one* airline, the definition is [0..1] or, abbreviated, [1] (if the minimum value is omitted, the default value 0 is used). In this case, you don't have to specify the target cardinality; however, you should always specify it if you know it. The default value that is used if the target cardinality is omitted is [1].

Runtime Check of the Target Cardinality   [«]

The cardinality of the target data source isn't checked at runtime. Nevertheless, you should ensure that the specification is correct because as of AS ABAP 7.5, it's used to optimize SQL joins in SAP HANA. The cardinality is also used for syntax checks within the scope of the association's use. For example, only associations with cardinality [1] can be used in WHERE clauses.

Next, we define a Za4h_06_Flight CDS view for table SFLIGHT (see Listing 6.5). The Flightplan association uses the Za4h_06_Flightplan CDS view as the target data source. In the association definition, you can see the $PROJECTION keyword. It allows you to refer to fields of the SELECT list. If you've assigned aliases to your fields to improve readability, you can also use these aliases in your association definition via $PROJECTION.

$projection

```
@AbapCatalog.sqlViewName: 'ZA4H06FLIGHT'
define view Za4h_06_Flight as select from sflight
association [1..1] to Za4h_06_Flightplan
  as Flightplan on
    $projection.carrid = Flightplan.carrid and
    $projection.connid = Flightplan.connid
{
 carrid,
 connid,
 fldate,
 price,
 currency,
 planetype,
 seatsmax,
 seatsocc,
 paymentsum,
 seatsmax_b,
```

```
seatsocc_b,
seatsmax_f,
seatsocc_f,
//Display association for external usage
Flightplan
}
```

Listing 6.5 CDS View Za4h_06_Flight with Definition of the FLIGHTPLAN Association

[+]   **Modeling Associations**

When modeling associations, you should make the same considerations as when defining *foreign key* relationships in SQL. Associations are usually modeled from the transaction data level to the master data level. This means that associations are defined in the entity of the transaction data, and the entity of the master data is specified as the target data source.

Nevertheless, it's possible and often makes sense to describe relationships between entities using associations that don't meet the integrity condition. Similar to joins, associations aren't bound by referential integrity. Associations are supposed to provide easy and semantically reproducible access to the data model and to the relationships of the entities the data model contains.

However, you should make sure that the association definitions don't lead to cyclical dependencies between CDS views. At least in AS ABAP 7.4, these definitions can result in errors during the activation of the involved CDS sources.

Use of Associations

The Za4h_06_Flightplan and Za4h_06_Flight CDS views now form the interface for reading the flight data. Direct read accesses to the database tables of the flight data model are no longer necessary. You'll understand the benefits of using CDS views as interfaces to business data when we solve our initial problem with these views, that is, calling all flights of the airlines, including information on flight plans and names of the airlines. Listing 6.6 shows how we implemented this query using a CDS view and the Flightplan and Airline associations.

```
@AbapCatalog.sqlViewName: 'ZA4H06SFLIGHTSUA'
define view Za4h_06_Sflights_Using_Assocs
as select from Za4h_06_Flight as Flight {
    Flight.carrid,
    Flight.Flightplan.Airline.carrname,
    Flight.connid,
```

```
Flight.Flightplan.countryfr,
Flight.Flightplan.cityfrom,
Flight.Flightplan.airpfrom,
Flight.Flightplan.countryto,
Flight.Flightplan.cityto,
Flight.Flightplan.airpto,
Flight.fldate,
Flight.seatsmax,
Flight.seatsocc
}
```

Listing 6.6 CDS View Za4h_06_Sflights_Using_Assocs with Path Expressions

Compared to Listing 6.1, the view definition is definitely more intuitive. Because we use associations in path expressions, we don't need to know or specify the technical join conditions of the data sources used. We only have to determine the data source link in the association definition once so that the ABAP AS can interpret it by each time the association is used. This means that we can focus on the semantic relationships between the entities during the modeling process: "A flight has a flight plan, and a flight plan belongs to an airline." This way, our query better reflects the requirements of the users as shown in Table 6.2. To make the path expressions even more transparent, we assigned the Flight alias to the Za4h_06_Flight data source and used this alias in the SELECT list. This alias isn't mandatory and can also be omitted in the path expressions.

Benefits of associations

Requirement	Statement/Path Expression	Explanation
"I want to view all flights of the airlines …,	select from Za4h_06_Flight	Read all flights.
… including information on their flight plans …	Flight.Flight-plan.<detail>	Read the information from the flight plan of the flight. For this purpose, follow the path from the flight via the flight plan (association) to the information. Every piece of information is a field from the target data source of the Flightplan association.

Table 6.2 Power of Expression of CDS, Demonstrated Using CDS View Za4h_Sflights_Using_Assocs

Requirement	Statement/Path Expression	Explanation
... and including the names of the airlines."	`Flight.Flight-plan.Airline.carrname`	Read the name of the airline from the flight plan. For this purpose, follow the path from the flight via the flight plan and airline (associations) to the name.

Table 6.2 Power of Expression of CDS, Demonstrated Using CDS View Za4h_Sflights_Using_Assocs (Cont.)

[!] **Prefixes in Association Names**

The association name is a semantic alias for the target data source. In the `Flight.Flightplan` path, `Flightplan`, for example, represents the `Za4h_06_Flightplan` CDS view. The path is generated via the dot operator. The dot operator allows access to the elements in the `Za4h_06_Flightplan` view (including the associations defined there).

Consequently, it becomes superfluous to express in the association name that it's an association or a path (e.g., `Flight.toFlightPlan.toAirline.carrname`). Prefixes, such as `to`, impair the readability and are considered bad form. If you want to use prefixes to avoid naming conflicts with other fields of the `SELECT` list when defining associations, for example, you can use an underscore (e.g., `Flight._FlightPlan._Airline.carrname`). Underscores are used as prefixes in nearly all CDS data models provided by SAP to avoid conflicts and ensure a consistent format.

SQL view definition

Let's take a look at the corresponding SQL view definition in Listing 6.7, which was created in the database for the CDS view.

```
CREATE VIEW "ZA4H06SFLIGHTSUA" AS SELECT
  "FLIGHT"."MANDT" AS "MANDT",
  "FLIGHT"."CARRID",
  "=A1"."CARRNAME",
  "FLIGHT"."CONNID",
  "=A0"."COUNTRYFR",
  "=A0"."CITYFROM",
  "=A0"."AIRPFROM",
  "=A0"."COUNTRYTO",
  "=A0"."CITYTO",
  "=A0"."AIRPTO",
  "FLIGHT"."FLDATE",
```

```
    "FLIGHT"."SEATSMAX",
    "FLIGHT"."SEATSOCC"
FROM (
    "ZA4H06FLIGHT" "FLIGHT"
    LEFT OUTER JOIN "ZA4H06FLIGHTPLAN" "=A0" ON (
        "FLIGHT"."CARRID" = "=A0"."CARRID" AND
        "FLIGHT"."CONNID" = "=A0"."CONNID" AND
        "FLIGHT"."MANDT" = "=A0"."MANDT"
    )
) LEFT OUTER JOIN "SCARR" "=A1" ON (
    "FLIGHT"."MANDT" = "=A1"."MANDT" AND
    "=A0"."CARRID" = "=A1"."CARRID"
)
```

Listing 6.7 SQL View Definition for CDS View Za4h_06_Sflights_Using_Assocs

Because the database management systems don't provide native support for ABAP CDS entities, the entity names are replaced by their corresponding SQL view name and the ABAP AS converts the used associations into SQL joins. In the generated SQL statement, aliases (=A0 and =A1) were automatically defined for the ZA4H06FLIGHTPLAN and SCARR data sources, and the system generated left outer joins from the associations.

Which join type is generated for the associations depends on where the associations are used. Associations can be used in the SELECT list and in the FROM, WHERE, and GROUP BY clauses. If they are used in the FROM clause, an inner join is generated by default. In all other cases, left outer joins are generated. You can define the join type yourself by specifying the join operator and the target cardinality that is to be expected after the association name in the path expression, for example, Flight.Flightplan[1: inner].countryfrom.

Here, as well, you don't have to specify the target cardinality, but it does make sense to do so. If you use associations, you can only indicate the maximum target cardinality.

If you use associations, you should pay particular attention to the sequence of the generated joins. The ABAP AS translates the occurrences of associations from left to right. For more complex CDS views, you should take a look at the generated CREATE statement.

Join type when associations are used

[»] **Supported Join Types for Associations**

When assigning the join type, you can only use the INNER and LEFT OUTER operators. You can't specify RIGHT OUTER. If you require right outer joins, you first have to—if this is possible and makes sense from the technical modeling perspective—either reverse the direction of your association in the definition (source and target) and use a left outer join or define the links of the data sources via classic join definitions as shown earlier in Listing 6.1.

Association filter   You can also filter the data that are linked via associations. Association filters can be specified within square brackets and then affect the result set. For example, the following usage of an association allows you to view only the flights with Germany as the target country:

```
Flightplan[1: inner where countryto = 'DE'].countryfrom
```

If you define filter conditions together with a join type, the filter conditions must begin with the WHERE keyword. You can't use association filters in view definitions that form aggregations. The ABAP AS inserts the conditions of the association filters into the generated ON condition of the SQL join.

The system generates a join for each occurrence of an association. If no filter is specified, the ABAP AS aggregates similar joins in one join. If you use association filters, this is no longer done automatically. However, you can enforce this optimization by using the @AbapCatalog.compiler.CompareFilter: true annotation. This annotation must precede the DEFINE VIEW statement. The filters of the associations are then compared, and joins with the same filter are also aggregated. We recommend that you generally use this annotation for your CDS view definitions.

Views with Parameters

Transfer values   Using literals in view definitions, for example, in comparison expressions, is usually inflexible. If you want to transfer values to a CDS view when it's called, you can define parameters for this view. In Listing 6.8, we use parameters to transfer the target country to which the result list of the flights is supposed to be restricted only when the view query is executed.

```
@AbapCatalog.sqlViewName: 'ZA4H06SFLIGHTSUP'
@AbapCatalog.compiler.compareFilter: true
define view Za4h_06_Sflights_Using_Params
with parameters p_countryto : abap.char(3)
as select from Za4h_06_Flight as Flight {
    Flight.carrid,
    Flight.Flightplan.Airline.carrname,
    Flight.connid,
    Flight.Flightplan.countryfr,
    Flight.Flightplan.cityfrom,
    Flight.Flightplan.airpfrom,
    Flight.Flightplan.countryto,
    Flight.Flightplan.cityto,
    Flight.Flightplan.airpto,
    Flight.fldate,
    Flight.seatsmax,
    Flight.seatsocc
}
where Flight.Flightplan.countryto =
      $parameters.p_countryto
and   Flight.Flightplan.countryto is not null
```

Listing 6.8 CDS View Za4h_06_Sflights_Using_Params with Parameters

View parameters are defined before the SELECT statement using the WITH PARAMETERS keyword. The parameter definition includes the specification of the parameter name and type. The type needs to be scalar. You can define selected DDIC types and data elements from the DDIC as parameter types.

Definition and usage

In CDS views, DDIC types are prefixed with abap, for example, abap.int4. Parameter names commonly start with p_ to avoid naming conflicts. Although the $PARAMETERS keyword or scope operator (:) need to be used for parameters, the ABAP CDS Compiler reports a syntax error if parameters and elements of the SELECT list use the same names.

You can define several parameters in a CDS view that are separated by a comma. In general, you can use parameters everywhere in the view definition where literals can be used, in particular on the right side of comparison operators.

Database support CDS views with parameters can be used as data sources in other CDS views and in Open SQL statements. In AS ABAP 7.4, SAP HANA and many other database systems support CDS views with parameters. If CDS views with parameters aren't available, the execution of the view results in the CX_SY_SQL_UNSUPPORTED_FEATURE exception. As of AS ABAP 7.5, this feature is available for all database systems.

Version dependency If you use CDS views with parameters in Open SQL statements, AS ABAP 7.4 outputs a syntax warning indicating that these views aren't supported by all database versions. You can prevent this warning from being issued with the ##DB_FEATURE_MODE pragma. You can also use the CL_ABAP_DBFEATURES class to check at runtime whether CDS views with parameters are supported. If required, you can implement the function as an alternative.

Usage in Open SQL Listing 6.9 shows you how to use CDS views with parameters in Open SQL. Note that the more strict Open SQL syntax must be applied here. You need to prefix the lv_countryto and lt_flights ABAP variables with the escape character (@). For more information on the syntax, refer to Section 6.4.

```
DATA:
    lv_countryto TYPE za4h_06_flightplan-countryto,
    lt_flights   TYPE STANDARD TABLE OF
                      za4h_06_sflights_using_params
                      WITH EMPTY KEY.
lv_countryto = 'US'.
IF abap_true =
  cl_abap_dbfeatures=>use_features(
    requested_features =
    VALUE #( (
      cl_abap_dbfeatures=>views_with_parameters ) )
  ).
  SELECT *
  FROM za4h_06_sflights_using_params(
    p_countryto = @lv_countryto )
    INTO TABLE @lt_flights
    ##DB_FEATURE_MODE[VIEWS_WITH_PARAMETERS].
ELSE.
* Alternative implementation ...
ENDIF.
```

Listing 6.9 Using CDS Views with Parameters in Open SQL

You can provide parameters with literals or other parameters. If a CDS view with parameters is used as the target data source of an association, the parameter must be provided with a value if the association is used. However, in this case, you can also use a field of the data sources as the parameter value.

Support of Session Variables as of SAP NetWeaver AS ABAP 7.5   **[«]**

As of AS ABAP 7.5, you can also use *session variables* in CDS view definitions. These variables don't have to be transferred as parameters but can be addressed as global variables. The values for session variables are automatically set when using Open SQL. For example, for the `$session.user` session variable, the value from the `sy-uname` system field is set. If Open SQL isn't used, and the view isn't executed on SAP HANA, the values of the session variable aren't defined when the view is executed. Always keep this in mind when using session variables.

6.2.2 Code Pushdown

The previous sections introduced CDS and data modeling using ABAP CDS. However, ABAP CDS provides even more functions that enable you to implement calculations and application logic in your CDS views to support code pushdown. If you are familiar with the SQL-92 and SQL:1999 standards, you'll probably already know some of them.

This section provides you with an overview of these new functions and explains their usage by using examples. After reading this section, you should easily be able to determine which processing logic you can implement in ABAP CDS views. You can find a complete description of the individual functions in the ABAP help ([F1] help).

Table 6.3 through Table 6.8 provide you with an overview of the SELECT clauses, operators, and functions that ABAP CDS supports as of AS ABAP 7.4 SP 8. In addition, you can use CASE statements (simple case and searched case) in the SELECT list to define condition expressions. You can imagine simple CASE statements as SWITCH statements, whereas searched CASE statements behave like IF ... ELSE ... IF statements.

Keywords in AS ABAP 7.4

Clause/Operator	Usage/Remark
WHERE	Specifies filters for the result set. The filters are applied after all data sources have been linked. Subselects aren't supported.
GROUP BY	Specifies fields with which aggregations (AVG, SUM, MIN, MAX, COUNT) are supposed to be formed. Rows with the same values in the specified fields define a group and are summarized in one row in the result set.
AS	Specifies an alternative name (*alias*).
UNION	Merges the result sets of two SELECT statements in the same view definition. Duplicates in the merged result set are deleted.
HAVING	Specifies filters for the result set. In contrast to the WHERE clause, aggregation functions can be used in conditions here. If aggregation functions are used in conditions, the filters are applied after the filters in the WHERE clause have been applied.
UNION ALL	Like UNION, but keeps results that occur several times in the merged result set. UNION ALL is more efficient than UNION and should be used if you already know that there are no duplicates.

Table 6.3 SELECT Clauses

Function	Usage/Remark
AVG([DISTINCT] field)	Average value of field for each group. If DISTINCT is indicated, duplicates are ignored during the aggregation process.
MIN(field)	Minimum value of field for each group.
MAX(field)	Maximum value of field for each group.
SUM([DISTINCT] field)	Sum of the values of field for each group. If DISTINCT is indicated, duplicates are ignored during the aggregation process.

Table 6.4 Aggregation Functions

Function	Usage/Remark
COUNT(DISTINCT field)	Number of rows in the group. Duplicates aren't counted.
COUNT(*)	Number of rows in the group.

Table 6.4 Aggregation Functions (Cont.)

Function	Usage/Remark
CEIL(expr)	Smallest integer that is greater than or equal to the expr numeric expression.
MOD(expr1, expr2)	Divides numeric expression expr1 by expr2 and returns the remainder.
ABS(expr)	Absolute value of the expr numeric expression.
DIV(expr1, expr2)	Integer-based division of numeric expression expr1 by expr2.
DIVISION(expr1, expr2, dec)	Decimal-based division of numeric expression expr1 by expr2. The result is rounded to dec decimal places.
FLOOR(expr)	Greatest integer that is smaller than or equal to the expr numeric expression.
ROUND(expr, pos)	Rounded value of expr. pos numeric expression indicates the position of the rounding in relation to the decimal separator.

Table 6.5 Numeric Functions

Function	Usage/Remark
SUBSTRING(expr, pos, len)	Returns a part of the character string from the expr string expression. The part is determined by the position (pos) and length (len) in the character string.
LPAD(expr, len, literal)	Populates the right-aligned character string from the expr string expression with the characters from literal up to the length len from the left.
CONCAT(expr1, expr2)	Concatenates the character strings of the expr1 and expr2 string expressions.

Table 6.6 String Functions in ABAP CDS 7.4

Function	Usage/Remark
REPLACE(expr1, expr2, expr3)	Replaces all occurrences of the expr2 character string in the expr1 character string with the content of expr3. All specified character strings can be string expressions.

Table 6.6 String Functions in ABAP CDS 7.4 (Cont.)

Function	Usage/Remark
CAST(expr AS type)	Converts the result type of the expr expression into the defined type DDIC type. AS ABAP 7.4 supports only selected DDIC types. They are indicated with the abap prefix, for example, abap.int4 or abap.char(3).
COALESCE(expr1, expr2)	Returns the value of the expr1 expression if this isn't equal to NULL. Otherwise, the value of the expr2 expression is returned.
CURRENCY_CONVER- SION(...)	Performs a currency conversion.
UNIT_CONVERSION(...)	Performs a unit conversion.
DECIMAL_SHIFT(...)	Sets the decimal separator of a value according to the currency specified.

Table 6.7 Additional Functions in ABAP CDS 7.4

Operator Type	Operators	Usage/Remark
Boolean operators	NOT, AND, OR	AND and OR link logical expressions. NOT reverses the result of a logical expression.
Comparison operators	BETWEEN, =, <>, <, >, <=, >=, LIKE, IS [NOT] NULL	IS [NOT] NULL can only be used in WHERE clauses.
Arithmetic operators	+, -, *, /	The / operator is used for float-based divisions. It's generally not suitable for financial applications.

Table 6.8 Operators

To demonstrate the usage of these functions with an example, we implement a variant of the Open SQL query with aggregate functions from Listing 3.6 in Chapter 3, Section 3.2.2, as a CDS view. We want to find out if there are more bookings for the booking class of a flight (based on the entries in table SBOOK) than occupied seats (table SFLIGHT). The desired class is specified using a view parameter.

Listing 6.10 shows the CDS view. We only consider the bookings that haven't been canceled and restrict the bookings to the requested class in the WHERE clause. The actual check, whether there are more bookings than occupied seats, is performed in the HAVING clause. We implement the check separately for each class. In addition, we marked the key attributes of the view with the key keyword. In SAP NetWeaver 7.4, the specification of the key is mainly to help users understand the data model and isn't relevant for the execution of the view query in Open SQL. However, because there are ABAP frameworks that use this metadata, for example, SAP List Viewer with Integrated Data Access (ALV with IDA), you should always define the key attributes in your views.

CDS keyword KEY

```
@AbapCatalog.sqlViewName: 'ZA4H06BOOKCHKP'
@AbapCatalog.compiler.compareFilter: true
define view Za4h_06_Booking_Cchk_Params
with parameters p_Booking_Class : abap.char( 1 )
as select from sbook as booking
inner join sflight as flight
    on  booking.carrid = flight.carrid
    and booking.connid = flight.connid
    and booking.fldate = flight.fldate
{
    key booking.carrid,
    key booking.connid,
    key booking.fldate,
    case $parameters.p_Booking_Class
        when 'Y' //Economy Class
            then flight.seatsocc
        when 'C' //Business Class
            then flight.seatsocc_b
        else     //First Class
            flight.seatsocc_f
    end as count_Occupied_Seats,
    count( * ) as count_Bookings
}
```

```
where booking.cancelled <> 'X'
   and booking.class = $parameters.p_Booking_Class
group by
    booking.carrid,
    booking.connid,
    booking.fldate,
    booking.class,
    flight.seatsocc,
    flight.seatsocc_b,
    flight.seatsocc_f
having
    //Occupied seats < number of bookings
    ( booking.class = 'Y' and
      flight.seatsocc < count( * ) )
 or ( booking.class = 'C' and
      flight.seatsocc_b < count( * ) )
 or ( booking.class = 'F' and
      flight.seatsocc_f < count( * ) )
```

Listing 6.10 Consistency Check of Flight Bookings

UNION ALL keyword

Finally, we design a CDS view that checks all classes for inconsistencies and returns these inconsistencies in a result set. For each inconsistency, it should be transparent to which booking class it refers, and the difference between the number of bookings and the number of occupied seats should be determined. For this purpose, we first define the UNION ALL CDS view as shown in Listing 6.11.

```
@AbapCatalog.sqlViewName: 'ZA4H06BOOCKCHKA'
@AbapCatalog.compiler.compareFilter: true
define view Za4h_06_Booking_Check_All as
select from
  Za4h_06_Booking_Cchk_Params( p_Booking_Class: 'Y' )
{
  key carrid,
  key connid,
  key fldate,
  cast('ECONOMY' as abap.char( 8 )) as class,
  count_Bookings,
  count_Occupied_Seats,
  abs(count_Bookings - count_Occupied_Seats)
     as difference
}
union all
select from Za4h_06_Booking_Cchk_Params( p_Booking_Class: 'C' )
{
```

```
  carrid,
  connid,
  fldate,
  'BUSINESS' as class,
  count_Bookings,
  count_Occupied_Seats,
  abs(count_Bookings - count_Occupied_Seats)
    as difference
}
union all
select from Za4h_06_Booking_Cchk_Params( p_Booking_Class: 'F' )
{
  carrid,
  connid,
  fldate,
  'FIRST' as class,
  count_Bookings,
  count_Occupied_Seats,
  abs(count_Bookings - count_Occupied_Seats)
    as difference
}
```

Listing 6.11 Consistency Check for the Flight Bookings of All Classes

We define a separate query for each booking class. We merge the results using UNION ALL because there will hardly be any duplicates in the merged result set. We define a class field for each result, which maps the booked class. We use a literal to define the value of this field. It's important that each query has the same number of fields and that the corresponding fields are type-compatible in the individual queries. When merging the results, the first query always has the leading role; that is, the element names and element types as well as the annotations defined for the elements of the overall result are used from the first SELECT list. Consequently, we convert the class field of the first query to define an appropriate type for all literals.

Unions in CDS views

Further New Functions with AS ABAP 7.5   [«]

The following sections introduce additional code pushdown examples in CDS views, for example, the usage of the CURRENCY_CONVERSION function in Listing 12.5 from Chapter 12, Section 12.3.2. There are many more new developments to come in the future. As of AS ABAP 7.5, you can also use the following functions:

- ▶ String functions: `CONCAT_WITH_SPACE`, `INSTR`, `LEFT`, `LENGTH`, `LTRIM`, `RIGHT`, `RPAD`, `RTRIM`
- ▶ Byte chain functions: `BINTOHEX`, `HEXTOBIN`
- ▶ Date and time functions: `DATS_DAYS_BETWEEN`, `DATS_ADD_DAYS`, `DATS_ADD_MONTHS`, `DATS_IS_VALID`, `TIMS_IS_VALID`, `TSTMP_IS_VALID`, `TSTMP_CURRENT_UTCTIMESTAMP`, `TSTMP_SECONDS_BETWEEN`, `TSTMP_ADD_SECONDS`

6.2.3 View Extensions

The CDS specification also describes how you can extend CDS views free of modifications. These extensions enable you to include additional fields from data sources used in the view. You can also add calculated fields. You define view extensions in ABAP CDS in the same way you specify view definitions in a separate DDL source. For this purpose, the creation wizard provides the EXTEND VIEW template. Listing 6.12 shows an extension of the `Za4h_06_Sflights` CDS view from Listing 6.1.

```
@AbapCatalog.sqlViewAppendName: 'ZA4H06SFLIEXT'
@EndUserText.label: 'ZA4H_06_SFLIGHTS_EXTENSION'

extend view Za4h_06_Sflights with Za4h_06_Sflights_Extension {
  sflight.planetype,
  replace( scarr.url, 'http:', '' ) as protocol_relative_url
}
```

Listing 6.12 Extension of CDS View Za4h_06_Sflights

The `EXTEND VIEW` keyword extends the CDS view. The name of the CDS extension follows the `WITH` keyword. Technically, the extensions are implemented through the default extension mechanisms of the ABAP system. For each extension, an *append view* is generated and appended to the SQL view. The name of the append view is defined in the `@Abap-Catalog.sqlViewAppendName` annotation.

CDS extensions are always assigned to exactly one CDS view, but you can create more than one extension for a CDS view.

Specify fields clearly
Within the curly brackets, you can specify more fields that are supposed to be added to the CDS view. The name of the respective data source must precede the name of these fields to identify the fields clearly. If

naming conflicts arise, you can define aliases for the individual fields. In Listing 6.12, we added two fields to the `Za4h_06_Sflights` CDS view: `planetype` and `protocol_relative_url`.

You can also use the fields of the data sources in expressions and calculations. The `scarr.url` field, for example, is used to convert the absolute URL of the airline into a relative URL (without "http:").

Calculations

You can't use parameters, associations, or aggregation functions in CDS extensions; you can't define new join conditions.; and you can't extend CDS views with `GROUP BY` or `UNION` clauses. Some of the restrictions were removed in AS ABAP 7.5.

As shown in Figure 6.5, the symbol at the left side of the editor indicates whether a CDS view has been extended. Click on the symbol to view a list of the CDS extensions. The hyperlinks navigate you to the individual extensions. The ELEMENT INFO displays all elements of the selected CDS views, including extensions. To call the ELEMENT INFO, position the cursor on the entity name in the DDL source, and press F2.

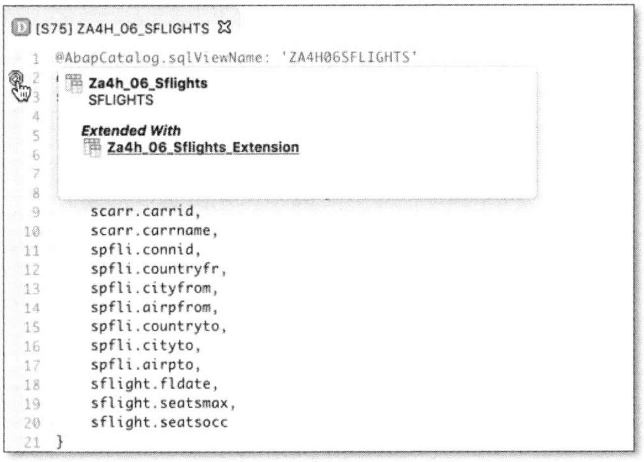

Element Info option in Eclipse

Figure 6.5 Extension Symbol at the Left Side of the DDL Editor

Figure 6.6 shows information on the `Za4h_06_Sflights` view. The ELEMENT INFO is available for all data sources and elements (including associations) that are used in the DDL source.

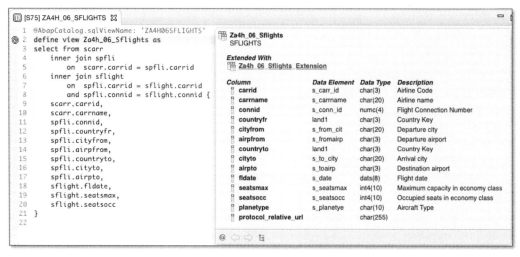

Figure 6.6 Element Info on an Extended CDS View

6.2.4 Annotations

Using annotations
In our examples of view definitions in this chapter, you already learned about four critical annotations with which you can add metadata on CDS objects: `AbapCatalog.sqlViewName`, `AbapCatalog.sqlViewAppendName`, `AbapCatalog.compiler.compareFilter`, and `ClientDependent`. In DDL sources, the @ symbol precedes these annotations. Furthermore, a value needs to be specified for the annotation if the annotation doesn't have a default value. Depending on the type of the annotation, truth values (`true` or `false`), literals (numeric or string literals), or enumeration values can be specified.

Scope
Annotations have a specific *scope* in which they can be used. In AS ABAP 7.4, annotations can be specified for views (scope: VIEW), view extensions (scope: EXTEND VIEW), or elements (scope: ELEMENT). Annotations with the VIEW or EXTEND VIEW scope must always precede the `DEFINE VIEW` or `EXTEND VIEW` statement. Annotations with the ELEMENT scope precede the element.

> **Post-Annotations** [«]
>
> You can also write element annotations directly after the element. In this case, they are prefixed with the @< symbol to define the annotations as *post-annotations*. However, this format is rather uncommon. We recommend first writing the annotation and then the element.

The specification of annotations in CDS is a generic concept to enhance the metadata of a data model. In AS ABAP 7.4, annotations are used to integrate ABAP CDS objects optimally into the existing infrastructure of the ABAP AS. The annotations map the functionality, which you already know from classic DDIC views and database tables. For your CDS views, you can define texts, buffer settings, and reference fields for fields with quantities (QUAN data type) or currency amounts (CURR data type).

Possible content of annotations

Table 6.9 through Table 6.11 list the annotations supported in AS ABAP 7.4.

Supported annotations

Annotation	Valid Values	Default Values for Usage	Effect
AbapCatalog. sqlViewName	String literal with a maximum of 16 characters	–	Specifies the SQL view name
AbapCatalog. compiler. compareFilter	true, false	true	Compares the annotation filters and optimization of SQL joins
ClientDependent	true, false	true	Defines a view as client-dependent
AbapCatalog. buffering. status	#ACTIVE, #SWITCHED_OFF, #NOT_ALLOWED	#SWITCHED_OFF	Determines whether the view is or may be buffered
AbapCatalog. buffering.type	#SINGLE, #GENERIC, #FULL, #NONE	#NONE	Determines the buffering type

Table 6.9 View Annotations (Scope "View")

Annotation	Valid Values	Default Values for Usage	Effect
AbapCatalog. buffering. numberOfKeys	Integer value between 0 and the number of key attributes minus 1	0	Defines the number of key attributes for generic buffering
EndUserText. label	String literal with a maximum of 60 characters	–	Specifies a translatable short text for the CDS view

Table 6.9 View Annotations (Scope "View") (Cont.)

Annotation	Valid Values	Default Values for Usage	Effect
EndUserText. label	String literal with a maximum of 60 characters	–	Specifies a translatable short text for the element
EndUserText. quickInfo	String literal with a maximum of 100 characters	–	Specifies a translatable tool tip for the element
Semantics. currencyCode	true, false	true	Defines the field as a currency key
Semantics. amount. currencyCode	Field name of a currency key	–	Defines the field as the currency field and assigns a currency key to it
Semantics. unitOfMeasure	true, false	true	Defines the field as a unit key
Semantics. quantity. unitOfMeasure	Field name of a unit key	–	Defines the field as a quantity field and assigns a unit key to it

Table 6.10 Element Annotations (Scope "Element")

Annotation	Valid Values	Default Value for Usage	Effect
AbapCatalog. sqlViewAppend- Name	String literal with a maximum of 16 characters	–	Specifies the append view name

Table 6.11 Annotations for View Extensions (Scope "Extend View")

In Listing 6.13, we used annotations to activate the CDS view buffering and assign the PRICE currency field a currency key. You can see the effect that the buffering annotations have on the SQL view in Figure 6.7. By default, in ABAP CDS, short texts for view fields are derived from the data element from the DDIC. You should use the @EndUserText.label annotation for view fields if the data element texts are supposed to be overwritten, the fields have been calculated, or the fields have been converted into integrated DDIC types.

```
@AbapCatalog.sqlViewName: 'ZA4H06FLIPRICE'
@EndUserText.label: 'Flight prices'
@AbapCatalog.buffering.status: #ACTIVE
@AbapCatalog.buffering.type: #FULL
define view Za4h_06_Flight_Price as
select from sflight {

    key carrid,

    @EndUserText.label: 'Flight Number'
    key connid,

    @EndUserText.quickInfo: 'Flight departure date'
    key fldate,

    @EndUserText.label: 'Airfare Currency'
    @Semantics.currencyCode: true
    currency,

    @EndUserText.quickInfo: 'Airfare Economy Class'
    @Semantics.amount.currencyCode: 'currency'
    price
}
```

Listing 6.13 Using Annotations in CDS Views

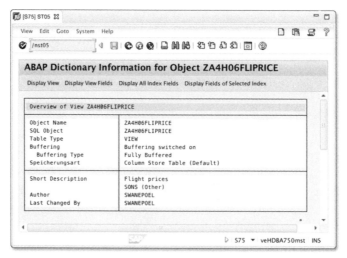

Figure 6.7 Effect of the Buffering Annotations on the SQL View (Transaction ST05)

[»] **New Annotations as of SAP NetWeaver AS ABAP 7.5**

As of AS ABAP 7.5, there are a lot of new annotations that enable you, for example, to define analytical queries, OData services, and models for SAP NetWeaver Enterprise Search.

6.2.5 Using Core Data Services Views in ABAP and in SAP List Viewer with Integrated Data Access

The CDS view name represents a structured data type in the DDIC that contains the fields of the CDS view as structural components. You can use the data type to enter variables and parameters in your ABAP programs. In general, you should always use the entity name (CDS view name) instead of the SQL view name in your ABAP programs. By using the CDS view name, AS ABAP can access CDS-specific metadata and perform many additional checks to ensure the quality of your developments. This is not possible if you use the SQL view name.

Use CDS entities   CDS entities can have the following functions:

- They can be used as data sources in CDS view definitions, in reading Open SQL statements, and in other ABAP frameworks.
- They can be used as standalone data types in ABAP programs.

They can't be used as data types for the definition of classic DDIC objects, such as table types.

Many existing ABAP frameworks support CDS entities. The new *SAP List Viewer with Integrated Data Access* (ALV with IDA) also supports CDS views. ALV with IDA enables you to process large data amounts and output the data on the UI. The ALV with IDA functions allow you to execute operations, such as sorting, grouping, paging (scrolling), aggregating, and filtering, in the database without having to load the data into internal tables on AS ABAP first.

ALV with IDA

You can use ALV with IDA via both SAP HANA and other SAP-supported databases. The static method DB_CAPABILITIES of the CL_SALV_GUI_TABLE class enables you to check which function you can use with your database. Using the statements from Listing 6.14, we have the system display the Za4h_06_Flight_Price CDS view from Listing 6.13 as an ALV list with IDA. Figure 6.8 shows the output.

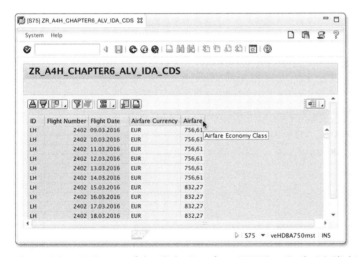

Figure 6.8 ALV Output of the Flight Data from CDS View Za4h_06_Flight_Price

The tool tip that we defined with the @EndUserText.quickInfo annotation is displayed here when the user moves the cursor over the AIRFARE column.

```
DATA(lo_alv_display) =
  cl_salv_gui_table_ida=>create_for_cds_view(
```

```
       CONV #( 'ZA4H_06_FLIGHT_PRICE' ) ).

lo_alv_display->fullscreen( )->display( ).
```
Listing 6.14 Displaying a CDS View with Parameters with ALV with IDA

ALV with IDA also supports CDS views with parameters. The IF_SALV_
GUI_TABLE_IDA~SET_VIEW_PARAMETERS interface method allows you to
set the values of the parameters. For more information on ALV with
IDA, go to the SAP Help Portal (*http://help.sap.com*), and search for "ALV
with IDA".

6.2.6 Tips for Using ABAP Core Data Services Views

To conclude this section on ABAP CDS, we'll provide you with some recommendations for their usage in real-life scenarios.

View-on-View Schema

Subselects Although ABAP CDS already provides an entire gamut of code pushdown options, some application scenarios still aren't supported. In
many cases, the *view-on-view schema* proves to be useful. With this modeling schema, you implement subtasks in your own CDS views, which
you then can use as data sources in other CDS views. For example, you
can reproduce SELECT statements with *subselects* by implementing the
subselect in your CDS view and linking this view to the data sources of
the main query using INNER JOIN.

[!] **Moderate Modularization**

The view-on-view schema enables you to modularize your data model into
smaller modules. This way, you can reuse parts of the model more easily to
define new queries. However, you should always follow the principle, "Modularize, don't atomize"; that is, you should always ensure that the individual
modules are semantically useful and contain sufficient logic.

Activation Log

In the case of activation errors, you should view the activation log of the
CDS view. It contains important information that can help you solve the

problem. You can directly navigate from the display of the DDL source to the activation log via NAVIGATE • OPEN ACTIVATION LOG. In the ABAP log, call the detailed log by pressing the ⌈Ctrl⌉ key and clicking on the hyperlink. Use the search function to find errors by activating the search toolbar via SHOW SEARCH TOOLBAR and searching for "error". Previously, you should ensure that all columns are displayed in the tool (Figure 6.9) by choosing VIEW MENU • SHOW ALL COLUMNS.

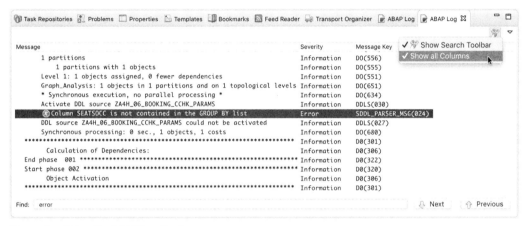

Figure 6.9 Using the ABAP Log Tool

Additional Information

You can find more information on ABAP CDS tools in the ABAP Development Tools under HELP • HELP CONTENTS • SAP – CORE DATA SERVICES FOR ABAP. For a detailed description of the ABAP CDS language features, you can call the ⌈F1⌉ help by positioning the cursor on a CDS keyword and pressing ⌈F1⌉.

6.3   SAP HANA Core Data Services

Although SAP HANA CDS currently plays a minor role in the development of ABAP applications on SAP HANA, we'll provide a brief overview on this variant. SAP HANA CDS is driven by the requirements of

Differences from ABAP CDS

the native application development for SAP HANA. SAP implements functions purposefully; that is, it provides functions that use the SAP HANA architecture and in-memory data processing optimally and support the application development in the SAP HANA environment.

Possible objects

Among other things, you can use SAP HANA CDS for the definition of the following CDS objects:

▸ Database tables

▸ SQL views

▸ Associations

▸ User-defined scalar and structured data types

You define SAP HANA CDS objects in a separate file. To do so, you need an SAP HANA database user with the corresponding authorizations. The object files and the SAP HANA catalog objects that were generated from them are subject to SAP HANA Lifecycle Management. This close integration of the CDS objects with SAP HANA means that they are difficult to consume in ABAP applications and synchronize with other ABAP objects. Therefore, ABAP CDS are usually used for application development in ABAP.

Syntax

Although SAP HANA CDS objects are usually not used in ABAP applications, we'll take a look at the SAP HANA CDS syntax for comparison reasons. In SAP HANA CDS, several CDS objects can be defined in a file. Listing 6.15 shows the definition of two database tables (`Address` and `Partner`) and one view (`Supplier`) in SAP HANA CDS. The semantically related objects are grouped in one context. The `@Catalog.tableType` annotation determines which table type is supposed to be created in the database. The relationship between the entities is modeled using the _ `Address` association.

```
context BusinessPartner {

@Catalog.tableType : #COLUMN
  define entity Address {
     key id        : Integer;
     city          : String(40);
     postalCode    : String(10);
     street        : String(80);
```

```
  countryCode : String(3);
};

@Catalog.tableType : #COLUMN
define entity Partner {
      key id          : Integer;
      addressId       : Integer;
      role            : String(3);
      companyName     : String(80);
      _Address: association[1] to Address
      on addressId = _Address.id;
};

define view Supplier as select from Partner {
  id,
  'SUPPLIER' as role,
  companyName,
  _Address.street,
  _Address.countryCode
} where role = '02';
};
```

Listing 6.15 Sample Syntax of SAP HANA CDS

Although the functional scope of ABAP CDS and SAP HANA CDS differs, the data model is easy to understand, and the syntax is consistent for the shared functions. We could define this view in the same way in ABAP CDS but would have to replace the `Partner` data source with a CDS view. This harmonization facilitates the access to the native SAP HANA data models and a migration to in-memory development, for example, in side-by-side scenarios.

Additional Information on SAP HANA CDS   [«]

You can find more information on SAP HANA CDS in the SAP HANA Developer Guide for SAP HANA Studio in the SAP Help Portal (*http://help.sap.com*).

6.4   Open SQL Enhancements

In Chapter 5, you were already introduced to Open SQL enhancements that enable you to use ABAP CDS views in Open SQL statements. As of AS ABAP 7.4 SP5, there are many more extensions you can use to query and process your persistent data. With these extensions, Open SQL further approaches the full functional scope of the SQL 92 standard. This section provides a brief overview of the new Open SQL features.

SQL expressions   One of the most significant extensions in Open SQL is the support of SQL expressions in the SELECT list and in the WHERE, GROUP BY, and HAVING clauses of SELECT statements. The operands of the expression can generally be fields of the data sources used, ABAP variables (*host variables*), or literals. In addition, new operators and SQL functions are supported, including the following:

▸ **Arithmetic operators:** +, -, *, /
The / operator is used for float-based divisions and isn't permitted in integer expressions. Overflows of integer expressions or floating point number expressions result in the CX_SY_OPEN_SQL_DB exception.

▸ **String operator:** &&
The && operator is used in string expressions and concatenates two character-type operands. As of AS ABAP 7.5, the following string functions are also available: CONCAT, LPAD, LENGTH, LTRIM, REPLACE, RTRIM, RIGHT, and SUBSTRING.

▸ **Unary negation operator:** -
The unary negation operator generates the negative value of a numeric operand.

▸ **Arithmetic functions:** ABS(expr), CEIL(expr), FLOOR(expr), DIV(expr1, expr2), MOD(expr1, expr2)
The DIV function is used for integer-based divisions of the numeric expressions expr1 and expr2. If the operand of an arithmetic function has the NULL value, the function returns NULL.

▸ **Additional functions:** CAST(expr AS fltp) and COALESCE(expr1, expr2)
In AS ABAP 7.4, operands in the CAST function can only be converted to FLTP. As of AS ABAP 7.5, additional DDIC types can be used.

▸ **Case distinctions: simple and searched CASE statements**
Simple CASE statements behave like SWITCH statements, whereas searched CASE statements behave like IF ... ELSE ... IF statements.

Compared to ABAP CDS, SQL expressions can also be used as operands in the `MAX`, `MIN`, `SUM`, and `COUNT( DISTINCT )` aggregation functions.

The definition of joins in `SELECT` statements also includes numerous extensions, for example:

New join types

- You can use `RIGHT OUTER JOIN` to link data sources.
- You can now use `LIKE` and `IN` operators in `ON` conditions.
- You can link individual comparisons in `ON` conditions with `OR` and negate them with `NOT`.
- You can also use literals as operands of an `ON` condition. By defining `ON` conditions, which always have the `true` truth value, for example, `ON 1 = 1`, you can also implement cross joins. Here, the involved data sources are linked to each other as a Cartesian product.

To facilitate the implementation of queries in `SELECT` Open SQL statements, you can now also use ABAP inline declarations for the target area of `SELECT` statements. For this purpose, use a declaration expression with the `DATA()` declaration operator in the `INTO` clause of the `SELECT` statement (see Listing 6.16). The abbreviated `<data_source>~*` form enables you to add all fields of a data source to the `SELECT` list.

Inline declarations

If you use one of the previously mentioned extensions in Open SQL, the syntax of the Open SQL statement is automatically checked in a strict mode. This includes stricter checks to ensure the accuracy of the statement. In the strict mode, previous syntax warnings are now syntax errors. It also includes new checks; for example, fields that are included in the `HAVING` clause of a `SELECT` statement must be listed in the `GROUP BY` clause. Furthermore, you must adhere to the following rules in the strict mode:

Strict mode

- Field lists, for example, in the `SELECT` and `GROUP BY` list, must be separated by commas.
- ABAP variables (host variables) that are used in Open SQL statements must precede the @ escape character.

The strict mode is not only available for `SELECT` statements but also for all Open SQL statements. However, it only applies to the currently used statement and not automatically to all Open SQL statements of the

Enable the strict mode

compilation unit. If you want to benefit from the strict checks in your existing Open SQL statements, you can enable the strict mode by implementing minor changes to your statements. To do so, you only have to meet one of the rules just mentioned, for example, by adding the @ escape character in front of the used host variables.

[»] **Strict Open SQL Mode**

We recommend always activating the strict Open SQL mode. You can use the strict mode in Unicode programs in which the *fixed point arithmetic* program attribute is activated.

Example   To demonstrate the usage of the new features, we check the total baggage weight of the individual flight classes of a flight through an Open SQL query (see Listing 6.16). The result includes all classes that exceed the maximum baggage weight. The flight that is to be checked and the upper limit for the baggage weight of a passenger of a class are specified in the `lv_flight` and `lv_max_luggweight` (economy class), `lv_max_luggweight_b` (business class), and `lv_max_luggweight_f` (first class) host variables. To make it easier to read the results, we transform the internal IDs of the flight classes into user-friendly constants using a `CASE` statement.

```
SELECT
    flight~carrid,
    flight~connid,
    flight~fldate,
    CASE booking~class
        WHEN 'Y' THEN 'ECONOMY'
        WHEN 'C' THEN 'BUSINESS'
        ELSE 'FIRST'
    END AS class,
    SUM( booking~luggweight ) AS luggage_weight
  FROM sflight AS flight
  RIGHT OUTER JOIN sbook AS booking
    ON      flight~carrid = @lv_flight-carrid
    AND     flight~connid = @lv_flight-connid
    AND     flight~fldate = @lv_flight-fldate
    AND     booking~class IN ( 'C', 'Y', 'F' )
  INTO TABLE @DATA(results)
WHERE booking~cancelled <> 'X'
GROUP BY
    flight~carrid,
    flight~connid,
```

```
    flight~fldate,
    booking~class
HAVING
    ( booking~class = 'Y' AND
      SUM( booking~luggweight ) >
      MAX( flight~seatsmax     * @lv_max_luggweight    ) )
 OR ( booking~class = 'C' AND
      SUM( booking~luggweight ) >
      MAX( flight~seatsmax_b  * @lv_max_luggweight_b ) )
 OR ( booking~class = 'F' AND
      SUM( booking~luggweight ) >
      MAX( flight~seatsmax_f * @lv_max_luggweight_f ) ).
```

Listing 6.16 New Open SQL Features

These Open SQL extensions provide you with numerous new options for accessing and manipulating your persistent data. In particular, the support of SQL expressions enables you to optimally leverage the strengths of your database for data processing.

6.5   ABAP Database Procedures

As you learned in Chapter 4, SQLScript and SAP HANA database procedures provide many benefits for the implementation of code push-downs from the application layer to the SAP HANA database.

The *ABAP Managed Database Procedure framework* (AMDP framework) manages database procedures and integrates them optimally into the ABAP programming language, development tools, and ABAP Lifecycle Management. The integration is implemented through the use of ABAP classes in which database procedures and their parameter interfaces are modeled as specific ABAP methods (AMDP methods). The processing logic of an AMDP is implemented in an AMDP method in SQLScript. This kind of integration has the following benefits:

Benefits of AMDPs

▶ You can implement database procedures in the normal development environment with an ABAP user without requiring an additional SAP HANA database user. The AMDP framework is responsible for the entire communication with the SAP HANA database and automatically creates the database procedures as SAP HANA catalog objects when the AMDP method is called for the first time.

- You can call AMDPs as ABAP methods with the normal ABAP syntax.

- To define the parameter interface, you only use ABAP and DDIC types. This ensures that only types are used in the AMDP that can also be mapped in ABAP.

- Database procedures are checked using the ABAP compilation unit. This makes errors in the procedure implementation transparent, even in the ABAP development environment.

- AMDPs are integrated fully with ABAP Lifecycle Management. You can easily synchronize and transport AMDPs with other ABAP objects.

- AMDPs provide the most comprehensive access to in-memory technologies of the SAP HANA database in your ABAP applications.

- You can enhance AMDPs using the *SAP Business Add-Ins* (*BAdIs*) framework.

6.5.1   Creating ABAP Managed Database Procedures

AMDP classes *AMDP classes* are created like normal ABAP classes in ABAP Development Tools. Similar to ABAP CDS, you can't create or modify AMDP classes in the Class Builder in SAP GUI (Transaction SE24).

AMDP classes are defined as such through the use of a specific ABAP interface, IF_AMDP_MARKER_HDB. You can only create AMDPs in ABAP classes that implement this interface. The interface itself is write-protected and doesn't define methods. It only serves to indicate ABAP classes as AMDP classes.

Listing 6.17 shows how you can implement the example from Listing 4.15 in Chapter 4, Section 4.3, as an AMDP method. The database procedure accesses the SFLIGHT database table and determines the average percentage utilization of flights for each flight connection for each requested airline. It assigns the result to the output parameter GET_UTI-LIZATION.

```
CLASS zcl_a4h_chapter6_flights_amdp DEFINITION
  PUBLIC
  CREATE PUBLIC .
  PUBLIC SECTION.
```

```
    INTERFACES: if_amdp_marker_hdb.
    TYPES: BEGIN OF ty_flight_utilization,
             carrid       TYPE s_carr_id,
             connid       TYPE s_conn_id,
             utilization TYPE p LENGTH 5 DECIMALS 2,
           END OF ty_flight_utilization.
    TYPES: tt_flight_utilization
           TYPE STANDARD TABLE OF
           ty_flight_utilization
           WITH EMPTY KEY.
    METHODS:
      get_utilization
        IMPORTING
          VALUE(iv_mandt)      TYPE mandt
          VALUE(iv_carrid)     TYPE s_carr_id
        EXPORTING
          VALUE(et_utilization) TYPE tt_flight_utilization.
ENDCLASS.

CLASS zcl_a4h_chapter6_flights_amdp IMPLEMENTATION.
  METHOD get_utilization
      BY DATABASE PROCEDURE
      FOR HDB LANGUAGE SQLSCRIPT
    OPTIONS READ-ONLY USING sflight.
    et_utilization =
        SELECT carrid,
               connid,
               avg(to_decimal(seatsocc + seatsocc_b +
                              seatsocc_f) /
                   to_decimal(seatsmax + seatsmax_b +
                              seatsmax_f) * 100 )
             AS utilization
        FROM sflight
        WHERE mandt  = :iv_mandt
          AND carrid = :iv_carrid
        GROUP BY carrid, connid;
  ENDMETHOD.
ENDCLASS.
```
Listing 6.17 Implementation of an AMDP Method

AMDP methods can be static or instance methods. They differ as follows AMDP methods
from normal ABAP methods:

► All parameters must be transferred per VALUE. IMPORTING, EXPORTING,
  and CHANGING parameters are supported.

► The keywords BY DATABASE PROCEDURE FOR HDB LANGUAGE SQLSCRIPT
  define a method as an AMDP method. The READ-ONLY addition is

optional and indicates that the database procedure only reads data. If the database procedure uses other DDIC objects or AMDPs, they must be listed after the USING keyword due to dependency management reasons. The FOR HDB and LANGUAGE SQLSCRIPT specifications define that it's an SAP HANA database procedure in SQLScript. Currently, only SAP HANA is supported, but more languages and databases might be supported in future.

▶ When AMDP methods are executed, exceptions of the basic CX_AMDP_ERROR class might occur. The following subclasses are the main error sources:

  ▷ CX_AMDP_VERSION_ERROR: AMDP version management error.

  ▷ CX_AMDP_CREATION_ERROR: Error during the creation of the procedure in the database.

  ▷ CX_AMDP_EXECUTION_ERROR: Error during the execution of the procedure in the database.

  ▷ CX_AMDP_CONNECTION_ERROR: Database connection error during the creation or execution of the procedure.

▶ The database procedure is implemented in SQLScript in the area between METHOD and ENDMETHOD. The procedure can access the parameters of the method definition.

Database proce-
dure names
As already mentioned, database procedures in the AMDP framework are only generated when the AMDP method is executed in the default schema of the ABAP system for the first time. The name of the generated procedure consists of the ABAP class name, the method name, and the => separator. In the preceding example, the generated database procedure is called ZCL_A4H_CHAPTER6_FLIGHTS_AMDP=>GET_UTILIZATION. This database procedure can even be called by other AMDPs in SQLScript. In this case, the AMDP must also be listed in the USING clause of the user. The explicit dependency specification in the USING clause additionally ensures that other used AMDPs are also generated. AMDP classes can also be transported and activated in system landscapes without SAP HANA. If AMDP methods are called in a non-SAP HANA system, the CX_AMDP_WRONG_DBSYS exception is returned. Listing 6.18 shows how you can call the AMDP method in ABAP.

```
TRY.
    DATA(lo_flights) =
        NEW zcl_a4h_chapter6_flights_amdp( ).
    lo_flights->get_utilization(
        EXPORTING
            iv_mandt = sy-mandt
            iv_carrid = 'AA'
        IMPORTING
            et_utilization = DATA(utilization) ).
  CATCH cx_amdp_error INTO DATA(error).
    "Error handling
ENDTRY.
```

Listing 6.18 Calling an AMDP Method in ABAP

> **Calling Database Procedures in the AMDP Framework** [«]
>
> Basically, you can call any database procedure in the AMDP framework even if it isn't ABAP managed. However, you should only call other AMDPs; otherwise, you can't benefit from the many advantages of AMDP, such as ABAP Lifecycle Management.

The AMDP framework also allows you to specify a database connection that is supposed to be used to execute the AMDP. For this purpose, you must additionally define an IMPORTING parameter with a predefined name, connection. The parameter must be of the dbcon_name type. When calling your AMDP method, you can assign the connection parameter either the default connection (DEFAULT) or a service connection to the default database (R/3*<connection_name>). The framework then uses this database connection to execute the database procedure. Currently, it isn't possible to use a secondary database connection to another database.

Database connection

6.5.2 Troubleshooting

If you implement AMDPs, tools for troubleshooting are available. First, you should analyze the errors reported by the SAP HANA server. The ABAP Development Tools PROBLEMS view displays these messages when the AMDP class is checked or activated. If the execution of an AMDP method leads to a short dump, the ABAP dump analysis (Transaction

SAP HANA server error messages

ST22) provides additional, AMDP-relevant information in the INFORMA-
TION ON DATABASE PROCEDURES (AMDP) area.

SQLScript
Debugger

The SQLScript Debugger in SAP HANA Studio is another troubleshooting option for AMDPs. If you want to debug AMDPs, you need an SAP
HANA database user with specific authorizations to debug database procedures of the default ABAP database user. All AMDPs are created with
the same ABAP database user, which is usually the SAP<SAPSID> user.
SAP Note 1942471 describes the required authorizations (*http://ser-
vice.sap.com/sap/support/notes/1942471*). Before you can perform the
debugging, you need to ensure that the database procedure has been
generated in the database. Here, it's sufficient to execute the AMDP
method at least once before the process. Alternatively, you can also use
ABAP Program RSDBGEN_AMDP to create the database procedure.

Setting
breakpoints

Now, you can set a breakpoint in the database procedure and debug the
external session of the default ABAP database user in the SAP HANA system. Navigate to the DEBUG perspective in SAP HANA Studio. Select
DEBUG • DEBUG CONFIGURATIONS, and create the new configuration for
debugging the SAP HANA STORED PROCEDURE. On the GENERAL tab,
select your SAP HANA system, and set a filter for the default ABAP database user (HANA USER) and optionally for the ABAP user (APPLICATION
USER). You should also specify the ABAP user to avoid accidentally inter-
rupting processes of other ABAP users who also access the database with
the default ABAP database user. You can start the debugger via the
DEBUG button. Figure 6.10 shows how you create a debug configuration.

If you now execute your AMDP method, the SQLScript Debugger stops
at your set breakpoint. Because some default debugger functions (e.g.,
STEP INTO or STEP OVER) aren't supported yet, you can set further breakpoints in your database procedure and use RESUME to execute the database procedure up to the next breakpoint. In the VARIABLES view, you
can analyze the variables of the procedure. For table-type variables, the
DATA PREVIEW tool is ideal (see Figure 6.11). You can start the tool in the
context menu of the variable (OPEN DATA PREVIEW). Select RUN • TERMI-
NATE to deactivate the Debugger in SAP HANA Studio.

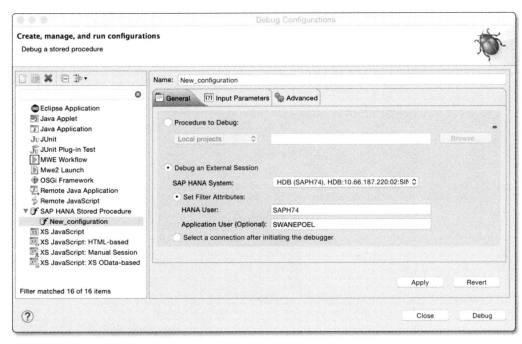

Figure 6.10 Creating a Debug Configuration

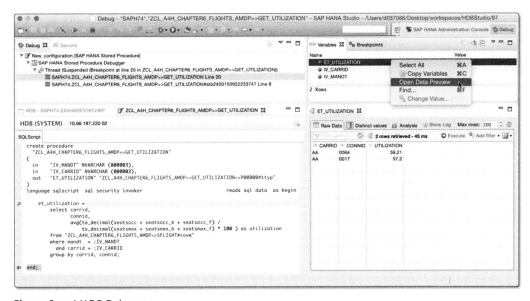

Figure 6.11 AMDP Debugger

[»]

AMDP Debugging as of SAP NetWeaver AS ABAP 7.5

As of AS ABAP 7.5, you can analyze AMDPs with your ABAP user directly in the ABAP Development Tools ABAP Debugger.

6.5.3   Enhancements

As already mentioned, you can enhance ABAP-managed database procedures with the BAdI framework. In this section, we'll explain how this works.

AMDP BAdIs   To enhance AMDPs free of modifications, specific AMDP BAdIs were introduced with AS ABAP 7.4 SP 8. In AMDP BAdIs, you can implement BAdI methods as AMDP methods. You can create AMDP BAdIs for enhancement spots in the Enhancement Builder (Transaction SE20) as usual.

Characteristics   AMDP BAdIs differ from BAdIs with regard to the following aspects:

- When using BAdIs, AMDP BADI needs to be selected.
- AMDP BAdIs don't support filters.
- You have to specify a fallback class.
- All implementations of the BAdI interface methods have to be AMDP methods.

We demonstrate the functionality of AMDP enhancements using a sample AMDP BAdI of the MULTIPLE USE setting for checking the flight data. You can see the ZA4H_06_FLIGHTS_CHECK BAdI definition and ZA4H_CHAPTER6_FLIGHTS_CHECK enhancement spot for managing the BAdI in Figure 6.12.

Listing 6.19 shows the respective BAdI interface ZIF_A4H_06_FLIGHTS_CHECK.

```
INTERFACE zif_a4h_06_flights_check
  PUBLIC .
  INTERFACES if_badi_interface .
  TYPES:
    BEGIN OF ty_finding,
      carrid    TYPE s_carr_id,
      connid    TYPE s_conn_id,
```

```
      fldate      TYPE s_date,
      class       TYPE s_class,
      error_code TYPE c LENGTH 30,
    END OF ty_finding .
  TYPES:
    ty_findings TYPE STANDARD TABLE OF ty_
finding WITH EMPTY KEY .
  METHODS check
    IMPORTING
      VALUE(i_clnt)      TYPE mandt
    CHANGING
      VALUE(c_findings) TYPE ty_findings
    RAISING
      cx_amdp_error .
ENDINTERFACE.
```

Listing 6.19 AMDP BAdI Interface ZIF_A4H_06_FLIGHTS_CHECK

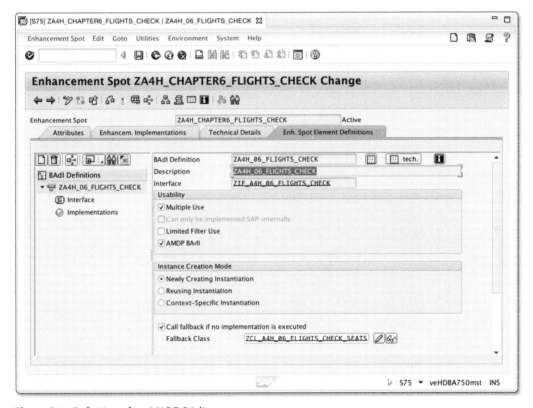

Figure 6.12 Definition of an AMDP BAdI

In the `ZCL_A4H_06_FLIGHTS_CHECK_SEATS` fallback AMDP class, the `CHECK`
BAdI interface method is implemented as an AMDP method. This BAdI
implementation checks the consistency of the flight bookings and the
occupied seats (see Listing 6.20). Let's take a closer look at how ABAP
`CHANGING` parameters are implemented in AMDPs. In the AMDP, an `IN`
parameter (`c_findings__in__`) and an `OUT` parameter with the same
name (`c_findings`) are created for the `CHANGING` parameter. The `IN`
parameter is always assigned the `__in__` suffix. The AMDP framework
ensures that the content of `c_findings__in__` is first automatically copied to `c_findings` when the procedure is called. This way, the `CHANGING`
behavior is emulated. As you can see in Listing 6.20, you have to be particularly careful when using `CHANGING` parameters. To enrich the results,
we have to use `UNION ALL`. This ensures that the results that the framework copied to `c_findings` and that are overwritten in the first `SELECT`
in our implementation are still included in the overall result.

```
METHOD zif_a4h_06_flights_check~check
BY DATABASE PROCEDURE FOR HDB LANGUAGE SQLSCRIPT
OPTIONS READ-ONLY USING sflight sbook.
  c_findings =
    select
        booking.carrid,
        booking.connid,
        booking.fldate,
        booking.CLASS as CLASS,
        'SEATSOCC_LT_BOOKINGS' as error_code
    from sbook as booking
    inner join sflight as flight
        ON  booking.mandt  = :i_clnt
        and booking.carrid = flight.carrid
        and booking.connid = flight.connid
        and booking.fldate = flight.fldate
    where booking.cancelled <> 'X'
    group by booking.carrid, booking.connid,
            booking.fldate, booking.CLASS,
            flight.seatsocc, flight.seatsocc_b,
            flight.seatsocc_f
    having
    ( booking.class = 'Y' and
      flight.seatsocc   < count(*) )
 or ( booking.class = 'C' and
      flight.seatsocc_b < count(*) )
 or ( booking.class = 'F' and
      flight.seatsocc_f < count(*) )
```

```
      union all
         SELECT * FROM :c_findings__in__;
   ENDMETHOD.
```
Listing 6.20 Fallback BAdI Implementation

You can now call the AMDP BAdI in ABAP with `GET BADI/CALL BADI` as usual (see Listing 6.21).

Using AMDP BAdIs

```
DATA:
 lo_flights_check TYPE REF TO za4h_06_flights_check,
 lt_findings TYPE zif_a4h_06_flights_check=>ty_findings.

GET BADI lo_flights_check.
CALL BADI lo_flights_check->check
  EXPORTING
    i_clnt     = sy-mandt
  CHANGING
    c_findings = lt_findings.
```
Listing 6.21 Calling an AMDP BAdI in ABAP

You can also call AMDP BAdIs in other AMDP methods. The AMDP frameworks generates a database procedure for each AMDP BAdI. The name of the BAdI database procedure consists of the BAdI name, the BAdI interface method, and the => separator. In our example, the BAdI database procedure is called `ZA4H_06_FLIGHTS_CHECK=>CHECK`. The call is shown in Listing 6.22.

AMDP BAdIs in AMDP methods

```
METHOD amdp_badi_call
  BY DATABASE PROCEDURE FOR HDB LANGUAGE SQLSCRIPT
  OPTIONS READ-ONLY
  USING za4h_06_flights_check=>check.
    CALL  "ZA4H_06_FLIGHTS_CHECK=>CHECK"(
        i_clnt          => :i_clnt,
        c_findings__in__ => :c_findings,
        c_findings       => :c_findings );
ENDMETHOD.
```
Listing 6.22 Calling an AMDP BAdI in an AMDP Method

If there is more than one implementation for the BAdI, the generated BAdI database procedure `ZA4H_06_FLIGHTS_CHECK=>CHECK` delegates the call to the active BAdI implementations. It considers the switches of the `SWITCH` framework for the call. This allows you to create enhancement options in your SQLScript code and implement the AMDP enhancement options provided by SAP.

[»] **AMDP Classes and Implicit Enhancement Options**

Implicit enhancement options in AMDP classes and methods, such as at the beginning and at the end of a method, aren't supported.

You can find more information on BAdIs and the SAP Enhancement Framework in the SAP Help Portal (*http://help.sap.com*).

6.5.4 Practical Tips

SELECT-OPTIONS in AMDPs
The SELECT-OPTIONS function in ABAP declares a selection table, which can be linked to a field of a database table. In the selection table, complex selection criteria are defined that are directly used in the WHERE clause of an Open SQL SELECT statement. Here, the ABAP AS converts the selection criteria into SQL WHERE conditions.

If you want to use ABAP selection tables in AMDPs, you first have to convert the selection criteria into SQL WHERE conditions and transfer the conditions to the AMDP method as IMPORTING parameters. You can do this using the CL_SHDB_SELTAB=>COMBINE_SELTABS class method. In SQLScript, you can then use the APPLY_FILTER function to filter a data source using the conditions.

[»] **Availability of CL_SHDB_SELTAB**

If CL_SDHB_SELTAB isn't available in your AS ABAP 7.4 system yet, import SAP Note 2124672 as of SP 5 (*http://service.sap.com/sap/support/notes/2124672*).

The ABAP application server is home to a collection of powerful runtime and error analysis tools that can assist you in accelerating ABAP programs on SAP HANA. When used correctly, they make it easier to identify potential areas of optimization, implement changes, and test such changes.

7   Runtime and Error Analysis with SAP HANA

In the previous chapters, you learned about the various ABAP options available to you in relation to accessing the SAP HANA database. In addition to the already-familiar process of using SQL (Open SQL, including enhancements, and Native SQL) to access tables in the database, you learned various new ways to model and implement views and database procedures, as well as how to use ABAP to access these objects.

If you intend to develop a new application or to optimize an existing application for use with SAP HANA, you may be wondering which approach to adopt and which tools can support the undertaking. In this chapter, we'll provide you with an overview of the runtime and error analysis tools available. In particular, we'll focus on correct usage of these tools within the context of optimizing database accesses. As a result, we won't discuss any other usage scenarios (e.g., system administration) or configuration options in detail here. As an ABAP developer, you're already familiar with some of the tools that can be used for this purpose: For example, the SQL trace (Transaction ST05), ABAP runtime analysis (Transaction SAT), and the SAP Code Inspector. Therefore, we won't describe their use in any detail. Basic information about these tools is available in *ABAP Performance Tuning* by Hermann Gahm (SAP PRESS, 2009). If needed, check out the SAP training course BC490, in which you learn how to use the analysis tools. This chapter focuses on the new SAP HANA-specific analysis options that are available within these tools.

In this chapter, we'll use very simple examples to demonstrate the capabilities of and differences between each tool. Then, building upon this, we'll demonstrate the correct use of these tools (either individually or in combination) within the context of a fictitious optimization project for an overall scenario, which we'll discuss in Chapter 8.

7.1   Overview of the Tools Available

Before we introduce each tool, we'll provide an overview of all the tools available and classify them according to their usage scenario and primary user role. This overview also contains the release requirements for ABAP. We've classified the tools under the categories listed in Table 7.1.

Category	Purpose	Roles
Troubleshooting (Section 7.2)	To identify and resolve functional problems	▶ Developers ▶ Support
ABAP code analysis (Section 7.3)	To identify those parts of the ABAP program with potential for optimization	▶ Developers ▶ Quality managers
Runtime statistics and traces (Section 7.4)	To perform a detailed analysis of the runtime associated with an individual request (e.g., the runtime associated with a dialog step)	▶ Developers ▶ Performance experts
System-wide SQL analyses (Section 7.5)	▶ To determine the SQL profile of an application or system ▶ To perform runtime checks for specific SQL statements	▶ Administrators ▶ Performance experts
SQL Performance Optimization (Section 7.6)	To plan and perform an optimization	▶ Developers ▶ Performance experts

Table 7.1 Categorizing Runtime and Error Analysis Tools

If you optimize implementations on SAP HANA by transferring calcula-   Troubleshooting
tions to the database, this may lead to new sources of error. Within error
analysis, our primary goal is to introduce you to the options available in
relation to analyzing (and avoiding) program terminations associated
with database accesses. In particular, we'll discuss testing, analyzing,
and debugging SQL statements and SQLScript procedures from ABAP
programs.

A static *code analysis* provides clues about which parts of the ABAP pro-   Code analysis
gram have potential for optimization. This is known as a *static* analysis
because no runtime data is incorporated into it (e.g., the frequency with
which a program or function is called within a particular period), and no
dynamic calls are analyzed (e.g., SQL statements that are first generated
at runtime). For the code analysis, SAP NetWeaver AS ABAP has a *Code
Inspector* (Transaction SCI), which provides a set of checks that can be
grouped into check variants. You can use the ABAP Test Cockpit (Transaction ATC) or the Code Inspector to perform these checks in the development environment. To ensure efficient ABAP programming, some
new or improved checks have been added to ABAP 7.4.

AS ABAP contains a number of runtime analysis tools for a database   Runtime analysis
request (or a sequence of requests). The *statistic records* (Transaction
STAD) provide a simple overview of database times and are a useful
starting point. The *ABAP trace* (Transaction SAT) provides detailed
analysis options for individual statements. The new *ABAP profiler* in the
ABAP development environment in Eclipse, which provides additional
functions such as graphical representations, is also based on this infrastructure. In Chapter 3, we introduced you to the *SQL trace* (Transaction
ST05), which also provides other useful runtime analysis functions. *Single transaction analysis* (Transaction ST12) is a special tool that combines
Transactions STAD, SAT, and ST05 into one interface.

In SAP HANA, special tools are available for analyzing an individual SQL
statement or a more complex SQLScript implementation. The *explain
plan* provides information about the execution plan for an SQL statement, while SAP HANA Plan Visualizer (*PlanViz*) visualizes the execution
plans for SQL statements and combines them with additional runtime
information.

System analysis
and optimization

In Chapter 3, Section 3.2.5, we introduced you to the Database Administration Cockpit (DBA Cockpit; Transaction DBACOCKPIT). In addition to managing and configuring the database, the DBA Cockpit also provides some SQL performance analysis functions through, for example, the *SQL cache* and *expensive SQL statement trace*.

New tools

To determine a detailed SQL profile for applications within an SAP system, a new tool, the *SQL Monitor* (Transaction SQLM), is available as of AS ABAP 7.4. This tool monitors the production system and provides valuable performance optimization data.

The *runtime check monitor* is also new. You can use it to record specific SQL statements.

You can use the new *SQL performance tuning worklist tool* (Transaction SWLT) to combine the data from the SQL Monitor with the results of a code analysis and therefore make plans toward achieving a promising optimization. In the following sections, we'll explain how to use each of these tools.

7.2   Troubleshooting

Before we discuss performance optimization tools, we want to introduce some important error analysis tools. As the saying goes, "You can't make an omelet without breaking eggs," so functional problems may occur when making changes to a program or a new development, especially if the previous program code is very old, and the author is no longer available.

Testing, analyzing,
tracing, and
debugging

Therefore, in this section, we'll discuss some aforementioned elements, namely testing, analyzing program terminations, tracing, and debugging. Here, we'll focus on error analyses within the context of database accesses and the use of native implementations in SAP HANA.

We'll explain some approaches in relation to writing *unit tests* for SAP HANA views and procedures in ABAP, discuss the analysis of program terminations in the context of database accesses in Transaction ST22, and introduce the concept of tracing and debugging SQLScript.

7.2.1 Unit Tests

When making changes to program code, it's very helpful to have a set of tests (preferably automatic) that can be performed both before and after making the changes; this helps to identify errors as soon as possible. In this context, the approach of testing single objects (*units*), either individually or in combination, is known as *unit testing*. *ABAP Unit* is integrated into the ABAP language and development infrastructure, and it can be used to write unit tests. This tool is also integrated into the ABAP Test Cockpit, which we'll discuss in Section 7.3. In addition to the ABAP Unit tool, AS ABAP also provides support for further testing approaches, such as integration tests or simulated user interactions. However, these are beyond the scope of this book.

You should also conduct tests to safeguard complex implementations in SAP HANA (in SQL and SQLScript, in particular). The sophisticated test infrastructure in the ABAP AS provides a good framework here. We'll use the ABAP Managed Database Procedure (AMDP) `GET_UTILIZATION` method, which we introduced in Chapter 6, Section 6.5.1, as an example. This procedure determines the average percentage utilization of flights for each flight connection. A simple unit test for the AMDP method is shown in Listing 7.1.

Complex SQL/SQLScript operations

This test validates that the average utilization for the flight connection LH 0400 is calculated as expected.

```
CLASS ltcl_flights_amdp DEFINITION FINAL FOR TESTING
  DURATION SHORT
  RISK LEVEL HARMLESS.

  PRIVATE SECTION.
    DATA:
      flights_under_test TYPE REF TO zcl_a4h_chapter6_flights_
amdp,
      act_utilization    TYPE zcl_a4h_chapter6_flights_amdp
=>tt_flight_utilization.
    METHODS:
      setup,
      flights_gt_0_utilization_gt_0 FOR TESTING RAISING cx_
static_check.
ENDCLASS.

CLASS ltcl_flights_amdp IMPLEMENTATION.
```

```
METHOD setup.
  CREATE OBJECT flights_under_test.
ENDMETHOD.

METHOD flights_gt_0_utilization_gt_0.

  flights_under_test->get_utilization(
      EXPORTING
          iv_mandt = sy-mandt
          iv_carrid = 'LH'
      IMPORTING
          et_utilization = act_utilization ).

  READ TABLE act_utilization
      WITH KEY connid = '0400'
      ASSIGNING FIELD-SYMBOL(<connection>).

  cl_abap_unit_assert=>assert_subrc(
    act = sy-subrc
    msg = 'Test data not installed correctly. Flights not
found for LH 0400.'
      level = if_aunit_constants=>tolerable ).

  cl_abap_unit_assert=>assert_equals(
      act = <connection>-utilization
      exp = '48.44'
      msg = 'Incorrect utilization for LH 0400.' ).

  ENDMETHOD.

ENDCLASS.
```
Listing 7.1 Unit Test for an AMDP Method

Test data To gauge whether the calculation within the procedure is correct, the exact output data must be known. In general, it pays to have different sets of stable, consistent test data that can be used in different systems for different purposes (e.g., mass data for conducting performance tests). You can also use the ABAP client concept to generate suitable test data constellations in special clients.

[+] **Design Patterns Make It Easier to Write Tests**

The use of suitable *design patterns* makes it easier to write unit tests. These include modularization and decoupling as a result of well-defined interfaces, as well as avoiding dependencies in relation to specific system statuses.

For example, when testing database procedures, it makes sense to avoid reading directly from a Customizing table or application context within the procedure and instead transfer the required values as parameters. Such (generic) implementations are easier to test and increase the potential for reuse in other contexts.

Furthermore, it's generally recommended to use a suitable interface to abstract a calculation in the ABAP application and therefore encapsulate an SAP HANA-specific implementation.

7.2.2 Dump Analysis

If a program terminates during a transaction (known as a *dump*), Transaction ST22 provides valuable troubleshooting information. In this section, we'll explain the information you obtain when an error occurs with a database access.

For SQL statements, different types of runtime errors can occur and trigger a dump. Many of these errors can be caught within the application by means of a class-based exception. Table 7.2 groups together the most important exceptions. Here, special runtime error types exist for each category.

Runtime errors and exceptions

Category	Exception	Example
Error during Open SQL access	CX_SY_OPEN_SQL_DB	Use of an invalid cursor (see also Chapter 3, Section 3.2.2)
Syntactical error in dynamic Open SQL	CX_SY_DYNAMIC_OSQL_SYNTAX	Invalid, dynamically generated WHERE condition (see also Chapter 3, Section 3.2.2)
Semantic error in dynamic Open SQL	CX_SY_DYNAMIC_OSQL_SEMANTICS	Aggregation by means of a nonnumerical, dynamically specified column (see also Chapter 3, Section 3.2.2)
Error during ABAP Database Connectivity (ADBC) access	CX_SQL_EXCEPTION	Syntactical error in a Native SQL statement (see also Chapter 3, Section 3.2.4)
Error while calling a database procedure	CX_SY_DB_PROCEDURE	Runtime error in SQLScript (see Chapter 4)

Table 7.2 Error Categories for SQL Accesses

Category	Exception	Example
Errors in the context of AMDP	CX_AMDP_ERROR (and subclasses)	Runtime errors in SQLScript (see Chapter 6, Section 6.5)
Noncatchable errors	None	Internal error during a database access

Table 7.2 Error Categories for SQL Accesses (Cont.)

SQL error number and error text in the database

In Transaction ST22, the short text is the initial starting point for an analysis, in addition to the exception that occurred and the runtime error type (e.g., DBIF_RSQL_SQL_ERROR). The short text contains, for example, information such as SQL ERROR <NUMBER> OCCURRED WHILE ACCESSING TABLE <TABLE>. Figure 7.1 shows an example of an error that occurred while accessing an SAP HANA view that doesn't exist. In most cases, this error text contains enough information to enable you to localize and resolve the problem.

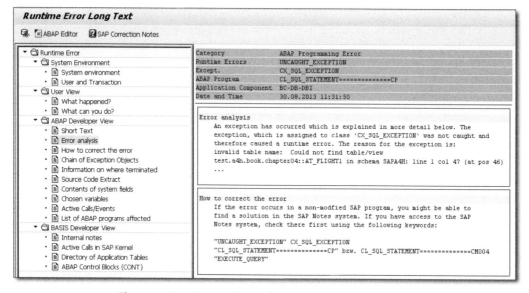

Figure 7.1 Error Text in the Database

Further contextual information in relation to an ABAP program is available in the following sections in Transaction ST22:

▸ Information on which statement caused the dump

▸ Source code extract

▸ Contents of system fields

▸ Chosen variables

▸ Active calls/events

Error When Accessing SAP HANA Views and Database Procedures   **[+]**

When you use external views and database procedure proxies (see Chapter 5), development errors can occur as a result of inconsistencies (e.g., if the view or the procedure was changed without updating the proxy). In most cases, this situation causes an exception of the type CX_SY_OPEN_SQL_DB (with the error text INVALIDATED VIEW ...). In this case, you need to synchronize the objects across the development environment as described in Chapter 5.

If you require further information from the database, the analysis must continue there. The information in Transaction ST22 is no longer sufficient, particularly for more extensive implementations within the database (e.g., a database procedure that calls an additional procedure). In such cases, however, you can use the information available to reconstruct the call that triggered the error and then use debugging and tracing to continue the analysis.

Restrictions associated with dump analysis

7.2.3 Debugging and Tracing in SQLScript

If you analyze an error within an implementation in SQLScript, you may want to view certain interim results or trace them successively in the implementation. For this purpose, you can either debug SQLScript or store it as an interim result in temporary tables using the TRACE statement.

We already described the debugging of AMDP in detail in Chapter 6, Section 6.5.2. You can precisely track the SQLScript execution by setting breakpoints in the implementation and inspecting the variable values. For debugging of native SAP HANA procedures, refer to the SAP HANA development guide at *http://help.sap.com/hana*.

Debugging

Tracing Additionally, SQLScript contains the TRACE calculation engine (CE) plan operator , which enables you to log the contents of a local table variable (displays an interim result for a database procedure) in a local temporary table. It allows you to test calls using various combinations of parameters.

CE Plan
Operator TRACE For the GET_AGENCIES_FOR_CONNECTIONS database procedure, which we used as an example in Chapter 4, Section 4.2.1, the TRACE plan operator can look like the following:

```
LT_AGENCIES = SELECT...
LT_AGENCIES = TRACE(:LT_AGENCIES);
ET_AGENCIES = SELECT...
```

The system automatically creates the local temporary table when it calls the database procedure. This table has the same structure as the table variable. To determine its name, you can read the SQLSCRIPT_TRACE monitoring view after you call the database procedure. Because this is a *local* temporary table, it can only be viewed within the same database connection. Note that the system doesn't undertake some optimizations when the TRACE CE plan operator is used. Furthermore, logging the contents of the table has a negative impact on runtime. Therefore, don't use the TRACE CE plan operator in productive code.

7.3 ABAP Code Analysis

The Code Inspector can support you in identifying those parts of the program that have potential for improvement. With this in mind, the Code Inspector has a series of checks that you can perform on your development objects. You then receive a prioritized list of messages, each assigned to the relevant check. Because false alarms can occur with these checks, you can insert special comments in the code to prevent a message from being issued. In the case of a code analysis, bear in mind that SAP doesn't allow standard SAP code to be scanned.

Extensive
check options Because the Code Inspector has very extensive functions, we can't cover them in detail here. If you're interested in learning more about the Code Inspector, we recommend *ABAP Performance Tuning* by Hermann Gahm (SAP PRESS, 2009). Here, we'll describe the new and revised Code

Inspector checks that are relevant for SAP HANA. You'll learn how to perform checks in the development environment and how to check the entire system.

7.3.1   Checks and Check Variants

When the Code Inspector performs a code analysis, it executes a check-list that comprises a defined set of development objects. Here, you can use *check variants* to configure the list of checks to be performed and their settings.

Checklist

In this section, we'll introduce those checks that can support you in migrating to or optimizing SAP HANA. These checks primarily relate to the following areas: robust programming, security checks, and performance checks. The Code Inspector also contains a large number of additional checks that we won't discuss here in detail. Accurate technical documentation on all checks is available in Transaction SCI, which is used to configure the check variants that you'll learn about in this section.

Relevant Checks when Migrating to SAP HANA

During migration, the main priority is to ensure that you don't experience any functional setbacks, including program terminations and unwanted changes to the behavior of an application. In general, thanks to the compatibility and portability of ABAP code, no adjustments are required.

An exception here is any part of a program where you used database-dependent implementations in the past. These include the use of Native SQL and database hints. The following two check options can help you locate such parts within a program: USE OF ADBC INTERFACE and CRITICAL STATEMENTS.

Native SQL/ database hints

The sorting behavior may also require adaptations, particularly if no explicit sorting is specified in the program code, for example, using ORDER BY or SORT. If no ORDER BY clause is specified, the database returns the data in an unsorted sequence. In classic databases, the sequence might involve a database index if it was used for the query. The ABAP

Sort behavior

program frequently received the data in the desired sequence. However, this was rather coincidental, and there was no guarantee for this sorting. For stable programming, you had to specify the ORDER BY addition here.

In SAP HANA, there are considerably fewer database indexes, and most of them differ from those of classic databases. To receive the read data in the desired sequence, you must use the ORDER BY addition or subsequently sort in the ABAP program using SORT as was the case for classic databases. You can use the check option SEARCH PROBLEMATIC STATEMENTS FOR RESULT OF SELECT/OPEN CURSOR WITHOUT ORDER BY to find those parts of the program for which a result set that requires a sorting (e.g., in a binary search) is processed using an ABAP command and for which a sorting can't be determined in the program via ORDER BY or SORT.

Depooling/ declustering

A further example involves pool/cluster tables, which, when migrated to SAP HANA, are converted into transparent tables (discussed in Chapter 3, Section 3.2.1). This doesn't require any change to the application. However, you must consider that when data is selected in Open SQL without any specified sorting, the documentation states that the user can't rely on sorting (e.g., according to the primary key). For pool/cluster tables, however, the database interface always supplements the ORDER BY PRIMARY KEY addition internally. If you've relied on this behavior (i.e., you chose not to specify a particular sorting), you may have to add an ORDER BY statement after the migration. In the ROBUST PROGRAMMING category, a check is available to help you find the relevant parts within the program. SAP recommends that you adjust these parts of the program irrespective of a migration to SAP HANA because this is a programming error. In Chapter 14, we'll give further recommendations for existing ABAP code when migrating to SAP HANA.

Relevant Checks during Optimization for SAP HANA

To identify optimization potential in the context of database accesses, you have a range of checks at your disposal. These checks essentially reflect the performance recommendations for Open SQL, which are explained in detail in Chapter 14. In the next section, we'll introduce some important checks, including some key enhancements and improvements in AS ABAP 7.4.

Unsecure Use of FOR ALL ENTRIES

The performance optimization in which you convert a nested SELECT statement into a FOR ALL ENTRIES statement or a join is frequently successful. For a FOR ALL ENTRIES expression, the *driver table* must never be empty. Otherwise, all the data records are read from the database, which generally isn't desired. Therefore, a check to determine whether the driver table is empty must always be performed before a FOR ALL ENTRIES statement is executed. The check to detect unsecure use of FOR ALL ENTRIES searches for parts of the program in which the driver table doesn't appear to be checked.

Empty driver table

Searching FOR ALL ENTRIES Clauses to Be Transformed

In many situations, a join offers additional performance advantages over a FOR ALL ENTRIES clause. For this reason, the system performs a check on those FOR ALL ENTRIES clauses to be transformed and finds clauses that can be converted to joins. This is only the case if a database access was used to determine the driver table for the FOR ALL ENTRIES expression.

SELECT Statements that Bypass the Table Buffer

The ABAP table buffer still plays an important role when using SAP HANA as a database. To avoid an increased database load, you shouldn't bypass this buffer if buffering has been switched on for a table. To this end, a check is performed on SELECT statements that ignore the buffer. Note that this check can't support you in finding the right buffer setting for a table.

Problematic SELECT* Statements

You should avoid reading database columns that you don't need. To this end, a check is available to find SELECT statements for which too many fields are selected. Frequently, this concerns pure *existence checks*—where all fields are selected, even though the return code for the SELECT statement is sufficient. However, there are also scenarios in which only a small part of the fields is actually used. With AS ABAP 7.4, these

Reading volumes of data that are too large

checks are also able to identify usage in another *modularization unit* (e.g., in another ABAP class or another function module). Therefore, the entire call sequence is analyzed, which means you can set the depth of search when configuring this check.

Searching SELECTs in Loops in Modularization Units

Usually, performance problems aren't caused by a single database access but rather a large number of accesses in succession. For example, problems can occur with accesses that are executed in loops. Consequently, there is a range of checks that can find such loops. In particular, they include a check that finds SELECT statements that are executed in loops. As of AS ABAP 7.4, searches can also extend beyond modularization units. Consequently, the triggering part of the program for a SELECT statement can also be determined for complex implementations.

Change Database Accesses in Loops

For change operations, you should also favor array processing (see also Chapter 3, Section 3.2.2) over individual operations at all times, if possible. To this end, a check is available to find individual INSERT, UPDATE, or DELETE statements that are executed in loops.

EXIT/CHECK in SELECT… ENDSELECT loop

If you use EXIT to exit a SELECT… ENDSELECT loop, a large number of data records may be read unnecessarily because the data are transferred in blocks. A CHECK statement that immediately follows a SELECT statement indicates that a filter isn't used until the data has been read. Frequently, these two expressions can be converted into a suitable WHERE condition.

Configuring Check Variants

Default variants
You can configure check variants in Transaction SCI or in the ABAP Test Cockpit. SAP provides a range of default variants. Figure 7.2 shows the PERFORMANCE_DB check variant, which is available in AS ABAP 7.4. It provides a useful default configuration and contains the checks introduced in this section.

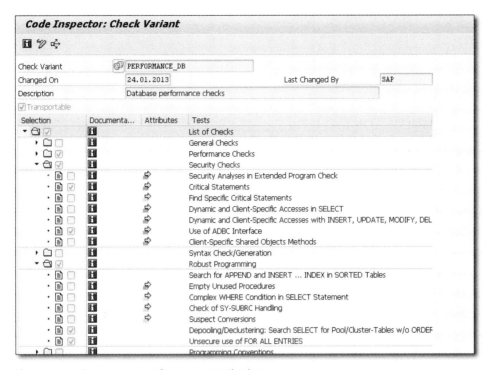

Figure 7.2 Code Inspector: Performance_DB Check Variant

However, you can also define custom check variants by selecting and configuring suitable checks from the directory tree. Furthermore, you can define check variants specifically for one system user or globally for all system users.

Configure custom variants

7.3.2 Checks in the Development Infrastructure

In this section, we'll explain how you, as the developer, can check individual objects. This enables you to perform a static code analysis before you release a new development or change to find errors before they are transported to a test system.

In the ABAP Workbench (Transaction SE80), you can use the context menu option, CHECK • ABAP TEST COCKPIT, to perform a check on a development object or package. The results are displayed in a list. From here, you can navigate to the relevant parts of the program (see Figure 7.3).

Code check in Transaction SE80

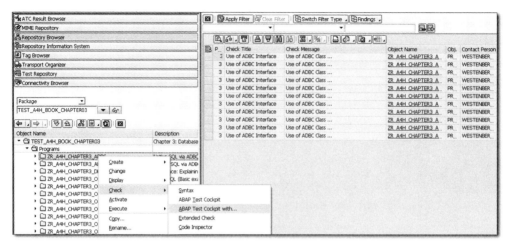

Figure 7.3 Code Check in Transaction SE80

Code check in Eclipse   The checks are also natively integrated into the ABAP Development Tools in Eclipse, which offers some advantages. Here, you use the context menu option, RUN AS • ABAP TEST COCKPIT, to start the check. Figure 7.4 shows the result of a check performed using the example from Listing 3.10 in Chapter 3, Section 3.2.2. The relevant parts of the program are highlighted clearly, and it's easy to navigate via the found locations.

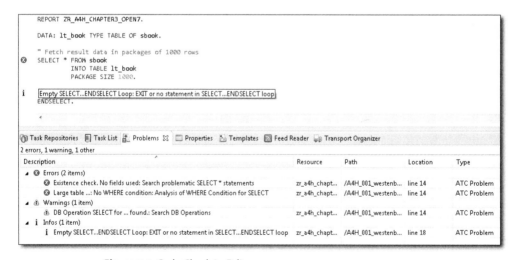

Figure 7.4 Code Check in Eclipse

The system default check variant is used first. However, you can use the project setting in Eclipse to replace the default variant with a custom variant, as shown in Figure 7.5.

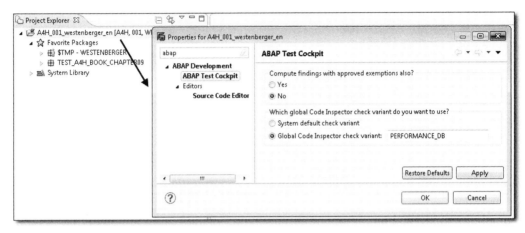

Figure 7.5 Selecting a Check Variant in Eclipse

7.3.3 Global Check Runs in the System

In the previous section, you learned how to check individual development objects or an entire development package. To ensure systematic use of such checks within a quality management process, it makes sense to perform the checks automatically at certain times for all developments (or selected parts) and to analyze the results.

In this section, we'll show you how to perform code checks in the *ABAP Test Cockpit*, which offers considerable advantages over the Code Inspector. You can manage the results of check runs, replicate them to other systems, manage exceptions, and automatically send results by email. Furthermore, the ABAP Test Cockpit is integrated into the ABAP Workbench (by means of a special browser) and into SAP Solution Manager.

Using the ABAP Test Cockpit

To start the ABAP Test Cockpit, call Transaction ATC. Here, you can configure the cockpit, schedule check runs, and analyze results. Figure 7.6 shows the initial screen for the transaction. You can use the SCHEDULE RUNS option to configure a check run. To do this, select a Code Inspector check variant and a set of objects. Figure 7.7 shows a configuration for the `PERFORMANCE_DB` variant (introduced in Section 7.3.1) checking the `TEST_A4H_BOOK*` packages, which contain examples from this book.

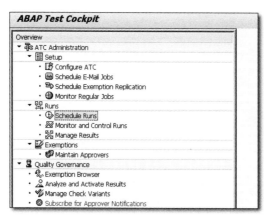

Figure 7.6 ABAP Test Cockpit: Initial Screen

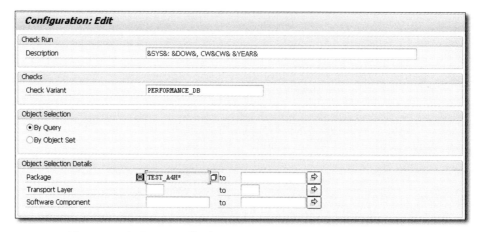

Figure 7.7 Configuring a Check Run

You can now schedule such a check run (either once or at specific times), which is then executed asynchronously in the background. You can then view the result under ANALYZE AND ACTIVATE RESULTS in the ABAP Test Cockpit or in the ATC RESULT BROWSER in the ABAP Workbench (see Figure 7.8). To do this, you may first have to activate this browser in the workbench settings for your user.

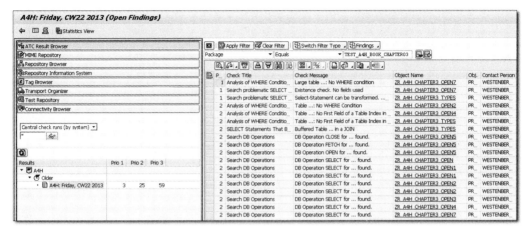

Figure 7.8 Result of an ABAP Test Cockpit Check Run in Transaction SE80

In Section 7.6, we'll show you how to merge the results of an ABAP Test Cockpit run with runtime data from the SQL Monitor for performance optimization.

7.4   Runtime Statistics and Traces

Runtime statistics and traces are used if a long-running program is already known, and you want to analyze its runtime behavior more closely. Runtime statistics provide you with an initial overview of where the time was consumed, that is, whether this time was consumed on the database or in the application server. The traces record the ABAP or SQL execution in detail and help you identify expensive statements, while the explain plan and PlanViz show in detail how a certain SQL statement was executed.

7.4.1   Runtime Statistics

In the SAP system, statistical data is collected and persisted for each *request*. Examples of a request include the execution of a program, dialog step, or Remote Function Call (RFC). These data are collected from the application server where the request is executed and are then written to the local file system. By default, the files are available for 48 hours before they are overwritten. These statistics include data about the overall runtime, CPU time, database time, and time associated with SAP locks, as well as other values (e.g., for memory usage).

Selection   After the program to be analyzed has been executed, you can select the statistical records in Transaction STAD. On the initial screen, you specify the required time frame. Note, however, that the statistic record isn't written until the request has been fully executed. You can also specify other filters here. Examples include the user name, program or transaction, task type (dialog, RFC, background, etc.), and different thresholds (e.g., minimum response time or minimum database time).

Analysis   The basic list (see Figure 7.9) contains some key performance indicators (KPIs) such as RESPONSE TIME, CPU TIME, and DB REQ. TIME (database request time).

When you double-click a statistical record in the basic list, further information appears in the detail display (see Figure 7.10 later in this section). Note the database-relevant topics such as response time (TIME), database time (DB), and database procedures and tables (DB PROCEDURES and TABLE).

SAP Workload: Single Statistical Records - Overview

Download ⊞ ⊞ ≜ ▲ ▼ ¥ ⊞Disp. mode ⊞Sel. fields ¥ Server ID ⊙

System: A4H   Number of RFCs which responded (without errors):   1 (1)
Analysed time: 28.06.2013 / 00:00:00 - 28.06.2013 / 23:50:00
Display mode: All statistic records, sorted by time

Started Server	Transaction	Program	T Scr. Wp	User	Response time (ms)	Time in WPs (ms)	Wait time (ms)	CPU time (ms)	DB req. time (ms)
	*	*	*	*	1.000			0	0
19:00:34 a4hhost_A4H_00	SE38	ZR_A4H_CHAPTER8_TOP_CUST_2	D 0120 7	SCHNEIDERTHO	23.030	23.030	0	10	2
19:31:17 a4hhost_A4H_00		RSAL_BATCH_TOOL_DISPATCHING	B 11	DDIC	30.293	30.293	0	230	50
19:35:17 a4hhost_A4H_00		RFC	R 3004 8	DDIC	1.192	1.192	0	890	344
19:35:17 a4hhost_A4H_00		SWNC_TCOLL_STARTER	B 12	DDIC	2.060	2.060	0	20	10
19:37:13 a4hhost_A4H_00	SE38	ZR_A4H_CHAPTER8_TOP_CUST_2	D 0120 2	SCHNEIDERTHO	23.468	23.468	0	0	1
19:39:19 a4hhost_A4H_00	SE38	ZR_A4H_CHAPTER8_TOP_CUST_1	D 0120 7	SCHNEIDERTHO	76.257	76.257	0	55.040	25.353
20:00:25 a4hhost_A4H_00	SE38	ZR_A4H_CHAPTER8_TOP_CUST_2	D 0120 9	SCHNEIDERTHO	22.930	22.930	0	0	2
20:24:01 a4hhost_A4H_00	SE38	ZR_A4H_CHAPTER8_TOP_CUST_2	D 0120 0	SCHNEIDERTHO	23.062	23.062	0	20	2
20:31:17 a4hhost_A4H_00		RSAL_BATCH_TOOL_DISPATCHING	B 12	DDIC	30.314	30.314	0	230	55
20:32:23 a4hhost_A4H_00	SE16	/1BCDWB/DBSPFLI	D 1000 1	SCHNEIDERTHO	1.163	33	0	30	8
20:35:17 a4hhost_A4H_00		SWNC_TCOLL_STARTER	B 12	DDIC	2.065	2.064	1	20	10
21:31:17 a4hhost_A4H_00		RSAL_BATCH_TOOL_DISPATCHING	B 11	DDIC	30.315	30.314	1	230	57
21:35:17 a4hhost_A4H_00		SWNC_TCOLL_STARTER	B 12	DDIC	2.058	2.057	1	20	11
21:38:21 a4hhost_A4H_00	SE24	SEO_STARTUP	D 0200 1	SCHNEIDERTHO	1.387	70	1	50	21
21:54:47 a4hhost_A4H_00	SE16	/1BCDWB/DBSBOOK	D 1000 3	GAHM	637.030	637.030	0	401.800	40.290
22:04:43 a4hhost_A4H_00	STAD	RSSTAT26	D 0120 4	GAHM	2.105	2.105	0	2.090	3
22:05:14 a4hhost_A4H_00	STAD	RSSTAT26	D 0120 9	GAHM	2.187	2.187	0	2.190	0
22:05:33 a4hhost_A4H_00	STAD	RSSTAT26	D 0120 4	GAHM	2.088	2.088	0	2.080	0

Figure 7.9 Basic List in Transaction STAD

Times

Table 7.3 lists the components of the RESPONSE TIME. For SAP HANA, the database time and the time for database procedures are of particular interest.

For the most part, the CPU time is generally consumed during the processing time. However, it also occurs in all of the other time components listed in Table 7.3. RFC+CPIC TIME (Figure 7.10) is the time associated with RFCs. It's consumed during the *processing* or *roll-in* and *roll wait time*, depending on whether or not the work process was rolled out. The upper half of the screen shown in Figure 7.10 contains a detailed analysis of the individual times.

Time	Explanation
WAIT FOR WORK PROCESS	Time spent waiting for a work process to become available (in the dispatcher queue).
PROCESSING TIME	Uses the response time as the basis for calculating all other times named here. Generally contains the time associated with ABAP processing and CPU consumption, but also wait times (e.g., RFC time, update time, and roll wait time) if the work process isn't rolled out.
LOAD TIME	Time taken to load programs.
GENERATING TIME	Time taken to generate programs.
ROLL (IN+WAIT) TIME	Times when the work process was rolled out and the time for the subsequent roll-in (loading of the user context).
DATABASE REQUEST TIME	Time consumed for database accesses (Open SQL and Native SQL).
ENQUEUE TIME	Time for lock requests in relation to the SAP enqueue service.
DB PROCEDURE CALL TIME	Time taken to call database procedures (e.g., CALL DATABASE PROCEDURE, see Chapter 5, Section 5.2.3), or AMDP.

Table 7.3 Time Components in Transaction STAD

Database Times

Access times   In the DB view, the DATABASE REQUEST TIME is broken down further. Here, you see how the database time is divided into different access types (READ, INSERT, UPDATE, DELETE). For each access type, you see how many rows were processed and how much time was needed to process them. The lower half of Figure 7.10 contains detailed information about the database.

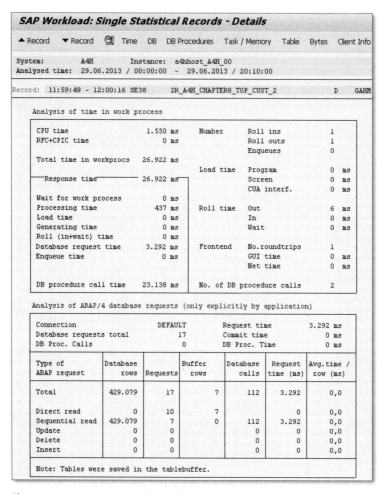

Figure 7.10 Transaction STAD: DB View Details

[«]

Useful Parameters for Transaction STAD

You can use the stat/max_files parameter to extend the default analysis time frame of 48 hours up to 99 hours. The detailed data introduced here at the table and database procedure level are displayed only if the two stat/tabrec and stat/dbprocrec parameters are set to values greater than zero. You can use the following path in Transaction ST03 to change these parameters dynamically for a specific time frame: COLLECTOR & PERF. DB • STATISTIC RECORDS AND FILE • ONLINE PARAMETERS • DIALOG STEP STATISTICS.

Database Procedures and Tables

In the DB PROCEDURES and TABLE views, you see those database procedures and tables that required the most time. The maximum number of procedures and tables displayed here is configured in the stat/dbprocrec and stat/tabrec profile parameters.

The following information is displayed for each procedure: the name of the procedure, the database connection, the number of calls, and the time (see Figure 7.11).

DB procedures (list might be incomplete!)

DB procedure	Log. DB connection	No. of exec.	Exec. time (ms)	Time / exec. (ms)
"_SYS_BIC"."test.a4h.book.chap	R/3	1	23.137	23.137,0
GET_OBJECT_VERSION	R/3	1	1	1,0

Figure 7.11 Transaction STAD: DB Procedures View

For tables or views, you see the name of the table (or view), the number of data records processed, and the time required (see Figure 7.12).

Table accesses (list might be incomplete!)

	Number of rows accessed				
Table name	Total	Dir. reads	Seq. reads	Changes	Time (ms)
TOTAL	429.079	0	429.079	0	3.292
SBOOK	429.079	0	429.079	0	3.292
AAB_ID_ACT	0	0	0	0	0
VARID	0	0	0	0	0

Figure 7.12 Transaction STAD: Table Details

[»] **Alternative Interface for Statistic Data**

In Transaction STATS, the functionality described previously is available in a modernized interface. Transaction STATS doesn't make any measurements; it only displays the statistical data recorded by the kernel.

The SAP List Viewer (ALV) is used in the basic list of the transaction. You thus have various options, for example, for sorting, grouping, or summarizing. The display of the details also varies slightly. For example, the data are grouped by various criteria, such as times, database, storage, and so on. For times, the hierarchical presentation helps you easily identify the times that are contained in other times.

7.4.2 ABAP Trace and ABAP Profiler

The *ABAP trace* (Transaction SAT) is a powerful runtime analysis tool for ABAP applications and, as of SAP NetWeaver Release 7.02, it's the successor to Transaction SE30. Based on this infrastructure, its new interface (the *ABAP profiler*) forms part of the ABAP development environment in Eclipse. The interface provides developers with a clear results overview, including a graphical representation. In this section, we'll discuss both variants.

ABAP Trace

Configuration and recording
To record the ABAP trace, a measurement variant is configured first, and then the trace is recorded. In a measurement variant, you define the following:

▶ The type of recording and its length (DURATION AND TYPE tab page)

▶ What will be recorded (STATEMENTS tab page, see Figure 7.13)

You then use the configured measurement variant to execute the program that will perform the recording.

Analysis
To perform an analysis, double-click a trace on the ANALYZE tab page. Four or six views are available for analysis, depending on whether the trace was created with or without aggregation. All of the views are linked to each other. In other words, you can open the context menu for an event in one view and display that event in another view.

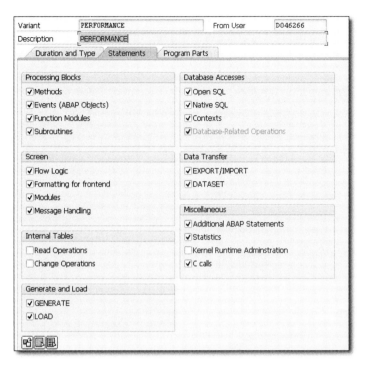

Figure 7.13 Measurement Variant in the ABAP Trace

The following views are available:

▶ HIT LIST
Displays all trace events with details about the number of calls, gross time, and net time. The gross time roughly corresponds to the TOTAL TIME, while the net time corresponds to the OWN TIME associated with the ABAP profiler (see Figure 7.17 later in this section).

▶ DB TABLES
Displays all accesses to database tables and corresponds to the DATABASE ACCESSES view in the ABAP profiler (see Figure 7.20 later in this section).

▶ PROFILE
Displays the events according to different profiles. The following views are available for selection: EVENTS, PACKAGES, COMPONENTS, and PROGRAMS.

▶ PROCESSING BLOCKS

Displays an interactive, hierarchical representation of events with details about the gross and net times. The various levels of the call hierarchy can be analyzed arbitrarily. An automatic analysis that displays critical processing blocks is also available here. For example, all modularization units that occupy more than 5% of the net time are highlighted.

▶ CALL HIERARCHY

Displays the events with details about the call level, gross time, and net time.

▶ TIMES

Displays a detailed list of events whereby the time is further subdivided into components such as database time, database interface time, time for internal tables, and so on.

ABAP Profiler

Recording options   In this section, we'll show you how to use the ABAP profiler in Eclipse to create an ABAP runtime analysis.

If you want to use the ABAP profiler to create a trace, choose the PROFILE icon ⬛ ▾ (see Figure 7.14), which starts a trace with default settings.

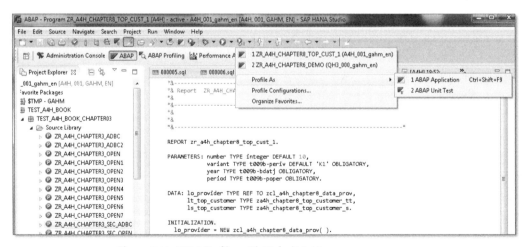

Figure 7.14 ABAP Profiler with Default Settings

In the dropdown menu for the profile icon, you can use the PROFILE CONFIGURATIONS menu option to select some recording options. To do this, make the necessary settings on the TRACING tab page, and click the PROFILE button to confirm your entries (see Figure 7.15).

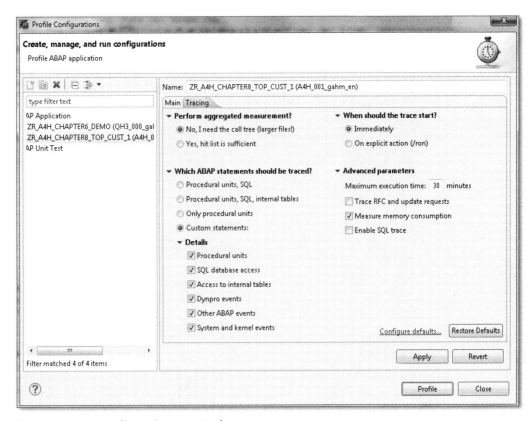

Figure 7.15 ABAP Profiler with a Trace Configuration

The basic settings are summarized in Table 7.4.

Category	Setting	Explanation
When?	WHEN SHOULD THE TRACE START (IMMEDIATELY/ON EXPLICIT ACTION [/RON])?	Defines whether the trace is to be started immediately or only when an explicit action is performed.

Table 7.4 Settings for the ABAP Profiler

Category	Setting	Explanation
How?	PERFORM AGGREGATED MEASUREMENT (YES/NO)?	Defines the level of detail for the recording. This setting has a major impact on the trace scope. The call hierarchy isn't available for an aggregated measurement (see Figure 7.18 later in this section).
What?	WHICH ABAP STATEMENT SHOULD BE TRACED?	Determines which calls are to be traced: ▸ PROCEDURAL UNITS, SQL ▸ PROCEDURAL UNITS, SQL, INTERNAL TABLES ▸ ONLY PROCEDURAL UNITS ▸ CUSTOM STATEMENTS
Additional parameters	ADVANCED PARAMETERS	Determines the following additional settings: ▸ MAXIMUM EXECUTION TIME ▸ TRACE RFCs AND UPDATE REQUESTS ▸ MEASURE MEMORY CONSUMPTION ▸ ENABLE SQL TRACE

Table 7.4 Settings for the ABAP Profiler (Cont.)

Trace analysis

If you want to analyze a trace you've created, switch to the ABAP PROFILING perspective. In the lower screen area, update the list on the ABAP TRACES tab page. The system then displays a list of trace files. Double-click to open your trace.

An overview screen is displayed. In the GENERAL INFORMATION area of the screen, you can see what was recorded, and when, where, and how it was recorded. The ANALYSIS TOOLS area contains different detail views, which we'll explain in greater detail next. Finally, the RUNTIME DISTRIBUTION area provides an initial overview of the runtime. A graphical representation of the amount of time consumed for ABAP statements is shown (e.g., processing of internal tables, the database [Open SQL, etc.], and the system [e.g., loading processes]). Figure 7.16 shows a representation of a trace in the ABAP profiler. The overview area shows you the overall runtime and how it's distributed between the database and application server.

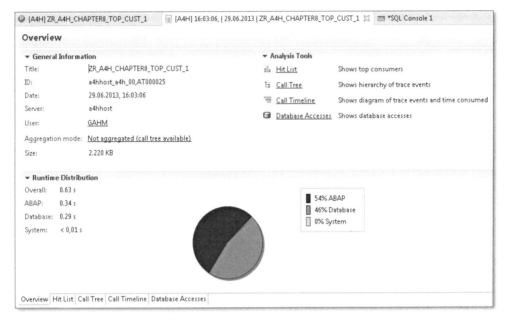

Figure 7.16 ABAP Profiler Initial Screen

We'll now explain the different detail views available, starting with the Hit List view shown in Figure 7.17. All recorded trace events are displayed in the HIT LIST, which is sorted in descending order according to OWN TIME, that is, the time consumed by the relevant event itself. This time excludes calls that were called within the event and that were subsequently measured. The TOTAL TIME, on the other hand, includes all calls and specifies the total amount of time consumed by the event itself and the calls executed by the event.

Detail views

The HIT LIST view also shows you the frequency with which an event was executed and the program in which it was called. For calls concerning modularization units, you see which program was called. If you sort this list according to the OWN TIME column, you see the most expensive executions associated with the statements recorded. If you sort this list according to the TOTAL TIME, you see the most expensive modularization units in the program.

Hit List view

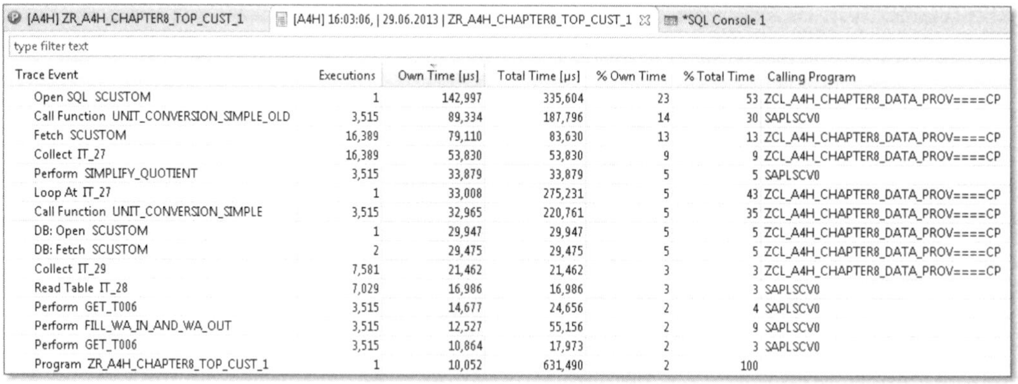

[A4H] ZR_A4H_CHAPTER8_TOP_CUST_1
[A4H] 16:03:06, | 29.06.2013 | ZR_A4H_CHAPTER8_TOP_CUST_1
*SQL Console 1
type filter text
Trace Event | Executions | Own Time [µs] | Total Time [µs] | % Own Time | % Total Time | Calling Program
Open SQL SCUSTOM | 1 | 142,997 | 335,604 | 23 | 53 | ZCL_A4H_CHAPTER8_DATA_PROV====CP
Call Function UNIT_CONVERSION_SIMPLE_OLD | 3,515 | 89,334 | 187,796 | 14 | 30 | SAPLSCV0
Fetch SCUSTOM | 16,389 | 79,110 | 83,630 | 13 | 13 | ZCL_A4H_CHAPTER8_DATA_PROV====CP
Collect IT_27 | 16,389 | 53,830 | 53,830 | 9 | 9 | ZCL_A4H_CHAPTER8_DATA_PROV====CP
Perform SIMPLIFY_QUOTIENT | 3,515 | 33,879 | 33,879 | 5 | 5 | SAPLSCV0
Loop At IT_27 | 1 | 33,008 | 275,231 | 5 | 43 | ZCL_A4H_CHAPTER8_DATA_PROV====CP
Call Function UNIT_CONVERSION_SIMPLE | 3,515 | 32,965 | 220,761 | 5 | 35 | ZCL_A4H_CHAPTER8_DATA_PROV====CP
DB: Open SCUSTOM | 1 | 29,947 | 29,947 | 5 | 5 | ZCL_A4H_CHAPTER8_DATA_PROV====CP
DB: Fetch SCUSTOM | 2 | 29,475 | 29,475 | 5 | 5 | ZCL_A4H_CHAPTER8_DATA_PROV====CP
Collect IT_29 | 7,581 | 21,462 | 21,462 | 3 | 3 | ZCL_A4H_CHAPTER8_DATA_PROV====CP
Read Table IT_28 | 7,029 | 16,986 | 16,986 | 3 | 3 | SAPLSCV0
Perform GET_T006 | 3,515 | 14,677 | 24,656 | 2 | 4 | SAPLSCV0
Perform FILL_WA_IN_AND_WA_OUT | 3,515 | 12,527 | 55,156 | 2 | 9 | SAPLSCV0
Perform GET_T006 | 3,515 | 10,864 | 17,973 | 2 | 3 | SAPLSCV0
Program ZR_A4H_CHAPTER8_TOP_CUST_1 | 1 | 10,052 | 631,490 | 2 | 100

Figure 7.17 ABAP Profiler: Hit List View

Call hierarchy

The *call hierarchy* (also known as the CALL TREE; see Figure 7.18) displays statements in a hierarchy. In other words, you see which statements were called at which level in the call hierarchy. Statements that occur directly within a modularization unit are hidden initially. However, you can choose SHOW to display them. The ALL STATEMENTS WITHIN row specifies the duration of those statements that weren't recorded separately. These times are included in OWN TIME for the modularization unit selected.

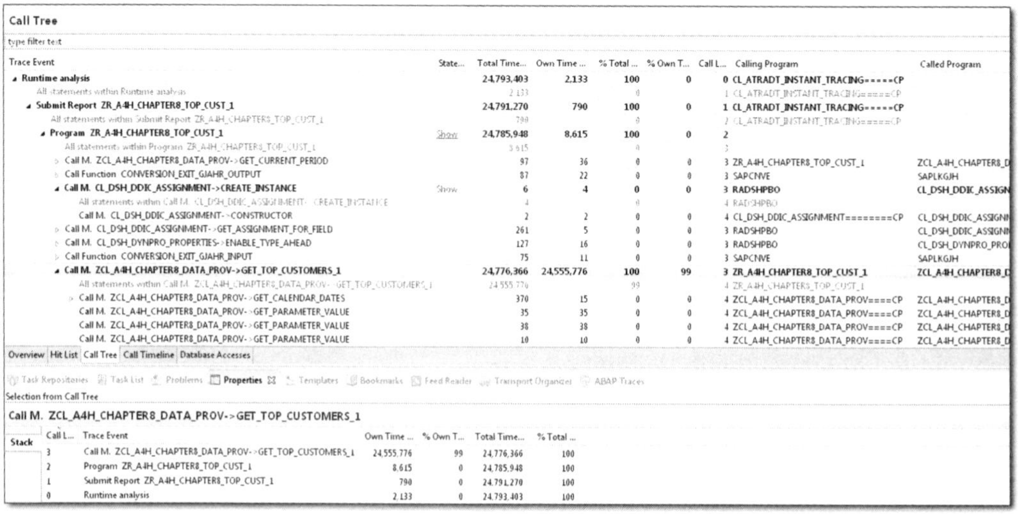

Call Tree
type filter text
Trace Event | State... | Total Time... | Own Time ... | % Total ... | % Own T... | Call L... | Calling Program | Called Program
Runtime analysis | 24,793,403 | 2,133 | 100 | 0 | 0 CL_ATRADT_INSTANT_TRACING=====CP
Submit Report ZR_A4H_CHAPTER8_TOP_CUST_1 | 24,791,270 | 790 | 100 | 0 | 1 CL_ATRADT_INSTANT_TRACING=====CP
Program ZR_A4H_CHAPTER8_TOP_CUST_1 | Show | 24,785,948 | 8,615 | 100 | 0 | 2
Call M. CL_DSH_DDIC_ASSIGNMENT->CREATE_INSTANCE
Call M. ZCL_A4H_CHAPTER8_DATA_PROV->GET_TOP_CUSTOMERS_1 | 24,776,366 | 24,555,776 | 100 | 99 | 3 ZR_A4H_CHAPTER8_TOP_CUST_1
Overview | Hit List | Call Tree | Call Timeline | Database Accesses
Selection from Call Tree
Call M. ZCL_A4H_CHAPTER8_DATA_PROV->GET_TOP_CUSTOMERS_1
Stack | Call L... | Trace Event | Own Time ... | % Own T... | Total Time... | % Total ...
3 | Call M. ZCL_A4H_CHAPTER8_DATA_PROV->GET_TOP_CUSTOMERS_1 | 24,555,776 | 99 | 24,776,366 | 100
2 | Program ZR_A4H_CHAPTER8_TOP_CUST_1 | 8,615 | 0 | 24,785,948 | 100
1 | Submit Report ZR_A4H_CHAPTER8_TOP_CUST_1 | 790 | 0 | 24,791,270 | 100
0 | Runtime analysis | 2,133 | 0 | 24,793,403 | 100

Figure 7.18 ABAP Profiler: Call Hierarchy

The CALL TIMELINE view displays the call hierarchy in the form of a time-line (see Figure 7.19). Each call is displayed as a horizontal bar whose length corresponds to the call duration. Calls made within a call are displayed below this bar. The depth of the call hierarchy (known as the *call stack*) is shown from top to bottom. These bars are color-coded according to the call type, thus making it possible for you to identify items immediately (e.g., database calls). You can use the black square in the lower area of the graphic to maximize or minimize the area shown. If you move the mouse over a bar, a dialog box displays information about the event, TOTAL TIME, and OWN TIME. When you right-click a bar, you can execute the following actions:

Call Timeline view

▶ Navigate to the same event in the hit list.

▶ Display the call stack for this event.

▶ Display the event in the database accesses.

▶ Navigate to the call point in the ABAP program.

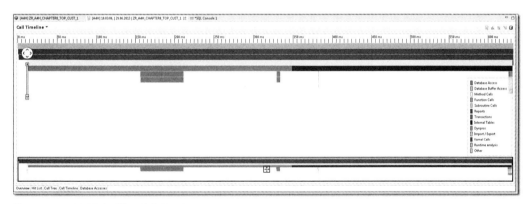

Figure 7.19 ABAP Profiler: Call Timeline

You can also adjust the color-coding used in the diagram.

The DATABASE ACCESSES view shows you which tables were accessed using which statements (see Figure 7.20). Here, you see the number of executions (divided into database accesses and table buffer accesses) and

Database Accesses view

the time required. You also obtain information about the table type, a short description, and the package to which the table is assigned.

Table Name	SQL Statement	Access Type	Executions	Buffered Acce...	Positions	Total Time [µs]	% Tota...	Buffer Settings	Table T...	Short Text	Package
SCUSTOM	select	OpenSQL	1	0	1	281,774	44	Single Entries bu	TRANSP	Flight customers	SAPBC_DATAMODEL
SCUSTOM	select single	OpenSQL	10	10	1	5,390	1	Single Entries bu	TRANSP	Flight customers	SAPBC_DATAMODEL
<DB Time of S			0	0	0	2,464	0				
<DB Access fr			2	0	0	134	0				
ZA4H_C8_PAR	select single	OpenSQL	4	4	1	105	0	Entirely buffered	TRANSP	Parameters for miles calcula	TEST_A4H_BOOK_CHAPTER8
T006	select single	OpenSQL	2	2	1	84	0	Generically buffe	TRANSP	Units of Measurement	SZME
T009Y	select	OpenSQL	1	1	1	79	0	Generically buffe	TRANSP	Shortened fiscal years in Ass	SFBX
T006D	select	OpenSQL	1	1	1	44	0	Entirely buffered	TRANSP	Dimensions	SZME
T009	select single	OpenSQL	1	1	1	34	0	Entirely buffered	TRANSP	Fiscal Year Variants	SFBX
T006A	select single	OpenSQL	1	1	1	26	0	Generically buffe	TRANSP	Assign Internal to Language	SZME

Figure 7.20 ABAP Profiler: Database Accesses

7.4.3 SQL Trace

Transaction ST05 contains various functions, one of which—the SQL trace—we want to examine in greater detail. In Chapter 3, we used the SQL trace to explain how Open SQL is translated to Native SQL statements. In this section, we'll explain how to use the SQL trace as a runtime analysis tool.

Recording

On the main screen, select SQL TRACE as the TRACE TYPE. On the right-hand side of the screen, you can also activate a stack trace recording, which enables you to record not only the SQL statement itself, but also information about the call stack. To record an SQL trace, choose ACTIVATE TRACE or ACTIVATE TRACE WITH FILTER. With the first option, the trace is activated for your user. With the second option, you can activate the trace with different filters. Figure 7.21 shows the trace recording with filter options. Execute the desired program upon activating the trace recording. Choose DEACTIVATE TRACE as soon as the program ends.

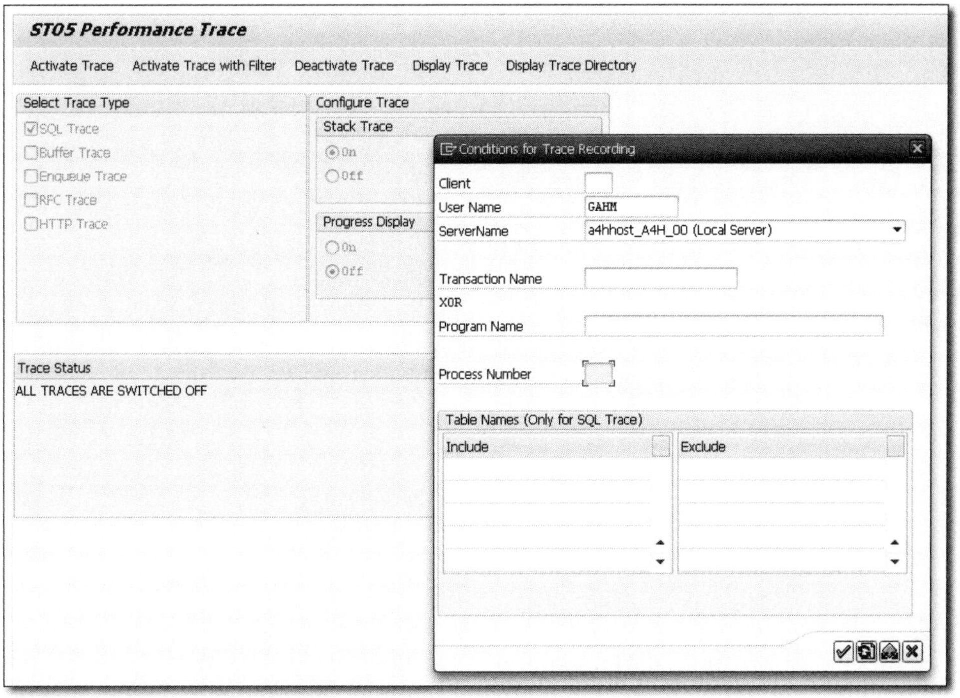

Figure 7.21 Trace Recording in Transaction ST05

Analysis

To display the trace, choose DISPLAY TRACE. In the next dialog box, the filters are predefined in accordance with the settings for the recording. In other words, you generally don't have to change anything here if you want to display the trace immediately after the recording. However, if you want to display the trace at a later time, or you want to display a trace associated with another user, you must ensure the following:

▸ You're logged on to the server on which the trace was saved.

▸ The filters for the user and time frame correspond to those for the trace recording.

You can choose between different views by clicking the relevant icon on the icon bar (see Figure 7.22).

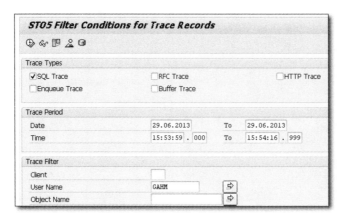

Figure 7.22 Displaying the SQL Trace

The following views are available for selection:

▶ SUMMARIZED STATEMENTS
An SQL statement corresponds to a row in the trace. In other words, detailed information such as OPEN, FETCH, and CLOSE are aggregated into one row. From this list, you can navigate to a list of detailed statements, a list of identical statements, or an aggregated view for each table.

▶ DETAILED STATEMENTS
All of the calls that were sent to the database are shown here. An SQL statement is displayed, for example, in an OPEN statement, one or more FETCH statements, or a CLOSE statement.

▶ STRUCTURE-IDENTICAL SUMMARY
All SQL statements with an identical structure are summarized here. Therefore, if there are similar SQL statements at different call points within a program, these are displayed in aggregated form.

▶ TRACE OVERVIEW
A summary of the entire SQL trace is shown here.

▶ SAVE
In addition, a function is available for saving the SQL trace in the database.

Next, we'll show you the structure-identical summary and an analysis of the call hierarchy (*stack trace*).

First, display the structure-identical statements (see Figure 7.23). We recommend that you start your analysis with this list because it provides the best overview of the most expensive SQL statements. You see which statement had the longest duration overall, the frequency with which it was executed, and whether there were redundant accesses (known as *identical selects*). This information is made available to you both in absolute figures and as a percentage.

Structure-identical statements

You also see all execution times (for each execution and data record), and the number of data records—both in total and for each execution. Finally, you obtain buffering information from the ABAP Data Dictionary (DDIC; see Figure 7.23).

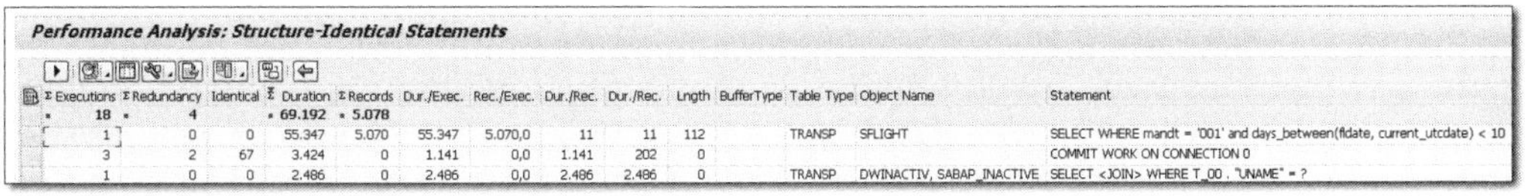

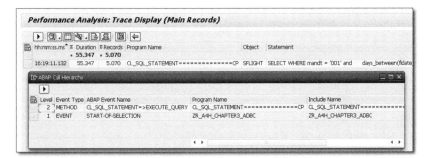

Figure 7.23 Structure-Identical Statements

If you double-click the number of executions, you branch to a list of summarized statements in which one row corresponds to one execution. You can display the call hierarchy for this execution. The ABAP call stack for this statement is then displayed in a dialog box (see Figure 7.24). This function is very helpful in the case of ADBC calls, for example. The SQL statement is executed first in the ADBC classes, while the actual execution occurs at a higher level in the call stack. The stack trace enables you to navigate to any level within the call stack. To do this, double-click the relevant row.

Stack trace

Figure 7.24 Call Hierarchy for an SQL Statement

353

Identical selects

If you want to display identical selects from within the list of summarized statements, select the menu option, TRACE • VALUE-IDENTICAL STATEMENTS. Here, you see those statements that are executed repeatedly in the WHERE condition with exactly the same values. You also see their duration and the number of data records that were read.

Statement details

If you double-click the text for a SQL statement contained in the list of summarized statements, you see the entire statement as well as the parameters used to execute the statement.

[!] **Overwriting Trace Data**

The SQL trace is a part of the database interface and is therefore specific to a particular application server. The trace itself is written to files on the relevant application server. These files have a size restriction. Therefore, if all of the files are full, the first file is overwritten again. If traces are very large, data may be overwritten in this way. If this situation arises, you're notified in Transaction ST05 that some files may have been overwritten. You can also save the contents of the files to the database before they are overwritten.

7.4.4 Single Transaction Analysis

Transaction ST12 combines Transactions SAT, ST05, and STAD into one interface and, thanks to this combination, offers some advantages in terms of recording and analyzing traces during performance analysis.

Requirements

Transaction ST12 is an additional development within the context of service tools for applications (ST-A/PI). SAP Active Global Support (AGS) makes this software available as an add-on, and SAP Note 69455 explains how to obtain and import this software. This software package doesn't form part of the standard SAP delivery. It isn't formally documented and is only available in English. AGS originally developed Transaction ST12 for its own use within the context of the services it offers. Essentially, however, all SAP customers can use this transaction.

Advantages

The following advantages are associated with combining the various transactions into one interface:

▸ During an analysis, the ABAP trace and SQL trace can be activated together and then deactivated. If you don't know which application server is associated with a particular request, you can start the recording on all application servers simultaneously.

▶ The trace data and the data from Transaction STAD are collected and stored in the database, thus making subsequent analyses easier because all the data is stored in one central location and is no longer overwritten.

▶ The trace data can be combined with other data. For example, in the ABAP trace for a SELECT statement, you can display related data from Transaction ST05. For data from Transaction ST05, you can specify which percentage of the overall runtime can be attributed to a SELECT statement. You can also call the Code Inspector for individual results.

▶ In the case of ABAP traces, additional functions (which aren't possible in Transaction SAT) are available for analyzing aggregated traces. For example, it's possible to draw conclusions about call hierarchies.

If you perform a large number of performance analyses, single transaction analysis can offer some advantages over the standard delivery. Further information is available in SAP Note 7559777 and in the SCN at *http://wiki.sdn.sap.com/wiki/display/ABAP/Single+Transaction+Analysis.*

7.4.5 Explain Plan

The *explain plan* is a database function that can be used to display an execution plan, which is a textual or graphical description of how an SQL statement was executed. The database optimizer always creates this description when the function is executed. The decision made by the optimizer is based on the system status at the time the plan was created.

You can call the explain plan from various locations (e.g., in the SQL trace in Transaction ST05 or in the EXPENSIVE STATEMENTS or SQL CACHE areas in Transaction DBACOCKPIT). This function is also available in SAP HANA Studio. Here, for example, the explain plan is available in the SQL console.

To call the execution plan in SAP HANA Studio, enter an SQL statement in the SQL console, and right-click to select the EXPLAIN PLAN function in the context menu for the statement.

Calling the execution plan in SAP HANA Studio

From an analysis perspective, the following columns are of interest:

▶ OPERATOR_NAME
Name of the operation executed (e.g., access to a column table, row table, or join).

▶ OPERATOR_DETAILS
Additional information about the operation (e.g., filter or join conditions).

▶ TABLE_NAME
Name of the database object referenced by the operator.

▶ EXECUTION_ENGINE
The engine that executes the operator.

▶ SCHEMA_NAME
Name of the database schema.

▶ TABLE_TYPE
The type of table used (e.g., column table, row table, OLAP view, calculation view, etc.).

▶ TABLE_SIZE
Estimated size of the table for this step (the number of rows for column tables, or the number of pages for row tables).

▶ OUTPUT_SIZE
Estimated number of rows for the result set associated with this step.

A sample execution plan output is shown in Figure 7.25.

Figure 7.25 Explain Plan in SAP HANA Studio

A graphical variant of the execution plan is also available. In the execution plan, you can see how an SQL statement is executed (in particular, which engine is responsible for which parts of the execution). If you require a more in-depth look at the execution details, you can use Plan-Viz (see the next section).

7.4.6 SAP HANA Plan Visualizer

SAP HANA Plan Visualizer (PlanViz) provides a graphical representation of an SQL statement or database procedure execution. You can also execute the statement and collect runtime data here if you have the required permissions.

If you want to use PlanViz to analyze an SQL statement or procedure, open the SQL console in SAP HANA Studio, and insert the statement (or procedure) that you want to analyze. Choose VISUALIZE PLAN • EXECUTE in the context menu for the SQL console. If the SQL statement contains parameters, the PREPARED SQL tab page is displayed after you choose EXECUTE. Specify the necessary input parameters here. The return parameter fields are left blank. Then, choose the EXECUTE icon 🔾 ▾ at the upper-right of the screen. Runtime data are collected internally and presented in a graphic on the EXECUTION tab page after the query has ended.

Recording

In the PlanViz perspective, the OVERVIEW tab provides an overview of the execution. You can determine how much time was required for compilation and execution. Below that area, you can view the operators that required the most time. Additionally, you can find information on distributed execution (if available), the data flow, number of tables involved, maximum number of processed rows, and the number of results rows. The STATEMENT STATISTICS tab provides further KPIs from the SQL cache on the executed SQL statements.

Analysis

You can run a detailed analysis on the EXECUTED PLAN tab. Here, you see nodes (known as *plan operators* in technical terms), which are connected to each other by arrows. These, in turn, represent the flow of data from one node to another. The volume of data actually transferred is displayed at the arrow itself, The nodes also contain additional information about tables, columns, filters, execution times, and CPU times. You can use the icon displayed on the upper-right border of a node ▶ to open the relevant node. If you move the mouse over a node in the main screen, a dialog box opens to reveal detailed information that has been recorded for the node. Depending on the node, this box contains different values, such as the execution time and CPU time, and information about tables, columns, and filters.

The following section describes detailed analyses using the following tools: TIMELINE, TABLES USED, and OPERATOR LIST.

Timeline tool   The TIMELINE is a very helpful tool because you can see the call sequence and duration of database operations. To display this tool (or any of the other tools), choose WINDOW • SHOW VIEW • OTHER, select TIMELINE (or the other tools) under SAP HANA PLANVIZ, and choose OK to confirm your entry.

In the TIMELINE, each node is displayed as a bar, and the length of the bar corresponds to the runtime for that particular node. You therefore easily see the start time, runtime, and end time associated with executing the node. You also see which nodes were processed parallel to one other.

Tables Used tool   The TABLES USED tool shows all the tables used, the maximum number of processed data records for each table (possibly added up using various operators), the number of accesses, and the time required for each table. This view also shows temporary tables that can contain interim results.

Operator List tool   The OPERATOR LIST shows the individual operators of the execution plan in a list, which you can filter, sort, and aggregate. This tool is very useful if there isn't one time-consuming operator but many different time consumers. For example, you can determine the operators that process the most data and subsequently check whether more filters can be applied.

Analyzing a Database Procedure

Finally, we'll show you how to analyze a database procedure. using the sample procedure `DETERMINE_TOP_CONNECTIONS`, which you learned about in Chapter 5, Section 5.2.3. Three additional procedures, namely `DETERMINE_TOP_CONNECTIONS`, `GET_KPIS_FOR_CONNECTIONS`, and `GET_AGENCIES_FOR_CONNECTIONS`, are called within this procedure.

To analyze the main procedure, enter the following call in the SQL console (note that `'001'` stands for the client; if you use a different client, please change this entry accordingly):

```
call "test.a4h.book.chapter05::GET_DATA_FOR_TOP_
CONNECTIONS"('001', 'LH', ?, ?)
```

Choose VISUALIZE PLAN • EXECUTE in the context menu for the SQL console. Click on EXECUTE in the context menu of the EXECUTED PLAN tab. The analysis starts on the OVERVIEW tab (see Figure 7.26).

In the top-left area, you can view the times for execution and compilation. Under that, you find the most expensive operators and information on distributed execution (in this case, it isn't distributed because NUMBER OF NODES = 1). On the right-hand side of the screen, you find information on the data flow.

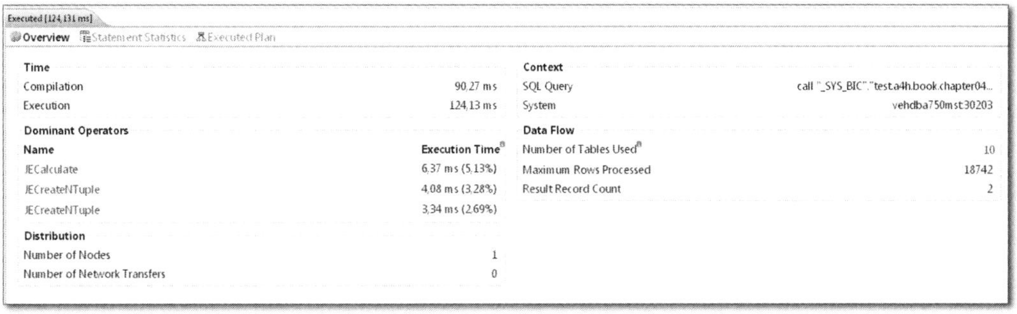

Executed [124.131 ms]				
⊚ Overview ≣Statement Statistics 吕 Executed Plan				
Time			**Context**	
Compilation		90.27 ms	SQL Query	call "_SYS_BIC"."test.a4h.book.chapter04...
Execution		124.13 ms	System	vehdba750mst30203
Dominant Operators			**Data Flow**	
Name		Execution Time	Number of Tables Used	10
JECalculate		6.37 ms (5.13%)	Maximum Rows Processed	18742
JECreateNTuple		4.08 ms (3.28%)	Result Record Count	2
JECreateNTuple		3.34 ms (2.69%)		
Distribution				
Number of Nodes		1		
Number of Network Transfers		0		

Figure 7.26 PlanViz: Overview

The TABLES USED tool (see Figure 7.27) shows the database tables `SFLIGHT`, `STRAVELAG`, and `SBOOK`, which are used in the procedure. In addition, some temporary tables were required for processing the procedure. You can see the number of accesses to the tables, how many data records were processed, and how much time was consumed.

Tables Used tool

In the TIMELINE tool (see Figure 7.28), you can analyze the runtime of the individual steps and operators in more detail. Here you can see that the first node is a CALCULATION NODE that contains a ceLJitPop, which in turn contains another node to our `DETERMINE_TOP_CONNECTIONS` procedure. If you click on this node in the TIMELINE, the system directly navigates to the respective node in the top area of the screen. In the detail

Timeline tool

view (the yellow dialog box that appears if you move the mouse over this node), you ascertain that it concerns the `DETERMINE_TOP_CONNECTIONS` procedure, whose runtime is 18 milliseconds (see Figure 7.28).

Timeline | Operator List | Tables Used | Performance Trace | Network

Showing 10 item(s)

Table Name	Max. Entries Processed	Number of Accesses	Max. Processing Time
SAPH74.SFLIGHT	94	8	1
SAPH74.0x00007f342f906580:2:0:#400000004d12292	5	1	0
SAPH74.vehdba750mst:30203:COL_0x7f350da2a4c00...	5	1	0
SAPH74.STRAVELAG	4	2	1
SAPH74.SBOOK	18.742	15	6
SAPH74.IT_0x00007f342f913f40:2:0	5	1	0
SAPH74.0x00007f342f913f40:2:0:#400000004d122aa	5	1	0
SAPH74.IT_0x00007f350da2a4c0:2:0	5	1	0
SAPH74.Temporary Table(s)	5	6	0
SAPH74.0x00007f350da2a4c0:2:0:#400000004d122c3	5	1	0

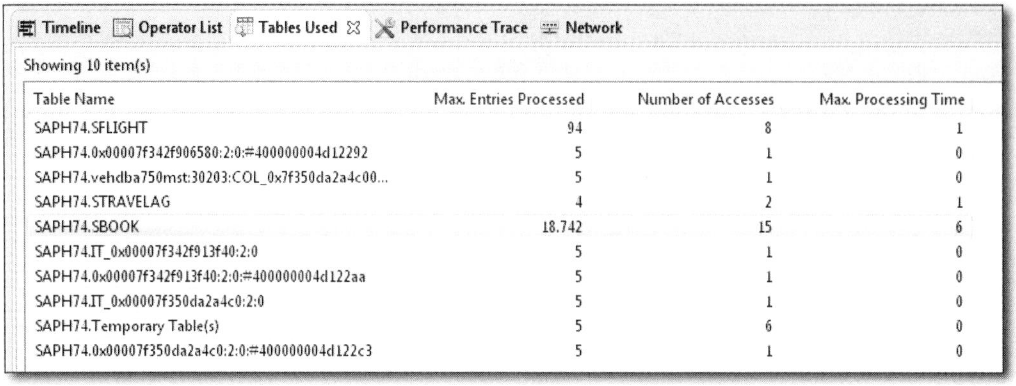

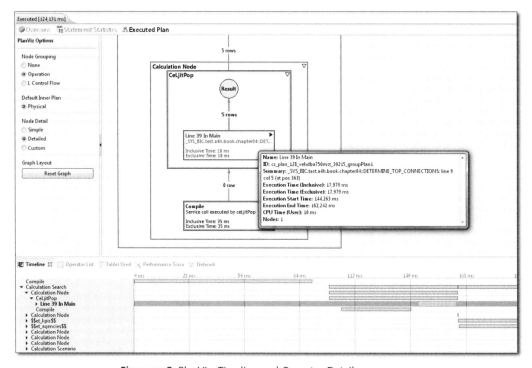

Figure 7.27 Plan Viz: Tables Used

Figure 7.28 PlanViz: Timeline und Operator Details

After this procedure is completed, the results are transferred to two additional nodes that run parallel to one other.

In the detailed information for each node, you see that it concerns two procedures, namely GET_KPIS_FOR_CONNECTIONS and GET_AGENCIES_FOR_CONNECTIONS. You also see the duration of each execution. In the TIME-LINE, you can see that these two procedures were executed in parallel because the two blue bars start almost simultaneously and run in parallel (see Figure 7.29).

Parallel execution

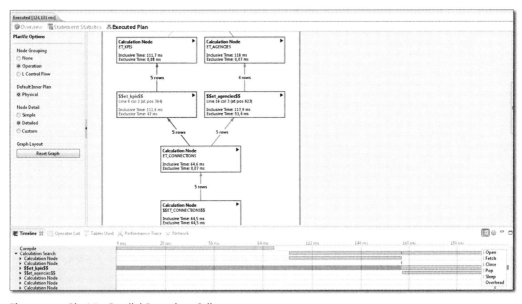

Figure 7.29 PlanViz: Parallel Procedure Calls

You can sort, filter, and aggregate the OPERATOR LIST by different fields (see Figure 7.30). You can analyze by time or by the number of processed data records. The node name enables you to draw conclusions in relation to the engine or process in which the node is executed. For example, CE stands for the calculation engine, BW for the OLAP engine, and JE for the join engine. You also see which type of operation it concerns (e.g., aggregation, sorting, etc.).

Operator List tool

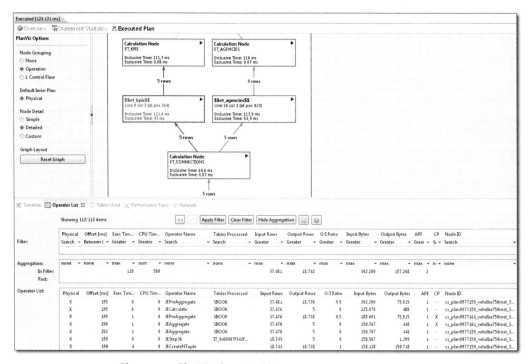

Figure 7.30 PlanViz: Operator List

7.5   System-Wide Analyses

System-wide SQL analyses help you identify expensive SQL statements in the entire system. At first, you don't require any information about the application. During the optimization process, however, you may find such information helpful or even necessary. In this section, we'll show you how to conduct such analyses in the DBA Cockpit. You'll also learn about the SQL monitor for system-wide SQL analysis and the runtime check monitor, which are both available as of AS ABAP 7.4.

7.5.1   Database Administration Cockpit

The DBA Cockpit contains all the functions needed for database monitoring and database administration. Here, you find an overview of the current database status as well as error messages and warnings.

Functions are also available for performance analysis, configuration, database jobs, diagnostics, and system information. These are a subset of the functions available in SAP HANA Studio for analyzing the SAP HANA database. The following sections present the most critical functions of the DBA Cockpit.

[«]

> **Note**
>
> SAP HANA Studio and other tools for system administration are presented in *SAP HANA Administration* by Richard Bremer and Lars Breddemann (SAP PRESS, 2014).

Under CURRENT STATUS • OVERVIEW, you can find information about the current database status. For example, you'll see the current CPU and memory consumption in the database. Current warnings are displayed on the ALERTS screen.

Overview and alerts

The PERFORMANCE area provides various monitors for performance analysis. Under THREADS, you see those threads that are currently active on the database. JOBS provides which database jobs are currently active and their current processing status. The EXPENSIVE STATEMENTS view contains a list of SQL statements if this particular trace is activated. This trace records SQL statements that exceed a specific runtime specified by the database administrator. The SQL PLAN CACHE area displays aggregated information about the SQL statements that have been executed. This information is taken from the SQL cache in the database. All executed SQL statements are stored in the SQL cache, and the runtime data associated with these statements are entered there. If, however, some data is displaced due to a lack of space or because new SQL statements are created, the data may be incomplete. In other words, only some of the execution data created since the database started is available. We'll take a closer look at these two functions. The SYSTEM LOAD HISTORY view enables you to display different KPIs graphically, such as CPU or memory consumption of the database. You can choose different periods of time and display the data of previous hours or days.

Performance

The CONFIGURATION area contains information about the HOSTS of the database, the SERVICES available, trace configurations, and configuration files.

Configuration

Jobs The JOBS area contains information about jobs for database administration. There is as central calendar and a DBA SCHEDULING CALENDAR. The results of these jobs are also available in the DBA LOGS.

Diagnostics The DIAGNOSTICS area contains a range of expert functions. For example, the SQL EDITOR can be used to execute read-only SQL statements. Queries in relation to monitoring views and application tables can be executed in this way if the relevant authorization exists. The TABLES/VIEWS area contains the definition and runtime information for database objects. Here, you can use the PROCEDURES function to view the database procedures available. The DIAGNOSIS FILES and MERGED DIAGNOSIS FILES areas enable you to view important trace and diagnosis files in the database and to merge them together to arrange information from different files in chronological order. You can use the BACKUP CATALOG function to view information about database backups. You'll also find various pieces of information about locks and other different trace CE plan operators, which we won't describe in greater detail here.

The LOCK subfolder provides different views of database locks. The following monitors are available, for example: BLOCKED TRANSACTIONS, TABLE LOCKS, and RECORD LOCKS.

System information In the SYSTEM INFORMATION area, you can query different monitoring views. Information about CONNECTIONS, CONNECTION STATISTICS, TRANSACTIONS, CACHES, LARGE TABLES, SQL WORKLOAD, LICENSE, and DATA BROWSER FOR SYSTEM TABLES is available here.

System landscape The SYSTEM LANDSCAPE area provides information on the system configuration and the database connections.

Now we'll show you how you can use the overview, threads, SQL cache, and the expensive statement trace in the DBA Cockpit to analyze the load on the SAP HANA database.

Transaction ST04 overview The upper area of the overview (GENERAL SYSTEM INFORMATION), which you call using Transaction ST04, shows whether all of the database services are active and when they were started, as well as whether they concern a distributed system. Furthermore, you obtain information about the database version and operating system. The upper-right area shows any current alerts. If there are, you can click the information displayed here to navigate directly to the alerts.

The middle and lower areas of the overview contain information about the current load on the main memory and CPU (on the basis of the database and the host on which the database is running). These areas also contain information about the hard drive or data, log, and trace areas (Figure 7.31). All of this information is based on the time you called the overview or chose UPDATE.

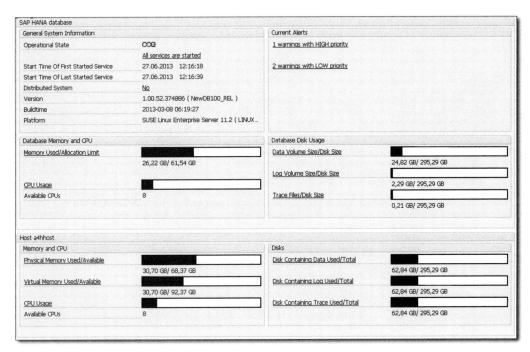

Figure 7.31 Transaction ST04: Overview

In the THREADS area, you see which threads are active in the database. **Threads** This area also contains information about the service, type, and method executed. The recently executed SQL statement, previous runtime, caller, and the name of the user who executed the statement are displayed. An example of a thread is shown in Figure 7.32.

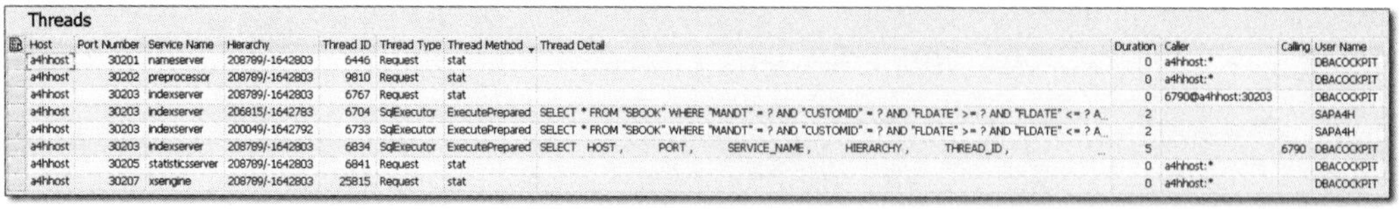

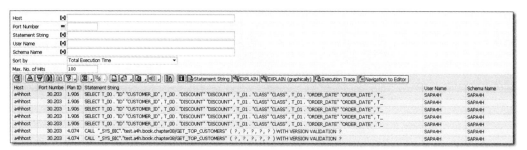

Figure 7.32 Transaction ST04: Threads

SQL cache
In the upper area of the SQL cache, you can specify filters for the SQL statements to be displayed (see Figure 7.33).

Figure 7.33 SQL Cache

Functions
You can execute the following functions for each SQL statement:

▶ STATEMENT STRING
Displays the entire SQL statement.

▶ EXPLAIN
Displays the execution plan as a piece of text.

▶ EXPLAIN (GRAPHICALLY)
Displays the execution plan graphically.

▶ EXECUTION TRACE
Generates a file that can be analyzed further using PlanViz (see Section 7.4.6) in SAP HANA Studio. This works for SELECT statements only, which the trace executes in the background if the relevant authorizations exist.

▶ NAVIGATION TO EDITOR
Displays the call point of the ABAP program within the program.

Information in the SQL cache
The SQL cache contains an entry for each unique SQL string. Therefore, different call points within ABAP programs can be aggregated into one

entry if they concern exactly the same SQL statement. A large amount of information can be retrieved for each entry (e.g., the number of executions, the execution times, the number of data records transferred, the time when the last execution was performed, and the times relating to database locks).

The EXPENSIVE STATEMENTS view contains similar functions to the SQL cache, but it works according to the trace principle. In other words, you must configure which SQL statements you want to record (e.g., all SQL statements that take longer than three seconds to execute). Such statements are written to a restricted memory area within the database. Whenever this area is full, old entries are simply overwritten, so space is always available. This particular function has the advantage over the SQL cache in that individual statements that satisfy the configuration criteria are recorded without needing to be aggregated. Therefore, information about the application user (the user in the SAP system) is also available here.

Expensive statements

7.5.2   SQL Monitor

SQL Monitor is a new development that is available as of AS ABAP 7.4 and was ported up to Release 7.00 (see SAP Note 1885926). SQL Monitor basically collects, aggregates, and persists runtime information about SQL statements in the database interface (DBI). The SQL cache in the database provides database-specific information about the SQL statement (e.g., the number of pages read or the I/O and CPU times required), but information about the ABAP program and the call context in which the statement was executed is available in the SQL Monitor. Consequently, these two data sources complement each other and provide specific additional information about SQL statements. In this section, we'll show you how to activate the SQL Monitor and explain which data is available for analysis.

Recording

To launch the SQL Monitor, call Transaction SQLM. Here, you can activate the SQL Monitor on every application server or on specific application servers only. You can also define both the period in which the recording will take place and an upper limit for the number of records. Data recording stops as soon as the date or number of records has been reached. Figure 7.34 shows the initial screen of the SQL Monitor after it has been activated.

Figure 7.34 SQL Monitor: Activation

Once activated, data are collected and aggregated for each SQL statement executed (Open SQL, Native SQL, database procedures such as AMDP, `EXPORT` and `IMPORT` statements, and system activities such as loading table buffers). The data are collected in the main memory and written asynchronously to a database table. The data are available for analysis in Transaction SQLM about an hour after recording. The data are also provided in a background job for analysis to make a minimal impact on the runtime.

Analysis

To analyze the data, choose DISPLAY DATA. The selection screen shown in Figure 7.35 appears.

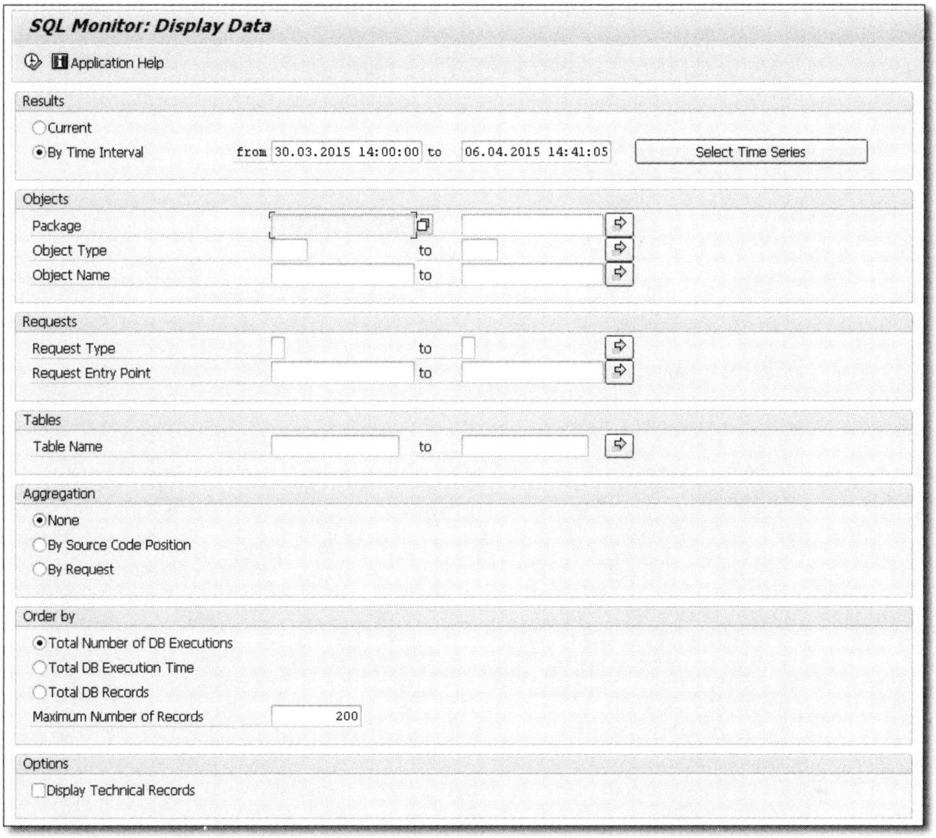

Figure 7.35 SQL Monitor Analysis

In the results area, you can set a time restriction:

Restrictions and filters

▶ CURRENT
Current measurement.

▶ BY TIME INTERVAL
Specific time window.

In the areas below, you can filter data according to the following information:

369

- PACKAGE
  Software package.

- OBJECT TYPE
  Program, function module, and so on.

- OBJECT NAME
  Name of the object.

- REQUEST TYPE
  Type of entry point.

- REQUEST ENTRY POINT
  Name of entry point.

- TABLE NAME
  Name of the table.

[»] **Entry Point**

The entry point (request) is the first entry in the ABAP call hierarchy that is deemed to be of semantic importance. Entry points can include transactions, RFC modules, URLs, or ABAP reports.

For example, Program ZR_A4H_CHAPTER8_TOP_CUST calls a method of the `ZCL_A4H_CHAPTER8_DATA_PROV` class in which a `SELECT` statement is executed. The object name for this statement is `ZCL_A4H_CHAPTER8_DATA_PROV`, while Program ZR_A4H_CHAPTER8_TOP_CUST is the entry point. Without this entry point, it may not be possible to establish a reference to the ABAP report nor to assign the SQL statement to a business process. If a function module now calls this method via RFC, a new entry is created and receives the object name `ZCL_A4H_CHAPTER8_DATA_PROV`. Furthermore, its entry point bears the name of the RFC function module. Consequently, `SELECT` statements can be assigned easily to a business process—even if they are called in modularization units that don't recognize such an assignment.

You can choose from the following settings in the AGGREGATION area:

- NO
  A separate entry is created for each call point, entry point, and table.

- BY SOURCE CODE POSITION
  Dynamic SQL is summarized across tables for each call point.

- BY REQUEST
  See the preceding information box.

Finally, you can also sort by various criteria and restrict the number of data records displayed. DISPLAY TECHNICAL RECORDS enables you to specify whether system activities, such as loading table buffers, are displayed.

Results lists

The *results list* provides different information depending on the aggregation you selected. We'll describe the most critical columns of each list.

Aggregation by request

The following columns are particularly important for the aggregation by request (see Figure 7.36):

- TOT DB E
  Number of executions of all SQL statements from the request.
- TOTAL DB TIME
  Total database time consumed by all executed SQL statements from the request.
- TOTAL TIME
  Total time of request in the ABAP work process.
- DB TIME/TOTAL TIME
  Percentage of database time in the total time.
- TOTAL RECORDS
  Number of all data records processed by the request.
- SESSIONS
  Number of calls in the request.
- REQUEST TYPE
  Type of request: transaction, batch job, report, and so on.
- REQUEST ENTRY POINT
  Name of request.

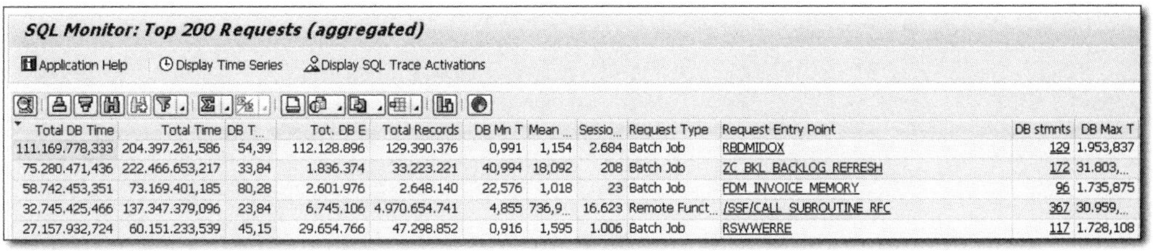

Total DB Time	Total Time	DB T...	Tot. DB E	Total Records	DB Mn T	Mean ...	Sessio...	Request Type	Request Entry Point	DB stmnts	DB Max T
111.169.778,333	204.397.261,586	54,39	112.128.896	129.390.376	0,991	1,154	2.684	Batch Job	RBDMIDOX	129	1.953,837
75.280.471,436	222.466.653,217	33,84	1.836.374	33.223.221	40,994	18,092	208	Batch Job	ZC_BKL_BACKLOG_REFRESH	172	31.803,...
58.742.453,351	73.169.401,185	80,28	2.601.976	2.648.140	22,576	1,018	23	Batch Job	FDM_INVOICE_MEMORY	96	1.735,875
32.745.425,466	137.347.379,096	23,84	6.745.106	4.970.654.741	4,855	736,9...	16.623	Remote Funct...	/SSF/CALL_SUBROUTINE_RFC	367	30.959,...
27.157.932,724	60.151.233,539	45,15	29.654.766	47.298.852	0,916	1,595	1.006	Batch Job	RSWWERRE	117	1.728,108

Figure 7.36 Transaction SQLM: Results List by Request

The other columns show the number of SQL statements as well as various statistics (minimum, mean, and maximum values as well as standard deviation for various columns).

If you double-click a row in this view, the system takes you directly to the nonaggregated list of SQL statements for this request. The columns of this list are presented in the following.

Aggregation by source code position The following columns are particularly important for aggregation by source code position or if no aggregation takes place (see Figure 7.37):

▶ DB EXECUTIONS
Number of SQL statement executions.

▶ DB EXECUTIONS %
Percentage of the SQL statement in the total number of SQL statement executions in the request.

▶ TOTAL DB TIME
Time consumption of all SQL statement executions.

▶ DB TIME %
Percentage of the statement's time in the total database time of SQL statement executions in the request.

▶ DB TIME/TOTAL TIME %
Percentage of the statement's time in the total time of SQL statement executions in the request.

▶ TOTAL RECORDS
Total number of processed records in the SQL statement.

▶ RECORDS %
Percentage of processed SQL statement records in the total number of records of all SQL statements in the request.

▶ DB MN TIME
Average time for executing the SQL statement.

▶ MEAN DB RECORDS
Average number of records for the execution of the SQL statement.

▶ TABLE NAMES
In the case of joins, the list of tables is separated by commas.

▶ SQL Operation
   Type of SQL statement.

▶ Type, Name, Include, Include Line
   Information about the object.

▶ ABAP Source Code Fragment
   Extract of the SQL statement in the ABAP program.

▶ Changed
   Shows whether the call point was changed since the recording.

▶ Int.Sess
   Number of sessions.

▶ Execution/Session
   Number of executions per session.

Internal Sessions and Executions per Session [«]

The Int. Sess and Exe/Sess. fields enable you to analyze the number of executions in greater detail. Here, you see whether the total number equates to one program run (session) in which the same statement is executed several times (sessions = 1; number of executions per session = 1,000) or to a large number of sessions in which the statement is executed once in each session (sessions = 1,000; number of executions per session = 1).

Figure 7.37 shows a sample result list in the SQL Monitor.

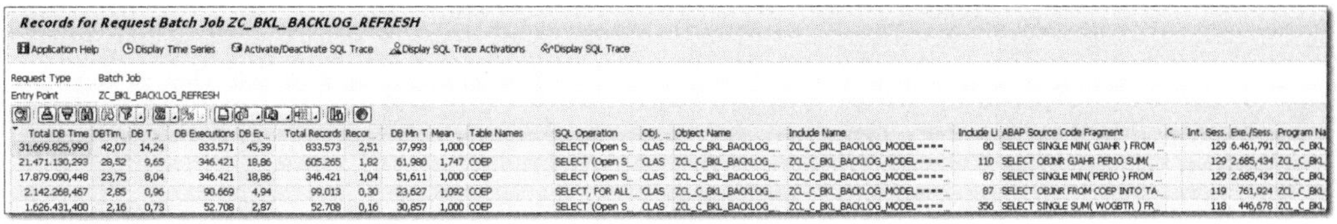

Figure 7.37 Transaction SQLM Results List by Call Position

The columns include information about the program, package, and the modularization unit as well as various statistics (minimum, mean, and maximum values as well as standard deviation for various columns).

Time Series

If you selected a specific time window (By Time Interval in the selection screen), the Display Time Series function is available (see Figure 7.37), which allows you to view the most critical KPIs of an SQL statement aggregated by hours. This function is very helpful to evaluate whether an SQL statement always behaves the same or is subject to changes in the timeline. This function isn't available if you analyze the current measurement only.

Integration of the SQL trace (Transaction ST05)

The integration of the SQL trace (Transaction ST05) is a very powerful function of the SQL Monitor. A prerequisite for this function is that you have the authorization (create, activate, etc.) for logpoints (S_DYNLGPTS authorization object). This function permits the activation of an SQL trace for a specific call point of the SQL statement. The distinguishing feature is that you can now activate several SQL traces for each application server. Only the SQL statements activated in the SQL Monitor are written to the SQL trace. However, the limits of Transaction ST05 still apply, which means that the trace file can still be overwritten if a high number of trace records exists. We'll show you how to activate and analyze the SQL trace for a specific SQL statement from SQL Monitor.

Activating the SQL trace

To activate an SQL trace, click on the Activate/Deactivate SQL Trace button (refer to Figure 7.37). Note that this button is only available if you have the authorization for logpoints. In the following dialog window (see Figure 7.38), you can restrict the trace to users or application servers and specify a time for trace deactivation. You can also determine whether the SQL trace will be recorded with a call stack. The Filter by Request setting defines that the selected SQL statement is recorded at the selected entry point in the SQL trace. With Maximum Executions per Session, you can specify that the system records only a specific number of executions of the SQL statement. Note that this isn't a global counter per application server but only a counter per session. Consequently, many sessions will record the number of executions specified here. This is important, for example, if the SQL statement to be recorded is located in an RFC function module that is called frequently. Click on Save to activate the SQL trace.

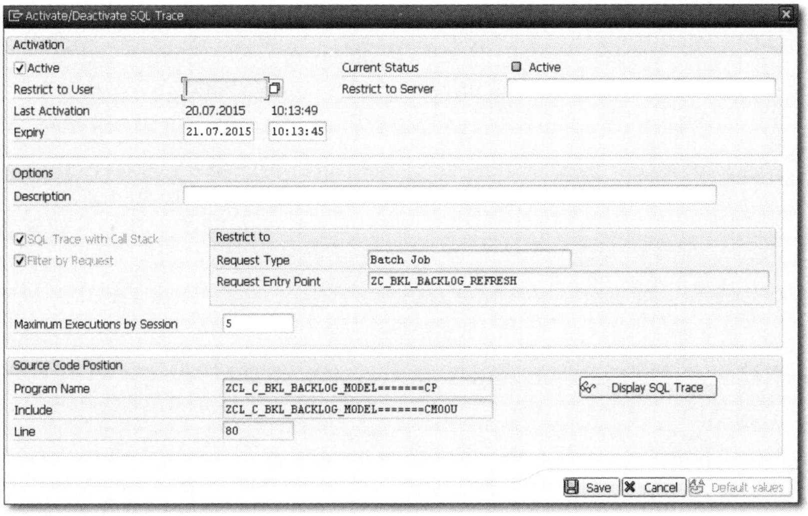

Figure 7.38 Activating the SQL Trace

After you've activated an SQL trace, the DISPLAY SQL TRACE ACTIVATIONS and DISPLAY SQL TRACE buttons are displayed. In addition, the rows for which an SQL trace was activated are displayed in green (if the trace is deactivated again, the rows are displayed in yellow).

If you click on the DISPLAY SQL TRACE ACTIVATIONS button, the system takes you to the dialog window shown in Figure 7.39. Here, you can deactivate the SQL trace again, change the settings, or delete an entry.

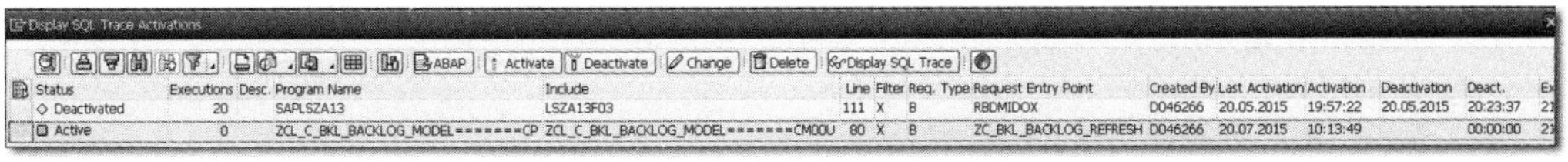

Managing and displaying the SQL trace

Figure 7.39 Activated SQL Traces

The EXECUTIONS column in Figure 7.39 shows how often an SQL statement has been executed since the activation of the trace. When you select DISPLAY SQL TRACE, the system takes you to the analysis in Transaction ST05. The system may prompt you for which server the trace records are to be displayed if the trace has been activated for several servers and if the SQL statements have been recorded on more than one server. Transaction ST05 then starts on the server selected and includes all necessary filters to display the selected SQL statement. You don't need to make any changes to the selection and can run the statement directly. Note that the data recorded may have been overwritten by other Transaction ST05 traces (from the SQL Monitor or directly in Transaction ST05) if no trace records are displayed. It's therefore important to keep the number of executions to be recorded as low as possible (refer to Figure 7.37).

Analysis examples You can use the SQL Monitor to conduct some interesting analyses. The following examples serve to give you some points of reference:

- **Requests that consumed the most database time**
  Aggregation by request, sorted according to time.

- **Statements that took the longest to execute**
  no aggregation, sorted according to time.

- **Statements executed most often**
  No aggregation, a large number of sessions, or a large number of executions per session.

- **Statements executed directly within a specific function module (e.g., ZFUNC2)**
  Selection according to the object name ZFUNC2.

- **Statements called directly within and below a specific function module (e.g., ZFUNC2) that was called by RFC and by other function modules, methods, or programs called by the function module**
  Selection according to the request entry point = ZFUNC2.

- **Statements relating to customer tables called within and below a specific transaction (e.g., Transaction VA01)**
  Selection according to the request entry point = VA01 and table name = Z*.

- **Programs accessed a specific table (e.g., table ZTAB1)**
  Selection according to table ZTAB1.

Advantages of the SQL Monitor The SQL Monitor helps you quickly analyze the points at which database tuning is necessary and promising.

Because the data in the SQL Monitor is periodically stored in a database table, no data is displaced here (which is the case with the SQL cache).

You can link the data in the SQL Monitor to the results of a static code analysis, thus providing runtime information for the static check results. Consequently, it becomes apparent quickly where an optimization would be most beneficial. We'll show you how to do this in Section 7.6.

Integrating the SQL trace (Transaction ST05) in the SQL Monitor is a very powerful function that allows you to record only the interesting parts of an application in the SQL trace.

The SQL Monitor is a comprehensive tool for determining an SQL profile for an application or an entire system. For each call point, an entry is created for each table and application. Because the data are written asynchronously to the database tables, performance isn't negatively affected. Furthermore, no information is lost, and the additional information makes it possible to draw more accurate conclusions in relation to the ABAP program and the context in which it was executed.

7.5.3 Runtime Check Monitor

The runtime check monitor (Transaction SRTCM) lets you activate specific checks that are run at the runtime of ABAP programs. You can then analyze the results of these checks.

The transaction currently comprises the following two checks:

Checks

▸ **Empty table in** FOR ALL ENTRIES **clause**
This check records all executions of SELECT statements in which the internal table of the FOR ALL ENTRIES clause is empty. This check lets you identify problems in which too many records are read from the database (refer to Section 7.3.1).

▸ **Missing** ORDER BY **or** SORT **after** SELECT
This check records all executions of SELECT statements without ORDERBY or subsequent SORT statements for which the internal table requires a subsequent sorting. This is the case, for example, if you work with the READ .. BINARY SEARCH statement or other statements (refer to Section 7.3.1).

The following shows how to activate the monitor and then analyze the data.

Recording

After you've started Transaction SRTCM, you receive an overview of the status of available checks (see Figure 7.40).

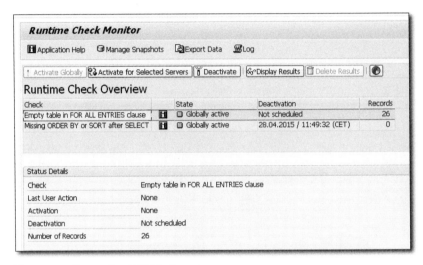

Figure 7.40 Transaction SRTCM: Overview

You can view the activation status and further information on the two checks. You can select the information icon to go to the documentation of the checks. To activate a check, click on ACTIVATE GLOBALLY or ACTIVATE FOR SELECTED SERVERS, depending on whether you want to run the check on all servers or specific servers only. In the dialog window that appears, you can specify the time at which the check is to be deactivated again.

Analysis

Click on DISPLAY RESULTS (refer to Figure 7.40) to analyze the data. A selection screen appears in which you must select the desired check in the RUNTIME CHECK SELECTION area and then click DISPLAY RESULTS (see Figure 7.41). Alternatively, you can call Transaction SRTCMD to start directly from here.

This results in a list of check results (see Figure 7.42). When you click on the link in the INCLUDE or INCL.LINE columns, you can directly navigate to the ABAP source code. The CHANGED column indicates whether the ABAP source code was changed between the check and the analysis.

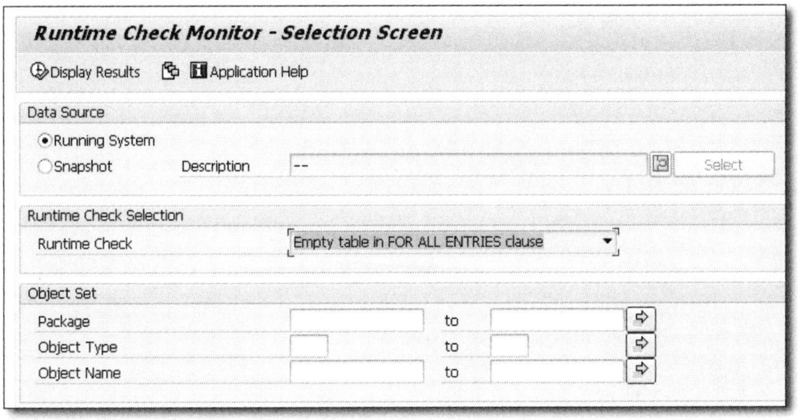

Figure 7.41 Transaction SRTCM: Selecting Results

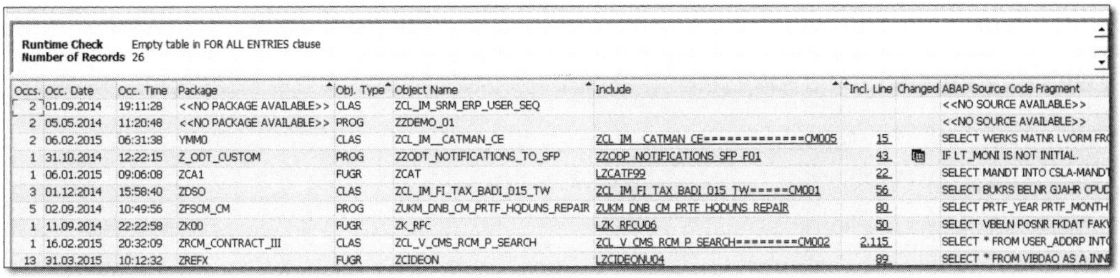

Runtime Check Empty table in FOR ALL ENTRIES clause
Number of Records 26

Occs.	Occ. Date	Occ. Time	Package	Obj. Type	Object Name	Include	Incl. Line	Changed	ABAP Source Code Fragment
2	01.09.2014	19:11:28	<<NO PACKAGE AVAILABLE>>	CLAS	ZCL_IM_SRM_ERP_USER_SEQ				<<NO SOURCE AVAILABLE>>
2	05.05.2014	11:20:48	<<NO PACKAGE AVAILABLE>>	PROG	ZZDEMO_01				<<NO SOURCE AVAILABLE>>
2	06.02.2015	06:31:38	YMM0	CLAS	ZCL_IM__CATMAN_CE	ZCL_IM__CATMAN_CE==============CM005	15		SELECT WERKS MATNR LVORM FR
1	31.10.2014	12:22:15	Z_ODT_CUSTOM	PROG	ZZODT_NOTIFICATIONS_TO_SFP	ZZODP_NOTIFICATIONS_SFP_F01	43		IF LT_MONI IS NOT INITIAL.
1	06.01.2015	09:06:08	ZCA1	FUGR	ZCAT	LZCATF99	22		SELECT MANDT INTO CSLA-MAND
3	01.12.2014	15:58:40	ZDSO	CLAS	ZCL_IM_FI_TAX_BADI_015_TW	ZCL_IM_FI_TAX_BADI_015_TW=====CM001	56		SELECT BUKRS BELNR GJAHR CPU
5	02.09.2014	10:49:56	ZFSCM_CM	PROG	ZUKM_DNB_CM_PRTF_HQDUNS_REPAIR	ZUKM_DNB_CM_PRTF_HQDUNS_REPAIR	80		SELECT PRTF_YEAR PRTF_MONTH
1	11.09.2014	22:22:58	ZK00	FUGR	ZK_RFC	LZK_RFCU06	50		SELECT VBELN POSNR FKDAT FAK
1	16.02.2015	20:32:09	ZRCM_CONTRACT_III	CLAS	ZCL_V_CMS_RCM_P_SEARCH	ZCL_V_CMS_RCM_P_SEARCH========CM002	2.115		SELECT * FROM USER_ADDRP INT
13	31.03.2015	10:12:32	ZREFX	FUGR	ZCIDEON	LZCIDEONU04	89		SELECT * FROM VIBDAO AS A INN

Figure 7.42 Transaction SRTCM: Displaying Results

7.6 SQL Performance Optimization

The SQL performance optimization tool—the *SQL Performance Tuning Worklist*—is a new development available as of AS ABAP 7.4 and was ported up until Release 7.02. It can be used to combine data from a static code analysis (e.g., the data associated with a check run in the ABAP Test Cockpit) with runtime measurements from the SQL Monitor (or Coverage Analyzer [Transaction SCOV]) to determine the points where optimization is promising for SAP HANA. We'll now show you how to link the results of a static analysis with the results of the SQL Monitor. This link uses a join that is based on the call point.

Linking data from
SQL Monitor and
Transaction SCI

In Section 7.3, you learned how to perform static code analyses, and, in Section 7.5.2, we explained how to use Transaction SQLM to collect data. These two pools of data can now be linked to each other in Transaction SWLT.

Don't make any restrictions or changes on the GENERAL tab. Then, on the STATIC CHECKS tab (see Figure 7.43), select the USE STATIC CHECK DATA checkbox. Then select an ABAP Code Inspector or ABAP Test Cockpit check that was run previously. A check run can be used both from the local and from a remote system (using the RFC DESTINATION field).

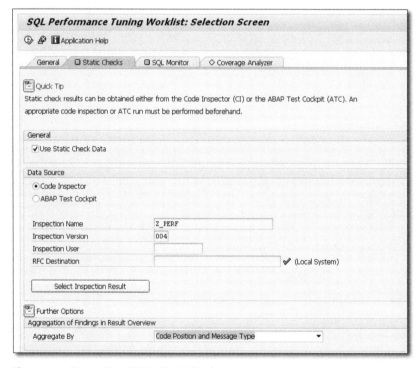

Figure 7.43 Transaction SWLT: Static Checks

Then select the USE SQL MONITOR DATA checkbox on the SQL MONITOR tab (see Figure 7.44). To select a snapshot, click on MANAGE/CREATE SNAPSHOT. You can use the local system, a remote system that is connected via RFC, or a file import as the data source. An SQL Monitor snapshot must have been created first, however.

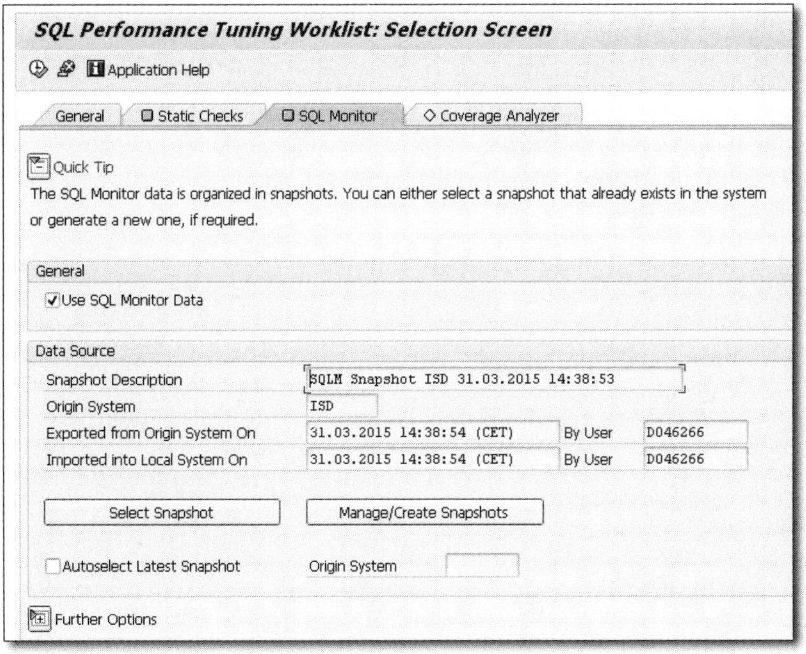

Figure 7.44 Transaction SWLT: SQL Monitor Data

You can now run the analysis by clicking on the ⊕ icon.

The result list includes a screen that is divided into three sections (see Figure 7.45):

Analysis

▶ RESULT OVERVIEW
This area contains the data from the SQL Monitor. As soon as you double-click a data record in this area, the data is filled in the lower screen areas. If you select an entry in the INCLUDE NAME column, you navigate directly to the call point in the ABAP program.

▶ SQL MONITOR RESULTS
In the list on the lower left-hand side of the screen, you see the relevant caller for the SQL statement (REQUEST ENTRY POINT, first program in the ABAP call hierarchy) and the most important measurement

readings for this from the SQL Monitor. When you select the table name, you call Transaction SE12 (ABAP Data Dictionary) for this table.

▶ STATIC CHECK FINDINGS

In the list on the lower right-hand side of the screen, you see the consolidated results from the Code Inspector and the ABAP Test Cockpit. From here, you can call the documentation for the check, or you can select the entry in the ADDITIONAL INFORMATION column to navigate directly to detailed information about the results in the Code Inspector or the ABAP Test Cockpit.

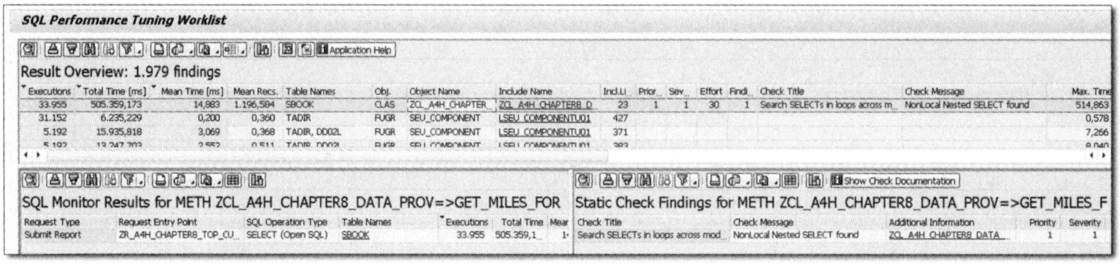

Figure 7.45 Transaction SWLT: Analysis

Data from the DDIC

The upper area of the screen shows the data from the SQL Monitor and the corresponding results of the ABAP Code Inspector check (both aggregated by call point; see the top right area of Figure 7.45). When you click on the INCLUDE NAME field, the system takes you directly to the call point of the SQL statement. If you double-click a row of the results overview, you receive the SQL Monitor results in the bottom left area (not aggregated). Clicking on REQUEST ENTRY POINT or TABLE NAMES takes you to the request entry point or DDIC. The ABAP Code Inspector results are displayed in nonaggregated form in the STATIC CHECK FINDINGS area. When you click on the link in the ADDITIONAL INFORMATION field, the system takes you to the results of the Code Inspector check, for example, the call hierarchy of an SQL statement in loops.

The SQL Performance Tuning Worklist is a very powerful tool that can be used to plan optimization projects for SAP HANA very efficiently. If SQL statements are assigned to applications, they can also be assigned to business processes. Runtime measurements show which SQL statements require a large amount of time or run very frequently. The static analysis shows where there is potential for optimization and how time-consuming such an optimization would be. Combining this data into one transaction is extremely useful for detecting the source code with the best cost-benefit ratio for applying optimizations.

Compared to the SQL Monitor, the main result list contains some additional columns. From the DDIC, you obtain the following information for the database tables:

▶ BUFFERING TYPE
Buffering type associated with the table.

▶ COLUMNS
Number of columns in the table.

▶ KEY COLUMNS
Number of key columns.

▶ WIDTH IN BYTES
Row length in bytes.

▶ STORAGE TYPE
Table type (COLUMN STORE and ROW STORE).

▶ SIZE CATEGORY
Size category for the table.

▶ TABLE CLASS
Table type (TRANSPARENT, POOL, and CLUSTER).

You also obtain information about the Code Inspector checks:

Information from the Code Inspector

▶ PRIORITY
This is the priority of the message as configured in the Code Inspector.

▶ SEVERITY
This value depends on the relevant check. (For more information, refer to the documentation for the Code Inspector.) It specifies the severity of the result. For the SELECT * check, this column specifies how many superfluous columns were read. In general, the following applies: the higher this value, the greater the negative impact on performance.

▶ EFFORT

This value depends on the relevant check (see the documentation for the Code Inspector) and is an estimate of the effort associated with the correction. In general, the following applies: the higher this value, the greater the effort.

▶ FINDINGS

This is the number of Code Inspector results for this SQL statement.

You can use these columns to compare the results and prioritize where an optimization would be most beneficial.

By optimizing existing ABAP programs, you can achieve signifi-
cant performance gains. As an ABAP developer, you can identify
programs that are suitable candidates for optimization and then
modify them so that they benefit from the SAP HANA architec-
ture.

8   Sample Scenario: Optimizing an Existing Application

In the previous chapters, we described the basic principles of the in-memory technology and ABAP development on SAP HANA. You now know how to move portions of the application logic (especially complex calculations with large amounts of data) to the database layer. In addition, you learned which tools SAP NetWeaver AS ABAP provides to identify optimization potential in programs.

This chapter now deals with combining and using the individual techniques and tools in sample scenario in which an application is optimized for SAP HANA.

This chapter is divided into three parts. We'll start with a description of the necessary steps to optimize systems and applications. The second part introduces the sample scenario and optimization requirements. To conclude the chapter, you'll learn how to optimize the sample program. In this part, we won't explain every step in detail, but we'll focus on the most important excerpts that are relevant for optimization. You can download the application and its source code in the download area for this book at *www.sap-press.com/3973* (see Appendix E).

8.1 Optimization Procedure

This section presents the general procedure in optimization projects. We'll discuss the following scenarios:

- Migrating to SAP HANA
- System optimization
- Application optimization

Every scenario has a different focus and different roles of responsibility. This chapter lists and describes the most important tools for every scenario. Some tools are used in several scenarios, with a different focus in each case.

8.1.1 Migrating to SAP HANA

When performing a migration to SAP HANA, you want to make sure that all programs continue to run as before. You also might want to identify optimization potential with regard to database access before or during the migration, and implement the necessary adjustments. These tasks are mainly the responsibility of ABAP developers and quality managers for ABAP programs. In addition, process owners may also need to work with these employees to prioritize possible performance optimizations based on the importance of the respective business process.

Steps for analyzing and optimizing ABAP code

When migrating to SAP HANA, the following steps are necessary to analyze and possibly modify or optimize ABAP code:

- Collect respective data information.
- Analyze ABAP code (in combination with the collected data).
- Prioritize the applications identified as relevant for optimization.
- Adjust the programs accordingly.

Data collection

You should examine the coding statically and combine the analysis results with runtime data to facilitate prioritization, so the first step is to schedule a data collection. To do this, activate the SQL Monitor in the production system for a period of time where all important business

386

processes are run (refer to Chapter 7, Section 7.5.2). For the month-end closing processes to be considered, this time period should contain at least one period-end. We recommend a time period of at least six weeks.

While collecting the data, you can simultaneously use the SAP Code Inspector and the ABAP Test Cockpit to analyze ABAP code. When doing so, a distinction is made between functional checks and performance checks (refer to Chapter 7, Section 7.3.1). Run the tests on a development system that has developments and coding that are comparable to the production system.

Run the checks

We recommend that you prioritize the results of the performance checks based on their importance in the business process, the impact on the system, and the required effort for the optimizations. For prioritization, combine the results of the ABAP code analysis with the runtime data in the SQL performance optimization tool:

Prioritization

- The Code Inspector provides information on the SQL statements that have optimization potential, on the impact on performance, and on the effort for modifying these statements.

- The SQL Monitor indicates whether or not an SQL statement was executed, the number of executions, and the time needed for execution. Information on the entry point is also provided so that you can identify the business process affected. This makes it possible to consider the business-process relevance when prioritizing the results of the performance tests and to discuss the weighting with the respective process owners.

While adjusting programs, suitable measures can be derived from the results of the functional checks and the performance checks:

Adjusting programs

- To make sure that all programs continue to run in the same way after the migration, we recommend that you consider the results of functional checks in all cases—independent of runtime measurements—and implement the necessary corrections. Because these adjustments are independent of the runtime analysis, you can start implementation at the same time as data collection.

▶ If the performance checks indicate optimization potential, you should optimize the affected programs in order according to their prioritization. We describe how to identify the exact modifications that are necessary for each program in Section 8.1.3.

8.1.2 System Optimization

System optimization considers the system as a whole. Its focus is highly technical, and SAP system and database administrators usually perform the required steps. When dealing with applications that system and database administrators can't optimize directly, ABAP developers will also be involved in the optimization measures. System optimization has priority if a large number of system processes are too slow, and the runtime problems can't be narrowed down to one or a few applications.

There are two possible approaches for system optimization: analysis of system settings and hardware resources on the one hand, and application and SQL analysis on the other. In this context, note that the two subject areas are interdependent, which means that nonoptimal system settings or resource bottlenecks can lead to slow applications. Slow applications (e.g., with high resource consumption), in turn, can lead to resource bottlenecks.

System settings and hardware resources
When analyzing the system settings and hardware resources, the system settings are checked using different configuration parameters (for memory size, number of processes, CPU, etc.). A tool also verifies whether the available hardware resources are sufficient for the workload or whether the system is overloaded and needs more hardware. Tools used for these analyses are typically the SAP memory settings in Transaction ST02, the database performance monitor (Transaction ST04 or Transaction DBACOCKPIT), and the Operating System Monitor (Transaction ST06). In addition to this, the system load can be analyzed in SAP HANA Studio.

Application and SQL analysis
Another approach is to analyze which applications or SQL statements are resource intensive enough to have a negative impact on the entire system. For this task, you can use the Workload Monitor (Transaction ST03), the SQL Monitor, the SQL cache of the database, and the expensive statement trace.

If necessary, resource-intensive applications can be further analyzed using the tools described in Section 8.1.3. For resource-intensive SQL statements, the following cases in particular are possible:

▶ SQL statements used to transfer a large number of records from the database to the application server

▶ SQL statements that have fast execution times when contemplated individually but which still take up a lot of time in total because they are executed frequently

▶ SQL statements that are executed rarely and transfer only a few records from the database to the application server but which have a long runtime

In the first and second case, often the applications must be optimized to solve the problem. In the third case, the access path to the database must be analyzed. In some cases, SAP system or database administrators can optimize the runtime of those statements (e.g., with an index).

With system optimization, you can identify configuration problems, resource bottlenecks, and expensive ABAP programs or SQL statements. This type of optimization is described in detail in *SAP Performance Optimization Guide: Analyzing and Tuning SAP Systems* by Thomas Schneider (7th ed., SAP PRESS, 2013) and included in the learning content of the SAP ADM315 course on workload analysis.

8.1.3 Application Optimization

The goal of application optimization is to optimize the performance of an existing application or of individual programs of that application. Concrete complaints by end users often motivate an organization to optimize an application.

ABAP developers usually optimize applications. In some cases, SAP system or database experts give consulting guidance on technical aspects. It may also be necessary to work with business-process specialists to discuss design changes or questions regarding a given business process.

Application optimization is an iterative process that mainly consists of three phases: Phases

- Analysis
- Adjustment
- Comparison

Analysis

During the analysis, you try to identify reasons for performance problems and determine possible performance optimizations.

Runtime statistics We recommend starting the analysis of a program by first evaluating the runtime statistics, that is, by using Transaction STAD (refer to Chapter 7, Section 7.4.1). This will provide early hints on the areas that constitute large portions of the runtime and on the tools that are best suited for a more comprehensive analysis. Three distinct types of cases emerge:

- CPU time constitutes the largest portion of the runtime.
- Database time constitutes the largest portion of the runtime.
- Wait times constitute the largest portion of the runtime.

CPU time If the largest portion of the runtime is CPU time, we recommend continuing the analysis with an ABAP trace (Transaction SAT or ABAP Profiler).

Database time If the database time is the problem, Transaction STAD already provides further information on the database accesses (e.g., with regard to the affected database tables). If this information isn't sufficient, you can run an SQL trace in the next step. This delivers detailed information on the number of executions of an SQL statement on the database and the number of records processed. In addition to that, you can use the SQL Monitor and the SQL Performance Tuning Worklist to create an SQL profile of the application and combine this profile with the data from a static code analysis. If necessary, you can then run further analyses using the execution plan and/or the SAP HANA Plan Visualizer (PlanViz). However, both tools require very good knowledge of the SAP HANA database.

Wait time If the largest portion of the runtime is neither CPU time nor database time, there are usually long wait times, which can be caused by synchronous Remote Function Calls (RFC), the ABAP WAIT statement, or synchronous updates. In this case, you should analyze the causes of the wait times. When dealing with RFC or update modules, you should first evaluate the runtime statistics of the function that was called and then examine the CPU and database time based on those results.

Adjustment

The analysis results are used to adjust the program. You have very distinct options for program adjustments. You might, for example, be able to increase the performance by changing the table type of an internal table or by making a few simple changes to a data selection. In other cases, fundamental modifications might be necessary to accelerate the program.

For every modification, you should consider possible side effects. After adjusting a program, make sure to run functional tests. By executing unit tests, you can make sure that a given adjustment won't lead to regression.

Functional testing

Comparison

After or during adjustments, you compare the runtime of the optimized program with the runtime from when you performed the analysis. If the performance didn't increase at all or not to the extent expected, you can run another analysis with further adjustments before comparing the programs again. Figure 8.1 shows the sequence of application optimization.

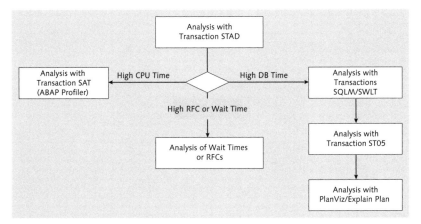

Figure 8.1 Application Analysis

8.2   Scenario and Requirements

Now that you have an overview of the required steps for system and application optimization, we'll introduce the sample application that you'll optimize for SAP HANA in this chapter.

8.2.1   Initial Situation

Initial situation   The focus of our sample scenario is a network of airlines that provides a variety of services for the connected airlines based on a central database. This includes regularly generating reports on flight occupancy, sales figures, and the booking behavior of customers. Moreover, the network provides a bonus system that allows customers of the connected airlines to earn and spend miles.

Reporting

Available reports   The following reports are provided via the network:

▸ Utilization per flight connection for a fiscal year or a fiscal year period

▸ Miles earned per customer within a fiscal year or a fiscal year period

▸ List of premium customers (customers with the highest numbers of earned miles within a period of 24 months)

▸ Average use, total turnover, and booking behavior for each flight connection per fiscal year period and in comparison to the previous period

Calculation of Miles

Calculation of miles   Miles are calculated based on a set of rules that was agreed upon by the connected airlines. The following formula is used to determine the miles earned for a flight booking:

Miles = (distance of flight connection booking class factor
+ distance of flight connection early booking factor)
× (100 – customer-specific discount rate) / 100

Using the *booking class factor*, customers earn more miles when booking business or first class than when booking an economy class flight. The following factors are currently used:

▸ Business class factor: 1,2

▸ First class factor: 1,5

The *early booking factor* is an incentive for customers to book their flights early. For flights that are booked at least 100 days before the flight date, this factor is 0.1. In all other cases, the factor is 0.

Some customers receive *customer-specific discounts* when booking a flight. In this case, the miles earned are reduced by the same percentage as the airfare. If a customer receives a 30% discount so that he only pays 70% of the regular airfare, he only earns 70% of the miles that are earned by a customer who pays the full price.

To illustrate and explain these rules, let's consider a flight booking by customer Tom Peterson (customer number 178; the customer-specific discount is 20%) from Frankfurt to New York flying business class. The distance of this connection is 6,162 kilometers. This corresponds to 3,829 miles. The flight took place on 8/20/2012 and was booked on 7/24/2012. Mr. Peterson earns the following miles for this flight:

Miles = (3,829 1.2 + 3,829 0) (100 − 20) / 100 = 3,676

8.2.2 Technical Implementation

The airline network uses an ABAP-based IT system. The tables and data within this system are based on the SFLIGHT data model.

Database Tables

The airlines connected to the system transfer all relevant data to a central system in real time. The relevant database tables of the SFLIGHT data model are listed in Table 8.1.

Table	Description
SCARR	Airlines
SPFLI	Flight schedule
SCUSTOM	Customer data
SFLIGHT	Flights
SBOOK	Flight bookings

Table 8.1 Relevant Database Tables of the SFLIGHT Data Model

Other database
tables

There are also two extensions of the SFLIGHT data model, as shown in Table 8.2.

Table	Description
ZA4H_C8_PARAMS	Parameters for mile calculation
ZA4H_C8_STATIST	Storage of static data regarding the flight connections

Table 8.2 Other Database Tables

Reports

ABAP program

All reports needed are executable ABAP programs with corresponding transaction codes (see Table 8.3).

ABAP Program	Transaction	Description
ZR_A4H_CHAPTER8_ UTILIZATION	ZR_A4H_C8_UTIL	Use per flight connection
ZR_A4H_CHAPTER8_ MILES	ZR_A4H_C8_MILES	Miles earned per customer
ZR_A4H_CHAPTER8_ TOP_CUST	ZR_A4H_C8_TOP_CUST	List of premium customers
ZR_A4H_CHAPTER8_ FILL_STATISTIC	ZR_A4H_C8_FILL_STAT	Fills database table ZA4H_C8_STATIST
ZR_A4H_CHAPTER8_ READ_STATISTIC	ZR_A4H_C8_READ_ STAT	Analyzes database table ZA4H_C8_STATIST

Table 8.3 Required ABAP Programs

For visualization, the ABAP programs use classic ABAP lists. Figure 8.2 shows a sample output of Program ZR_A4H_CHAPTER8_TOP_CUST.

```
00000828 Carmel Simonen          3.071.664  MI
00002679 Kurt Trensch            3.049.846  MI
00004485 Fabio Deichgraeber      3.010.440  MI
00002619 August Deichgraeber     3.009.718  MI
00002888 Guenther Matthaeus      2.992.177  MI
00000989 Amelie Legrand          2.978.668  MI
00004670 Carmel Sommer           2.978.114  MI
00004096 Lee Kreiss              2.973.046  MI
00001868 Kurt Eichbaum           2.970.285  MI
00001627 Mathilde Deichgraeber   2.945.687  MI
```

Figure 8.2 Output of Program ZR_A4H_CHAPTER8_TOP_CUST

Customizing

The parameters for mile calculation are stored in the customizing table ZA4H_C8_PARAMS. The system stores the following values in this database table:

Parameters for mile calculation

▶ FACTOR_C
Factor for business-class flights.

▶ FACTOR_F
Factor for first-class flights.

▶ EARLYB_D
Minimum time difference between booking date and flight date to earn additional miles.

▶ EARLYB_F
Factor for early bookings.

The customer-specific discount is derived from the DISCOUNT field in database table SCUSTOM.

Miscellaneous

In addition to the executable ABAP programs, the application includes a Web Dynpro ABAP application and an RFC interface:

Web Dynpro, RFC

▶ The Web Dynpro application ZWD_A4H_CHAPTER8_APP can be used to evaluate the miles earned per customer via the browser (Figure 8.3).

▶ The remote-enabled function module ZA4H_CHAPTER8_GET_UTILIZA-TION can be used by all airlines connected to the network to query the utilization of flight connections.

Figure 8.3 Web Dynpro Application ZWD_A4H_CHAPTER8_APP

Central class Internally, the ABAP programs, the Web Dynpro application, and the function module use methods of the ZCL_A4H_CHAPTER8_DATA_PROV class.

8.2.3 Current Problems

Bad performance The connected airlines have been complaining about the network service for some time. The necessary reports typically have long delays, and end users aren't satisfied with the response time.

Migrating to SAP HANA Due to these complaints, the system was migrated to SAP HANA. Although the migration was performed without any issues and some of the reports are now generated faster (e.g., Program ZR_A4H_CHAPTER8_TOP_CUST had a runtime of 1,491 seconds before the migration; with SAP HANA, it now runs within 567 seconds), not all problems could be solved by merely migrating the system.

To determine how you can improve the response-time behavior of the system, you should follow the application and process-optimization procedure now. Due to time constraints, you'll limit this analysis to

Program ZR_A4H_CHAPTER8_TOP_CUST to determine the premium customers. You should suggest and implement possible modifications as quickly as possible while avoiding any unnecessary risks.

8.3 Meeting the Requirements

As you've learned in the previous chapters, an existing ABAP application can only benefit from SAP HANA if it uses the *code-to-data paradigm*. To avoid any risks, however, you should modify as few parts of the existing system as possible. To ensure portability of the system, you also only want to use SAP HANA views and SQLScript if necessary or if it leads to significant performance gains in comparison with Open SQL.

In the following sections, you'll learn how to determine the extent to which Program ZR_A4H_CHAPTER8_TOP_CUST uses the SAP HANA database and which modifications you can implement to accelerate the program.

8.3.1 Narrowing Down the Problem Using Runtime Statistics

When analyzing Program ZR_A4H_CHAPTER8_TOP_CUST, you start by using Transaction STAD. Within this transaction, you call the runtime statistics for a program execution to analyze the program's runtime and determine the amount of data processed by the program.

The runtime statistics in Figure 8.4 show that Program ZR_A4H_CHAP-TER8_TOP_CUST was executed in 547 seconds (RESPONSE TIME). This runtime is made up of 475 seconds PROCESSING TIME and 71 seconds DATABASE REQUEST TIME. This means that the largest portion of the runtime is attributed to the ABAP program itself and not the time needed for database access. However, database access also takes too long for a dialog program.

Time distribution

The lower part of Figure 8.4 shows detailed information on the database accesses. As you can see, a little over 5.2 million records were read within the database request time of 71 seconds.

Details on data-base access times

```
┌─────────────────────────────────────────────────────────────────────────────┐
│  Analysis of time in work process                                             │
│                                                                               │
│    CPU time                488.850 ms   Number     Roll ins           2       │
│    RFC+CPIC time                 0 ms              Roll outs          2       │
│                                                    Enqueues           2       │
│    Total time in workprocs 547.004 ms                                         │
│                                         Load time  Program            2  ms   │
│   ┌─Response time──────────547.005 ms─┐            Screen             0  ms   │
│                                                    CUA interf.        0  ms   │
│    Wait for work process         1 ms                                         │
│    Processing time         475.465 ms   Roll time  Out                0  ms   │
│    Load time                     2 ms              In                 0  ms   │
│    Generating time               0 ms              Wait               0  ms   │
│    Roll (in+wait) time           0 ms                                         │
│    Database request time    71.536 ms   Frontend   No.roundtrips      0       │
│    Enqueue time                  0 ms              GUI time           0  ms   │
│                                                    Net time           0  ms   │
└─────────────────────────────────────────────────────────────────────────────┘

   Analysis of ABAP/4 database requests (only explicitly by application)
┌─────────────────────────────────────────────────────────────────────────────┐
│  Connection                   DEFAULT        Request time       71.536 ms     │
│  Database requests total      4.706          Commit time             3 ms     │
│  DB Proc. Calls                   0          DB Proc. Time           0 ms     │
```

Type of ABAP request	Database rows	Requests	Buffer rows	Database calls	Request time (ms)	Avg.time / row (ms)
Total	5206.001	4.706	24	4.672	71.536	0,0
Direct read	0	24	23		0	0,0
Sequential read	5205.988	4.669	1	4.659	71.528	0,0
Update	8	8		8	5	0,6
Delete	1	1		1	0	0,0
Insert	4	4		4	3	0,8

```
  Note: Tables were saved in the tablebuffer.

  No database procedure statistics for this record.
```

Figure 8.4 Runtime Statistics from Transaction STAD

Table access statistics

Because the table access statistics (refer to Chapter 7, Section 7.4.1) was activated during the selected execution of the program, you also examine the five tables where the program took the longest time for read accesses (see Figure 8.5). The access time of 71 seconds was almost exclusively used for accesses to table SBOOK (with 5,201,341 records read from this table). Accesses to table SCUSTOM only took 0.02 seconds (with a total of 4,637 records read from this table).

```
Table accesses    (list might be incomplete!)

                           ─────── Number of rows accessed ───────
Table name                    Total Dir. reads Seq. reads   Changes  Time (ms)

TOTAL                     5.205.989        0  5.205.981         8    71.531
SBOOK                     5.201.341        0  5.201.341         0    71.491
SCUSTOM                       4.637        0      4.637         0        29
TSP01                             3        0          1         2         5
TST01                             7        0          1         6         3
TPRI_DEF                          1        0          1         0         2
```

Figure 8.5 Table Access Statistics

The preceding analysis results have shown that most of the execution time of the ABAP program wasn't used within database accesses. Only 13% (71 seconds) of the runtime was used within the database to read about 5.2 million records. In the next steps, you must therefore analyze the ABAP processing and further analyze the database accesses.

Next steps

8.3.2 Detailed Analysis of the ABAP Program Using Transaction SAT

To learn more about the ABAP processing, you now analyze Program ZR_A4H_CHAPTER8_TOP_CUST in more detail using the ABAP runtime analysis in Transaction SAT. Figure 8.6 shows the result of the program execution using Transaction SAT. The program was executed in 545 seconds.

The results of the runtime measurement can be evaluated as follows:

Evaluation of the runtime measurement

▶ **Function modules for conversions**
About 30% (162 seconds) was needed for internal processing blocks, particularly for calling function modules and subprograms. You'll immediately notice that the UNIT_CONVERSION_SIMPLE function module, which is used for unit conversions, was called more than 2 million times. This function module thus accounts for 22% (123 seconds) of the total runtime.

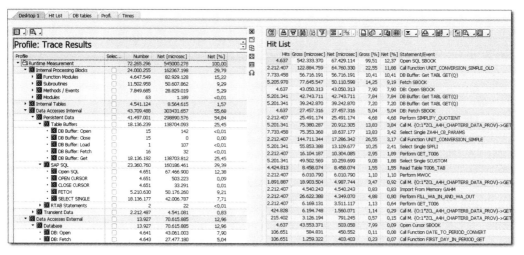

Figure 8.6 ABAP Trace in Transaction SAT

▸ **Database interface and table buffer**

Transaction SAT differentiates between internal (INTERNAL DATABASE ACCESSES) and external database time (EXTERNAL DATABASE ACCESSES). Internal database time refers to the time needed by SQL statements within the ABAP work process and accesses to the table buffer. In our example, about 56% (303 seconds) of the total runtime can be attributed to the internal database time. It distributes to the time for SQL statements within the ABAP work process (160 seconds) and accesses to the table buffer (138 seconds).

You'll immediately notice the high number of accesses to the database and the table buffer. The analysis results show 23 million executions of SQL statements and 18 million accesses to the table buffer. When double-clicking a row within the hit list for a buffer access, the source code is displayed (not shown in Figure 8.6). From this source code, you can see that the accesses to the table buffer were mainly done for tables ZA4H_C8_PARAMS, SCUSTOM, and SPFLI.

The external database time refers to the time needed for SQL statements outside the ABAP work process. In our example, the external database time accounts for about 13% (70 seconds) of the total runtime.

8.3.3 Detailed Analysis of Database Accesses

Before further analyzing the program using the SQL trace, you should check the SQL profile of the application and compare this with static code analyses.

Code Analysis Using SQL Monitor

You first use the SAP Code Inspector to examine the performance of the TEST_A4H_BOOK_CHAPTER08 package. The results are then linked to the existing data from the SQL Monitor in Transaction SWLT. In this transaction, runtime data for the entire system is displayed for access to table SBOOK. Figure 8.7 shows that the SELECT statement was executed 33,000 times with an average execution time of 14.8 milliseconds and 1,196 records read. If you scroll to the right of the screen, the TYPE and NAME OF PROCESSING BLOCK columns (not displayed in Figure 8.7) show that the SELECT statement is run in the GET_MILES_FOR_CUSTOMER method.

SQL profile

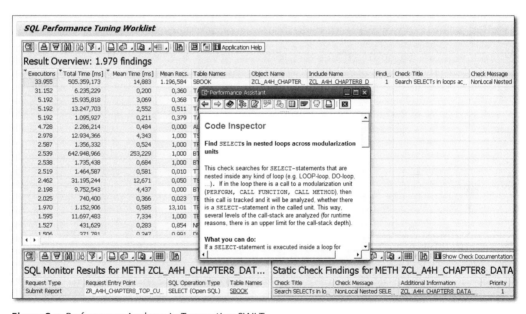

Figure 8.7 Performance Analyses in Transaction SWLT

The CHECK TITLE and CHECK MESSAGE columns also display a Code Inspector check for this method, which indicates that this is a SELECT statement within a loop (with the loop not being present within the same modularization unit as the database access).

When clicking the ADDITIONAL INFORMATION column, the system displays the different levels of the call hierarchy (not shown in this screen). This allows you to navigate easily to the different levels of the call hierarchy where you'll find the loop in the GET_TOP_CUSTOMERS method. When clicking the SHOW CHECK DOCUMENTATION button (shown in Figure 8.7), a document with optimization tips appears. This documentation contains a description of the problem together with possible optimization measures.

You know now that accesses to table SBOOK are caused by a very frequently executed SQL statement, and you also know where this statement is executed and where to find the loop responsible for its execution. Because you also want to know if the SQL statement is executed with identical values each time, you'll record an SQL trace.

SQL Trace with Transaction ST05

You run Program ZR_A4H_CHAPTER8_TOP_CUST again while creating an SQL trace. This will show you how often each statement was executed, if there were identical executions, the execution times, the number of data records read, and the text of the SQL statement that was transferred to the database.

Figure 8.8 and Figure 8.9 show you the list of structure-identical SQL statements and the call hierarchy (call stack) for the SQL statement used to access table SBOOK. The REDUNDANCY and IDENTICAL columns show that the statements weren't executed with identical values and that all bookings within a certain time period that weren't canceled are read for a customer.

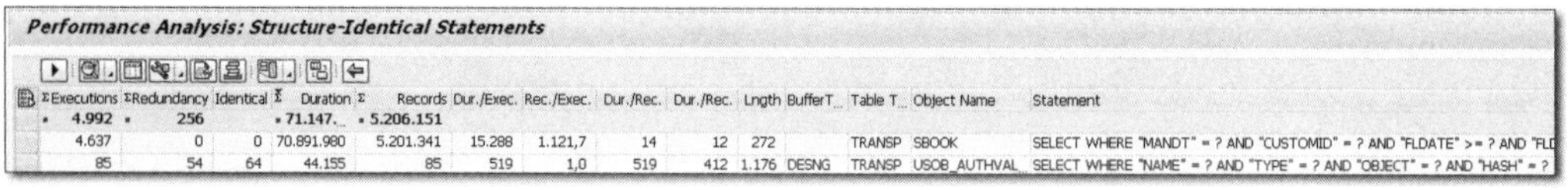

Figure 8.8 SQL Trace: SQL Statements with the Same Structure

You must execute 4,637 SQL statements for this purpose. Using the stack trace from the main records, you can display how the statement for table SBOOK was used via the ABAP stack. By double-clicking an entry, you can easily navigate between the levels of the call hierarchy.

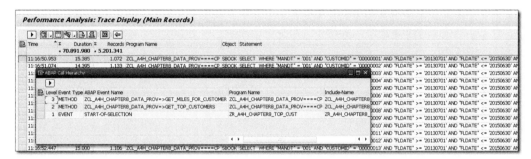

Figure 8.9 SQL Trace: Call Hierarchy

8.3.4 Analysis Result

The analysis of Program ZR_A4H_CHAPTER8_TOP_CUST described in the previous sections has shown that the long runtime can be attributed mainly to a large number of SQL statement and function module executions (particularly for unit conversion). The reason for this is the large number of records that are transferred from the database to the application.

Separate processing of flight bookings

When analyzing the source code, you'll notice that by using the GET_TOP_CUSTOMERS method, the flight bookings are read and processed separately for each customer. Due to the large number of flight bookings (in our example, more than 5 million bookings were read), the database and table buffer are accessed frequently, and there are many function module calls.

Records are often processed individually if function modules and methods are used or reused that aren't suitable for mass data. In our example, each customer's miles are determined using the GET_MILES_FOR_CUSTOMER method to identify the premium customers.

8.3.5 Optimization Using Open SQL

In the first step, you'll try to accelerate the identification of premium customers without using SAP HANA views and SQLScript. For this purpose, you'll create Program ZR_A4H_CHAPTER8_TOP_CUST_1 and call the GET_TOP_CUSTOMERS_1 method within this program.

Code optimizations The new implementation differs from the original program in the following ways:

► Nested SELECT statements are avoided (because these are disadvantageous both in general and especially for SAP HANA).

► Structures are used instead of the SELECT * statement.

► The number of buffer accesses is minimized (in particular by reading Customizing table ZA4H_C8_PARAMS only once).

► The number of function module calls is minimized; the new implementation converts units only at the end of the algorithm, after the bookings are already aggregated (wherever possible).

Coding before optimization Listing 8.1 shows the original implementation of the code for identification of premium customers as pseudo code.

```
"Selecting customers
SELECT * FROM scustom ...
  ...
  "Determining miles per customer by re
  "using the method GET_MILES_FOR_CUSTOMER
  CALL METHOD GET_MILES_FOR_CUSTOMER(...)
    ...
    "Selecting the bookings for the customer
    SELECT * FROM sbook...
      ...
      "Selecting the connection master data for the
      "bookings
      SELECT SINGLE * FROM spfli...
      ...
      "Unit conversion per booking
      CALL FUNCTION 'UNIT_CONVERSION_SIMPLE'...
      ...
      "Reading the Customizings per booking
      CALL METHOD GET_PARAMETER_VALUE(...)
      ...
      "Selecting the master data for the customer
      SELECT SINGLE * FROM scustom...
```

```
    ...
  ENDSELECT.
  ...
  ...
ENDSELECT.
```
Listing 8.1 Original Implementation

Listing 8.2 shows the optimized coding for determining the premium
customers.

```
"Single reading operation for the Customizing
CALL METHOD GET_PARAMETER_VALUE(...)

"Reading all customers, bookings, and master data of the
"connections using a JOIN and a
"field string
SELECT... FROM scustom
  INNER JOIN sbook...
  INNER JOIN spfli...
  WHERE...
  ...
  "Calculating the miles in accordance with the
  "Customizing
  IF class = 'C'.
    lv_miles = ...
  ELSEIF class = 'F'.
    lv_miles = ...
  ELSE.
    ...
  ENDIF.
  ...
  COLLECT ls_miles INTO lt_miles.
ENDSELECT.

"One-time unit conversion per customer and
"for the unit used for this customer
LOOP AT lt_miles INTO ls_miles.
  ...
  CALL FUNCTION 'UNIT_CONVERSION_SIMPLE'...
  ...
ENDLOOP.
```
Listing 8.2 Coding Optimized with Open SQL

Despite the optimization, premium customers are still identified in
ABAP because the logic described in Section 8.2.1 can't be expressed
using Open SQL.

8.3.6   Analysis of the First Optimization

You now run Program ZR_A4H_CHAPTER8_TOP_CUST_1, which runs much faster. A runtime analysis using Transaction STAD confirms the positive impact of the modifications (see Figure 8.10). The program is now executed within only 71 seconds. The database portion was reduced to about 25 seconds. However, a large number of records (more than 5.2 million records) are still read from the database.

```
Analysis of time in work process

CPU time                  50.660 ms     Number     Roll ins            1
RFC+CPIC time                  0 ms                Roll outs           1
                                                   Enqueues            0
Total time in workprocs   71.474 ms
                                        Load time  Program          0  ms
 ┌─Response time────────── 71.474 ms─┐             Screen           0  ms
                                                   CUA interf.      0  ms
Wait for work process          0 ms
Processing time           46.794 ms     Roll time  Out              0  ms
Load time                      0 ms                In               0  ms
Generating time                0 ms                Wait             0  ms
Roll (in+wait) time            0 ms
Database request time     24.679 ms     Frontend   No.roundtrips       1
Enqueue time                   0 ms                GUI time         0  ms
                                                   Net time         0  ms


Analysis of ABAP/4 database requests (only explicitly by application)

Connection                    DEFAULT        Request time      24.679 ms
Database requests total            14        Commit time            0 ms
DB Proc. Calls                      0        DB Proc. Time          0 ms

Type of        Database           Buffer   Database  Request  Avg.time /
ABAP request       rows  Requests    rows     calls  time (ms)  row (ms)

Total          5201.342        14       11       359   24.679       0,0

Direct read           0        10       10         0        0       0,0
Sequential read 5201.342        4        1       359   24.679       0,0
Update                0         0                  0        0       0,0
Delete                0         0                  0        0       0,0
Insert                0         0                  0        0       0,0

Note: Tables were saved in the tablebuffer.
```

Figure 8.10 Runtime Statistics after the First Optimization

Function module calls

The ABAP trace (Transaction SAT) clearly shows these improvements. From Figure 8.11, you can see that the UNIT_CONVERSION_SIMPLE function module was called only once per customer (4,637 times) and that the table buffers weren't accessed as frequently. However, the same number of records was read from the database so that the related load of the database interface remained unchanged.

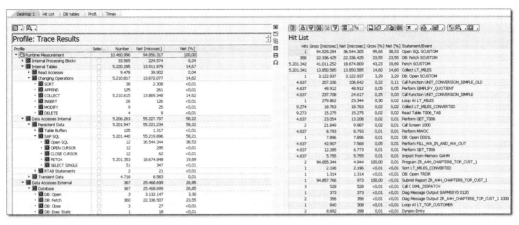

Figure 8.11 ABAP Trace after the First Optimization

The SQL trace in Transaction ST05 shows the improvement as well. A join is now executed only once to transfer all records (more than 5.2 million) to the program in one operation (see Figure 8.12).

Join to transfer data records

Figure 8.12 SQL Trace after the First Optimization

8.3.7 Analysis Result

The analysis using Transactions STAD, SAT, and ST05 shows that despite the adjustment, more than 5.2 million records are still transferred from the database server to the application server. The reason for this is primarily that some of the calculations are done for individual bookings, which are listed here:

Individual bookings

▶ Application of the booking-class factor

▶ Application of the early-booking factor

▶ Application of the customer-specific discount

In particular, the application of the early-booking factor can only be done for individual bookings because it depends on the time difference between booking date and flight date. To optimize the program further, you have to avoid transferring every individual booking from the database to the application server. Basically, there are two options to reach this goal:

- Implementing a database procedure with ABAP Managed Database Procedures (AMDP) and SQLScript (or calculation engine [CE] functions)
- Modeling a view in SAP HANA Studio

8.3.8 Optimizing a Database Procedure

You'll optimize the program using an AMDP. To do this, you'll create Program ZR_A4H_CHAPTER8_TOP_CUST_2. This program calls the GET_TOP_CUSTOMERS_2 method, which calls the AMDP GET_TOP_CUSTOMERS method of the ZCL_A4H_CHAPTER8_TOP_CUST_AMDP class implemented in SQLScript (see Listing 8.3). Here, the values are read from the Customizing and stored in variables that are required in the subsequent step. Then the program reads the bookings and calculates the surcharges for the booking classes and the early bookings (values from Customizing). The data are aggregated per customer and unit for the distance flown taking into account the reduction for any discounts. You then implement the conversion of all distances into miles. Subsequently, you determine the top customers and transfer them to the procedure's return structure. As a result, the system only transfers the required data of the top customers to the ABAP application server.

```
METHOD get_top_customers
BY DATABASE PROCEDURE FOR HDB LANGUAGE SQLSCRIPT
    USING za4h_c8_params scustom sbook spfli.

    declare lv_factor_c decimal := 0;
    declare lv_factor_f decimal := 0;
    declare lv_earlyb_d integer := 0;
    declare lv_earlyb_f decimal := 0;

/* Get the customizing */
select value into lv_factor_c from za4h_c8_params
where mandt = :iv_mandt and name = 'FACTOR_C';
select value into lv_factor_f from za4h_c8_params
where mandt = :iv_mandt and name = 'FACTOR_F';
select value into lv_earlyb_d from za4h_c8_params
```

```
where mandt = :iv_mandt and name = 'EARLYB_D';
select value into lv_earlyb_f from za4h_c8_params
where mandt = :iv_mandt and name = 'EARLYB_F';

/* Calculate the miles and read additional data
which is needed later */
lt_miles = select s.mandt as mandt, s.id as customer_id,
s.discount as discount, i.distid as miles_unit,
( case b.class when 'Y' then i.distance
  when 'C' then i.distance * :lv_factor_c
  when 'F' then i.distance * :lv_factor_f end )
as miles_with_factor,
( case when days_between(b.order_date, b.fldate)
< :lv_earlyb_d then 0
  when days_between(b.order_date, b.fldate)
>= :lv_earlyb_d then i.distance * :lv_earlyb_f end )
as miles_earlyb
from scustom as s
inner join sbook as b ON b.mandt = s.mandt
and b.customid = s.id
inner join spfli as i ON i.mandt = b.mandt
and i.carrid = b.carrid and i.connid = b.connid
                      where s.mandt = :iv_mandt
                        and b.fldate >= :iv_date_from
                        and b.fldate <= :iv_date_to
                        and b.cancelled != 'X';

/* Aggregate the data and consider the discount */
lt_miles_aggregated = select mandt, customer_id,
miles_unit as unit_code,
sum( ( miles_with_factor + miles_earlyb ) * ( 100 -discount ) /
 100 ) as unit_value
from :lt_miles
group by mandt, customer_id, miles_unit;

/* Do the conversion    */
lt_miles_converted = CE_CONVERSION(
          :lt_miles_aggregated,
          [ error_handling = 'set to null',
          client = :iv_mandt,
          family = 'unit',
          method = 'ERP',
          erp_rate_lookup = 'ERP_DIMENSION_ONLY',
          target_unit = 'MI',
          source_unit_column = "UNIT_CODE",
          output_unit_column = "UNIT_CODE_CONVERTED",
          output = 'input,converted,output_unit' ],
          [ "UNIT_VALUE" as "UNIT_VALUE_CONVERTED" ]
        );
/* Fill the output parameter     */
et_top_customer = select top :iv_number customer_id,
```

```
s.name, sum(round(unit_value_converted, 0)) as miles,
unit_code_converted as miles_unit
from :lt_miles_converted as c
inner join scustom as s on s.mandt = c.mandt
and s.id = c.customer_id
group by customer_id, name, unit_code_converted
order by miles desc;

ENDMETHOD.
```
Listing 8.3 AMDP GET_TOP_CUSTOMERS Method

8.3.9   Analysis of the Second Optimization

The second optimization is once again analyzed using Transaction STAD. Figure 8.13 shows that the runtime is now only 2.3 seconds and is determined almost completely by the time in the database. Only 11 data records were transferred.

```
Analysis of time in work process

CPU time                  10 ms    Number     Roll ins          1
RFC+CPIC time              0 ms               Roll outs         1
                                              Enqueues          0
Total time in workprocs  2.328 ms
                                    Load time  Program          0  ms
 ┌─Response time          2.328 ms─┐          Screen            0  ms
                                              CUA interf.       0  ms
Wait for work process      0 ms
Processing time            9 ms     Roll time  Out              0  ms
Load time                  0 ms                In               0  ms
Generating time            0 ms                Wait             0  ms
Roll (in+wait) time        0 ms
Database request time      2 ms     Frontend   No.roundtrips     1
Enqueue time               0 ms               GUI time          0  ms
                                              Net time          0  ms

DB procedure call time   2.317 ms   No. of DB procedure calls   1
```

```
Connection               DEFAULT      Request time      2 ms
Database requests total     12        Commit time       1 ms
DB Proc. Calls               0        DB Proc. Time     0 ms
```

Type of ABAP request	Database rows	Requests	Buffer rows	Database calls	Request time (ms)	Avg.time / row (ms)
Total	11	12	10	2	2	0,2
Direct read	0	10	10		0	0,0
Sequential read	11	2	0	2	2	0,2
Update	0	0		0	0	0,0
Delete	0	0		0	0	0,0
Insert	0	0		0	0	0,0

```
Note: Tables were saved in the tablebuffer.
```

Figure 8.13 Eleven Records Read from the ZEV_A4H_MILES View

Regarding the table accesses in Figure 8.14, you can see that only 10 records are now read by the ZCL_A4H_CHAPTER8_TOP_CUST_AMDP=>GET_TOP_CUSTOMERS method. This is the aggregated final result.

Aggregated records

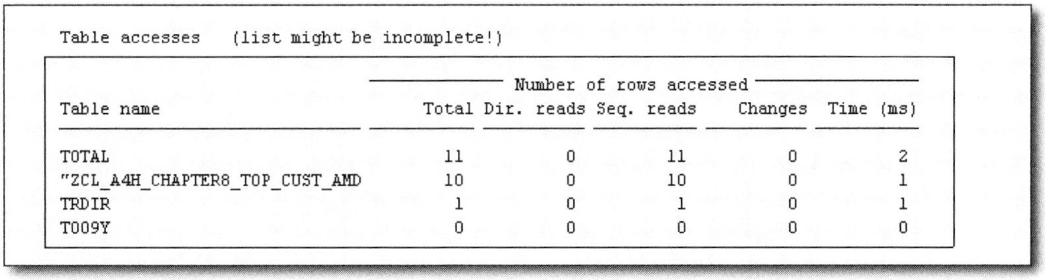

Table accesses (list might be incomplete!)

Table name	Number of rows accessed: Total	Dir. reads	Seq. reads	Changes	Time (ms)
TOTAL	11	0	11	0	2
"ZCL_A4H_CHAPTER8_TOP_CUST_AMD	10	0	10	0	1
TRDIR	1	0	1	0	1
T009Y	0	0	0	0	0

Figure 8.14 Runtime Statistics: Table Accesses

Due to the smaller result set, the number of calls of the internal database statements in the ABAP program can be dramatically reduced. As you can see from the ABAP trace (Figure 8.15), the program is now executed almost entirely in the database (98%).

Program execution moved to the database layer

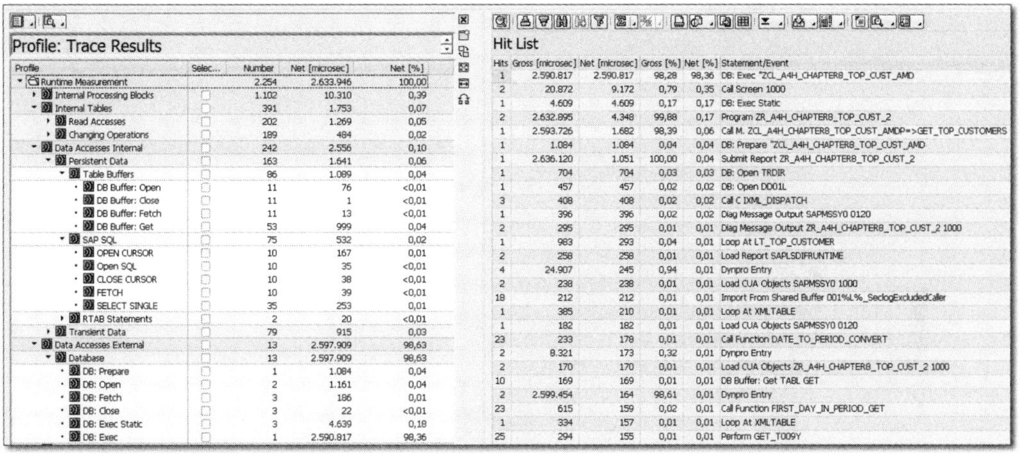

Profile: Trace Results

Profile	Selec...	Number	Net [microsec]	Net [%]
Runtime Measurement		2.254	2.633.946	100,00
Internal Processing Blocks		1.102	10.310	0,39
Internal Tables		391	1.753	0,07
Read Accesses		202	1.269	0,05
Changing Operations		189	484	0,02
Data Accesses Internal		242	2.556	0,10
Persistent Data		163	1.641	0,06
Table Buffers		86	1.089	0,04
DB Buffer: Open		11	76	<0,01
DB Buffer: Close		11	1	<0,01
DB Buffer: Fetch		11	13	<0,01
DB Buffer: Get		53	999	0,04
SAP SQL		75	532	0,02
OPEN CURSOR		10	167	0,01
Open SQL		10	35	<0,01
CLOSE CURSOR		10	38	<0,01
FETCH		10	39	<0,01
SELECT SINGLE		35	253	0,01
RTAB Statements		2	20	<0,01
Transient Data		79	915	0,03
Data Accesses External		13	2.597.909	98,63
Database		13	2.597.909	98,63
DB: Prepare		1	1.084	0,04
DB: Open		2	1.161	0,04
DB: Fetch		3	186	0,01
DB: Close		3	22	<0,01
DB: Exec Static		3	4.639	0,18
DB: Exec		1	2.590.817	98,36

Hit List

Hits	Gross [microsec]	Net [microsec]	Gross [%]	Net [%]	Statement/Event
1	2.590.817	2.590.817	98,28	98,36	DB: Exec "ZCL_A4H_CHAPTER8_TOP_CUST_AMD
2	20.872	9.172	0,79	0,35	Call Screen 1000
1	4.609	4.609	0,17	0,17	DB: Exec Static
2	2.632.895	4.348	99,88	0,17	Program ZR_A4H_CHAPTER8_TOP_CUST_2
1	2.593.726	1.682	98,39	0,06	Call M. ZCL_A4H_CHAPTER8_TOP_CUST_AMDP=>GET_TOP_CUSTOMERS
1	1.084	1.084	0,04	0,04	DB: Prepare "ZCL_A4H_CHAPTER8_TOP_CUST_AMD
1	2.636.120	1.051	100,00	0,04	Submit Report ZR_A4H_CHAPTER8_TOP_CUST_2
1	704	704	0,03	0,03	DB: Open TRDIR
1	457	457	0,02	0,02	DB: Open DD01L
3	408	408	0,02	0,02	Call C IXML_DISPATCH
1	396	396	0,02	0,02	Diag Message Output SAPMSSY0 0120
2	295	295	0,01	0,01	Diag Message Output ZR_A4H_CHAPTER8_TOP_CUST_2 1000
1	983	293	0,04	0,01	Loop At LT_TOP_CUSTOMER
2	258	258	0,01	0,01	Load Report SAPLSDIFRUNTIME
4	24.907	245	0,94	0,01	Dynpro Entry
2	238	238	0,01	0,01	Load CUA Objects SAPMSSY0 1000
18	212	212	0,01	0,01	Import From Shared Buffer 001%L%_SeclogExcludedCaller
1	385	210	0,01	0,01	Loop At XMLTABLE
1	182	182	0,01	0,01	Load CUA Objects SAPMSSY0 0120
23	233	178	0,01	0,01	Call Function DATE_TO_PERIOD_CONVERT
2	8.321	173	0,32	0,01	Dynpro Entry
2	170	170	0,01	0,01	Load CUA Objects ZR_A4H_CHAPTER8_TOP_CUST_2 1000
10	169	169	0,01	0,01	DB Buffer: Get TABL GET
2	2.599.454	164	98,61	0,01	Dynpro Entry
23	615	159	0,02	0,01	Call Function FIRST_DAY_IN_PERIOD_GET
1	334	157	0,01	0,01	Loop At XMLTABLE
25	294	155	0,01	0,01	Perform GET_T009Y

Figure 8.15 ABAP Trace after the Second Optimization

The SQL trace in Transaction ST05 (see Figure 8.16) also confirms the good result. This trace also shows that the ZCL_A4H_CHAPTER8_TOP_CUST_AMDP=>GET_TOP_CUSTOMERS method is accessed only once.

Single access

Performance Analysis: Structure-Identical Statements

ΣExecutio	ΣRedunda	Identi	Duration	ΣReco	Dur./Exec.	Rec./Ex	Dur./Rec.	Dur./Rec.	Lngth	BufferT	Table T	Object Name	Statement
18	3		2.321.485	18									
1	0	0	2.306.720	0	2.306.720	0,0	2.306.720	2.306.720	0			"ZCL_A4H_CHAP	CALL "ZCL_A4H_CHAPTER8_TOP_CUST_AMDP=>GET_TOP_CUSTOMERS#stb2#20150614202022" (?, ?, ?, ?)
3	2	67	3.676	0	1.225	0,0	1.225	1.136	0				COMMIT WORK ON CONNECTION 0
2	1	50	2.773	2	1.387	1,0	1.387	802	342		VIEW	PROGDIR	SELECT WHERE "NAME" = ? AND "STATE" = ?

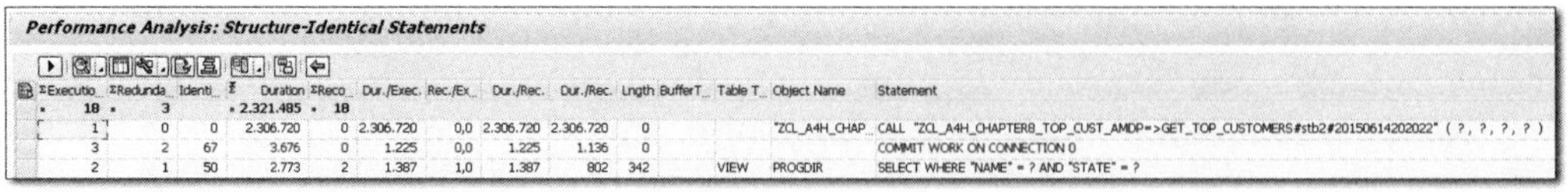

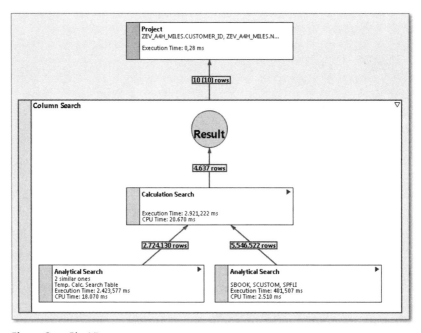

Figure 8.16 SQL Trace after the Second Optimization

Displaying the SQL statement

For a detailed analysis of the SQL statement using PlanViz, you now take the call from Transaction ST05, which may look like Listing 8.4. You then run the statement in the SQL Console in SAP HANA Studio.

```
CALL  "ZCL_A4H_CHAPTER8_TOP_CUST_AMDP=>GET_TOP_
CUSTOMERS#stb2#20150614202022"  ('001',10,'20130701',
'20150630')
```

Listing 8.4 Call of Procedure

Analytical search and CPU time

The analysis result of PlanViz is displayed in Figure 8.17. As you can see, an *analytical search* was performed, which means that the Online Analytical Processing (OLAP) engine was used. You can see the execution time and the CPU time in microseconds for each node.

Figure 8.17 PlanViz

The fact that the value for CPU time is higher than the value for execution time shows that the respective nodes ran in parallel. This means that several threads started and ran on several CPUs so that about 20 seconds of CPU time were used within the runtime of 2.9 seconds.

Sample Execution Times	[«]
Note that our sample program and the optimized versions were run on a small system in the cloud and didn't use very powerful hardware. If these sample programs were run on a more powerful system with more CPUs, a runtime of about one second or less would be possible for this procedure.	

8.3.10 Analysis Result

The identification of premium customers was optimized in two steps: **Runtime improvement**

▶ By optimizing the program using Open SQL, the runtime was reduced from 547 seconds to 71 seconds. This is a factor of about 7.5.

▶ In the subsequent optimization steps using a database procedure, the runtime was reduced to 2.3 seconds. In comparison to the original runtime, this corresponds to a factor of about 230.

By optimizing both the program and the database access, premium customers can now be identified at much higher speeds. Figure 8.18 shows a graphical representation of the runtimes.

Due to this improvement, the code can now be used in dialog programs, and you benefit from a range of new possibilities and options. You can, for example, use the database procedure for planning and simulation purposes to analyze the impact of changed parameters for mile calculation. **Summary**

With this sample scenario, we were able to illustrate the following:

▶ How to use the optimization tools presented in Chapter 7

▶ How you can write fast programs using Open SQL and good ABAP programming techniques

▶ How, in some cases, performance gains only occur when using native functions from SAP HANA

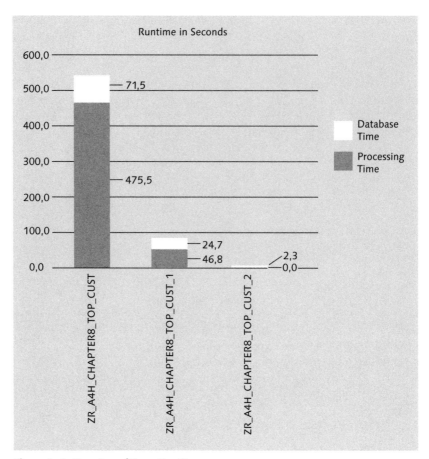

Figure 8.18 Overview of Execution Times

You can now also further analyze the other programs from the TEST_
A4H_BOOK_CHAPTER08 package and try to accelerate them using your technical options.

PART III

Advanced Techniques for ABAP Programming for SAP HANA

Using SAP HANA, you can expand transactional applications through analytical functionality. Varied technologies and tools are available for this purpose, which—in many cases—allow you to add analytical functions with very little programming effort.

9   Integrating Analytical Functionality

In Chapter 1, you learned that you can combine transactional and analytical functionality or add analytical capabilities to existing transactional applications using SAP HANA. This chapter describes this topic in more detail. From our point of view, this is important to avoid investments in the development of analytical functionalities that are already provided out of the box.

We'll start by explaining important concepts and terms used in this context. Then we provide an overview of the SAP BusinessObjects portfolio and describe the options provided by the Analytic Engine of SAP Business Warehouse (SAP BW). Finally, we'll introduce possible architectures that can be used to expand transactional, ABAP-based systems by analytical functionality, along with their advantages and disadvantages.

Due to space constraints, however, the presented technologies and tools can't be explained in detail. Therefore, you won't be able immediately to use all of the methods presented for integrating analytical functionality in transactional applications after reading this chapter.

9.1   What Is Analytical Functionality?

To understand the options described in this chapter, you need to understand *analytical functionality* and how the integration of analytical capabilities in transactional applications differs from a data warehouse.

Reporting vs.
data analysis Analytical functionality is more than just reporting. Reporting helps you present and format data. Data analysis should then help you understand correlations and causes so you can determine necessary measures based on this information (*insight to action*). Ideally, these measures should have a positive impact for your organization (e.g., higher revenues, lower cost, improved customer retention). Figure 9.1 shows how these concepts correlate.

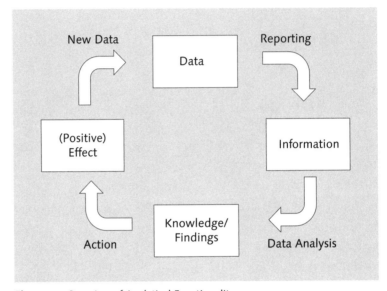

Figure 9.1 Overview of Analytical Functionality

Levels of reporting
and data analysis Reporting and data analysis tasks can be performed at different levels (Figure 9.2):

- ▶ **Strategic level**
  The strategic level deals with basic questions that have a long-term impact on an organization. Using the SFLIGHT data model from the previous chapters, possible strategic questions for an airline include the following: Which flight connections should be expanded? How should the miles program be enhanced?

- ▶ **Tactical level**
  The tactical level deals with questions that have a medium-term impact on the organization or individual areas within the company.

Possible tactical questions include the following: How should ticket prices be adjusted starting January 1 of the following year if kerosene prices continue to develop as they have in the past three months? How will the operating result in the next three years be affected by the new air-traffic tax?

▶ **Operational level**
The operational level deals with short-term questions regarding day-to-day operations. Possible operational questions include the following: Which duty-free products should be replaced due to lack of demand? Which customers should be approached to improve the business-class utilization of a certain flight connection?

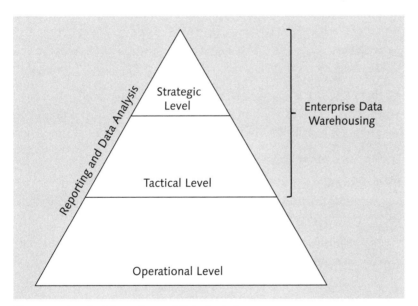

Figure 9.2 Levels of Reporting and Data Analysis

While small time delays in data provisioning usually aren't problematic for reporting and data analysis at the strategic and tactical level—and it may not be possible to avoid such delays, as data from different systems must be consolidated—latency-free data provisioning is often of paramount importance at the operational level. Imagine a travel agent who is on the phone with a customer who wants to book a flight. Ideally, the travel agent should not only know the current use of the desired flight

Time delay in data provisioning

but should also be able to offer alternative flights on other dates and possibly on better terms. The travel agent should also know the current status and bonus-mile count of the customer, the discounts granted, and so on. In this example, time delays when providing this data aren't acceptable.

OLTP and OLAP In addition to *transactional systems* for their business processes (e.g., SAP ERP), organizations often use separate *analytical systems* referred to as *data warehouses* (e.g., SAP BW). Transactional systems are systems for Online Transaction Processing (OLTP). As a synonym for analytical systems, the term Online Analytical Processing (OLAP) is often used. The latter isn't entirely correct because OLAP describes multidimensional analyses based on a star schema, while data in a data warehouse can also be organized in flat database tables (in SAP BW, for example, in the form of *operational data store (ODS) objects*—see Section 9.3). Some background information on OLAP is also provided in Chapter 4, Section 4.4.

Usage for operative scenarios In recent years, SAP BW was used not only for strategic and tactical analyses in the SAP environment but often also for operational reports and data analyses for the following reasons:

- Load reduction on transactional systems
- No significant enhancements of Report Painter, drilldown reporting, Logistics Information System (LIS), and other existing reporting tools within transactional systems
- Extensive business intelligence (BI) content (i.e., preconfigured data transformations and information models for SAP BW)

This meant that the required data wasn't always provided in real time for the end users.

Analyses on the fly Today, you have the option to implement operational reporting where it belongs: within the transactional systems. Analyses that could only be run during the night and after several data transformations in the past can now be done on the fly based on the original data and, for instance, using the tools of the *SAP BusinessObjects portfolio*.

9.2   SAP BusinessObjects Portfolio

The SAP BusinessObjects portfolio provides numerous tools for the different levels of reporting. Each tool is used for different application cases and has specific advantages and disadvantages. A detailed description of all tools is beyond the scope of this chapter, so we'll only categorize the tools and give you a general overview here.

In Table 9.1, the tools of the SAP BusinessObjects portfolio are subdivided into three categories: reporting, data analysis, and data exploration.

Categorization

Reporting	Data Analysis	Data Exploration
SAP Crystal Reports	SAP BusinessObjects Analysis, edition for Microsoft Office	SAP Business Explorer (SAP BEx)
SAP BusinessObjects Web Intelligence	SAP BusinessObjects Analysis, edition for OLAP	SAP Lumira
SAP BusinessObjects Dashboards		
SAP BusinessObjects Design Studio		

Table 9.1 Overview of the SAP BusinessObjects Portfolio

Reporting

The reporting tools will help you gather and format data. The most commonly known tool used for this purpose is probably *SAP Crystal Reports* with which you can create, format, and print reports with precise pixel values. This tool is the de facto standard for formatted reporting.

SAP Crystal Reports

Figure 9.3 shows the preview of a report created with SAP Crystal Reports that breaks down the sales of the airlines by connection.

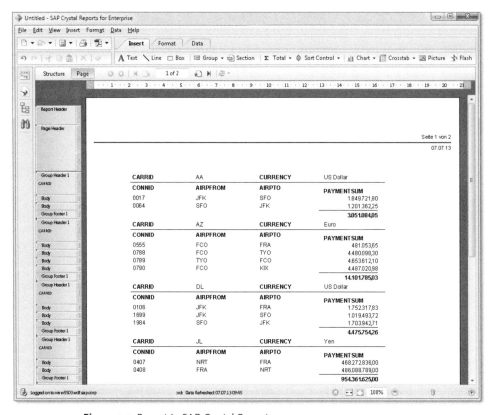

Figure 9.3 Report in SAP Crystal Reports

Web Intelligence   *SAP BusinessObjects Web Intelligence* can also be used to generate formatted reports. However, this tool doesn't provide the same scope of formatting and printing options as SAP Crystal Reports. Web Intelligence,
however, is better suited if end users from the individual departments
want to create their own reports (*self-service BI*).

Dashboards   *Dashboards* summarize important key figures for decision makers. *SAP
BusinessObjects Dashboards* provides a series of components that can be
used to create appealing dashboards. Using these dashboards, you can
visualize *what-if scenarios* as well as use them offline, if necessary.
Although SAP BusinessObjects Dashboards is still maintained and partially improved, *SAP BusinessObjects Design Studio* is the strategic tool
recommended by SAP for creating dashboards (described briefly in the
next section).

Data Analysis

This brings us to the tools for data analysis. With *SAP BusinessObjects Analysis, Edition for Microsoft Office*, you can analyze multidimensional datasets interactively and based on Microsoft Excel. This makes the tool particularly useful for employees in individual departments who are often well-practiced with Excel. SAP BusinessObjects Analysis, edition for Microsoft Office, is similar to the *SAP BEx Analyzer*. However, SAP BusinessObjects Analysis, edition for Microsoft Office, provides more functions and a better user experience. In addition to Excel, data also can be embedded in Microsoft PowerPoint.

SAP Business-Objects Analysis, edition for Microsoft Office

Figure 9.4 shows the formatted view of a SAP BW query using SAP BusinessObjects Analysis, edition for Microsoft Office.

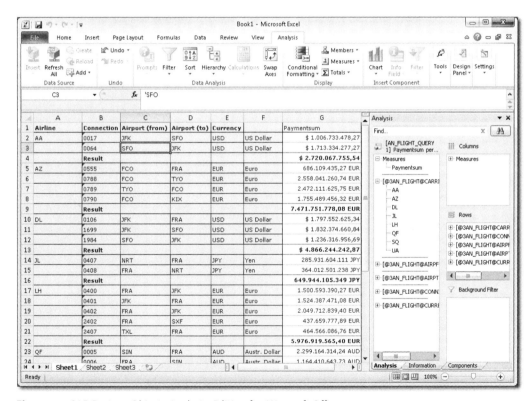

Figure 9.4 SAP BusinessObjects Analysis, Edition for Microsoft Office

SAP Business-
Objects Analysis,
edition for OLAP

The web-based variant for analyses of multidimensional datasets is *SAP BusinessObjects Analysis, edition for OLAP*. Alternatively, you can also analyze multidimensional datasets in SAP BusinessObjects Design Studio.

SAP Business-
Objects
Design Studio

SAP BusinessObjects Design Studio is a tool used to create analytical applications and dashboards. Using SAP BusinessObjects Design Studio, you can create pixel-perfect analytical applications and dashboards. This tool provides a variety of charts and comprehensive *theming*. In addition, it also supports mobile scenarios.

Figure 9.5 shows the design of a simple analytical application in SAP BusinessObjects Design Studio.

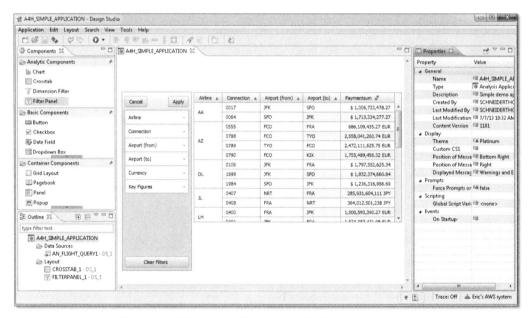

Figure 9.5 SAP BusinessObjects Design Studio

Data Exploration

SAP Business
Explorer and
SAP Lumira

A special case of data analysis is data exploration (i.e., the interactive analysis of a dataset). For data exploration, end users need tools that can be used intuitively and provide high-quality visualizations. The SAP BusinessObjects portfolio includes two tools: SAP Business Explorer

(SAP BEx) and SAP Lumira. Although SAP BEx is still maintained and partially improved, SAP recommends SAP Lumira as the strategic tool for data exploration.

For more detailed information, see the following information sources:

▶ The SAP Community Network and SAP Service Marketplace provide full information on the various products of the SAP BusinessObjects portfolio and their roadmaps.

▶ *SAP NetWeaver BW and SAP BusinessObjects* by Heilig, Kessler, Knötzele, John, and Thaler-Mieslinger (SAP PRESS, 2012) provides comprehensive descriptions of the various tools.

▶ You can find useful information on the web, for example, at *http:// blogs.sap.com/analytics/2014/06/25/run-simple-convergence-of-the-sap-businessobjects-bi-product-portfolio/*.

9.3   Digression: SAP Business Warehouse

Two questions that come up on a regular basis are as follows:

▶ Does SAP HANA replace SAP BW?

▶ Is it true that every SAP NetWeaver AS ABAP has SAP BW functionality?

We'll discuss these two questions in this section.

9.3.1   SAP HANA Versus SAP Business Warehouse

In answer to the first question, SAP HANA does *not* replace SAP BW. Even though SAP HANA is more than just a database, it isn't a data warehouse on its own.

However, some scenarios that were implemented using SAP BW in the past will be possible without this data warehouse in the future. Instead of setting up extraction, transformation, loading (ETL) processes for these scenarios, you'll use the original data from the transactional systems (if SAP HANA is the primary database), or you'll replicate the required data to a secondary SAP HANA database (i.e., you use SAP HANA as a data mart).

Other scenarios will still benefit from the capabilities of a data warehouse in the future. Using SAP BW (based on a traditional database or an SAP HANA database), you can do the following:

▸ Reduce the load of transactional systems.

▸ Create data models that are better suited than the original data for strategic and tactical reports and data analyses.

▸ Harmonize and integrate data from different data sources.

▸ Keep historical data available without using the capacity of transactional systems.

From our point of view, SAP HANA should be used instead of SAP BW in particular for operational reports and data analysis and, in some cases, for system landscapes where only a single transactional system is connected to the data warehouse today. For enterprise data warehousing at the tactical and strategic level, you should still use SAP BW (based on SAP HANA, if possible).

This takes us to the second question: Is it true that every AS ABAP has SAP BW functionality? The answer to that question is yes because every AS ABAP includes the `SAP_BW` software component as of Release 6.40. Therefore, every up-to-date ABAP system, including SAP ERP or SAP Customer Relationship Management (SAP CRM), includes the *Analytic Engine* from SAP BW. You can also use the SAP BW functionality in SAP ERP or SAP CRM (i.e., directly in the OLTP system). This way of using SAP BW is referred to as *Embedded Reporting* (as opposed to Enterprise Data Warehousing) and is especially suitable for operational reports and data analyses.

Using SAP BW can provide some benefits if you want to expand transactional applications through analytical functionality. These benefits are discussed in more detail in Section 9.4. Before we discuss those benefits, however, we want to explain some basic SAP BW terms and discuss how to access data in SAP HANA using *InfoProviders*.

9.3.2 Overview of Terminology

To understand how you can access data in SAP HANA using InfoProviders, you must know some terms and concepts of SAP BW. If you've never worked with SAP BW, Figure 9.6 provides an overview of the most important concepts.

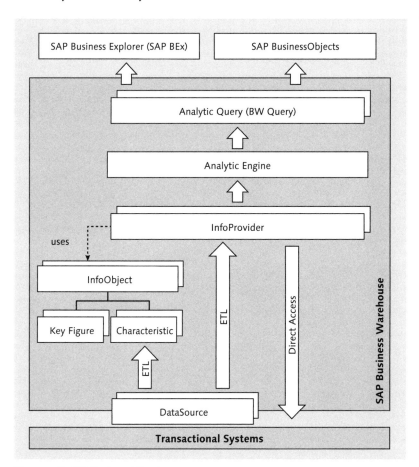

Figure 9.6 SAP Business Warehouse

InfoProviders are used for data access in SAP BW. The system differentiates between InfoProviders where data are actually loaded physically via ETL processes and InfoProviders that only provide a logical view of the data. Examples for InfoProviders are *InfoCubes*, *ODS objects*, *InfoObjects*, *transient* and *virtual InfoProviders*, and *MultiProviders*.

InfoProvider

InfoObjects
Put simply, *InfoObjects* can be subdivided into key figures (e.g., revenue) and characteristics (e.g., an airline). InfoObjects are used to model Info-Providers. However, characteristics can also be used as InfoProviders themselves (and usually provide access to master data in this case).

DataSources
DataSources transfer data in SAP BW (e.g., from a transactional system such as SAP ERP).

SAP BW queries
Analytic queries (also referred to as *SAP BW queries*) describe data queries executed on InfoProviders. They define rows and columns, filters, threshold values (to highlight specific records), and so on. To define analytical queries, you use the SAP BEx Query Designer, which is part of the SAP *BEx*. Analytical queries are executed via the *Analytic Engine*, which supports reporting and multidimensional analyses.

SAP Business Explorer
SAP BEx provides reporting and analysis tools for SAP BW:

▶ **SAP BEx Query Designer**
To define SAP BW queries.

▶ **SAP BEx Analyzer**
For analyses based on SAP BW queries in Excel.

▶ **SAP BEx Web Application Designer**
To create browser-based analytical applications based on SAP BW queries.

SAP Business-Objects
As an alternative to the SAP BEx Analyzer and the SAP BEx Web Application Designer, you can also use the tools provided by SAP BusinessObjects:

▶ *SAP BusinessObjects Analysis, Edition for Microsoft Office* is an alternative to the SAP BEx Analyzer (see Section 9.2).

▶ An alternative to the SAP BEx Web Application Designer is SAP Design Studio (also described in Section 9.2).

For further information on SAP BEx, go to *http://scn.sap.com/community/business-explorer*.

9.3.3 InfoProviders When Using SAP HANA

This section explains how you can access data views in SAP HANA using transient and virtual InfoProviders. In addition to that, we'll introduce further transient InfoProviders for accessing data on the SAP HANA database. We'll then provide an example to describe how to use InfoProviders in SAP BW queries.

Transient InfoProviders Based on Views

Transient InfoProviders are generated based on a data source at runtime and without modeling in the Data Warehousing Workbench. This type of InfoProvider doesn't contain any data. When accessing transient InfoProviders, the system reads the data from the underlying data source.

When using SAP HANA as a primary database, you can access SAP HANA views via transient InfoProviders. To do so, you must first publish the views. Suitable candidates are analytic views and calculation views (see Chapter 4, Section 4.4).

Publishing

Use Transaction RSDD_HM_PUBLISH to publish SAP HANA views. This transaction creates an *analytical index* for an SAP HANA view and subsequently a transient InfoProvider @3<Name of the analytical index> based on this index. For an analytic view, the characteristics and key figures of the transient InfoProvider are derived from the fact table (*data foundation*) and the dimension tables (e.g., the linked attribute views).

Figure 9.7 shows the analytical index and the transient InfoProvider for the analytic view AN_FLIGHT.

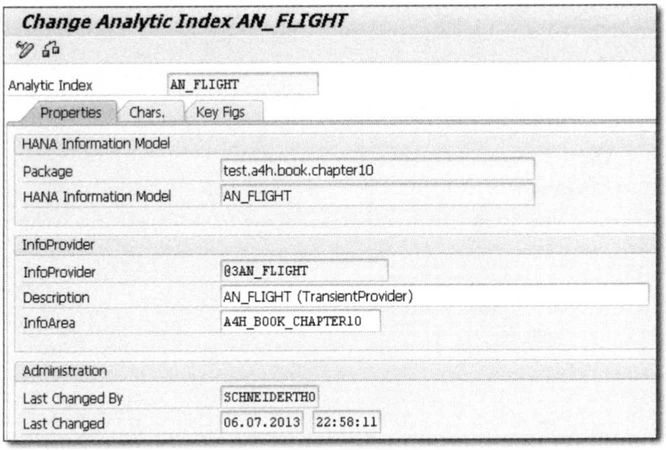

Figure 9.7 Creating an Analytical Index

Assigning InfoObjects

Optionally, you can assign InfoObjects defined in the Data Warehousing Workbench to the characteristics and key figures of the transient Info-Provider. You can thus add further metadata to the InfoProvider that can, for example, be used for authorization checks. It's currently not possible to use the navigation attributes of the referenced InfoObjects.

Advantages and disadvantages

The biggest advantage of a transient InfoProvider is that it's regenerated at runtime by the system if necessary. This means that the InfoProvider and the SAP BW queries that are based on this provider are usually changed automatically if you modify the underlying analytic view or cal-culation view.

A disadvantage is that transient InfoProviders can't be transported, so they must be created manually in every system (development, quality assurance, production).

Virtual InfoProviders Based on Views

Instead of working with a transient InfoProvider, you can also define a virtual InfoProvider. In contrast to transient InfoProviders, virtual Info-Providers are modeled in the Data Warehousing Workbench (Transac-tion RSA1). Like transient InfoProviders, virtual InfoProviders don't contain any data. When accessing virtual InfoProviders, the system reads the data from the underlying data source. When using SAP HANA as a primary database, you can use virtual InfoProviders to access ana-lytic and calculation views.

Creating virtual InfoProviders

The example in Figure 9.8 shows how the AN_FLIGHT virtual InfoPro-vider is created.

Characteristics and key figures of vir-tual InfoObjects

If you want to access virtual master data when defining a virtual InfoPro-vider, you can use *virtual InfoObjects*. Like virtual InfoProviders, virtual InfoObjects are modeled in the Data Warehousing Workbench but don't contain any data. When accessing virtual InfoObjects, the system reads the data from the underlying data source.

Figure 9.8 Creating a Virtual InfoProvider

When defining a virtual InfoObject, you can refer to an attribute view in the primary SAP HANA database. The example in Figure 9.9 shows how this is done using the InfoObject CARRID and the attribute view AT_AIR-LINE.

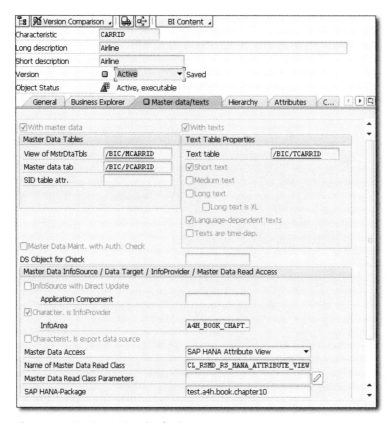

Figure 9.9 Creating a Virtual InfoObject

Virtual InfoProviders have several advantages over transient InfoProviders: they support navigation attributes, can be transported, and can be used in MultiProviders. A disadvantage is that virtual InfoProviders must be modeled in the Data Warehousing Workbench. If you modify the underlying analytic view or calculation view, you might also have to change the virtual InfoProvider. The effort is thus a little greater than in the case of a transient InfoProvider.

Other Transient InfoProviders

For the sake of completeness, note that there are further transient InfoProviders that are also available in traditional databases:

▸ Transient InfoProviders based on classic InfoSets

▸ Transient InfoProviders based on Operational Data Provisioning (ODP)

Long before developing SAP BW, SAP already provided the reporting tool *SAP Query*. In contrast to other reporting tools (e.g., Report Painter and drilldown reporting for Financial Accounting (FI) and Controlling (CO), or the LIS for purchasing and sales), SAP Query can be used universally.

Classic InfoSets

Reports created with SAP Query (i.e., *queries*, which must not be confused with SAP BW queries) are based on *classic* InfoSets (not to be confused with the InfoSets in SAP BW). Classic InfoSets provide a view of certain data. The data sources used for classic InfoSets are often database tables or *joins* defined for several database tables. However, classic InfoSets can also be based on a logical database or on a data-retrieval program.

If you release a classic InfoSet for use via the Analytic Engine in Transaction SQ02, the system creates the @1<Name of the classic InfoSet> transient InfoProvider based on the classic InfoSet.

ODP is part of the infrastructure that is provided for *Search and Operational Analytics* as of AS ABAP Release 7.31. In the context of Enterprise Data Warehousing, *DataSources* (see Section 9.3.2) are used to load data from transactional systems in SAP BW.

Operational Data Provisioning

The basic idea of ODP is to define a search-and-analysis model by linking and enhancing DataSources by analytical properties in the transactional system. You can then create an *operational data provider* based on this search-and-analysis model. This operational data provider is made available via a transient InfoProvider for operational reports and data analyses without having to perform an extraction to a data warehouse. Optionally, the data can be indexed in a secondary SAP HANA database or in the *SAP BW Accelerator* (BWA) based on the infrastructure of the ABAP AS.

Using the InfoProviders in SAP BW Queries

All InfoProviders described previously can be used when creating a SAP
BW query. A SAP BW query describes a data query to an InfoProvider.
SAP BW queries are defined using the SAP BEx Query Designer.

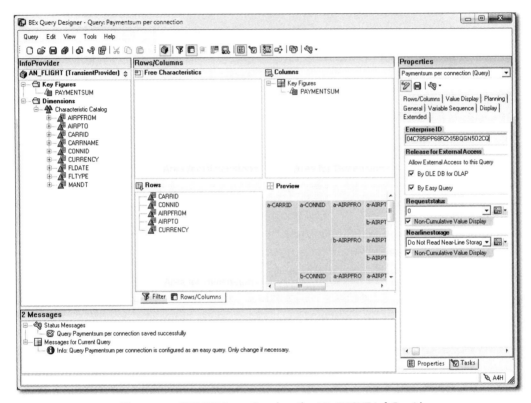

Figure 9.10 SAP BW Query Based on the AN_FLIGHT InfoProvider

The example in Figure 9.10 shows the SAP BW query AN_FLIGHT_QUERY1
(PAYMENT SUM PER CONNECTION) that is based on the AN_FLIGHT transient
InfoProvider. The SAP BW query describes a report that indicates the
sales per flight connection. You can run a first test for your query in
Transaction RSRT.

9.4 Overview of Possible Architectures

This last section is based on the basic principles of the previous chapters and describes the two basic architectures to add analytical functionality to transactional, ABAP-based systems:

- *Direct access* to analytical functions in SAP HANA and integration of analytical functionality in a transactional, ABAP-based application via user interface (UI) integration (e.g., using the SAP Enterprise Portal or SAP Business Client).

- *Access via the AS ABAP* to analytical functions, in particular through the Analytic Engine in SAP BW, and integration of analytical functionality in a transactional, ABAP-based application at different levels. In this case, the SAP BW infrastructure is used via the Analytic Engine without having to operate a separate SAP BW system.

When doing so, we'll focus only on the operational level for reporting and data analysis while assuming that SAP HANA is used as the primary database. In some cases, however, the two approaches can also be used if SAP HANA is implemented as a secondary database.

9.4.1 Direct Access to Analytical Functionality in SAP HANA

Direct access to analytical functionality in SAP HANA refers to data analysis via SAP BusinessObjects tools without using an AS ABAP. Moreover, this also includes the provisioning of analytical functionality via *SAP HANA Extended Application Services* (SAP HANA XS Engine, which is described in Chapter 1, Section 1.1.4).

The architecture for direct access to analytical functions in SAP HANA is displayed in Figure 9.11. In this architecture, end users communicate with the SAP HANA database either directly or via the SAP Business-Objects portfolio but without using the ABAP AS.

Direct communication

435

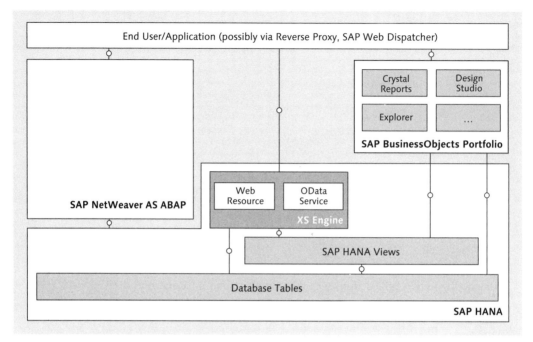

Figure 9.11 Direct Access to SAP HANA

[»]   **SAP HANA Live**

One scenario for direct access to SAP HANA for operational reporting is the implementation of *SAP HANA Live* (previously *SAP HANA Analytics Foundation*). Put simply, SAP HANA Live provides a virtual, multilevel data model (*Virtual Data Model*) consisting of SAP HANA views based on the database tables of the SAP Business Suite.

SAP HANA Live can be accessed using the SAP BusinessObjects tools or using special HTML5 applications based on SAP HANA XS. You can use SAP HANA Live both with a primary and a secondary SAP HANA database.

Advantages and disadvantages

The advantages and disadvantages of analytical functions in SAP HANA are obvious:

▸ One of the biggest advantages of the SAP BusinessObjects portfolio is that many of the requirements with regard to reporting and data analysis are met by default (see Section 9.2). Reports can be created without any programming efforts, and you can save the generated reports in a central repository to make them accessible to a large number of end users. Alternatively, end users can create their own reports and data analyses (provided they have the necessary authorizations).

The disadvantage of this approach is that for certain tools, a Java server (with its own administration and lifecycle management) is needed in addition to AS ABAP.

The advantages and disadvantages of using SAP BusinessObjects tools also apply to access to analytical functions via AS ABAP, which is described in the following section.

▶ If you decide to develop reports and data analyses via SAP HANA XS, you have the flexibility to adapt the analytical UIs exactly to the end users' requirements. Especially when using SAP HANA as a secondary database, this approach has already proven itself in practice because this architecture was used in many of the first customer projects with SAP HANA (SAP HANA as a data mart). A disadvantage is that hardly any functions for reporting and data analysis are provided out of the box. Another disadvantage is that every end user needs both a user account for the AS ABAP and a corresponding user account for the SAP HANA database, which is assigned the required authorizations for accessing the relevant data models.

9.4.2 Access via SAP NetWeaver AS ABAP

Instead of using the SAP BusinessObjects portfolio or the SAP HANA XS Engine to access SAP HANA directly, you can provide analytical functions via AS ABAP. In addition to the SAP BusinessObjects tools, you can use further options to add analytical functions to transactional applications when choosing this approach. A central infrastructure component of this approach is the Analytic Engine we mentioned earlier.

The architecture for accessing analytical functions via AS ABAP is shown in Figure 9.12. With this architecture, the application server is used for all communications with the SAP HANA database.

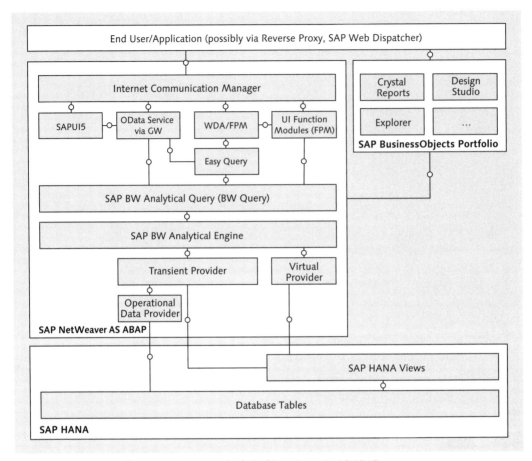

Figure 9.12 Access to Analytical Functions via AS ABAP

Access to SAP HANA via AS ABAP and using the Analytic Engine provides some important advantages over direct access to SAP HANA to integrate analytical functionality in transactional applications.

User administration First, in contrast to direct access to SAP HANA, you can maintain and administer users and authorizations in a single system when accessing analytical functionality via the Analytic Engine. End users need only one user account for AS ABAP. As described in Chapter 3, communication with the SAP HANA database is done via a technical database user. In addition, you might have to create users in the SAP BusinessObjects BI server.

Second, when using the Analytic Engine, you benefit from some additional functions that SAP HANA doesn't currently provide:

▶ **Hierarchy processing**
As already described in Chapter 4, Section 4.4, SAP HANA provides basic support for simple hierarchies. If your hierarchy-processing requirements aren't met by this basic support, you can probably meet them by modeling the hierarchy using the SAP BW functionality. SAP BW currently provides the following functions, but they aren't available directly in SAP HANA: hierarchy versions, time-dependent hierarchies, plus/minus sign reversal, and elimination of internal business volume.

▶ **Formulas**
The SAP BEx Query Designer provides some functions that aren't available directly in SAP HANA when defining calculated fields and key figures. In the SAP BEx Query Designer, you can, for instance, use functions to calculate the percentage share of a result in an interim result or in the overall result of the SAP BW query. Or, you might want to display both the absolute sales per flight connection and the relative percentage share of the sales in the total sales of the respective airline.

▶ **Report-report interface**
The *report-report interface* (RRI) allows you to navigate from a SAP BW query to other SAP BW queries, transactions, and reports of an ABAP system or any web address. No comparable function is provided directly in SAP HANA.

Third, the infrastructure of AS ABAP provides some interesting approaches for integrating analytical functions with transactional applications. Although we can't describe them in detail here, we'll mention them briefly:

▶ **Easy Query**
Using the *Easy Query interface*, you can expose the result of SAP BW queries via function modules, web services, or the OData protocol (the latter is done in connection with the SAP Gateway).

▶ **SAP Gateway**
The SAP Gateway allows you to make business data available as an

 OData service. Within OData services, you can address the Analytic Engine either via multidimensional expressions (MDX; not described in any detail within this book) or via the Easy Query interface. Based on an OData service and using SAPUI5, you can implement HTML5-based UIs.

▶ **UI building blocks**
The SAP Business Suite (or, more precisely, the software component SAP_BS_FND) includes some reusable UI building blocks for Floorplan Manager that allow you to directly access SAP BW queries (when performing your development tasks in an SAP Business Suite system).

These approaches that go beyond the tools of the SAP BusinessObjects portfolio are particularly suitable to extending existing applications easily and without risk, such as by providing analytical side panels in the SAP Business Client for your end users.

Many of the technologies and tools mentioned in this chapter were only described very briefly, but this information will help you with some ideas for adding analytical functions to transactional, ABAP-based applications.

SAP HANA offers a function for analyzing unstructured data. By leveraging this capability, you can considerably improve the user friendliness of search scenarios within business applications. In addition, you can gain further insight by recognizing patterns in existing datasets.

10 Text Search and Analysis of Unstructured Data

Hardly any other functionality has experienced as great a boost from the Internet in recent years as the search within large datasets—irrespective of whether you search through a product catalog, the telephone book, or the entire Internet. This chapter introduces options provided by SAP HANA to search and analyze texts and documents. These options open up many ways to employ the SAP HANA platform, particularly in business applications, which haven't been extensively equipped with these kinds of functions until now.

Input helps represent a simple usage scenario for text searches in SAP HANA. SAP applications contain input helps in many different places. When using input helps, users sometimes search for an entry in a large dataset without knowing the details of the entry, or at least without having these details at hand. For example, you may be searching for a specific customer in Argentina who is based in Buenos Aires and works in the telecommunications industry. Because his customer number isn't available to you, you enter information such as the company name, country, location, and industry into a complex input template, You often have to enter this data several times using *wild cards* such as the asterisk (*). In addition, if you mistype an entry or the data is stored in a different way in the database (e.g., if the name of the location was entered using the country-specific spelling), you usually won't obtain any results.

Input help use scenario

441

The text search function in SAP HANA allows you to develop search helps that work similarly to modern Internet searches. They provide a certain error tolerance and are able to process multilingual terms and synonyms. In the preceding example, such a search help might consist of an input field that *correctly* interprets a user request such as "buenes eires tele", despite the incorrect spelling and the search via multiple columns. However, users can't always easily determine whether the returned result is the expected one in this type of error-tolerant search, also referred to as a *fuzzy search*. Have you ever asked yourself why you sometimes obtain unexpected results when performing a search on the Internet?

Pattern recognition usage scenario

The recognition of patterns in texts and documents represents an entirely different kind of text-analysis function. You can use this feature in many different scenarios, some of which are presented in the following sections. For example, to avoid having duplicate business partners in your master data, you may want to check in the system whether a similar client already exists in the dataset prior to creating a new client, and, if so, notify the application user about it. In this context, being "similar" might mean that the last name and address of an existing and new client are almost identical. As it often happens that names and addresses in particular are entered with different kinds of spellings, a simple check for identical entries rarely returns satisfactory results.

The text analysis function in SAP HANA not only allows you to run searches within texts but also to extract additional information from the texts. For example, you can recognize relationships and even intentions or emotions within texts. Let's suppose you run a web store that enables clients to order products online as well as to post comments about the products and the vendor. The *sentiment analysis* is part of the text engine functionality in SAP HANA and enables you to recognize patterns in these types of unstructured data. In the context of the online store, for instance, it would allow you to analyze whether a specific product evokes more positive or negative comments.

Chapter overview

This chapter begins by introducing some of the basic technical principles and prerequisites for using the text search in SAP HANA. This is followed by a description of how to call the function using SQL and how to use it in ABAP, with a special focus on embedding the text search function in input helps. In addition to using the text search function directly, you'll learn about several existing SAP components that support the implementation of complex searches. Moreover, the chapter contains practical examples of pattern recognition within texts. Finally, you'll become acquainted with nonfunctional aspects such as resource consumption, performance, and error analysis.

The practical examples will be used to implement search runs across airline names (table SCARR), flight schedule data (airports and locations from tables SPFLI and SAIRPORT), and the flight passenger address data (name, address, town, and country from table SCUSTOM).

Reference example for this chapter

10.1   Basic Principles of the Text Search in SAP HANA

The main purpose of the text search function in SAP HANA is to provide users with an optimized usability of search interfaces. In addition to various features common in Internet search engines, this includes functions with special significance for business applications, such as industry-specific lists of synonyms.

This involves the following characteristics that are usually deployed in combination:

Characteristics of the SAP HANA text search

- ▶ **Freestyle search**
  The user doesn't need to know the exact database columns in which the search is supposed to be carried out. For example, you can implement an address search across a single input field and include all technical characteristics such as street name, ZIP code, town, country, and so on.

- ▶ **Error-tolerant search (fuzzy search)**
  The user may vary the spelling slightly in his search requests.

- ▶ **Linguistic search and synonym search**
  Linguistic variants and synonymous terms are included.

- ▶ **Value suggestions**
  The system efficiently identifies probable search results while the user is typing and presents these to the user in real time.

▶ **Results ranking**
The sequence of the search results is optimized so that results with the highest probability rate are presented at the top of the list.

▶ **Search facets**
The search results are counted and grouped according to specific criteria. For example, when searching for airlines, you can view the distribution of the airlines per country.

▶ **Text analysis (particularly sentiment analysis)**
Additional information is extracted from texts, which allows you to gain insights on semantical aspects.

10.1.1 Technical Architecture

The following sections describe how you can use the text search and text analysis functions. To provide you with an idea of which components are involved in SAP HANA, Figure 10.1 shows the architecture of the text search functionality. The column store supports the data types and operations that are required for the search, which are described in further detail in Section 10.2 and Section 10.3. To perform complex text analyses and to extract information, the column store draws on the *preprocessor server*. In this context, the system uses the *Document Analysis Toolkit*.

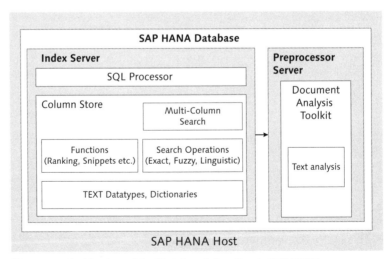

Figure 10.1 Architecture of the Text Search Function in SAP HANA

Section 10.1.3 provides further details on other text search components.

[«]

10.1.2 Error-Tolerant Search

The error-tolerant or fuzzy search involves the search for character strings (i.e., the search request) in text-based data, where the data doesn't have to correspond exactly to the search request; this way, sufficiently similar entries are also included in the result set. This section provides an overview of the techniques used for the fuzzy search in SAP HANA.

Fuzzy search

Mathematical algorithms that form the basis of the fuzzy search determine the degree to which a data record must correspond to the search request. The result of the calculation is often a numerical value used to decide whether a data record is sufficiently similar to the search request. With regard to texts, the simplest type of such an algorithm consists of determining the minimum number of operations (such as replacing and moving characters) that are required to generate a section of the actual data record from the search request. In practice, it's very complicated to determine the degree of similarity between texts, and it involves using variants and heuristics that all have their pros and cons depending on the scenario in which they are used.

Algorithms

The text search function in SAP HANA determines a value between 0 and 1 that marks the degree of similarity. As a programmer, you must define a threshold value (e.g., 0.8) from which a value of the dataset that has been searched is categorized as matching the search request.

In addition, the functionality of the fuzzy search can be adapted for specific (semantic) data types. For example, the fuzzy search for a date can include date values that are several days before or after the specific date

Semantic fuzzy search

being searched. In this case, the similarity criterion is the period rather than the similarity of the character string (so, according to this criterion, the date 01/01/1909 isn't similar to 01/01/1990, although the position of only one character has been changed).

Another example involves the search for a town on the basis of a ZIP code. In most countries, ZIP codes are structured in such a way that a similarity of the code's first digits tells more about geographical proximity than a similarity of the last digits.

Expressions used in searches

When running a fuzzy search, you can use a set of simple *expressions* that enable an expert to formulate more precise search requests. For example, this includes the option to enforce an exact search for a specific portion of the search request or to use logical expressions. Table 10.1 contains some sample expressions of the SAP HANA text search based on the example of an airline search.

Search Request	Explanation
lufthansa OR united	Results that are similar either to "Lufthansa" or to "United".
airline—united	Results that are similar to "airline," but not to "united".
"south air"	Results that are similar to the entire expression, "south air", and not only to its components, "south" and "air". In this example, "South African Airways" isn't returned as a result.

Table 10.1 Using Expressions in the SAP HANA Text Search

Linguistic search

To determine the degree of similarity, it's also useful to include grammatical and other linguistic aspects. In this context, terms are reverted to their word stem so that word variants such as "house," "houses," "housing," and so on, are recognized. In addition, the linguistic search provides opportunities for handling multilingual texts and search requests.

Lists of synonyms

The fuzzy search can also be extended by lists of synonyms. In this context, you can store a list of terms that are equivalent to a specific term; the search request can then draw upon this list. For example, "notebook" might be regarded as a synonym of "laptop," or "monitor" as a synonym of "screen." This feature is particularly useful for industry-specific abbreviations and concepts.

Another option to implement a more intelligent search is to familiarize the system with semantic characteristics of specific terms. In this context, it's important to know that not every term in a search request has the same *selectivity*. For example, terms such as "Inc." or "LLC" aren't as selective as the actual company name when you search for a specific company. It's therefore usually more important to enter a company name similar to the one you're searching for than to enter that the search result is an "Inc.," for example.

Stop words

Likewise, in longer texts such as product descriptions, similarities in certain parts of speech such as articles or pronouns are less important than similarities in names within the text (e.g., in brand names). When you run a search request in SAP HANA, you can enter a list of so-called *stop words* (also referred to as noise words) that are considered less important than other words.

Because the text search function is based on a number of rather complex algorithms, it may be necessary to create specific *fuzzy search indexes* to accelerate the search runs and thus optimize the system performance, particularly if large amounts of data are involved. However, these indexes require additional memory. Section 10.6 provides some recommendations on how to use them.

Fuzzy search index

10.1.3 SAP Components and Products for Search

In Section 10.3, you'll learn in detail how to access the search features of SAP HANA directly through SQL. In addition, SAP provides specific components and frameworks that support you in the creation of search runs, but because these aren't the focus of this book, they are mentioned only briefly in the following paragraphs.

Since release 7.0, SAP NetWeaver AS ABAP contains the *Embedded Search*. This component allows users to extract data for indexing via the *TREX Search and Classification Engine*, which represents an SAP NetWeaver component that can be installed separately (*standalone engine*).

Embedded Search

Embedded Search provides interfaces that enable a more efficient search within the extracted data of an application.

SAP NetWeaver Enterprise Search However, Embedded Search is limited to searches within an SAP system. To run searches across different systems (e.g., in an application portal), you can use the *SAP NetWeaver Enterprise Search* solution. This is based on the capabilities of the local Embedded Search functionality in integrated systems.

TREX Because SAP HANA supports most of the functions of the TREX engine, you can use these functions directly in SAP HANA and without a separate TREX installation. This means you can use existing Embedded Search models in SAP HANA, while, by default, the data continues to be extracted and replicated within SAP HANA. SAP currently plans to enable direct searches in tables via Embedded Search in SAP HANA without the requiring the data to be replicated.

UI Toolkit for Information Access (InA) Since SPS 5, SAP HANA also provides the *UI Toolkit for Information Access* (*InA*), which allows you to create simple HTML5-based search interfaces. Based on attribute views, you can use HTML and JavaScript as well as the *UI templates* contained in InA to build a simple search application according to the modular design principle. This application employs SAP HANA Extended Application Services (SAP HANA XS).

10.2 Types of Text Data and Full Text Indexes in SAP HANA

The fuzzy search in SAP HANA is based on the data types in the column store. Here, TEXT and SHORTTEXT represent two specific data types that are dedicated for text searches (and text analyses). The SHORTTEXT data type is used for character strings of a given length (similar to NVARCHAR), whereas TEXT represents a *large object* (similar to NCLOB—the SQL data type for a string in the ABAP Data Dictionary [DDIC]). In this context, texts are internally fragmented into *tokens* that form the basis for searches and analyses. The following sections provide detailed information about this subject.

Unfortunately, however, there is currently no native support available in ABAP for the TEXT and SHORTTEXT data types, which makes it impossible to create a table via the DDIC that uses these data types. In addition, although the fuzzy search function is also supported for other data types (e.g., VARCHAR and NVARCHAR), this support isn't extensive enough. Without the ability to split the texts into searchable tokens, the system can't recognize a permutation of words, which is a standard in modern search applications. Similarly, the reversion to their word stem doesn't work directly with these data types.

Support in ABAP

What you can do, however, is add the functionality offered by the text data types to a specific column by creating a full text index. In this way, you can enable the text search and text analysis functions for the majority of character-type DDIC types (including CHAR, STRING, DATS, etc.). When you create a full text index for a table column, the system creates an internal, invisible column (*shadow column*) of the TEXT type, which contains the same data but in a presentation optimized for search requests. In this context, the text is fragmented into tokens, and an additional dictionary is generated.

Full text index

Figure 10.2 shows the internal presentation in a schema based on the example of airline names.

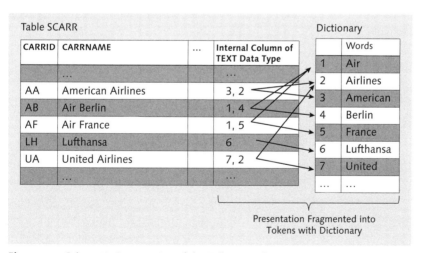

Figure 10.2 Schematic Presentation of the Full Text Index

Note that the shadow column exists only transiently in the main memory. When you load the table into the memory (e.g., after a database restart), this data structure is created anew. Section 10.6 contains further details about the memory consumption of a full text index.

Using SQL for the creation You can create the full text index using the CREATE FULLTEXT INDEX SQL statement:

```
CREATE FULLTEXT INDEX <index name>
ON <table name> ( <column name> )
[<parameter list>]
```

Here, you can use numerous optional settings, as described in the following using examples. However, you can obtain comprehensive documentation from *http://help.sap.com/hana*. You should also note that the name of the full text index must be unique within a schema, so it makes sense to prefix the index name with the table name to avoid name clashes.

Creation in the DDIC The following SQL statement defines a full text index for the CARRNAME column of table SCARR:

```
CREATE FULLTEXT INDEX scarr~name ON scarr(carrname);
```

Because you can't create full text indexes via the DDIC (Transaction SE11) prior to ABAP Release 7.4, these indexes can't be transported automatically. As of ABAP Release 7.4, it's also possible to create a full text index via the DDIC using common parameters. For this purpose, you must define a new index for a table using Transaction SE11 or, rather, an *extension index* (for a modification-free extension of an SAP standard table). This contains only the required column as a field and is created exclusively in the SAP HANA database. Figure 10.3 shows this type of index in the CITY column of table SCUSTOM.

Via GOTO • FULL TEXT INDEX, you can then activate the full text index and set a variety of parameters (see Figure 10.4). The parameters correspond to the CREATE FULLTEXT INDEX statement parameters mentioned earlier. The standard settings and a language configuration (using a column of the table or a fixed language) are usually sufficient for a fuzzy search.

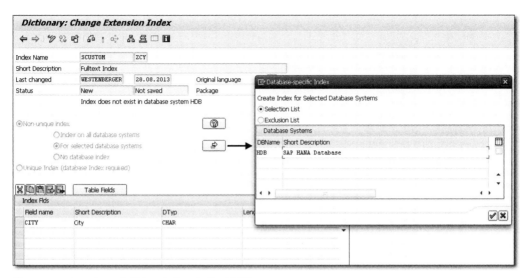

Figure 10.3 Creating a Full Text Index via the DDIC

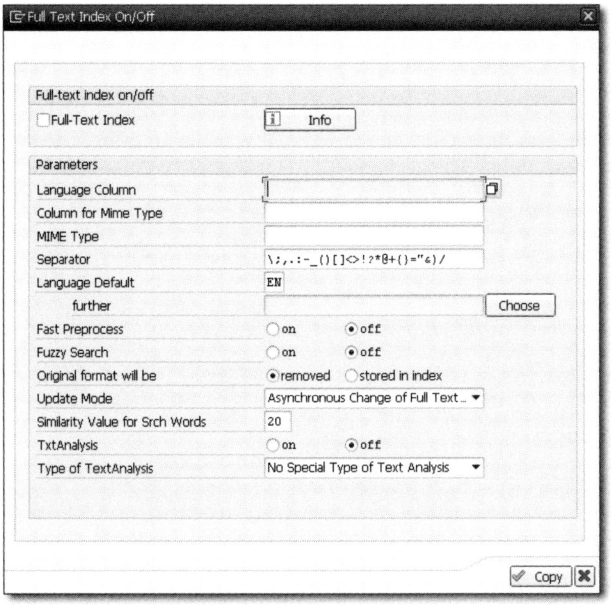

Figure 10.4 Configuring a Full Text Index via the DDIC

In addition to using the DDIC, you can also use Native SQL in an ABAP program to create a full text index. This allows you to use the entire

Creation via ADBC

range of options available for a text search (also those that can't be selected via the configuration screen in Transaction SE11); however, this method requires you to manage the index in a system landscape yourself. This variant can also be useful in older ABAP releases or in side-by-side scenarios. Listing 10.1 shows how you can create and remove full text indexes using the ABAP Database Connectivity (ADBC) interface:

```
REPORT zr_a4h_chapter9_adbc_ft_index.

" Configuration
PARAMETERS:
 table LIKE dd02l-tabname DEFAULT 'SCUSTOM',
 column LIKE dd03l-fieldname DEFAULT 'NAME',
 fzyidx TYPE abap_bool AS CHECKBOX DEFAULT abap_false,
 ta TYPE abap_bool AS CHECKBOX DEFAULT abap_false,
 taconfig TYPE string DEFAULT 'EXTRACTION_CORE',
 drop TYPE abap_bool AS CHECKBOX DEFAULT abap_true,
 create TYPE abap_bool AS CHECKBOX DEFAULT abap_true.

" Index name (<table>~<column>)
DATA(lv_idx) = table && '~' && column.

" SQL statement for creating a full text index
DATA(lv_sql) = |CREATE FULLTEXT INDEX { lv_idx } |
          && |ON { table }({ column })|.

" Additional fuzzy search index
IF ( fzyidx = abap_true ).
  lv_sql = lv_sql && ' FUZZY SEARCH INDEX ON'.
ENDIF.

" Text analysis
IF ( ta = abap_true ).
 lv_sql = lv_sql && ' TEXT ANALYSIS ON'.

 " Special configuration of text analysis
 IF ( taconfig IS NOT INITIAL ).
  lv_sql = lv_sql && | CONFIGURATION '{ taconfig }'|.
 ENDIF.
ENDIF.

IF ( drop = abap_true ).
  TRY.

    " Remove index
    cl_sql_connection=>get_connection(
      )->create_statement( )->execute_ddl(
        |DROP FULLTEXT INDEX { lv_idx }|
```

```
      ).

    WRITE: / |Fulltext index { lv_idx } removed|.
  CATCH cx_sql_exception INTO DATA(lo_ex).

    " Error handling
    WRITE: / | Error: { lo_ex->get_text( ) }|.
  ENDTRY.
ENDIF.

IF ( create = abap_true ).
  TRY.

    " Create text index via ADBC
    cl_sql_connection=>get_connection(
        )->create_statement(
        )->execute_ddl( lv_sql ).

    WRITE: / |Fulltext index { lv_idx } created|.
  CATCH cx_sql_exception INTO DATA(lo_ex1).

    " Error handling
    WRITE: / | Error: { lo_ex1->get_text( ) }|.
  ENDTRY.
ENDIF.
```

Listing 10.1 Creating a Text Index via ADBC

You can view existing full text indexes when you open a table and click on the INDEXES tab in SAP HANA Studio (see Figure 10.5). Here you can view technical characteristics such as the synchronization behavior.

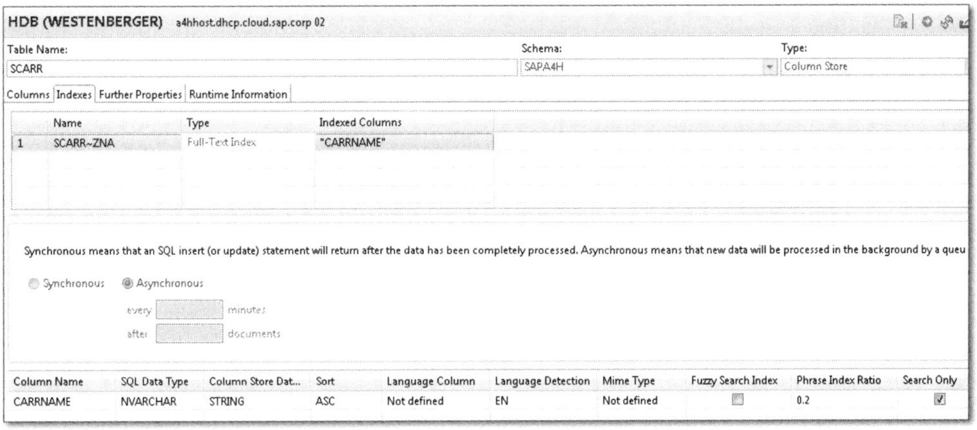

Display full text indexes

Figure 10.5 Displaying a Full Text Index in SAP HANA Studio

453

10.3   Using the Text Search via SQL

CONTAINS
keyword

As is the case with the majority of functions in SAP HANA, you can invoke the text search via SQL. To do this, you must use a SELECT statement with the keyword CONTAINS keyword, which enables you to call the manifold variants of the text search. The standard syntax is as follows:

```
SELECT <field list>
FROM <table or view>
WHERE CONTAINS (<columns>,<search request>,<parameter>);
```

The following example provides an initial idea of how you can use the CONTAINS clause for a fuzzy search:

```
SELECT * FROM scarr WHERE CONTAINS( carrname, 'lusthansa',
FUZZY(0.8));
```

Here, we run a search for airlines whose names are *sufficiently similar* to the search request, 'lusthansa'. Although the search request contains two errors (the search term starts with a lowercase letter and contains one incorrect letter), the system returns the expected data record, "Lufthansa."

FUZZY parameter

The following sections discuss the definition of similarity in detail. At this point, you should know that the FUZZY(0.8) parameter defines the threshold value, where a value between 0.7 and 0.8 is usually a good standard value to obtain results that are relatively similar to the search request. In addition to the threshold value, the FUZZY parameter provides many other setting options.

Exact search/
linguistic search

Apart from its use with the FUZZY parameter, you can use the CONTAINS statement in two other variants: EXACT and LINGUISTIC. In searches with the addition EXACT, the system searches for exact matches for the search request with entire words (based on the tokenization of the text in the database). EXACT also represents the default value if you don't enter any parameter. In this case, you can also use wildcards such as '*' in the search request. In contrast to a LIKE in standard SQL, the CONTAINS clause allows you to perform searches across multiple columns. The following example shows an exact search for airlines whose names or web addresses contain "Airlines" or "Airways" or end with ".com".

```
SELECT * FROM scarr WHERE CONTAINS ((carrname,url), 'Airlines
OR Airways OR *.com', EXACT)
```

This example is also useful for demonstrating the effects of a missing full text index. If no full text index exists for the `carrname` column, the names won't be split into words (tokens); consequently, there will be no exact match between the search request `'Airlines'` and an entry such as "United Airlines".

If you run an additional analysis of the word stems via a text analysis (see Section 10.5), the `LINGUISTIC` parameter allows you to obtain additional results in which only the word stems must match.

Limitations to the Text Search in SAP HANA SQL	[«]
As already mentioned, you can use SQL for text searches in SAP HANA. However, there are currently a couple limitations with regard to the supported combinations: ▶ You can apply the CONTAINS clause only to text searches in tables of the column store. ▶ You can't apply the text search function to calculated attributes of a view.	

This book focuses primarily on the subject of fuzzy searches because it's difficult to implement an intuitively usable search function with the exact or linguistic search within an ABAP application. In both cases, fewer results are often found than in a classic ABAP input help.

10.3.1   Fuzzy Search

The following section describes how you can use the fuzzy search function for a simple search run across one or several columns of a table or view. Section 10.3.2 and Section 10.3.3 will then provide details about the specific search variants that use additional semantic information about the data.

The examples used in this context involve the airline names (CARRNAME column in table SCARR) and the locations from the flight schedule (CITYFR and CITYTO columns in table SPFLI). For this purpose, a full text index is defined for each attribute using DDIC, as described in Section 10.2.

Searching across Multiple Columns

Multiple columns within a table

The CONTAINS statement allows you to specify multiple columns to be considered during the search run. The following example indicates a search in the flight schedule to "Tokio":

```
SELECT * FROM spfli WHERE CONTAINS ((cityfrom,cityto),
'Tokio', fuzzy(0.8))
```

The result will contain all flights departing from and arriving in Tokyo, even though the spelling of the city's name deviates slightly (in some languages, this is the common spelling of this city), as shown in Figure 10.6. Instead of the individual column names, you can also use an asterisk (*) to run the search across all columns that support a text search.

Multiple columns in multiple tables

If you want to run the search across multiple columns in different tables that are linked through foreign key dependencies, you can either write an SQL join or use a view.

	MANDT	CARRID	CONNID	COUNTRYFR	CITYFROM	AIRPFROM	COUNTRYTO	CITYTO	AIRPTO
					select * from sapa4h.spfli where contains ((cityfrom,cityto), 'Tokio', fuzzy(0.8))				
1	001	AZ	0789	JP	TOKYO	TYO	IT	ROME	FCO
2	001	JL	0407	JP	TOKYO	NRT	DE	FRANKFURT	FRA
3	001	JL	0408	DE	FRANKFURT	FRA	JP	TOKYO	NRT
4	001	AZ	0788	IT	ROME	FCO	JP	TOKYO	TYO
5	001	SQ	0988	SG	SINGAPORE	SIN	JP	TOKYO	TYO

Figure 10.6 Fuzzy Search across Multiple Columns

To include the airline name in addition to the departure and destination names in the flight schedule search, you can use a simple Core Data Services (CDS) view, DEMO_CDS_SCARR_SPFLI, as illustrated in Figure 10.7. The name of the appropriate database view is DEMO_CDS_JOIN.

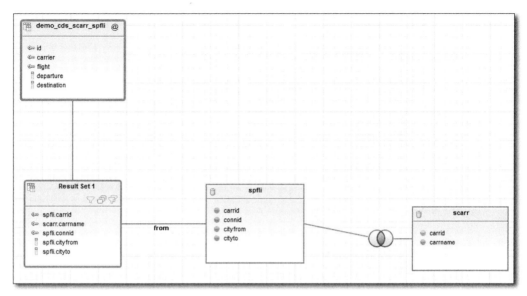

Figure 10.7 CDS View as the Basis for a Fuzzy Search via Two Tables

In a view, the fuzzy search via SQL is carried out in the same manner as within a table. Thus, the result of the following SELECT statement contains all flights from or to Singapore, as well as all flights operated by Singapore Airlines:

```
select * from DEMO_CDS_
JOIN WHERE CONTAINS(*, 'singapore', fuzzy(0.8))
```

Fuzzy search in CDS view

Similarly, you can also use other view types such as attribute views.

Special Functions

Special scalar functions are available that enable you to retrieve additional information for individual data records in the result set. SAP HANA currently provides the score(), highlighted(), and snippets() functions, as described in the following sections.

The score() function provides information about the degree of similarity between the search result and the search request. This value ranges between 0 and 1, with higher values indicating a higher degree of similarity. Normally, the function is used for sorting the search results so

Score

that results with a higher degree of similarity are displayed at the top of the list:

```
SELECT * FROM scarr WHERE CONTAINS( carrname, 'airways',
fuzzy(0.8)) ORDER BY score() desc;
```

[!] **Difference between SCORE() and Threshold Values for Searches**

The return value of the `score()` function doesn't directly correspond to the threshold value in the `fuzzy()` statement. Consequently, it's conceivable to obtain search results in which the value of the `score()` function is lower than the transferred threshold value.

Highlighted and snippets
In searches through longer texts, it's particularly useful for users if the exact found location of a search request is highlighted in the text. For this purpose, SAP HANA SQL offers the `highlighted()` and `snippets()` functions. If the former is used, the system returns the entire text with the found location highlighted; if `snippets()` is used, only an extract of the text around the found location is returned. Note that there is no difference between the two with regard to shorter texts such as the airline names, for example.

When using these functions, you must specify the column as shown in the following example:

```
SELECT *, highlighted(carrname) FROM scarr
   WHERE CONTAINS( carrname, 'airways', fuzzy(0.8))
   ORDER BY score() desc;
```

The result contains the found location enclosed by *markups* that use the HTML tag `<b>...</b>` (see Figure 10.8). If you plan to implement your own type of search result display, you may want to replace these tags accordingly.

```
SQL   Result
SELECT *, highlighted(carrname) FROM sapa4h.scarr
   WHERE CONTAINS( carrname, 'airways', fuzzy(0.8))
   ORDER BY score() desc
```

	MANDT	CARRID	CARRNAME	CURRCODE	URL	HIGHLIGHTED(CARRNAME)
1	001	BA	British Airways	GBP	http://www.british-airways.com	british \airways\
2	001	QF	Qantas Airways	AUD	http://www.qantas.com.au	qantas \airways\

Figure 10.8 Highlighting the Found Location Using the HIGHLIGHTED() Function

<table>
<tr><td>

Limitations of HIGHLIGHTED() and SNIPPETS()

The `highlighted()` and `snippets()` functions can only highlight hits within one column. If you run a search across multiple columns, you can query the value of individual attributes only. Thus, if no found location exists in a column, you won't find any highlight in the value of the function. Moreover, you only get the first found location in a document and not all occurrences.

</td><td>**[«]**</td></tr>
</table>

Other Parameterizations

The parameterization of the fuzzy search hasn't yet been discussed in detail, and it's beyond the scope of this book to describe all options and variants related to this topic. However, you should be familiar with some of these aspects, which are essential to using fuzzy search correctly. These involve, first and foremost, the `similarCalculationMode` and `textSearch` parameters. You must transfer these types of parameters by means of a character string in which you use commas to separate individual parameters, as shown in the following example:

```
SELECT * FROM scarr WHERE
  CONTAINS(carrname, 'lusthansa',
  fuzzy(0.8, 'similarCalculationMode=search'));
```

The `similarCalculationMode` parameter enables you to check how the fuzzy score (i.e., the degree of similarity) is calculated. In this context, you must distinguish between two scenarios. In a text comparison, the request and the text in the database as a whole should be similar; however, in a normal search run, it should be sufficient that the search request is part of the text. For this reason, you use the `compare` parameter value for text comparisons, and you use `search` for search runs. The following section describes how you can manually create a specific full text index and discusses the differences between the parameter values.

Parameter similarCalculation-Mode

In addition, the `textSearch` parameter is important for the description of some of the more complex search options in the following sections; this parameter switches between separate technical implementations in SAP HANA. The details of this parameter and its use are described in Section 10.3.2.

Parameter textSearch

10.3.2 Synonyms and Noise Words

Lists of synonyms and stop words (also called noise words) represent an option to implement a more intelligent search. To do this, you must store the additional data in tables of a predefined structure, and the names of these configuration tables must be included in the search requests.

Stop word table

Let's first consider the use of noise words. Names of airlines, for example, frequently contain the word "air," which, compared to other words, presumably plays a minor role in search runs. For this reason, we want to include this term in the list of stop words. This doesn't mean that the word will be completely ignored or even that the search will terminate, but merely that the system will attach less importance to the term.

The structure of the configuration table is shown in Table 10.2.

Column	SQL Data Type	Example
stopword_id	VARCHAR(32)	"1"
list_id	VARCHAR(32)	"airline"
language_code	CHAR(2)	
term	NVARCHAR(200)	"Air"

Table 10.2 Structure of the Configuration for Stop Words

Configuration table columns

Here, the stopword_id field represents the unique key. The list_id column allows for storing multiple individual lists for different usage scenarios in the table. In addition, you can store words that are relevant only for specific languages (this value has been left empty in this example of airline names).

Search within sample table

Figure 10.9 shows a table called ZA4H_BOOK_STOPW in the DDIC with a matching structure.

Now the sample data record from Table 10.2 is entered into this table. If you want to include the list of stop words in a fuzzy search, you must use the stopwordTable and stopwordListId parameters. The example in

Listing 10.2 shows the search for the terms "air" and "united" and uses the previously generated stop word table.

```
SELECT * FROM scarr WHERE CONTAINS( carrname, 'air
OR united', fuzzy(0.8, 'textsearch=compare,
stopwordTable=ZA4H_BOOK_STOPW, stopwordListId=airline,
similarCalculationMode=search')) ORDER BY score();
```
Listing 10.2 Fuzzy Search with Stop Word Table

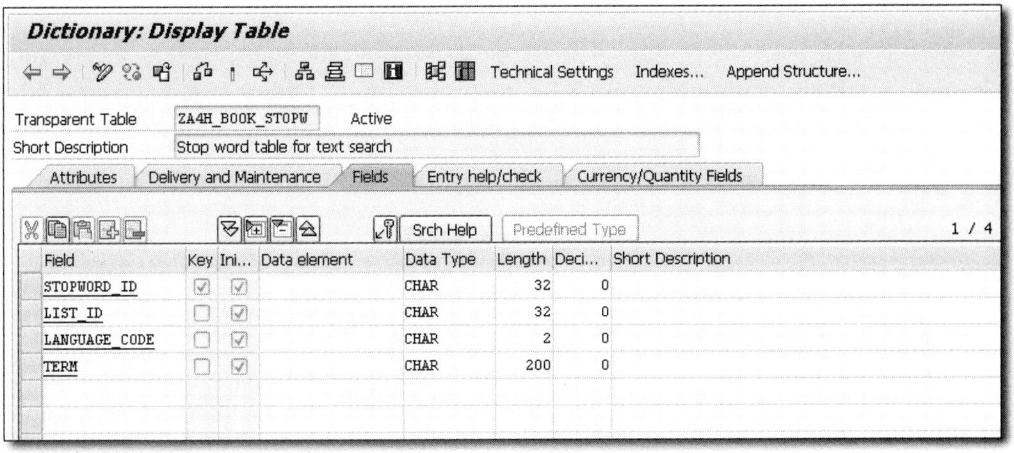

Figure 10.9 Stop Word Table in DDIC

The `textsearch=compare` parameter is necessary if you want to use these search variants. The result contains the entry "United Airlines", but not "Air Canada", for example, because due to the stop word table, a lower degree of importance has been attached to the term "Air".

This describes how you can use synonyms in your search requests. To do this, you must map those terms you want to treat as synonyms in a configuration table (*term mapping*). As is the case with stop words, you can store these terms based on individual languages and in multiple lists. In addition, you can store a weighting between 0 and 1 to indicate the extent to which the finding of a synonym is supposed to reduce the value of similarity. Table 10.3 shows the structure of the corresponding configuration table.

Lists of synonyms

461

Column	SQL Data Type	Example
mapping_id	VARCHAR(32)	"1"
list_id	VARCHAR(32)	"airline"
language_code	CHAR(2)	
term_1	NVARCHAR(255)	"Airways"
term_2	NVARCHAR(255)	"Airlines"
weight	DECIMAL	0.8

Table 10.3 Structure of the Configuration for Synonyms

[»] **Client-Dependent Stop Word and Synonym Lists**

Although the table structures for stop words and synonyms don't have any client column in SAP HANA, you can add such a table in ABAP tables and then simply put a view on the tables by taking this column from the projection list.

Similar to the previous example, we create an ABAP table ZA4H_BOOK_ TMAP with the structure from Table 10.3 and enter the sample value from Table 10.3. The example in Listing 10.3 describes the search for the term, "United Airways".

```
SELECT * FROM scarr WHERE CONTAINS( carrname,
'united airways', fuzzy(0.8, 'textsearch=compare,
termMappingTable=ZA4H_BOOK_TMAP, termMappingListId=airline,
similarCalculationMode=search')) ORDER BY score();
```
Listing 10.3 Fuzzy Search with List of Synonyms

The specification of the mapping table via the termMappingTable and termMappingListId parameters causes the fuzzy search to analyze the list of synonyms so that the result contains the expected entry, "United Airlines".

Hypernyms, hyponyms

In addition to terms with identical meaning (i.e., synonyms), you can use the mapping mechanism to include *hypernyms* and *hyponyms*; that is, more general or more concrete terms, which can be particularly useful with large, unstructured texts. This enables you, for example, to recognize the occurrence of the hypernym "airline" when searching for the term "Lufthansa" in a text. To achieve this, you have to choose a low value (e.g., `0.2`) as the weight (`WEIGHT`).

You also can use a combination of stop words and synonyms in a search request; in that case, the system calculates the synonymous variants first, followed by the stop words.

10.3.3 Searching across Date Fields and Address Data

Finally, this section describes some of the more comprehensive options we introduced in Section 10.1.2 so that you can get an idea of how to use them. This section focuses on fuzzy searches in date fields as well as on the search for ZIP codes. Unfortunately, both options can't be used directly from within ABAP because they require specific data types and column definitions. These kinds of native developments in the database require additional design concepts.

For this reason, we will manually create a table for our scenario in a separate database schema. This table will store customer addresses as well as the date and time of the last booking from within the ABAP tables where native SAP HANA types were used. We'll then run a fuzzy search across this data in which the semantic characteristics of dates and ZIP codes will be used.

Sample scenario

For the sake of convenience, the scenario is implemented here exclusively via the SQL console in SAP HANA Studio. Of course, you can also execute these native SQL statements from within an ABAP program through the ADBC interface.

The table is created via SQL, as shown in Listing 10.4. Here, you must replace `<schema>` with your own database schema.

Native database table with SQL

```
create column table <schema>.custom_fuzzy (
 mandt NVARCHAR(3) DEFAULT '000' NOT NULL ,
 id    NVARCHAR(8) DEFAULT '00000000' NOT NULL ,
 name  NVARCHAR(25) DEFAULT '' NOT NULL ,
 city  NVARCHAR(25) DEFAULT '' NOT NULL ,
 postcode NVARCHAR(10) FUZZY SEARCH MODE 'postcode',
 lastbooking DATE
 );
```

Listing 10.4 Creating a Table with Customer Addresses and Booking Dates via SQL

For the date, we use the native data type `DATE`, and specify a fuzzy search mode for the ZIP code. Both these settings can't be used in the same manner for a DDIC table.

After that, the table is populated based on the data from tables `SCUSTOM` and `SBOOK` using the SQL statement in Listing 10.5.

```
INSERT INTO <schema>.custom_fuzzy
SELECT c.mandt, c.id, c.name, c.city, c.postcode,
       to_date( MIN ( b.order_date ) ) as lastbooking
FROM   sbook as b INNER JOIN  scustom as c
       ON b.mandt = c.mandt and b.customid = c.id
GROUP BY c.mandt, c.id, c.name, c.city, c.postcode;
```
Listing 10.5 Populating the Database Table with Data

Fuzzy search for a date

In a fuzzy search for a date field, the degree of similarity is impacted by the time difference between the date values and by typical typing errors in date entries. You don't need to create a full text index for this kind of fuzzy search because a fragmentation into tokens (words) isn't needed here.

In Listing 10.6, we search for customers whose last booking was carried out on or around November 13, 2015. The `maxDateDistance=3` parameter specifies the maximum difference in days. In addition, the system also returns results that contain an incorrect number, for example, or in which the day and month have been exchanged.

```
SELECT lastbooking, score() FROM <schema>.custom_fuzzy
   WHERE CONTAINS(lastbooking, '2015-11-13',
        FUZZY(0.9, 'maxDateDistance=3'))
ORDER BY score() DESC;
```
Listing 10.6 Fuzzy Search for a Date

Fuzzy search for a ZIP code

As described in Section 10.1.2, in the fuzzy search for a ZIP code, the degree of similarity is determined through the geographical proximity, which is indicated by the internal structure of the ZIP codes. Listing 10.7 searches for codes close to '69190'.

```
SELECT postcode, score() FROM custom_fuzzy
  WHERE CONTAINS( postcode, '69190', fuzzy(0.7))
ORDER BY score() desc;
```
Listing 10.7 Fuzzy Search for ZIP Codes

Figure 10.10 shows the result of a combined search for customers close to Walldorf, Germany (ZIP code 69190), whose last booking was carried out on or around January 31, 2016.

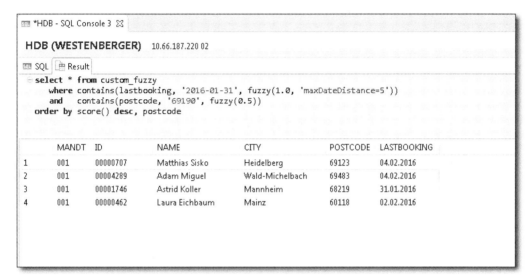

Figure 10.10 Fuzzy Search for a Date and ZIP Code

In addition to ZIP codes, you can also run fuzzy searches for house numbers containing specific characteristics such as number ranges (e.g., "8–10") or letters ("8a").

10.4   Using the Text Search in ABAP

As you've seen, the fuzzy search function in SAP HANA provides many innovative options to run searches on existing data. Some of these scenarios require you to format or transform the data to take advantage of all the options. In the following sections, you'll learn how to use ABAP to call the text search function. We'll detail the direct usage *within* an application, for example, in an input help for a form's field.

In some scenarios, the direct use of the text search function from within ABAP currently requires a few technical tricks (particularly prior to

Mind the lifecycle management

ABAP 7.4 SP 06). As a result, you must carefully think about the design of your development before you can use the function in a production system. Some of these design aspects are discussed in Chapter 14 as part of our recommendations on using the advanced SAP HANA functions.

10.4.1 Direct SQL Access from ABAP

Because the text search function in SAP HANA isn't part of the standard features of a traditional database, the CONTAINS statement is unfortunately not yet supported in Open SQL. However, you can still employ the text search directly from within ABAP if you use ABAP Managed Database Procedures (AMDP) or Native SQL via ADBC.

Access via a database procedure
To use the text search via AMDP, all you need to do is include the CONTAINS statement in the Native SQL statement, as shown in the example in Listing 10.8.

```
CLASS zcl_a4h_chapter9_amdp_contains DEFINITION
  PUBLIC CREATE PUBLIC .

  PUBLIC SECTION.
    INTERFACES: if_amdp_marker_hdb.
    TYPES: tt_result_cust TYPE STANDARD TABLE OF scustom.

    METHODS search_customer
      IMPORTING
              VALUE(iv_client) TYPE mandt
              VALUE(iv_search) TYPE string
      EXPORTING VALUE(et_result) TYPE tt_result_cust.

  PROTECTED SECTION.
  PRIVATE SECTION.
ENDCLASS.

CLASS zcl_a4h_chapter9_amdp_contains IMPLEMENTATION.

  METHOD search_customer BY DATABASE PROCEDURE
    FOR HDB LANGUAGE SQLSCRIPT OPTIONS READ-ONLY
    USING scustom.

    et_result = SELECT * FROM SCUSTOM
        WHERE mandt = :iv_client
        AND CONTAINS(*, :iv_search,
          fuzzy(0.8,'similarCalculationMode=search') )
        ORDER BY score() desc, id;
```

```
    ENDMETHOD.
ENDCLASS.
```
Listing 10.8 Using the Text Search in AMDP

You can also trigger search requests on CDS views or attribute views, although CDS views are recommended.

Search request via views

10.4.2 Embedding Input Helps

As mentioned at the beginning of this chapter, input helps (also referred to as search helps) provide good options for using text search in SAP HANA. Figure 10.11 shows this on the basis of a free text search for a passenger based on the passenger's name and place of residence. In this section, you'll learn about the various options for implementing an input help in the SAP GUI and Web Dynpro ABAP.

You define an input help in the DDIC. In general, these input helps can then be used in both classic Web Dynpro-based applications and in application interfaces that have been created using Web Dynpro ABAP or the Floorplan Manager. In this context, you can either create single (called *elementary*) search helps or combine multiple input helps into a *collective search help*. Usually, the individual search helps are then displayed on separate tabs. Collective search helps are particularly useful if you want to extend an existing search help by an optimized variant in SAP HANA (this variant is hidden in other databases).

Test Program for Value Help with Fuzzy Search

Customer name					
	mannheimer				
	Customer name	Cust. No.	Street	City	Ctry
	Motomarkt GmbH	00000253	**Mannheimer** Str. 14	Heidelberg	DE
	Dr. Ricken & Partner	00000302	**Mannheimer** Str. 118	Karlsruhe	DE
	Alpha Dienstleistungen	00000078	Kurpfalz-Straße	**Mannheim**	DE
	Anna Babilon	00000661	N7, 215	**Mannheim**	DE
	Anna Barth	00004657	N7, 36	**Mannheim**	DE
	Anna Benjamin	00003366	N7, 236	**Mannheim**	DE
	Anna Benz	00003526	N7, 111	**Mannheim**	DE
	Anna Buchholm	00002210	N7, 159	**Mannheim**	DE
	Anna Buehler	00000789	N7, 123	**Mannheim**	DE
	Anna Cesari	00000723	N7, 36	**Mannheim**	DE
	Not all search results shown...				

Figure 10.11 ABAP Search Help with Fuzzy Search across Multiple Columns

ABAP 7.4 provides various enhancements beyond the support of a fuzzy search. For example, it's now possible in SAP GUI to display values directly to users while they are still making entries (see Figure 10.11).

[»] **Prerequisites for Advanced Search Helps in SAP GUI**

Using the advanced options of the search help in ABAP 7.4 requires the following minimum system requirements:

▸ ABAP 7.4 SP 06 or higher is required.

▸ Multicolumn full text search is only supported for the SAP HANA database on ABAP systems.

▸ The presentation of values requires SAP GUI 7.30 for Windows (Patch Level 6 or higher) or SAP GUI 7.40 for Java/HTML. You should use the current version of SAP GUI because the usability has been steadily improving.

Create fuzzy search help declaratively

As a developer, you can define a search help declaratively in such a way that you specify the name of a table or view and select the fields for the dialog. As of ABAP 7.4 SP 06, you can also specify the parameters for a fuzzy search here. For this purpose, you can use Transaction SE80 or Transaction SE11 to create a new input help and select a table or view as the data source. In the advanced options, you can select whether values are displayed directly (supported for all databases), whether a cross-column full text search is run, and which level of detail is applied (only possible in SAP HANA). Figure 10.12 shows a simple configuration based on table SCUSTOM. You don't necessarily need to create a full text index for this purpose.

After activation, you can integrate the input help with a test program (Listing 10.9), and you receive the display shown previously in Figure 10.11. Note that the test environment for input helps doesn't support values and fuzzy search yet.

```
REPORT zr_a4h_chapter9_valuehelp.

PARAMETERS: cust_id TYPE s_customer
                    MATCHCODE OBJECT za4h_book_f4_fuzzy.
```

Listing 10.9 Test Program for Input Help

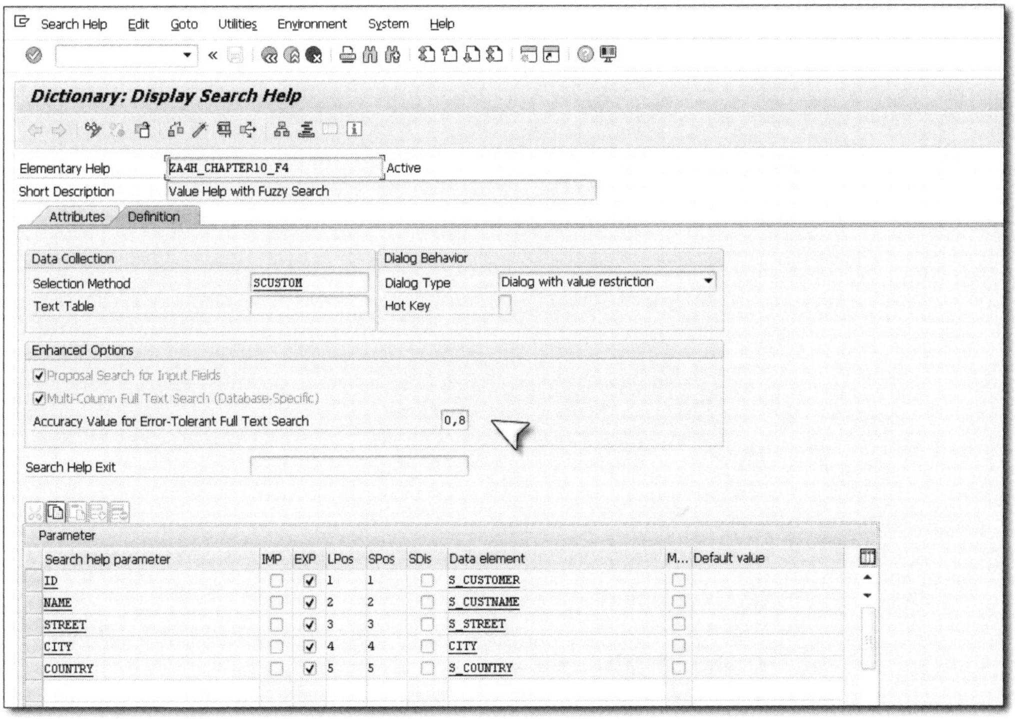

Figure 10.12 Declarative Definition of a Fuzzy Search Help

As a selection method for an input value, you can also use views instead   Views
of tables, for example, to read possible values for a search field from
another table. Unfortunately, the classic help views in DDIC don't support fuzzy searches (see the following information box).

Using CDS Views Instead of Help Views   [+]

As presented in Chapter 3, Section 3.2, the classic DDIC offers a special view
type (help view) that SAP provided specifically for use in input helps. Because
normal database views didn't support outer joins at that time, the join in the
database interface was implemented in the ABAP kernel. Thus, these views
don't support any flexible SQL access as is necessary for a fuzzy search. However, because outer joins can also be implemented via CDS views as of ABAP
7.4, you should also use them as a consistent view technology for input helps.

In addition, you can implement the data retrieval process using a *search*   Search help exit
help exit, which offers you a higher degree of freedom. To define a

search help exit, you must first create a function module that contains the interface shown in Listing 10.10. A simple search help exit is contained in the `F4IF_SHLP_EXIT_EXAMPLE` function module in the standard SAP system.

```
FUNCTION z_a4h_book_chapter9_exit_cust
  CHANGING
    VALUE(shlp) TYPE shlp_descr
    VALUE(callcontrol) LIKE ddshf4ctrl
  TABLES
    shlp_tab TYPE shlp_desct
    record_tab LIKE seahlpres.

  " ...
ENDFUNCTION.
```

Listing 10.10 Interface for Search Help Exits

Creating and testing an input help

Prior to implementing the function module, you should familiarize yourself with the processes of creating and testing an input help in the DDIC, including the specification of such an exit. All you have to do is open Transaction SE11 and create a new search help. Then enter the relevant display and search help exit parameters. Figure 10.13 shows the configuration of the search help in Transaction SE11.

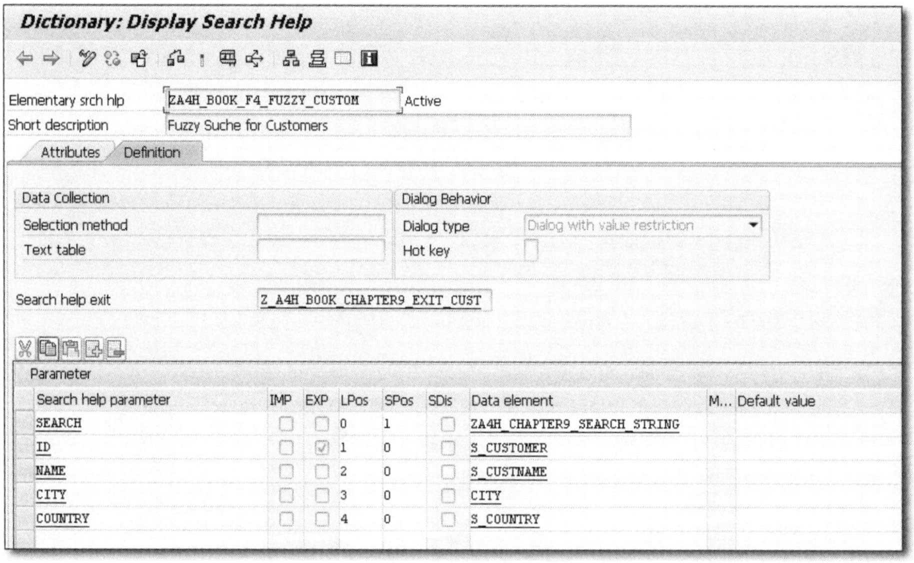

Figure 10.13 Configuring the Search Help in Transaction SE11

The search help framework calls the function module several times, and it's during these phases that you can manipulate the behavior of the system. The `callcontrol-step` value allows you to query the current phase. Table 10.4 provides an overview of the phases with a focus on those operations that are available in the context of a fuzzy search.

Call times for search help exits

Phase	Explanation
SELONE	This phase is relevant only for collective search helps. It enables you to manipulate the number and sequence of elementary search helps. In particular, it allows you to hide SAP HANA-specific search helps in systems running on other databases.
PRESEL	This phase enables you to manipulate the selection conditions so that you can replace certain special characters (such as a "*") in the context of a fuzzy search, for example.
SELECT	This phase enables you to implement your own selection of data and thus run a fuzzy search via ADBC, for example.
DISP	This phase once again allows you to manipulate the data and run an authorization check, for example, or change the presentation mode. The following examples don't use this phase.

Table 10.4 Phases of a Search Help Exit

Listing 10.11 shows the complete implementation of the search help exit. The data is read from Listing 10.8 in the SELECT phase using the database procedure and written to the target structure using the F4UT_RESULTS_MAP function module.

Implementing a search help exit

```
FUNCTION Z_A4H_BOOK_CHAPTER9_EXIT_CUST
  CHANGING
    VALUE(SHLP) TYPE SHLP_DESCR
    VALUE(CALLCONTROL) LIKE DDSHF4CTRL
  TABLES
    SHLP_TAB TYPE SHLP_DESCT
    RECORD_TAB LIKE SEAHLPRES.

  DATA: lt_data TYPE TABLE OF scustom.

  IF callcontrol-step <> 'SELECT'.
    EXIT.
  ENDIF.

*"------------------------------------------------------
```

```
* STEP SELECT    (Select values)
*"-------------------------------------------------------
  IF callcontrol-step = 'SELECT'.
    " Search request
    DATA: lv_value TYPE string.
    TRY.
        lv_value =
          shlp-selopt[ shlpfield = 'SEARCH' ]-low.
      CATCH cx_sy_itab_line_not_found.
        " Ignore
    ENDTRY.
    " Selecting data via AMDP
    NEW zcl_a4h_chapter9_amdp_contains( )->search_customer(
      EXPORTING
        iv_client = sy-mandt
        iv_search = lv_value
      IMPORTING
        et_result = lt_data
    ).

    CALL FUNCTION 'F4UT_RESULTS_MAP'
      EXPORTING
        source_structure = 'SCUSTOM'
      TABLES
        shlp_tab         = shlp_tab
        record_tab       = record_tab
        source_tab       = lt_data
      CHANGING
        shlp             = shlp
        callcontrol      = callcontrol.
    callcontrol-step = 'DISP'.
  ENDIF.

ENDFUNCTION.
```
Listing 10.11 Search Help Exit with Fuzzy Search across Name and Place of Residence

Usage in Web Dynpro ABAP   To conclude this section, we'll describe how you can use search helps created in the DDIC in Web Dynpro ABAP. This is a standard Web Dynpro functionality, independent of SAP HANA, and we can only introduce some of the details in the following sections. You should also have some basic development knowledge using Web Dynpro ABAP.

Data model of a Web Dynpro component   The data model of a Web Dynpro component must be defined using the *context*, which in turn can be defined either manually or based on a DDIC structure (table or view). When you define the context, the system transfers the associated search helps by default; however, you can also use your own DDIC search help for an attribute in the Web Dynpro context. Figure 10.14 shows a Web Dynpro context with an attribute for the customer ID (SCUSTOM-ID). At this point, we're using the new Eclipse-based development environment for Web Dynpro ABAP. However, you can make the setting as well via Transaction SE80.

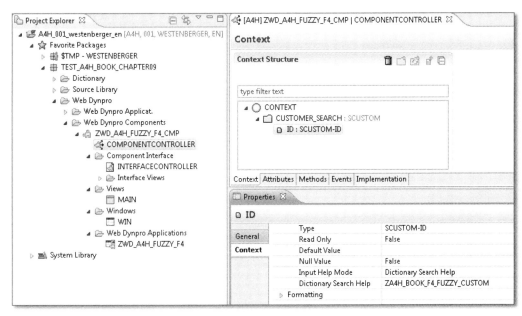

Figure 10.14 Web Dynpro ABAP Context Attribute with Fuzzy Search Help

---

Web Dynpro ABAP Development in Eclipse   [«]

In addition to tools that are used for pure ABAP developments, the ABAP Development Tools for SAP NetWeaver also contain other tools that are integrated natively in Eclipse—one of them being the development environment for Web Dynpro ABAP. You can use this tool in the same manner as other ABAP development objects. Specific editors are available for the Web Dynpro objects (e.g., Web Dynpro components) as well as for the related subobjects (such as *views* or *windows*). These editors can be created or opened through the PROJECT EXPLORER view in Eclipse, similar to the way you work with ABAP reports or classes.

If you link this context attribute to an input field in a Web Dynpro view, you'll obtain a Web Dynpro application with a search help similar to the one shown in Figure 10.11. This is illustrated in Figure 10.15.

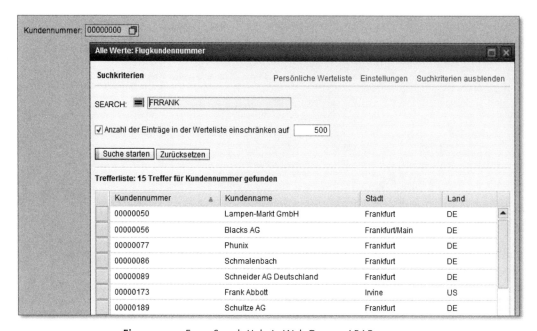

Figure 10.15 Fuzzy Search Help in Web Dynpro ABAP

Suggesting values   In addition, you can also view default values directly via Web Dynpro ABAP at the same time the user enters data. With this combination of an error-tolerant intelligent search and immediate display, you can create search helps for your end users that are in no way inferior to modern Internet searches.

10.4.3 ABAP Source Code Search

This last section presents another useful application of the SAP HANA text search: a free text search across the entire source code of an ABAP system as part of the ABAP-in-Eclipse environment.

Necessary Configuration and Memory Consumption

[«]

Because the memory consumption for indexes that are required for a search across the entire ABAP source code is rather high (some gigabytes of memory in SAP HANA), they aren't created automatically. You must activate the SRIS_SOURCE_SEARCH business function in Transaction SFW5 for this purpose. Indexing after activation is done in the background and takes several hours. You can check the status using Report SRIS_CODE_SEARCH_PREPARATION. More information is available in SAP Note 1918229.

To search for a text in the ABAP source code, use the  icon in the toolbar to open the general search dialog in Eclipse. Select the ABAP SOURCE SEARCH tab (see Figure 10.16) to search, for example, for all locations in the source code that were marked with "TODO". By means of the filter function, you can additionally restrict the search to packages, objects, or users. You can simply double-click to go directly from the search results to the source code.

Usage in Eclipse

Figure 10.16 ABAP Source Code Search in Eclipse

The free search on the ABAP source code allows for scenarios that clearly go beyond the "where-used" options. Besides the option of searching for comments (e.g., "TODO", "FIXME", "WORKAROUND", or

Application examples

similar comments that are commonly used among developers), you can also search for special calls or character strings, for example, "CALL FUNCTION" or the name of an Remote Function Call (RFC) destination.

10.5 Text Analysis

Semantic characteristics

In addition to running pure searches, you can use the text analysis to extract further insights. Based on the splitting of texts into *tokens*, these tokens are then assigned additional semantic characteristics (see Section 10.1). The semantic principles include the following, for example:

▶ Which language does the term come from? What is the word stem or basic grammatical form? Is it an abbreviation?

▶ Is the term a technical term? If so, which subject area or industry does it come from?

▶ Does the term implicitly contain an emotional statement; that is, does the term have a positive (e.g., "ideal") or negative (e.g., "unbearable") connotation?

For the purpose of the text analysis, it's necessary for the system to know the characteristics and specifics of the respective language pretty well. SAP HANA has dictionaries containing terms from more than 20 languages. Then, in a text analysis, the system extracts and categorizes metadata from the texts.

You can use the text analysis function for all types of data that allow for the creation of a full text index (such as columns of the following types: NVARCHAR, VARCHAR, CLOB, NCLOB, etc.). Note that when creating a full text index, you must specify the TEXT ANALYSIS ON option as well as an option for the analysis.

Text analysis options

SAP currently supports the options listed in Table 10.5. You can find information on the languages supported by each option in the developer documentation at *http://help.sap.com/hana/*.

Option	Description
LINGANALYSIS_BASIC	Fragments a text into its components (individual words with normalization of umlauts, accented characters, etc.)
LINGANALYSIS_STEMS	Fragments a text into its components and identifies the word stem of each word
LINGANALYSIS_FULL	Acts similar to LINGANALYSIS_STEMS, with additional grammatical categorization of terms
EXTRACTION_CORE	Extracts terms from the text and categorizes them semantically (e.g., into persons, organizations, locations, etc.)
EXTRACTION_CORE_VOICEOFCUSTOMER	Analyzes texts according to patterns that indicate emotions and desires of the writer (*sentiment analysis*)

Table 10.5 Text Analysis Options

You can employ the text analysis function in two different ways: via a linguistic variant and a semantic variant. The linguistic analysis is useful in scenarios where you want to analyze texts according to grammatical aspects. In particular, this variant is a prerequisite for the linguistic search described in Section 10.3. The semantic analysis, in turn, can be used to extract additional information. In many cases, the EXTRACTION_CORE option is sufficient for this.

Linguistic and semantic analysis

The following example defines a full text index with text analysis for the airline names. To define the index in DDIC, use the settings shown in Figure 10.17.

Example: Full text index with text analysis

When you create a full text index with text analysis, the system creates a technical table with the prefix $TA_ in the same schema, whose content is shown in Figure 10.18. In addition to the extracted information, this table also contains the primary keys of the original table, so that it can be embedded easily in joins and used accordingly. Because the DDIC doesn't know this table, you must revert to native technologies, such as SAP HANA views, AMDP, or ADBC.

Table $TA_*

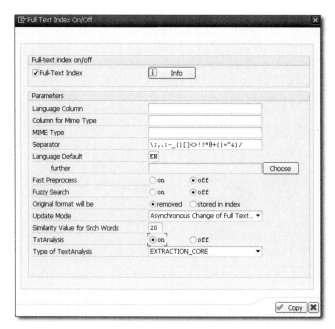

Figure 10.17 Creating a Full Text Index with Text Analysis

	MANDT	CARRID	TA_RULE	TA_COUNTER	TA_TOKEN	TA_LANGUAGE	TA_TYPE
1	000	AF	Entity Extraction	1	Air France	en	ORGANIZATION/COMMERCIAL
2	001	AA	Entity Extraction	1	American Airlines	en	ORGANIZATION/COMMERCIAL
3	001	AF	Entity Extraction	1	Air France	en	ORGANIZATION/COMMERCIAL
4	001	AZ	Entity Extraction	1	Alitalia	en	ORGANIZATION/COMMERCIAL
5	000	AC	Entity Extraction	1	Air Canada	en	ORGANIZATION/COMMERCIAL
6	000	LH	Entity Extraction	1	Lufthansa	en	ORGANIZATION/COMMERCIAL
7	001	AC	Entity Extraction	1	Air Canada	en	ORGANIZATION/COMMERCIAL
8	001	BA	Entity Extraction	1	British Airways	en	ORGANIZATION/COMMERCIAL
9	001	FJ	Entity Extraction	1	Air Pacific	en	ORGANIZATION/COMMERCIAL
10	001	CO	Entity Extraction	1	Continental Airl...	en	ORGANIZATION/COMMERCIAL
11	001	DL	Entity Extraction	1	Delta Airlines	en	ORGANIZATION/COMMERCIAL
12	001	AB	Entity Extraction	1	Air Berlin	en	ORGANIZATION/COMMERCIAL
13	001	NG	Entity Extraction	1	Lauda Air	en	ORGANIZATION/COMMERCIAL
14	001	JL	Entity Extraction	1	Japan Airlines	en	ORGANIZATION/COMMERCIAL
15	001	SA	Entity Extraction	1	South African Air	en	ORGANIZATION/COMMERCIAL
16	001	LH	Entity Extraction	1	Lufthansa	en	ORGANIZATION/COMMERCIAL
17	001	NW	Entity Extraction	1	Northwest Airli...	en	ORGANIZATION/COMMERCIAL
18	001	QF	Entity Extraction	1	Qantas Airways	en	ORGANIZATION/COMMERCIAL
19	001	SQ	Entity Extraction	1	Singapore Airlin...	en	ORGANIZATION/COMMERCIAL
20	001	SR	Entity Extraction	1	Swiss	en	PEOPLE
21	001	UA	Entity Extraction	1	United Airlines	en	ORGANIZATION/COMMERCIAL

Figure 10.18 Result of a Text Analysis for Airline Names Using the EXTRACTION_CORE Configuration

The system has recognized that the data are related to commercial organizations (TA_TYPE column in Figure 10.18). However, one entry was misinterpreted due to ambiguity, which is a clear indication that most of the time, you can't rely on a completely automatic treatment of the results. In general, the text analysis function is a powerful tool that enables you to detect indicators and trends, but a data scientist must always analyze and calibrate the results.

Analysis result

10.6 Resource Consumption and Runtime Aspects of the Text Search

In this chapter, we've discussed the basic architecture and use of the text search and text analysis functions in SAP HANA. You've learned that the column store contains specific data types (TEXT and SHORTTEXT) that provide powerful functions for searching and analyzing unstructured data. For ABAP text types, you can use a full text index to create a virtual column of the TEXT type. If you employ an additional fuzzy search index, you also can accelerate a fuzzy search run.

This section provides essential background information on the functionality of the text data types, as well as recommendations concerning the use of indexes. In particular, you'll learn how to use SQL queries to analyze the memory consumption.

Depending on the configuration, special dictionaries are created for text data types and full text indexes. These dictionaries store the fragmentation into tokens and linguistic information (e.g., word stems) in an efficient way. This process involves the same mechanisms and memory structures as other functions of the column store. If you want to learn more about the technical details of building and accessing such dictionary structures, you can find additional information in Appendix C.

Functionality of text data types

As described in Section 10.2, texts are fragmented into words (tokens), and then normalized and stored in the dictionary vector of the column (*word dictionary*). In addition to this, word stems can optionally be stored in a second dictionary, where inflected verbs, for example, are reverted to their basic form, or umlauts are replaced. All this information isn't persisted on the disk but generated only when the table is loaded into the main memory.

Fuzzy search index/
phrase-index ratio
You can use additional memory structures (optional) to accelerate text searches further; however, this will have an impact on the required memory size. Currently, two options are available: an additional fuzzy search index, or an increase of the *phrase-index ratio*. Using a fuzzy search index means that certain data are precalculated instead of being determined at the start of a search request. Additionally, in the phrase index, frequently occurring word constellations (phrases) are stored in a separate dictionary. The higher the specified phrase-index ratio value, the more storage space is reserved in relation to the actual memory consumption of the column (currently, the default value of this ratio is 0.2, i.e., 1:5).

Recommendations
As you can see, many setting options are available. Using the search and analysis options described here will increase the memory requirements for the required columns, and usually ABAP-based text data require twice as much memory space. Therefore, it's advisable to use the default settings first and to employ additional tuning options—such as fuzzy search indexes or changing the phrase-index ratio—only after you encounter performance problems.

Monitoring views
For you to get a better picture of this, we'll now describe how you can use *monitoring views* via the SQL console to obtain detailed information on the indexes and system memory consumption.

The FULLTEXT_INDEXES view in SAP HANA enables you to view the configuration of all full text indexes in the system. Figure 10.19 shows the full text indexes for the flight data model tables created in the preceding sections, as well as some other predefined indexes in the SAP HANA repository.

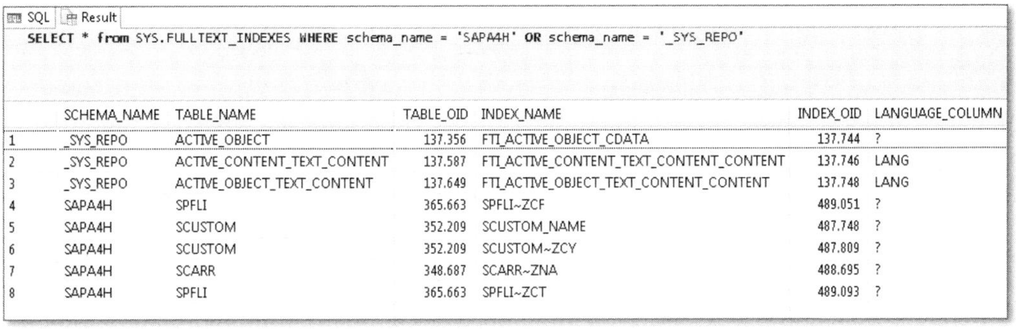

SQL | Result

```
SELECT * from SYS.FULLTEXT_INDEXES WHERE schema_name = 'SAPA4H' OR schema_name = '_SYS_REPO'
```

	SCHEMA_NAME	TABLE_NAME	TABLE_OID	INDEX_NAME	INDEX_OID	LANGUAGE_COLUMN
1	_SYS_REPO	ACTIVE_OBJECT	137.356	FTI_ACTIVE_OBJECT_CDATA	137.744	?
2	_SYS_REPO	ACTIVE_CONTENT_TEXT_CONTENT	137.587	FTI_ACTIVE_CONTENT_TEXT_CONTENT_CONTENT	137.746	LANG
3	_SYS_REPO	ACTIVE_OBJECT_TEXT_CONTENT	137.649	FTI_ACTIVE_OBJECT_TEXT_CONTENT_CONTENT	137.748	LANG
4	SAPA4H	SPFLI	365.663	SPFLI~ZCF	489.051	?
5	SAPA4H	SCUSTOM	352.209	SCUSTOM_NAME	487.748	?
6	SAPA4H	SCUSTOM	352.209	SCUSTOM~ZCY	487.809	?
7	SAPA4H	SCARR	348.687	SCARR~ZNA	488.695	?
8	SAPA4H	SPFLI	365.663	SPFLI~ZCT	489.093	?

Figure 10.19 FULLTEXT_INDEXES Monitoring View

Memory consumption

Moreover, you can query the memory consumption of the special fuzzy search indexes separately using the M_FUZZY_SEARCH_INDEXES monitoring view. The memory consumption depends on various factors but predominantly on the number of different values within the column. The following SQL statement allows you to query the current memory consumption of all data structures available for the fuzzy search in the system:

```
SELECT * FROM m_heap_memory
WHERE category LIKE '%FuzzySearch%'
```

Write operations

To conclude this chapter, we'll briefly discuss the topic of write operations, especially in the context of tables, which are both frequently modified and can be used for text searches and analyses. Full text indexes can be updated synchronously and asynchronously. If an index is updated synchronously, write operations take slightly longer because the creation of dictionary and index structures is part of the write operation. Usually, the effects should be minimal with small data types (e.g., with character strings of a fixed length). For larger documents that are stored as *large objects* in the database (e.g., STRING), an asynchronous update can be advantageous.

Delta store

In addition, when write operations are carried out in the column store, the data is first stored in the *delta store* and is automatically integrated into the *main store* only at specific *merge times* (see also Appendix C). The bigger the delta store gets in this process, the more costly the merging of results in SQL queries. This can significantly impact the system runtime, particularly in complex operations such as those described in this chapter. If you want to run text analyses across large datasets that are carried out asynchronously at fixed points in time, for example, it makes sense to implement *delta merge* manually, which is supposed to be executed on the relevant tables prior to the text analyses. For this purpose, you could, for example, use the `MERGE DELTA OF <Table>` SQL statement.

Decoupling decision rules from the actual program logic is an important trend in modern business applications. By providing options for modeling decision tables, SAP HANA makes it easy to control parts of an application flexibly via rules.

11   Decision Tables in SAP HANA

Because parameters of business processes are often changed, business applications must be modified from time to time throughout their life-cycle. The complexity and, thus, the cost, of such modifications are often higher than the original cost of introducing the software into an environment. This is especially true if the application wasn't designed to support flexible adaptation. In addition to the cost, the speed of implementations and adjustments is also a decisive factor. If a business unit must first submit a development request to the internal IT team, which is then implemented and validated in practice, the *turnaround times* are often too long for today's business environment. That is why *business rule management systems* are gaining more and more importance, as they make it possible to control and easily adjust certain parts of an application via rules. *Decision tables* are a typical element of such systems. These tables are used to define simple "if-then" rules. As of SPS 5, SAP HANA provides native support for modeling decision tables, which is introduced in this chapter.

SAP HANA Rules Framework   [«]

In addition to decision tables as part of the standard modeling options, an advanced environment available for defining business rules via the *SAP HANA Rules Framework* (*HRF*) must be installed separately.

Because the HRF hasn't been released for general usage yet, we won't discuss this component in more detail in this edition.

In addition, the ABAP AS comprises established environments for modeling, testing, and executing complex business rules. In current releases, SAP recommends the usage of the *Business Rules Framework plus (BRFplus)*, which is also deployed in numerous SAP applications (see the following information box). If you're interested in this topic, we recommend *BRFplus—Business Rule Management for ABAP Applications* by Thomas Albrecht and Carsten Ziegler (SAP PRESS, 2012). We can't present the topic of business rules comprehensively within the scope of this book. Instead, we limit our descriptions to native decision tables in SAP HANA that you can use for modeling very simple rules.

[»]   **BRFplus and SAP Decision Service Management**

With BRFplus, SAP NetWeaver AS ABAP provides a powerful tool for defining and executing business rules. Using the *SAP Decision Service Management (DSM)* tool, you can distribute and use these rules in a heterogeneous landscape. Specialist departments can then execute a large number of operations without help from the IT department.

SAP plans to facilitate the use of SAP HANA capabilities in BRFplus or DSM incrementally and to offer an integration of the modeling options described in this chapter. As a variant, DSM offers the option to establish a connection between BRFplus expressions and data sources in SAP HANA via *dynamic database views*. Refer to the DSM documentation at *http://help.sap.com/nwdsm100*.

11.1   Basic Principles of Decision Tables

We'll explain the concept of decision tables via an example. If you, for example, need to verify whether an air passenger's profile data is complete, you can specify the conditions for this check via ABAP code. The example in Listing 11.1 shows how to check if a private customer has both an email address *and* a phone number, while business customers need only either an email address *or* a phone number.

```
METHOD is_profile_complete.
  IF ( is_customer-custtype = 'B' ).

    " Business customers
    IF ( is_customer-email IS NOT INITIAL ).
      rv_complete = abap_true. " Complete
```

```
      ELSEIF ( is_customer-telephone IS NOT INITIAL ).
        rv_complete = abap_true. " Complete
      ELSE.
        rv_complete = abap_false. " Incomplete
      ENDIF.
    ELSE.
      " Private customer
      IF ( is_customer-email IS NOT INITIAL ).
        IF ( is_customer-telephone IS NOT INITIAL ).
          rv_complete = abap_true. " Complete
        ELSE.
          rv_complete = abap_false. " Incomplete
        ENDIF.
      ELSE.
        rv_complete = abap_false. " Incomplete
      ENDIF.

    ENDIF.
  ENDMETHOD
```

Listing 11.1 Decision Rule as ABAP Code

If a company changes its criteria for verifying the completeness of an air passenger's profile, the code must be modified. As a first step to avoid such complicated changes, you can decouple the parameters via a configuration (e.g., via Customizing settings). Even with the advantage this provides, the implementation process for changes is still complex, and the structure of the rules is still inflexible in this Customizing approach.

Decision tables can be used to clearly describe the decisions (*actions*) to be taken based on several parameters (*conditions*). Table 11.1 shows a decision table using the same criteria as Listing 11.1. The last column, CUSTOMER PROFILE, represents the action; the other columns define the conditions. When changing the rules or parameters, only the structures and values in the decision table must be modified.

Decision tables

Decision tables are structured case distinctions for mapping input parameters (conditions) and decision values (actions). Conditions can be either columns of a database table or the result of calculations. The actions that constitute the decision table's output are determined by applying certain regulations (*rules*). This set of rules is represented by a table, as shown in Table 11.1. One of the main goals of decision tables is to define the dependencies of conditions and actions clearly and consistently. Each rule management system provides different options for

Conditions and actions

defining rules. The current options available in SAP HANA are described in detail in Section 11.2.

Customer Type	Email Address	Phone Number	Customer Profile
Business customer	Present	Any	Complete
	Missing	Present	Complete
		Missing	Incomplete
Private customer	Present	Present	Complete
		Missing	Incomplete
	Missing	Any	Incomplete

Table 11.1 Simple Decision to Check the Completeness of Customer Profiles

Decision table as a view or procedure
In SAP HANA, decision tables are development objects that can be created via the MODELER perspective in SAP HANA Studio, similar to views and procedures. Tables or views can be used as a data basis. The conditions and actions are physical or calculated fields of these objects. When activating a decision table, runtime objects (e.g., views or procedures) are generated.

There are two alternative scenarios:

▸ Column values of a database table will be changed using a decision table.

▸ The value of a view's calculated column will be determined using a decision table.

In the following section, we'll focus mostly on the second alternative. This is because we recommend in general modifying ABAP tables only from ABAP. It's also often not necessary to persist such results on SAP HANA (just like it isn't always necessary to materialize aggregates on SAP HANA). Accessing decision tables using ABAP is described in more detail in Section 11.5.

Limits
Decision tables in SAP HANA are somewhat limited because rules can be based only on table content (or views). It's currently not possible to

486

make decisions based on rules *prior* to saving a data record. Furthermore, no direct integration in process management systems is possible. For special scenarios, SAP offers the *SAP Operational Process Intelligence* tool.

> **SAP Operational Process Intelligence**
>
> SAP Operational Process Intelligence powered by SAP HANA is a tool for intelligent process analysis. This analysis covers process visibility (current state of the processes) and decision support for continuous improvement. The tool is integrated with different data sources such as SAP Process Observer, SAP Business Process Management (SAP BPM), and SAP Business Workflow. Decision tables are an important tool used internally by SAP Operational Process Intelligence.

[«]

In this chapter, we'll first create a simple decision table DT_PASSENGER_PROFILE that can be used to classify the air passengers from table SCUSTOM in Table 11.1. In the second example, decision table DT_DISCOUNT, we'll use a view as the data basis to implement a more complex scenario. We'll determine a proposed value for a new discount for air passengers based on the customer type (private customer, business customer), the frequent flyer miles earned in the past year, and the present discount value. For the required calculations (especially for calculating the miles), we'll create an analytic view called AN_MILES used for unit conversion of flight routes into miles, as seen in Chapter 8.

Reference examples for this chapter

11.2   Creating Decision Tables in SAP HANA Studio

Like other development objects, decision tables are created via the MODELER perspective in SAP HANA Studio. To do so, you select NEW • DECISION TABLE in the context menu of a package as shown in Figure 11.1.

In the next step, you specify the name for the decision table and a description (see Figure 11.2).

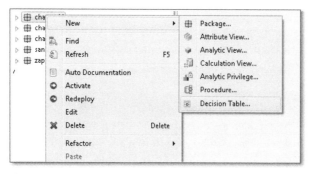

Figure 11.1 Creating a Decision Table (Part 1)

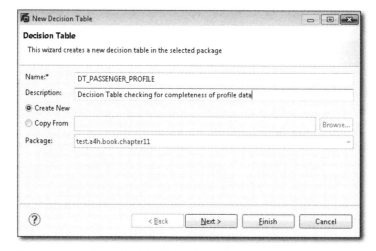

Figure 11.2 Creating a Decision Table (Part 2)

Selecting a
data basis

As with view modeling (see Chapter 4), you now have to select the data basis for the decision table. You can choose between tables or previously defined views (e.g., an attribute view).

The editor for decision tables (Figure 11.3) consists of two sections that are opened via the DATA FOUNDATION and DECISION TABLE tabs. The DATA FOUNDATION tab is used to define the conditions and actions used in the decision table, whereas the DECISION TABLE pane is used to maintain the actual rule values.

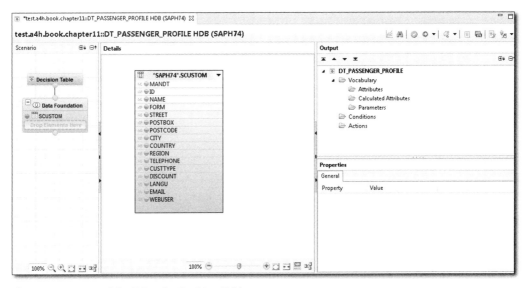

Figure 11.3 Layout of the Editor for Decision Tables

To get started, we want to classify air passengers directly based on columns of table SCUSTOM and add them to the DATA FOUNDATION tab. Because we want to access the attributes CUSTTYPE, EMAIL, and TELEPHONE in addition to the name of the passenger, we add these as attributes of the decision table. To use the named attributes as conditions, they must be flagged as such (ADD AS CONDITION). As for all other modeled objects in SAP HANA, you can also add calculated fields to decision tables.

Flag attributes as conditions

In our example, we want to determine a classification with the help of a calculated attribute. To do so, we first define a new parameter via the PARAMETERS context menu, for which we specify a data type CHAR(1) and static fixed values—T for True (Complete) and F for False (Incomplete)—as shown in Figure 11.4.

Define actions

Because this parameter should be used as the result, we flag it as ACTION (ADD AS ACTION). The final structure of the decision table is shown in Figure 11.5.

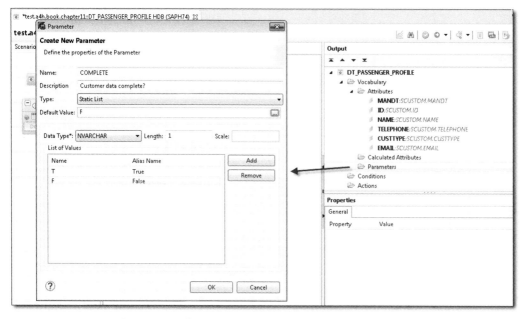

Figure 11.4 Defining a Parameter for the Output Value

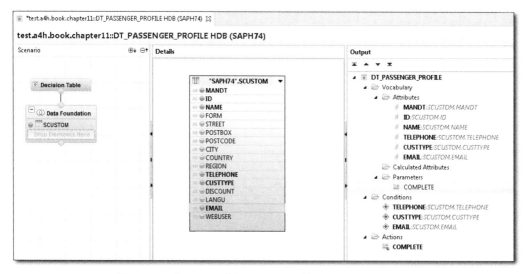

Figure 11.5 Structure of the Decision Table

Using the DECISION TABLE node, you can now specify the classification
rules for the decision table, as shown earlier in Table 11.1. To define the
conditions (e.g., CUSTTYPE), you select a cell and then choose ADD CON-
DITION VALUES from the context menu. This opens a dialog where you
can either enter a condition or select a fixed value from a list. To specify
actions (in our example, COMPLETE), you can select either SET INITIAL
VALUE for fixed values or SET DYNAMIC VALUE for calculated values from
the context menu. Figure 11.6 shows the resulting set of rules, where it
depends on the customer type and the availability of an email address or
telephone number whether the profile is complete. With this rule set,
the Like _* expression is used to verify if a nonempty string is present.
The static True and False action values were set using SET INITIAL VALUE.

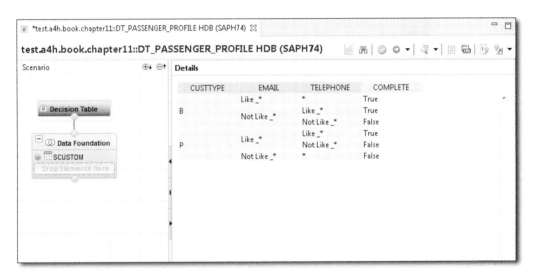

Figure 11.6 Rules of the Decision Table

After saving and activating the decision table, you can display the result
using the DATA PREVIEW. Decision tables are activated the same way as
views. Figure 11.7 shows that, according to the defined rules, 6% of the
system's roughly 4,800 customer profiles are incomplete.

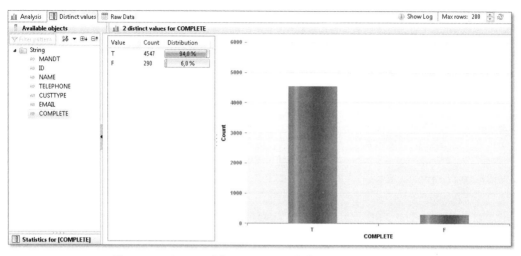

Figure 11.7 Output of the Decision Table for Profile Analysis

Exporting and importing values
You can also export or import the values for decision tables to or from Microsoft Excel. This especially facilitates collaboration between IT experts and business departments. To export or import values, use the context menu in the DECISION TABLE editor pane.

Expressions for decision rules
SAP HANA currently supports the expressions listed in Table 11.2 to define decision rules. You can then logically link such expressions via And and Or.

Expression	Supported SQL Data Types	Example
Not equal (!=)	Any	!= Lufthansa
Greater Than (>), Greater Than Or Equals (>=), Less Than (<), Less Than Or Equals (<=)	Strings and numeric types	Greater Than 20
In, Not In	Strings and numeric types	In AA;LH
Like, Not Like	Strings	Like Lufthansa*

Table 11.2 Available Expressions for Decision Rules

Expression	Supported SQL Data Types	Example
Between	Numeric types	Between 100 and 200
After, Before, Between	Date (DATE)	Before 2016-01-01 Between 2015-01-01 and 2016-01-01

Table 11.2 Available Expressions for Decision Rules (Cont.)

Once again, correct handling of data types can be somewhat tricky, and ignoring these aspects may cause problems. In particular, you must first convert data types in some cases. For example, to compare dates (After, Before, Between with an ABAP date (DATS, i.e., NVARCHAR(8) in the database), you first have to convert this date into a field of type DATE. For this purpose, you usually create a calculated attribute and use a conversion function such as to_date().

Data types

Another example is numeric data stored in a character-type field. If you used the NUMC data type for a numeric value in your ABAP data model, for instance, this is a NVARCHAR type in the database (see Chapter 3, Section 3.1.3). An example for this is the DISCOUNT column in table SCUSTOM. As a result, a rule such as >20 is interpreted as a comparison of strings by the decision table, that is, as >'20' instead of a numeric comparison. Once again, the value must be converted first.

Consider Data Types When Designing Decision Tables

[!]

To avoid unexpected consequences when evaluating rules, you must carefully define the structure and semantics of a decision table. For a successful design, you must have the required development skills and understand the technological aspects and semantics of the data structures and types. In combination with a thorough documentation, this makes it possible for the specialist department to define the set of rules correctly.

11.3 Decision Tables Based on SAP HANA Views

Rules are often based on different parameters from several database tables, with certain calculations and expressions potentially also playing a role. Let's consider the following example (see Table 11.3): To determine the discount for a flight customer, the miles earned within the past year should be considered in addition to the customer type. Based on the current discount, either a higher or a lower discount should be proposed.

Customer Type	Miles Earned within the Past Year	Current Discount	Proposed Discount Change for the Next Year
Business customer	<10,000 MI	<5%	reduced discount rate of 0%
		between 5% and 15%	–1%
		>15%	–2%
	>=10,000 MI	<15%	+1%
		>=15%	unchanged
Private customer	<20,000 MI	0%	unchanged
		>0%	–1%
	>=20,000 MI	<20%	+1%
		>=20%	unchanged

Table 11.3 Decision for Passengers Based on Calculated Key Figures

Calculating frequent flyer miles

To determine the frequent flyer miles, we'll once again use the bookings and flight plan from tables SBOOK and SPFLI and convert the flight route into miles. To do this, we'll use the techniques described in Chapter 4, Section 4.4.2, to create a new analytic view called AN_MILES. This view is called from a calculation view, CA_MILES_LAST_YEAR, where we determine the air miles per passenger within the past year using SQLScript. Listing 11.2 shows the SQLScript coding and uses the known columns from tables SBOOK and SPFLI, in addition to the distance_mi column (containing the distance in miles) and the discount_dec column (containing the current customer discount as decimal value—type DECIMAL).

```
var_out =
   select mandt, name, country, city,
          custtype, sum(distance_mi) as miles,
          discount_dec as discount
```

```
from "test.a4h.book.chapter11::AN_MILES"
where year(fldate) = year(current_utcdate) - 1
group by mandt, name, country, city,
        custtype, discount_dec;
```
Listing 11.2 Determining Miles Earned within a Year

We'll now create a new decision table DT_DISCOUNT and add the CA_MILES_ LAST_YEAR calculation view to the DATA FOUNDATION. Subsequently, we'll define the conditions and actions as described in the previous section. When doing so, we'll define a DISCOUNT_NEW parameter of type DECIMAL as the action.

To determine the proposed value for the new discount, you need to access the existing discount value. To do so, you specify a dynamic value for the calculated column (using the context menu item SET DYNAMIC VALUE). Figure 11.8 shows the resulting decision table with dynamic values for the DISCOUNT_NEW column (e.g., "DISCOUNT" –1).

Dynamic values

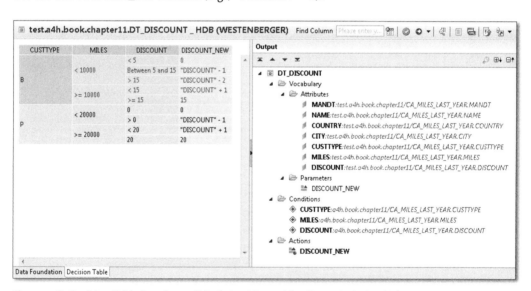

Figure 11.8 Decision Table Based on a Calculation View with a Dynamic Action Value

After successfully activating the decision table, the proposed values for a new discount are displayed as the result (see Figure 11.9). In the following sections, we'll show you how this result is embedded into an ABAP application.

Analysis | Distinct values | Raw Data

200 rows retrieved - 4 sec, 353 ms

MANDT	NAME	COUNT...	CITY	CUSTTYPE	MILES	DISCOUNT	DISCOUNT_NEW
001	Eastland Trade	CA	Vancouver	B	3.506.347	18	15
001	Compu Tech	US	San Fransisco	B	3.407.565	18	15
001	Roberta Energy Ltd	CA	Calgary	B	2.895.695	18	15
001	PH Keyboard Corporation	US	Boston	B	3.715.827	17	15
001	Infix Co.	US	San Mateo	B	3.092.348	17	15
001	ABC Dienstleistungen Gm...	DE	Kaiserslautern	B	3.418.927	17	15
001	British Railways	GB	Manchester	B	3.431.930	16	15
001	Marta Buchholm	ES	Barcelona	P	3.475.776	15	16
001	Sophie Kramer	DE	Schifferstadt	P	2.930.768	15	16
001	Theresia Jacqmain	DE	Gaertringen	P	3.508.064	15	16
001	Johann Lindwurm	DE	Berlin	P	3.326.360	15	16
001	Peter Hoffen	DE	Potsdam	P	3.396.326	15	16
001	Irmtraut Sudhoff	DE	Heusenstamm	P	3.240.690	15	16
001	Astrid Buehler	DE	Mannheim	P	3.576.481	15	16
001	Stephen Montero	DE	Schwetzingen	P	3.362.443	15	16
001	Andrej Goelke	SI	Ljubljana	P	3.327.847	15	16
001	Fabio Detemple	IT	Roma	P	3.539.698	15	16
001	Kurt Sessler	DE	Kurt	P	3.278.721	15	16
001	Florian Illner	DE	Wiesloch	P	3.501.449	15	16
001	Adam Eichbaum	DE	Wald-Michelba...	P	3.391.883	15	16
001	Fabio Cesari	IT	Roma	P	3.381.861	15	16

Figure 11.9 Result of the Decision Table Based on Calculated Key Figures and Dynamic Action Values

11.4 Runtime Objects and SQL Access for Decision Tables

When activating a decision table, several objects are created in the database catalog (schema `_SYS_BIC`). To start, a database procedure to implement the rules in SQLScript and the corresponding table types are created. If the actions are virtual parameters so that the database procedure doesn't modify any data, a result view is also created (i.e., a column view that contains the result of the decision table and that can be addressed via standard SQL in SAP HANA like other views).

Result view The name of this result view is composed of the package name, the name of the decision table, and the suffix `RV`, for example, `"test.a4h.book.chapter13/DT_PASSENGER_CLASS/RV"`

If the data basis of the decision table itself is a column view, the same limitations apply for accessing the decision table via SQL as for the view (see Chapter 4).

11.5   Access to Decision Tables from ABAP

Because the result views generated from a decision table and other views can be addressed via SQL, they can also be accessed from ABAP using Native SQL. Unfortunately, it's not currently possible to define an external view in the ABAP Data Dictionary (DDIC) directly for result views. Instead, you must first *wrap* the result view via a calculation view. This can also be necessary for other reasons, such as to remove an unsupported data type from the projection list. For simple scenarios, you can graphically model the calculation view so that you simply add the generated view (via drag and drop from the database catalog) and select the desired column (see Chapter 4, Section 4.4.3). The example in Figure 11.10 shows how our sample result view is wrapped by another calculation view, CA_DISCOUNT_PROPOSAL.

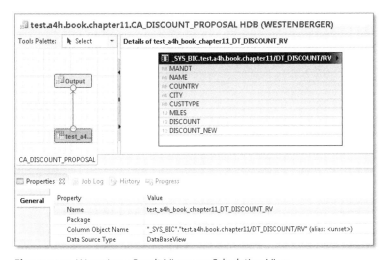

Figure 11.10 Wrapping a Result View as a Calculation View

As described in Chapter 5, Section 5.1.2, you can now define an external view for this additional calculation view in the DDIC, which can be accessed via Open SQL. Alternatively, you can also embed the decision table's view in an SQLScript procedure (or in an SQLScript calculation view), which can then be accessed from ABAP.

For our example, we'll define the external view ZEV_A4H_DISCOUNT and display the results in an SAP List Viewer (ALV) list. When doing so, we'll

Decision table in ALV list

497

use a new variant of the ALV grid with integrated data access that moves all operations to the database layer (see the upcoming information box). Listing 11.3 shows the coding for the *process before output (PBO) module* when initializing the dynpro.

```
MODULE pbo OUTPUT.

  " Create ALV with external view as data basis
  DATA(lo_alv_display) =
    cl_salv_gui_table_ida=>create(
      iv_table_name = 'ZEV_A4H_DISCOUNT'
      io_gui_container =
      NEW cl_gui_custom_container( lv_container ) ).

  " Initial sorting
  lo_alv_display->default_layout( )->set_sort_order(
    VALUE #( ( field_name = 'DISCOUNT_NEW'
               is_grouped = abap_false
               descending = abap_true ) )
  ).

  ENDIF.
ENDMODULE.
```

Listing 11.3 Using the ALV with Integrated Data Access

As a result, the proposed discounts are displayed in an ALV list (see Figure 11.11). To enhance this scenario further, we could add an option, accept or adjust the proposed values, and then update them in the system.

Proposals for discount adaptation

Customer name	Country	City	B/P customer	Old discount	New discount	Miles
Helmle	US	chicago	P	20,00	20,00	2.564.285,42
Andreas Klotz	DE	Walldorf	P	20,00	20,00	2.686.584,22
Tom Peterson	US	Pascadenia	P	20,00	20,00	2.506.358,63
Jean Cosman	CA	Kitchener	P	20,00	20,00	2.626.146,57
Laura Deichgraeber	DE	Mainz	P	15,00	16,00	2.631.673,07
Roland Hansmann	DE	Waldshut	P	15,00	16,00	2.512.746,45
Adam Koller	DE	Wald-Michelbach	P	15,00	16,00	2.506.038,20
Salvador Henry	ES	Sevilla	P	15,00	16,00	2.388.808,27
Anneliese Rahn	DE	Buxtehude	P	15,00	16,00	2.552.791,77
Mathilde Weiss	DE	St. Leon-Rot	P	15,00	16,00	2.498.420,39
Johann Heller	DE	Berlin	P	15,00	16,00	2.372.632,26
Guillermo Koller	ES	Madrid	P	15,00	16,00	2.847.052,88
Annemarie Sessler	DE	Kaiserslautern	P	15,00	16,00	2.342.770,99
Lee Barth	US	Boulder	P	15,00	16,00	2.860.875,31
Guillermo Benz	ES	Madrid	P	15,00	16,00	2.564.367,61
Laura Meier	DE	Mainz	P	15,00	16,00	2.436.550,95
Fabio Henry	IT	Roma	P	15,00	16,00	2.672.419,00
Juan Mechler	ES	Madrid	P	15,00	16,00	2.619.877,98

Figure 11.11 Output of the Proposed Discounts in an ALV List

ALV with Integrated Data Access

[«]

ALV is a powerful component for displaying data in ABAP AS; just about every SAP user and ABAP developer has already worked with ALV lists. In addition to the display functionality, ALV offers many other functions (e.g., for sorting, aggregation, personalization, and data export). When using this viewer, you can choose between several display variants for different scenarios and user interfaces (SAP GUI, Floorplan Manager for Web Dynpro ABAP). However, the same programming model is used in all cases. The data are first read into an internal table and then passed on to the ALV.

As of ABAP 7.4, a new option is available that allows you to describe only the data source for the ALV and let the viewer make the selections independently on the database. We've used this option in Listing 11.3 by displaying the discount information of all passengers, whereas end users can only see a portion of the list. When scrolling or sorting the result list, the system determines the required portion of the result data.

To conclude this chapter, we'll briefly mention the transport of decision tables. Like views and procedures, you can transport decision tables within an ABAP system landscape using the SAP HANA transport container introduced in Chapter 5, Section 5.3. Because the transport container automatically includes all package contents, there are no special aspects to consider.

Transport of decision tables

As mentioned at the beginning of this chapter, decoupling rule maintenance and rule usage within an ABAP application represents an important aspect of these decision tables. The interface is defined by the structure of the generated result view. For this reason, structural changes to a decision table should only be implemented in the development system and then transported consistently.

Function libraries add specific business and mathematical operations to the functionality of SAP HANA. They are integrated into special products but can also be used directly within an application via SQLScript. This provides new analysis options, especially in the context of statistical predictions.

12   Function Libraries in SAP HANA

This book has already presented several options for analyzing operational business data using SAP HANA. Depending on the usage scenario, you can use direct native database functions in SAP HANA (e.g., via views and procedures) or benefit from the advanced SAP Business Warehouse (SAP BW) infrastructure (see Chapter 9). Regardless of the technology, analyses based on real-time data allow users to respond quickly to current developments. It's a relatively new trend in business intelligence to take this approach one step further by using statistical models to make predictions on future developments. Such *predictive analysis* is used to enable decision makers to act before an event occurs, rather than to react after the fact. The mathematical models are quite complex, and the interpretation and calibration of the results generally require a good understanding of the business domain as well as the statistical algorithms. For this reason, data scientists have taken on increasingly important roles in recent years.

For many scenarios, you currently have to use special third-party software. Particularly for operational scenarios where time is important, this approach introduces a number of challenges. Due particularly to the required data extraction and conversion, a significant time delay and complexity are introduced to the process chain. SAP HANA offers special *function libraries* called Application Function Libraries (AFL) to provide an integrated option for some scenarios, which are based directly on the business data from the ABAP system. Before we discuss these libraries in more detail, we'll present three specific application scenarios.

Forecast creation

A classic usage scenario for statistical models is the creation of forecasts, such as predictions on the development of revenue, sales, or costs. Certain scenarios can also be created using forecasts for customer movements or business environments, which can play an important role within the strategic planning of a company.

Integration of risk assessment and planning

The assessment and response to risks in live operations plays a major role in many industries today. You can imagine, for example, assessing the likelihood of potential defaults on payments but also analyzing the risks in a complex production process. Here, frequent use is made of *key performance indicators* (KPIs) and *scorecards*, which define limits and assess impacts. The use of statistical predictions enables early detection of exceptional situations and signals in running business processes. This results in new options for closer integration of operational planning, risk analysis, and control options, which opens up great potential for increased efficiency.

Deriving business rules

Another trend that is currently increasing in importance is related to the derivation of business rules from existing business processes (*business rule mining*). This approach can particularly support the modernization of a legacy application by identifying execution patterns and decision points. This allows the use of a service-oriented approach within the application that is controllable via business rules. An integrated solution has the advantage of being able to base itself directly on the existing application code.

Application Function Libraries

The required functions are implemented in SAP HANA in *function libraries*. These libraries are written in C++ and provide highly optimized access to functions for advanced calculations and data-analysis scenarios. With SAP HANA SPS 5, the AFL package provides the following two libraries, which have been released for customer developments:

▸ **Business Function Library (BFL)**
This library contains a variety of complex business functions (e.g., for determining annual depreciation) as well as reusable basic functions (e.g., a weighted average).

▸ **Predictive Analysis Library (PAL)**
This library contains statistical functions with which you can recognize patterns based on historical datasets (e.g., customer groups with similar purchasing behavior) and make predictions (e.g., about the development of revenue).

In the meantime, additional libraries are available, for example, the *Data Quality Library* that is used for SAP HANA within the scope of the Enterprise Information Management (EIM) module. Product-specific AFLs are also available, that is, libraries that are only deployed in combination with a special product and aren't part of the SAP HANA delivery. Ultimately, a Software Development Kit (SDK) is available that allows partners to develop their own function libraries and have them certified by SAP.

Additional libraries

We can't present the full range of functions within the scope of this book. The number of functions is too great, and, as mentioned, some of the algorithms are quite complex or require mathematical knowledge of the statistical models. We'll thus limit the discussion to individual examples to give you an overview.

Objective of the chapter

SAP Predictive Analytics 2.0   **[«]**

With *SAP Predictive Analytics 2.0*, SAP provides a powerful tool for advanced analyses, for example, for creating forecast models. This product is the successor of SAP Predictive Analysis and SAP InfiniteInsight, which originate from SAP's acquisitions (Business-Objects and KXEN).

Using SAP Predictive Analytics, even nondevelopers can run advanced statistic analyses. When used in combination with SAP HANA, various function libraries are deployed to execute mathematical algorithms entirely in the SAP HANA database in the ideal case.

Because this involves separate products that are subject to licensing, we won't discuss this solution in further detail in this book. For further information, refer to the SAP Community Network at *http://scn.sap.com/community/predictive-analytics*.

As an application scenario, we'll again consider simple examples from the flight-data model in this chapter. We'll determine a special key figure for seat utilization in the `LINEAR_AVERAGE_UTILIZATION` database

Reference examples

procedure using a BFL function to illustrate the development of utilization over time by placing more emphasis on recent results than on those of the past. Furthermore, we'll perform a segmentation of passengers into target groups in the CUSTOMER_SEGMENTATION procedure using a PAL function, which could provide helpful information, for example, in an airline's customer rewards program.

Structure of the chapter

We'll first give you a brief overview of the functions and installation of standard AFL in the next section. Then, in Section 12.2 and Section 12.3, we'll provide examples to describe how you can use AFL functions in your own implementations. For this purpose, we'll create Core Data Services (CDS) views, respectively, to prepare the data in the required input format and ABAP database procedures for calling the functions.

12.1   Basics of the Application Function Library

In this section, we'll give you a technical overview of the functions of the standard AFL and introduce an example of one function from each of the two libraries: BFL and PAL.

Installation of AFL

The AFL library is dynamically linked to the index server of the SAP HANA database. Although it's part of the delivery and license of the SAP HANA appliance, the hardware partner doesn't preinstall it by default. However, it can be set up on the customer side using the *SAP HANA Database Lifecycle Manager (hdblcm)*. (You'll find the necessary documentation in the SAP HANA installation guide at *http://help.sap.com/hana*.) If you as the administrator want to check whether the AFL is installed in the system, you can use the system overview in SAP HANA Studio or Transaction ST04 (DBA Cockpit) in ABAP (see Figure 12.1 under INSTALLED PLUG-INS).

After the installation, you as an administrator have to perform some configuration steps, which we'll discuss briefly now.

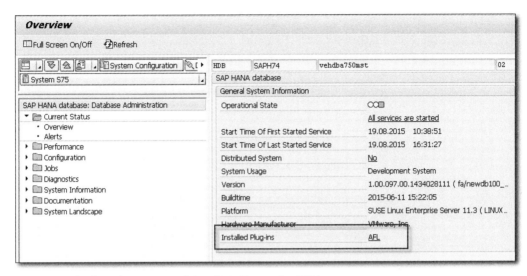

Figure 12.1 Checking the Presence of the AFL in Transaction ST04

You must configure a separate *script server* because the AFL functions for large datasets may take up a lot of resources (see SAP Note 1650957 for more information). The script server is a special index server process that doesn't perform any tasks during normal database operations. This ensures that the execution of AFL functions doesn't interfere with the operation of a standard application on SAP HANA.

Activating script server

The installation of the AFL results in the creation of the _SYS_AFL technical schema, which contains the AFL procedures. In addition, the administrator must assign a user (the database user of the SAP NetWeaver AS ABAP, in the case of access via ABAP) the following two roles for the execution of AFL functions in SAP HANA:

Authorizations

▸ AFL__SYS_AFL_AFLBFL_EXECUTE (for the BFL)

▸ AFL__SYS_AFL_AFLPAL_EXECUTE (for the PAL)

Some functions of the BFL and virtually all functions of the PAL are implemented as *generic functions*; that is, the structure of the input and output parameters (number of fields, column names, data types) isn't defined a priori. This allows flexible usage but has the disadvantage that you, as a developer, can't call these functions directly after the installation. Instead, you first have to generate a special form of the function—

Generating AFL functions

known as a *wrapper function*—using a special database procedure. To generate procedures, you as the developer additionally require the `AFLPM_CREATOR_ERASER_EXECUTE` role. In earlier versions (up until SAP HANA SPS 7), you had to create them manually via SQL. Now you can leverage the *Application Function Modeler (AFM)* as a graphical tool, which we'll introduce based on a PAL function in Section 12.3.

12.2 Business Function Library

Examples of functions

The Business Function Library (BFL) provides a range of specific business functions mainly from the internal cash flow statement. Table 12.1 contains some examples of calculations that are implemented in the BFL.

Function	Corresponding Database Procedure
Annual Depreciation	`AFLBFL_DBDEPRECIATION_PROC` `AFLBFL_SLDEPRECIATION_PROC` `AFLBFL_SOYDEPRECIATION_PROC`
Internal Rate of Return	`AFLBFL_INTERNALRATE_PROC`
Rolling Forecast	`AFLBFL_FORECAST_PROC`

Table 12.1 Some Functions of the Business Function Library

The underlying algorithms and data models are quite extensive, and it's beyond the scope of this book to introduce them in detail. In addition to calculations based on a fixed process, the BFL also exposes specific mathematical functions that are used within complex algorithms but can also be called independently.

Example: weighted average

For example, `AFLBFL_LINEARAVERAGE_PROC` is such a function, which can be used to determine a *weighted average*. The individual variables are weighted differently here compared to the standard arithmetic average. You can, for example, let values from the recent past play a greater role in the result than older values, which can be useful for some forecasts.

The following is the mathematical definition of the weighted average of the numeric values *x1* to *xn* with the corresponding weights *w1* to *wn*:

$$(w1 \times x1 + \ldots + wn \times xn) \div (w1 + \ldots + wn)$$

Let's take as an example the seat utilization of flights of a fixed flight connection with sample data from Table 12.2.

Period	Year	Average Use (Percent)
1	2012	87.5%
2	2013	95%
3	2014	91%
4	2015	60%

Table 12.2 Sample Data for Weighted Average

We use the period as a weighting factor and thus get the following weighted average:

$$(1 \times 0.875 + 2 \times 0.95 + 3 \times 0.91 + 4 \times 0.6) \div (1 + 2 + 3 + 4) = 0.7905$$
$$\sim 79\,\%$$

The normal average is approximately 83%. The lower value is due to the low utilization during the past year, which has more of an impact on the weighted average. The interface of the AFLBFL_LINEARAVERAGE_PROC function has the structure shown in Table 12.3.

Parameter	Explanation	Column Structure (Name, Type)	
Input: Database table	Original data	VALUE	DOUBLE
Output: Result	In row N, the weighted average of the values up to the period N	AVERAGED_ RESULT	DOUBLE

Table 12.3 Interface of the LINEAR_AVERAGE Function from the BFL

As an application example, we want to use this function to determine the weighted average of seat utilization for all flights of one airline. The result should be a time-based progression over the years, which can provide a better data basis for a flight-utilization forecast than the normal calculation of the average because the current data are valued higher than results of the past. To determine the required values, we use the ZA4H_SEAT_UTIL CDS view as the data source from Listing 12.1. We

Weighted average of seat utilization

determine the percentage utilization using a calculated field (utiliza-tion). Here, we consider the economy, business, and first class seats and convert the result to an ABAP floating-point number (abap.fltp), which corresponds to the SQL type DOUBLE.

```
@AbapCatalog.sqlViewName: 'ZA4H_SEAT_UTIL'
@EndUserText.label: 'CDS Views in Chapter 12'
define view Za4h_Cds_Seat as select from sflight {
  carrid,
  fldate,
  case
    when seatsmax = 0 then 0
    else ( cast ( ( seatsocc + seatsocc_b + seatsocc_f )
            as abap.fltp ) )
      / ( cast ( ( seatsmax + seatsmax_b + seatsmax_f )
            as abap.fltp ) )
  end as utilization
}
```
Listing 12.1 CDS View for Determining the Seat Utilization

Implementation as AMDP

Now we create an ABAP Managed Database Procedure (AMDP), to which we transfer the current client and the airline as inputs; as outputs, we expect a table with the normal and the weighted average of seat utilization for all years for which data are available in the system. In Listing 12.2, you see the SQLScript implementation for calling the AFLBFL_LIN-EARAVERAGE_PROC BFL function. We first select the average seat utilization using the CDS view grouped by year that we defined previously, and thus call the BFL function. Finally, we use the calculation engine (CE) plan operator CE_VERTICAL_UNION (see Chapter 4, Section 4.2.2) to transfer the columns of the two internal tables to the result structure. The result of the calculation is displayed in Figure 12.2.

```
CLASS zcl_a4h_chapter12_linavg DEFINITION
  PUBLIC
  CREATE PUBLIC .

  PUBLIC SECTION.
    INTERFACES: if_amdp_marker_hdb.

    TYPES: BEGIN OF ty_utilization,
        year           TYPE i,
        average        TYPE p LENGTH 4 DECIMALS 2,
        linear_average TYPE p LENGTH 4 DECIMALS 2,
      END OF  ty_utilization.
```

```
    TYPES tt_utilization TYPE TABLE OF ty_utilization.

    METHODS: linear_average_utilization
        IMPORTING
            VALUE(iv_mandt)  TYPE mandt
            VALUE(iv_carrid) TYPE s_carrid
        EXPORTING
            VALUE(et_utilization) TYPE tt_utilization.

  PROTECTED SECTION.
  PRIVATE SECTION.
ENDCLASS.

CLASS zcl_a4h_chapter12_linavg IMPLEMENTATION.

  METHOD linear_average_utilization BY DATABASE
  PROCEDURE FOR HDB LANGUAGE SQLSCRIPT OPTIONS READ-ONLY
  USING ZA4H_SEAT_UTIL.

    lt_data = select 100 * to_double(avg(utilization))
        as "VALUE", year(fldate) as "YEAR"
          from ZA4H_SEAT_UTIL
          where mandt = :iv_mandt and carrid = :iv_carrid
          group by year(fldate);

    call _SYS_AFL.AFLBFL_LINEARAVERAGE_PROC(:lt_data,:lt_avg );

    et_utilization = CE_VERTICAL_UNION(
     :lt_data, [ "YEAR", "VALUE" as "AVERAGE"],
     :lt_avg, [ "AVERAGED_RESULT" as "LINEAR_AVERAGE"]);

  ENDMETHOD.
ENDCLASS.
```

Listing 12.2 ABAP Managed Database Procedure with Access to the BFL Function

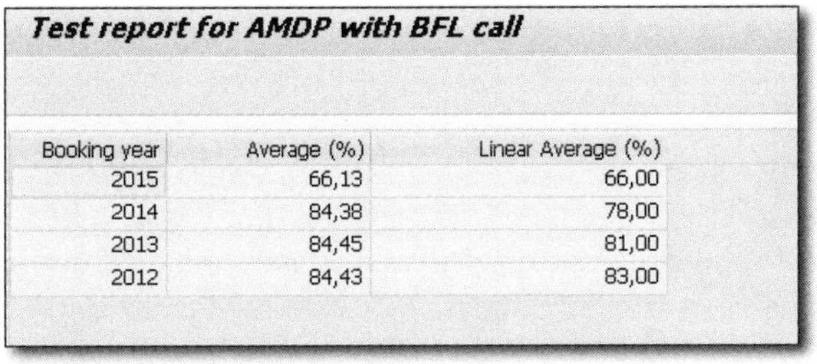

Test report for AMDP with BFL call

Booking year	Average (%)	Linear Average (%)
2015	66,13	66,00
2014	84,38	78,00
2013	84,45	81,00
2012	84,43	83,00

Figure 12.2 Result of the Database Procedure in the ALV Table

509

12.3 Predictive Analysis Library

Examples of functions

In comparison to the BFL, the Predictive Analysis Library (PAL) provides a series of generic, statistical algorithms that can be used on any data models. Table 12.4 contains some examples of algorithms you can implement in PAL.

Function	Description	Sample scenario
Anomaly detection	Determination of outliers	Detecting unusual system behavior: long response times despite normal system load
A priori	Detection of correlations for deriving rules	Analysis of purchasing behavior: "Customers who have purchased products A and B often purchase product C also"
K-means	Classification of data into groups	Segmentation of a customer base into target groups for promotions

Table 12.4 Some Functions of the Predictive Analysis Library

Predictive Model Markup Language

Not all PAL functions are provided for direct use. For example, some of the more complex PAL functions provide as a return value a description in the *Predictive Model Markup Language* (PMML) format, a standardized XML format for statistical models. Such functions are aimed at exchange options with other products, such as SAP Predictive Analytics, which was described initially.

[»] **Background: Training and Execution of Statistical Models**

In real life, there are only a few cases where you can apply standard algorithms to an existing dataset for gaining new information. Usually, you first have to prepare the data elaborately and determine the right input and output variables in modeling so that these models can then be *trained* using datasets and the resulting algorithm can be run (*scoring*). To keep the examples comprehensible, this chapter is restricted to the technical call of PAL functions.

In this section, we'll demonstrate a PAL function that you can use to segment general datasets: the *K-means function*. Here, a dataset is divided into a specified number (K) of groups (or *clusters*). We won't discuss the underlying mathematical algorithm in detail at this point. However, the basic idea is based on assigning an initial selection of centers of data records to the cluster whose center is closest. This enables you to identify patterns and classify datasets (e.g., customers, products, and so on). Figure 12.3 visualizes sample values and displays the corresponding cluster.

Example: clustering via K-means

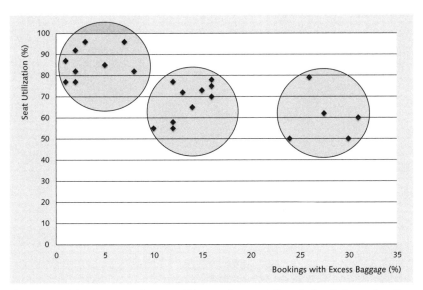

Figure 12.3 Schematic Visualization of Dataset Segmentation via the K-Means Function

As sample values, you can imagine that each point represents a flight connection, and the values on the axes represent the average seat utilization (Y-axis) and the percentage share of bookings with excess baggage (X-axis) in a period of time. Via the segmentation, you get a classification of flights into different categories. Flight connections with a high utilization and low excess baggage may indicate, for example, very frequent usage by business travelers (left upper cluster).

Table 12.5 shows the input and output parameters of the interface of the K-means function, where this segmentation is based on two numeric values (V000 and V001).

Interface

511

Parameter	Explanation	Column Structure	
Input: Database table	The dataset to be classified, consisting of ID and numeric values	ID	INTEGER
		V000	DOUBLE
		V001	DOUBLE
Input: Parameter table	Parameterization of segmentation by name/value pairs, for example, cluster number (GROUP_NUMBER)	NAME	NVARCHAR (50)
		INTARGS	INTEGER
		DOUBLEARGS	DOUBLE
		STRINGARGS	NVARCHAR (100)
Output: Cluster assignment	Assignment of data records to a cluster	ID	INTEGER
		CENTER_ASSIGN	INTEGER
		DISTANCE	DOUBLE
Output: Cluster data	List of centers of the groups (cluster ID and coordinates of the center)	CENTER_ID	INTEGER
		V000	DOUBLE
		V001	DOUBLE

Table 12.5 Interface of K-Means Function from PAL

12.3.1 Generating the K-Means Function via the SQL Console

As described in Section 12.1, you as an administrator must first generate this interface. In this section, we'll show you how to do this using Native SQL. Then, we'll discuss the graphical AFM so that you as the developer no longer need to use manual generation. However, we'll show the functioning because you'll get a better understanding of the procedures behind the scenes of AFM and because generation the procedures from a program is beneficial in some generic cases.

Generating the K-means function via the SQL console
To generate the K-means function with the interface from Table 12.5, execute the SQL statements from Listing 12.3 using the SQL console in SAP HANA Studio. Here, table types for the input and output parameters from Table 12.5 are first created in the _SYS_AFL schema, and then the desired interface is created using the AFL_WRAPPER_GENERATOR database procedure. After the successful execution of these SQL statements, the _SYS_AFL schema contains a procedure named PAL_KMEANS. For

more information on generating database procedures for the BFL and PAL libraries, see the reference documentation of these libraries at *http://help.sap.com/hana.*

```
SET SCHEMA _SYS_AFL;

-- Create table types for interface
CREATE TYPE PAL_KMEANS_ASSIGNED_T AS TABLE(
"ID" INT,
"CENTER_ASSIGN" INT,
"DISTANCE" DOUBLE);

CREATE TYPE PAL_KMEANS_DATA_T AS TABLE(
"ID" INT,
"V000" DOUBLE,
"V001" DOUBLE,
primary key("ID"));

CREATE TYPE PAL_KMEANS_CENTERS_T AS TABLE(
"CENTER_ID" INT,
"V000" DOUBLE,
"V001" DOUBLE);

CREATE TYPE PAL_CONTROL_T AS TABLE(
"NAME" VARCHAR (50),
"INTARGS" INTEGER,
"DOUBLEARGS" DOUBLE,
"STRINGARGS" VARCHAR (100));

-- Define interface
DROP TABLE PDATA;
CREATE COLUMN TABLE PDATA(
"ID" INT,
"TYPENAME" VARCHAR(100),
"DIRECTION" VARCHAR(100) );

INSERT INTO PDATA VALUES (1,'_SYS_AFL.PAL_KMEANS_DATA_T','in');
INSERT INTO PDATA VALUES (2,'_SYS_AFL.PAL_CONTROL_T','in');
INSERT INTO PDATA VALUES (3,'_SYS_AFL.PAL_KMEANS_ASSIGNED_T',
 'out');
INSERT INTO PDATA VALUES (4, '_SYS_AFL.PAL_KMEANS_CENTERS_T',
 'out');

-- Generate K-means function
call SYSTEM.AFL_WRAPPER_GENERATOR ('PAL_KMEANS', 'AFLPAL',
 'KMEANS', PDATA);
```

Listing 12.3 Generation of an Interface for the K-Means Function

To test the generated function via the SQL console in SAP HANA Studio, you can execute the statements in Listing 12.4.

```
; Configuration table: 4 clusters
CREATE LOCAL TEMPORARY COLUMN TABLE #PAL_CONTROL_TBL like
 PAL_CONTROL_T;
INSERT INTO #PAL_CONTROL_TBL VALUES ('GROUP_
NUMBER', 4, null, null);

; Create data table and insert sample values
CREATE COLUMN TABLE PAL_KMEANS_DATA_TBL LIKE PAL_KMEANS_DATA_T;
INSERT INTO PAL_KMEANS_DATA_TBL VALUES (0, 0.5, 0.5);
INSERT INTO PAL_KMEANS_DATA_TBL VALUES (1, 0.5, 1);
INSERT INTO PAL_KMEANS_DATA_TBL VALUES (2, 1, 0.5);
INSERT INTO PAL_KMEANS_DATA_TBL VALUES (3, 1, 1);

; Create output tables
CREATE COLUMN TABLE PAL_KMEANS_ASSIGNED_TBL LIKE PAL_KMEANS_
ASSIGNED_T;
CREATE COLUMN TABLE PAL_KMEANS_CENTERS_TBL LIKE PAL_KMEANS_
CENTERS_T;

; Call K-Means function
CALL PAL_KMEANS( PAL_KMEANS_DATA_TBL,
                #PAL_CONTROL_TBL,?,?);
```

Listing 12.4 Testing the K-Means Function via the SQL Console

The result of the calculation is shown in Figure 12.4. As expected, the four sample values were distributed to the four clusters, and the values form the center of the cluster.

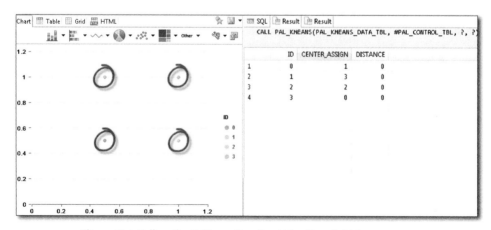

Figure 12.4 Calling the K-Means Function Using Sample Values

As you've seen, both the steps for generating and the parameterization of a PAL function are very comprehensive. By means of the AFM, you can define the generation and the call from Listing 12.3 and Listing 12.4 in graphical form to a great extent and even model complex call sequences.

12.3.2 Using the Application Function Modeler

The Application Function Modeler (AFM) is a tool that supports the generation of AFL procedures. Published with SAP HANA SPS 7, AFM initially supported the generation of individual PAL or BFL functions only. The first version was some kind of graphical interface for the `AFLLANG_WRAPPER_PROCEDURE_CREATE` procedure, which we presented in the previous section. With SPS 9, the AFM has been revised significantly and now allows for modeling of entire *flowgraphs*, that is, an entire sequence of operations. This results in a database procedure that you can reuse in your own programs or other tools. In this section, we'll present the basic usage of this tool. All detail options are described in the development guide available at *http://help.sap.com/hana*.

Overview

As an application example, we want to perform a segmentation of flight customers using the Kmeans function in a `CUSTOMER_SEGMENTATION` procedure, while considering the following input variables:

Example

▸ Total of booking prices (in EUR) in one year
▸ Total of baggage weight (in KG) in one year

We create two CDS views to determine the required values. Initially, we convert the data types, currencies, and units in the first view (see Listing 12.5).

CDS view as the data source

```
@AbapCatalog.sqlViewName: 'ZA4H_BOOK_CONV'
@EndUserText.label: Conversions and type casts'
define view Za4h_Cds_Booking
   as select from sbook {
   cast ( customid as abap.int4) as id,
   cast ( unit_conversion(
     quantity => luggweight,
     source_unit => wunit,
     target_unit => cast( 'KG' as abap.unit(3) ),
     error_handling => 'SET_TO_NULL' )
   as abap.fltp) as weight_kg,
```

```
    cast ( currency_conversion(
      amount => sbook.loccuram ,
      source_currency => loccurkey,
      target_currency => cast( 'EUR' as abap.cuky ),
      exchange_rate_date =>
 cast( '20150819' as abap.dats ),
      error_handling => 'SET_TO_NULL' )
      as abap.fltp) as price_eur
};
```

Listing 12.5 Currency and Unit Conversion

In another view, we use this as the basis to perform aggregations (see Listing 12.6).

```
@AbapCatalog.sqlViewName: 'ZA4H_KMEANS_IN'
@ClientDependent: false
@EndUserText.label: 'Input for KMeans-Clustering'
define view Za4h_Cds_Kmeans as select from za4h_book_conv {
    id,
    sum ( weight_kg ) as weight,
    sum ( price_eur ) as price
} group by id;
```

Listing 12.6 Aggregation and Type Conversion

As a result of this application, we expect a division of flight passengers into groups (with gradations and combinations), of which passengers are more likely to be business (many flights, little baggage) or private (fewer flights, more baggage). From this information and its corresponding time-based development, an airline could design a bonus system that is tailored to the needs of these groups (e.g., higher baggage allowance for frequent travelers).

Diagram presentation

Before we describe the actual usage of the AFM, we first want to explain the associate diagram presentation (see Figure 12.5). You define the specific data sources and target structures as well as the mapping to the respective columns (in the AFM, you select the arrows to perform this configuration). For a single function call, the presentation simply corresponds to the interface of the function. However, in the AFM, you can also use the output of a function directly as an input for another call.

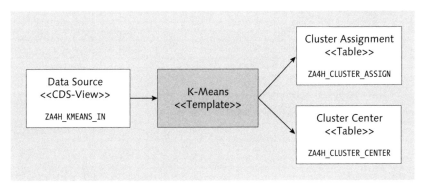

Figure 12.5 Flow Chart of the K-Means Function

To use the AFM in SAP HANA Studio as a developer, you must first create an SAP HANA Extended Application Services (SAP HANA XS) project. We discussed this procedure in Chapter 4, Section 4.3. Now create an object of the *flowgraph model* type in your package, and enter a name (see Figure 12.6).

Creating an SAP HANA XS project

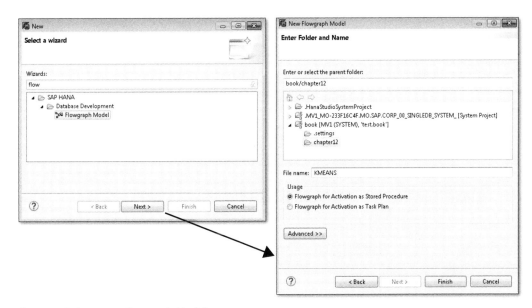

Figure 12.6 Creating a Flowgraph Model

Select FLOWGRAPH FOR ACTIVATION AS STORED PROCEDURE to generate a database procedure as the result of modeling. Alternatively, you can generate a *task plan* that can be configured for automatic execution within the scope of the package SAP HANA Enterprise Information Management.

Again, we consider the K-means function from the previous section as an example. Now we want to implement the generation via the AFM. Figure 12.7 shows a graphical model of the desired function. By means of the palette on the right-hand side ❶, you add the K-means function from the PREDICTIVE ANALYSIS LIBRARY area and a DATA SOURCE as well as two result structures (DATA SINK [TEMPLATE TABLE]) to the editor area ❷. Now select the ZA4H_KMEANS_IN CDS view as the data source, and define tables in the _SYS_BIC schema as target tables, which the AFM automatically creates when you establish a connection with the right structure of the output tables. Under PROPERTIES ❸, you can specify the parameters, for example, the number of clusters.

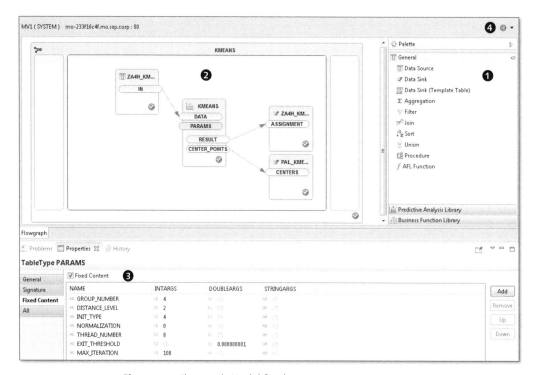

Figure 12.7 Flowgraph Model for the K-Means Function

In the settings, choose 4 as the number of desired clusters (GROUP_NUM-BER=4), and enforce a normalization of values (NORMALIZATION=1) because the values for weight and price have different value ranges, and the price would otherwise dominate the analysis too much. It's necessary here to find the right calibration. In real life, however, this involves far more than playing with the values mentioned.

Configuration

After you've concluded the definition with no errors found (indicated by green icons), you must activate the model (using the Activate SAP HANA Development Object button). The database procedure is then generated in the selected schema (e.g., _SYS_BIC). Next, you can test the procedure by selecting the Execute in SQL Editor entry from the top right selection area ❹. This opens the SQL console, and you can query the values in the target tables.

Generating and testing

> **Advantages and Disadvantages of the AFM** [«]
>
> As you've seen, the AFM provides much simpler access to using the AFL functions compared with manual generation. Because the models are defined as SAP HANA development objects, you can transport them with your application.
>
> However, you must define both the data sources and the target structures as static tables or views. Moreover, if the AFM is used, the technical _SYS_REPO user requires specific authorizations for the objects involved.
>
> There are advantages and disadvantages, but the AFM is the method of choice for most scenarios.

As in the previous section, we use an ABAP database procedure to integrate the procedure we've previously generated with ABAP (see Listing 12.7). We only want to assign the datasets to the clusters (and additionally *join* the input values). Note that we don't use the OPTIONS READ-ONLY addition for this procedure because the K-means function writes data to the output tables.

Using an AMDP

```
CLASS zcl_a4h_chapter12_kmeans DEFINITION
  PUBLIC CREATE PUBLIC.

  PUBLIC SECTION.
    INTERFACES: if_amdp_marker_hdb.
```

```
      TYPES: BEGIN OF ty_center_assign,
         id            TYPE s_customer,
         weight        TYPE s_lugweigh,
         price         TYPE s_price,
         center_assign TYPE i,
         distance      TYPE p LENGTH 6 DECIMALS 2,
       END OF  ty_center_assign.
      TYPES tt_center_assign TYPE TABLE OF ty_center_assign.

      METHODS: kmeans
        EXPORTING
          VALUE(et_center_assign) TYPE tt_center_assign.

    PROTECTED SECTION.
    PRIVATE SECTION.
  ENDCLASS.

  CLASS zcl_a4h_chapter12_kmeans IMPLEMENTATION.

    METHOD kmeans BY DATABASE PROCEDURE /FOR HDB
    LANGUAGE SQLSCRIPT USING ZA4H_KMEANS_IN.

      CALL "_SYS_BIC"."test.a4h.book.chapter12::kmeans"();

      lt_center_assign = select * from
          _sys_bic.za4h_cluster_assign;

      et_center_assign = select r.id, i.weight, i.price,
                  r.center_assign, r.energy as distance
              from :lt_center_assign as r
              inner join ZA4H_KMEANS_IN as i on r.id = i.id
              order by center_assign, distance;
    ENDMETHOD.
  ENDCLASS
```

Listing 12.7 Calling the K-Means Function from an ABAP Database Procedure

Visualization We use a sample report to save the result in an ABAP table and then use the data display in SAP HANA Studio for an initial analysis of the entries (see Figure 12.8). We added the customer type (CUSTTYPE) and the customer discount (DISCOUNT) to the result structure to filter by these values. Of course, you can also use the results in ABAP applications, for example, using Web Dynpro ABAP, SAPUI5, and so on, to implement a graphical display.

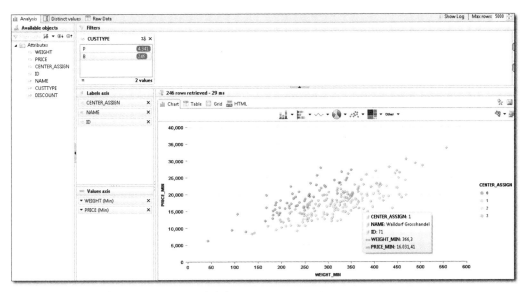

Figure 12.8 Result of the Segmentation of Flight Customers via K-Means

By means of the libraries presented in this chapter, you can access com-   Additional options
plex statistical functions to deploy individually or in combination with
an ABAP program. For more detailed analyses, SAP HANA provides
additional integration options (particularly with the open-source statistics software R).

R-Integration	[«]

In addition to PAL, SAP HANA also contains an adapter for integrating the
open-source software system R (*www.r-project.org*). You have an additional
range of statistical operations available via this adapter. We won't discuss R
integration in detail within this book. However, it's used in a similar manner
to how the AFL functions are used via database procedures in SAP HANA.
AFM also permits the integration of nodes that are implemented via an R
script.

You must note, however, that the R server isn't part of SAP HANA for licensing reasons, and it must be installed separately on a dedicated server. More
information is available in the SAP HANA R Integration Guide at *http://
help.sap.com/hana*.

Business data with geographical relevance play a significant role in many scenarios, particularly in logistics. SAP HANA provides native support for saving and calculating geoinformation that you can use for innovative ABAP applications.

13   Processing Geoinformation

In real life, large parts of business data refer to a geographical location such as fixed locations of factories or subsidiaries. The geographical data might also have a time reference, for example, the current position of a parcel delivery to the end customer. Today, such information is often available in real time and can be used for applications and analyses thanks to the proliferation of GPS and the increasing cross-linking of systems via the Internet. This results in new options for planning, monitoring, and controlling logistic processes.

Motivation

A class of software systems—referred to as *geoinformation systems (GIS)*—has emerged for handling spatial information. They usually support the definition, calculation, and visualization of geographical data and are used in logistics as well as in the insurance industry, traffic control, urban planning, and environmental research.

Geoinformation systems

Many geographical calculations require rather complex algorithms that must be able to handle various coordinate systems and units of measures around the globe. In this chapter, we only impart the basic principles and restrict the corresponding mathematics to a minimum.

Mathematical background

Section 13.1 provides a short overview of the GIS capabilities. Section 13.2 then describes the capabilities of the *Geo-Spatial Engine* in SAP HANA. Here, we'll take a detour and show how you can import external maps to SAP HANA because this is a prerequisite for many application scenarios. Finally, Section 13.3 provides an example of how you can use SAP HANA to calculate geoinformation in ABAP applications.

Structure of the chapter

Example The examples in this chapter are based on the data model SFLIGHT. Table SGEOCITY contains longitude and latitude of cities that we'll use for calculating distances in our scenario.

13.1 Basic Principles of Geoinformation Systems

Data models Geoinformation systems (GIS) initially permit the modeling of spatial data. A GIS thus has an "understanding" of basic geographical formations such as points, routes, areas, and so on, which are usually available as native data types. You can use them within the scope of a data model.

Algorithms Based on these data types, a GIS enables you to answer geographically related questions. These include the following operations, for example:

▸ **Is a geographical location included in an outline?**
Application example: In which state is a vehicle currently located based on its GPS coordinates?

▸ **Which entry from a list of locations has the shortest distance to a given position?**
Application example: calculation of the nearest gas station (linear distance).

▸ **Is a route included in an area?**
Application example: determination of highway miles, grouped by state.

▸ **What is the surface area of an object?**
Application example: determination of a plot area for a factory location.

Coordinate systems and unit of measures The presentation in a coordinate system plays a critical role for calculations using geographical information. This coordinate system is also referred to as a *spatial reference system* (SRS) and includes the following information:

▸ **Identifier**
Each SRS has a unique identification in the form of a figure (*spatial reference identifier*, SRID). There are several standardized SRSs, some of which will be presented in this section.

▶ **Coordinates**

Geographical information can be indicated in various units. Usually, a geographical location on earth is specified using longitude and latitude (and possibly height information). Alternatively, other coordinate systems are possible, for example, for the floor area of a warehouse, with coordinates given in meters and with an artificial origin. An SRS must exactly define the underlying coordinate system.

▶ **Algorithms and units of measure**

For operations on geographical coordinates, it's essential to determine whether the calculations take place at a two-dimensional level or in spatial coordinates (see Figure 13.1). As you can clearly see, distortion causes considerable differences with regard to the determination of distances or areas, depending on the presentation in which the calculation takes place. An SRS defines in detail whether a flat or spatial presentation is to be used and in which units the calculations' results are to be provided (e.g., meters for distances).

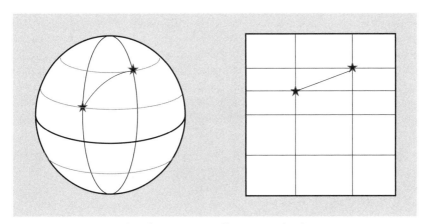

Figure 13.1 Distance and Surface Areas in Different Spatial Reference Systems

The following information box lists some coordinate systems supported in SAP HANA. The next section describes how you use them to define tables.

Coordinate systems in SAP HANA

[+]   **Spatial Reference Systems Supported in SAP HANA**

By default, SAP HANA supports several SRSs, which you can query in the ST_ SPATIAL_REFERENCE_SYSTEMS system view. The most critical systems are the following:

▸ **Standard (SRID 0)**
A flat (Cartesian) coordinate system without geographical reference that uses meters as the unit of measure.

▸ **WGS84 (SRID 4326)**
A spatial presentation of the earth, which uses longitude (value range between –180 and 180) and latitude (value range between –90 and 90). WGS84 is the global standard that is also used within the scope of GPS. In this presentation, Berlin has the approximate coordinates 13.33, 52.51.

▸ **WGS84 (Planar) (SRID 1000004326)**
Similar to WGS84, just with projection on a flat plain. The coordinates are indicated in longitude and latitude. In this SRS, however, the calculation of distances and areas is very imprecise due to projection and shouldn't be used (refer to Figure 13.1). This system can be used to check whether a location is included in an area.

From the three SRSs mentioned, WGS84 (SRID 4326) has the most accurate mapping and should be used as the standard for storing real geographical information. You can also deploy other systems for special scenarios or for accelerating some calculations. Moreover, the Geo-Spatial Engine in SAP HANA SPS 9 still has some restrictions with regard to the calculation of spatial presentations (e.g., for surface areas). The usage of a projected presentation may be necessary here.

13.2   Geodata Types and Geo-Spatial Functions in SAP HANA

The previous section provided a brief general overview of GISs. Let's now discuss the support in SAP HANA. We'll first present the relevant data types and then use some examples to discuss the SQL functions for geographical calculations.

Geo-Spatial Engine   The Geo-Spatial Engine included in SAP HANA is a special engine for operations using geoinformation, and it supports both flat and spatial presentations. The individual geographical formations are represented as data types which you can use via special SAP HANA SQL statements.

Geo-Spatial Support in Other Databases and Underlying SQL Standards [«]

In addition to SAP HANA, other relational database systems also provide support for geoinformation. Most implementations, including SAP HANA, use the related standards of the *Open Geospatial Consortium* (OGC) and the *International Organization for Standardization* (ISO) for the SQL interfaces and the exchange formats. If you're interested in the particular specifications of the formats and types, refer to ISO/IEC 19125 and 13249.

13.2.1 Data Types

The abstract ST_Geometry data type forms the basis for processing geoinformation in SAP HANA. Seven data types are derived from this data type that comprise different geometrical information (see Figure 13.2). The most important types include ST_Point (a geographical point on the map), ST_LineString (a route, e.g., a highway or a river, that is defined by several points), and ST_Polygon (an outline, e.g., of a state). The other types are joins of points, routes, and outlines. They are necessary because geographical formations are often incoherent. For example, if you consider the outlines of states, you must compose the outline of various partial polygons (ST_MultiPolygon) for associated islands.

Overview

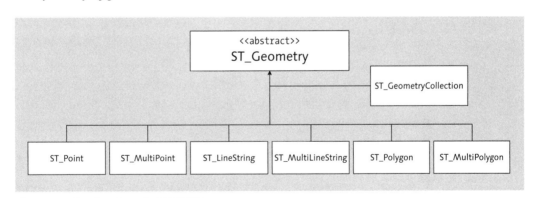

Figure 13.2 Geodata Types in SAP HANA

By means of these data types, you can create, for example, tables that map a highway system. In one table, you can store the routing (each table line contains the name of a highway and the route in the form of

Example

an object of the type ST_MultiLineString) and important points such as junctions or exits (ST_Point) in another table.

Because objects such as routes or areas consist of many points in real life, SAP HANA and other GISs efficiently store and index objects.

13.2.2 Creating Tables and Reading Data

In this section, we'll show you how to create database tables in SAP HANA that use the data types presented in the previous section. In this context, we use native SAP HANA statements for creating the tables. We'll explain the options for using the Geo-Spatial Engine from ABAP later in this chapter.

Create a table — In the following example, we use SQL to create two tables in a separate test schema using different geodata types. In SAP HANA Studio, open an SQL console, and run the data definition language (DDL) statement from Listing 13.1.

```
create column table CITY (
  name NVARCHAR(30),
  location   ST_Point(4326),
  location_f ST_Point(1000004326)
);
```
Listing 13.1 Table with Geographical Information

The 4326 and 1000004326 parameters specify the coordinate systems (see the information box in Section 13.1). We save a spatial and a flat presentation separately; in both cases, the coordinates are specified in longitude and latitude.

Insert values — Internally, geodata types use a binary presentation for efficient saving. To add values to a table, you usually use *constructors* (similar to object-oriented programming). To create, for example, an entry in the previously created table, use the new ST_POINT() function, as shown in Listing 13.2.

```
insert into CITY values ( 'Frankfurt' ,
  new ST_POINT( 8.61, 50.07 ) ,
  new ST_POINT( 8.61, 50.07 ));
```

```
insert into CITY values ( 'Hamburg' ,
  new ST_POINT( 10.03, 53.56 ) ,
  new ST_POINT( 10.03, 53.56 ));
insert into CITY values ( 'Berlin' ,
  new ST_POINT( 13.33, 52.51 ) ,
  new ST_POINT(13.33, 52.51));
```

Listing 13.2 Adding Geographical Places to the Table

In the same way, there are functions for creating the other data types illustrated in Figure 13.2. To create a route, for example, you must use the `new ST_LineString()`function and transfer the points as parameters.

To select entries from the table, you use special functions in `SELECT` statements. You can control the presentation for these functions. For a point, for example, you can query the individual coordinates (`ST_X()` and `ST_Y()`) or present the entire object in a special output format (see Figure 13.3). The coordinate system used can be queried using `ST_SRID()`.

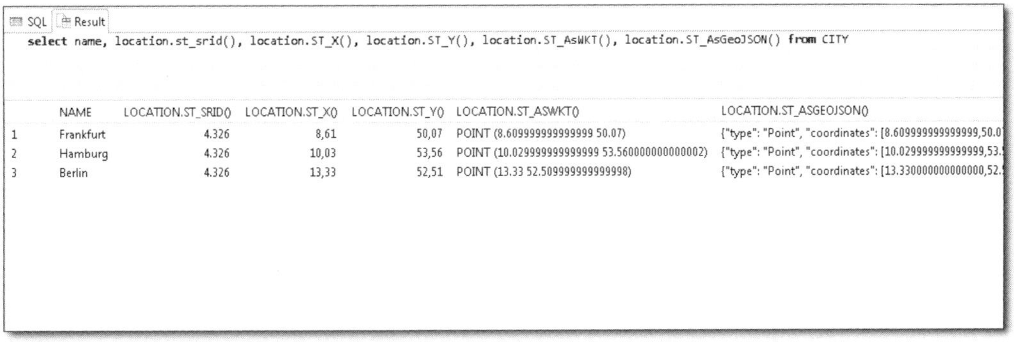
SQL | Result

```
select name, location.st_srid(), location.ST_X(), location.ST_Y(), location.ST_AsWKT(), location.ST_AsGeoJSON() from CITY
```

	NAME	LOCATION.ST_SRID()	LOCATION.ST_X()	LOCATION.ST_Y()	LOCATION.ST_ASWKT()	LOCATION.ST_ASGEOJSON()
1	Frankfurt	4.326	8,61	50,07	POINT (8.609999999999999 50.07)	{"type": "Point", "coordinates": [8.609999999999999,50.0
2	Hamburg	4.326	10,03	53,56	POINT (10.029999999999999 53.560000000000002)	{"type": "Point", "coordinates": [10.029999999999999,53.
3	Berlin	4.326	13,33	52,51	POINT (13.33 52.509999999999998)	{"type": "Point", "coordinates": [13.330000000000000,52.

Figure 13.3 Selection of Geodata in Various Output Formats

Presentation formats

Various standard formats used to facilitate the exchange of information have established themselves for the presentation of geoinformation. SAP HANA supports the Well-Known Binary and Well-Known Text (WKB/WKT) formats, *GeoJSON*, as well as ESRI Shapefiles. Figure 13.3 shows an example of the WKT and GeoJSON presentation. We'll use ESRI shapefiles as the import format in Section 13.2.4.

13.2.3   Operations on Geographical Structures

The previous example familiarized you with the basic principles. We'll now show you some operations that you can run on geographical data. We'll restrict our descriptions to some common functions and refer you to the reference documentation at *http://help.sap.com/hana* (SAP HANA Spatial Reference) to learn about the full functional scope.

Conversions   Some useful conversion functions allow you to convert data from tables that don't use the geodata types of SAP HANA. This is particularly important for later usage in ABAP because the ABAP Data Dictionary (DDIC) can't support the geodata types of SAP HANA as they aren't available for all databases. The following example shows the usage based on ABAP table SGEOCITY, whose flight data model contains the locations of cities with airports.

```
select city, new ST_Point(longitude, latitude)
as location from SGEOCITY;
```

You can also run conversions for other geodata types. Of course, you can also transform geodata types back to normal coordinates.

ST_Distance and
ST_WithinDistance   In many cases, you want to determine the geographical distance between two objects. For this purpose, you use the ST_Distance function, which you can apply to points, routes, and areas, whereas the distance always refers to the minimum value. The example of Listing 13.3 determines the distances between all places from the table in Listing 13.1 both in spatial and projected presentation. Figure 13.4 shows the calculation's result.

```
select c1.name as "City 1", c2.name as "City 2",
  c1.location.st_distance(c2.location, 'kilometer')
          as "Distance(km), round earth",
  c1.location_f.st_distance(c2.location_f, 'kilometer')
          as "Distance (km), flat earth"
from CITY as c1, CITY as c2
  where c1.name <= c2.name order by c1.name
```
Listing 13.3 Determining the Distance between Two Points

As you can see, there are major differences between determining the distances in the various reference systems.

```
SQL  Result
  select c1.name as "City 1", c2.name as "City 2",
        c1.location.st_distance(c2.location, 'kilometer')        as "Distance (km), round earth",
        c1.location_flat.st_distance(c2.location_flat, 'kilometer') as "Distance (km), flat earth"
        from CITY as c1, CITY as c2 where c1.name <= c2.name order by c1.name
```

	City 1	City 2	Distance (km), round earth	Distance (km), flat earth
1	Berlin	Frankfurt	426,5841649609653	590,4227121432871
2	Berlin	Hamburg	250,28625450081648	384,81066169627013
3	Berlin	Berlin	0	0
4	Frankfurt	Frankfurt	0	0
5	Frankfurt	Hamburg	400,4454223436375	418,6806367962063
6	Hamburg	Hamburg	0	0

Figure 13.4 Distances between All Cities of Table CITY

If you only want to check whether the distance between two objects doesn't exceed a certain threshold value, you can also use the ST_WithinDistance function .

As you've seen, it's very easy to calculate with individual points. The calculation is somewhat more complex for routes and areas because the individual objects consist of a large number of points (e.g., state borders). In the following, we discuss some simple examples that each consist of few objects only.

ST_Length and ST_Area

By means of the ST_Length() function, you can determine the length of a route (ST_LineString or ST_MultiLineString). In the same way, you can calculate the content of areas using the ST_Area() function. The example in Figure 13.5 shows the calculation of the circumference and the area of a triangle that stretches among the cities of Frankfurt, Hamburg, and Berlin.

```
SQL  Result
  SELECT new ST_LineString('LineString (8.61 50.07, 10.03 53.56, 13.33 52.51, 8.61 50.07)' , 4326).ST_Length('kilometer')
        as "Circumference in km (Frankfurt, Hamburg, Berlin, Frankfurt)",
        new ST_Polygon(   'Polygon(   (8.61 50.07, 10.03 53.56, 13.33 52.51, 8.61 50.07))', 1000004326).ST_Area('kilometer')
        as "Area in qkm (Frankfurt, Hamburg, Berlin, Frankfurt)"
  FROM dummy
```

Circumference in km (Frankfurt, Hamburg, Berlin, Frankfurt)	Area in qkm (Frankfurt, Hamburg, Berlin, Frankfurt)
1	1.077,3158418054197	80.309,14419705012

Figure 13.5 Determining the Circumference and Area

For the area, we must use the projection on a plain (SRID 1000004326) because the ST_Area() method in SAP HANA SPS 9 isn't available for SRSs yet.

ST_Contains

If you want to find out whether an object is included in another object, you can use the ST_Contains() function. So if you want to check whether a location from the table in Listing 13.1 is contained in the geographical object from the previous example, proceed as shown in Listing 13.4.

```
SELECT *, new ST_Polygon( 'Polygon(
  (8.57 50.02,
   10.03 53.56,
   13.33 52.51,
   8.57 50.02))', 1000004326)
.ST_Contains(location)
FROM city;
```

Listing 13.4 Using the ST_Contains() Function for Checking whether a City Is Contained in an Area

Additional options

Several useful functions are available for handling geographical data, whereas we've only scratched the surface so far. Besides the additional geofunctions, you can also use combinations with normal SQL operations, such as aggregations or joins, to have many more options at hand for answering complex questions. For real-life usage, however, you usually require *geographical master data*, in particular, outlines of countries, states, and so on. The next section provides an example of how you can import such data to SAP HANA and use the data in queries.

13.2.4 Integration of External Maps

External maps

In addition to your own business data with geographical references, you also require information on geographical or political structures as well as transport infrastructure as a reference for many scenarios. This includes, for example, the outlines of countries and regions, coordinates of cities, and road and rail networks. Additionally, industry-specific data records can be relevant, for examples, routes of container ships, no-fly zones, and so on.

Because the recording of such information involves some time and effort, most of these data records are commercial and must be licensed.

Various established providers partner with SAP to offer maps that are certified for SAP HANA. If you have an SAP HANA license that includes the geo-spatial option (e.g., the Platform or Enterprise license), you can download various map packs for almost any region around the globe from the SAP Service Marketplace. In SAP HANA Studio, you can import these files to SAP HANA using special SQL statements. Detailed information about the installation is available in the SAP HANA Spatial Reference (and in SAP Note 1928222).

The example of Listing 13.5 shows the import of a data package for Germany (packages for other countries can be imported analogously). For this purpose, you must copy the underlying files to the file system of the SAP HANA server. As you can see, you can transfer the reference system as a parameter in the form of its `SRID` during import.

```
IMPORT "SAP_SPATIAL_POSTAL"."DEU_GEN" AS SHAPEFILE FROM
'/usr/sap/MV1/HDB00/work/DEU_2013Q3_PCB_PLY_GEN' WITH SRID
1000004326;
```

Listing 13.5 Importing Geographical Data of Germany

The structure of the table generated and some data records are illustrated in Figure 13.6. The SHAPE column contains the respective geographical structure as `ST_MultiPolygon`.

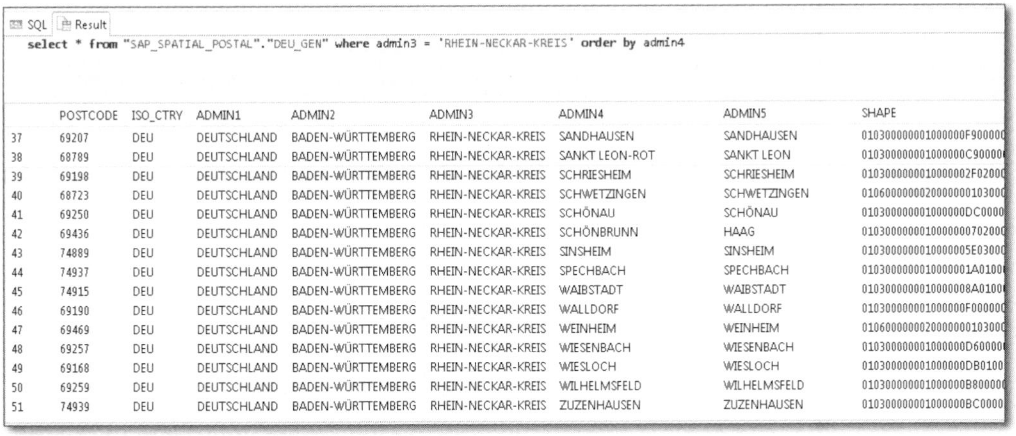
SQL | Result

```
select * from "SAP_SPATIAL_POSTAL"."DEU_GEN" where admin3 = 'RHEIN-NECKAR-KREIS' order by admin4
```

	POSTCODE	ISO_CTRY	ADMIN1	ADMIN2	ADMIN3	ADMIN4	ADMIN5	SHAPE
37	69207	DEU	DEUTSCHLAND	BADEN-WÜRTTEMBERG	RHEIN-NECKAR-KREIS	SANDHAUSEN	SANDHAUSEN	01030000000100000F900000
38	68789	DEU	DEUTSCHLAND	BADEN-WÜRTTEMBERG	RHEIN-NECKAR-KREIS	SANKT LEON-ROT	SANKT LEON	010300000001000000C90000
39	69198	DEU	DEUTSCHLAND	BADEN-WÜRTTEMBERG	RHEIN-NECKAR-KREIS	SCHRIESHEIM	SCHRIESHEIM	0103000000010000002F0200
40	68723	DEU	DEUTSCHLAND	BADEN-WÜRTTEMBERG	RHEIN-NECKAR-KREIS	SCHWETZINGEN	SCHWETZINGEN	010600000002000000010300
41	69250	DEU	DEUTSCHLAND	BADEN-WÜRTTEMBERG	RHEIN-NECKAR-KREIS	SCHÖNAU	SCHÖNAU	010300000001000000DC0000
42	69436	DEU	DEUTSCHLAND	BADEN-WÜRTTEMBERG	RHEIN-NECKAR-KREIS	SCHÖNBRUNN	HAAG	010300000001000000702000
43	74889	DEU	DEUTSCHLAND	BADEN-WÜRTTEMBERG	RHEIN-NECKAR-KREIS	SINSHEIM	SINSHEIM	0103000000010000005E0300
44	74937	DEU	DEUTSCHLAND	BADEN-WÜRTTEMBERG	RHEIN-NECKAR-KREIS	SPECHBACH	SPECHBACH	0103000000010000001A0100
45	74915	DEU	DEUTSCHLAND	BADEN-WÜRTTEMBERG	RHEIN-NECKAR-KREIS	WAIBSTADT	WAIBSTADT	0103000000010000008A0100
46	69190	DEU	DEUTSCHLAND	BADEN-WÜRTTEMBERG	RHEIN-NECKAR-KREIS	WALLDORF	WALLDORF	010300000001000000F00000
47	69469	DEU	DEUTSCHLAND	BADEN-WÜRTTEMBERG	RHEIN-NECKAR-KREIS	WEINHEIM	WEINHEIM	010600000002000000010300
48	69257	DEU	DEUTSCHLAND	BADEN-WÜRTTEMBERG	RHEIN-NECKAR-KREIS	WIESENBACH	WIESENBACH	010300000001000000D60000
49	69168	DEU	DEUTSCHLAND	BADEN-WÜRTTEMBERG	RHEIN-NECKAR-KREIS	WIESLOCH	WIESLOCH	010300000001000000DB0100
50	69259	DEU	DEUTSCHLAND	BADEN-WÜRTTEMBERG	RHEIN-NECKAR-KREIS	WILHELMSFELD	WILHELMSFELD	010300000001000000B80000
51	74939	DEU	DEUTSCHLAND	BADEN-WÜRTTEMBERG	RHEIN-NECKAR-KREIS	ZUZENHAUSEN	ZUZENHAUSEN	010300000001000000BC0000

Figure 13.6 Data Structure of the Imported Maps

Example

After these data are available, you can run meaningful requests with geographical reference. For example, if you want to determine the number of locations from table CITY in Listing 13.1 grouped by state, you can use joins and aggregations (see Listing 13.6). Note that we use the ST_CONTAINS()function as a join condition in this case.

```
select r.admin2 as "state", count(*) from CITY as c
inner join "SAP_SPATIAL_POSTAL"."DEU_GEN" as r on r.shape.
st_contains(c.location_f) = 1 group by r.admin2
```
Listing 13.6 Determining the Number of Locations, Grouped by State

[»] **Geo-Coding and Geospatial Indexes**

Additionally, you have another option to enrich existing business data with geographical coordinates. If you already have address information (country, city, ZIP code, street, house number) in your system, you can add the associated geoinformation using Internet services. Here, SAP HANA offers an option to add this information to tables in virtual format as a shadow column, which is created via a special index. This procedure is similar to the full-text indexes presented in Chapter 10. Refer to the SAP HANA spatial documentation for more details.

13.3 Integrating Geoinformation with ABAP Applications

This last section now presents an example to show a possible application of geoinformation in an ABAP program. As mentioned initially, we use the contents of tables SGEOCITY and SPFLI for this purpose.

Sample scenario

In the following, we implement two simple scenarios in which we enrich the data from the previously mentioned tables with further geographical information. Based on the imported map information, we first want to determine the state and the ZIP code for each city from table SGEOCITY using the longitudes and latitudes that are available in the table. In the second sample program, we calculate the geographical distance between the start point and end point of all flights from table SPFLI and compare the value with the flight route contained (DISTANCE column).

To implement the two functions, we use ABAP Managed Database Pro-   Design
cedures (AMDP), respectively. Because we can't use the geodata types in
the ABAP tables directly, we perform conversions at runtime. To determine the state and the ZIP code, we use the same approach as in Listing
13.6. To calculate the distances, we don't need any external data but
only the ST_Distance() function, which we presented in Section 13.2.3.

To implement the procedures, we create an ABAP class zcl_a4h_chap-   Class definition
ter13_geoamdp and define the required types and methods. For using
the database procedures, we must utilize the if_amdp_marker_hdb
marker interface (see Chapter 6). Listing 13.7 shows the full definition
of the class.

```
CLASS zcl_a4h_chapter13_geoamdp DEFINITION
  PUBLIC FINAL CREATE PUBLIC .

  PUBLIC SECTION.
    INTERFACES if_amdp_marker_hdb .

    TYPES:
      BEGIN OF ty_city_info,
        city     TYPE sgeocity-city,
        state    TYPE scustom-region,
        postcode TYPE scustom-postcode,
      END OF ty_city_info,
      tt_city_info TYPE STANDARD TABLE OF ty_city_info.

    TYPES: BEGIN OF ty_distance,
             carrid       TYPE spfli-carrid,
             connid       TYPE spfli-connid,
             cityfrom     TYPE spfli-cityfrom,
             cityto       TYPE spfli-cityto,
             flt_distance TYPE spfli-distance,
             geo_distance TYPE spfli-distance,
           END OF ty_distance,
         tt_distance TYPE STANDARD TABLE OF ty_distance.

    METHODS get_city_info
      IMPORTING
        VALUE(iv_mandt)   TYPE mandt
        VALUE(iv_country) TYPE sgeocity-country
      EXPORTING
        VALUE(et_result) TYPE tt_city_info
      RAISING
        cx_amdp_error .

    METHODS get_distance_info
```

```
      IMPORTING
        VALUE(iv_mandt)  TYPE mandt
      EXPORTING
        VALUE(et_result) TYPE tt_distance
      RAISING
        cx_amdp_error .

    PROTECTED SECTION.
    PRIVATE SECTION.
  ENDCLASS.
```

Listing 13.7 Definition of Types and Methods

Implementation
To implement the procedures, you must enter the additions, which we presented in Chapter 6 (BY DATABASE PROCEDURE FOR HDB LANGUAGE SQLSCRIPT) and declare the used ABAP tables, respectively. There's a little pitfall when you calculate the longitude information from table SGEOCITY: You must multiply the longitude information from table SGEOCITY with -1 because otherwise the coordinate systems don't match.

The full implementation is shown in Listing 13.8. As you can see, the two procedures each consist of one single SQL statement.

```
CLASS zcl_a4h_chapter13_geoamdp IMPLEMENTATION.
  METHOD get_city_info BY DATABASE PROCEDURE FOR HDB
                          LANGUAGE SQLSCRIPT
                          USING sgeocity.

  et_result = select c.city, r.admin2 as state,
    r.postcode as postcode from sgeocity as c
    inner join "SAP_SPATIAL_POSTAL"."DEU_GEN" as r
    on r.shape.st_contains( new st_point(
       'POINT(' || -c.LONGITUDE || ' ' || c.LATITUDE ||')'
       , 1000004326) ) = 1
  where c.mandt = :iv_mandt
    and c.country = :iv_country;

  ENDMETHOD.

  METHOD get_distance_info BY DATABASE PROCEDURE FOR HDB
                          LANGUAGE SQLSCRIPT
                          USING spfli sgeocity.

    et_result = select carrid, connid, cityfrom, cityto,
                       distance as flt_distance,
    new st_point(
```

536

```
  'POINT(' || -c1.LONGITUDE || ' ' || c1.LATITUDE ||')'
        ,4326).st_distance(
    new st_point(
  'POINT(' || -c2.LONGITUDE || ' ' || c2.LATITUDE ||')'
        ,4326) ) / 1000 as geo_distance4326
        from spfli as s
        inner join sgeocity as c1 on s.mandt = c1.mandt
              and s.countryfr = c1.country
              and s.cityfrom = c1.city
        inner join sgeocity as c2 on s.mandt = c2.mandt
              and s.countryto = c2.country
              and s.cityto = c2.city
        where s.mandt = :iv_mandt;
  ENDMETHOD.
ENDCLASS.
```
Listing 13.8 Implementation of Database Procedures

To display the results, we use a simple ABAP report that calls the proce-   Call
dure and outputs it in an SAP List Viewer (ALV) list (see Listing 13.9 for
calculating the distance). Here, we use the new language elements of
ABAP 7.4 again.

```
REPORT zr_a4h_chapter13_distance.

TRY.
    NEW zcl_a4h_chapter13_geoamdp( )->get_distance_info(
        EXPORTING iv_mandt = sy-mandt
        IMPORTING et_result = DATA(lt_distance)
    ).
  CATCH cx_amdp_error INTO DATA(lo_exc).
    WRITE: | { lo_exc->get_text( ) } |.
ENDTRY.

" Display in ALV table
IF ( lt_distance IS NOT INITIAL ).
  cl_salv_table=>factory(
      IMPORTING r_salv_table = DATA(lo_alv)
      CHANGING t_table  = lt_distance
  ).
  lo_alv->display( ).
ENDIF.
```
Listing 13.9 Display of Results in an ALV List

Figure 13.7 and Figure 13.8 show the results of the calculations, based
on the SFLIGHT sample data.

Data enrichment via geo-coding for cities (SGEOCITY)

City	Federal State	ZIP Code
BERLIN	BERLIN	10587
HAMBURG	HAMBURG	22089
FRANKFURT	HESSEN	64546
WALLDORF	BADEN-WÜRTTEMBERG	69254
MUNICH	BAYERN	80331

Figure 13.7 Advanced City Information

As you can see, the state and ZIP code were determined for all cities based on the GPS coordinates. Figure 13.8 shows that some distances in table SPFLI vary considerably from the real geographical distances, which indicates errors in the flight schedule data.

Comparisson of distance values (data model vs. geographic)

Airline	Flight Number	Depart. city	Arrival city	Flight distance (KM)	Geo-Distance (KM)
LH	2407	BERLIN	FRANKFURT	555,0000	433,4749
UA	3517	FRANKFURT	NEW YORK	6.162,0000	6.216,8374
QF	0006	FRANKFURT	SINGAPORE	10.000,0000	10.264,2023
JL	0408	FRANKFURT	TOKYO	9.100,0000	9.370,6488
LH	0402	FRANKFURT	NEW YORK	6.162,0000	6.216,8374
LH	0400	FRANKFURT	NEW YORK	6.162,0000	6.216,8374
LH	2402	FRANKFURT	BERLIN	555,0000	433,4749
UA	0941	FRANKFURT	SAN FRANCISCO	5.685,0000	9.160,8489
UA	3516	NEW YORK	FRANKFURT	6.162,0000	6.216,8374
AA	0017	NEW YORK	SAN FRANCISCO	2.572,0000	4.140,0174
LH	0401	NEW YORK	FRANKFURT	6.162,0000	6.216,8374
DL	0106	NEW YORK	FRANKFURT	3.851,0000	6.216,8374
DL	1699	NEW YORK	SAN FRANCISCO	2.572,0000	4.140,0174
AZ	0790	ROME	OSAKA	6.030,0000	9.718,1234
AZ	0788	ROME	TOKYO	6.130,0000	9.875,5238
AZ	0555	ROME	FRANKFURT	845,0000	958,3922
AA	0064	SAN FRANCISCO	NEW YORK	2.572,0000	4.140,0174
DL	1984	SAN FRANCISCO	NEW YORK	2.572,0000	4.140,0174
UA	3504	SAN FRANCISCO	FRANKFURT	5.685,0000	9.160,8489
SQ	0015	SAN FRANCISCO	SINGAPORE	8.452,0000	13.598,2741
SQ	0002	SINGAPORE	SAN FRANCISCO	8.452,0000	13.598,2741

Figure 13.8 Flight Rout and Geographical Distance

If you use the Geo-Spatial Engine in SAP HANA, you can integrate a GIS in ABAP with little effort. This enables many new application cases that go beyond pure visualization of geoinformation.

Best practices play an important role, especially when using new technologies. Even if something is technically possible, it may not be practical or useful in each scenario. You should review old rules and explore new design patterns.

14   Practical Tips

We've presented a variety of options within this book for calling functions in SAP HANA from ABAP systems. In addition to normal database access, we've discussed modeling views, SQLScript-based views, and database procedures, as well as some advanced technologies such as text analysis, function libraries, and decision tables. Moreover, you've learned a lot about the new options of database programming using ABAP 7.4 (Core Data Services [CDS] views and ABAP database procedures).

In this chapter, we'll present some practical tips on topics that are particularly important when developing ABAP applications on SAP HANA. These are subdivided into the following topic areas:

Structure

▶ **General recommendations**
We'll first provide you with some general recommendations for developing ABAP on SAP HANA. We primarily discuss details that you should consider for the migration and optimization of ABAP programs.

▶ **Conventions**
We present some conventions that, from our perspective, are useful but optional. These include naming conventions, encapsulating and packaging conventions, distributed development guidelines, and similar topics.

▶ **Quality aspects**
For implementations in the database, nonfunctional criteria such as robustness, testability, and security should play an important role in

addition to performance. We introduce some measures that will help ensure high quality in development.

▶ **Performance guidelines**
The execution speed of programs naturally plays a crucial role in the context of SAP HANA. Many usage scenarios involve access to large datasets in real time. A solid understanding of the guidelines and techniques for achieving optimal performance is essential here. We provide an overview of existing and new recommendations, and we particularly discuss changes in comparison to traditional databases.

We'll also enhance programming recommendations via positive and negative examples.

14.1   General Recommendations

In this first section, we've compiled some general recommendations that you should follow for migration and development on SAP HANA. This involves functional aspects in particular. We'll return to nonfunctional topics such as conventions, quality aspects, and performance in subsequent sections.

We'll start with recommendations for the use of column stores or row stores in SAP HANA. We'll then discuss possible design patterns for the encapsulation of SAP HANA-specific implementations and provide a checklist for relocating calculations to SAP HANA.

14.1.1   Recommendations for Column Stores and Row Stores

You can look in the technical settings of the ABAP Data Dictionary (DDIC) to see whether a table should be created in the row store or column store of SAP HANA (see Chapter 3, Section 3.2.1). The column store is the default setting here.

Column store   You can analyze large datasets more efficiently in the column store. Thus, SAP recommends that you store every table in the column store, as long as there is no dedicated reason for storing it in the row store. Tables that contain application data are always stored in the column store because it's very likely that this data are will also be used in analysis scenarios. This applies particularly to tables that contain a large number of data records because the column store provides better compression properties. This also applies to tables that are will be used for text searches (see Chapter 10, Section 10.3).

Still, you have reason to use the row store if, for example, a table is accessed predominantly by time-critical data manipulation language (DML) statements (i.e., UPDATE, INSERT, or DELETE). In addition, this can't be an application table on which you subsequently want to perform analyses. Therefore, primarily technical, internal SAP tables are eligible for the row store. Examples include tables for update processing (STSK package) or for Remote Function Call (RFC) processing (SRFC package). These tables are typically accessed with a SELECT SINGLE.

Row store

> **Use the Column Store!**   [+]
>
> In general, you should store all tables in the column store for SAP HANA unless more technical tables are involved, as just described.

14.1.2 SAP HANA-Specific Implementations

With the ABAP development on SAP HANA, we must distinguish between two scenarios:

▸ Database-independent implementations (e.g., Open SQL or CDS views)

▸ Implementations using SAP HANA-specific functions (e.g., Native SQL, column views, and database procedures)

In the first case, you don't have to consider anything special from a software logistics perspective. You use SAP HANA like any other database, but you benefit directly from the high processing speed of SAP HANA in many scenarios. Your developments are executable on all database systems supported by SAP.

Independent implementations

When using native SAP HANA functions, the same implications as usual initially apply if you define parts of an application specifically for a database system (e.g., via Native SQL, hints, or other techniques). When designing the application, you should consider the following questions:

SAP HANA-specific implementations

▸ Are there systems with a different database system in your landscape or in your customers' landscapes? Is an alternative implementation of the functions required for other database systems?

▸ How fundamental are database-specific functions to your application scenario? Is the central quality of the application involved, or is it just the "teasing out" of the optimal performance?

▸ Is the development in SAP HANA to be called solely via ABAP-based applications or via other channels as well (e.g., SAP BusinessObjects tools)?

Optimization initially via Open SQL

It's difficult to give a general recommendation as to when exactly it makes sense to use a database-specific implementation. For pure performance optimization of an existing ABAP application, we recommend that you initially proceed by using standard tools. The following guidelines provide help here:

▸ **First open, then native**
Preferably use Open SQL and CDS views before you deploy Native SQL, SAP HANA views, or database procedures. Open features are integrated optimally with the ABAP development environment and the ABAP runtime. The ABAP application server comprehensively checks your development objects, and you don't need any additional user for the SAP HANA database. Client handling is also automatic.

▸ **First ABAP managed, then database managed**
Use ABAP database procedures instead of SAP HANA database procedures. Development objects that are managed by ABAP AS are optimally linked with ABAP Lifecycle Management. You can easily synchronize ABAP database procedures with other ABAP objects and transport them. You also benefit from the strengths of the ABAP enhancement concept.

In Section 14.4, we provide special performance recommendations for the use of Open SQL on SAP HANA.

ABAP interface

If you use the techniques in this book to relocate operations to SAP HANA and ensure that they can be called via ABAP, it's often useful to encapsulate access to these functions via an interface in ABAP (thus, an ABAP interface). This enables the use of the *factory pattern*—a standard design pattern in software development—which is used for decoupling. Listing 14.1 shows sample code in which data retrieval was abstracted via the `lif_data_provider` interface (the exact appearance of this interface is irrelevant to understanding this example). The factory class provides a method that transfers an instance of an SAP HANA-specific implementation (`lcl_hana_provider`) to an SAP HANA system, while an alternative implementation is created in systems with a classic database. The test on SAP HANA is done via the `CL_DB_SYS` class, which has advantages over a test on the `sy-db` *system field* because you can easily make a where-used list for a class to find all parts of the program that perform such a distinction.

```
" Factory class
CLASS lcl_factory DEFINITION.
  PUBLIC SECTION.
    CLASS-METHODS: get_instance
                     RETURNING VALUE(ro_instance)
                       TYPE REF TO lif_data_provider.
ENDCLASS.

" Implementation of the factory class
CLASS lcl_factory IMPLEMENTATION.
  METHOD get_instance.
    IF ( cl_db_sys=>is_in_memory_db = abap_true ).
      ro_instance = NEW lcl_hana_provider( ).
    ELSE.
      ro_instance = NEW lcl_standard_provider( ).
    ENDIF.
  ENDMETHOD.
ENDCLASS.
```
Listing 14.1 Example of Factory Design Pattern Use for Decoupling SAP HANA-Specific Implementations

This approach can also be combined with Business Add-Ins (BAdIs) because the concept of an (abstract) factory class is also used in this case.

BAdIs

Optimization Procedure	**[+]**

Try to implement local performance optimization initially via Open SQL and CDS views. For major program changes and relocation of operations to SAP HANA, invest in decoupling, for example, via the aforementioned factory approach.

14.1.3   Checklist for Database-Specific Implementations

In this section, we'll provide a checklist of what you should consider when relocating program code to the database. This helps you avoid errors related to internationalization or localization.

Date/time

Dates play an important role in business data and processes (e.g., when a booking was made). You must of course pay attention to using the respective time zones correctly. If you use the time zone to which the server is set, you must note that the database server's time zone is used for SQLScript, while the time zone of AS ABAP is crucial in ABAP implementations. SAP recommends that you always make sure these time zones are identical during the installation.

Calculating with date fields

To determine the period between two calendar dates, there are special calculation rules for some business processes and in some global regions (e.g., using a fiscal year with 360 days or combining the days of a weekend into one day). Depending on the context, you must ensure that such calculations are interpreted correctly from a business perspective. The days_between SQL function supported by SAP HANA doesn't know these specifics.

Currencies and units

When handling currencies, you must ensure that some amounts are stored in the database with displaced decimal places (e.g., for Japanese yen). When calculating with such values, you must ensure that this displacement is taken into account before an output for an end user. This takes place in ABAP, for example, via specific conversion functions or the WRITE statement. If you work with currencies in analytical models in SAP HANA and want to consume them externally, you should mark these key figures as such and specify that the decimal displacement is taken into account (see Chapter 4, Section 4.4). In SQLScript procedures, you should clearly define whether you're working with internal or external formats in the definition of the interface, so each user knows how to interpret the values.

Conversion exits

There may be differences between internal and external presentations for other data types also. An example of this is the flight time in the flight plan of our sample data model (FLTIME column in table SPFLI). The flight time is stored internally in minutes as an INTEGER in the database, while it's presented externally via a conversion exit as a character string consisting of hours and minutes. If you're thus using a data model in different user interfaces (UIs), we recommend you ensure that it's treated uniformly.

When calculating with decimals, rounding behavior plays an important role, especially for monetary amounts. Small rounding differences can have a major impact on totals, so you should make sure to minimize rounding errors. When converting a currency, you should, if possible, only perform the conversion after an aggregation, which is also advantageous from a runtime perspective.

Rounding behavior

The sorting of texts depends on the current language settings. In the ABAP SORT command, therefore, the AS TEXT addition sorts the character strings alphabetically according to the set text environment. If you sort content in an SQL statement via the ORDER BY addition, however, it's sorted in a binary manner according to the internal presentation. Figure 14.1 shows an example using German umlauts. Here, the name "Möller" appears after "Muller," although it should appear alphabetically after "Moller." For this reason, we recommend that you usually sort texts, which you present in an ABAP application for an end user, in an application server.

Text sorting

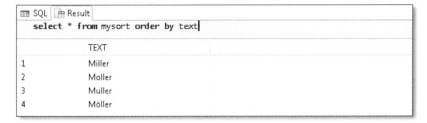

Figure 14.1 Sorting Texts in the Database

Handling Data Correctly from a Business Perspective   [+]

For time stamps, currencies, units, and texts, pay particular attention to the correct treatment of the business data in the context of native implementations in the database.

14.1.4 Recommendations for Migration

In this section, we give you some tips to consider when migrating an existing system to SAP HANA. A basic rule is that ABAP applications are fully compatible. There are a few fine points to note, which we'll discuss here:

▸ **Database-dependent ABAP code**
If you use database-dependent ABAP code in existing developments, you must test it as with any data migration and adjust it for the SAP HANA database if necessary.

▸ **Converting pool and cluster tables**
When converting pool and cluster tables to transparent tables, problems may occur if you've relied on an implicit sort behavior in your developments or if you directly accessed the internal physical clusters or pools.

▸ **Sort behavior**
If no ORDER BY was specified in the SQL statement, the sequence in which the records are read is unpredictable.

Database-Dependent Code

If your existing applications have database-dependent code—for example, Native SQL via the EXEC SQL statement , the ABAP Database Connectivity (ADBC) interface, or database *hints*—these positions in the code must be checked. While database hints are no longer executed on the new platform when you migrate to another database, an exact check is always required for database-dependent SQL because errors may occur here unless you intervene.

Hints Hints to the database (or also the database interface [DBI]) are given a database indicator in ABAP. This generally looks as follows:

```
SELECT ... %_HINTS <DB> 'db_specific_hint'.
```

The hint is sent only to the database specified instead of the <DB> placeholder. This means that when the additional statement to the optimizer of the old database platform is converted to the new platform, it's no longer sent to the optimizer of the new database. This concerns not only hints for the database but also specific instructions to the DBI. For a conversion, you must thus check whether the desired behavior on the old database platform should also be defined again by a hint on the new database platform. This is generally unnecessary for SAP HANA due to the modified architecture. Usually, no adjustment is necessary for the hints to the DBI, either. Here, we recommend that you use the default values for SAP HANA for the DBI.

You must always check database-dependent code for a conversion, even if standard SQL is involved. For database-specific SQL, you must first clarify what the code is to achieve. An SQL statement must then be written to deliver the same result on SAP HANA. If possible, you should use Open SQL for this.

Native SQL

Sort Behavior

Access to former pool or cluster tables, which we've already discussed in Chapter 7, Section 7.3.1, is a point that should be emphasized separately. For pool and cluster tables, the DBI always performs an implicit sorting. This is lost after the conversion to a transparent table because no automatic ORDER BY is added here to the statement. Therefore, access to pool and cluster tables must be analyzed with regard to their sorting during a migration. In this case, the Code Inspector provides a separate check—FIND SELECT FOR POOL/CLUSTER TAB WITHOUT ORDER BY—so you can quickly and easily find such critical points in your own developments.

Pool and cluster tables

However, changes can also occur in the implicit sort behavior for existing transparent tables. Classic row-oriented databases are usually accessed via a primary or secondary index. Here, the data are often read in the desired sequence because they are read from the database in the sequence stored there when you use an index. However, this isn't guaranteed, and this behavior isn't a documented feature of Open SQL. The selected access path and the associated sorting can thus change at any time. You must use the ORDER BY addition instead if the data is to be selected in a specific sorting. This rule applies in particular to SAP HANA because the data are column-oriented, there is no secondary index, and

Sort explicitly when sorting is necessary

the data can be read in parallel. Thus, such places involve a programming error that you should correct regardless of a migration to SAP HANA. The Code Inspector and the runtime check monitor (Transaction SRTCM) provide separate checks (see Chapter 7, Section 7.3.1 and Section 7.5.3).

Possible effects

Problems may occur if a certain sorting is assumed in program sequences. This is the case, for example, when working with searches in internal tables with the BINARY SEARCH addition because a relevant sorting is essential there. However, there may also be surprises with the output of data if it's suddenly not appearing in the desired sort order.

[+] **Don't Rely on Implicit Sortings**

If you require a specific sorting of data when you access a database, use the ORDER BY addition explicitly.

14.1.5   Development in Landscapes

In a standard SAP development scenario, multiple systems are generally used, and even entire landscapes are often included in larger developments. To ensure that no problems occur during the transition from a development system to another system (e.g., a test or production system), you should follow some guidelines for implementations in the database.

Schema and client handling

First, review the correct handling of schema names and the client field, which we discussed in Chapter 5, Section 5.1.4. During modeling or SQLScript implementation, avoid referencing schema names directly because these names are no longer valid after a transport to a different system. Thus, for procedures and calculation views, use the settings for a standard schema, and define appropriate *schema mappings* as described in Chapter 5, Section 5.3.1. As with SQLScript and Native SQL, you should always ensure that you handle the client field correctly. One option is to store different data configurations in various clients in the development or test system, and test them explicitly. For SAP HANA views, you should generally select the DYNAMIC DEFAULT CLIENT setting to use the current client of the ABAP session (see Chapter 5, Section 5.1.4).

For the transport of ABAP applications that directly reference SAP HANA objects such as views or procedures, we recommend the techniques described in Chapter 5, Section 5.3. You should use a common transport to ensure that inconsistencies don't occur in a target system (e.g., a missing database procedure that is accessed from ABAP). When using external views, database procedure proxies, and SAP HANA transport containers, you should also ensure that you've synchronized the content prior to a transport.

Transport

If you've mixed development landscapes in which some systems don't run on SAP HANA (yet), you can transport ABAP developments on SAP HANA through these systems without any problems. We recommend you always ensure that SAP HANA-specific implementations—which can't run in such systems—don't lead to uncontrolled program terminations if they are called (also see Section 14.3.2).

Mixed landscapes

Development in System Landscapes

Avoid direct accesses to schema names in SQLScript, and ensure correct client handling. Dependent ABAP and SAP HANA developments should be transported together consistently.

[+]

14.1.6 Modifying Data in SQLScript or Native SQL

We recommend in general that you largely avoid write operations on ABAP tables via SQLScript (including ABAP Managed Database Procedures [AMDPs]) or Native SQL EXEC SQL or ADBC). If you nevertheless modify database contents via these mechanisms, you should be particularly careful. We'll give you some important relevant information in this section.

Such accesses are sent virtually unchanged via the DBI to the database, so the SAP services on the application server—for example, for locking (see Chapter 3, Section 3.1) and table buffering (see Chapter 3, Section 3.2)—and their synchronization are completely bypassed. Such changes may lead to inconsistent data, as the following examples show.

Bypassing ABAP services

If, for example, data that is in the SAP table buffer is changed via SQLScript or Native SQL, the change is made only in the database. The data in the local table buffer (on the server on which the change was

Changes to buffered tables

made) won't be changed. Synchronization entries won't be written in table DDLOG, where other application servers are informed of changes in buffered tables and then can synchronize them. The data in the table buffer are no longer consistent with the data in the database because the changes were made directly via Native SQL or SQLScript while bypassing the table buffer. Thus, tables that are in the SAP table buffer must always be changed via Open SQL; otherwise, the data can't be changed or synchronized in the buffers.

In Figure 14.2, you can see the differences between changes via SQLScript (or Native SQL) and the standard variant via Open SQL statements. In the former case, the calls are forwarded directly via the DBI to the database while bypassing the table buffer, and the changes are made in the database.

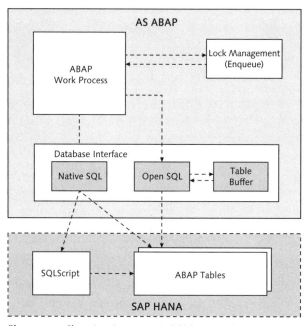

Figure 14.2 Changing Accesses via SQLScript or Native SQL

Changes without enqueue service   The system behavior is similar for locks. Data protected from change in parallel in the ABAP system via the enqueue service can still be changed directly in the database if SAP lock management is bypassed. This can also lead to inconsistent data if, for example, an ABAP application has set a lock to perform consistent calculations while another application is covertly changing this data directly in the database. Changes that were already made may also be lost if a lock on data records is ignored.

> **Avoiding Modification of ABAP Tables via SQLScript and Native SQL** [+]
>
> You should avoid changing data via SQLScript or Native SQL if possible. If you can't avoid this, ensure that the data isn't subject to table buffering or protected via the SAP enqueue service. Otherwise, data inconsistencies may occur.

14.2 Conventions

Conventions are helpful, particularly when distributing development projects among one or more teams. In this section, we'll discuss the following topics:

- Possible naming conventions for SAP HANA objects, including parameters in interfaces and ABAP proxies
- Recommendations for the encapsulation of developments, such as using packages in SAP HANA repository and granularity of the SAP HANA transport container

14.2.1 Naming Conventions

In contrast to ABAP, the names of development objects in the SAP HANA repository have to be unique only within a package. Some types of objects share a namespace: For example, it isn't possible to create an attribute view and an analytic view with the same name in a package. For this reason and for easy readability, we recommend that you use *prefixes* for SAP HANA development objects. Table 14.1 lists established naming conventions.

Naming conventions for SAP HANA objects

Object	Prefix	Example
Attribute view	AT_	AT_FLIGHT
Analytic view	AN_	AN_BOOKING_AMOUNTS

Table 14.1 Naming Conventions for SAP HANA Development Objects

Object	Prefix	Example
Calculation view	CA_	CA_PASSENGER_MILES
Procedure	–	EXECUTE_SEGMENTATION
Decision table	DT_	DT_PASSENGER_CLASS

Table 14.1 Naming Conventions for SAP HANA Development Objects (Cont.)

The package in the SAP HANA repository assumes the role of the namespace. You'll find the SAP standard development in subpackages of the sap package.

Naming conventions for ABAP proxies

The corresponding ABAP objects (external views, procedures) are subject to the ABAP naming restrictions. This includes the ABAP namespace concept in addition to the global uniqueness of names. Due to the length of name restrictions for ABAP development objects, the names of SAP HANA objects (including the package) can't always be adopted. Often, they must be abbreviated. Table 14.2 includes our recommendations for naming ABAP objects (Z namespace).

Object	Prefix	Example
External view	ZEV_	ZEV_AT_FLIGHT
Database procedure proxy	ZDP_	ZDP_EXECUTE_SEGMENTATION
Interface for the database procedure proxy	ZIF_	ZIF_EXECUTE_SEGMENTATION

Table 14.2 Naming Conventions for ABAP Proxies

Simple assignment

We recommend that you create only one corresponding external view or procedure proxy for each SAP HANA object and reuse them in ABAP. This facilitates the necessary adjustments, particularly in the event of changes.

Input and output parameters

For naming input and output parameters of a database procedure, you can use the conventions provided in Table 14.3, for example.

Type	Prefix	Example
Scalar input parameter	IV_	IV_CLIENT
Tabular input parameter	IT_	IT_FLIGHT
Scalar output parameter	EV_	EV_CARRNAME
Tabular output parameter	ET_	ET_FLIGHT
Local scalar variable	LV_	LV_COUNT
Local table variable	LT_	LT_FLIGHT

Table 14.3 Naming Conventions for Input and Output Parameters

You can also use the conventions of Table 14.3 for your ABAP database procedures.

The conventions listed in Table 14.4 are common for ABAP CDS views.

Type	Prefix	Example
Association	_	_Flightplan
Parameter	p_	p_countryto

Table 14.4 CDS Naming Conventions

It's recommended that the data definition language (DDL) source has the same name as the CDS view, which is defined in this source.

14.2.2 Encapsulating SAP HANA Packages

In principle, you can create objects anywhere in the SAP HANA repository (outside the SAP namespace). However, we recommend that you clearly encapsulate components of applications in packages. Pay attention to the following aspects:

Delivery unit

▶ Local developments and developments to be transported must be in separate packages because delivery units always contain full packages.

▶ A delivery unit should ideally include a package tree, that is, a superpackage and all subpackages.

553

▸ Cyclical dependencies between delivery units must be avoided; otherwise, an automatic import isn't possible. You should also avoid cyclical dependencies between packages.

▸ Those objects that are accessed externally (e.g., via ABAP code) should be marked because changes to the interface usually require adjustments and synchronization of the user. One option is to encapsulate these objects in a separate package.

14.3 Quality Aspects

In this section, we've compiled some recommendations you can use when implementing native views and procedures in SAP HANA; these guidelines will help increase the quality of your own developments. We'll discuss three aspects here: testing views and procedures, robust programming, and security aspects.

14.3.1 Testing Views and Procedures

Design   It's particularly important to ensure a stable design and good test coverage for the definition of data models and implementations near the database. First, functional errors can have potentially expensive implications (such as data inconsistencies or incorrect business results). Additionally, changes to database objects are always more complex than small adjustments to a UI. For this reason, you should pay great attention to these design aspects, especially for SAP HANA views and database procedures.

Testing   Tests are an essential tool for verifying whether the interfaces are usable and cover all special cases. We've already discussed the technical options for testing views and procedures in Chapter 7, Section 7.2.1. Let's review the two most important test recommendations:

▸ Enable the writing of unit tests for individual parts of your application by modularization and decoupling. If parts of the application can't be tested automatically, testing becomes more difficult, and you run the risk of overlooking important special cases.

▸ Create appropriate test data in realistic dimensions. You can either use anonymous copies from a production system or data generators.

If you optimize an existing implementation and want to make sure that the optimized version is the functional equivalent of the old version, the system provides automatic tests that compare the results of both implementations. You can also determine runtime improvements here.

SAP HANA Test Tools

[«]

With SAP HANA SPS 09, SAP delivers a separate unit test framework (XSUnit) and a mocking framework (Mockstar), which you can use to test SAP HANA views procedures. To use these tools, you must install the HANA_TEST_TOOLS delivery unit. You can find more information on the SAP HANA test tools in the SCN (*http://scn.sap.com/community/developer-center/hana/blog/2014/12/09/sap-hana-sps-09-new-developer-features-hana-test-tools*).

14.3.2 Robust Programming

If an implemented function is used in practice, configurations can always occur for which the function wasn't intended (e.g., a call with invalid parameters). Such situations can be dealt with via *robust programming*. This should be an important design goal for implementations near the database because problems can have potentially serious consequences for data consistency or system stability. We'll give you some recommendations for robust programming within the context of SAP HANA.

Robust programming guarantees well-defined and deterministic behavior in all situations. Assumptions with regard to the value range of input parameters should be tested explicitly. If an input table of an SQLScript procedure shouldn't be empty, it must be clearly defined whether this is to lead to a program termination or a specific output (e.g., an empty output table). In other words, the interfaces of database functions should be fully defined. Using unit tests, you should review the behavior for invalid input data as well.

In addition to well-defined behavior, dealing with error situations is essential for a robust implementation. Terminations shouldn't lead to unwanted side effects on data consistency, system stability, or other users. Such situations can potentially arise, particularly with write accesses to ABAP tables outside of the logical unit of work (LUW) concept in ABAP systems. When calling read operations only, you should always provide clear error handling—even if, from an ABAP code perspective, it's only a simple call such as a `SELECT` statement on an external view. You should decide whether there must be a controlled program termination (*dump*) or whether a meaningful error message for the user (along with a log entry for subsequent analysis) is possible.

Avoiding dynamic SQLScript

In SQLScript, there is the option of using the `EXEC` command to execute a programmatically generated SQL statement in the form of a character string. This is a powerful tool for generating flexible and generic instructions at runtime but has disadvantages with regard to robustness, security (see Section 14.3.3), and performance (see Section 14.5.3). We recommend that you largely avoid dynamic SQLScript, particularly to ensure robust behavior.

[+] **Robust Programming**

Pay particular attention to robustness for implementations in the database. Every possible data configuration should lead to a well-defined result or error. Program terminations should be avoided.

14.3.3 Security Aspects

Secure ABAP programming

If you follow the classic ABAP development model and the associated guidelines, this will provide you with protection against most security risks.

Security for native implementations

When changing to native implementations for SAP HANA and using native database calls from ABAP, you should always incorporate security considerations. We'll discuss two important aspects: authorization checks and SQL injection attacks.

Authorization check

With critical business data, you must always ensure that no user has access to data for which he has no authorization. To do this, you must know and protect the possible access channels. For ABAP applications, you should implement authorization checks via ABAP authorization objects and the assignment to roles. If you relocate operations via views and procedures to SAP HANA, you should secure the call paths in ABAP using appropriate `AUTHORITY-CHECK` statements. If you also want to release these data models in SAP HANA directly for end users (e.g., via the Microsoft Excel client presented in Chapter 4, Section 4.4.5, or via the SAP BusinessObjects tools presented in Chapter 9), you should restrict access by means of analytical authorizations (see Chapter 2, Section 2.4.3). For information about authorization checks in the context of native developments in SAP HANA using SAP HANA Extended Application Services (SAP HANA XS), see the development documentation at *http://help.sap.com/hana*.

Especially when using Native SQL or SQLScript, you should always check or mask external inputs (e.g., by a user or via an external interface) to avoid an injection of unwanted SQL code (SQL injection) by an attacker. We recommend that you keep the level of free input of such Native SQL statements as small as possible and check them against *white lists* as much as possible. For Native SQL accesses via ADBC, the use of prepared statements (see Chapter 3, Section 3.2.4) can provide certain protection here. Just like for other interfaces, in SQLScript implementations, you should take care that the calculations necessary for execution are clear from a business perspective. We advise against creating excessively "powerful" procedures that read a combination of business data, which no end user may see in this form.

Avoid SQL injection

Secure Programming	[!]
Native implementations increase the responsibility for ensuring security. Be sure to protect all access paths with authorization checks and check all user input.

14.4 Performance Recommendations for Open SQL

In this section, we'll provide performance recommendations for developing ABAP applications on SAP HANA. We'll discuss the most important, frequently asked questions related to SAP HANA. If you want to delve more extensively into the topic of SAP or ABAP performance, we recommend *SAP Performance Optimization Guide: Analyzing and Tuning SAP Systems* by Thomas Schneider (SAP PRESS, 2013), *ABAP Performance Tuning* by Hermann Gahm (SAP PRESS, 2009), in which the topic of performance is discussed in great detail. Here, we'll describe the most important rules and any changes in the context of SAP HANA. In addition, there are some new performance topics with SAP HANA that we'll consider here.

First, we'll discuss the golden rules for database programming and whether or how these change for SAP HANA. The time-tested golden rules for database programming are as follows:

1. Keep the result set as small as possible.

2. Keep the transferred dataset as small as possible.

3. Reduce the number of query executions.

4. Minimize the search effort.

5. Reduce the load on the database.

In the next sections, we'll describe each rule and illustrate some with examples. We'll then explain the extent to which these rules are relevant for SAP HANA or what has changed.

14.4.1 Rule 1: Keeping Result Sets Small

The first golden rule recommends that you keep the result set (i.e., the number of selected rows) as small as possible when reading data from the database. You can minimize the result set using various measures:

▶ Using a WHERE clause

▶ Working with the HAVING clause

▶ Transferring only required rows

WHERE condition

In ABAP, the number of transferred data records is controlled by the WHERE condition. You should read only those data records that you actually need. The WHERE condition may be waived only if all records are required for each access. Waiving the WHERE clause is particularly problematic for database tables that increase over time because increasing volumes of data are then transferred over time.

The following examples show this in comparison. All customers are selected in Listing 14.2, and then the selection is restricted to the data records actually required. In Listing 14.3, only the data records actually required are read from the database.

SELECT with and without WHERE clause

```
SELECT id name discount custtype
    FROM scustom
    INTO (lv_cust-id, lv_cust-name,
    lv_cust-discount, lv_cust-custtype).
      IF lv_cust-custtype = 'B'.
        WRITE: / lv_cust-id,
        lv_cust-name, lv_cust-discount.
      ENDIF.
ENDSELECT.
```
Listing 14.2 Missing WHERE Clause

```
SELECT id name discount
    FROM scustom
    INTO (lv_cust-id, lv_cust-name, lv_cust-discount)
    WHERE custtype = 'B'.
        WRITE: / lv_cust-id,
        lv_cust-name, lv_cust-discount.
ENDSELECT.
```
Listing 14.3 Query with WHERE Clause

HAVING Clause

Use of the HAVING clause provides another option to reduce the transferred rows. It's used if there is a GROUPBY clause, and you want to transfer only certain groups by making restrictions to the grouped rows, for example, in the aggregate values.

The following examples illustrate this option. In Listing 14.4, the minimum use of all flight connections is determined and transferred. In Listing 14.5, only the flight connections with a minimum use greater than zero are transferred.

GROUP BY expression with and without HAVING

```
SELECT carrid connid MIN( seatsocc )
  FROM sflight
  INTO (lv_sflight-carrid, lv_sflight-connid, lv_min)
  GROUP BY carrid connid.
    IF lv_min > 0.
      WRITE: / lv_sflight-carrid,
      lv_sflight-connid, lv_min.
```

```
    ENDIF.
ENDSELECT.
```
Listing 14.4 Missing HAVING Clause

```
SELECT carrid connid MIN( seatsocc )
  FROM sflight
  INTO (lv_sflight-carrid, lv_sflight-connid, lv_min)
  GROUP BY carrid connid
  HAVING MIN( seatsocc ) > 0.
    WRITE: / lv_sflight-carrid,
    lv_sflight-connid, lv_min.
ENDSELECT.
```
Listing 14.5 GROUP BY Expression with HAVING Clause

Transferring Only Required Rows

You should always transfer only data records that you actually require. You should never remove data that you don't require in the application server in the ABAP program and thus transfer it unnecessarily from the database.

Select specific data instead of deleting

Two examples were listed previously. Another example that falls under this rule concerns the selection of data in internal tables, from which unnecessary data records are then deleted using DELETE (see Listing 14.6). CHECK statements or filtering by means of IF may also indicate the transfer of too many rows. In the example in Listing 14.7, the selection is restricted instead to the required data.

```
SELECT id name discount custtype
    FROM scustom
    INTO CORRESPONDING FIELDS OF TABLE lt_scustom
    WHERE country = 'DE'.
DELETE lt_scustom WHERE custtype = 'P'.
LOOP AT lt_scustom INTO ls_cust.
  WRITE: / ls_cust-id, ls_cust-name,
  ls_cust-discount, ls_cust-custtype.
ENDLOOP.
```
Listing 14.6 Subsequent Deleting

```
SELECT id name discount custtype
    FROM scustom
    INTO CORRESPONDING FIELDS OF TABLE lt_scustom
    WHERE country = 'DE'
    AND custtype <> 'P'.
```

```
LOOP AT lt_scustom INTO ls_cust.
  WRITE: / ls_cust-id, ls_cust-name,
  ls_cust-discount, ls_cust-custtype.
ENDLOOP.
```
Listing 14.7 Selecting Only Required Data

Summary and Significance for SAP HANA

A consistent application of this rule for classic databases leads to reduced I/O effort, optimized memory consumption in the cache, reduced CPU consumption, and an optimized network transfer because less data is transferred.

Significance of Rule #1 for SAP HANA	[«]

This rule applies unchanged and with the same priority to SAP HANA. CPU and main memory resources are also conserved on SAP HANA if fewer data records have to be read. There is no change in the transfer of data via the network.

The Code Inspector (see Chapter 7, Section 7.3) provides support here with the following checks:

- Analysis of the WHERE condition for a SELECT
- Analysis of the WHERE condition for the UPDATE and DELETE statements
- Search for SELECT statements with DELETE
- SELECT statements with subsequent CHECK

These checks are described in more detail in Chapter 7, Section 7.3.1.

14.4.2   Rule 2: Keeping Transferred Datasets Small

The second golden rule recommends that you transfer as little data as possible between the database and the application server. The data are transferred from the database to the application server in blocks. The network load can be reduced by transferring fewer blocks.

As a programmer, you can do this by influencing the number of selected rows and columns via restrictions that go beyond the WHERE condition. We'll discuss these aspects in the following subsections:

Number of selected rows and columns

- ► Using the UP TO n ROWS addition
- ► Working with DISTINCT
- ► Reducing the number of columns
- ► Using aggregate functions
- ► Performing existence checks efficiently
- ► Changing only required columns

Using UP TO n ROWS

If you require only a certain number of rows, you can use the UP TO n ROWS addition to restrict the number of rows further. The following examples illustrate how you can use UP TO n ROWS to reduce the number of transferred data records further. The business customers with the highest discounts are selected. In Listing 14.8, the system terminates in a loop after the tenth data record (example of a bad process). Because SELECT ... ENDSELECT reads the data in blocks from the database, however, more data records than necessary were already transferred in the first block. In Transaction ST05 (see Chapter 7, Section 7.4.3), you can see how many data records were transferred in the first block (corresponds to a FETCH). Exactly 10 records are transferred in Listing 14.9 because the statement—the statement saying only 10 records were required—was transferred to the database (example of a good process).

```
SELECT id name discount
    FROM scustom
    INTO (ls_cust-id, ls_cust-name, ls_cust-discount)
    WHERE custtype = 'B'
    ORDER BY discount DESCENDING.
  IF sy-dbcnt > 10. EXIT.
  ENDIF.
  WRITE: / ls_cust-id, ls_cust-name, ls_cust-discount.
ENDSELECT.
```
Listing 14.8 Without UP TO n ROWS

```
SELECT id name discount
    FROM scustom UP TO 10 ROWS
    INTO (ls_cust-id, ls_cust-name, ls_cust-discount)
    WHERE custtype = 'B'
    ORDER BY discount DESCENDING.
```

```
    WRITE: / ls_cust-id, ls_cust-name, ls_cust-discount.
ENDSELECT.
```
Listing 14.9 With UP TO n ROWS

Using DISTINCT

If the system calculates with a certain WHERE condition that has unnecessary duplicate entries regarding the selected columns, the DISTINCT statement should be used to remove the duplicate entries already in the database.

In the following example, a list is created of discounts that were granted. In Listing 14.10, the duplicate entries are deleted after the selection. In Listing 14.11, only the required data is read from the database.

Example with and without DISTINCT

```
SELECT custtype discount
    FROM scustom
    INTO CORRESPONDING FIELDS OF TABLE lt_scustom
    WHERE discount > 0
    ORDER BY custtype discount DESCENDING.

DELETE ADJACENT DUPLICATES FROM lt_scustom.

LOOP AT lt_scustom INTO ls_cust.
  WRITE: / ls_cust-custtype, ls_cust-discount.
ENDLOOP.
```
Listing 14.10 Query without DISTINCT

```
SELECT DISTINCT custtype discount
    FROM scustom
    INTO CORRESPONDING FIELDS OF TABLE lt_scustom
    WHERE discount > 0
    ORDER BY custtype discount DESCENDING.

LOOP AT lt_scustom INTO ls_cust.
  WRITE: / ls_cust-custtype, ls_cust-discount.
ENDLOOP.
```
Listing 14.11 Query with DISTINCT

Reducing the Number of Columns

You should select only columns in a database table that are also required in the ABAP program. Here, you should list the columns individually in the field list after `SELECT`, if possible. The selection of all columns using `SELECT *` should only be used if all columns are actually required.

Although the `INTO CORRESPONDING FIELDS OF` addition selects only the columns that are also in the preceding objective when * is specified, extra effort is involved in comparing names in the DBI. Thus, this addition should only be used sparingly and for larger result sets because the effort involved in comparing names can be relatively high for very quick `SELECT` statements.

In the following example, the system determines the days on which a certain flight connection exists in 2013. In Listing 14.12, all columns of table `SFLIGHT` are read, although only the flight date is required. In Listing 14.13, only the required column is read.

```
SELECT * FROM sflight
    INTO ls_sflight
    WHERE carrid = 'LH'
      AND connid = '0300'
      AND fldate LIKE '2013 %'.
  WRITE: / ls_sflight-fldate.
ENDSELECT.
```
Listing 14.12 Query without Field List

```
SELECT fldate FROM sflight
    INTO (lv_sflight-fldate)
    WHERE carrid = 'LH'
      AND connid = '0300'
      AND fldate LIKE '2013 %'.
  WRITE: / lv_sflight-fldate.
ENDSELECT.
```
Listing 14.13 Query with Field List

Another option for reducing the dataset is the use of aggregate functions.

Using Aggregate Functions

If data are required only for calculations, it's better to perform these calculations in the database and transfer the results rather than transferring all data and performing the calculation in the ABAP program. The available aggregate functions are COUNT, MIN, MAX, SUM, and AVG for the number, the minimum value, the maximum value, the sum of the values, and the average value, respectively.

In the following example, the system determines the sum of the reserved seats of an airline in a specific year. In Listing 14.14, all reservations of flights are selected and added up in the ABAP program. In Listing 14.15, the sum of the reservations is calculated in the database, and only this sum is transferred to the ABAP program.

Determine data with and without aggregate function

```
lv_sum = 0.
SELECT seatsocc
    FROM sflight INTO lv_seatsocc
    WHERE carrid = 'LH'
      AND fldate LIKE '2013 %'.
  lv_sum = lv_sum + lv_seatsocc.
ENDSELECT.
WRITE: / lv_sum.
```
Listing 14.14 Query without Aggregate Function

```
SELECT SUM( seatsocc )
  FROM sflight INTO lv_sum
  WHERE carrid = 'LH'
    AND fldate LIKE '2013 %'.
WRITE: / lv_sum.
```
Listing 14.15 Query with Aggregate Function

Performing Existence Checks Efficiently

You should use these aggregate functions only if you need such a calculation. To determine whether there is a data record for a specific key, for example, you shouldn't use SELECT COUNT(*) because the number is irrelevant in this case. For such an existence check, you require only a single field of the data record you seek, and this should be a field of the index that is in use.

In the example, the system is to check whether there were flights for a specific flight connection in a specific year. In Listing 14.16, this is checked using a COUNT(*). Here, all data records in the database that meet the condition are counted. The UP TO 1 ROWS addition doesn't change anything because it's only executed after counting. In Listing 14.17, the data records aren't counted because the number of records is

Existence check without counting the data records

irrelevant. Only one field is selected—there should be no `SELECT *` here either—and the result set is restricted to one row with `UP TO n ROWS`. This ensures that only one data record is read. After the database has determined a record that meets the conditions, the processing is terminated.

```
SELECT count(*) UP TO 1 ROWS
    FROM sflight INTO lv_cnt
    WHERE carrid = 'LH'
      AND connid = '0400'
      AND fldate LIKE '2013 %'.
IF lv_cnt > 0.
...
```

Listing 14.16 Existence Check with COUNT(*)

```
SELECT carrid INTO lv_sflicht-carrid
    UP TO 1 ROWS
    FROM sflight
    WHERE carrid = 'LH'
      AND connid = '0400'
      AND fldate LIKE '2013 %'.

ENDSELECT.
IF sy-subrc = 0.
...
```

Listing 14.17 Existence Check without COUNT(*)

Changing Only Required Columns

For changes with the `UPDATE` statement, only the desired columns are to be changed with the `SET` statement. When changing rows from work areas, too much data is usually transferred and columns that haven't changed are also overwritten.

Complete and specific change

The connection number of a specific flight is to be changed in the example. In Listing 14.18, the rows to be changed are first read, then a column is changed with a new value in the work area, and finally the entire row is written back to the database. Here, an unnecessarily large number of columns is transferred and all columns are overwritten in the database, even if their values haven't changed. In Listing 14.19, an `UPDATE ... SET` overwrites only the desired column with a new value. Therefore, the records aren't read at all, and far less data are transferred to the database. In addition, the database has to change only the transferred column.

```
SELECT * FROM sbook
    INTO ls_sbook
    WHERE carrid  = 'LH'
      AND connid  = '0400'
      AND fldate >= '20140101'.
  ls_sbook-connid = '0500'.
  UPDATE sbook FROM ls_sbook.
ENDSELECT.
```
Listing 14.18 Changing the Entire Row

```
UPDATE sbook
  SET connid = '0500'
  WHERE carrid  = 'LH'
    AND connid  = '0400'
    AND fldate >= '20140101'.
```
Listing 14.19 Changing the Desired Columns

Summary and Significance for SAP HANA

The effects of rule #2 are very similar those of rule #1. The consistent application of these rules leads to reduced resource consumption in the classic database.

> **Significance of Rule #2 for SAP HANA**   **[«]**
>
> This rule applies unchanged to SAP HANA because the resources are con-served in a similar manner here. The priority of the rule is slightly higher than for other databases. This can be attributed to the different storage of data. If data records are stored in a row-based manner, all columns in a block are close together. In column-oriented storage, each column is a separate storage structure. Although these storage structures can be processed in parallel, the time required for multiple columns is slightly higher. Even if the differences aren't very large, you should pay special attention to these rules and check time-critical applications for optimization with regard to this rule.
>
> The Code Inspector (see Chapter 7, Section 7.3) provides support here with the following checks:
>
> ▶ Problematic SELECT * statement
>
> ▶ EXIT or no statement in SELECT ... ENDSELECT loop
>
> These checks are described in more detail in Chapter 7, Section 7.3.1. With regard to the aggregate functions, these are very well supported by SAP HANA. However, you should only use them where you actually require the calculations.

14.4.3 Rule 3: Reducing the Number of Queries

The third rule recommends reducing the number of queries to the database. Each SQL statement in an ABAP program that is sent to the database involves a certain degree of effort in the database. Thus, the statement and its associated parameters are transferred to the database where the statement is analyzed in terms of the syntax and search by hash function in the SQL cache, or where the statement is stored when it's first executed. In addition, authorizations and the existence of database objects (tables, views, etc.) must be checked to ensure they are present. The results of the query must also be transferred. To reduce the load on the database, you should keep the number of accesses as low as possible. In ABAP programs, you can influence the number of statements by the following measures:

▸ Using set operations instead of individual operations

▸ No longer performing multiple accesses

▸ No longer using nested SELECT loops

▸ Not executing SELECT statements in the LOOP via internal tables

▸ Using buffers

Using Set Operations Instead of Individual Operations

When reading with SELECT, you should choose the INTO TABLE addition instead of the SELECT ... ENDSELECT loop if all the data to be read must fit into the main memory. The SELECT ... ENDSELECT also reads the data in blocks from the database to the DBI. From there, the data are transferred in single records to the ABAP program. The SELECT ... ENDSELECT loop is thus useful if the available memory is insufficient for all data or if the read data is accessed once only.

For write accesses, you should rely wherever possible on set operations with internal tables. The number of database queries is greatly reduced, and the database can perform more optimizations with the data that was transferred all at once.

In the following two examples, data records are inserted in table SBOOK. In Listing 14.20, the data records are inserted record by record in a loop.

```
LOOP AT lt_sbook INTO ls_sbook.
  INSERT INTO sbook VALUES ls_sbook.
ENDLOOP.
```
Listing 14.20 Inserting in a Loop

With the following statement, all data records are inserted at once in a set operation:

```
INSERT sbook FROM TABLE lt_sbook.
```

No Longer Performing Multiple Accesses

You should make sure you don't repeatedly access the same data. For example, avoid a SELECT before a DELETE for the same data record (see Listing 14.21). You've already seen an example with UPDATE in Listing 14.18. Listing 14.22 shows a DELETE operation without a preceding SELECT statement.

Deleting without a SELECT statement

```
SELECT SINGLE * FROM sflight INTO lv_sflight
  WHERE carrid = 'SQ' AND connid ='0002'.

IF sy-subrc = 0.
  DELETE FROM sflight
  WHERE carrid = 'SQ' AND connid = '0002'.
    IF sy-subrc = 0.
      COMMIT WORK.
    ENDIF.
  ENDIF.
```
Listing 14.21 Deleting after SELECT

```
  DELETE FROM sflight
  WHERE carrid = 'SQ' AND connid = '0002'.
    IF sy-subrc = 0.
      COMMIT WORK.
    ENDIF.
  ENDIF.
```
Listing 14.22 Deleting without SELECT

No Longer Using Nested SELECT Loops

For nested SELECT loops, the inner SELECT statement is executed once for each data record that the outer SELECT loop returns. The number of records in the outer data records' result set thus determines the executions of the inner SELECT statement. Therefore, such a construct should only be used if the result set of the outer loop contains very few rows.

For merging data sets, we recommend that you use the following options:

- ▶ Views (see Chapter 3, Section 3.2.3, and Chapter 4)
- ▶ Joins
- ▶ FOR ALL ENTRIES
- ▶ Subqueries
- ▶ Cursors

Views and joins

The runtime of views and joins depends greatly on the execution plan selected by the database optimizer. Accesses to views and joins are still usually faster than nested loops. If this isn't the case, the execution plan must be analyzed more precisely, which requires good knowledge of the respective database. The optimizer may not be able to determine the optimal sequence of the tables. Joins and views have a disadvantage in that the data of the outer table are redundant in the result set with a 1:n relationship between the outer and inner table. Thus more data than necessary may be transferred. You must make sure to select only the fields that are actually required. In extreme cases, a FOR ALL ENTRIES (see next section) can be better.

SELECT loop and inner join

The following is an example where the data from tables SFLIGHT and SBOOK are merged. All bookings from table SBOOK for a specific aircraft type are to be read from table SFLIGHT. In Listing 14.23, this is implemented via nested SELECT loops. Here, the SELECT statement is executed once in table SBOOK for each data record that was read from table SFLIGHT. In Listing 14.24, the data are read using a join, and only one statement is sent to the database.

```
SELECT carrid connid fldate FROM sflight
    INTO (lv_carrid, lv_connid, lv_fldate)
    WHERE planetype = '727-200'.
  SELECT bookid FROM sbook INTO lv_bookid
    WHERE carrid = lv_carrid
      AND connid = lv_connid
      AND fldate = lv_fldate.
    WRITE: / lv_carrid, lv_connid, lv_bookid.
```

```
   ENDSELECT.
ENDSELECT.
```
Listing 14.23 Nested SELECT Loops

```
SELECT f~carrid f~connid b~bookid
    INTO (lv_carrid, lv_connid, lv_bookid)
    FROM sflight AS f INNER JOIN sbook AS b
        ON f~carrid = b~carrid AND
           f~connid = b~connid AND
           f~fldate = b~fldate
    WHERE planetype = '727-200'.
  WRITE: / lv_carrid, lv_connid, lv_bookid.
ENDSELECT.
```
Listing 14.24 Inner Join

Nested loops can also be avoided via the FOR ALL ENTRIES construct. **FOR ALL ENTRIES** Here, the data of the outer table are stored in an internal table, and then the inner SELECT statement is executed once with the FOR ALL ENTRIES addition. The internal table is thereby divided into blocks, and a statement is executed for each block. That means the transfer of redundant data from the outer table can be avoided, which can lead to better performance in certain cases. Generally, a JOIN should be selected wherever possible because the number of statements sent to the database is smaller than with FOR ALL ENTRIES. You'll find an example of a FOR ALL ENTRIES statement in the following section.

With subqueries, you can also access multiple tables in a single state- **Subqueries** ment. The data of the subquery isn't transferred at all but is used only within the query in the database itself.

The following example shows the flight data of the busiest flights, based **Nested and** on the maximum number of occupied seats. In Listing 14.25, the inner **subquery** SELECT statement is sent for each data record of the outer to the database. For Listing 14.26, only a single statement is sent to the database.

```
SELECT carrid connid MAX( seatsocc )
  FROM sflight
  INTO (lv_carrid, lv_connid, lv_max)
  GROUP BY carrid connid.
    SELECT fldate FROM sflight
        INTO lv_fldate
        WHERE carrid   = lv_carrid AND
              connid   = lv_connid AND
```

571

```
            seatsocc = lv_max.
      WRITE: / lv_carrid, lv_connid, lv_fldate.
    ENDSELECT.
ENDSELECT.
```
Listing 14.25 Nested SELECT Statements

```
SELECT carrid connid fldate
    FROM sflight AS f
    INTO (lv_carrid, lv_connid, lv_max)
    WHERE seatsocc IN
    ( SELECT MAX( seatsocc ) FROM sflight
        WHERE carrid = f~carrid
          AND connid = f~connid ).
  WRITE: / lv_carrid, lv_connid, lv_fldate.
ENDSELECT.
```
Listing 14.26 Subquery

Not Executing SELECT Statements in the LOOP via Internal Tables

Similar to nested loops, you shouldn't execute SELECT statements in the LOOP via internal tables. Here, the FOR ALL ENTRIES addition is useful for reducing the number of executions. In this case, you should ensure that the internal table is never empty and doesn't contain duplicates with FOR ALL ENTRIES.

In the example, the corresponding booking data is determined for all flights that are in internal table LT_SFLIGHT. In Listing 14.27, a SELECT is executed for each data record in the LOOP loop via internal table LT_SFLIGHT. In Listing 14.28, the number of executed SELECT statements is reduced by FOR ALL ENTRIES.

```
LOOP AT lt_sflight INTO lv_sflight.
    SELECT SINGLE bookid customid FROM sbook
    INTO lv_sbook
      WHERE carrid = lv_sflight-carrid
        AND connid = lv_sflight-connid
        AND fldate = lv_sflight-fldate.

      WRITE: / lv_sflight-carrid,
      lv_sflight-connid, lv_sflight-fldate,
      lv_sbook-bookid, lv_sbook-customid.
ENDLOOP.
```
Listing 14.27 SELECT in the LOOP

```
IF lines( lt_sflight ) > 0.
  SELECT carrid connid fldate bookid customid
  FROM sbook
  INTO CORRESPONDING FIELDS OF TABLE lt_sbook
  FOR ALL ENTRIES IN lt_sflight
    WHERE carrid = lt_sflight-carrid
      AND connid = lt_sflight-connid
      AND fldate = lt_sflight-fldate.
ENDIF.
```
Listing 14.28 Restriction with FOR ALL ENTRIES

Using Buffers

The use of the SAP table buffer and other buffers (see Section 14.4.5) also contributes to minimizing the number of SQL statements that are sent to the database.

Summary and Significance for SAP HANA

The consistent application of this rule leads to reduced CPU consumption for classic databases. Network resources are also used in a better way because the number of sent blocks can be optimized.

Significance of Rule #3 for SAP HANA [«]

This rule has a higher priority for SAP HANA than for other databases. The effort involved in the execution of a statement is currently slightly higher in SAP HANA than in classic databases. However, this will be optimized in the future. Applications that send a very large number of quick queries to the database are thus to be examined in terms of optimization potential, based on the approaches presented in the examples in this section.

The SAP Code Inspector provides support here with the following checks:

▶ Searching for SELECT ... FOR ALL ENTRIES clauses to be transformed

▶ Searching for database operations in LOOPS within modularization units

▶ Changing database accesses in loops

These checks are described in more detail in Chapter 7, Section 7.3.1.

14.4.4 Rule 4: Minimizing Search Effort

This section is about the effort involved in selecting the dataset that was restricted via the WHERE and HAVING clauses. You can minimize the effort of the data search with an index. As in the previous sections, we'll first discuss the recommendations for classic databases before we turn to the recommendations for SAP HANA.

Database Index in Classic Databases

An index consists of selected fields of the database table, which are copied in a sorted sequence into a separate structure. A distinction is made between the *primary index* and the *secondary index*. The primary index contains the primary key fields. Thus, this index is *unique*, and there can be only one data record for any combination of the fields of this index. It's always created automatically in SAP systems when you create a table. Then there are the secondary indexes, which can be unique or nonunique. Secondary indexes are created in the DDIC. They are usually used to optimize performance but can also have semantic motives for unique indexes if, for example, only unique values may be in a column that isn't part of the primary key.

Recommenda-
tions for classic
databases

The correct formulation of WHERE or HAVING clauses and a suitable secondary index definition can minimize the search effort significantly because only part of the data has to be read.

Our recommendations for creating indexes are as follows:

- Secondary indexes are to be created only for database tables where the read accesses are more time critical than the write accesses because each created index has to be maintained for write accesses.

- The number of created indexes and fields in the index should be kept as small as possible. Otherwise, it takes more effort to change database accesses, and the optimizer is likelier to make wrong decisions.

- The fields on which indexes are created should only be in one index if possible. Overlaps should be avoided.

- The fields in a secondary index should be fields through which you often select. These fields should also be selective; that is, the percentage of data records selected by the index should be small.

- The fields that are most likely to be queried with the = operator should be at the beginning of the index.

To formulate the WHERE clauses, these are our main recommendations: WHERE condition

- The = operator or EQ operator and AND links are always supported efficiently in the index. That is, the optimizer can thus reduce the I/O effort whenever it's technically possible. An IN list also falls into this category because it represents, in principle, a multiple = for the column. Thus, you should use = and IN conditions wherever possible.

- Avoid negative conditions (<>, NE, NOT) because they can't be supported efficiently in the index. If possible, rewrite such conditions as positive conditions. If this isn't possible, you should still specify the conditions in the WHERE condition and not omit them completely. This is the only way in which the required data records will be selected. Otherwise, you read unnecessary records that you then have to remove in the ABAP program, which contradicts the first golden rule.

- If you don't specify all fields in the index, make sure that you enclose the initial section of the index in the WHERE condition. Otherwise, the use of an index isn't possible in many cases.

Database Index in SAP HANA

There has been much development in this area for SAP HANA. This section involves the question of how and when indexes should be created in SAP HANA. In Appendix C, we explain the background of read accesses and write accesses for column-based data storage. We also explain why it's no longer necessary in many cases to create an index here, even though an index had to be created in other databases. With SAP HANA, we distinguish between *inverted* and *composite indexes* (see Appendix C).

Composite indexes have a higher memory requirement due to the memory structures for an additional internal column. Thus, we recommend that you work as much as possible with inverted indexes. That is, an index should be created in each case for the column that has the most selective condition. Composite indexes should be created only in exceptional cases—for example, when data from different columns correlates Inverted versus composite index to such an extent that only certain combinations are selective. The maintenance of indexes results in increased costs for write accesses in SAP HANA also. However, these costs are significantly less for inverted indexes than for composite indexes, for which multiple memory structures must be maintained.

Index creation in SAP HANA

If you're migrating an existing system to SAP HANA, all existing secondary indexes for column store tables are no longer created. Technically, they are included in the exclusion list for SAP HANA in the DDIC (see Chapter 3, Section 3.2.1). In principle, additional indexes should only be created if the access times are insufficient without an index. In this case, an index should be created for the selective conditions, provided these aren't already covered by the primary index.

[+]   **SAP Note for Analyzing and Creating Column Store Indexes**

SAP Note 1794297 describes a method recommended by SAP for analyzing and creating indexes in column store tables. The note also provides the necessary programs for analyzing and creating the indexes. We recommend you use this method when creating additional secondary indexes.

Summary and Significance for SAP HANA

A consistent application of this fourth rule for classic databases leads to reduced I/O effort, optimizes memory consumption in the cache, reduces CPU consumption, and optimizes the network transfer because less data is transferred.

[»]   **Significance of Rule #4 for SAP HANA**

The fourth rule changes in SAP HANA, and its observance has a lower priority because no index at all is required in SAP HANA in many cases. If an index is required for very large tables, the rules for the index definition change. In these cases, the CPU consumption is reduced by the index.

In SAP HANA, indexes are usually created for individual columns. Indexes that span multiple columns are the exception. The Code Inspector supports you here with the ANALYSIS OF THE WHERE CONDITION check.

14.4.5 Rule 5: Reducing the Load on the Database

The fifth rule summarizes the aforementioned rules and recommends reducing the load on the database wherever possible. The database is a central resource in the SAP system. For this reason, you should keep the load for repeated operations on the database as small as possible. We'll describe some measures that contribute to reducing the load on the database:

- Using buffers
- Sorting
- Avoiding identical accesses

Using Buffers

Because the data for SAP HANA are stored in the main memory, you may have wondered whether the buffers on the application server or in programs are still required. The following cross-user buffers are available on the application server:

Cross-user buffer

- Shared objects
- Shared buffer
- Shared memory
- Table buffer

The following user-specific buffers are also available within a user session:

User-specific buffers

- SAP memory
- ABAP memory
- Program-specific buffering in internal tables

The most important properties of this buffer are summarized in Table 14.5.

Cross-User Buffering				
	Table Buffer	**Shared Objects**	**Shared Memory**	**Shared Buffer**
Possible Purpose	Simple table data	Complex data, object nets	Extracts, metadata	Extracts, metadata
Copy-Free Access	No	Yes	No	No
Compression	No	No	Optional	Optional
Synchronization	Yes	No	No	No
Displacement	Yes	No	No	Yes
ABAP Statement	Open SQL	Methods of the `cl_shm_area` class	▸ EXPORT TO SHARED MEMORY ▸ IMPORT FROM SHARED MEMORY ▸ DELETE FROM SHARED MEMORY	▸ EXPORT TO SHARED BUFFER ▸ IMPORT FROM SHARED BUFFER ▸ DELETE FROM SHARED BUFFER

User-Specific Buffering			
	Internal Tables	**ABAP Memory**	**SAP Memory**
Possible Purpose	Smaller amounts of master data	Extracts, metadata	Parameter
Copy-Free Access	Yes, if implemented appropriately	No	No
Compression	Yes, if implemented appropriately	Optional	No
ABAP Statement	Statements for internal tables (READ, LOOP, etc.)	▸ EXPORT TO MEMORY ID ▸ IMPORT FROM MEMORY ID ▸ DELETE FROM MEMORY ID	▸ SET PARAMETER ID ▸ GET PARAMETER ID

Table 14.5 Properties of Cross-User and User-Specific Buffers

There are no changes to the recommendations for buffering data when using SAP HANA. Accessing the buffer on the application server is still faster than accessing the database also for SAP HANA. This is because, among other things, the main memory in the application server is on the same server on which the ABAP program is running. For the main memory in the database, however, a network is located between the application server and the database. In addition, several software layers are involved in accessing the database. We'll highlight the table buffer in particular because it's one of the most important buffers.

Accessing the table buffer is approximately 10 times faster than accessing data in the database. Tables that are frequently read, rarely changed, and aren't too big should be buffered. When doing so, you should consider the following:

Table buffer

▸ Due to the synchronization between the application servers, there may be a delay in the availability of the changed data for other users. This must be acceptable from the application perspective. Thus, tables where the latest level is always required shouldn't be buffered.

▸ Tables that are frequently changed (> 0.1% to 1% of all accesses), shouldn't be buffered because performance tends to deteriorate rather than improve due to the synchronization effort and reloading.

▸ A buffered table should only occupy a small percentage (up to 5%) of the table buffer.

▸ In SAP NetWeaver 7.4, both primary and secondary keys are used efficiently in the table buffer for the search. In earlier releases, this was true only for the primary key, and accesses via the secondary key weren't optimized.

When accessing buffered tables, you must ensure that the SQL statements can use the buffer. Accesses pass the table buffer if the WHERE condition applies to more than one buffer object. Thus, all fields of the generic key must be specified for generically buffered tables, and all fields of the primary key must be specified for single-record buffered tables. In addition, a number of statements still read past the buffer:

Accesses that read past the buffer

▸ Accesses with the BYPASSING BUFFER addition

▸ Accesses with IN lists in key fields that contain more than one element

▸ Accesses with the FOR UPDATE addition in the SELECT clause

▸ Accesses with aggregate functions

▸ Accesses with the DISTINCT addition

- ▶ Accesses with the IS NULL operator

- ▶ Accesses with subqueries

- ▶ Accesses with ORDER BY (except for ORDER BY PRIMARY KEY)

- ▶ Accesses with JOIN

- ▶ Accesses with the CLIENT SPECIFIED addition if the client isn't specified

- ▶ Accesses that were written in Native SQL

- ▶ Accesses that are executed after calling the DB_SET_ISOLATION_LEVEL function module (see SAP Note 1376858)

The Code Inspector helps you search for such statements with the check SELECT STATEMENTS THAT BYPASS THE BUFFER.

Other buffers The rules remain the same for the other buffers (e.g., shared objects, shared memory, shared buffer, internal tables, ABAP memory, and SAP memory). This means you should continue to store in such buffers any data that are time-consuming to obtain or calculate and any data used more than once. This will relieve the database of repeated costly queries. These include, for example, the results of analytic views or database procedures that you've created using code pushdown.

If you need the results several times in the application context, it's better just to read the data once from the database and then to buffer it in the application server. The buffers you choose will depend on whether the data are required across multiple users or only within an application. You'll find the most important properties of the various buffers in Table 14.5 at the beginning of this section. Through this, you can relieve the database of unnecessary multiple accesses that are repeated with the same parameters.

Sorting to Improve Performance

Sorting in database or application server In Section 14.1.4, we discussed the functional aspects of sorting for the database migration. The question remained open as to whether you should sort in the database or in the ABAP program. The rules haven't changed here. If the sorting in the database can't be mapped via an index that is used for the selection, you should sort in the ABAP AS—

especially if the total dataset to be sorted is required by the application. If, however, the sorting of a large dataset is required to calculate a smaller result (e.g., determining the five best customers in relation to order value), the sorting should be left to the database. If the sorting is part of the calculation or can be performed cost-effectively in the database, it should also take place in the database.

Avoiding Identical Accesses

Another measure is avoiding identical accesses—that is, you should avoid the multiple reading of identical data. This not only reduces the number of accesses to the database (see golden rule #3) but also avoids unnecessary loads on the database. Usually, internal tables or even buffers are used to avoid identical accesses.

Summary and Significance for SAP HANA

A consistent application of this fifth rule for classic databases leads to reduced CPU consumption and to a reduced load on the network. The I/O effort may also be reduced by avoiding multiple accesses.

Also with SAP HANA, the buffers on the application server continue to be justified because they offer faster access times and can relieve the database of unnecessary accesses. This means, for example, that you can execute complex calculations via code pushdown in the database on SAP HANA, but you only call these calculations as often as necessary. If a result has to be queried multiple times, it should be stored in a buffer.

Buffering calculations called frequently

Significance of Rule #5 for SAP HANA **[«]**

The central strength of SAP HANA lies in the execution of complex calculations on large datasets. You should execute such calculations in the database. However, it doesn't make sense to always send the same calculations or accesses to the same data to the database. For this reason, you can formulate the fifth rule for SAP HANA as follows: Relieve the database of unnecessary accesses. Thus formulated, this rule applies unchanged and with the same priority to SAP HANA because CPU and network resources can be relieved here, too.

> The buffering rules also remain unchanged when using SAP HANA. All buffers continue to be used in those places where the database can be relieved from repeated accesses. Sortings can also provide relief if they are executed on the application server, where this is useful. Identical requests should always be avoided to relieve the database.

14.4.6 Summary of Rules

Same rules, changed priorities

As you've seen in the previous sections, most golden rules for database programming also apply to SAP HANA. Only a few priorities change. Therefore, the number of accesses to the database is more important for SAP HANA than it is in classic databases. Thus, rule #3 has a higher priority. On the other hand, indexes are required on SAP HANA only under certain circumstances, so rule #4 has a lower priority. To sum up, observing the golden rules means fewer adjustments to ABAP programs for performance optimization.

14.5 Performance Recommendations for Native Implementations in SAP HANA

Now that we've discussed performance recommendations for working with Open SQL, we'll provide some recommendations for working with Native SQL, modeled and implemented SAP HANA views, and SQLScript.

14.5.1 Recommendations for Native SQL

In connection with the use of Native SQL via ADBC, we'll refer—in addition to the recommendations for Open SQL, which apply in the same way as Native SQL—to two topics separately. This involves the use of prepared statements and mass operations. We've presented both in Chapter 3, Section 3.2.4, so we only want to discuss the performance aspects here. For the topics presented here (and for others), there is an example in the INSERT_ROWS and INSERT_ITAB subroutines in ABAP test Program ADBC_DEMO, which is provided with the standard SAP.

Prepared Statements

Unlike Open SQL, which is optimized for performance by the SAP Kernel, the programmer must ensure optimal use when using Native SQL via ADBC. If the `CL_SQL_STATEMENT` class is used, this involves a dynamic statement that is transferred to the database for each execution with the `EXECUTE_QUERY` method, which analyzes the SQL statement in turn as a character string. The parameters are included in the analysis. The following two SQL statements are thus different for the database because two different character strings are involved:

```
SELECT * FROM scarr WHERE carrid = 'AA';
SELECT * FROM scarr WHERE carrid = 'UA';
```

For each of these two statements, the database must perform, among other things, the following steps:

▶ Parse the statement (e.g., for the syntax).

▶ Reserve memory for the statement and the execution plan.

▶ Create the execution plan and store it in the SQL cache.

These steps are known as the *prepare phase* because the statement for execution is prepared here. If a very large number of SQL statements is sent to the database, which differ only in the parameters that are used, the database has to make a relatively large effort in preparing each statement. The time required can lie in the mid-three-digit microsecond range and thus may be as high as the time required for actually executing the statement. Frequent executions therefore quickly involve additional effort, which can constitute a significant part of the runtime.

Prepare phase

If only the parameters of an SQL statement change, the statement can be transferred to the database using the `CL_PREPARED_STATEMENT` class with a *parameter marker*. The transferred statement looks, for example, as follows:

Advantage of prepared statements

```
SELECT * FROM scarr WHERE carrid = ?;
```

This statement is prepared once only and is stored in the SQL cache. Immediately before execution, the parameters that were set with the `SET_PARAM` method are used instead of the parameter marker when you call the `EXECUTE_QUERY` method of the `CL_PREPARED_STATEMENT` class. That means you can reduce the effort in preparing the SQL statements to the bare minimum. After you no longer require the prepared SQL statement, you should use the CLOSE method to close the CL_PREPARED_STATEMENT class, so you can release the resources required by the SQL statement as soon as possible.

You should use the CL_SQL_STATEMENT class to execute statements that are executed only once. For SQL statements that you want to execute several times, you should use the CL_PREPARED_STATEMENT class and pass the different parameters separately. That helps keep the effort in preparing SQL statements as low as possible and contributes to relieving the database.

Mass Operations

As of SAP NetWeaver AS ABAP 7.4, an array interface is available for modifying SQL statements via ADBC. You can add, for example, multiple rows at once, and you don't have to proceed row by row. Because a reduced number of statements has a positive effect on the performance of an application, we recommend that you use this option not only for read accesses but also for write accesses. As discussed in Section 14.1.6, however, you should modify data via the ADBC interface only in exceptional situations.

14.5.2 Recommendations for SAP HANA Views

Chapter 4 introduced you to various view types. When modeling and implementing SAP HANA views, you can make certain errors that have a particularly adverse effect on performance. We'll provide a few basic recommendations for modeling SAP HANA views.

Selecting the Correct View Type

First, it's incredibly important to select the correct view type when modeling in SAP HANA Studio. Your options are shown in Figure 14.3, which is derived from the SAP HANA SQLScript Reference that supports you in decision making.

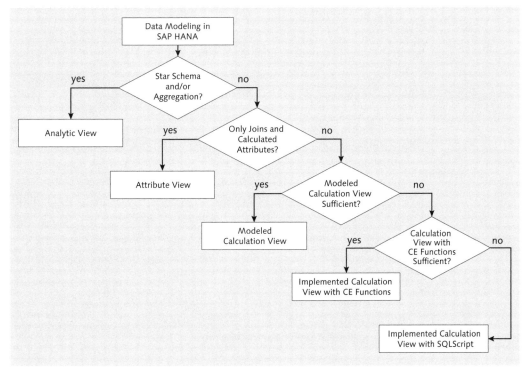

Figure 14.3 Selecting the View Type in SAP HANA

When selecting the view type, you should first check whether you need a star schema to map a given requirement and/or want to aggregate a large number of data records. If this is the case, we recommend that you use an analytic view. Otherwise, you can first use an attribute view. An attribute view allows you to relate multiple tables to each other using joins. If necessary, you can also define calculated fields.

Analytic and attribute views

If you can't map a given requirement through an analytic view nor an attribute view, use a calculation view. You can use a modeled calculation view if you want to use only the operations JOIN, PROJECTION, AGGREGA-TION, and UNION. Otherwise, you must implement the calculation view and either use only calculation engine (CE) functions or rely on the additional options of SQLScript.

Calculation views

585

Modeling/Implementation

In addition to selecting the correct view type, you should consider some other recommendations for modeling and implementing SAP HANA views to achieve optimum performance.

Combination of several views
You very often need several SAP HANA views (see Figure 14.4) to solve a given requirement, as in the following situation:

- You aggregate various key figures with different analytic views (e.g., an analytic view based on table SFLIGHT and a second analytic view based on table SBOOK; the first analytic view determines the load, while the second determines the sum of baggage weights per flight connection).

- You then combine the interim results of the analytic views for the final result (by using the UNION operation within a calculation view).

- Finally, you can enrich the final result with additional master data (e.g., by using the JOIN operation and an attribute view based on table SPFLI within the calculation view to read the master data of the flight connections).

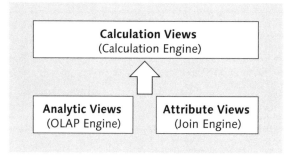

Figure 14.4 Combination of SAP HANA Views

In such a case, several engines (see Chapter 1, Section 1.3) are involved in calculating the final result. This is illustrated schematically in Figure 14.4.

Important rules for SAP HANA views
You can support the engine involved in solving a given task by following some rules:

▶ **Keeping datasets small**
As when using Open SQL within ABAP applications, we recommend that you minimize the dataset that is read *and* exchanged between the engines for modeling SAP HANA views. You achieve this by filtering data as soon as possible (by defining a suitable filter or WHERE conditions) and aggregating (especially via analytic views). In addition, you should read only the columns that are actually required.

▶ **Aggregating data as soon as possible and performing calculations on aggregated data**
By aggregating data as soon as possible and performing calculations on aggregated data, you achieve two things: First, you reduce the dataset for further processing and thus also the dataset, which must, for example, be transferred from the OLAP engine to the Calculation Engine. Secondly, you minimize the number of calculations under certain circumstances (e.g., for currency conversions).

▶ **Avoiding complex joins**
Avoid complex joins, that is, long concatenations of JOIN operations and joins between very large database tables. These can be very expensive. Alternatively, in some cases, you can first aggregate key figures from different fact tables independently of each other via different analytic views, and then combine the interim results via the UNION operation.

▶ **Reading master data as late as possible**
Read master data as late as possible, if it isn't required for the previous calculation steps.

▶ **Following recommendations for SQLScript**
When using implemented calculation views, also note the following recommendations for SQLScript.

14.5.3 Recommendations for SQLScript

If you have to use SQLScript to implement a requirement (because the requirement can't be mapped by modeling an SAP HANA view), note the following rules (already discussed to some extent in Chapter 4, Section 4.2):

Important rules for SQLScript

- **Minimizing complexity of SQL statements**
  You can break down complex SQL statements using table variables. This makes it easier for you to read the code and also facilitates the work of the SAP HANA database optimizer. It makes it easier in some cases, for example, by decomposing complex database queries, to identify redundant subqueries and to avoid calculating them several times.

- **Avoiding dependency of SQL statements**
  As described in Chapter 4, multiple SQL statements within a database procedure or a calculation view are executed in parallel by the database as often as possible. However, this assumes that these statements are independent of each other. Thus, avoid *unnecessary* dependencies between SQL statements.

- **Avoiding usage of CE functions**
  As we've already mentioned in Chapter 4, Section 4.2.2, it's no longer recommended to use CE functions for implementing database procedures, so you should avoid them.

- **Avoiding imperative programming**
  Imperative language elements (especially loops and cursor processing) make the parallelization more difficult or may prevent it completely. Try to work with declarative language elements. For data-intensive calculations, use loops and cursors in particular only if you can't solve a requirement in a different way.

- **Using strengths of OLAP and the join engine**
  If you need SQLScript to implement a requirement, it doesn't necessarily mean that you have to implement the requirement solely with SQLScript. You can often delegate parts of the task within a database procedure or a calculation view to analytic views and attribute views. Check this option because it allows you to use the strengths of Online Application Processing (OLAP) and the join engine.

- **Avoiding dynamic SQL**
  The optimization options of dynamic SQL are restricted. Dynamic SQL must be recompiled for each call under certain circumstances. Avoid dynamic SQL where it isn't necessarily required.

▶ **Using ABAP database procedures systematically**
If you use ABAP database procedures, you should ensure that you only call further ABAP database procedures in your SQLScript code. Only then can you benefit from ABAP Lifecycle Management.

For more information, refer to SAP HANA SQLScript Reference in the SAP online help.

14.6 Summary of Recommendations

At the end of this chapter (and the book), we again compile the five main recommendations for successful ABAP development on SAP HANA in a more concentrated and striking form:

▶ **Tip 1: Don't see the database as a black box.**
Our first recommendation is more theoretical and involves the interaction between application server and database. You should no longer see the database as a pure black box that provides only the basic create, read, update, delete (CRUD) functions for you as a developer. Instead, it provides a rich platform that offers a variety of services. There are various channels for using these services, of which SQL is the most important. For this reason, the SQL knowledge and related database programming concepts, which you've acquired within this book, are very important.

Another change from the past is that the database platform is no longer used solely by an ABAP system but also by other users such as SAP BusinessObjects Business Intelligence tools or the SAP HANA XS Engine.

▶ **Tip 2: Perform performance optimizations as much as possible with standard tools.**
For an optimization, we always recommend that you proceed gradually. After an analysis of the status quo, the optimization potential of Open SQL, CDS views, and standard ABAP programming (and standard ABAP components) should be used in the first step. Ideally, you can already change the ABAP code in this step so that further potential optimization of database accesses can be easily performed by a native

implementation. For a native implementation, you should choose ABAP database procedures over SAP HANA database procedures.

The performance recommendations for Open SQL in ABAP don't change fundamentally on SAP HANA but are mainly weighted differently (see Section 14.4). Familiarize yourself with the rules and the new tools for performance analyses.

▶ **Tip 3: Encapsulation and testing are essential for implementations in the database.**
If you can't solve a requirement (whether in terms of performance or functions) with standard tools, use SAP HANA-specific functions. Bear in mind that a clean encapsulation and good test coverage are important, especially for implementations near the database. Define appropriate test cases, provide appropriate test data, and run automated tests if possible to make sure that the system still responds correctly, even after an adjustment is made to an SAP HANA view or a database procedure.

▶ **Tip 4: Maintainability, correctness, and robustness are ultimately more important than optimal performance.**
The relocating of application code from the application layer to the database layer provides a lot of potential. However, it may also increase the complexity of ABAP programs—for example, if you also have to reserve an implementation for traditional databases in addition to the optimized implementation of a program for SAP HANA. In addition, the result of a program can change due to the relocation of the application code in the database, if you're not careful (see Section 14.1.3). Always ensure that the data are handled correctly from a business perspective.

We recommend that you not relocate application code unnecessarily in SAP HANA views and database procedures. Only do so where there is a real benefit in terms of performance and functions. Not every ABAP program is performance-critical and must provide a result within a fraction of a second.

▶ **Tip 5: Recognize new opportunities and application patterns beyond performance optimizations.**
Consider SAP HANA as more than a technology to accelerate programs. Particularly in the third part of this book, you encountered a

number of techniques through which you can gain new insights from existing databases. OLTP and OLAP become blurred due to the possibilities of SAP HANA, and new application patterns emerge. These sometimes allow companies to achieve far more than just performance improvements—they can develop new business models and differentiate themselves from competitors.

The opening of the ABAP programming model with regard to SAP HANA's native database technologies is a major step that will create new opportunities for ABAP developments together with further innovations in SAP HANA. We hope that the recommendations in this book have made it easier for you to get the maximum out of the SAP HANA platform within ABAP developments or enhancements.

Opening of the ABAP programming model

Appendices

A Flight Data Model

In this book, we use the SAP NetWeaver flight data model as our data basis (with some slight extensions). Therefore, information about the structure of the flight data model is provided in this appendix as reference material.

The flight data model, often known as the SFLIGHT model, is a simple example of classic application development using SAP NetWeaver AS ABAP. It also provides the basis for numerous specialist books, training courses, and documentation relating to SAP software. Essentially, the data model comprises a set of database tables. An understanding of these tables and their content is helpful to understand the examples in this book. As an ABAP developer, you've almost certainly worked with the SFLIGHT model at some time or another. Therefore, we'll focus our attention on the relationships that exist between the tables used in this book.

First, we'll briefly outline the simple underlying business process. Then, we'll explain the structure of and relationships between the most important database tables used in this book. Finally, we'll discuss the various options associated with generating mass data.

A.1 Basic Principles of the Flight Data Model

The flight data model can be used to simulate various business scenarios within the context of bookings for scheduled flights. Essentially, two scenarios are considered here:

Scenarios

▸ **Operating an airline**
An airline operator sells tickets either directly to customers or through a travel agent. The system contains only data relating to this airline, albeit for all bookings.

▸ **Simulating a travel agency**
A travel agency sells tickets on behalf of multiple airlines. The system contains the complete flight schedule. Furthermore, bookings for all

595

flights can be made here. This scenario is based on the assumption that the system contains the latest booking information from the airlines so that the number of seats available on a flight is always known locally. Only bookings made through a travel agent are held in the system.

The flight data model is fully presented and documented in the *Data Modeler* (Transaction SD11) for the BC_TRAVEL model. In addition to individual flights, this model also makes it possible to combine multiple flights (e.g., flights with stops en route). However, this variant is beyond the scope of this book.

A.2   Database Tables for the Flight Data Model

There are approximately 25 database tables for business data that relate to the flight data model. Standard configurations and Customizing also play a role (e.g., the client configuration, customizing for currencies, etc.). These are stored in additional tables.

In this section, we'll discuss the structure of and relationships between approximately 10 tables used in this book. We'll classify these tables on the basis of Customizing, master data, and transaction data. After we've introduced you to the main tables associated with the SFLIGHT model and their role within the business scenario, we'll discuss some general design decisions in relation to the data model and evaluate them in the context of SAP HANA.

A.2.1   Customizing

Settings for ABAP AS   The flight data model uses the following settings for ABAP AS:

- The client configuration, which is stored in table T000 and is used as a check table for the client field associated with other tables.

- Customizing for currencies and conversion variants, which are stored in tables TCURR and TCURX. At this point, we must mention that for training purposes, the flight data model uses a separate currency-conversion variant based on tables SCURR and SCURX. Because particularly

Chapter 4 uses the standard variant, we won't discuss the special variant of the flight data model. Instead, we'll implicitly assume that the data (e.g., the currencies available) are identical.

► Customizing for units of measure (lengths, weights, etc.) from table T006.

A.2.2 Master Data

In this book, we use the SFLIGHT model master data listed in Table A.1.

Table	Description	Important Content
SCARR	Airlines	Airline code and name
SPFLI	Flight schedule	Flight connection with information about the origin/destination as well as the flight duration
SAIRPORT	Airports	Airport names and time zones
SGEOCITY	Cities	Cities, including their geographical data (longitude and latitude)
SCUSTOM	Customer data	Name, address, email address, and authorized price reduction
SAPLANE	Aircraft	Information about the number of seats available, as well as aircraft usage and speed

Table A.1 Master Data for the Flight Data Model

Because this book primarily considers the scenario involving a travel agent who sells tickets directly to customers, we won't use the tables for configuring different travel agents (e.g., table STRAVELAG) and business partners (e.g., table SBUSPART), which would be important in the scenario that simulates operating an airline.

From a master data perspective, important relationships exist among the flight schedule, the airlines, the airports, and the cities. Figure A.1 shows the relevant tables and foreign key relationships in the form of an attribute view in SAP HANA Studio.

The other two tables—SCUSTOM and SAPLANE—have, above all, connections to the transaction data, which we'll show in the next section as dimensions of a star schema.

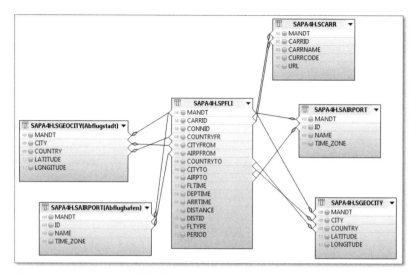

Figure A.1 Master Data Tables for the Flight Schedule in the SFLIGHT Model

A.2.3   Transaction Data

The flight data model primarily has two tables that contain transaction data: the flight bookings table (SBOOK) and the flights table (SFLIGHT). Table A.2 summarizes the contents of each. In certain respects, table SFLIGHT plays a dual role here. On one hand, it contains transaction data because it represents an actual flight. On the other hand, it can also be regarded as a dimension of the bookings.

Table	Description	Important Content
SFLIGHT	Flights	Information about a specific flight (flight connection, time, and seats occupied) **Key performance indicators:** ▸ Flight price ▸ Seats occupied/available
SBOOK	Flight bookings	Information about a flight booking in relation to passenger information **Key performance indicators:** ▸ Booking price ▸ Luggage weight

Table A.2 Transaction Data in the Flight Data Model

The business logic for creating transaction data is relatively simple. For a   **Business logic**
flight booking for a customer, both the flight and the customer must
exist in the system. Then, before making a flight booking, a check is performed to determine whether any seats are available, and, if so, the
number of seats available is reduced over the course of the transaction.
The booking price is also calculated from the passenger discount and the
previously configured flight price. This logic is encapsulated in a Business Application Programming Interface (BAPI) (`FlightBooking` business object) and can be called within function modules.

At this point, we won't discuss the transaction logic in any further detail.
Instead, we'll consider how it interacts with the master data. The cardinality of the transaction data (❶ in Figure A.2) with respect to the master
data is n:1 because the master data is used in different transactions (each
booking ❷ for a flight ❸ involves a customer ❹ who can make multiple
bookings). Figure A.2 shows a section of the data model in which the
additional master data associated with a flight schedule in ❺ (previously
in Figure A.1) aren't shown again.

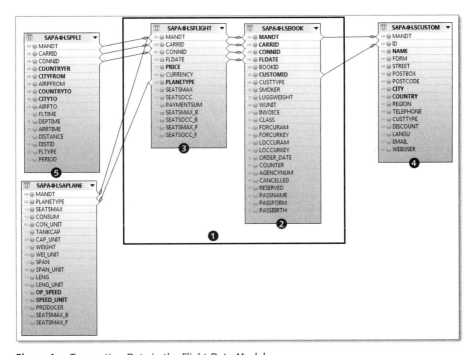

Figure A.2 Transaction Data in the Flight Data Model

The attribute view model shown here is a simple, graphical representation of the relationships between the tables. When analyzing the transaction data in real life, it's better to use an analytic view in SAP HANA.

A.2.4   Designing the SFLIGHT Data Model

In this section, we'll discuss some design considerations associated with the SFLIGHT data model. It's obvious that the tables used here were developed prior to SAP HANA, which is the case with most tables in an SAP system. Next, we'll discuss the technical structure of the tables (primary and foreign keys, data types, indexes, and normalization), along with the semantics of their contents.

Table structure

Technical modeling of the SFLIGHT tables is typical of SAP R/3. This includes the following structural characteristics:

- Tables generally have a set of character-like key fields. No *Globally Unique Identifiers* (GUID) are used as generated, technical keys. Foreign key relationships therefore comprise multiple conditions (refer to Figure A.1 and Figure A.2).

- A date is recorded in the date and time fields (DATS, TIMS). Time stamps aren't used (TIMESTAMP and TIMSTAMPL data elements).

- Some numeric fields are recorded as a character-like field (NUMC) to ensure that the display is formatted consistently (including leading zeros). One example of this is the customer number in table SCUSTOM.

- The model isn't completely normalized. In other words, the tables contain certain redundancies. In particular, this is a direct consequence of avoiding technical keys. For example, a flight is defined using three attributes (CARRID, CONNID, and FLDATE), which also exist in other tables.

Newer SAP Business Suite modules have pursued other approaches. Interestingly, however, the aforementioned structural characteristics are also well-suited to the SAP HANA architecture. On the other hand, GUIDs, which often exist in the database as RAW types, don't have an optimal compression behavior, and the performance of join operations can be negatively impacted. In the SFLIGHT data model, however, there are also some design decisions that are unreservedly not recommended for new developments within the context of SAP HANA.

For example, some calculated values are materialized as physical columns. The booking price, for example, is stored twice in table SBOOK—once in the airline currency and once in the local currency. Such a field can also be recorded as a calculated field within a view. You learned about this in Chapter 4, Section 4.4.1. Furthermore, numerical values that potentially play a role for calculations shouldn't be modeled as character strings (NUMC) because the database can't differentiate between these and other texts. The DISCOUNT value in table SCUSTOM is one such example.

Table content

A.3 Data Generation

To become familiar with the opportunities presented by SAP HANA, you should always work with large volumes of data. Even though the SAP NetWeaver flight data model is a very simple data model, there are, in reality, extremely large volumes of data in the underlying business scenario. In 2011, for example, approximately 56 million flight passengers passed through Frankfurt Airport (source: The Statistics Office for the State of Hesse).In 2014, for example, the Federal Aviation Authority found that approximately 46.5 million flight passengers enplaned at Hartsfield-Jackson Atlanta International Airport.

To have a large volume of data available during training, the development of a prototype (or any productive development) tools for data generation are often used. These tools help to generate a consistent and realistic volume of records for a data model. ABAP Report SAPBC_DATA_GENERATOR is available in the flight data model for this purpose. At present, however, it can't generate data volumes of arbitrary size (e.g., the number of bookings is currently limited to a maximum of 1.4 million).

Data generator

Therefore, for this book, we developed a data generator that was suitable for our examples—namely, ABAP Report ZR_A4H_BOOK_GENERATE_MASS_DATA. It draws on data generated by ABAP Report SAPBC_

Mass data

DATA_GENERATOR and generates additional flights and flight bookings. In other words, you must call this ABAP report first. At present, our data generator works as follows:

- In the first step, the data generator deletes the flights and flight bookings generated by ABAP Report SAPBC_DATA_GENERATOR.

- It then generates flights (i.e., entries in database table SFLIGHT). For each connection (each entry in database table SPFLI), the program generates one flight for each day that falls within the dates entered on the selection screen. Flight capacity fluctuates between 70% and 100%. In some months (e.g., during the Christmas period), a higher average capacity is assumed than in other months. During these months, the flight price is also higher than in other months.

- Finally, the program generates the flight bookings in database table SBOOK and uses a random algorithm to determine the customers and travel agencies associated with the bookings. The data generator determines the booking date on the basis of three hard-coded distribution functions that are selected at random for each flight. There is a maximum of 180 days before the flight date.

ABAP Report ZR_A4H_BOOK_GENERATE_MASS_DATA generates, on average, approximately 3 million bookings each year. Therefore, if you schedule the program for a period of 10 years, you obtain a volume of data that equates to approximately 30 million bookings. Because these are distributed across approximately 4,500 customer master records, many more bookings are accepted here for individual customers than would be the case in reality. However, this isn't a problem for our examples. For more information about generating data, see Appendix E.

B Enhancements to the ABAP Programming Language (as of SAP NetWeaver 7.4)

Since SAP NetWeaver 7.4, a number of compatible enhancements have been made to the ABAP programming language. Thanks to a greater orientation toward expressions, these enhancements enable you to write shorter, more legible ABAP code.

In the context of ABAP development on SAP HANA, the options associated with expressions make it possible to reduce ABAP code to the essential intention. The code pushdown paradigm discussed in this book can be used to perform calculations within the database, and (by using the components contained in the ABAP AS) the application can be orchestrated using considerably less application code.

In this appendix, we'll briefly introduce some ABAP language features that are used throughout this book. For comprehensive information, refer to the ABAP language documentation (see *http://help.sap.com/abapdocu_740/en/*).

B.1 Inline Declarations

Previously in ABAP, you always had to use a DATA statement to declare variables before you could use them. Furthermore, you always had to specify the data type—even if, during an assignment, this was canonical from the context. Let's take a look at the example in Listing B.1.

Variables

```
" Data declaration without inline declaration
DATA: lo_alv TYPE REF TO cl_salv_table,
      lo_exc TYPE REF TO cx_salv_msg.

TRY.
    " Generate table ALV in factory
    cl_salv_table=>factory(
      IMPORTING r_salv_table = lo_alv
      CHANGING t_table = lt_data ).
```

```
    " Display ALV
    lo_alv->display( ).
  CATCH cx_salv_msg INTO lo_exc.
    MESSAGE lo_exc TYPE 'I' DISPLAY LIKE 'E'.
ENDTRY.
```
Listing B.1 Classic Example without Inline Declaration

To define the corresponding variables, you have to know or find out the names of the CL_SALV_TABLE and CX_SALV_MSG classes.

DATA() statement With an inline declaration using the DATA() statement, you can make an implicit declaration and specify a type for a variable directly (inline) during the assignment. Listing B.2 demonstrates this using the same example.

```
" Data declaration with inline declaration
TRY.
    " Generate table ALV in factory
    cl_salv_table=>factory(
      IMPORTING r_salv_table = DATA(lo_alv_inline)
      CHANGING t_table       = lt_data ).

    " Display ALV
    lo_alv_inline->display( ).
  CATCH cx_salv_msg INTO DATA(lo_exc_inline).
    MESSAGE lo_exc_inline TYPE 'I' DISPLAY LIKE 'E'.
ENDTRY.
```
Listing B.2 Example with Inline Declaration

Here, the variables for the SAP List Viewer (ALV) table and the CX_SALV_MSG exception in the CATCH block are defined directly (*inline*) during the assignment. Inline declarations can be used not only for classes and interfaces but also for structures, table types, data references, and so on.

Field symbols It's also possible to declare field symbols inline, as shown in Listing B.3.

```
LOOP AT lt_data ASSIGNING FIELD-SYMBOL(<line>).
  " ...
ENDLOOP.
```
Listing B.3 Inline Declaration of a Field Symbol

When using inline declarations, you must consider the following:

▸ Inline declarations don't change the *scope* of ABAP variables. Therefore, it's not possible to use the same variable name multiple times within a method, even if you seem to define it locally—as is the case with the `lo_exc_inline` variable in Listing B.2, for example.

We recommend that you continue to define, at the very start of a method implementation, variables that you want to use in several places within an extensive method. Inline declaration is useful for variables with a local, limited usage context (e.g., the loop in Listing B.3).

▸ Inline declarations can't be used in all situations. In particular, it's not possible yet to use an inline declaration to define the result of a `SELECT` statement (`INTO`, `INTO TABLE`).

B.2 Constructor Expressions

Constructor expressions enable you to create and initialize ABAP objects, data structures, and data references by means of an expression. The benefit of such expressions lies in the reduction of statements needed, as well as compatibility with inline declarations.

Traditionally, ABAP objects can be created using the following statement:

```
CREATE OBJECT <variable> [ TYPE <type> ].
```

Of course, the variable must be declared beforehand and adjusted to the   **NEW operator**
instantiation. When we introduced you to inline declaration in the previous section, you may have asked yourself whether it can be used in connection with creating an object instance. This can be done using the `NEW` operator, which enables you to declare an object instance directly inline. The parameters for the constructor are transferred when the method is called. For example, the following assignment is possible:

```
DATA(lo_object) = NEW lcl_my_class( iv_param = 1 ).
```

Of course, you can also define the `lo_object` variable separately.

VALUE operator   In addition to objects, you can also use expressions to initialize structures and even internal tables. In this case, the VALUE operator shown in
the example in Listing B.4 is used.

```
DATA: ls_carr TYPE scarr.

" Classic initialization of a structure
ls_carr-carrid   = 'LH'.
ls_carr-carrname = 'Lufthansa'.

" Alternative using the constructor expression
ls_carr = VALUE #( carrid   = 'LH'
                   carrname = 'Lufthansa' ).
```
Listing B.4 Using VALUE to Initialize a Structure

One benefit of the VALUE expression is that it can be combined with an
inline declaration. In this case, however, you must specify the exact data
type:

```
DATA(ls_carr) = VALUE scarr( carrid   = 'LH'
                             carrname = 'Lufthansa').
```

You can also use the VALUE operator to initialize internal tables, as shown
in Listing B.5.

```
DATA: lt_carrier TYPE TABLE OF scarr.
lt_carrier = VALUE #(
    ( carrid = 'AA' carrname = 'American Airlines' )
    ( carrid = 'LH' carrname = 'Lufthansa' ) ).
```
Listing B.5 Using VALUE to Initialize an Internal Table

In this example, it's particularly evident that less code is needed, and
code is more legible, compared to using multiple APPEND statements to
perform a classic initialization of structures or to set up an internal table.

REF operator   The final element we want to mention is the REF operator, which is an
expression-oriented alternative to generating a data reference (TYPE REF
TO DATA) with the GET REFERENCE ABAP statement. The example in Listing
B.6 uses this operator and inline declarations for an ABAP Database Connectivity (ADBC) access (see Listing 3.12 in Chapter 3, Section 3.2.4).

```
TRY.
 " Prepare SQL connection and statement
 DATA(lo_result_set) =
         cl_sql_connection=>get_connection(
```

```
                    )->create_statement(
                    )->execute_query( lv_statement ).

  lo_result_set->set_param_table( REF #( lt_result ) ).

  " Get result
  lo_result_set->next_package( ).
  lo_result_set->close( ).
CATCH cx_sql_exception INTO DATA(lo_exc).
  " Error handling
ENDTRY.
```
Listing B.6 ABAP Expressions in an ADBC Context

In addition to NEW, VALUE, and REF, there are many more operators such as conversions (CONV) or type conversions (CAST). For more information, refer to the documentation at *http://help.sap.com/abapdocu_740/en/*.

When you use constructor expressions, you shouldn't overlook runtime considerations or the elegance of the code. If you require an object in several places, for example, you should not initialize it twice.

Performance considerations

B.3   Internal Tables

Traditionally, READ TABLE statements were used to access the content of internal tables, which facilitated the use of a key or line index to read individual lines.

This can be done using expressions that you assign directly or process further. Listing B.7 shows an example of such use.

Access via an index or key

```
DATA: lt_carrier TYPE TABLE OF scarr WITH KEY carrid.
lt_carrier = VALUE #(
    ( carrid = 'AA' carrname = 'American Airlines' )
    ( carrid = 'LH' carrname = 'Lufthansa' ) ).

" Read first entry from the internal table
DATA(ls_carrier) = lt_carrier[ 1 ].

" Access with a key and use of an
" attribute
DATA(lv_name) = lt_carrier[ carrid = 'LH' ]-carrname.
```
Listing B.7 Expressions for Access to Internal Tables

These expressions also facilitate direct access in the case of multidimensional structures, that is, if an internal table in a column also contains a table.

Performance considerations

As is the case with constructor expressions, you should always bear performance in mind and avoid unnecessary accesses with expressions for internal tables. The following example demonstrates *unfavorable* usage of table expressions because the same line is read multiple times. Instead, you should temporarily store the line in a variable.

```
DATA(lv_carrid)   = lt_carrier[ 1 ]-carrid.
DATA(lv_carrname) = lt_carrier[ 1 ]-carrname.
```

C Read and Write Access in the Column Store

Having some technical background knowledge of the structure of the column store will help you understand the concept of read and write access in SAP HANA. In this appendix, we'll give you some key information about the column store, as well as some background information about processing accesses in the column store. First, we'll examine the concept of accesses without indexes. Then, we'll outline the basic principles of indexes in SAP HANA and explain how to use indexes to optimize accesses.

C.1 Basic Principles

In Chapter 1, Section 1.2.2, you learned that a column in a column store is stored internally in at least two structures: the *dictionary vector* and the *attribute vector*. Figure C.1 shows a sample table that comprises three columns: *ID*, *Name*, and *Gender*. The data stored in this table are contained in Table C.1.

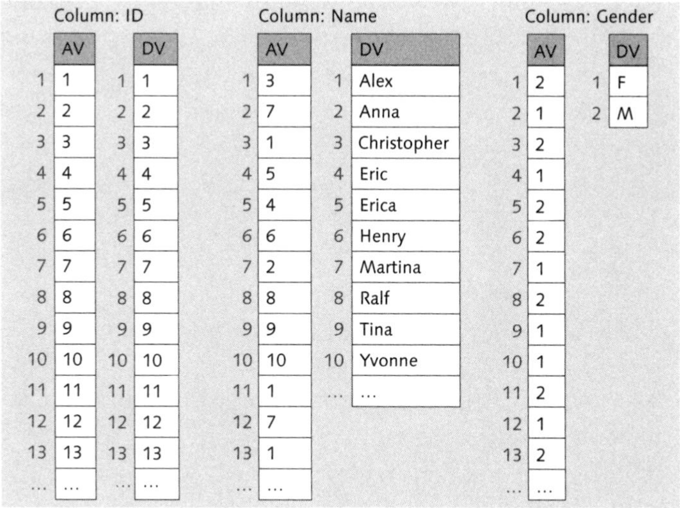

Dictionary and attribute vectors

Figure C.1 Column Store with a Dictionary Vector and Attribute Vector

ID	Name	Gender
1	Christopher	M
2	Martina	F
3	Alex	M
4	Erica	F
5	Eric	M
6	Henry	M
7	Anna	F
8	Ralf	M
9	Tina	F
10	Yvonne	F
11	Alex	M
12	Martina	F
13	Alex	M

Table C.1 Sample Data for this Appendix

Each column has one dictionary vector and one attribute vector. In the dictionary vector, the distinct contents of the column are saved once. The data are held in the dictionary vector in sorted order, thus making it possible to find relevant entries quickly through a binary search. A value is assigned to an entry's position in the dictionary vector, and this value is stored in the attribute vector instead of the actual value. In our example, the name "Martina" occupies seventh position in the dictionary vector. In the attribute vector, the number 7 occupies second and twelfth position because "Martina" is both the second and the twelfth data record in Table C.1's data.

C.2   Read Access without an Index

The dictionary vector and attribute vector make it possible to store data efficiently and therefore process this data quickly. Very little data needs to be transferred from the main memory to the CPU. Consequently, in SAP HANA, indexes aren't required in many cases that previously would have needed them. In this section, we'll explain how a read access in the column store is processed and how the dictionary vectors and attribute vectors are used.

We'll now use an example that illustrates the column store's search function in detail. Figure C.2 shows a table that comprises the following three columns: *ID*, *Name*, and *Gender*. The dictionary and attribute vectors are shown for each column. To make it clearer, we've displayed the row ID for each vector on the left-hand side of the figure. This is implicitly determined by the value's position in the vector. It isn't persisted and doesn't use any memory. Furthermore, no indexes are defined. For the purpose of our example, we'll use the WHERE NAME = 'Alex' condition.

Read access in the column store

1. First, a binary search is performed in the dictionary vector to determine the value for "Alex". Because the dictionary vector has been sorted, an optimized binary search can be used. "Alex" occupies first position in the dictionary vector ❶. Therefore, the value for Alex is "1".

2. The attribute vector is then searched for the value "1" ❷.

3. Then, the row IDs are used to reconstruct the rows for all hits. In other words, in our example, the third, eleventh, and thirteenth entries in the other columns are read ❸.

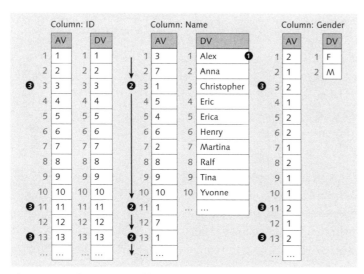

Figure C.2 Column Store Table with Three Columns

Performance

Thanks to data compression, a relatively small volume of data needs to be searched, and the search mainly compares integers. Because you can parallelize the search across multiple CPU cores, the speed is usually sufficient, and an index isn't required. For tables with fewer than half a million entries, there is very little difference between having an index and not having an index. If, on the other hand, the table has hundreds of millions of entries, accessing a highly selective column without an index is slower by a factor of 100 or more compared to accessing it with an index. This factor increases as the table grows in size. If such an access is performed very frequently, as may be the case in an Online Transaction Processing (OLTP) system, for example, an index is vital for good performance.

Main store and delta store

Up to now, we've discussed only the concept of the *main store*, which has been optimized for read accesses (see also Chapter 1, Section 1.2.2). However, data can also be stored in a *delta store*, which is generated by write accesses and optimized for such accesses. In the next section, we'll discuss the differences between the main store and the delta store. We'll also explain how to transfer data from one to another.

C.3 Write Access without an Index

Write accesses in the delta store

Because the dictionary vector in the main store has been sorted, and this data needs to be held in sorted order, it would be very time-consuming to have direct write accesses to the main store. If the name "Adrian" was inserted in the example in Section C.2, all existing values in the dictionary vector have to move one place. Therefore, the value for "Alex" changes from 1 to 2, the value for "Anna" changes from 2 to 3, and so on. Then, the entire attribute vector has to be changed to include the new values.

To prevent this, write accesses are executed in the delta store. As is the case with the main store, good data compression is facilitated by having one dictionary vector and one attribute vector for each column in the delta store. Unlike the main store, however, the dictionary vector in the delta store isn't sorted. As a result, a new value can be inserted quickly by simply appending it to the end of the dictionary vector. However, a binary search can no longer be performed in the dictionary vector. For this reason, each column has a B* tree index that makes it possible to quickly find existing values in the dictionary vector. These structures also make it possible to insert and compress data quickly. A schematic representation of a main store and delta store is provided in Figure C.3. To improve legibility, we've abbreviated the dictionary and attribute vectors and omitted the implicit row IDs for each vector.

All change accesses are processed in the delta store. In the example shown in Figure C.3, the following data records were added to in Table 1.1: "14−Tanya−F" and "15−Tara−F".

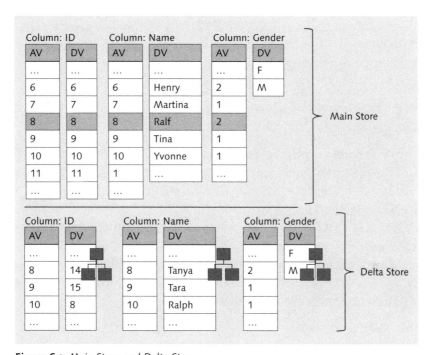

Figure C.3 Main Store and Delta Store

The following change was made to the "8−Ralf−M" data record: "Ralf" was changed to "Ralph." In SAP HANA, such an UPDATE is made using the following sequence: SELECT (to find the old data record and mark it for   **INSERT ONLY** deletion) and `INSERT`. This action is known as `INSERT ONLY` because a change to a data record only ever results in a new version of the data record being inserted. The deletion indicators are managed in another internal structure not shown in Figure C.3. The old version of the data record is deleted later when the merge action is performed.

Read accesses in the delta store While the main store is searched (or afterwards, depending on the complexity of the SQL statement), the delta store must also be searched because data records that correspond to the search request may have been written to the delta store. The delta store has been optimized for write accesses, so searches performed in the delta store are more time-consuming. This is because, for example, the delta store contains an additional memory structure—the B* tree—which references the unsorted dictionary vector. It's therefore desirable to keep the delta store quite small and to transfer it to the main store regularly. This action is known as *merge*.

Merge action generates a new main store When the merge is performed, the data in the delta store is transferred to the main store asynchronously. Old versions of data records are deleted if there are no open transactions for these records.

During the merge process, data from the delta store are incorporated into the main store's dictionary and attribute vectors, so these vectors are reorganized and assigned a new structure. A new main store (Main 2) is generated from the old main store (Main 1) and delta store (Delta 1). Data records that have an open transaction aren't transferred to the new main store but to a new delta store (Delta 2). After the transfer and building of the new main store (Main 2) is complete, the old main store (Main 1) and the old delta store (Delta 1) are rejected. New queries then read from the new main and delta store.

Write accesses in the new delta store This process occurs at the table level. During the merge, the data from the old main store and delta store are transferred to a new main store, and data from the old main store is still readable. However, write accesses occur in the new delta store (Delta 2) while the merge is still running and Delta 1 is being processed. A schematic representation of the merge is shown in Figure C.4.

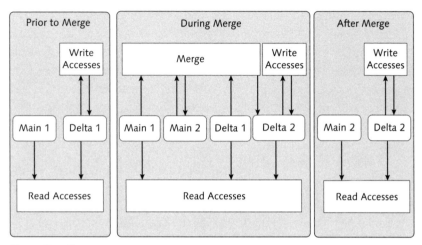

Figure C.4 Merge

You can use different parameters to configure the execution times for merge processes. Such parameters can take into consideration, for example, the size of the delta store, the system load, and the number of entries or the time since the last merge was performed. Therefore, a new main store is created on a regular basis, and changes are bundled together and transferred as efficiently as possible from the delta store to the main store.

Figure C.3 and Figure C.5 in the next section show the dictionary and attribute vectors both before and after the merge.

C.4   Read Accesses with an Index

Now that you've learned about accesses without an index, we'll turn our attention to accesses with an index. As mentioned, read accesses involving very large tables can, despite compression and parallelism, be too slow if these are executed very frequently. In such cases, an index should be created so you won't have to scan the entire column. In SAP HANA, a distinction is made between the following two types of indexes:

▸ **Inverted index**

Inverted indexes refer to only one column. Here, the index data are stored in internal memory structures that belong to the respective column—namely, the index offset vector and the index position vector. For each value in the dictionary vector, the index offset vector stores the position of this value's first occurrence in the index position vector. The index position vector contains the row ID assigned to the data record in the attribute vector. The index position vector is sorted according to the indexed column and uses the row ID to reference the attribute vector.

▸ **Composite index**

Composite indexes refer to more than one column. First, the contents of these columns are grouped together in an internal column, and an inverted index is then created for this internal column.

Let's discuss read accesses for these two index categories.

Inverted index   As an example, we'll create an index for the *Name* column. Because it concerns only one column, we'll create an inverted index as shown in Figure C.5.

Column: ID		Column: Name		Inverted Index: Name		Column: Gender	
AV	DV	AV	DV ❶	IO ❷	IP	AV	DV
1	1	3	Alex	1	3	2	F
2	2	7	Anna	4	11	1	M
❹ 3	3	1	Christopher	5	13	2	
4	4	5	Eric	6	7	1	
5	5	4	Erica	7	1	2	
6	6	6	Henry	8	5	2	
7	7	2	Martina	9	4	1	
8	8	8	Ralph	11	6	2	
9	9	11	Tanya	12	2	1	
10	10	12	Tara	13	12	1	
❹ 11	11	1	Tina	14	8	2	
12	12	7	Yvonne	15	14	1	
❹ 13	13	1	...	...	15	2	
14	14	9			9	1	
15	15	10			12	1	
...	...	...			...	...	

Figure C.5 Inverted Index for the "Name" Field

We'll continue to use the example from the previous sections, namely the WHERE NAME = 'Alex' condition. When there is no index, the entire attribute vector must be searched for the value determined from the dictionary vector.

With an inverted index, however, this is no longer necessary. The search process is then as follows:

❶ First, in the dictionary vector, a binary search is performed to determine the value for "Alex". This concerns the value "1" because "Alex" occupies first position in the dictionary vector.

❷ Then, the index offset vector is checked to see which value occupies first position (and therefore contains information about the first value in the dictionary vector). In this case, the number "1" is stored there, which means that the positions of the value we require are stored in the first position in the index position vector.

❸ Here, you find the following values in succession: "3" (in first position), "11" (in second position), and "13" (in third position). These values are the positions (row IDs) in the attribute vector occupied by "Alex" (the value "1").

❹ The search ends with the fourth entry in the index position vector because position 4 describes the end of the section being searched within the index offset vector. In other words, the value that lies after the value "Alex" in the dictionary vector occupies position 4 in the index position vector. Now, only the required columns from the other attribute vectors need to be read using the predetermined row IDs.

In the next example, we'll create a composite index for the *Gender* and *Name* columns. In this case, an additional column is created in SAP HANA, and the contents of the *Gender* and *Name* columns are stored there together (see Figure C.6). As described earlier, an inverted index is created for this internal column, which isn't visible in the ABAP Data Dictionary (DDIC).

Search process

Composite index

Column: ID		Column: Name		Column: Gender		Concat. Index: Gender, Name			
AV	DV	AV	DV	AV	DV	AV	DV	IO	IP
1	1	3	Alex	2	F	9	fAnna	1	7
2	2	7	Anna	1	M	3	fErica	2	4
3	3	1	Christopher	2		8	fMartina	3	2
4	4	5	Eric	1		2	fTanya	5	12
5	5	4	Erica	2		10	fTara	6	14
6	6	6	Henry	2		11	fTina	7	15
7	7	2	Martina	1		1	fYvonne	8	9
8	8	8	Ralph	2		12	mAlex	9	10
9	9	11	Tanya	1		6	mChristopher	12	3
10	10	12	Tara	1		7	mEric	13	11
11	11	1	Tina	2		8	mHenry	14	13
12	12	7	Yvonne	1		3	mRalph	15	1
13	13	1	...	2		8	..	...	5
14	14	9		1		4			6
15	15	10		1		5			8
...	...	...		...		...			...

Figure C.6 Composite Index for the "Gender" and "Name" Fields

In our example, we'll search the database table using the WHERE GENDER ='W' AND NAME = 'Tina' condition. When there was no index, the entire attribute vector for the *Name* column had to be searched.

Search process   This is no longer necessary. The search process is as follows:

❶ In the dictionary vector for the internal column composed from the *Gender* and *Name* fields, a binary search is performed to determine the position. The required value occupies position 6.

❷ In the index offset vector, the reference to the position in the index position vector (position 7 in our example) is obtained from position 6.

❸ In the index position vector, the reference to the position in the attribute vector (position 9 in our case) is at position 7.

❹ We've now determined row IDs for the attribute vectors whose columns are required for the SELECT.

Write Accesses with an Index [«]

Inverted and composite indexes occur in both the main store and the delta store. As with classic databases, write accesses in the delta store are more labor-intensive because the indexes have to be maintained. For a composite index, write accesses require more time and effort than with an inverted index because composite indexes require that more memory structures be maintained.

D   SAP Business Application Accelerator Powered by SAP HANA

Using the SAP Business Application Accelerator powered by SAP HANA, you can accelerate existing programs by executing specific SQL accesses on SAP HANA without having to change the programs. Because the redirection is done via Customizing, there is no need to change the program itself. This appendix explains how to use the SAP Business Application Accelerator.

SAP Note 1694697 details how to obtain the software, which comprises the SAP Kernel and add-on.

Technical Requirements   [«]

To install the SAP Business Application Accelerator, SAP Kernel Version 7.21 or higher and the SAP Business Application Accelerator add-on SWT2DB are required. For the kernel, check SAP Notes 1713986 and 1716826; for the add-on, read SAP Notes 1694697 and 1597627.

To use the SAP Business Application Accelerator, you'll need an SAP HANA database connected to your SAP system via a secondary connection (side-by-side scenario). SAP Note 1597627 explains how to create a secondary connection.

Tables are also needed on SAP HANA that are replicated by the SAP system that will be used with the SAP Business Application Accelerator. This is usually done via the SAP Landscape Transformation Replication Server (SAP LT Replication Server).

One of the prerequisites for redirecting a program using the SAP Business Application Accelerator is a large database time-share in the program runtime. Only programs reading from the tables that are replicated by the SAP system can be redirected. These are typically programs used in reporting. When reading from replicated tables, note that the data are presented in *near real-time*; that is, there may be smaller delays until the data are replicated. Because it's possible that position data are replicated prior to header data, transactional consistency can't be guaranteed for short periods of time. You should therefore carefully assess which programs are suitable candidates for redirecting access to the data replicated

Programs and accesses for redirection

in SAP HANA. You should then evaluate which accesses would greatly benefit from being redirected to SAP HANA.

To identify programs that are good candidates for redirection, we recommend the *SAP HANA Feasibility Check* (*HFC*) service from SAP Active Global Support (AGS) (also check SAP Note 1694697). Based on the preceding criteria, this service identifies the programs where redirection is possible and useful.

Customizing   In Customizing, you can maintain a *context* for the program to be redirected. This is where entries for the combination of program, background job, and table/view are entered. For example, for each program, you specify the tables for which reading accesses should be redirected. By maintaining a background job, you can also specify whether this should only be done if the program runs in the background. This customizing is evaluated during runtime, and all accesses are redirected accordingly. Figure D.1 illustrates this process.

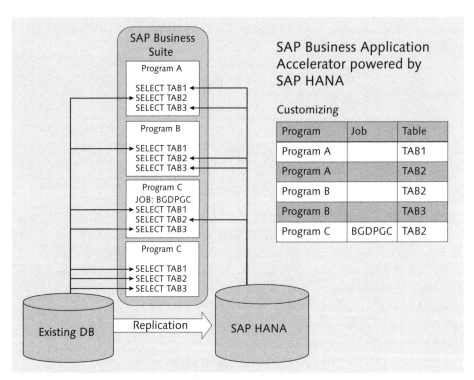

Figure D.1 Redirecting Specific Table Accesses

Redirection can only be done on application servers with the `rsdb/rda =`   **Technical details**
`on` profile parameter set. If this parameter is set, access to the following objects can be redirected:

▸ Transparent tables

▸ Cluster tables (converted into transparent tables during replication)

▸ Database views (if all underlying tables are replicated and the view exists in SAP HANA)

Access to pool tables, table pools (the actual database tables containing the pool tables), and table clusters (the actual database tables containing the cluster tables) can't be redirected.

There are also limitations with regard to the statements that can be redi-   **Limitations**
rected. The following Open SQL statements can be redirected:

▸ `SELECT` statements

▸ `OPEN CURSOR ... FETCH`

However, the following accesses can't be redirected:

▸ `SELECT` statements with the `CONNECTION` addition (secondary connections)

▸ `SELECT ... FOR UPDATE`

▸ `OPEN CURSOR WITH HOLD...`

See SAP Note 1694697 for further details on the customizing of the SAP Business Application Accelerator.

The SAP Business Application Accelerator can be used to accelerate programs where the runtime is dominated by read accesses without having to change the program itself. The extent to which accesses can be accelerated depends on the specific SQL statement. In several projects, customers observed performance increases of 20% to 300% compared to the original performance.

E   Installing the Sample Programs

Together with this book, several sample programs are available to help you better understand the explanations and content in each chapter. These sample programs are provided in the download area for this book at *www.sap-press.com/3973*. In this download area, you'll find the code used in this book and details regarding the subsequent steps that must be executed for your system.

All ABAP development objects are included in the `TEST_A4H_BOOK` package, and all SAP HANA development objects are included in the `test.a4h.book` package. These packages include subpackages for each chapter of this book.

Packages

For all sample programs, SAP NetWeaver AS ABAP 7.4 (SP 10), ABAP Development Tools for SAP NetWeaver 2.7, and SAP HANA 1.0 (SPS 8) are required. For our tests, we used SAP HANA 1.0 Revision 97.

Requirements

If your system doesn't meet these requirements, you can also install the sample programs on a hosted test system. As of July 2013, you can have an Infrastructure as a Service (IaaS) provider (currently Amazon Web Services) provision such a test system as a virtual appliance for you. This system is comprised of SAP NetWeaver AS ABAP 7.4 and the SAP HANA database. This offer is based on a free 90-day Test and Evaluation License Agreement. However, you must pay for all costs incurred for the infrastructure services of the IaaS provider. For further information, refer to the SAP Community Network at *http://scn.sap.com/docs/DOC-41566*.

Hosted test system

After importing the code, make sure to generate sufficient data for your tests. For this purpose, use ABAP Report ZR_A4H_BOOK_GENERATE_MASS_DATA. Details can be found in the download area.

Test data

F   The Authors

Hermann Gahm is a principal consultant in the performance CoE of SAP Global IT Application Services. In this position, he is primarily responsible for performance analysis and optimization of the internal SAP ABAP systems powered by SAP HANA. Between 2006 and 2012, Hermann worked as an SAP technology consultant at SAP SI AG and as an SAP support consultant in the Technology & Performance division of the Active Global Support SAP department. In this position, his main responsibilities were helping major SAP customers solve performance problems in the context of ABAP developments and system, database, and ABAP program tuning. During his in-service studies of information management, he worked as an ABAP developer in one of the largest commercial enterprises in Germany and as an SAP system administrator for a market-leading industrial mortgage company between 1998 and 2006. During this time, his main responsibilities were performance analysis and optimization of mass data processing in SAP systems.

Thorsten Schneider is a product manager in the Product & Innovation HANA Platform department at SAP SE. In this position, he deals with application development using the new in-memory database technology. His main focus is the implementation of business applications based on ABAP and SAP HANA. Prior to working as a product manager, Thorsten was a consultant at SAP Deutschland AG & Co. KG for several years. During this time, he advised national and international organizations on product lifecycle management and project portfolio management matters.

Christiaan Swanepoel has worked for SAP SE since 2003. He is currently Product Owner in the area of ABAP development tools for Core Data Services (CDS) in Eclipse. Prior to that, he worked in the area of

ABAP programming language development and was part of the ABAP for SAP HANA integration team that deals with the software development based on ABAP and SAP HANA. Another focus of his work is agile software development. This includes agile testing of CDS objects in ABAP.

Dr. Eric Westenberger has been working for SAP SE since 2005, where he is currently a product manager for SAP HANA and SAP NetWeaver. Prior to this, he was involved in the development of several components of the SAP NetWeaver basis technology as a developer and software architect for several years. He studied mathematics at the University of Kaiserslautern, Germany, where he was awarded his doctorate degree in the field of singularity theory.

Index

- ▶ Get instructions for SUM migration with DMO and SWPM

- ▶ Understand how to test and monitor your new system once live

- ▶ Learn how to optimize your new setup for SAP HANA

Michael Pytel

Implementing SAP Business Suite on SAP HANA

If you're thinking about moving to SAP S/4HANA, your first step is getting SAP ERP on SAP HANA—and this book will serve as your go-to guide. Understand and complete all steps of the migration process, from planning the transition to making the move and going live. Then discover how to optimize your system for SAP HANA by activating enhancements and installing SAP S/4HANA Finance (SAP Simple Finance) and SAP HANA Live. Detailed instructions and guiding screenshots will help get your new platform up and running in no time!

597 pages, pub. 11/2015

E-Book: $69.99 | **Print:** $79.95 | **Bundle:** $89.99

www.sap-press.com/3895

- ▶ Discover the latest and greatest features in the ABAP universe

- ▶ Explore the new worlds of SAP HANA, BRFplus, BOPF, and more

- ▶ Propel your code and your career into the future

Paul Hardy

ABAP to the Future

ABAP has been around for a while, but that doesn't mean your programming has to be stuck in the past. Want to master test-driven development? Decipher BOPF? Manage BRF+? Explore ABAP 7.4? With clear explanations, engaging examples, and downloadable code, this book is your ride to the future. After all: If you're going to build something with ABAP, why not do it with some style?

727 pages, pub. 3/2015

E-Book: $59.99 | **Print:** $69.95 | **Bundle:** $79.99

www.sap-press.com/3680

- ► Learn the basics of ABAP and write your first program

- ► Set up an ABAP trial system and master the integrated development environment (IDE)

- ► Develop an example application using strings and text, dates and times, and more

Brian O'Neill

Getting Started with ABAP

Learn to code in ABAP, SAP's programming language! This book is a beginner's guide to all things ABAP. You'll become familiar with core language concepts, develop your first application, and learn key advanced programming techniques. Step-by-step instructions and hands-on exercises help ensure that you can apply the skills you learn to real-life scenarios.

451 pages, pub. 10/2015

E-Book: $44.99 | **Print:** $49.95 | **Bundle:** $59.99

www.sap-press.com/3869

Rheinwerk
Publishing

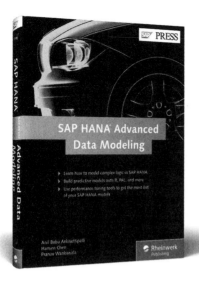

- ▶ Learn how to model complex logic in SAP HANA
- ▶ Build predictive models with R, PAL, and more
- ▶ Use performance tuning tools to get the most of out of your SAP HANA models

Anil Babu Ankisettipalli, Hansen Chen, Pranav Wankawala

SAP HANA Advanced Data Modeling

Move past the SAP HANA basics and into some real data model design, with this book! Discover how to build and design predictive, simulation, and optimization models straight from the experts via step-by-step instructions and screenshots. From information views to AFL models, you'll learn to scale for large datasets and performance tune your models to perfection.

392 pages, pub. 10/2015
E-Book: $69.99 | **Print:** $79.95 | **Bundle:** $89.99

www.sap-press.com/3863

James Wood, Joseph Rupert

Object-Oriented Programming with ABAP Objects

There's more to ABAP than procedural programming. If you're ready to leap into the world of ABAP Objects—or are already there and just need a refresher—then this is the book you've been looking for. Thanks to explanations of basic concepts, practical examples, and updates for AS ABAP 7.4, you'll find answers to questions you didn't even know you had.

470 pages, 2nd edition, pub. 10/2015

E-Book: $59.99 | **Print:** $69.95 | **Bundle:** $79.99

www.sap-press.com/3597

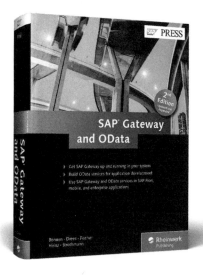

Interested in reading more?

Please visit our website for all new
book and e-book releases from SAP PRESS.

www.sap-press.com